INVESTIGATING
SCIENCE

FOR JUNIOR CYCLE

**STEPHEN COMISKEY,
SEÁN KELLEHER & SINÉAD KELLY**

ST. OLIVER'S BOOK SCHEME	
YEAR	NAME

ⓖ GILL EDUCATION

Gill Education
Hume Avenue
Park West
Dublin 12
www.gilleducation.ie

Gill Education is an imprint of M.H. Gill & Co.

ISBN: 978-0-7171-67500

Design and layout: Charles Design Associates
Cover design: Martin O'Brien

At the time of going to press, all web addresses were active and contained
information relevant to the topics in this book. Gill Education does not, however,
accept responsibility for the content or views contained on these websites.
Content, views and addresses may change beyond the publisher or authors'
control. Students should always be supervised when reviewing websites.

The paper used in this book is made from the wood pulp of managed forests. For every tree felled, at
least one tree is planted, thereby renewing natural resources.

Contents

Introduction

Investigating Science is a three-year textbook designed to meet all the requirements of the new **Junior Cycle Science Specification**.

There are forty-six learning outcomes in the Specification across the unifying strand, **Nature of Science (NOS)**, and the four contextual strands: **Earth and Space (ES), Chemical World (CW), Physical World (PW)** and **Biological World (BW)**. All learning outcomes are rigorously covered in *Investigating Science*, with Nature of Science outcomes embedded throughout the other strands.

The **inquiry-based approach** in *Investigating Science* emphasises the practical experience of science for each student. It supports the use of a wide range of teaching, learning and assessment approaches that provide opportunities for students to develop a range of inquiry skills.

Investigating Science provides opportunities for students to engage with contemporary issues in science that affect everyday life. They will **learn**, **interpret** and **analyse data** – a skill that has a value far beyond science wherever data is used as evidence to support argument. In **presenting evidence and findings**, they will engage in objectively discussing and justifying conclusions.

Investigating Science affords a reasonable degree of **flexibility for teachers and students** to make their own choices and pursue their interests, and offers many possible routes for an integrated science approach, including class-based extension work and outside school discussions/projects.

Using this book

Learning Outcomes
BWLO 1. Investigate the structures of animals and plants and relate them to their functions.

LEARNING INTENTIONS
At the end of this unit you should:
1. Be able to draw and identify parts of a plant and animal cell.
2. Be able to state the functions of plant and animal cells.

The **Learning Outcomes** are referenced for the teacher at the beginning of each unit. These have been translated into easy-to-follow **Learning Intentions** for the student.

How do plants move or excrete? Apart from breathing, how do we know we are alive?

Lightbulb questions throughout the topics use assessment for learning (AfL) strategies to encourage students to explore their prior knowledge and to predict before they read/listen/watch.

✓ Checkpoint 2

(a) List the food groups that provide the essential nutrients for survival and the function of each group.
(b) Deficiency of which food group can result in anaemia?
(c) Why is water included in the food groups table?

Checkpoint questions throughout the units can be used as a form of assessment for learning (AfL) and as homework.

Demonstration 06.01.01 – Making a cloud in a bottle

Instructions: Using a small amount of water, a 2-litre bottle and a match, your teacher will show you how a cloud in a bottle can be made to appear and disappear.

What did you learn?
1. Were the substances that made up the cloud destroyed each time the cloud disappeared?
2. Were the substances that made up the cloud created each time the cloud appeared?

Fig. 06.01.02 The stages of making a cloud in a bottle.

Demonstrations can be carried out by the teacher, but some are easily converted into whole-class exercises at the teacher's discretion. (Direction is given in the Teacher's Resource Book.)

🔍 Investigation 06.01.02: Testing the compression of solids, liquids and gases

Instructions: Using a disposable syringe, water, a marshmallow and the air in the room, can you suggest how you could show the compression of a solid, a liquid and a gas. You may need to add other equipment to this list.

What did you learn?
1. Explain whether the changes you see are physical or chemical, and why the changes happen.
2. How might you measure these changes?
3. Can you explain what might happen if you put a piece of marshmallow into a sealed syringe and pushed the plunger down? What might happen if you drew the plunger out?

Investigations allow students to develop their understanding of scientific processes, to use evidence to support explanations and to develop their inquiry skills.

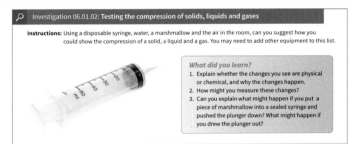

WHAT I HAVE LEARNED...

- Evolution is a slow, ongoing change in an organism over a very long time.
- Many scientists promoted the idea of the theory of evolution, but it was Charles Darwin who produced evidence to support the theory.
- Darwin proposed the theory of natural selection to explain the theory of evolution.

The **What I Have Learned** summary at the end of each unit allows students to assess their progress.

Question Time

Copy and Complete

In this unit I learned that a _____ can be made by _____ a _____ into a _____. A strong solution can be called a _____ solution and a weak solution is called a _____ solution. _____ solutions have the maximum amount of _____ that is possible at a _____ _____. The solubility of a solid _____ as _____ increases. The solubility of a _____ decreases with the increase of temperature. Crystals are formed when _____ solutions are _____.

Questions

1. Can you list four substances that are insoluble in water?
2. *Fig. 06.02.09* shows three solutions of copper sulfate. Decide which diagram, A, B or C, is the **dilute** solution. Also decide which diagram is the **saturated** solution.

Question Time at the end of each unit provides a variety of question types.

The **Copy and Complete** task is ideal for revision and as an exercise for those at different learning levels.

General contextual questions bring topics together.

Inquiry

A **Research** the answers to the following questions:
   (i) Why would a muscle need many mitochondrion?
   (ii) Which part of a plant cell absorbs energy from the sun?
   (iii) The heart muscle is called cardiac muscle and it never tires. How is cardiac muscle different from all the other muscles in the body?
   (iv) Which of the following animals are vertebrates? Why? Which is an invertebrate? Why?
   dog • snake • butterfly • frog • turtle • whale

Inquiry questions allow for further investigation while preparing students for their classroom-based assessment, the EEI and SSI. Key action words linked to Bloom's taxonomy are highlighted.

Other features to help the student in *Investigating Science*:

KEYWORDS

concentrated
concentration
crystallisation
dilute
dissolve
insoluble
saturated
solubility
solubility curve
soluble

Keywords are given at the start of units to assist with literacy strategies.

Saturated: A solution that has the maximum amount of solute dissolved into the solvent at a given temperature.

Concise and student-friendly **definitions** of key concepts present appropriate and suitable information.

Did you know?
Across the world, many people eat insects as they are a great source of protein. In some countries you can even buy chocolate-covered ants!

Did you know? boxes include fun and interesting additional information to engage students as they work through topics.

For the teacher:

The symbol **R** appears in this book where there are additional resources available to support teaching, such as background information, tips and photocopiable worksheets, which offer differentiated learning opportunities.

What About Electrons?

R Scientists were certain that the protons and neutrons sat as a solid mass in the centre of the atom (the nucleus), but where did the negative sub-atomic particles – the electrons – fit?

The **Teacher's Resource Book** provides support material to enable active, yet focused, lessons and investigations.

- A detailed planning section includes practical guidelines and advice.
- Detailed information and conclusions are given for each demonstration and investigation.
- Additional context and clarification notes assist with new topics/activities.
- Differentiated worksheets facilitate mixed-ability teaching.

On GillExplore.ie:

- Curriculum-focused videos
- Selected PhET interactive simulations
- Unit PowerPoints, which provide support in the laboratory when undertaking demonstrations and investigations. Including click-by-click solutions to all Lightbulb, Checkpoint and end-of-chapter questions, they are a great classroom aid.
- Additional resources to support teaching and learning.

Assessment Focus

Science Assessment for the Junior Cycle Profile of Achievement (JCPA) will have the following components:

- Two Classroom-Based Assessments (CBAs), one to be carried out in second year and the other in third year, to be evaluated by the class teacher.
- A written Assessment Task (AT), based on the second CBA. This will be submitted to the State Examinations Commission (SEC) for marking.
- A final written exam, of not more than two hours, to be taken in June of third year.

Remember:

- All assessment components are at common level.
- All assessment and exam formats may change from year to year.

Classroom-Based Assessments

The following table gives some detail on the current requirements for the CBAs.

CBA	Format	Student preparation	Completion of assessment
Extended Experimental Investigation (EEI)	Reports which may be presented in a wide range of formats	Students will, over a three-week period, formulate scientific hypotheses, plan and conduct an experimental investigation to test their hypotheses, generate and analyse primary data, and reflect on the process, with support/guidance by the teacher.	End of second year
Science in Society Investigation (SSI)	Reports which may be presented in a wide range of formats	Students will, over a three-week period, research a socio-scientific issue, analyse the information/ secondary data collected, and evaluate the claims and opinions studied and draw evidence-based conclusions about the issues involved, with support/guidance by the teacher.	End of term 1 or early term 2 of third year

Presentation formats can vary and may include handwritten/typed reports, model building, multimodal presentations, webpages, podcasts, etc.

Assessment Task (AT)

The formal written Assessment Task will be based on the topic or task undertaken in the second Classroom-Based Assessment. This Assessment Task will be submitted to the SEC to be marked along with the state-certified examination in the subject.

State Exam

There will be a written examination completed at the end of third year. Examinations will be set, administered, marked and resulted by the SEC. The written examinations will be of no longer than two hours.

All elements of assessment will be recorded in the Junior Cycle Profile of Achievement (JCPA).

Investigating Science and Assessment

- The inquiry questions at the end of each unit in *Investigating Science* are designed to prepare students for their CBAs and to give ideas for **topics/ approaches**.

- Students will experience a variety of **presentational formats** through completion of checkpoint questions and through the inquiry section.

- Throughout *Investigating Science*, extensions to investigations encourage and spark ideas for the **Extended Experimental Investigation**.

- Throughout the inquiry sections, students are offered opportunities to develop skills for both the **Extended Experimental** and **Science in Society** investigations. The inquiry tasks are diverse as they can require research and/or further experimental activities to be carried out.

Laboratory Equipment and Student Diagrams

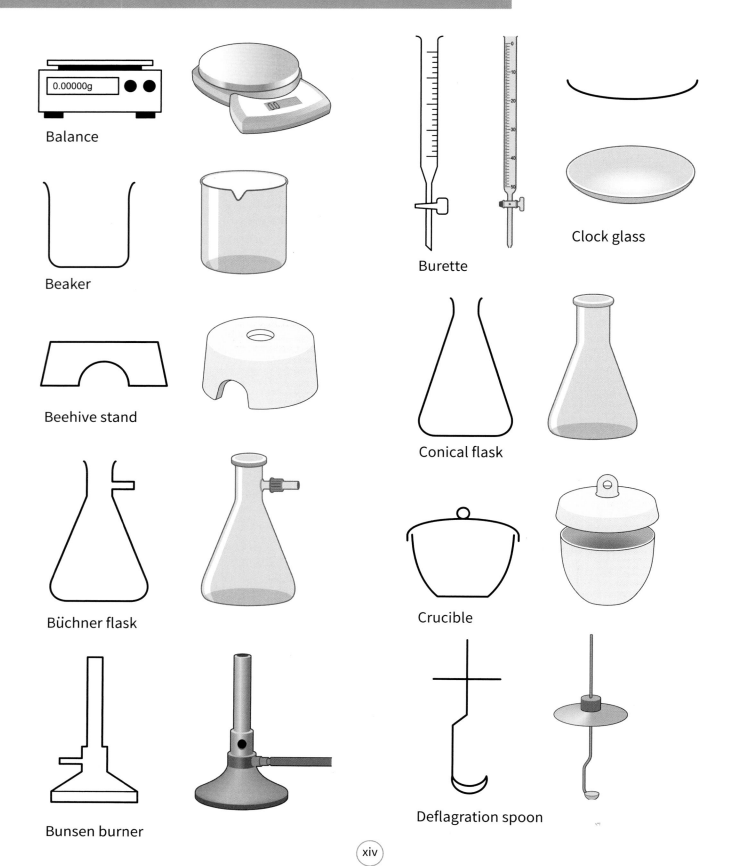

Balance

Beaker

Beehive stand

Büchner flask

Bunsen burner

Burette

Clock glass

Conical flask

Crucible

Deflagration spoon

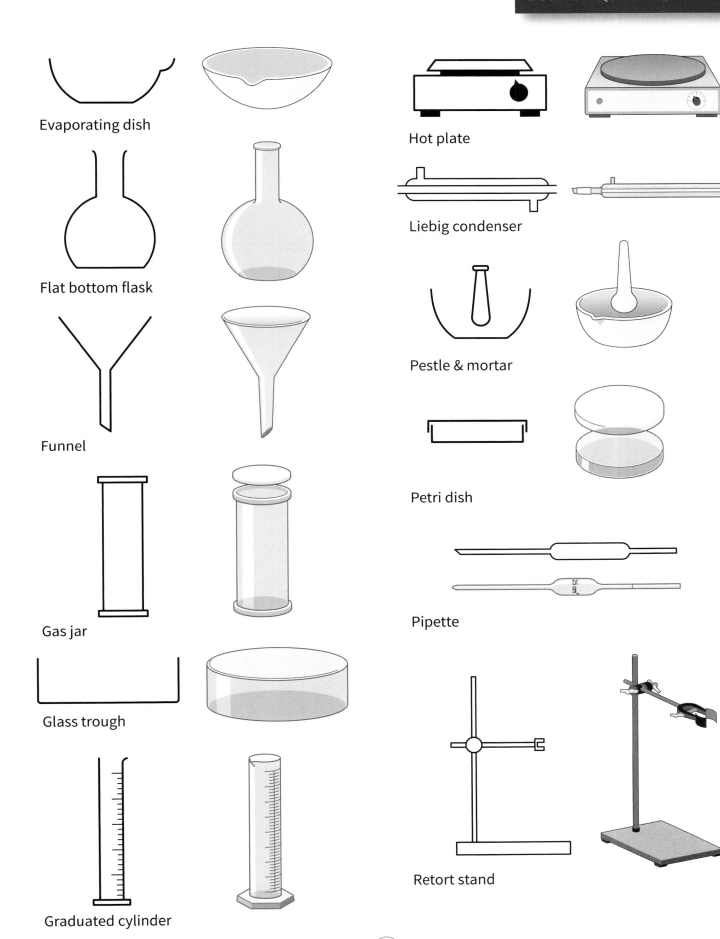

Evaporating dish

Flat bottom flask

Funnel

Gas jar

Glass trough

Graduated cylinder

Hot plate

Liebig condenser

Pestle & mortar

Petri dish

Pipette

Retort stand

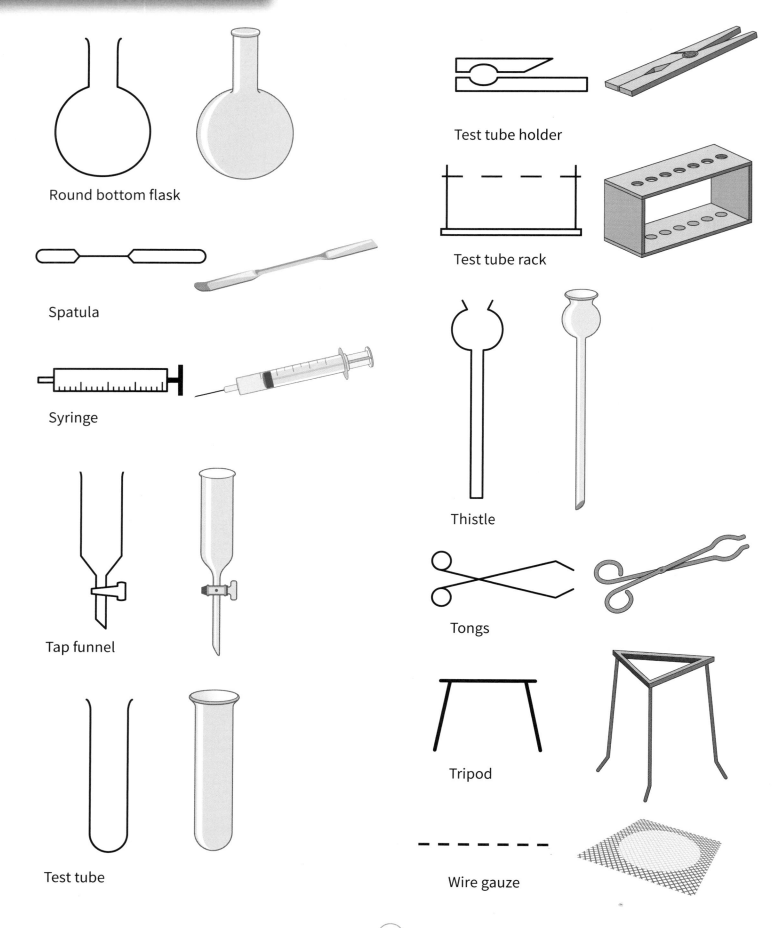

Round bottom flask

Spatula

Syringe

Tap funnel

Test tube

Test tube holder

Test tube rack

Thistle

Tongs

Tripod

Wire gauze

1.1

Cells and Living Things

Learning Outcomes

BWLO 1. Investigate the structures of animals and plants and relate them to their functions.

NSLO 1. Appreciate how scientists work and how scientific ideas are modified over time.

NSLO 6. Conduct research relevant to a scientific issue, evaluate different sources of information including secondary data, understanding that a source may lack detail or show bias.

NSLO 7. Organise and communicate research and investigative findings in a variety of ways fit for purpose and audience, using relevant scientific terminology and representations.

(R) Teacher's reference

KEYWORDS

biconcave	nutrition
cell	organ
cell membrane	organism
cell wall	palisade
characteristics	reproduction
chlorophyll	respiration
chloroplast	sensitivity
classified	specialised
cytoplasm	system
excretion	tissue
growth	unicellular
haemoglobin	vacuole
invertebrate	vertebrate
mitochondrion	
multicellular	
nucleus	

LEARNING INTENTIONS

At the end of this unit you should:

1. Be able to draw and identify parts of a plant and animal cell.
2. Be able to state the functions of plant and animal cells.
3. Know how to compare the structures of and differences between a plant and animal cell.
4. Know the difference between a unicellular and a multicellular organism.
5. Know the sequence of cell organisation.
6. Understand that some cells are specialised and perform a specific function, and be able to give two examples of such cells.
7. Be able to list the seven characteristics of life and understand the meaning of each.
8. Understand the difference between an invertebrate and a vertebrate.

What Are Cells?

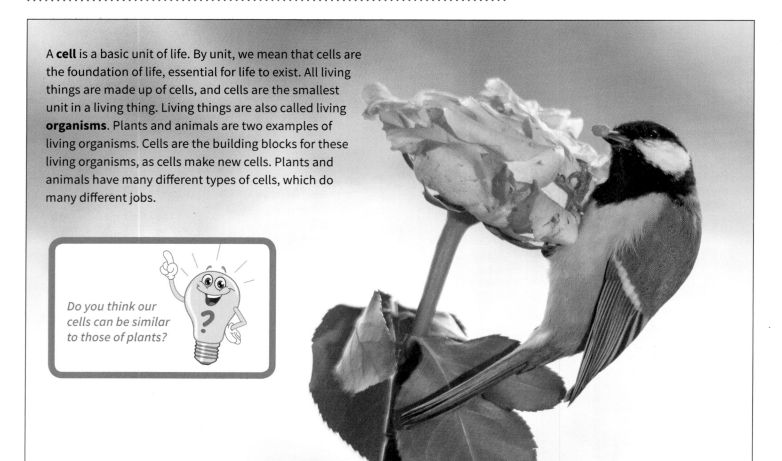

A **cell** is a basic unit of life. By unit, we mean that cells are the foundation of life, essential for life to exist. All living things are made up of cells, and cells are the smallest unit in a living thing. Living things are also called living **organisms**. Plants and animals are two examples of living organisms. Cells are the building blocks for these living organisms, as cells make new cells. Plants and animals have many different types of cells, which do many different jobs.

Do you think our cells can be similar to those of plants?

ROBERT HOOKE
1635 – 1703

Did you know?
In 1665, scientist Robert Hooke used a microscope to examine a thin piece of bark from a cork tree. He saw small 'boxes' in the structure and called them 'cells'. This discovery of cells formed the basis of cell theory.

Fig. 01.01.01 Robert Hooke, and the type of microscope he would have used.

Similarities and Differences Between the Cells

Plant and animal cells have similarities and differences. *Fig. 01.01.02* and *Fig. 01.01.03* represent typical plant and animal cells. There are a lot more parts in cells, but we'll look at the parts shown here. Later in the unit we will take a closer look at these cells using a microscope.

> **For further information on cells, check out this animated video on YouTube:** *'Animals Cells Structure & Functions'.*

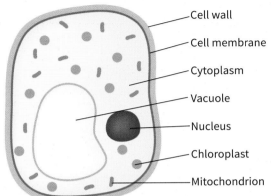

Fig. 01.01.02 A plant cell.

Fig. 01.01.03 An animal cell.

 **Checkpoint 1**

Copy the Venn diagram in *Fig. 01.01.04* and complete it by referring to *Fig. 01.01.02 and Fig. 01.01.03.*

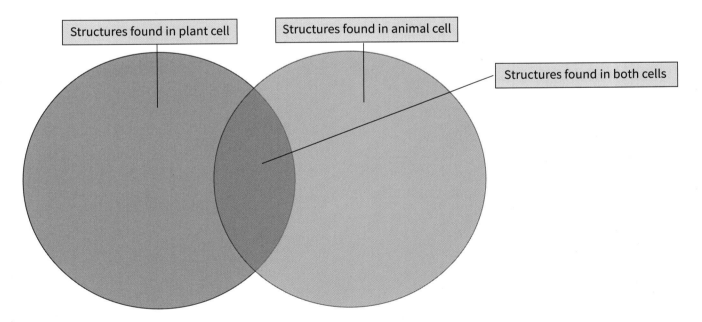

Fig. 01.01.04 List the similarities and differences between a plant and an animal cell.

Functions of the Parts of Cells

Table 01.01.01 lists the structures of plant and animal cells and their functions.

Structures	Functions
Nucleus	Contains the genetic material that controls what the cell does (genetic material = chromosomes or genes).
Cell membrane	Holds the cell together and controls what passes in and out of the cell.
Cell wall	A rigid coat of cellulose that gives the plant cell its shape and supports and strengthens the cell.
Cytoplasm	A jelly-like substance where chemical reactions take place, e.g. breaking down nutrients for energy.
Large vacuole	Filled with cell sap, which is a weak solution of salt and sugars, and stores food or waste products.
Mitochondrion	Place or site where energy is released from nutrients by **respiration**.
Chloroplast	Where photosynthesis occurs. Contains **chlorophyll**, a green pigment that traps the light energy from the sun.

Table 01.01.01 Functions of the parts of plant and animal cells.

⊘ **Checkpoint 2**

(a) In your copy, draw a labelled diagram of a plant cell and an animal cell. In your labels, include the functions of each part of the cell.

(b) Individually or with classmates, put together a cell song or rap. Check out the YouTube video 'Mr. W's Cell Song' to help you get started!

Unicellular and Multicellular Organisms

Different organisms have different numbers of cells. Some plants and animals are made up of only one cell. These are known as **unicellular** organisms. All of the organism's activities are carried out by this single cell. Examples of unicellular organisms are bacteria, yeast and amoebae.

Most plants and animals have lots of cells. These are known as **multicellular** organisms. The cells group together to carry out different functions. When a cell can only carry out one particular function, we call it a **specialised** cell, e.g. brain cells only work in the brain; leaf cells will only do their job in the leaf.

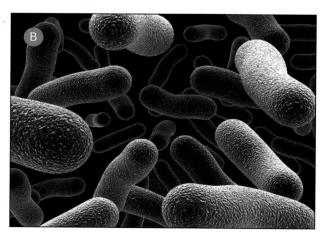

Fig. 01.01.05 Unicellular organisms: (a) an amoeba cell; (b) bacteria cells.

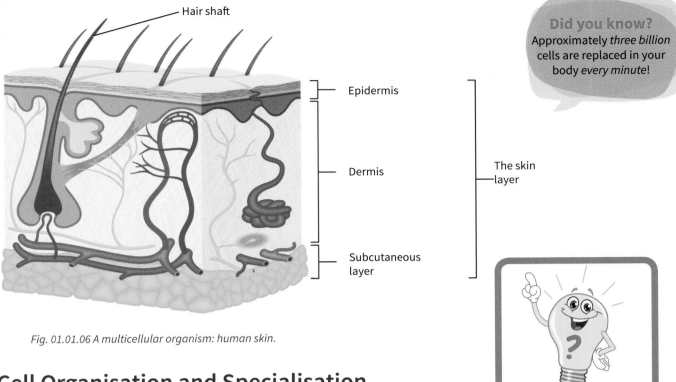

Hair shaft

Epidermis

Dermis

The skin layer

Subcutaneous layer

Fig. 01.01.06 A multicellular organism: human skin.

Did you know?
Approximately *three billion* cells are replaced in your body *every minute*!

R *Where do your body cells come from?*

Cell Organisation and Specialisation

How Cells Are Organised

Cells can be grouped together to carry out different functions. These **groups of cells** make a **tissue**; layers of tissues make an **organ**; and many organs, together with the tissues and cells, make a **system**. They all work together to make an **organism**.

Tissue: A group of similar cells carrying out the same function.

Organ: A group of different tissues working together.

System: A group of organs working together.

Organism: A plant or animal, which is made up of many cells, tissues, organs and organ systems.

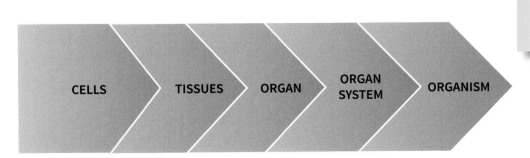

CELLS → TISSUES → ORGAN → ORGAN SYSTEM → ORGANISM

Cell Organisation in a Human

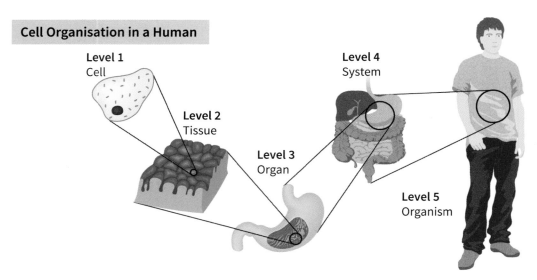

Fig. 01.01.07 Cell organisation in a human. The cells are gastric cells. These gastric cells make up gastric tissue, which forms the stomach (an organ), which is part of the digestive system.

Cell Organisation in a Plant

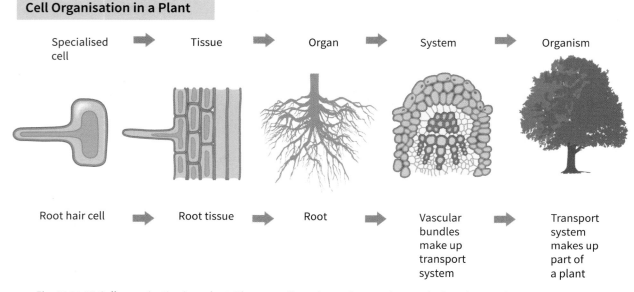

Fig. 01.01.08 Cell organisation in a plant. The root cells make up the root tissue, which makes up the organ of the root, which is part of the transport system of the plant.

✓ Checkpoint 3

(a) Make a list of tissues, organs and organ systems in your body.
(b) Are any of the tissues you have listed made from specialised cells? Which ones?
(c) Name any cells you know that are found in a plant.
(d) Name any of the organs of a plant.

Specialised Cells

As you can see, the plant and animal cells in *Fig. 01.01.02* and *Fig. 01.01.03* look very different to those in *Fig. 01.01.08* and *Fig. 01.01.09*. These particular cells have different jobs to do, so they are **specialised cells**.

Specialised Cell: A cell that is specifically adapted to carry out its function.

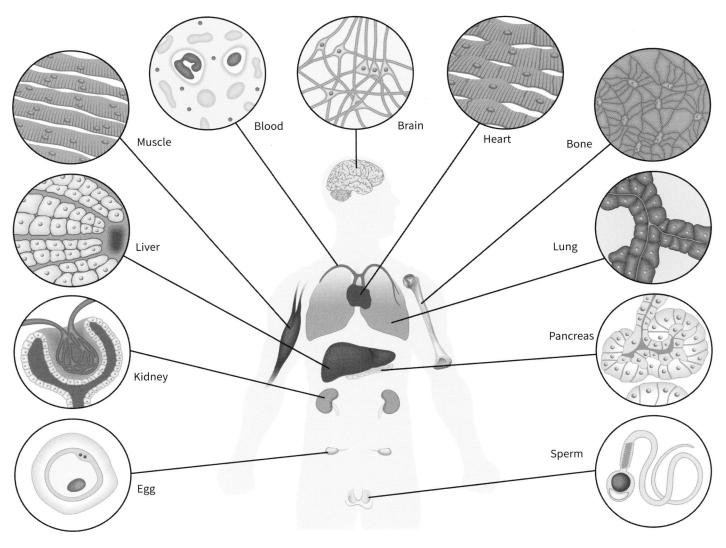

Fig. 01.01.09 Specialised animal cells in the human body. They look different from each other because they have different features, shapes and functions. We can therefore refer to them as 'specialised cells'.

Ⓡ Stem Cells

Stem cell research is a topic you often hear in the news. But what is a stem cell and what does it do? As you can see in *Fig. 01.01.10*, a stem cell is a single cell that can copy itself and can then specialise into other cell types. Stem cells often divide to repair and replace worn-out or damaged cells or tissues. These cells are only found in multicellular organisms.

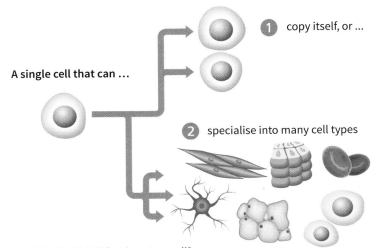

Fig. 01.01.10 What is a stem cell?

Specialised cell	Plant or animal cell?	How is it different?
Palisade Cell	Plant	*Structure:* A tall cell, giving it a large surface area; many **chloroplasts** *Found:* In the top layer of the leaf *Function:* Holds chloroplasts to allow photosynthesis
Root Hair Cell	Plant	*Structure:* Large surface area; thin walls *Found:* At the roots *Function:* Absorbs water and minerals from the soil
Red Blood Cell	Animal	*Structure:* No nucleus; contains a red pigment called **haemoglobin**. **Biconcave** in shape (the top and bottom of the cell curve inwards), allowing more space for carrying oxygen *Found:* In the blood *Function:* Haemoglobin in the cell allows blood to carry oxygen around the body
Muscle Cell	Animal	*Structure:* Three types of muscle: *Skeletal muscle tissue* (e.g. biceps, triceps, abdominals, any voluntary muscle) *Smooth muscle tissue* (e.g. muscles behind the eye, muscles of the digestive system, any involuntary muscle) *Cardiac (heart) muscle tissue* Each tissue is made up of different cell shapes which are formed to help with their function *Found:* All over the body *Functions:* Contract and relax to enable the body to move or parts of the body to function

Table 01.01.02 Specialised cells.

✓ Checkpoint 4

(a) Why do you think the root cell has thin walls?

(b) Since red blood cells do not have a nucleus, what is present in them to enable them to carry out their function?

(c) Why do you think the palisade cells are found in the top layer of the leaf?

(d) What do you think we mean by 'large surface area'? What will a large surface area allow to happen?

(e) Can you list any other skeletal or smooth muscles in the body?

Are you similar to a plant? If no, why not? If yes, how?

Living Things

What is a living thing? Remember, a living thing is also known as an organism – a plant or an animal that has **structures** in it that depend on each other to function, the basis of these structures being cells.

What Makes a Thing 'Living'?

To be **classified** as a living thing, or alive, the organism must have all seven of the **characteristics** of life (life processes):

1. **Movement**
2. **Respiration**
3. **Sensitivity/response**
4. **Growth**
5. **Reproduction**
6. **Excretion**
7. **Nutrition**

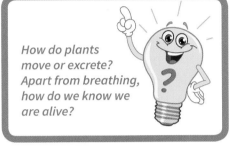

How do plants move or excrete? Apart from breathing, how do we know we are alive?

The acronym **'Mrs Gren'** will help you remember them!

Characteristics of Life Explained

1. **Movement**

The ability of an organism to move all or part of its structure.

- Animals move from place to place, whether they walk, run, swim, jump, etc.
- Plants move towards light and water, and due to gravity. For example, plants bend towards light, roots grow down towards water.

Fig. 01.01.11 Various organisms exhibiting movement – one of the characteristics of life.

2. *Respiration*

The ability to take in oxygen and release energy from food.

- All living things, plants and animals, break down food in their cells to release energy.

3. *Sensitivity or response*

An organism responds to changes in its surroundings.
- Animals use their sense organs to respond to changes. The sense organs are: eyes, ears, nose, skin and tongue.
- Plants respond to light, water, gravity, touch and chemicals.

 **Checkpoint 5**

(a) Use *Table 01.01.03* to list what each sense organ responds to.

Sense organ	Eyes	Ears	Nose	Skin	Tongue
Response					

Table 01.01.03.

(b) How do plants respond to light and water?
(c) There is a piece of gone-off food on your plate. Which of your senses could you use to tell you that the food is off?
(d) Suggest how animals use the energy that is released during respiration.
(e) Discuss with a classmate how the Venus flytrap plant traps tiny insects.

4. *Growth*

The increase in size of an organism.
- Living organisms produce new cells which cause **growth**.

5. *Reproduction*

The ability to produce new cells and therefore a new organism.
- Cells in plants and animals reproduce. This allows life to continue from generation to generation.

Fig. 01.01.12 Young trees grow into mature trees.

Fig. 01.01.13 Animals and their offspring.

6. **Excretion**

Removal of waste from a cell and from the organism.
- Plants mainly excrete oxygen and water.
- Animals excrete products such as carbon dioxide, water and salt.

7. **Nutrition**

How a living organism obtains its food.
- Plants make their own food.
- Animals take in their food by eating other animals and plants.
- Food helps with the workings of other life processes in plants and animals.

 Checkpoint 6

(a) List the seven characteristics of life. Remember **Mrs Gren**!
(b) Choose one plant and one animal from the list in *Table 01.01.04* and produce a fact card about how they carry out all seven life characteristics.
(c) Using the seven characteristics of life, describe two ways in which a strawberry plant and a horse are similar, and two ways in which they are different.

Plants	Animals
Daffodil	Lion
Venus flytrap	Snail
Oak tree	Cat

Table 01.01.04.

Invertebrate: An animal without a backbone

Vertebrate: An animal with a backbone.

Classifying Animals

Animals can be categorised as either **invertebrates** or **vertebrates**.
These groups can then be further divided into categories as shown in *Fig. 01.01.14*.

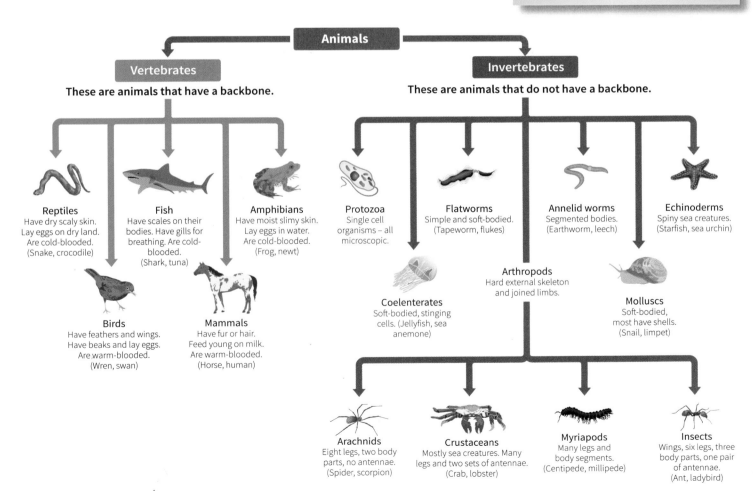

Fig. 01.01.14 Classification of animals.

WHAT I HAVE LEARNED...

- A cell is a basic unit of life.
- A typical plant and animal cell have four elements in common: nucleus, cell membrane, cytoplasm and mitochondrion.
- A plant cell differs from an animal cell in that it also has a large vacuole, cell wall and chloroplasts.
- The functions of plant and animal cell structures.
- A unicellular organism has one cell. A multicellular organism has more than one cell.
- The sequence of cell organisation: cell, tissue, organ, organ system, organism.
- The seven characteristics of life: movement, respiration, sensitivity, growth, reproduction, excretion and nutrition.
- An invertebrate is an animal without a backbone.
- An vertebrate is an animal with a backbone.

 ## Question Time

Copy and Complete

In this unit I learned that living things are made up of _____. Plants and _____ are two examples of living things. Animal and plant cells are similar as they both have a _____, _____ _____, _____ and _____. But only plant cells have a large vacuole, _____ _____and _____. An organism with one cell is called _____. An organism with many cells is called _____. An organism is made up of cells, _____, organs and a _____. A specialised cell is a cell that is _____ adapted to carry out its _____. An example of a specialised cell in an animal is a _____ _____. An example of a specialised cell in a plant is a _____ _____. I also learned that living things can be divided into two categories: _____ and _____. The difference between a living thing and a non-living thing is that a living thing has _____ characteristics of life. They are m_____, r_____ , s_____, g_____ , r_____, e_____ and n_____ . M_____ means that the plant or animal is able to move all or part of its structure. Respiration is being able to take in oxygen and release _____from food. S_____/response is how they react to any changes. Growth is when the plant or animal produces new _____. Reproduction is how new _____are made. Excretion is the _____ of waste. Nutrition is how an organism makes or takes in _____.

Questions

1. Where do most cell reactions take place?
2. Where is energy released in the cell?
3. Which part of both a plant and animal cell passes genetic information on to new cells?
4. What is a specialised cell? Name two examples, one from a plant and one from an animal.
5. What is the main difference between a unicellular organism and a multicellular organism?
6. How does the shape of a red blood cell help it carry out its function?
7. What is missing in a red blood cell that most other cells in the human body have?
8. (R) Using the information previously given on cell organisation, draw what you think the sequence of cell organisation in a plant would be, starting with a leaf cell.

9. Copy and fill in *Table 01.01.05*. A brief description of the characterisation is needed, as well as an example of the plant and animal carrying out this characteristic.

Characteristic	Brief description of characteristic	Example of how a plant carries out this characteristic	Example of how an animal carries out this characteristic
Sensitivity			
Reproduction			
Respiration			
Movement			
Nutrition			
Growth			
Excretion			

Table 01.01.05.

10. What is the name given to animals with a backbone?
11. What is the name given to animals without a backbone?
12. List four things that are non-living, giving a reason why you have chosen them.

Inquiry

A **Research** the answers to the following questions:
   (i) Why would a muscle cell need many mitochondrion?
   (ii) Which part of a plant cell absorbs energy from the sun?
   (iii) The heart muscle is called cardiac muscle and it never tires. How is cardiac muscle different from all the other muscles in the body?
   (iv) Which of the following animals are vertebrates? Why? Which is an invertebrate? Why?
   dog • snake • butterfly • frog • turtle • whale

B Robert Hooke, Marcello Malpighi and Antonie van Leeuwenhoek were some of the first scientists to work with microscopes and cells. They helped us understand cells and construct cell diagrams. It is said that van Leeuwenhoek was the first person to observe a red blood cell and a sperm cell. Choose one of these scientists and **design** a poster on their work and their discoveries.

C **Create** a cell of your own, with its structures. Make a 3-D cell structure using Lego pieces, a cereal box, a jam jar with a plastic bag, lime jelly, Play-Doh, etc. Get creative!

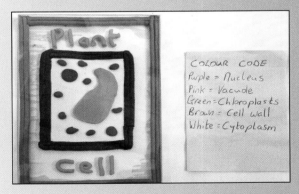

D Ⓡ 'Stem cell treatment and research may be vital in the replacement of cells/organs for future generations.' Do you agree or disagree with this statement? **Debate** this statement and explore the issues that have arisen in the stem cell research controversy.

1.2

The Microscope

Learning Outcomes

BWLO 1. Investigate the structures of animals and plants and relate them to their functions.

NSLO 1. Appreciate how scientists work and how scientific ideas are modified over time.

NSLO 5. Review and reflect on the skills and thinking used in carrying out investigations, and apply learning and skills to solving problems in unfamiliar contexts.

NSLO 7. Organise and communicate research and investigate findings in a variety of ways fit for purpose and audience, using relevant scientific terminology and representations.

NSLO 9. Research and present information on the contribution that scientists make to scientific discovery and invention, and its impact on society.

(R) Teacher's reference

KEYWORDS

beams
coarse
  adjustment
condenser
diaphragm lever
eyepiece
fine adjustment
magnification
microscope
nosepiece
objective lens
organism
resolution
specimen
stage
stains
structure

LEARNING INTENTIONS

At the end of this unit you should:

1. Be able to identify the parts of the scanning electron microscope.
2. Be able to identify parts of the light microscope and understand their functions.
3. Be able to identify parts of a plant and animal cell.
4. Be able to compare the parts of a plant and animal cell.
5. Understand magnification and how to calculate it.

The Microscope

. . . .

The naked eye (our eye alone) allows us to see objects, but with a **microscope** we can see these objects in much greater detail. In *Fig. 01.02.01* we can see the **magnification** of an image using different settings on a microscope. The greater the magnification, the more specific the detail we can see.

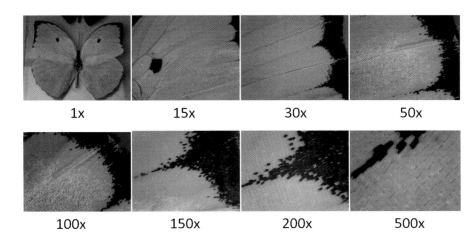

| 1x | 15x | 30x | 50x |
| 100x | 150x | 200x | 500x |

Fig. 01.02.01 What we can see of a butterfly's wing using the different magnification settings of a microscope.

A microscope is a tool that allows us to investigate objects. As we now know, plants and animals have many cells, each with different functions to help carry out the different jobs within an **organism**. We also know what the **structure** of a typical plant or animal cell looks like. In the seventeenth century, scientists such as Antonie van Leeuwenhoek and Robert Hooke developed and used microscopes to view and examine actual cells in an organism.

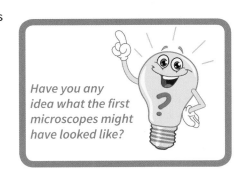

Have you any idea what the first microscopes might have looked like?

What structure do you want to see?

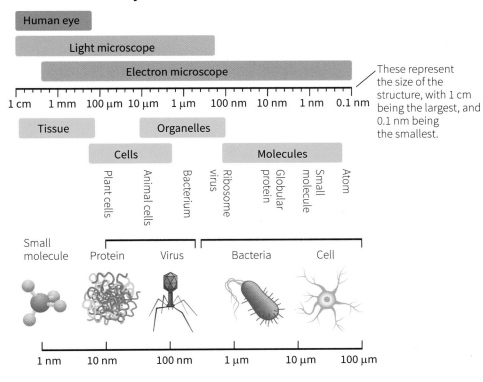

Fig. 01.02.02 What we can use to see different structures.

The History of the Microscope

Leeuwenhoek microscope (circa late 1600s)

Hand-held microscope (circa early 1700s)

✓ **Checkpoint 1**

Take a look at these microscopes. Do you think they have changed much over the centuries? What are your first impressions of them?

British microscope (circa 1865)

Winkel-ZEISS Dissecting microscope (circa 1927)

ZEISS Primo Star (circa 2010)

Fig. 01.02.03 Microscopes over the centuries.

Today's Microscopes

Several different types of microscope are used today. We will take a look at:

1. The light microscope
2. The electron microscope

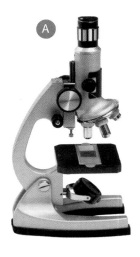

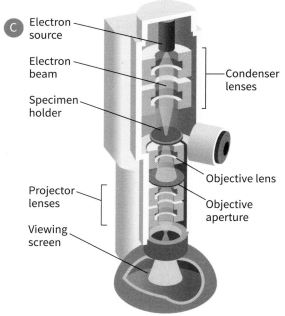

A

B

C

Electron source

Electron beam

Specimen holder

Condenser lenses

Objective lens

Projector lenses

Objective aperture

Viewing screen

Fig. 01.02.04 (a) A light microscope; (b) An electron microscope; (c) The inside of an electron microscope (the word 'aperture' means an opening that allows light to travel through).

1. The Light Microscope

We use the light microscope to view the **surface structure** of cells of a **specimen**. As the name suggests, light microscopes use light to magnify the image. Moving from a low-powered **objective lens** to a medium- and then a high-powered objective lens, we can see a specimen in greater and greater detail. To help us see the images under the microscope we often use a **stain**. A stain colours the cell or cell parts, highlighting them and allowing us to get a clearer view or image. The type of stain used will depend on what you want to look at, as different cell parts absorb different stains.

Stains: Used to highlight a cell or cell part, allowing a clearer view of the image.

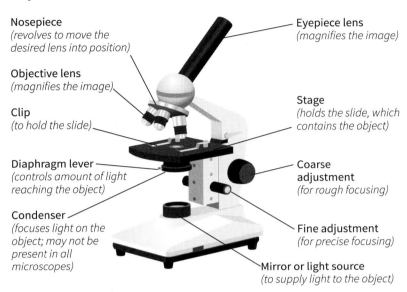

Nosepiece *(revolves to move the desired lens into position)*

Objective lens *(magnifies the image)*

Clip *(to hold the slide)*

Diaphragm lever *(controls amount of light reaching the object)*

Condenser *(focuses light on the object; may not be present in all microscopes)*

Eyepiece lens *(magnifies the image)*

Stage *(holds the slide, which contains the object)*

Coarse adjustment *(for rough focusing)*

Fine adjustment *(for precise focusing)*

Mirror or light source *(to supply light to the object)*

Fig. 01.02.05 The microscopes you use in your school are light microscopes. As you can see, the light microscope has more than one lens: the eyepiece lens and the objective lens. Lenses are used to focus light, which makes the image sharper.

2. The Electron Microscope

The electron microscope is a high-powered microscope used by scientists in laboratories for very close analysis of cells. It allows the user to see greater surface detail or a closer internal view of the specimen than the light microscope. This is because the electron microscope has a much greater **resolution** and because it uses a **beam** of electrons rather than light alone. Examples of electron microscopes are the transmission electron microscope (TEM) and scanning electron microscope (SEM).

Table 01.02.01 shows some of the differences between the light and electron microscope.

Resolution: The ability to distinguish two objects as separate things, rather than blurred together in a single smudge.

Light microscope	Electron microscope
Inexpensive	Very expensive
No major running costs	High running costs
Live or dead specimens can be used/seen	Dead or dried specimens can be used/seen
Surface view of specimen	Good surface details (SEM) or internal view (TEM) can be seen
A light source needed to see specimen	Electron beams used
The eyepiece and objective lenses made of glass	Lenses used are electromagnets
Images seen by the eye through the lens	Images must be received on a screen or a photographic plate
Max. resolution of 200 nanometres (nm) (A nanometre is one-billionth of a metre)	Max. resolution of 50 picometres (pm) (A picometre is one-trillionth of a metre)
Max. magnification of 2000x	Max. magnification of 10 000 000x

Table 01.02.01 The differences between the light and electron microscope.

The following images show the difference in detail that can be seen using each type of microscope.

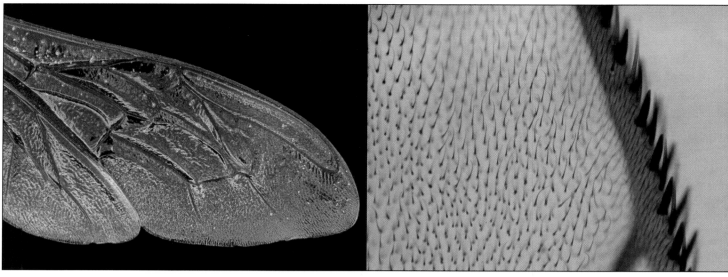

Fig. 01.02.06 (a) A fly's wing as viewed under a light microscope.

Fig. 01.02.06 (b) A fly's wing as viewed under an electron microscope.

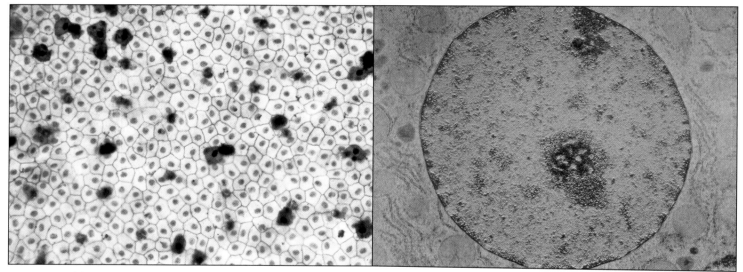

Fig. 01.02.07 (a) An animal cell as viewed under a light microscope.

Fig. 01.02.07 (b) An animal cell as viewed under an electron microscope.

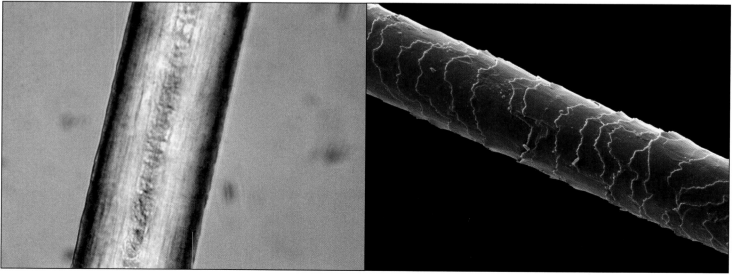

Fig. 01.02.08 (a) A strand of human hair as viewed under a light microscope.

Fig. 01.02.08 (b) A strand of human hair as viewed under an electron microscope.

 **Checkpoint 2**

(a) Looking at the microscope in your classroom, or using *Fig. 01.02.05*, answer these questions:
  (i) Which parts allow you to see the objects in greater detail?
  (ii) Which part allows the amount of light reaching the specimen to be adjusted?
(b) (R) Create a table in your copy listing the parts of the light microscope and their functions. You will need this table later for your investigation of a cell.
(c) Why are stains applied to specimens when viewing them under a microscope?
(d) We need a source of light to view specimen images under a light microscope. How are images projected using an electron microscope?

Magnification: What it is and How it is Calculated

When you use a microscope, magnification allows you to zoom in on your specimen to see it in greater detail. The light microscope has two lenses that allow you to do this: the eyepiece lens and the objective lens.

Each lens has a number printed on the side stating the strength of its magnification. Multiplying these two magnification numbers gives the total magnification of the microscope when you are looking at the image. By changing the magnification on the objective lens you change the total magnification, which means you are zooming in or zooming out on your specimen.

The magnification of an eyepiece lens is usually 10x, while the magnification of the objective lens can be 10x, 40x or 100x.

Fig. 01.02.09 (a) An eyepiece lens.

> **Magnification:** The use of lenses to see very small objects in greater detail.

Fig. 01.02.09 (b) Objective lenses at different magnifications.

Eyepiece lens magnification x objective lens magnification = total magnification
e.g.   10x   x   40x   =   400x

When your total magnification is high it means you have zoomed in, and when your total magnification is low it means you have zoomed out.

The images from an electron microscope can be magnified up to 10 000x or 250 000x. Some can be magnified by 1 million! *Fig. 01.02.10* shows how the different magnifications of the same slide can give different details.

  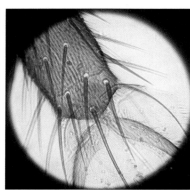

Fig. 01.02.10 A Varroa mite viewed at different magnifications.

✓ Checkpoint 3

(a) When you magnify something, what are you doing to the image? Will the physical size of what you are viewing change, or just its appearance?

(b) What is the symbol for magnification when using a microscope?

(c) How do you calculate the total magnification of the image or of your specimen?

(d) If you have an eyepiece with a magnification power of 10x and an objective lens of magnification 30x, what is your total magnification? Show your workings.

🔍 Investigation 01.02.01: **How to use a light microscope**

Equipment: Microscope, microscope slide or a ready-made sample slide, pencil.

Instructions: You may need to refer to the diagram of the microscope and its functions in *Fig. 01.02.05* to remind you of the names of the parts. Read through all the instructions before starting to use the microscope.

1. Make sure the stage is at its lowest point by turning the stage adjustor wheels (this makes sure that you do not break the glass microscope slide when you change the objective lens).
2. Turn the objective lens to the lowest power (e.g. 4x).
3. Place a microscope slide or a prepared microscope slide on the stage and fasten it with the stage clips (move the microscope slide around on the stage until you see an image).
4. Look at the microscope from the side – turn the focus wheel so you see the stage move upward.
5. Look through the eyepiece and move the focus wheel slowly – if using prepared slides, until an image comes into focus.
6. Adjust the condenser/diaphragm to allow the greatest amount of light in.
7. You may need to readjust the condenser/diaphragm or the focus wheels for the clearest image.
8. When you have a clear image of your specimen with the lowest power objective, change to the next objective lenses. *You must remember to adjust the height of the stage.*
9. When finished, lower the stage, click the low-power lens into position and remove the slide.
10. Repeat this technique using a pencil, placing it on the slide and starting with the lowest magnification view.

> #### *What did you learn?*
> 1. Which parts of the microscope allow you to change the magnification of the image?
> 2. Why is it important to always move the stage before you change objective lens?
> 3. What do you adjust to get a clearer view of the specimen image?
> 4. If there wasn't enough light reaching the specimen, what part would you adjust to increase the light?

Investigation 01.02.02: Preparing a slide for use under a microscope

Equipment: Microscope, microscope slide, cover slip, tissue paper, chosen cell, appropriate stain, a dropper, a probe.

Instructions: Choose from the list of cells below or use one your teacher gives you. Prepare a slide and apply the technique of using the microscope to view your cells. Your teacher may direct you, or alternatively research how to obtain the cells.

Cell list

- An onion cell (a plant cell)
- A cheek cell (an animal cell)
- Stomata/guard cells on the underside of a leaf (plant cell)
- Cells from the upper and lower side of a leaf (plant cell)

What did you learn?

1. Draw any image you see using the low-, medium- and high-powered lenses.
2. Write an observation that you noticed when changing between the magnifications.
3. What is the purpose of the stain?
4. What does the stain do to your cell when applied?
5. If you did not use a stain, would you be able to see the specimen image under the microscope?

WHAT I HAVE LEARNED...

- A microscope allows us to see small things that are not visible to the naked eye.
- The most commonly used microscopes are the light and electron microscopes.
- Stains are used to highlight a cell or cell parts, allowing a clearer view of the image.
- Magnification means using lenses to see very small objects in greater detail.
- The symbol for magnification is x.
- Eyepiece lens x magnification of objective lens = total magnification.
- The methods of preparing a slide and viewing a prepared slide under the microscope.

Question Time

Copy and Complete

In this unit I learned that a microscope allows us to see _____ parts of cells. The two main microscopes used today are the _____ microscope and the _____ microscope. The _____ microscope uses light to allow us to see the image; the electron microscope uses _____ of electrons. When looking through the microscope you can work out the total magnification used by reading the value on the _____ lens and the value on the objective _____ and then _____ them. To help us view the images under the microscope we often use _____ . The _____ highlights parts of the cell and then allows us to see a _____ image.

Questions

1. What does a microscope allow us to do that the naked eye cannot?
2. How are the light and electron microscopes different? Give a minimum of three points.
3. Number the statements in *Table 01.02.02* in order of the correct process of viewing a cell under a light microscope.
4. When preparing a specimen, what is used to allow a clearer view of the image?
5. What is the function or job of the cover slip, and why should the cover slip be lowered gently onto the slide?

Statement	Correct order
Use tissue to absorb any excess stain on slide	
Place cell on microscope slide	
Using a dropper, apply a drop of stain to the cell on your microscope	
Gently lower a cover slip at an angle over the cell	
Now look at cells using different lens powers	
Adjust stage and use the 10x objective lens to view cells	
While looking through the eyepiece, adjust the coarse and fine focus wheels	
Place slide on stage and secure with clips	

Table 01.02.02.

Inquiry

A   (R)   You are on work experience with your local newspaper. They would like to publish an article on 'The history of the microscope and its inventors'. **Research** and **write** a short article on the first scientists involved in using the microscope and how it has changed over the years. Include images of microscopes.

B   **Compare** the size and shape of the leaf stomata or guard cells of different plants.

C   Carry out **research** to create and design your own microscope.

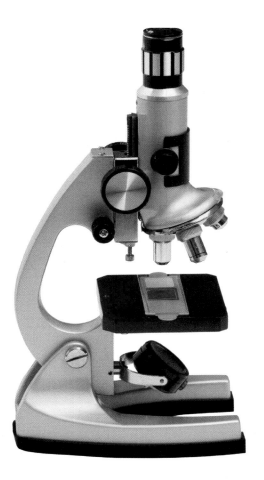

UNIT
2.1

Nutrition and Well-Being

Learning Outcomes

BWLO 6. Evaluate how human health is affected by inherited factors and environmental factors including nutrition, lifestyle choices; examine the role of micro-organisms in human health.

NSLO 3. Design, plan and conduct investigations; explain how reliability, accuracy, precision, fairness, safety, ethics and a selection of suitable equipment have been considered.

NSLO 4. Produce and select data (qualitatively/quantitatively), critically analyse data to identify patterns and relationships, **identify anomalous observations**, draw and justify conclusions.

NSLO 6. Conduct research relevant to a scientific issue, evaluate different sources of information including secondary data, understanding that a source may lack detail or show bias.

NSLO 7. Organise and communicate research and investigative findings in a variety of ways fit for purpose and audience, using relevant scientific terminology and representations.

R Teacher's reference

KEYWORDS

- artificially
- balanced
- calories
- carbohydrates
- cholesterol
- converted
- diet
- digestion
- environmental
- fats
- healthy
- inherit
- joules
- lifestyle
- micro-organisms
- minerals
- natural
- nutrients
- nutrition
- obesity
- preservatives
- proteins
- respiration
- vitamins
- well-being

LEARNING INTENTIONS

At the end of this unit you should:

1. Be able to name the food groups and list sources of each group.
2. Know the functions of the food groups.
3. Be able to recognise and understand the importance of a balanced diet.
4. Be able to recognise and understand the consequences of an unbalanced diet.
5. Be able to describe how to select foods from a food pyramid.
6. Be able to discuss our changing energy and nutritional needs at different stages of life.
7. Know how to read a food label and recognise the nutritional values on the label.
8. Understand that certain factors, including lifestyle, can affect and influence our food and drink choices.

The Need for Food

Animals and plants need food for survival. They take what they require from their surroundings. Plants make their own food and animals take in their food. Most foods that animals take in contain **nutrients**, which are essential for our body to function properly. Along with other functions, nutrients provide us with energy we need to survive. When food is taken in, it is broken down and **converted** into energy in the body. This process of an organism getting its energy from its surroundings is called **nutrition**. The energy that is released is mainly used for cell growth, movement, cell and tissue repair and fighting infection. The process of animals breaking down food is called **digestion** and the process of releasing the energy is called **respiration**.

The foods that nutrients are found in are divided into groups: **carbohydrates, proteins, fats, vitamins** and **minerals**.

By choosing the right foods we get the necessary nutrients to keep our bodies **healthy**, which then contributes to our **well-being**. It is a **lifestyle** choice. If we eat foods that are low in nutritional value, our bodies will not get enough of those vital nutrients.

What is a healthy lifestyle?

Nutrient: An essential substance for our bodies to function properly.

Nutrition: A process by which an organism gets its energy from its surroundings.

Digestion: The process of breaking down food.

Respiration: The release of energy from food.

Lifestyle: A particular way a person lives their life.

Well-being: A state of being content and healthy.

 **Checkpoint 1**

Will the food you have eaten today provide you with a good level of nutrients? Would you change your food choices in any way?

Fig. 02.01.01 Fuel to get you through the school day!

The Food Groups

As mentioned, the food groups are: carbohydrates, proteins, fats, vitamins and minerals. Foods that provide similar nutrients and functions for our body are grouped together. Water is not a food group, but it is essential for life and is present in most foods. Without water, we would not be able to absorb or digest food.

The Functions of the Food Groups

Protein Functions:	Growth and repair of cells
Fat Functions:	Stores energy and provides insulation
Carbohydrate Functions:	Provides energy
Vitamins Functions:	Keep the body's systems working
Minerals Functions:	Help the body to stay healthy

Carbohydrates

Carbohydrates are split into three groups: **sugar**, **starch** and **fibre**, and they can be either **simple** or **complex**. Simple carbohydrates are sugars that release energy quickly; complex carbohydrates are starchy foods that release energy more slowly and also provide fibre.

This means that starchy carbohydrates will keep you fuller for longer, while sugar-based carbohydrates provide a quick but short burst of energy.

Simple Carbohydrates: Give a quick release of energy in the body.

Complex/Starchy Carbohydrates: Give a slow release of energy in the body.

Proteins

Sources:
Meat, milk, eggs, fish, pulses (lentils, beans, peas), nuts, yams, cheese

Why the body needs proteins:
Growth and repair of body cells; cell replacement; creation of antibodies, hormones and enzymes

Lack of protein in the diet:
Cells would not form; illness due to lack of antibodies

Fig. 02.01.02 Foods that provide us with protein.

Did you know?

When carbohydrates are digested they are broken down into sugar units, but fibre cannot be digested fully by the body because it does not produce the enzymes to break up the sugar links, and so a lot of it passes through the body undigested. Fibre is very important for a healthy digestive system.

Carbohydrates (1) – Starches and Sugars

Sources:

Starch: Bread, pasta, rice, cereals, potatoes

Sugars: Cakes/biscuits, chocolate, jam, sweets, fizzy drinks

Why the body needs carbohydrate starches and sugars:

Provide energy – fuel for the body

Lack of carbohydrate in the diet:

Low energy

Too much sugar carbohydrate in the diet:

Weight gain; poor dental health

Fig. 02.01.03 Sources of starch carbohydrates.

Carbohydrates (2) – Fibre

Sources:

Fruit and vegetables, wholegrain foods (e.g. wholegrain rice, bread, pasta), lentils

Why the body needs fibre:

Maintains a healthy digestive system

Lack of fibre in the diet:

Constipation

Fig. 02.01.04 Sources of fibre.

Ⓡ Fats/Lipids/Oils

Fats are a misunderstood group. There are 'good' (unsaturated) fats and 'bad' (saturated) fats. Our bodies need fat, but we need to be aware of the amount of foods from this group we put into our bodies. Everything needs to be **balanced**.

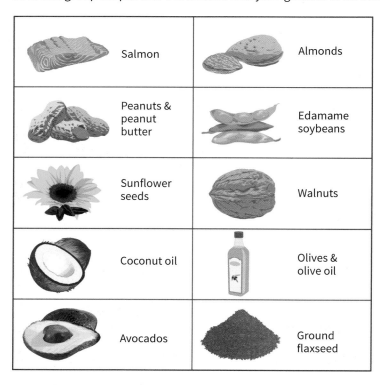

Salmon	Almonds
Peanuts & peanut butter	Edamame soybeans
Sunflower seeds	Walnuts
Coconut oil	Olives & olive oil
Avocados	Ground flaxseed

Fig. 02.01.05 (a) High-fat foods that are bad for you.

Fig. 02.01.05 (b) High-fat foods that are good for you.

Fats/Lipids/Oils

Two types of fat: unsaturated and saturated

Sources:

Unsaturated (*the good fat*): Olive oil, nuts, oily fish
Saturated (*the bad fat*): Butter, crisps, cakes/biscuits, burgers/kebabs

Why the body needs fats:
Store of energy; insulation/warmth; covers body organs

Lack of fat in the diet:
Body gets cold quickly; poor vitamin absorption

Too much fat in the diet:
Arteries can become blocked; high **cholesterol**

Minerals

Examples of minerals: calcium, iron

Sources:

Calcium: dairy products, tinned fish, green vegetables, cheese
Iron: red meat, fish, green vegetables, some breakfast cereals

Why the body needs calcium and iron:
Calcium: forms strong bones and teeth; helps blood to clot
Iron: helps formation of haemoglobin in the blood cells

Lack of calcium and iron in the diet/deficiency:
Calcium: weak bones
Iron: anaemia

Fig. 02.01.07 (a) Sources of calcium; (b) sources of iron.

Vitamins

Examples of vitamins: A, D, E, K, B, C

Sources:

A, D, E, K: green vegetables, meat, eggs, cheese, fish
B, C: vegetables, fruit, especially citrus fruits
D: sunshine

Why the body needs vitamins:
Only needed in small amounts but keep the body's systems functioning
A, D, E, K: healthy bones, protection against diseases
B, C: healthy immune system, keep skin healthy, healthy gums

Lack of vitamins C and D in the diet/deficiency:
Vitamin C: scurvy; bad skin, bad teeth and gums
Vitamin D: rickets in children results in softened and weakened bones

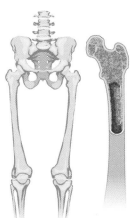
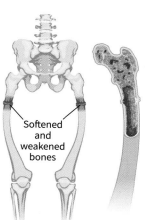

Fig. 02.01.06 Normal bone development (left) and poor bone development caused by rickets.

Water

Sources:
Fruit, vegetables, milk, etc.

Why the body needs water:
Hydration – every cell in the body needs water to function

Lack of water in the diet:
Inability of body to absorb nutrients from food; feeling of tiredness; headaches

Did you know?
Eighty per cent of your body is made up of water.

Checkpoint 2

(a) List the food groups that provide the essential nutrients for survival and the function of each group.
(b) Deficiency of which food group can result in anaemia?
(c) Why is water included in the food groups table?
(d) What is the result of a lack of fibre in the diet?
(e) List the sources of protein and carbohydrates you eat most often, dividing your list of carbohydrates into starch and sugary foods.
(f) Which type of carbohydrate releases energy into your body slowly and therefore keeps you fuller for longer?
(g) Which type of fat is better for you to eat?

The Effect of Inherited and Environmental Factors on Health

The factors that have a direct effect on our health and therefore our well-being can be:
- Inherited and/or
- Environmental.

You have no control over what you **inherit** as your genes are passed on from your parents. You may inherit disorders which require you to make different choices when it comes to food and lifestyle.

Environmental factors are what we choose to eat and what exercise to do, which can also be influenced by our surroundings. Other influences are peer pressure, health campaigns or initiatives, and how we are brought up.

Blood **cholesterol** level is an example of both an inherited and environmental factor. A person can have a history of high cholesterol in their family, but poor food and drink choices can contribute to a high blood cholesterol level. Cholesterol is a fatty substance. If a person has high blood cholesterol it means that there are high levels of this fatty substance in their blood vessels. This can lead to problems with blood flow and the heart.

Checkpoint 3

Describe how peer pressure affects the food choices young people make and the physical activities they take part in.

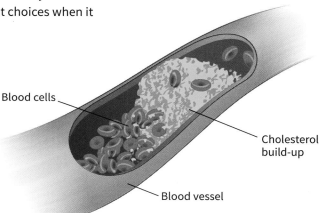
Blood cells
Cholesterol build-up
Blood vessel

Fig. 02.01.08 When there is a build-up of cholesterol in the blood vessels, the blood cells are not able to flow freely through the vessels.

The Nutritional Value of Food

The nutritional value of food is the amount of energy and nutrients a food provides. It is therefore important to know which foods contain which nutrients so that you can choose the right foods for a healthy and balanced **diet**.

- Eating too many starchy or sugary foods can lead to weight gain or **obesity**.
- Eating too much salt can lead to high blood pressure.
- Eating too much saturated fats can raise blood cholesterol levels.

Food is measured in the energy that it can provide: joules and **calories**. Both units will appear on food labels.

> 1000 joules is equal to 1 kilojoule (kJ)
> 1000 calories is equal to 1 kilocalorie (kcal)

Did you know?
Across the world, many people eat insects as they are a great source of protein. In some countries you can even buy chocolate-covered ants!

There are low-energy and high-energy foods. It is often thought that high-energy foods are bad for you. They are not, but you must use up the energy you take in or the result is weight gain or obesity.

| The *more* active you are | the *more* energy you need | the *more* high-energy value foods you need to eat |

Energy needs will also change depending on:

1. Age
2. Gender
3. Physical activity levels
4. Body size

Recommended daily kilojoule (KJ) intake, according to the Food Safety Authority of Ireland			
Boys (14–18)	**Boys (14–18)**	**Girls (14–18)**	**Girls (14–18)**
Not active	Moderately active	Not active	Moderately active
2200 kJ	2400–2800 kJ	1800 kJ	2000 kJ

Table 02.01.01.

✓ Checkpoint 4

(a) Write a short paragraph describing the energy requirements needed for the following stages in the life cycle, giving reasons to support your choices and comparing the requirements at all three stages:
   (i) A baby learning to crawl and walk
   (ii) A child who goes to school and plays with their toys when they get home
   (iii) A teenager who goes to school, has music practice after school and goes to scouts in the evening.

b) Using *Table 02.01.01*, answer the following questions:
   (i) What is the difference in the energy requirements of these three people:
   • A young person sitting exams
   • A young sports performer
   • A young person who plays video games in the evenings
   (ii) Of these three people, who needs to eat more? Who needs to eat less?

® What is a Food Label and How Do We Read it?

The **Food Safety Authority of Ireland** specifies that Irish food packaging must state:
• The name of the food
• If the food has been processed in any way. If so, the process must be included in the title, e.g. salted peanuts, smoked cheese, etc.

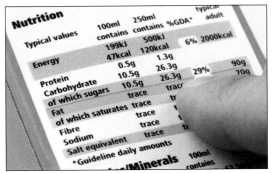

Fig. 02.01.09 All packaged foods must have a food label.

Food labels must, by law, list:
- The energy value of the product
- The amounts of fat and saturates, carbohydrate, sugars, protein and salt in the product.
- The information to back up any nutrition or health claim made.

Fig. 02.01.10 (a) A health claim ('actively lowers cholesterol'); (b) A nutrition claim ('Low fat/Low sugar').

What does a food label display?

Food labels display what is in the product and the recommended daily serving of the product, or 'reference intake'. This information helps the customer to make informed food choices.

Fig. 02.01.11 shows what 40 g of this particular food provides. 'Sugars' means simple sugar carbohydrates and not high-energy-value carbohydrates. The word 'saturates' means the amount of saturated fat. The reference intake states that this food per 40 g will provide 1.5 g of fat, which is 2% of the recommended daily intake. *Fig. 02.01.12* shows what a 100 g serving of this product will provide, as well as giving a more detailed nutritional guide.

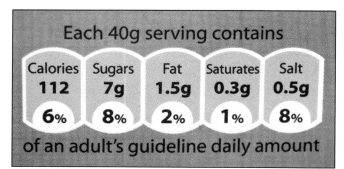

Fig. 02.01.11.

However, food labels can often be confusing and hard to read. To help consumers read these labels, governments have provided 'food shopping cards' (*Fig. 02.01.13*), which guide us on the nutritional information on food labels. These 'cards' have a traffic light code, indicating which amounts are considered high, medium and low in the various food groups.

Fig. 02.01.13 A food shopping card.

Watch out!
Don't forget to look at how many servings are in the package!

Nutrition Information

Typical Values	Per 100g	Per Serving with 125ml semi-skimmed milk
Energy	1632kJ	739kJ
	385kcal	174kcal
Protein	7.5g	6.6g
Carbohydrate	85.2g	31.7g
of which sugars	9.7g	9.0g
Fat	1.2g	2.3g
of which saturates	0.4g	1.5g
Fibre	1.5g	0.6g
Sodium	0.29g	0.15g
equivalent as salt	0.7g	0.4g
Vitamin D	5.0µg	1.5µg
	(100% RDA*)	(30% RDA*)
Thiamin (B1)	1.1mg	0.4mg
	(100% RDA*)	(35% RDA*)
Riboflavin (B2)	1.4mg	0.7mg
	(100% RDA*)	(46% RDA*)
Niacin	16.0mg	4.9mg
	(100% RDA*)	(31% RDA*)
Vitamin B6	1.4mg	0.5mg
	(100% RDA*)	(36% RDA*)
Folic Acid	200.0µg	68.0µg
	(100% RDA*)	(34% RDA*)
Vitamin B12	2.5µg	1.3µg
	(100% RDA*)	(50% RDA*)
Pantothenic Acid	6.0mg	2.2mg
	(100% RDA*)	(37% RDA*)
Iron	14.0mg	4.3mg
	(100% RDA*)	(30% RDA*)

*RDA: Recommended Daily Allowance

Guideline Daily Allowance for the Average Adult

Calories	2000
Sugar	90g
Fat	70g
Saturated fat	20g
Salt	6g

These figures are for average adults of normal weight. Requirements will vary with age, size and activity level.

This pack contains approximately 20 servings of 30g.

Fig. 02.01.12.

Checkpoint 5

(a) Looking back at *Fig. 02.01.12*, give a brief explanation of the amount and type of carbohydrates found in this food.

(b) You have been asked to carry out a nutritional analysis of the following three foods to determine their nutritional value.

1

COOKING INSTRUCTIONS

HOB: Empty contents into a saucepan and stir gently while heating. Do not boil or overcook as this will impair the flavour.

MICROWAVE (Category E - 850W):
Microwave ovens vary. The following is a guide only. Empty contents into a microwaveable container and cover. Heat on full power for 1½ minutes. Stir, then heat for a further 1 minute. Check that product is hot before serving.

INGREDIENTS

Beans (51%), Tomatoes (33%), Water, Sugar, Salt, Modified Cornflour, Spirit Vinegar, Spice Extracts, Herb Extract

NUTRITION INFORMATION

Typical Values	Per 100g	Per serving (207g)
Energy	309kJ/73kcal	640kJ / 151kcal
Protein	4.9g	10.0g
Carbohydrate (of which sugars)	12.9g (5.0g)	26.7g (10.4g)
Fat (of which saturates)	0.2g (Trace)	0.4g (Trace)
Fibre	3.8g	7.9g
Sodium	0.3g	0.7g
Salt equivalent	0.8g	1.7g

DIETARY INFORMATION

Suitable for a gluten free diet.

Suitable for vegetarians.

A low glycaemic index (GI) food.

No artificial colours, flavours or preservatives.
A serving contains 1.7g of an adult's recommended daily salt intake of 6g.

STORAGE

Empty unused contents into a suitable covered container. Keep refrigerated and use within 2 days.

2

Additional Information
• Suitable for vegetarians ⓥ

Typical Nutritional Information

	Cheese & Onion Per 100g	Per 25g Serving	%*	Salt & Vinegar Per 100g	Per 25g Serving	%*	Smokey Bacon Per 100g	Per 25g Serving	%*
Energy	2162kJ 519kcal	541kJ 130kcal	7%	2251kJ 540kcal	563kJ 135kcal	7%	2253kJ 541kcal	563kJ 135kcal	7%
Fat	34.3g	8.6g	12%	34.5g	8.6g	12%	34.4g	8.6g	12%
of which saturates	3.9g	1.0g	5%	3.5g	0.9g	4%	3.4g	0.9g	4%
Carbohydrate	46g	11.5g	5%	49.7g	12.4g	5%	49.6g	12.4g	5%
of which sugars	0.6g	0.2g	1%	2.1g	0.5g	1%	2.1g	0.5g	1%
Protein	5.8g	1.5g	3%	5.1g	1.3g	3%	5.6g	1.4g	3%
Salt	1.5g	0.4g	7%	2.3g	0.6g	9%	2.3g	0.6g	9%

*Reference Intake of an average adult (8400kJ / 2000kcal)

3

NUTRITIONAL INFORMATION

Typical values		Per 100 g	Per bar 21.5 g	% RI* per bar
Energy	kJ/kcal	2384/572	510/122	6
Fat of which Saturates	g g	37.3 17.3	8 3.7	11 19
Carbohydrates of which Sugars	g g	49.5 41.2	10.6 8.9	4 10
Protein	g	8.6	1.8	4
Salt	g	0.27	0.06	1

* Reference intake of an average adult (80 kJ / 2000 kcal)

(i) Analyse these foods' labels, including a bar chart in your analysis. Consider carefully what headings to use and how to present your findings.

(ii) Extend your work by comparing your findings against those of other students. Are some of them similar?

(c) Using the information you have gathered on food labels and nutritional values, discuss the following opinion and put forward your views.

• Enjoying a healthy diet is simply about getting the balance and choices right. There are no unhealthy or even healthy foods. It is rather a question of a healthy or unhealthy diet.

Food Additives and Preservatives

A food **additive** is a substance that can be either **naturally** or **artificially** made and is used in processing food to:

- preserve it
- improve or keep the nutrient value
- add flavour and aroma
- enhance colour (which enhances the appearance of the food)
- improve texture or taste (by the addition of flavours and spices).

Natural food additives include:

- Herbs or spices
- Vinegar
- Salt
- Some sugars

Preservatives are artificial additives which give processed foods a longer shelf life by stopping the growth of **micro-organisms**.

Food additives can also add to the nutrient value of foods. For example, some breakfast cereals are 'fortified with iron', which means that extra iron has been added. However, many artificial additives have *no* nutritional benefit. Some examples are:

- artificial sweeteners
- acid added to fruit juices
- dyes and colouring
- chemicals added to processed meat products
- stabilisers and emulsifiers (which retain the food's texture and stop some ingredients separating, especially in reduced-fat and low-fat foods).

With the increase in the availability and variety of processed foods, there has been a massive surge in the chemical misuse of additives to completely change the natural flavour and colour of foods, as well as to preserve them far beyond their natural shelf life. Food additives must be approved by food authorities, and some are only allowed to be added to a certain 'safe' level. To identify additives, they are given an 'E' number, which acts like a code. For example, E100 numbers identify colours and E200 numbers identify preservatives.

> **Preservatives:** Artificial additives which prevent food spoilage.

A Balanced Diet

A balanced diet is a diet that provides enough nutrients in the correct amounts to keep your body healthy. Our diet should include all five food groups – carbohydrates, fats, proteins, minerals and vitamins – and water. We need these foods for their energy values, to maintain the workings of our body and to allow new cells to be made. Crash diets or fad diets often omit some food groups, which ignores the fact that we need foods from all the food groups to stay healthy. If you are missing out on a food group (like carbohydrates or fats) or on vital vitamins and minerals, your health can suffer.

> **A balanced diet should include:**
>
> - A variety of foods from each of the levels of the food pyramid (*Fig. 02.01.14*).
> - Foods that are low in fat (especially saturated fats), sugar and salt.
> - At least five portions of fruit and vegetables daily.
> - Plenty of water – approximately 2 litres a day.

How Often and How Much?

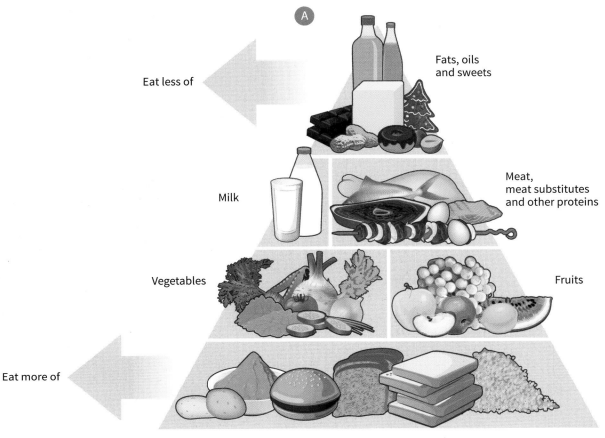

A

Eat less of

Fats, oils
and sweets

Milk

Meat,
meat substitutes
and other proteins

Vegetables

Fruits

Eat more of

Breads, grains and other starches

We need to eat foods from each level of the food pyramid every day (*Fig. 02.01.14 (b)*). We know the foods we should eat and how many servings we need, but what is the serving or the portion size that we should be eating? We could be eating the right foods every day but getting the portion size wrong! *Fig. 02.01.15* shows the European guide to portion sizes of some common foods.

*Fig. 02.01.14 (a) The food pyramid;
(b) Recommended servings of each food group.*

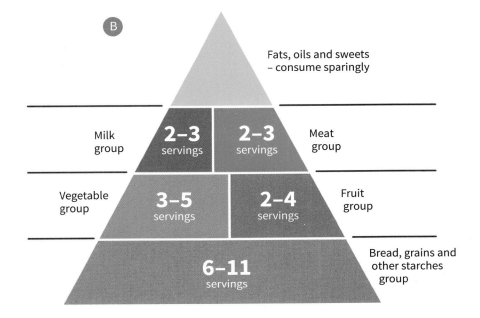

B

Fats, oils and sweets
– consume sparingly

Milk
group

2–3
servings

2–3
servings

Meat
group

Vegetable
group

3–5
servings

2–4
servings

Fruit
group

6–11
servings

Bread, grains and
other starches
group

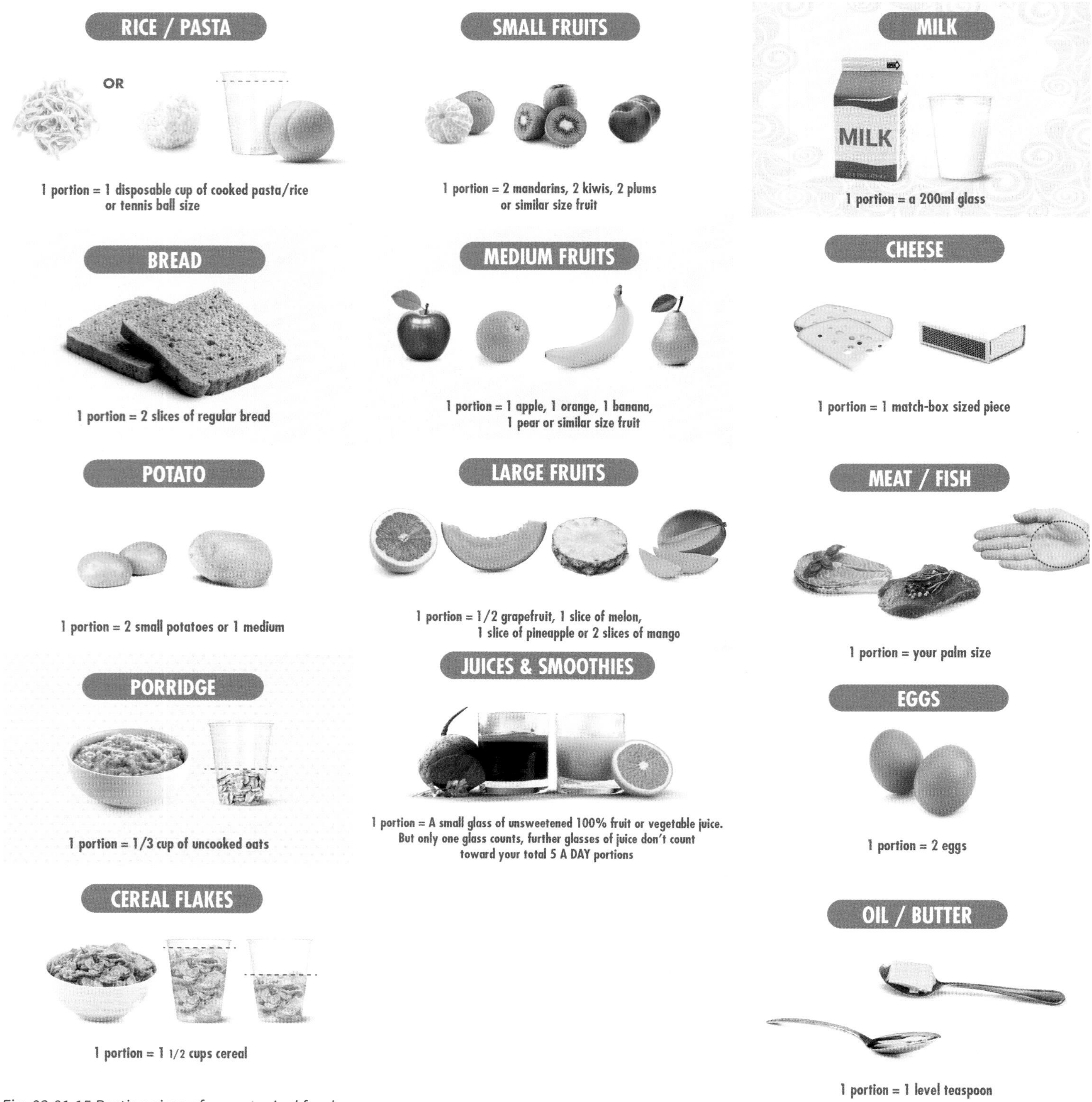

RICE / PASTA

OR

1 portion = 1 disposable cup of cooked pasta/rice or tennis ball size

SMALL FRUITS

1 portion = 2 mandarins, 2 kiwis, 2 plums or similar size fruit

MILK

1 portion = a 200ml glass

BREAD

1 portion = 2 slices of regular bread

MEDIUM FRUITS

1 portion = 1 apple, 1 orange, 1 banana, 1 pear or similar size fruit

CHEESE

1 portion = 1 match-box sized piece

POTATO

1 portion = 2 small potatoes or 1 medium

LARGE FRUITS

1 portion = 1/2 grapefruit, 1 slice of melon, 1 slice of pineapple or 2 slices of mango

MEAT / FISH

1 portion = your palm size

PORRIDGE

1 portion = 1/3 cup of uncooked oats

JUICES & SMOOTHIES

1 portion = A small glass of unsweetened 100% fruit or vegetable juice. But only one glass counts, further glasses of juice don't count toward your total 5 A DAY portions

EGGS

1 portion = 2 eggs

CEREAL FLAKES

1 portion = 1 1/2 cups cereal

OIL / BUTTER

1 portion = 1 level teaspoon

Fig. 02.01.15 Portion sizes of some typical foods.

Checkpoint 6

(a) What are food additives?

(b) Name some natural food additives.

(c) In pairs or individually, put together a daily menu for a student comprising breakfast, lunch, dinner and snacks. Aim for a nutritionally balanced menu. When your menu is complete, give a brief explanation as to why you have chosen the foods that you have.

An Unbalanced Diet

An unbalanced diet is a diet rich in foods that do not contain all the nutrients we need for our daily activities. Foods are eaten in the wrong portion sizes, and there are too many choices from the wrong area of the food pyramid (e.g. sugary foods and drinks). Foods high in sugar and fat often tend to be low in vitamins and minerals. Such foods are also low in nutritional value, and therefore do not satisfy our hunger in the long term, leading to more snacking and eating. Sustained consumption of such foods, as well as eating inappropriate portion sizes, will gradually lead to a person damaging their health, most evidently in obesity, but also in other health problems such as constipation, heart disease and diabetes.

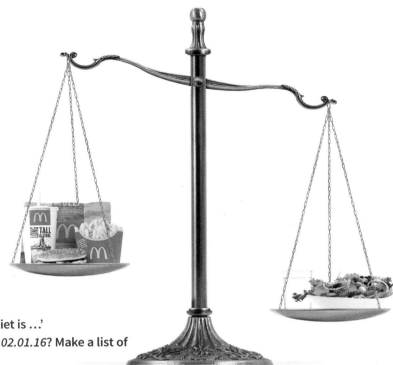

Fig. 02.01.16 Some healthy and unhealthy food choices.

⊘ Checkpoint 7

(a) Complete this sentence: 'In my opinion, an unbalanced diet is …'
(b) Why do you think the scales are tipped as they are in *Fig. 02.01.16*? Make a list of your points.
(c) Using the food pyramid in *Fig. 02.01.14 (a)*, draw what you think an unbalanced pyramid might look like.
(d) **R** What can an unbalanced diet lead to?

Avoiding Weight Gain

We know that if we take in more energy from food than we use up, we will gain weight. So we should aim for a balance.

Too much weight gain is referred to as **obesity**. Obesity can lead to illnesses that directly affect your health, such as heart disease, some cancers, type 2 diabetes and osteoarthritis.

So what can you do to ensure you follow a good eating regime?
* Follow the healthy food pyramid for a balanced diet.
* Have regular, small meals to prevent your body storing fat.
* Increase your physical activity levels to use up more energy.
* Reduce the amount of fat in the diet.
* Never skip meals.
* Avoid sugary drinks.

WHAT I HAVE LEARNED...

- Nutrients are substances essential for our body to function.
- Nutrition is a process whereby an organism gets its energy from its surroundings.
- 'Lifestyle' refers to a particular way a person lives their life.
- A state of well-being is a state of being content and healthy.
- There are five food groups: carbohydrates, proteins, fats, vitamins and minerals.
- The sources, functions and deficiency symptoms of the foods from the food groups.
- Sugar carbohydrates release energy into the body quickly; complex or starchy carbohydrates release energy slowly.
- Both inherited and environmental factors can affect the food choices we make.
- The nutritional value of food is the amount of energy and nutrients it provides, and is displayed on a food label.
- Food additives can be naturally or artificially made.
- A balanced diet is a diet that provides enough nutrients in the correct amounts to keep the body healthy.
- The consequences of an unbalanced diet can be weight gain and illness.

Question Time

Copy and Complete

In this unit I learned that making the right lifestyle choices is important. We need to eat food to release _____ in our cells that will allow us to carry out daily _____. The food we eat during the day must be from a variety of food _____ such as carbohydrates, _____, fats, _____ and minerals. This ensures that we eat a _____ diet that will keep us _____. Carbohydrates are found in _____ and pasta and they give us _____. _____ are found in eggs, meat and milk and help our _____ to grow. Healthy, _____ fats are found in olive oil, nuts and oily fish. They are important as they keep our bodies warm and our organs _____. Vitamins and minerals are found in _____ and _____. They are really important as they help our organ systems to work. A food _____ is found on all the packaged foods we eat and it tells us what is in the food, and how much _____ that food will give us. This then helps us eat a ____ _____diet and take in the energy that we need. Taking in more food than we need can result in _____ gain so the _____ size of the foods we eat is also important. Some foods have _____ and preservatives added to them to make them look appealing.

Questions

1. Copy *Table 02.01.02* and fill it in using the information you learned in this unit.

Food group/ Nutrient	Food source(s)	Function	Effect on health if not present in diet	Energy value (if known)
Protein				
Vitamins				
Fats				
Minerals				
Carbohydrates				
Fibre				
Water				

Table 02.01.02.

2. Which of the following people (all of a similar height and age) needs the most energy, and why?
   An artist • a builder • a teacher • a shopkeeper
3. Can you think of any examples of health problems that arise from not eating a balanced diet?
4. List two ways of maintaining a healthy weight.
5. Make a list of foods that an under-16 footballer or basketball player will need to eat consistently if they are training and hoping to make the team.

6. Make a list of the ingredients you would need to make a pizza from scratch, research the ingredients in a frozen pizza, and suggest the ingredients that would be in a takeaway pizza.

   (i) Compare and discuss your lists with the class.
   (ii) Why would the taste of the takeaway pizza be different from that of the home-made pizza?

Inquiry

A The Venus flytrap – is it a plant or an animal? **Research** the Venus flytrap – how they get their energy – and **present** your findings as a poster.

B **Investigate** the sugar content in the top three foods that your classmates enjoy. Remember, you will find the sugar content on the label of packaged foods.

   (i)   Design a survey.
   (ii) Present your results using a graph.
   (iii) Present your findings.

C Regarding these two plates of food, **place** each food you see in its food group and **list** the benefit of eating it. Confirm which meal, A or B, is of more nutritional value.

How Our Body Systems Interact

Learning Outcomes

BWLO 4. Describe the structure, function and interactions of the organs of the human digestive, circulatory and respiratory systems.

R Teacher's reference

KEYWORDS

circulatory system

digestive system

excretory system

hormonal system

immune system

muscular system

nervous system

reproductive system

respiratory system

skeletal system

LEARNING INTENTIONS

At the end of this unit you should:

1. Be able to identify the organ systems of the body and what these systems do.
2. Be able to identify how the different organs of the body interact with each other.
3. Be able to discuss how most organ systems depend on another system to function fully.
4. Be able to discuss some factors that can affect the workings of our body's systems.

What is a Body System?

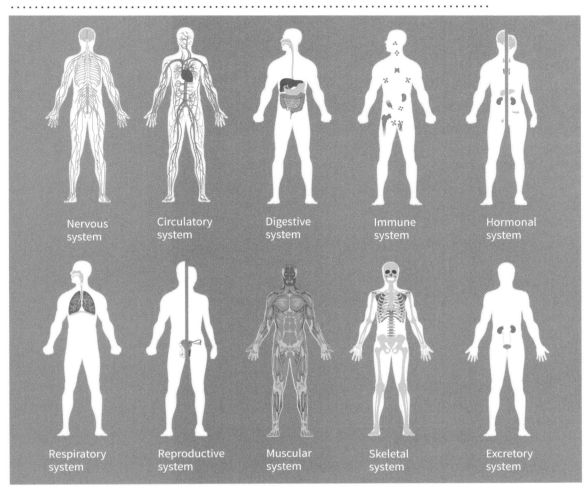

Nervous system

Circulatory system

Digestive system

Immune system

Hormonal system

Respiratory system

Reproductive system

Muscular system

Skeletal system

Excretory system

Fig. 03.01.01 Ten of the body's systems and their position in the body.

What body system(s) are you using to read this sentence?

Our body is made up of organ systems, which are made up of organs, which are made up of tissues, which are made up of specialised cells. Each cell, tissue, organ and system has a specific job or set of jobs to do. The systems in your body work together to enable your body to function. The systems depend on each other.

As we remember from *Unit 1.1*:

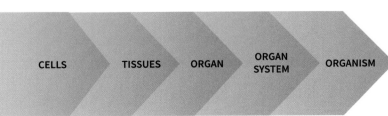

CELLS → TISSUES → ORGAN → ORGAN SYSTEM → ORGANISM

Organ System: A group of organs working together.

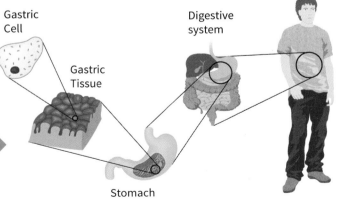

Gastric Cell

Gastric Tissue

Stomach

Digestive system

Fig. 03.01.02 The make-up of the digestive system.

R The following is an overview of systems in our body, their organs and body parts, functions and how they interact with other systems.

System	Organs and body parts involved in its function	Function of the system	How this system works with other systems within the body	
1. Nervous	• Brain • Spinal cord • Nerves	• Sends electrical impulses or messages to and from brain and spinal cord to all parts of the body • Picks up information for your senses • Controls the body	**Nervous & Circulatory:** • Brain controls heartbeat	**Nervous & all other systems** • Controls all the systems
2. Circulatory	• Heart • Blood vessels • Blood cells	• Transports substances around the body • Heart pumps blood around the body	**Circulatory & Respiratory:** • Blood transports oxygen to body cells **Circulatory & Digestive:** • Blood transports nutrients to body cells **Circulatory & Excretory:** • Blood is filtered by the kidneys	**Circulatory & Hormone:** • Blood transports hormones to organs **Circulatory & Immune:** • Blood transports white blood cells around the body **Circulatory & Nervous:** • The heartbeat is controlled by the brain
3. Digestive	• Mouth • Oesophagus • Stomach • Intestines • Anus	• Takes in and digests food • Absorbs nutrients into bloodstream • Glands – salivary, gall bladder and pancreas – release digestive juices into bloodstream to help break down food	**Digestion & Respiratory:** • Digested food and oxygen react to make energy at the body's cells **Digestive & Circulatory:** • Digested nutrients are transported to body cells via the blood **Digestive, Respiratory & Circulatory:** • Digested nutrients and oxygen are taken in; the blood in the circulatory system transports them to body cells	**Digestion & Excretory:** • Food taken into body is broken down, nutrients are released from the food and waste is excreted **Digestion & Muscular:** • Muscles are used to help move food through the digestive system
4. Immune/defence	• White blood cells • Lymph • Spleen • Tonsils • Bone marrow	• Protects the body against harmful organisms (bacteria and viruses)	**Immune & Circulatory:** • White blood cells are transported around the body in the blood **Immune & Skeletal:** • Bone marrow in the bones make the white blood cells	
5. Hormonal Pancreas	• Glands	• Releases hormones which help control the body's functions, e.g. controls growth with growth hormones, releases hormones that control the reproductive system	**Hormonal & Circulatory:** • Hormones are transported in the blood to target organs **Hormonal & Nervous:** • Nervous system controls hormone release **Hormonal & Reproductive:** • Hormones control the development of reproductive organs and control reproduction	

BIOLOGY

System	Organs and body parts involved in its function	Function of the system	How this system works with other systems within the body	
6. Respiratory	• Nose • Windpipe (trachea) • Lungs	• The exchange of gases (O_2 in, CO_2 out)	**Respiratory & Circulatory** • Takes in O_2, which is transported in the blood to cells • Removes CO_2 from the blood and from the body **Respiratory & Excretory** • Removes excretory waste via the lungs	**Respiratory & Nervous** • Controls breathing **Respiratory & Muscular** • The diaphragm and intercostal muscles control breathing
7. Reproductive	• Egg • Sperm • Sex organs	• Produce babies or young	**Reproductive & Hormonal:** • Hormones control the development of reproductive cells and organs **Reproductive & Muscular:** • Muscular movements allow baby to be born	
8. Muscular	• Muscles • Tendons	• Allows movement as the muscles contract and relax • Gives the body posture	**Muscular & Skeletal:** • Muscles are attached to bones via tendons, which allows movement **Muscular & Digestive:** • Muscles need the nutrients from the digestive system to work • Food moves through digestive system by muscular movements	**Muscular & Circulatory:** • The heart muscle pumps blood **Respiratory & Muscular:** • The diaphragm and intercostal muscles control breathing **Muscular & Nervous:** • The nerve cells in muscles control their movement
9. Skeletal	• All 206 bones • Cartilage • Ligaments	• Protects organs • Provides shape, support • Allows movement • Bone marrow produces blood cells	**Skeletal & Muscular** • Allows movement **Skeletal & Circulatory** • Bone marrow produces blood cells	**Skeletal & Immune:** • Bone marrow produces white blood cells **Skeletal & Circulatory & Respiratory:** • The bones protect these systems' organs
10. Excretory	• Kidneys • Bladder • Skin	• Filters blood • Removal of waste (substances the body does not need) • Releases sweat	**Excretory & Circulatory:** • Filter waste out of the blood at the kidneys	**Excretory & Respiratory:** • Removes CO_2 from body at the lungs

Table 03.01.01 An overview of body systems, parts, functions and how they work with each other.

✓ Checkpoint 1

(a) Make a list of the systems in the body. Beside each system, name the organs and tissues that are involved in its operation.

(b) Choose two systems that you find of interest and briefly describe how these systems work, and how they work with and interact with other systems.

(c) What system has the following organs and body parts: white blood cells, lymph, spleen, tonsils, bone marrow. What is the function of this system?

(d) What system has the following functions?
- Sends electrical impulses or messages to and from brain and spinal cord to all parts of the body.
- Picks up information for your senses.
- Controls your body.

What organs and body parts are involved in this system's workings? Name the other systems that it interacts with.

(e) Name the organ and body parts involved in the workings of the excretory system, its function and other systems it interacts with.

The Systems

Did you know?
A bone is an organ. It is made up of tissues and produces cells.

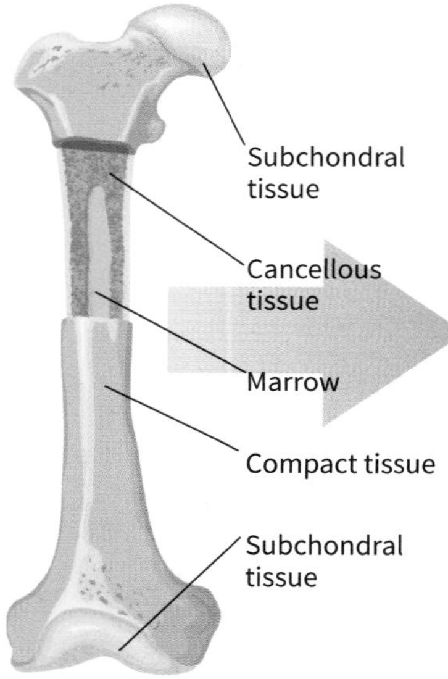

Fig. 03.01.03 (a) A bone and its tissues.

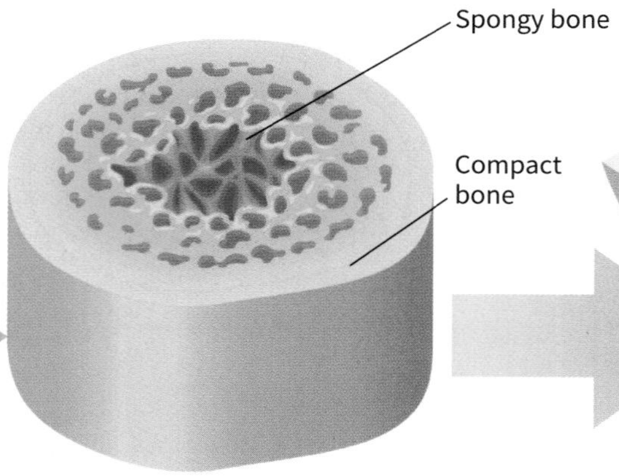

Fig. 03.01.03 (b) Transverse section of a bone.

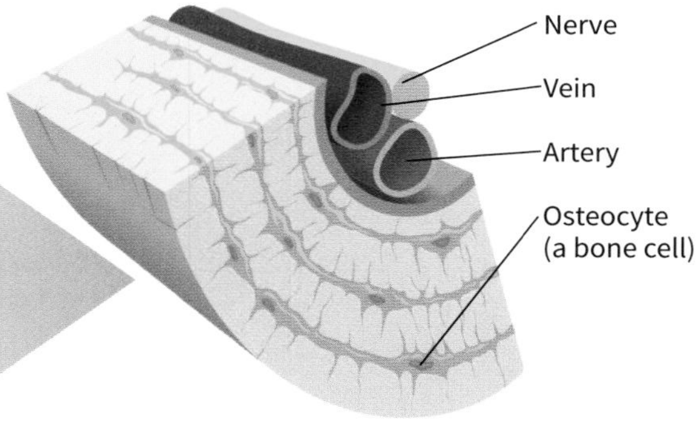

Fig. 03.01.03 (c) Section of compact bone showing bone cells.

How do the Body's Systems Work Together?

Most activities that our bodies carry out need the support of two or more organ systems working together. For example:

If you walk from the kitchen to the bathroom:

- Muscles and bones are needed to walk. The muscles are in the *muscular system* and the bones are in the *skeletal system*.

- The muscles need energy to move. This energy comes from nutrients broken down by the *digestive system* and oxygen from the *respiratory system*.
- Nutrients, oxygen and energy are transported to the muscles by the blood in the *circulatory system*.
- The *nervous system* tells your brain it needs to move and in turn it sends electrical messages to the muscles to enable them to move.

This simple task uses six systems!

 **Checkpoint 2**

With a partner or on your own, write a detailed list of the systems involved in two of the following four daily tasks, explaining how each of the systems are involved in the task.

- **Packing your school bag**
- **Eating your lunch**
- **Running a 5 km race**
- **Running for the bus**

Factors Affecting how Body Systems Function

Lifestyle choices (e.g. diet, exercise, drug use) and **disease** can affect body systems, how they carry out their functions and how they work together. For example, in the circulatory system, a healthy heart pumps blood around our body more efficiently than an unhealthy heart. A poor diet can cause blockages in the blood vessels and in turn force the heart to work harder (see *Unit 2.1*).

However, some factors that affect the workings and healthy function of the body systems are inherited conditions that people are born with. For example:

- *Asthma* causes difficulty in breathing. If the asthma is not controlled, less oxygen is taken in, which affects the respiratory system.
- *Cystic fibrosis* affects the lungs (part of the respiratory system) and the digestive system. The lungs can develop infections, and enzymes produced in the body are prevented from breaking down and absorbing food.
- *Sickle-cell anaemia* is a disorder of the circulatory system in which the red blood cells change shape and block the flow of blood in the blood vessels. This blockage can cause severe pain and organs can become damaged. It is most common in people with African ancestors, and it is also found in people from the Caribbean, Mediterranean countries and Asia.

Fig. 03.01.04 Think of all the body systems that need to work together for a simple walk from the kitchen to the bathroom.

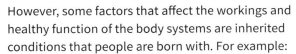 **WHAT I HAVE LEARNED...**

- There are many different organ systems in the body.
- The organ systems in the body depend on each other to function.
- How some of the systems interact with each other.
- Lifestyle choices can affect the workings of a healthy body system.
- Some factors that affect the workings of the body's systems are inherited. Others can be caused by disease or unhealthy lifestyle choices.

Question Time

Copy and Complete

In this unit I learned that our body is made up of cells, _____, organs and _____ _____. Each system has a _____ job within the body, and each system works _____ with other systems to allow them to function. Each system depends on each other to work properly. The circulatory system is made up of the _____, blood vessels, blood and _____. Its function is to _____ blood and _____ materials around the body. The nervous system is made up of the brain, _____ _____ and _____. Its function is to send _____ to and from the _____ and the spinal cord. The nervous _____ controls the activities of the body. When we take food into our body it is our _____ system that is involved. When we walk, talk, run and jump it is our _____ and _____ systems that are involved. A lot of our systems _____ with each other. For example: our digestive system breaks down _____ and it is carried in the _____ by the _____ system.

Questions

1. Which system is responsible for making our blood cells?
2. Which system controls our heartbeat?
3. ⓡ Study *Table 03.01.02*, which shows how the systems work together. Write down which system each number represents. Explain the interaction that is happening at each letter on the diagram.

Inquiry

ⓡ In your copy, draw three large outlines of the human body, numbering them 1, 2 and 3. **Draw** in and **label** the parts of (1) the respiratory system; (2) the circulatory system; and (3) the digestive system.

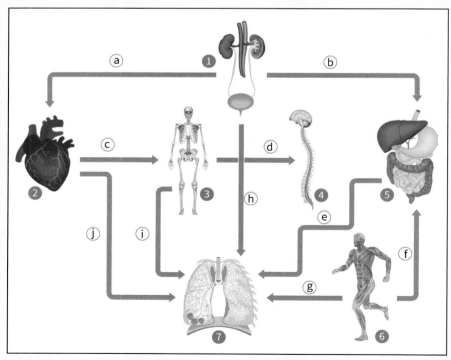

Table 03.01.02.

UNIT
3.2

The Digestive System

Learning Outcomes

BWLO 4. Describe the structure, function and interactions of the organs of the human digestive, circulatory and respiratory **systems.**

NSLO 3. Design, plan and conduct investigations; explain how reliability, accuracy, precision, fairness, **safety, ethics and a selection of suitable equipment have been considered.**

NSLO 4. Produce and select data (qualitatively/quantitatively), critically analyse data to identify patterns and relationships, identify anomalous observations, **draw and justify conclusions.**

NSLO 6. Conduct research relevant to a scientific issue, evaluate different sources of information including secondary data, understanding that a source may lack detail or show bias.

R Teacher's reference

KEYWORDS

absorption
amylase
appendix
bile
catalyst
chemical digestion
enzymes
faeces
gall bladder
gut flora
large intestine
liver
maltose
mechanical digestion
nutrients
oesophagus
pancreas
rectum
salivary glands
small intestine
soluble
stomach

LEARNING INTENTIONS

At the end of this unit you should:

1. Be able to describe what the word 'digestion' means.
2. Be able to distinguish between the two types of digestion.
3. Be able to discuss the role of the teeth, tongue and stomach in digestion.
4. Be able to describe mechanical and chemical digestion and the difference between them.
5. Know that digestion involves breaking down large molecules into smaller soluble ones.
6. Be able to describe what happens to food when it is broken down.
7. Be able to describe the role and the importance of enzymes in digestion.

The Digestive, Circulatory and Respiratory Systems

The digestive, circulatory and respiratory systems are very closely linked and they all depend on each other. If one system fails, so will the others. This knock-on effect can even permanently damage or cause another system to fail completely. For example, if the **liver** fails it can cause the kidneys to fail, soon followed by other body systems. The body's goal is to use the **nutrients** from food, and oxygen to make energy. Some nutrients are used for the growth and repair of cells. In this unit we shall focus on how the digestive system works, but first, examine *Fig. 03.02.01* to see the importance of the digestive, circulatory and respiratory systems to each other.

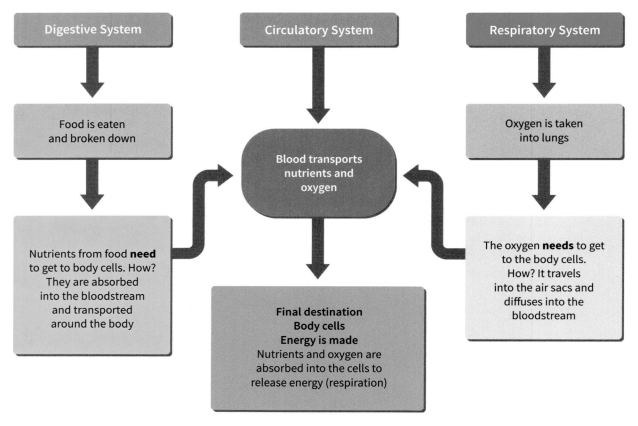

Fig. 03.02.01 How the digestive, respiratory and circulatory systems interact.

The Digestive System

Our digestive system is all about getting food into our body, breaking the food down, releasing the nutrients and absorbing them into our bloodstream to bring to our body cells. Once we put food into our mouth, the digestive process starts.

We need energy to break down our food. We also need food to give us energy. So why does digestion take so long? What happens to digested food after it has been absorbed into the blood?

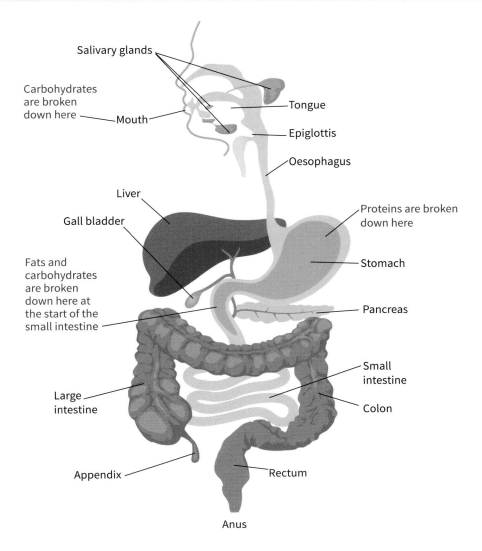

Salivary glands

Carbohydrates
are broken
down here

Mouth

Tongue

Epiglottis

Oesophagus

Liver

Gall bladder

Proteins are broken
down here

Fats and
carbohydrates
are broken
down here at
the start of the
small intestine

Stomach

Pancreas

Small
intestine

Large
intestine

Colon

Appendix

Rectum

Anus

Fig. 03.02.02 The structure of the digestive system. Different food groups are broken down in different parts of the system.

How is Food Broken Down?

The food we take in is broken down in two ways:

- Mechanical digestion
- Chemical digestion.

Mechanical digestion is the physical breaking down of food by the tongue, the teeth (by chewing) and the **stomach** (by churning).

In **chemical digestion**, **enzymes** or digestive juices are added to the food in the digestive system to help break it down. Enzymes speed up the breakdown of the food and are therefore known as biological **catalysts**.

 Checkpoint 1

You are about to eat a meal that consists of a homemade beef burger with a bread bun and a slice of cheese on top, served with a small side salad and no dressing. Give a detailed explanation of what happens to the food as it passes through the digestive system. For example, what happens in the mouth? Where does the food go then? Use *Fig. 03.02.02* to help you.

Part of Digestive System	Function	Food group broken down	Type of Digestion
Mouth	• Takes food in • Breaks food down, chemically and mechanically	Carbohydrates	• Mechanical – teeth grind, tear, bite and chew • Chemical – enzyme salivary amylase is released
Oesophagus	• A muscular tube that allows food to be passed to the stomach		
Stomach	• Churns food • Contains hydrochloric acid (HCl), which kills bacteria and allows enzymes to work • Enzymes are present to break down food	Proteins	• Mechanical – churning • Chemical – adding of enzyme pepsin
Liver	• **Bile** is made • Toxins are broken down	Bile breaks fat into smaller parts	
Pancreas	• Releases hormones such as insulin, which keeps our blood sugars at the right levels • Releases juices that contain enzymes into small intestine	The juices released contain enzymes to break down protein, fats and carbohydrates	• Chemical – releases digestive juices
Small intestine	• **Soluble** food is absorbed into the blood (**absorption**)	Fats and carbohydrates	
Large intestine	• Water is absorbed from the food (leaving **faeces**)		
Rectum	• Undigested food is stored here as faeces • It then gets moved out of the body through the anus		

R *Table 03.02.01 Functions of the digestive system.*

What is the Appendix?

The **appendix** is found at the **large intestine**. Recent research shows that the appendix could be a source of natural or good gut bacteria that live in our body. It was originally needed as our ancestors would have eaten a lot of plants and it helped with the digestion of tough fibre.

 **Checkpoint 2**

R Test your knowledge of the functions of the parts of the digestive system. See how many you can remember, then check *Table 03.02.01* to see how many you got right.

Digestion: The breaking down of food.

Catalyst: Speeds up a chemical reaction without being used itself in the reaction.

Enzymes and Absorption

The food molecules taken into our mouths are too big to be absorbed. The teeth, tongue and stomach make these molecules smaller, but the body needs more help to break them down. It gets this help from chemicals called **enzymes**.

Enzymes speed up the breakdown of the food molecules without being used up in the reaction, and are referred to as **catalysts**.

Each enzyme only breaks down one particular food group, in the way that a key only fits one lock. For example, the enzyme **amylase** breaks down starch into **maltose**. Amylase is found in saliva, which is produced by the **salivary glands**.

Absorption: The process in which the nutrients in the food are passed into the bloodstream at the small intestine.

Enzyme: A protein that speeds up a chemical reaction in an organism.

Food broken down	Enzyme involved	Product from the reaction
Starch	Amylase	Maltose
	Amylase breaks down starch into smaller molecules	

Table 03.02.02 Enzyme action on starch.

 **Checkpoint 3**

R *Table 03.02.03* shows the results of an investigation into how temperature can affect the speed at which the enzyme amylase works.

(i)   Study the results and suggest at which temperature the enzyme works best.
(ii) Give an explanation for your choice of temperature.
(iii) Present the results as a graph. (*Hint:* x axis = temperature; y axis = rate of amylase activity [how quickly it happens].)
(iv) Suggest a reason why you think enzymes may need a specific temperature to work at. Refer to your graph in your answer.

Amylase activity (rate of activity)	Temperature (°C)
0	0
1	10
2.5	20
5	30
7	40
4.5	50
0	60

Table 03.02.03 Results of an investigation into amylase.

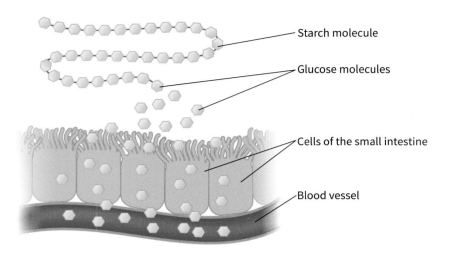

Fig. 03.02.03 Absorption of glucose into the walls of the small intestine and into the bloodstream.

Investigation 03.02.01: **Investigating what happens when food is taken into your body**

Equipment: A pop-sock, pestle and mortar, bin, clear plastic bag, funnel, hydrochloric acid, amylase solution, pepsin, water, a scissors, a sandwich (imagine a sandwich, halved, then halved again, then halved again: this is the size of your sample).

Instructions:
1. Working with a partner, match up each body part in the digestion list below with an everyday object in the equipment list that could represent it. (More than one body part can be matched with the equipment list.)
   Digestion list: Intestines • teeth • tongue • mouth • toilet • stomach • oesophagus
   Equipment list: Pop-sock • pestle and mortar • bin • clear plastic bag • funnel
2. Now that you have the equipment list linked to the digestive system and understand the need for the chemicals, plan an investigation to show what happens when food (your sandwich sample) enters your body.
3. Where would you find hydrochloric acid in your body?
4. What does the amylase solution represent?

What did you learn?
1. Explain what involvement the chemicals had in the breakdown of your food.
2. You needed to add water at different stages during the investigation. Can you link this to real-life experiences? Make a note of at least two links.
3. Explain how the pestle and mortar relates to your mouth, including references to the chemicals and the water.

Fig. 03.02.04 Pestle and mortar.

We Need Bacteria!

When we think of bacteria we think of diseases, but bacteria are essential to our health. Bacteria are found all over our body, for example on our skin and eyes, in our mouth and small intestine, but most of them are in the large intestine. The bacteria cells that live on us and in us are harmless most of the time. They help our bodies function, and in turn we give them a safe place to live. The bacteria in our digestive system are also called **gut flora**.

How do Bacteria Help Us?

- On our skin, some bacteria help keep other harmful bacteria out.
- Some bacteria produce enzymes that help break down fibre.
- Our gut bacteria can produce vitamin K and some B vitamins. One job of vitamin K is to help clot blood. One job of the vitamin B group is to promote healthy hair and nails.
- Bacteria help our immune or defence system prepare for when it needs to respond to harmful bacteria that may cause disease.
- Some break down hormones in the body when they are no longer needed.

The digestive system relies on the combination of bacteria, enzymes, blood and its own organs, all working together, to be an efficient system.

Have you ever been prescribed a course of antibiotics? An antibiotic is used to treat infections or a disease caused by bacteria, but it is actually made from micro-organisms such as bacteria and fungi that work to kill other micro-organisms or prevent them growing. We need bacteria!

> **Did you know?**
> We have approximately ten times more bacteria cells than human cells in our body: 100 trillion bacteria cells as compared to 10 trillion human cells!

WHAT I HAVE LEARNED...

- The digestive system breaks down food so that it can be used by the body.
- The order of the parts of the digestive system.
- The functions of the parts of the digestive system.
- The two different types of digestion: physical and chemical.
- Where each food group is broken down in the digestive system.
- Amylase is used in chemical digestion and is released into the mouth.
- Large molecules are broken down into smaller parts during digestion.

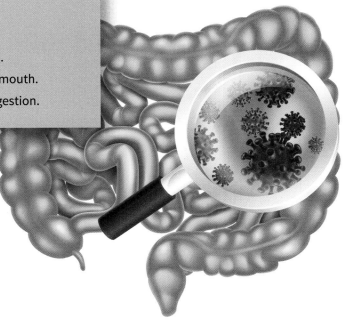

Question Time

Copy and Complete

In this unit I learned that the digestive system _____ _____ food. We take food into our mouths and this is where _____ starts. Your _____ and tongue break food down into smaller parts, but it is also broken down by an enzyme called _____, which is found in saliva. Enzymes help to _____ up the breakdown of food. After the mouth the ____ moves through the_____. It then moves into the stomach, which _____ and mixes the food with an _____. This kills any _____ that might be present in the food, and there are also enzymes in the stomach. After the stomach the food moves through the _____ _____. It is here that the nutrients from the food move across into the _____. This is called _____. The rest of the food parts move through the _____ intestine, where _____ is taken out of the food. The remaining substances leave the body through the _____.

Questions

1. Use the following keywords to describe what digestion is:

   • food breaks down   • mechanical
   • chemically   • nutrients

2. In your copy, name the parts labelled A–E in the diagram of the digestive system (*Fig. 03.02.05*).

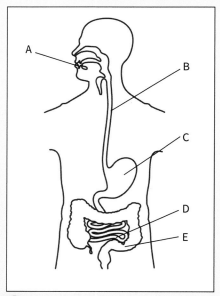

R   *Fig. 03.02.05 Name the labelled parts.*

3. Copy and complete *Table 03.02.04,* filling in the functions of the parts of the digestive system.

Parts of the Digestive System	Functions
Mouth	
Oesophagus	
Stomach	
Small intestine	
Large intestine	

Table 03.02.04.

4. Make a list of the main food groups and state where each group is broken down in the digestive system.
5. Explain what absorption is and why it is so important to the body.
6. Suggest a reason why the digestive system relies on the circulatory system.
7. How are the nutrients from the foods we digest used by the body?
8. Large food molecules cannot pass through the walls of the small intestine into the bloodstream. What chemicals help with the breakdown of these foods in the body? Give an example of this chemical action.

Inquiry

A   The national science museum has asked you to **produce** a 'travel guide' to the digestive system and how it breaks down food. Your guide must be colourful, feature pictures/diagrams, and include the following information:
   • What places you will visit after the mouth
   • What happens at the places you visit
   • If you will meet any other attractions on the way that might help food break down.

B   **Research** whether genetically modified foods have an effect on the bacteria that we need in our bodies.

C   **Design** a poster or IT information sheet on a disorder of the digestive system. You could choose one of the following: Crohn's disease; gastritis; coeliac disease. Include:
   • Name of disease or disorder
   • Symptoms
   • Causes
   • Treatment (if any)
   • How a person adapts to having the disorder.

3.3

The Circulatory System

Learning Outcomes

BWLO 4. Describe the structure, function and interactions of the organs of **the** human digestive, **circulatory**, and respiratory **systems.**

NSLO 3. Design, plan and conduct investigations; explain how reliability, accuracy, precision, fairness, safety, ethics and a selection of suitable equipment have been considered.

NSLO 4. Produce and select data (qualitatively/quantitatively), critically analyse data to identify patterns and relationships, identify anomalous observations, draw and justify conclusions.

NSLO 6. Conduct research relevant to a scientific issue, evaluate different sources of information including secondary data, understanding that a source may lack detail or show bias.

R Teacher's reference

KEYWORDS

- aorta
- artery
- atrium
- blood
- bone marrow
- capillaries
- carbon dioxide
- cardiac
- circulation
- clotting
- haemoglobin
- heart
- infection
- oxygen
- phlebotomist
- plasma
- platelets
- pulmonary
- pulse
- red blood cell
- septum
- vein
- vena cava
- ventricle
- white blood cell

LEARNING INTENTIONS

At the end of this unit you should:

1. Be able to list the parts of the circulatory system.
2. Be able to describe the functions of the blood and what the blood contains.
3. Know the functions of the parts of the blood.
4. Be able to explain the function of the heart and its interaction with the rest of the body systems.
5. Be able to identify the structures of the heart.
6. Be able to explain the directions of blood flow around the body.
7. Understand the positive effects of exercise on the heart.
8. Know what a pulse is and how to measure it.
9. Know that certain factors can affect the workings of the circulatory system.

What is the Circulatory System?

The circulatory system is a **transport system**. It includes:

- The **blood**
- The blood vessels:
  - Arteries
  - Veins
  - Capillaries
- The **heart**.

These parts of the system all work together to transport many substances around the body, the two most important of which are:

- Nutrients from the digestive system
- **Oxygen** from the lungs of the respiratory system.

The bloodstream carries nutrients and oxygen to the body's cells, which use them to release energy through the process of **respiration**. The bloodstream then transports the products – the products the body needs as well as waste products – from the cells.

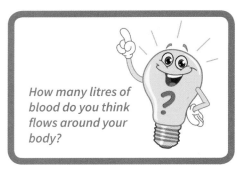

How many litres of blood do you think flows around your body?

Respiration: The release of energy from food through the intake of oxygen, and the release of carbon dioxide.

Did you know?
Blood is actually a type of tissue. Can you name any other tissues in the body?

Discovering that blood circulates

William Harvey, an English physician, made the discovery of the **circulation** of blood. Before this, most people believed that food was converted into blood when it was eaten. Harvey considered the heart as a pump and proved through investigations that the heart works to pump blood around the body.

Fig. 03.03.01 William Harvey (1578–1657).

Ⓡ What is Blood?

We all know that we cannot live without blood. For example, we would be unable to fight **infection**, keep warm, cool down, or get rid of our own waste products.

- Blood is a tissue, as it is made up of many different cells suspended in it, each with a specific function.
- It is carried by vessels.
- There is approximately five litres of blood flowing around the body, continuously pumped around the body by the heart.
- Blood has a liquid part called **plasma**, which is 90% water, that carries the substances around the body Some of the substances transported in the plasma are:
  - Nutrients
  - **White blood cells**
  - **Red blood cells**
  - **Platelets**
  - Hormones
  - **Carbon dioxide**
  - Enzymes
  - Salts
  - Urea

What are Blood Cells and Where Do They Come From?

There are cells within the blood — red blood cells, white blood cells and platelets — which are made in our bones at the **bone marrow**. The bone marrow is the soft tissue inside the bones which produces all the blood cells. Bones have blood vessels to carry the cells around the body.

Functions of blood
- To transport substances around the body
- To protect the body against infection
- To help keep the body temperature at 37°C.

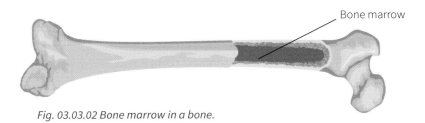

Fig. 03.03.02 Bone marrow in a bone.

✓ Checkpoint 1

(a) The nutrients released from digestion need to reach the body cells. What process in the body allows this to happen?

(b) How does the oxygen taken in by the lungs reach a body cell?

(c) Name the three types of blood vessel.

(d) Briefly outline what blood is and the functions of blood.

(e) Using a graduated cylinder and water, measure out five litres to give an indication of how much blood is flowing around the body.

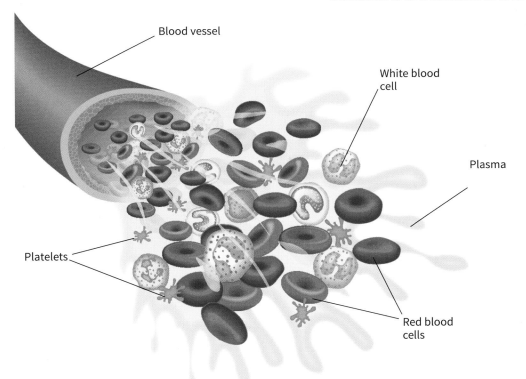

Fig. 03.03.03 The make-up of blood.

Part of the blood	Function	Part of the blood	Function
Red blood cells	*Transport* oxygen around the body. Red blood cells contain **haemoglobin**, a red pigment, which carries the oxygen.	**White blood cells**	*Protect* the body against infection (destroy bacteria that could cause disease) by making antibodies, which help destroy micro-organisms.
Platelets The yellow area is the platelet cells in action clotting blood	Tiny fragments of cells that help to *clot* blood.	**Plasma** The pale yellow liquid part of the blood, made up of 90% water Plasma (55%) White blood cells and platelets (<1%) Red blood cells (45%)	*Transports* substances around the body, e.g. nutrients, CO$_2$, hormones, enzymes, which are all dissolved in the plasma and carried around the body.

Table 03.03.01 Parts and functions of the blood.

⊘ Checkpoint 2

(a) A **phlebotomist** is a person who is trained to take blood from a patient.
   List what would be found in a typical blood sample.
(b) How do red blood cells transport oxygen around the body?
(c) What is the function of a white blood cell?
(d) When you cut yourself, a scab forms on your skin to stop the bleeding.
   Can you suggest what a scab is made of and why it is important that they form?
(e) Name four substances that are transported around the body in the plasma of the blood.

The Blood Vessels

The main function of the blood is to transport substances around the body. So how does it do this important job? It uses **blood vessels**: **arteries**, **veins** and **capillaries.**

The arteries – the thickest of the blood vessels – and the veins – thinner than arteries – never meet but have a capillary network from one to the other, allowing blood to flow through.

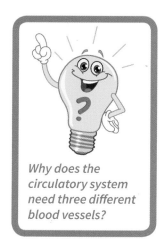

Why does the circulatory system need three different blood vessels?

Fig.03.03.04 shows the structure of the vessels. You will notice that different colours are used for different blood vessels. Red represents the arteries, which carry blood that is rich in oxygen; and blue represents veins, which carry blood that is rich in carbon dioxide. The arrows show the direction that blood flows in. Blood only flows in one direction around our bodies.

Table 03.03.02 gives a description of the vessels and visually shows the difference between them. Take a closer look at the difference between the images of the vessels and then read the descriptions.

In your body the blood that is rich in oxygen is bright red and the blood rich in carbon dioxide is a deeper, darker red.

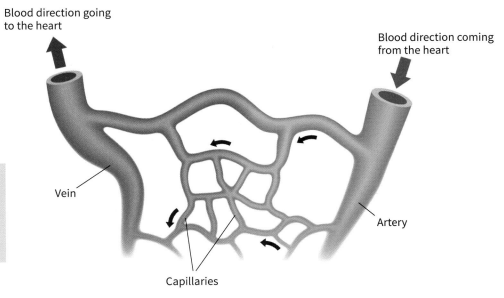

Blood direction going to the heart

Blood direction coming from the heart

Vein

Artery

Capillaries

Fig. 03.03.04 The blood vessel supply.

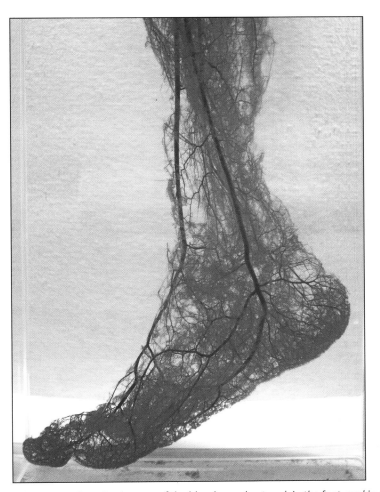

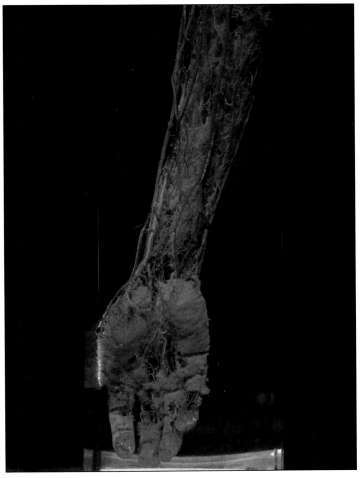

Fig.03.03.05 Amazing images of the blood vessel network in the foot, and in the arm and hand.

Blood vessel	Description	Blood vessel	Description
Artery  Small lumen · Thick wall	• Thick wall • Small lumen (area where blood flows) • Blood flows fast under high pressure • Carries blood away from the heart • Carries blood with oxygen in it • No valves	**Capillaries** One cell thick	• Very thin walls – one cell thick • Thin walls allow substances to pass across • Carries both blood rich in oxygen and blood rich in carbon dioxide • Capillary network surrounds organs
Vein Large lumen · Thin wall	• Thin wall • Large lumen • Blood flows slowly under low pressure • Carries blood into the heart • Carries blood with carbon dioxide in it • Has valves	Veins have **valves**. Why? To prevent the backflow of blood 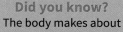 A valve in a vein ⬅ Direction of blood flow	

Table 03.03.02 Blood vessels.

Checkpoint 3

(a) Describe the job that each blood vessel carries out.
(b) Compare the pressure on the walls of an artery and that on a vein.
(c) Name the molecules that the artery and the vein carry.
(d) Why do capillaries have thin walls?

The Amazing Heart

Put your hand on your heart. Where did you place your hand? On your left side? The heart is actually in the centre and slightly to the left of the chest, as shown in *Fig. 03.03.06*. It is protected by the ribcage, and the heartbeats are controlled by signals from the brain.

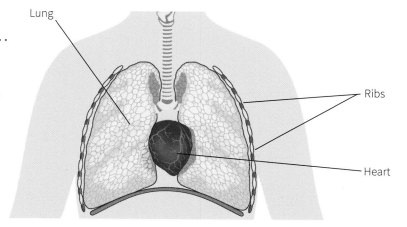
Fig. 03.03.06 The position of the heart in the body.

Function of the heart	To pump blood around the body
Protected by	The ribcage
What controls the heart?	The main controller of the heart is the brain
The muscle of the heart	The heart is made up of a muscle – the **cardiac muscle** – that never tires
Average number of heartbeats	In a day: approximately 100 000 times In a year: about 35 million times (The number of heartbeats varies with age and with a person's health and fitness levels)

Table 03.03.03 Some facts about the heart.

What the Heart Looks Like

Take a look at what a real sheep's heart looks like in *Fig. 03.03.07* (this is very similar to a human heart) and the structure of the heart in *Fig. 03.03.08*. Look closely at the arrows on the diagram. These show the direction in which the blood flows into and out of the heart.

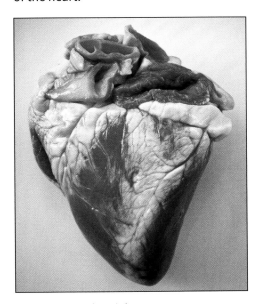

Fig. 03.03.07 A sheep's heart.

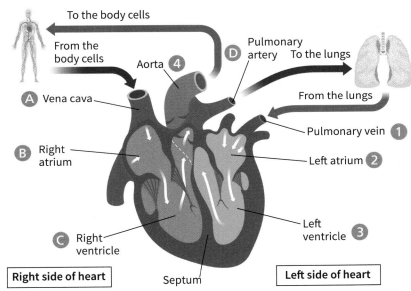

Fig. 03.03.08 The structure of the human heart and the direction of blood flow.

In *Fig. 03.03.08*, you will notice that the right side is on the left as you look at it and the left side is on the right. This is because you are looking at the heart as if you were looking in the mirror.

The heart is made up of four chambers:
* Two **atria**, one on the left and one on the right (atria is the plural of **atrium**)
* Two **ventricles**, one on the left and one on the right.

It has valves that control the blood flow from the atrium down into the ventricle.

The **septum** is the wall that separates the sides of the heart. But why do the two sides need separating? The heart is actually a double pump. It has to pump the blood along two pathways or circuits, and this happens at the same time, so the two circuits have to be separated.

Remember
L O R D
Left Oxygenated   Right Deoxygenated

Left & right swap sides
L = Left side of heart
O = Blood with oxygen
R = Right side of heart
D = Blood with carbon dioxide

✓ Checkpoint 4

(a) What is the muscle of the heart called?

(b) The heart is a pump. What is its function?

(c) What protects the heart in your body?

(d) Which organ controls the heart?

(e) List the four chambers of the heart.

(f) The right side of the heart carries blood rich in what?

(g) The left side of the heart carries blood rich in what?

The Flow of Blood

Blood flows along two pathways.
The heart pumps blood:

1. From the lungs → to the heart → to the body cells

and

2. From the body cells → to the heart → to the lungs

Along these pathways the blood picks up different molecules.

Pathway 1 takes oxygen from the lungs to the cells.

Pathway 2 takes carbon dioxide from the cells to the lungs.

Both pathways have to go through the heart – the heart is the pump that keeps the blood flowing.

Ⓡ The flow of blood goes into and out of the heart on the left and right side. Look again at the diagram of the human heart and the direction of blood flow, this time taking note of the numbers and letters.

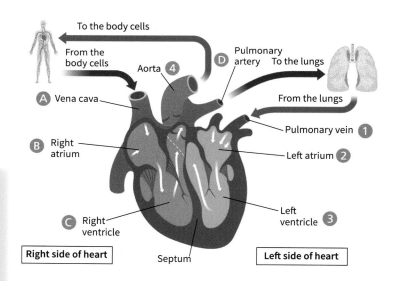

① The blood is coming from the lungs with lots of oxygen in it. It enters the heart through the **pulmonary** vein.

② The blood enters the left atrium and gets pushed down into the left ventricle.

③ At the left ventricle the blood gets pumped up and out with great force through the **aorta**.

④ The blood in the aorta is pumped to all the body cells.

Ⓐ In the **vena cava** there is blood from the body cells that contains carbon dioxide.

Ⓑ The blood enters the right atrium and gets pushed down into the right ventricle.

Ⓒ At the right ventricle, the blood gets pumped up and out through the pulmonary artery.

Ⓓ The blood in the pulmonary artery gets pumped to the lungs to get rid of the carbon dioxide.

Checkpoint 5

(a) The blood coming from the lungs contains lots of what molecule?

(b) What are the two reasons the blood leaves the heart and goes to the lungs?

(c) (R) Using the information from *Fig. 03.03.08* on blood flow, copy *Fig. 03.03.09* and fill in the labels.

(d) With the information you have learned about the blood flow within the circulatory system, write a story or comic strip on the following:
- You are an oxygen molecule that has just entered the lungs. Describe your journey around the circulatory system.

Exercise and the Heart

It is important to exercise regularly to maintain a healthy heart. Why is this so? The heart is a **muscle**, so the more exercise you do, the stronger your heart becomes and therefore the better it will work.

Every time the muscle of the heart contracts or beats, blood is forced through an artery. The pressure from this force is referred to as a **pulse**. The number of times the heart beats is known as a heart rate or pulse rate. A pulse rate depends on that person's age, gender, body size, health and whether the person is active or not.

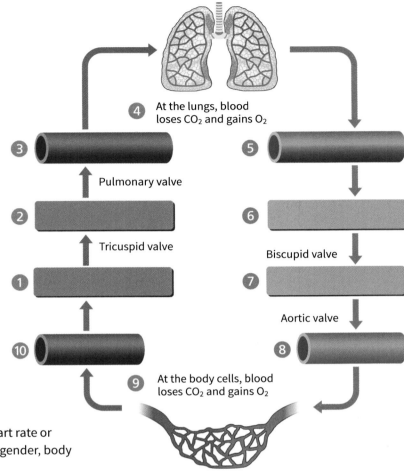

At the lungs, blood loses CO_2 and gains O_2

Pulmonary valve

Tricuspid valve

Biscupid valve

Aortic valve

At the body cells, blood loses CO_2 and gains O_2

Fig. 03.03.09 Blood flow through the heart.

🔍 Investigation 03.03.01: **How exercise affects your body**

Equipment: An area to exercise, a stopwatch.

Instructions: Plan and carry out an investigation on how exercise can directly affect your body.
Present your results both in a table and on a graph.

What did you learn?

1. Will exercise directly affect your body? Support your answer with an explanation.
2. Do you think there will be a pattern in your results?
3. Suggest a scientific explanation for the pattern.
4. Make a recommendation on how you could refine or extend your investigation if it were to be repeated.
5. The heart can beat up to 150–200 times per minute during intense exercise. Why do you think the average person's heart could not withstand this heart rate all the time?

The heart is a pump that needs to work efficiently to push the blood around the body. If the pump isn't working, the blood doesn't get pushed around. The heart can have trouble working if the vessels that transport the blood are blocked – this means that the heart has to work harder to pump the blood through the narrow vessels (see *Fig. 02.01.08* in *Unit 2.1*). If parts of the circulatory system are not working properly, this will have a knock-on effect on other systems.

Factors that can affect the circulatory system

- Smoking
- Poor diet, e.g. high cholesterol levels
- Little or no exercise
- Obesity
- Stress
- High blood pressure

Did you know?
All our blood passes through the heart, but the heart only uses 5% of the blood for itself. The kidney uses 25% and the liver uses 40%.

How the circulatory, digestive and respiratory systems are linked

Circulatory and digestive systems: Nutrient molecules from the digestion of food are transported to the circulatory system. This takes place across the wall of the small intestine, which has a large blood supply to allow this to happen.

Circulatory and respiratory systems: In the respiratory system there is an exchange of carbon dioxide and oxygen gases. Each alveolus in the lungs (see *Unit 3.4*) is surrounded by thin capillaries so that the gases can pass in and out of the blood. The blood transports the carbon dioxide to the lungs and the oxygen away from the lungs.

Why do these substances need to be transported? The body cells release energy to allow us to carry out daily activities. In order for our cells to make this energy they need a supply of nutrients and oxygen, and for carbon dioxide to be removed. The circulatory system transports the substances to the cells.

⊘ Checkpoint 6

Ⓡ Aidan is an office administrator who spends most of his day sitting at a desk. There is a lot of pressure in his job to meet deadlines and he manages a large number of staff.

For lunch he often eats from a nearby fast-food outlet or buys sandwiches from a nearby garage. His meals therefore contain a lot of fat and sugar. He likes to add salt and sauces to most of his food. He rarely eats salads or fruit and snacks on crisps or chocolate. He smokes about twenty cigarettes per day.

Although he lives within walking distance of work, he always uses his car for the short journey and does not take part in any fitness activities outside work.

(a) Examine Aidan's lifestyle. List the factors that you think would affect the health of his heart.

(b) Explain *how* each factor might affect his heart. You could present your answers as a table, using these headings:
- Factors affecting the heart
- Explanation

WHAT I HAVE LEARNED...

- The circulatory system is made up of the blood, the heart and blood vessels.
- The main function of the blood is to transport substances around the body.
- Blood is made up of cells (red and white blood cells and platelets), and a liquid called plasma.
- The job of the red blood cells is to carry oxygen around the body; the white blood cells protect the body against infection; and the platelets help clot blood.
- The three types of blood vessels are arteries, veins and capillaries. Arteries carry blood away from the heart and veins carry blood into the heart. Capillaries have thin walls to allow some substances to pass through them.
- The heart is protected by the ribcage.
- The function of the heart is to pump blood around the body.
- The heart has four chambers – two atria and two ventricles.
- Blood flows along two pathways: (1) from the lungs to the heart to the cells; and (2) from the cells to the heart to the lungs.
- Pulse rate is the number of times the heart beats. The heart beats because of the pressure of the force created when the muscle of the heart contracts, forcing blood through an artery.
- How to investigate the effect of exercise on pulse rate.

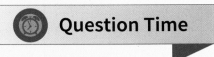

Question Time

Copy and Complete

In this unit I learned that the heart is part of the _____ system and is responsible for_____ blood around the body. It is made up of cardiac _____ that never _____ working. In the circulatory system there are three main blood vessels that work with the heart to transport blood around the body. These are _____, _____ and _____. The _____ are responsible for carrying blood away from the heart. The _____ carry blood to the heart and the _____ connect the arteries and the veins. The arteries have _____ walls. Veins have valves that prevent the _____ of blood. The heart has _____ chambers. The two at the top are called _____ and the two at the bottom are called _____. The wall that separates the two sides of the heart is called the _____. The job of the blood is to _____ substances around the _____ to the body cells. There are two pathways that the blood can take. The first one is where blood is _____ from the _____ to the heart to the _____ _____. Here the blood is rich in _____ as the body _____ need it to make energy. The second pathway is where the blood travels from the _____ to the heart and then to the _____. Here the blood is rich in carbon dioxide.

Questions

1. Using labelled diagrams, explain the parts of the circulatory system.
2. Explain why our body needs a circulatory system.
3. Copy and complete *Table 03.03.04* by matching each function with the correct part of the blood.

Parts of the blood	Functions	
A White blood cell	1 Helps clot the blood	A
B Plasma	2 Carries nutrients from the digestive system and other substances around the body	B
C Red blood cell	3 Produces antibodies	C
D Platelets	4 Transports oxygen around the body	D

Table 03.03.04.

4. Haemoglobin is the red pigment in red blood cells. Iron is the mineral that is essential in maintaining healthy levels of haemoglobin. What is the haemoglobin responsible for?

5. 'A capillary is a vessel with specialised cells.' Recalling information in *Unit 1.1*, suggest why this statement is true.

6. Copy and complete *Table 03.03.05* as instructed.

Blood vessel	Artery	Vein	Capillary
Draw a diagram of each vessel			
Describe the features	Lumen: Valves: Walls:	Lumen: Valves: Walls:	Lumen: Valves: Walls:
Substances flowing in vessels	Blood flow carried under _____ pressure. Carry blood with a high amount of _____	Blood flow carried under _____ pressure. Carry blood with a high amount of _____	Connect _____ to _____

Table 03.03.05.

7. What is the purpose of the valves in a vein?

8. Compare what is in the blood after it leaves the heart and when it returns to the heart.

9. If the blood did not contain platelets, what would happen when you cut yourself?

10. Suggest what might happen if blood did not contain white blood cells.

11. Explain each of the following statements.
    (i)   Our pulse increases when we exercise.
    (ii) Smoking affects the heart.
    (iii) High-cholesterol foods are bad for us.

12. (R) Sketch this diagram of the heart and name the parts labelled 1–12.

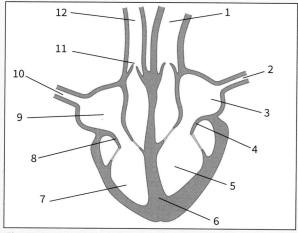

Fig. 03.03.10.

Inquiry

A You are visiting a primary school where you are explaining to the pupils what the circulatory system is. A pupil asks you, 'Where does the blood go after leaving the heart?'
Write what your response to the pupil would be.

B As a class or home task, **create** in a jar or bottle a sample of blood and all its components using different sweets or foods. (*Hint:* Buttons, Mentos sweets and runny jelly could be used, or red food colouring.)

C **Research** *and* **prepare** a presentation on factors that can affect the circulatory system.
    (i)   State how each factor can affect the workings of the circulatory system.
    (ii) Aim to use more than one source for your research.
    (iii) Do you agree with all the information you have sourced? When you were comparing the information you gathered and choosing what to present, did you think that the articles put their views on the factors across differently? Might there have been a reason behind this?

3.4

The Respiratory System

Learning Outcomes

BWLO 4. Describe the structure, function and interactions of the organs of the human digestive, circulatory, and **respiratory systems.**

NSLO 1. Appreciate how scientists work and how scientific ideas are modified over time.

NSLO 4. Produce and select data (qualitatively/quantitatively), critically analyse data to identify patterns and relationships, identify anomalous observations, draw and justify conclusions.

NSLO 5. Review and reflect on the skills and thinking used in carrying out investigations, and apply learning and skills to solving problems in unfamiliar contexts.

NSLO 6. Conduct research relevant to a scientific issue, evaluate different sources of information including secondary data, understanding that a source may lack detail or show bias.

NSLO 7. Organise and communicate research and investigate findings in a variety of ways fit for purpose and audience, using relevant scientific terminology and representations.

R Teacher's reference

KEYWORDS

alveoli
asthma
bronchiole
bronchitis
bronchus
carbon
  dioxide
diaphragm
emphysema
exhaling
gas exchange
inhaling
intercostal
  muscles

lung
  capacity
lungs
oxygen
respiration
ribcage
ribs
thoracic
  cavity
trachea

LEARNING INTENTIONS

At the end of this unit you should:

1. Be able to list the parts of the respiratory system and explain their function.
2. Know where in the body the lungs are located and what protects them.
3. Know what gases are exchanged at the lungs.
4. Know how gas exchange occurs.
5. Be able to distinguish between how we breathe in and how we breathe out.
6. Know the difference between the breath we take in and the breath we let out.
7. Be able to describe factors that affect the respiratory system.

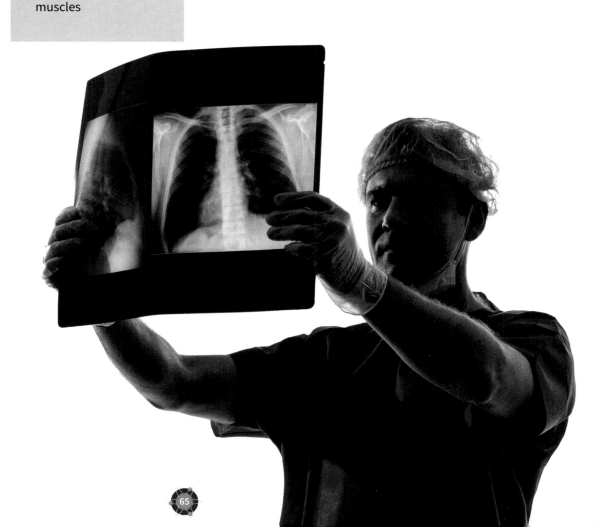

What is the Respiratory System?

Fig. 03.04.01 shows parts of the respiratory system, including inside our **lungs**. The main purpose of the respiratory system is to take air into our lungs and to get rid of a waste product, **carbon dioxide**. We are taking **oxygen** in and letting carbon dioxide out. There are two muscles that help our respiratory system work – the **diaphragm** and the **intercostal muscles**. The lungs are located in the chest area, known as the **thoracic cavity**, as shown in *Fig. 03.04.02*, and are protected by the **ribcage**.

Why do you breathe?

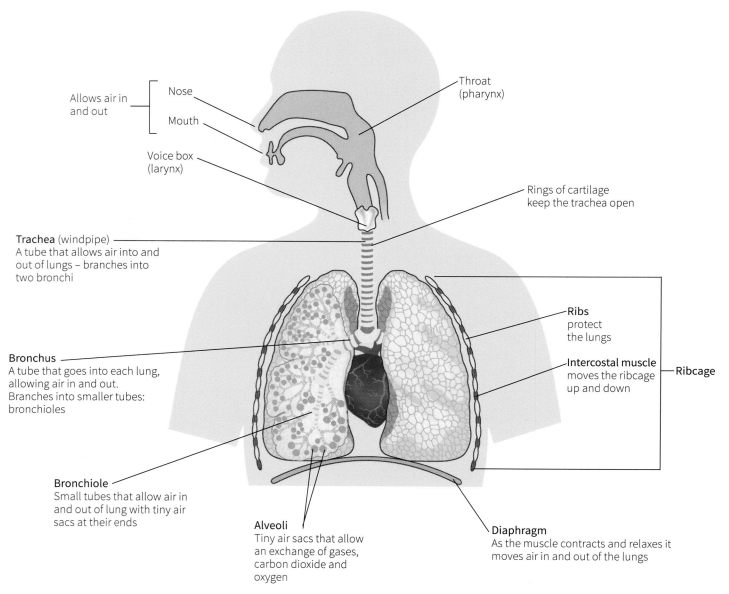

Allows air in and out

Nose

Mouth

Voice box (larynx)

Throat (pharynx)

Rings of cartilage keep the trachea open

Trachea (windpipe)
A tube that allows air into and out of lungs – branches into two bronchi

Bronchus
A tube that goes into each lung, allowing air in and out. Branches into smaller tubes: bronchioles

Ribs
protect the lungs

Intercostal muscle
moves the ribcage up and down

Ribcage

Bronchiole
Small tubes that allow air in and out of lung with tiny air sacs at their ends

Alveoli
Tiny air sacs that allow an exchange of gases, carbon dioxide and oxygen

Diaphragm
As the muscle contracts and relaxes it moves air in and out of the lungs

Ⓡ *Fig. 03.04.01 Parts of the respiratory system and their functions.*

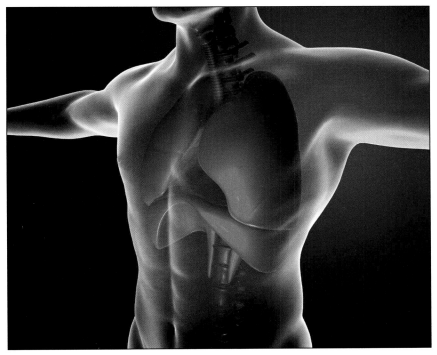

Fig. 03.04.02 The chest area/thoracic cavity.

(a) Copy *Table 03.04.01* and give the information needed.

Function of the respiratory system ...
Parts of the respiratory system ...
The muscles involved in breathing ...
The lungs are located in ...
They are protected by ...
Main gas taken in at the lungs ...
Main gas pushed out at the lungs ...

Table 03.04.01.

(b) Give a function for each part of the respiratory system.

How Does the Respiratory System Work?

At the lungs there is an **exchange of gases**. Oxygen is taken in and carbon dioxide is pushed out. This exchange is important because our body cells need the oxygen to release energy by **respiration** and our bodies need to get rid of the waste product carbon dioxide from our blood.

But how does this actually happen? In each lung there are lots of **alveoli** – tiny air sacs – at the end of the **bronchioles** (see *Fig. 03.04.03*). The alveoli are covered with a network of capillaries. The walls of the alveoli and capillaries are only one cell thick. This means that gases can easily pass through them.

The blood arriving at the lungs has a lot of carbon dioxide dissolved in it. The blood needs to get rid of this so it passes the carbon dioxide across into the air sac and exchanges it for an oxygen molecule. This oxygen then travels in the blood to the heart, from where it is pumped around the body.

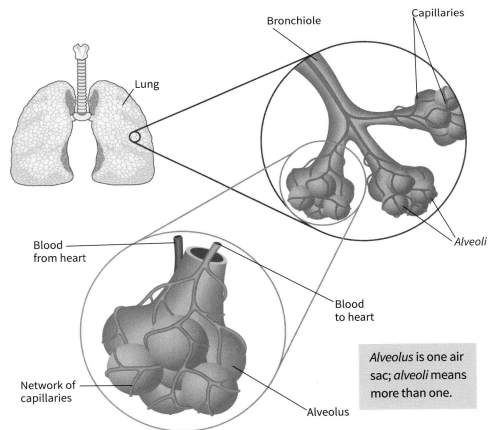

Alveolus is one air sac; *alveoli* means more than one.

Fig. 03.04.03 Alveoli at the end of the bronchioles.

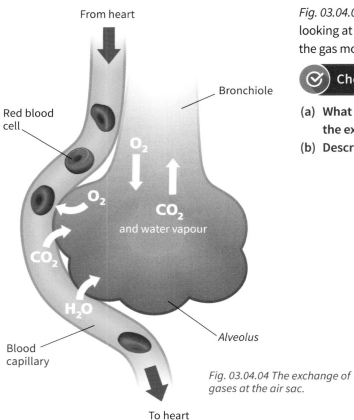

From heart

Red blood cell

Bronchiole

O_2

O_2

CO_2
and water vapour

CO_2

H_2O

Blood capillary

Alveolus

Fig. 03.04.04 The exchange of gases at the air sac.

To heart

Fig. 03.04.04 shows how this exchange of gases happens at the air sac. When looking at the diagram, pay attention to the arrows, which indicate the direction the gas molecule is travelling.

✓ Checkpoint 2

(a) **What is the name given to the part of the respiratory system that allows the exchange of gases to happen?**

(b) **Describe what the inside of the lung looks like.**

® Respiration and Breathing

At times we confuse the terms 'respiration' and 'breathing', but in science they do not mean the same thing.

Respiration is the process whereby our cells use oxygen to release energy from foods. Carbon dioxide is produced as a waste product.

Breathing is when we *take in* oxygen from the air and *push out* carbon dioxide.

Respiration is a *chemical* process. Breathing is a *mechanical* action.

Inhaling and Exhaling: Breathing In and Out

Refer to *Fig. 03.04.05* as you read the following to help you visualise what happens.

Inhaling

Breathing in is also referred to as **inhaling**.

- When we breathe in, the intercostal muscle contracts, causing the **ribs** to move up and outwards.
- The diaphragm muscle contracts and moves down.
- The volume inside the chest cavity (or thoracic cavity) increases – there is more room.
- This causes the air from outside to rush into the lungs.

The opposite happens when we exhale.

Did you know?
The lungs have no muscle tissue.

Exhaling

Breathing out is also referred to as **exhaling**.

- When we breathe out, the intercostal muscle relaxes, causing the ribs to move down and inwards.
- The diaphragm muscle relaxes and moves up (into a dome shape).
- The volume inside the chest cavity/thoracic cavity decreases – there is less room.
- This causes the air inside the lungs to be pushed out.

Fig. 03.04.05 Inhalation and exhalation.

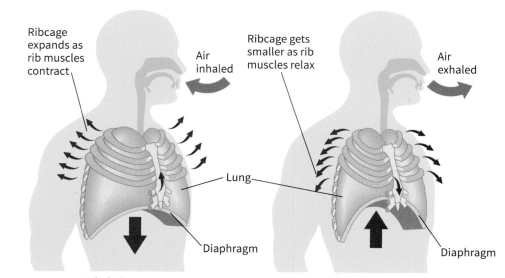

Ribcage expands as rib muscles contract

Air inhaled

Ribcage gets smaller as rib muscles relax

Air exhaled

Lung

Diaphragm

Diaphragm

Inhalation
Diaphragm contracts (moves down)

Exhalation
Diaphragm relaxes (moves up)

What happens to the air molecules?

Inhaling/breathing in:

* The air rushes in.
* The air molecules travel down into the **trachea**, then the **bronchus**, then into the bronchioli and into the air sacs.
* At the air sacs they cross over into the blood and travel to the heart. (Look back at *Fig. 03.04.04.*)

Exhaling/breathing out:

* Before the air is pushed out, the molecules must travel from the blood into the air sacs, then into the bronchioli, then up through the bronchus, then the trachea, and out of the nose or mouth.

Table 03.04.02 shows the differences between inhaled and exhaled air.

Inhaled air	Exhaled air
• High in oxygen	• High in carbon dioxide
• Low in carbon dioxide	• Low in oxygen
• Temperature of air can vary	• Warmer than inhaled air
• Less water vapour	• More water vapour

Table 03.04.02 Comparison of inhaled and exhaled air.

 **Checkpoint 3**

Using the words given, explain what happens when we take oxygen in and let carbon dioxide out. (All words must be used, they can be used more than once and they do not have to be used in the order given.)

> • inhale • exhale • muscles
> • diaphragm • ribcage
> • air in • air out

Lung Capacity

Lung capacity is the amount of air that you can hold in your lungs. People have different lung capacities. Do you know yours?

Investigation 03.04.01: **Finding out your lung capacity**

Equipment: An empty transparent plastic bottle (1 or 2 litres), a bendy straw or narrow tubing, a large deep bowl, water, masking tape and marker, a measuring cup/graduated cylinder.

Instructions:
1. Using the equipment as listed, devise an investigation to find your lung capacity.
2. Carry out the investigation three times and record your results.
3. Compare your results with your classmates' results.

> *What did you learn?*
> 1. Suggest why you were asked to carry out the investigation more than once.
> 2. Do you think there will be any variation within the class results? Support your answer with an explanation.
> 3. Make a list of factors that you think might affect lung capacity.

Factors that Affect the Respiratory System

- **Diseases** such as **emphysema**, **bronchitis**, **asthma** and heart disease can all have a direct effect on our respiratory system. For example, the heart's job is to pump blood around the body and deliver oxygen to the cells for respiration to take place. If the heart is unable to function at its best because of disease, this will have an effect on the respiratory system.

- **Drugs:** Some drugs *speed up* respiration at the cells. If this happens, the breathing rate needs to increase to deliver the oxygen. Examples: nicotine, cocaine, amphetamines. Some drugs *slow down* respiration and the breathing rate is also decreased. Examples: sleeping pills, alcohol.

- **Activity/exercise:** At night our breathing rate slows down as we are less active, so less oxygen is needed. When we increase our activity levels we increase the need for oxygen at our cells, so our breathing rate increases.

Checkpoint 4

(a) How do the oxygen molecules reach the body cells?

(b) Suggest why the oxygen is needed there.

(c) What would happen to a person's body if the heart was unable to work properly?

(d) There is an urgency or hurry of oxygen getting to the muscle cells. Will the need for oxygen to the muscles change if you are playing a game of hurling, for example? Explain your answer using as many of your new keywords as possible.

🔍 Investigation 03.04.02: **How do different levels of exercise affect breathing rate?**

Equipment: You and a partner, results table, stopwatch.

Instructions: Design and carry out an investigation to find out how different levels of exercise affect your breathing rate.

> ### *What did you learn?*
> 1. Predict what your results will be with different levels of exercise.
> 2. Why is it important to measure your breathing rate at rest before you start the investigation?
> 3. What would you expect to happen your breathing rate immediately after exercise? Support your answer with an explanation.
> 4. What happens when your exercise level is low?
> 5. Suggest a possible source of error during this investigation.

WHAT I HAVE LEARNED...

- The parts of the respiratory system are the nose, mouth, windpipe (trachea), bronchus, lungs, bronchioles and air sacs (alveoli).
- The function of each part of the respiratory system.
- The lungs are protected by the ribcage and located in the chest or thoracic cavity.
- Exchange of gases occurs at the alveoli, where oxygen is taken in and carbon dioxide is pushed out.
- Breathing in is inhalation and breathing out is exhalation.
- The air we take in has a high level of oxygen and low levels of carbon dioxide and water vapour. The air we breathe out has a high level of carbon dioxide, a low level of oxygen and more water vapour than inhaled air.
- Factors that affect the function of the respiratory system.
- Through investigation, that low levels of exercise result in low breathing rates, and as exercise levels increase, so too does breathing rate.

 Question Time

Copy and Complete

In this unit I learned that the respiratory system is made up of the mouth, nose, windpipe, lungs, bronchus, _____ and _____. The two muscles involved in the system are the _____ and the _____ _____. The lungs are _____ by the ribcage and they are in our chest area. At the air sacs, which are at the end of the small tube called the bronchiole, there is an exchange of _____: oxygen from the air goes from the air sac into the _____; _____ _____ goes from the blood into the air sac to be pushed out of the body. When we breathe in, our ribcage moves ____ and ____, and the _____ moves down, making more room in the chest area, which allows more air to come ____. When we breathe out, the _____ move down and in and the _____ moves up into a _____ shape. This makes the room inside the chest area _____, which causes the air to be pushed out. The oxygen molecules that we take in travel around the body in the _____.

Questions

1. Identify the parts of the respiratory system numbered in this diagram.

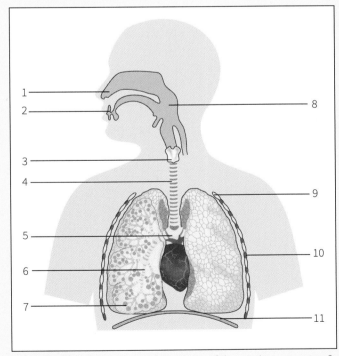

Fig. 03.04.06 Can you name all the parts of the respiratory system?

2. Describe the journey an oxygen molecule takes after it enters the nose.
3. Give another name for a) the windpipe; b) the chest area.
4. Using a diagram, describe what happens at the air sacs or alveoli.
5. Copy and complete the flow chart comparing what happens when you breathe in and out. Use the phrases in the list to help you.

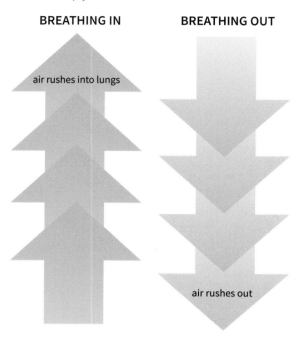

BREATHING IN   BREATHING OUT

air rushes into lungs

air rushes out

- air rushes out
- volume of chest cavity increases
- diaphragm moves down
- ribs move down and in

- air rushes into lungs
- ribs move up and out
- volume in chest cavity decreases
- diaphragm moves into a dome shape

6. How does the composition of blood change as it travels from the heart through the capillaries at the lungs? Can you explain why these changes occur?
7. What do you think might happen to your breathing rate if you were standing still and then started to run really fast?

Inquiry

A **R** **Build** a simple model of a lung.

B Smoking can cause many diseases, some of which have a direct effect on the respiratory system. **Research** two of these effects.

C **Produce** an information sheet on *either* asthma *or* bronchitis. Include the following headings:
- symptoms • causes • treatment

UNIT
3.5

The Reproductive System

Learning Outcomes

BWLO 9. Explain human sexual reproduction; discuss medical, ethical and social issues.

NSLO 6. Conduct research relevant to a scientific issue, evaluate different sources of information including secondary data, **understanding that a source may lack detail or show bias.**

NSLO 7. Organise and communicate research and investigate findings in a variety of ways fit for purpose and audience, using relevant scientific terminology and representations.

Ⓡ Teacher's reference

KEYWORDS

cervix	ovulation
conception	penis
condom	placenta
contraception	pregnancy
egg cell	progesterone
embryo	puberty
ethics	semen
Fallopian tube	sex cells
	sexual
fertilisation	intercourse
fertility	sperm cell
foetus	testes
fraternal	testosterone
gametes	umbilical
hormones	cord
implantation	uterus
IVF	womb
menstrual cycle	zygote
menstruation	
oestrogen	

LEARNING INTENTIONS

At the end of this unit you should:

1. Be able to explain what sexual reproduction is.
2. Be able to describe the human life cycle.
3. Be able to identify parts of the male and female reproductive system.
4. Know the functions of the parts of the male and female reproductive system.
5. Know what the male and female sex cells are.
6. Explain what puberty and contraception are.
7. Understand what happens during the female menstrual cycle.
8. Understand some of the ethical, medical and social issues surrounding human sexual reproduction.

Reproduction

All organisms reproduce to produce new individuals. There are two types of reproduction (discussed further in *Unit 4.2*):

- Sexual reproduction
- Asexual reproduction

In **sexual reproduction**, two different **sex cells** or **gametes** produce a new individual.

In **asexual reproduction**, a parent cell divides into two separate cells. Asexual reproduction does not involve gametes.

Sexual Reproduction in Humans

If humans did not reproduce, we would become extinct. Males and females have cells that allow reproduction to happen. These are referred to as **sex cells**, which fuse to form a new individual. The **genetic information** in each of these cells combines to produce a new person. Each individual is genetically different from their parents.

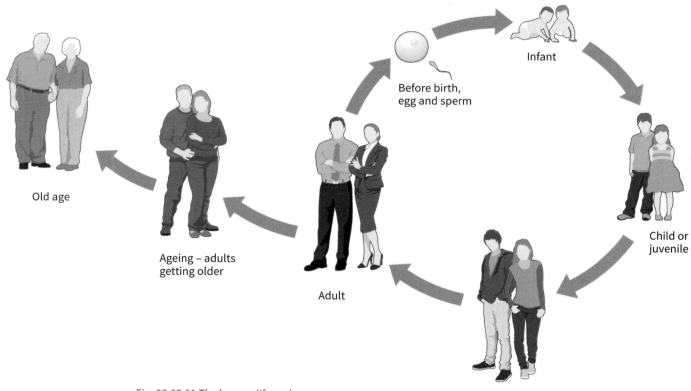

Fig. 03.05.01 The human life cycle.

As we grow from a baby to a child to a teenager, many changes happen in the body. When we reach **adolescence**, physical changes happen that prepare the body to become that of a young adult and ready to produce a baby.

This process starts with **puberty**.

The changes that happen between childhood and adolescence are collectively known as puberty. Everyone's body develops at a slightly different rate, so puberty happens at different times for different people. But all young people go through puberty and grow into young adults.

> **Puberty:** The period during which adolescents reach sexual maturity and become capable of reproduction.

What Happens During Puberty?

We are born with our reproductive organs, but they need to develop fully. Puberty is the final stage of sexual maturity; when we are sexually mature we are physically capable of **conception**. In puberty, **hormones** kick-start the changes that lead to sexual maturity. These are the chemical messengers that are sent from the brain to different parts of the body. The male hormone is **testosterone** and the female hormones are **oestrogen** and **progesterone**.

Our reproductive organs are referred to as our **primary sexual characteristics**.

During puberty the **secondary sexual characteristics** of the body develop. These changes are shown in *Table 03.05.01*.

	Boys	Girls
When do changes usually happen?	12–16 years old	10–15 years old
The changes	Growth of pubic hair	Growth of pubic hair
	Testicles and penis develop	Breast development
	Voice deepens	Menstruation (periods) begins
	Muscles develop	Eggs released
	Facial hair appears	Growth spurt (increase in height)
	Growth spurt (increase in height)	
Hormone(s) involved	Testosterone	Oestrogen Progesterone

Table 03.05.01 Changes at puberty.

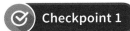 **Checkpoint 1**

(a) Explain in your own words what puberty is.
(b) List the changes that occur in boys and girls during puberty.
(c) What controls the start of these changes? List three of them.

Human Reproductive Systems

The human reproductive systems are different in males and females (*Fig. 03.05.03* and *Fig. 03.05.04*). The sex cells are also different: males have **sperm cells** and females have **egg cells**.

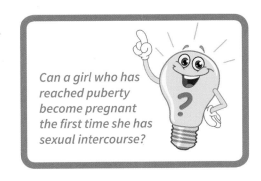

Can a girl who has reached puberty become pregnant the first time she has sexual intercourse?

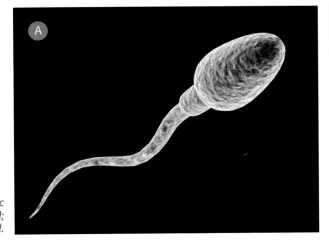

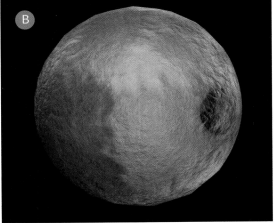

Fig. 03.05.02 Microscopic images of (a) a sperm cell; (b) an egg cell.

Conception: The action of conceiving a child or of one being conceived.

Fig. 03.05.04 also shows:

1. Where **fertilisation** occurs
2. Where **ovulation** occurs
3. Where the new cell attaches to the lining of the **womb** – that is called **implantation**.

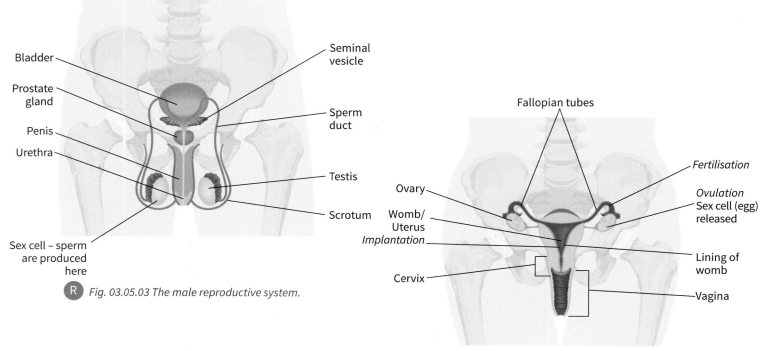

 *Fig. 03.05.03 The male reproductive system.*

R *Fig. 03.05.04 The female reproductive system.*

⊘ Checkpoint 2

(a) What term can also be used for 'sex cells'?
(b) Copy and complete *Table 03.05.02* by matching the functions given as follows with the body part listed in the table.

Male functions: Tube that transports **semen** out of the body; Sex cell that fertilises the egg; Allows sperm to travel through; Produces sperm; Holds **testes**; Allows semen (sperm in a fluid) to pass out of body and into female body

Female functions: Where implantation happens; Holds the baby as it develops; Tube that holds egg after being released and place of fertilisation; Opening of **uterus**,

Male reproductive part	Function	Female reproductive part	Function
Testicle		Ovary	
Sperm		Egg	
Scrotum		Fallopian tube	
Sperm duct		Womb/uterus	
Penis		Lining of womb/uterus	
Urethra		Cervix	
		Vagina	

Table 03.05.02.

How do the Sperm and the Egg Develop?

The sperm and egg cells have to **fertilise** to begin the development into a baby. Before this can happen, the sperm enters the vagina during **sexual intercourse** and begins the journey to the egg that has been released from the ovary and is now in the fallopian tube (see *Fig. 03.05.05*). **Fertilisation** happens in the **fallopian tubes**. Once the sperm and egg fuse or join, a new cell is produced – the **zygote**. The zygote then divides to form an **embryo**, which attaches to the lining of the mother's **uterus** or **womb**. The mother provides nourishment to the embryo via the **placenta**, which allows it to develop into a **foetus** and then a baby.

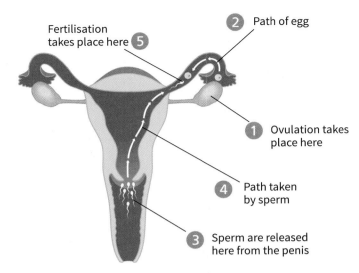

Fertilisation takes place here 5

2 Path of egg

1 Ovulation takes place here

4 Path taken by sperm

3 Sperm are released here from the penis

Fig. 03.05.05 Pathway of the sperm.

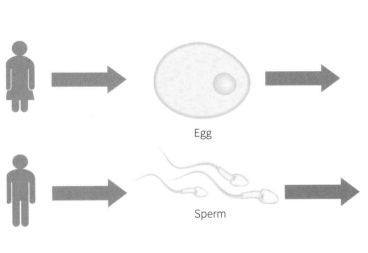

Egg

Sperm

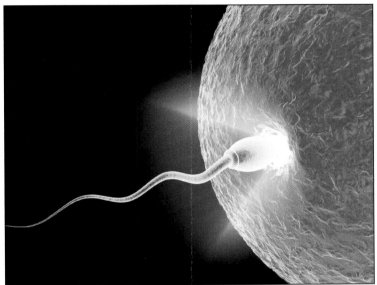

Fig. 03.05.06 Sperm and egg cells fertilising.

The Menstrual Cycle

The female body goes through **menstruation** to prepare for **pregnancy**.

When a girl reaches puberty the body will begin to go through a **menstrual cycle**, which normally lasts about 28 days – sometimes a few days more or less.

During the cycle the body goes through a sequence of changes that prepares it for the possibility of **pregnancy**.

How?
- Menstruation occurs, also referred to as the 'period'. During menstruation the lining of the womb or uterus breaks down and leaves the body.
- The uterus lining builds up, preparing itself to receive a fertilised egg, the zygote.
- An egg is released from an ovary (this is called **ovulation**), and waits to be fertilised.
- If the uterus does not receive a fertilised egg (zygote), menstruation occurs.

The menstrual cycle does not occur during pregnancy.

Table 03.05.03 shows the sequence of events during the 28-day cycle.

		What happens?	Why does this happen?	Where does this happen?
1	Days 1–5	Bleeding starts (the 'period') as the lining of the uterus breaks down	No fertilised egg or zygote has arrived in the womb	In the uterus – passes out through the vagina
2	Days 6–13	Lining of the uterus starts to build up again (get thick)	The uterus is getting ready for a fertilised egg	Lining of the womb
3	Day 14	Egg is released from ovary – this is called ovulation	Uterus is ready to receive a fertilised egg	From the ovary, then moves into the fallopian tube
4	Days 15–28	Lining of uterus stays in place	In case it receives a fertilised egg	Uterus

Table 03.05.03 Stages in the menstrual cycle.

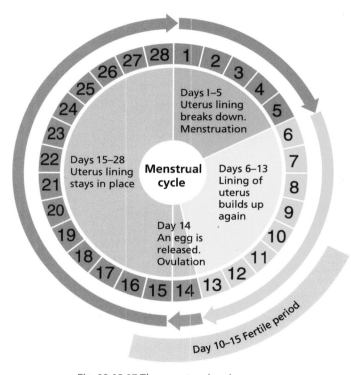

Fig. 03.05.07 The menstrual cycle.

Checkpoint 3

(a) How many days are there in a 'normal' menstrual cycle?
(b) Give a more commonly used word for 'menstruation'.
(c) What happens in the uterus after a woman's period? Why does this happen?
(d) Explain how the female body prepares itself for a baby to develop in the womb.
(e) On which day in an average menstrual cycle is the egg released from the ovary?

The Fertile Period

Since the sperm can live for five days and the egg lives for two days, including the day it is released, the fertile period in an average 28-day cycle is (approximately) between days 10 and 15, as shown in Fig. 03.05.07.

A woman is most likely to fall pregnant during this time, which means having sexual intercourse then increases the chances of having a baby. But because every woman's cycle will start on a different day, every woman's fertile period will be different. Also, some women have shorter or longer cycles.

Menstrual Cycle: A sequence of changes that occur in the female body roughly every 28 days.

Ovulation: When an egg is released from the ovary.

Menstruation: When the lining of the uterus breaks down and leaves the body.

What Happens to the Zygote?

1. **Implantation:** We know that when the sperm and egg fuse, a zygote is formed. This happens in the fallopian tube. Now the woman is pregnant. The zygote grows into a larger clump of cells and is now called an **embryo**. The embryo travels down into the **uterus** where it attaches itself into the lining of the uterus. This attachment is called implantation (*Fig. 03.05.08*).

2. **R** The **placenta** is attached to the lining of the uterus of the mother and is the lifeline that allows the embryo to develop into a baby. It is made up of blood vessels from the mother, which allow substances to pass from the mother's blood to the embryo's blood and from embryo to mother.

3. The embryo is attached to the placenta by the **umbilical cord**. This forms from the belly button of the embryo (baby) to the lining of the womb. The embryo's blood and the mother's blood never mix. The umbilical cord and placenta are shown in *Fig. 03.05.10 (a)*.

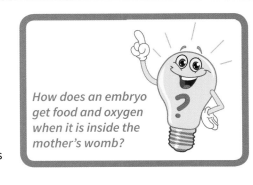

How does an embryo get food and oxygen when it is inside the mother's womb?

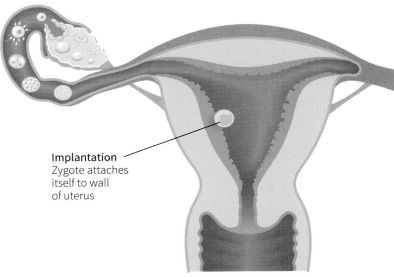

Implantation
Zygote attaches itself to wall of uterus

Fig. 03.05.08 Implantation.

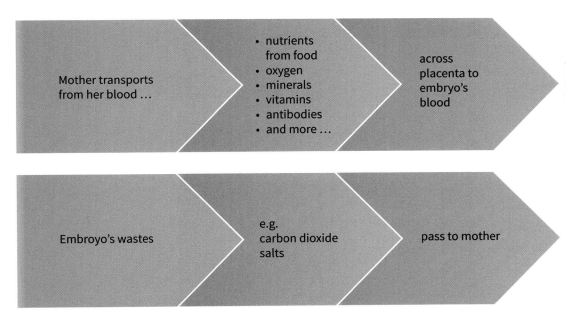

Mother transports from her blood …

- nutrients from food
- oxygen
- minerals
- vitamins
- antibodies
- and more …

across placenta to embryo's blood

Embroyo's wastes

e.g. carbon dioxide salts

pass to mother

4. With the nourishment that it needs, the embryo develops into a **foetus** and then into a baby.

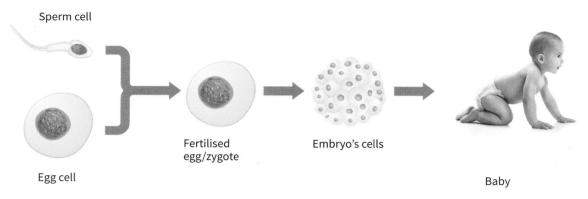

Fig. 03.05.09 Development of the zygote into a baby.

Checkpoint 4

(a) **R** **Identify the numbered parts in *Fig. 03.05.10 (b)*.**

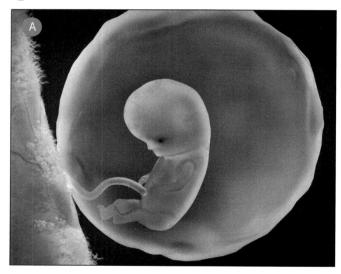

Fig. 03.05.10 (a) An image of the developing foetus.

Fig. 03.05.10 (b) Identify the numbered parts in this diagram.

(b) *Fig. 03.05.10 (a)* shows the amniotic sac. This is a sac that forms around the embryo and fills with amniotic fluid. Why would the embryo need this? Suggest what its purpose would be.

(c) Why is the placenta referred to as the baby's 'lifeline'?

(d) Make a list of substances that travel (i) from the mother to the baby; (ii) from the baby to the mother.

(e) Do you think the placenta is able to stop harmful substances from travelling across to the baby?

> **Implantation:** When the embryo becomes attached to the lining of the uterus.

Birth

Pregnancy lasts 39 weeks or nine months. Near the end of pregnancy the female body gets ready to give birth. Birth happens in three stages.

> **Pregnancy:** The carrying of an embryo in the female body.

Stage 1: Labour

- The uterus contracts.
- The amniotic sac bursts (the woman's waters break).
- The cervix begins to widen or dilate.

Stage 2: Birth
- The cervix is fully dilated.
- The baby is pushed out by the mother's muscular contractions.
- The umbilical cord is clamped, then cut.

Stage 3: Afterbirth
- The uterus contracts again.
- The placenta and umbilical cord are pushed out of the body (this is the afterbirth).

Multiple Births

How do multiple births happen?

Multiple births are when two or more babies develop inside the womb at the same time. These babies have come from either the same egg or different eggs. A common mistaken belief is that twins develop when two sperm fertilise an egg. This cannot happen. Only one sperm can fertilise one egg.

- **Identical twins, triplets, etc.:** Babies who are identical to each other have come from the same egg. The sperm only fertilises one egg, but this egg splits into more than one embryo, which then results in more than one baby.

- **Non-identical (fraternal) twins, triplets, etc.:** Babies who are not identical come from different eggs. More than one egg is released and a sperm has fertilised each egg.

Fig. 03.05.11 Example of multiple births.

Issues in Human Sexual Reproduction

Ⓡ Ethics

Your **ethics** are your own moral beliefs or personal views about how you should behave. Your beliefs may be different from other people's, but we all have the right to our own beliefs.

Our beliefs lead us to make different choices as we progress through adult life. Some of these choices might include using **contraception** to prevent pregnancy or using technology to aid or enable pregnancy (e.g. **IVF** – in vitro fertilisation – relates to ethics, medicine and technology. It is an individual's or couple's choice whether to go through the procedure of IVF).

> **Contraception:** Preventing the sperm and egg fertilising.

Contraception

If a couple do not want to have a child they can use contraception or birth control. Contraception means preventing the sperm and the egg fusing together (i.e. avoiding fertilisation) or preventing implantation.

Not having sex during the fertile period is also a form of contraception as the sperm and egg do not fertilise outside the fertile period.

Ⓡ Methods of contraception are listed in *Table 03.05.04.*

Method of contraception	Explanation	How does it work?
Natural	Avoid intercourse on fertile days of the menstrual cycle	No sperm is present to fertilise a viable egg
Mechanical	Example: **Condoms** create a barrier between the sperm and the egg	Sperm contained, so egg cannot be fertilised
Chemical	Example: Using hormones (the 'pill') to prevent ovulation	Some types of pill prevent implantation
Surgical	Prevents pregnancy. Surgery can be carried out on the man or woman or on both. In males, it prevents the emission of sperm; in females, it prevents the egg entering the fallopian tubes	Sperm and egg never have the opportunity to fertilise

Table 03.05.04.

Ⓡ Medical and Technological Issues

Medical research and technology have allowed people to:

- Have babies they might otherwise not have been able to. (Some of these methods are called 'assisted reproductive technology'.)
- Prevent or plan a pregnancy.
- Treat infertility using IVF (technology) and **fertility** drugs (medicines).
- Use contraceptive methods to control the number of children produced.

Infertility

What is infertility and what causes it?

Infertility is when the male or female is not able to have a baby.

There are many reasons why infertility might occur, for example:

- **In men:**
  - ◆ low sperm count
  - ◆ blocked sperm ducts
  - ◆ problems with the sperm being able to move.

- **In women:**
  - ◆ problems with ovulation
  - ◆ blocked fallopian tubes
  - ◆ problems with implantation.

Some infertility reasons may arise from poor lifestyle habits such as smoking, drinking too much and taking drugs.

> **Did you know?**
> Smoking damages male sperm, lowering the sperm count and the quality of the sperm.

Treating infertility

There are many ways to treat infertility. We are going to take a brief look at IVF treatment.

IVF

IVF stands for 'in vitro fertilisation'. What happens in IVF? Eggs are removed from a woman's body, and sperm is taken from the man. They are fertilised in a laboratory. The fertilised egg is monitored to see if it has developed into an embryo. If it has, it is then implanted into the woman's uterus. The pregnancy then continues in a natural way. Usually more than one egg is taken from the female, and when fertilised, implanted back into the female.

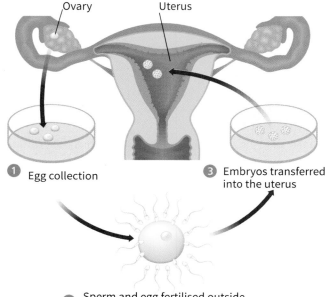

Ovary Uterus

1 Egg collection

3 Embryos transferred into the uterus

2 Sperm and egg fertilised outside the body; embryo forms

Fig. 03.05.12 IVF procedure.

WHAT I HAVE LEARNED...

- Sexual reproduction is when sex cells fuse together to form a new individual.
- The stages of the human life cycle are: infant; child; adolescent or young adult; older adult.
- Puberty is the final stage of sexual maturity. Hormones kick-start the physical changes that lead to puberty.
- The parts and functions of the male and female reproductive system.
- The male sex cell is the sperm and the female sex cell is the egg.
- When the sperm and egg fertilise, a zygote is produced.
- The menstrual cycle normally occurs over a 28-day cycle and there is a fertile period during which the female can become pregnant if sexual intercourse takes place.
- Ethical, medical and social issues arise when considering human sexual reproduction

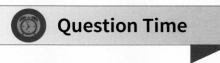

Question Time

Copy and Complete

In this unit I learned that sexual reproduction in humans needs to happen to stop humans becoming _____. Humans develop from a baby to a child to a young adult, to an adult and an _____ adult, and then death. During the teenage years _____ happens. This is when the bodies of boys and girls go through _____. The male produces a sex cell called the _____ and the female produces the _____. When sexual intercourse happens, the male sperm and the female egg _____ together. This is called _____. This egg develops and _____ itself to the lining of the woman's _____. This attachment allows a _____ between the mother and embryo. From the mother's placenta and _____ cord, _____ and _____ are transferred to the embryo, and the embryo transfers waste products to the _____ . After nine months the baby is ready to be born. The birth of a baby happens in three stages: _____; _____; and the _____.

Questions

1. Name two types of reproduction. From which type are new individuals produced?
2. Explain what the primary and secondary sexual changes are in the male and female body.
3. Draw up a table listing the parts of the female and male reproductive systems and their functions. In the table, indicate where the male and female sex cells are produced.
4. Explain, using information from *Unit 1.1*, why sex cells are referred to as specialised cells.
5. (R) Give an account of what is happening at each step in *Fig. 03.05.13*.

6. Explain how an embryo is formed.
7. What is the difference between an embryo, a foetus and a baby?
8. How does an embryo or foetus get the nourishment it needs from the mother?
9. Use some of the following words to explain contraception:

   • control   • prevent   • fertilisation   • fusing

10. What does the term 'infertility' mean?

Inquiry

A It is said that adolescent girls are at risk of anaemia. **Why** do you think this is?

B A mother's breast milk helps to protect her baby from infection. This protection can last for up to six months. **Research** how this protection happens.

C **Create** a leaflet giving advice to pregnant women about nutrition, and the effects of smoking and drinking alcohol during pregnancy.

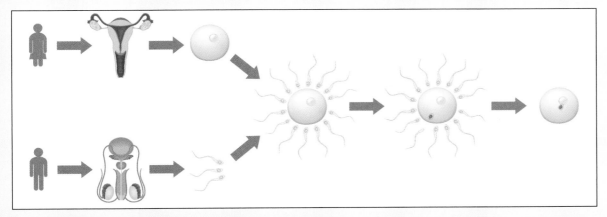

Fig. 03.05.13 What's happening here?

Variation and Reproduction

Learning Outcomes

BWLO 2. Describe asexual and sexual reproduction; explore patterns in the inheritance and variation of genetically controlled characteristics.

NSLO 3. Design, plan and conduct investigations; explain how reliability, accuracy, precision, fairness, safety, ethics and a selection of suitable equipment have been considered.

NSLO 4. Produce and select data (qualitatively/quantitatively), critically analyse data to identify patterns and relationships, identify anomalous observations, draw and justify conclusions.

NSLO 5. Review and reflect on the skills and thinking used in carrying out investigations, and apply learning and skills to solving problems in unfamiliar contexts.

Ⓡ Teacher's reference

KEYWORDS

asexual
characteristics
chromosome
clones
DNA
environmental
fertilised
fuse
gamete
genes
genetic
germinate
inherited
offspring
reproduction
sexual
traits
variation
zygote

LEARNING INTENTIONS

At the end of this unit you should:

1. Be able to describe what is meant by variation and describe variation in plants and animals.
2. Understand the differences between inherited and environmental variations.
3. Know that asexual reproduction results in new individuals that are genetically identical to the parent.
4. Identify that sexual reproduction results in new individuals that are not genetically identical to the parent.
5. Understand why plants and animals have features similar to their parents.
6. Know where chromosomes and genes are found in the body.

Variation

Fig. 04.01.01 Different types of species.

Variation is all about differences. There are differences between plants and animals, and between the plants and the animals themselves. All living things or organisms are different.

Take a look at *Fig. 04.01.02 (a)*. There are two animals, but with variations between them, one of the variations being that they are two different types of animal or organism. *Fig. 04.01.02 (b)* shows variation in plants. See how many variations you can spot between the animals and between the plants.

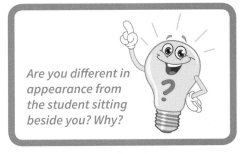

Are you different in appearance from the student sitting beside you? Why?

Variation: Any difference between organisms (or groups of organisms of any type).

Fig. 04.01.02 (a) Two animals, but two different organisms.

Fig. 04.01.02 (b) Two different plants.

Fig. 04.01.03 shows variations within one group of organisms – humans. List any variations that you can see.

Fig. 04.01.03 Variance is very easy to see in the human race.

Fig. 04.01.04 also shows variations within the same type of plant, insect or animal. Look closely at the images. What differences can you see?

Fig. 04.01.04 (a) Variation in a plant; (b) different butterfly wing designs; (c) variation in dogs.

Types of Variation

Variation can be **genetic** or **environmental**.

- **Genetic** means variations that are passed on or **inherited** from parents.
- **Environmental** means variations that are **learned**, **chosen** or a **response** to events/the environment.

A lot of variations are a mixture of genetic and environmental factors. What does this mean? Take heart disease as an example. Some people are more likely to have heart disease as it can be passed on or inherited, but your lifestyle choices (e.g. eating a lot of fatty foods) can also affect your chances of having heart disease. This is an environmental variation. Environmental factors also affect plants: some plants get more sunlight, nutrients and water than other plants, depending on where they are growing.

Variations: Examples and Explanations

Variation (Difference between two organisms)	Inherited (Passed on from a parent)	Environmental (Learned, chosen or has happened)	Both Inherited and Environmental	Variation explained
Hair colour	Original colour of hair – brown	Dyed blonde hair	Hair colour is either its natural colour (inherited) or dyed (environmental)	Brown hair colour was inherited from a parent; the person chose to dye it blonde – an environmental change
Height of an oak tree	Height to which the oak tree can grow	Having sunlight and water to make food	Making enough food to grow to its potential height	The height the oak tree can grow to is inherited, but whether the tree can make enough food to grow to that height will determine whether it actually grows to that height

Table 04.01.01.

 **Checkpoint 1**

(a) **Copy and fill in *Table 04.01.02* by writing 'Yes' under the correct heading for each variation – inherited, environmental or both. Explain your choice in the last column. Use *Table 04.01.01* as a guide.**

Variation	Inherited?	Environmental?	Both?	Explain your choice
Blue eyes				
Speaks Spanish				
Favourite colours are green and pink				
A long narrow leaf shape				
Tall, thin yellow leaves, drooping over side of flower pot				

Table 04.01.02 Inherited, environmental, or both?

(b) **Compare the physical appearance of the following pairs. How are they different? How are they similar?**
  (i) **A snail and a robin**
  (ii) **A beech tree and a dandelion**

Two examples of variation in plants or animals are:
- Physical appearance
- Type of reproduction

Physical appearance might include colour, height, width; plants with thin leaves, thick leaves, no leaves; long roots, shallow roots; animals with two legs, four legs, eight legs; wings, no wings; fur, no fur; people who are tall, people who are short. The list is endless. Can you suggest any other different physical appearances?

What is Reproduction?

All organisms reproduce. **Reproduction** is the process of making new individuals or offspring. Organisms make more of themselves!

Types of reproduction
- **Asexual**
- **Sexual**
- Budding in bacteria
- Production of spores

Here we will look at the two main types of reproduction:
- Asexual reproduction
- Sexual reproduction

Asexual Reproduction

- Asexual reproduction is when cells make a copy of themselves by dividing into two. (See *Fig. 04.01.05*.)
  - Only one parent cell is needed.

- There is no joining or fusing together of sex cells.
- The new cells are genetically identical to the parent.

- Asexual reproduction therefore does not give rise to variation.
- Therefore there is a chance of extinction.
- Both plants and animals produce cells by asexual reproduction.

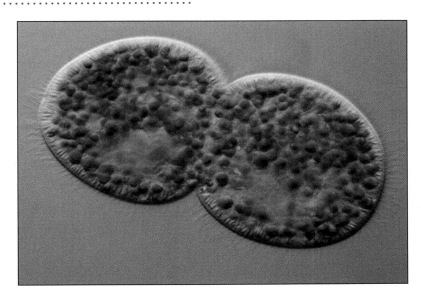

Fig. 04.01.05 A plant cell during asexual reproduction.

Asexual Reproduction in Plants

Many plants are able to reproduce copies or **clones** of themselves by asexual reproduction.

The plant does not have to produce flowers to attract animals to pollinate it, or produce or disperse any seeds. Asexual reproduction usually involves the plant's structures. The new plant grows from parts of the parent plant – the root, stem or leaves.

These plants are usually multicellular.

Asexual reproduction in plants with a stem is shown in *Fig. 04.01.06 (a)* and *(b)*, *(a)* being an artist's impression of asexual reproduction and *(b)* an actual strawberry plant. The new plant grows as a 'runner' from the base of the stem and it in turn will produce a new bud that will grow into a new strawberry plant.

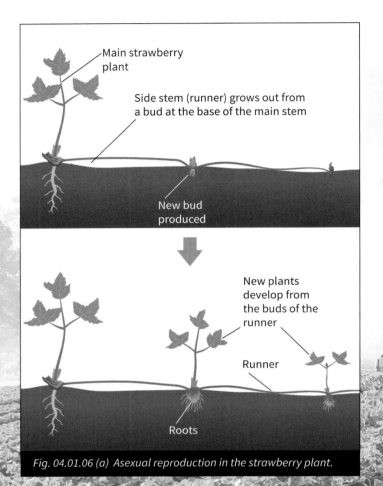

Main strawberry plant

Side stem (runner) grows out from a bud at the base of the main stem

New bud produced

New plants develop from the buds of the runner

Runner

Roots

Fig. 04.01.06 (a) Asexual reproduction in the strawberry plant.

Fig. 04.01.06 (b) The growing strawberry plant.

Investigation 04.01.01: **Showing how asexual reproduction happens in a potato**

Equipment: A large see-through glass jar, a potato or a sweet potato and some water.

Instructions: 1. Design an investigation to show asexual reproduction in a plant, using either a potato or a sweet potato.

2. Write down your observations as the potato grows.

What did you learn?

1. What predictions can you make about what will happen?
2. What conclusions can you draw from the fact that the potato grows?
3. If you placed the potato in soil and not a glass jar, would new potatoes grow?

Asexual Reproduction in Animals

Some invertebrate animals (remember that 'invertebrate' means 'without a backbone') reproduce **asexually**, for example, starfish and some fish.

In asexual reproduction, identical copies of the parent are produced – these are sometimes called **clones**. We can clone plants by taking cuttings or **grafts**, and scientists have been able to clone animals. We will be looking at cloning in more detail in the next unit.

Scientists are also now able to clone human organs, which are grown on animals, removed and transplanted to humans. This process is called **skin tissue cloning**.

Fig. 04.01.07 This invertebrate sea creature – a starfish – reproduces asexually.

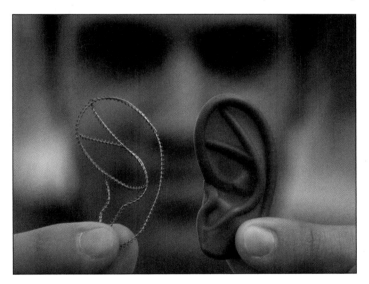

Fig. 04.01.08 A scaffold for a human ear. This is implanted in a lab rat, which grows the structure of a new ear on its back.

✓ Checkpoint 2

(a) **What is reproduction? Name two types of reproduction.**

(b) **How many parents are involved in asexual reproduction?**

(c) **There is a risk that at some point an organism that reproduces asexually could become extinct. Can you explain this possibility?**

(d) **Why is the process of asexual reproduction an advantage to a plant?**

(e) **Explain briefly what a clone is.**

Sexual Reproduction

- Sexual reproduction is when the male and female sex cells **fuse** or join with each other, producing a **fertilised** egg.
- The fusing of the sex cells is called **fertilisation**.

- Sex cells are called **gametes**.
- **In the human:** egg is the female gamete and sperm the male.
- **In the plant:** egg is the female gamete and pollen the male.

- The fertilised egg is called a **zygote**.
- The zygote develops into an embryo and then into a new individual.

- The new individual is genetically different from the parents.
- We say that the new individuals that are produced from sexual reproduction are *genetically unique*.
- This uniqueness allows for variation in organisms.

- Sexual reproduction can happen in animals and plants.
- Variation in organisms helps organisms to survive if their environment changes, and it can help to prevent extinction. But if no partner is found for reproduction, extinction can happen nonetheless.

Reproduction in Flowering Plants

We looked at sexual reproduction in humans in the previous unit. Sexual reproduction happens in flowering plants too.

Each flower contains both the male and female parts of the plant. The gametes, the egg and pollen, fuse together to produce a zygote. This cell then develops into a seed which, when given the correct environment – water, oxygen and a suitable temperature – will **germinate** and develop into a young seedling.

Reproducing sexually for a plant means that they will bear flowers, fruits and seeds. This then means that they increase their chances of survival as new plants develop, decreasing the chances of extinction.

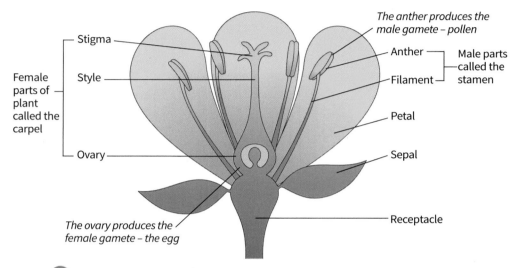

R   Fig. 04.01.09 Location of the male and female gametes in a flower.

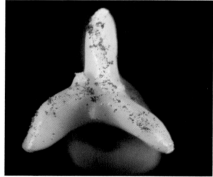

Did you know?
Different organisms have different numbers of chromosomes. An adder's-tongue fern has 1260 chromosomes, a rattlesnake fern 184, a dog 78, and a human 46.

Fig. 04.01.10 (a) Grains of pollen (male) on the stigma (female) of a lily.

Fig. 04.01.10 (b) Grains of pollen on a hibiscus flower.

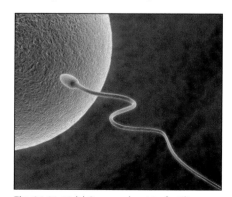

Fig. 04.01.10 (c) Sperm about to fertilise an egg.

Checkpoint 3

(a) What is another name for the sex cells in plants and animals?

(b) Name the specific sex cells in plants and animals.

(c) Describe what fertilisation means in plants and animals.

(d) What is the name of a fertilised egg?

(e) What are the advantages of new cells produced from sexual reproduction?

Inheritance

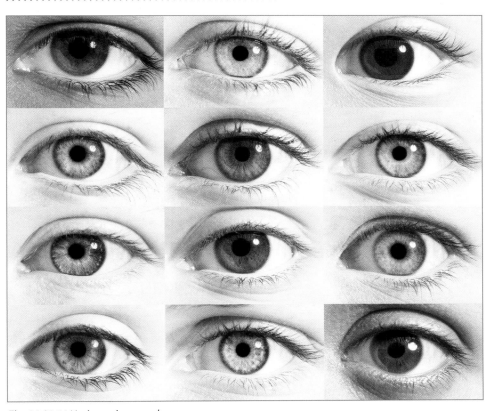

Fig. 04.01.11 Variance in eye colour.

Where did the colour of your eyes or hair come from?

Inheritance: The passing on of characteristics from generation to generation.

Characteristic: A distinguishing feature or quality that helps us to tell organisms apart.

Your eye colour, hair colour and many other of your features – your **characteristics** – were passed on – **inherited** – from your parents. Your parents got their characteristics from their parents, who got theirs from their parents, and so on. But you as a person are **unique**. Even though we share some characteristics with our family members and our classmates, every one of us has a unique combination or mix of characteristics. Our own unique mix of characteristics shows **variance** amongst humans.

Here is a list of some characteristics that make humans different:
• eye colour • hair colour • height • weight • body shape • length of fingers • earlobe attachment • being able to roll your tongue • having dimples

Here is a list of some characteristics that make plants different:
• height • flower colour • number, length and shape of leaves • whether flower has a scent • the way it reproduces • thickness of bark

Genes: What Are They?
Where Do They Come From?

When we take a closer look at these characteristics we find that they are controlled by **genes**. It is these genes that are passed on from parent to baby, from plant to seedling.

- Our parents in turn got their genes from their parents, and so on all the way back. The genes carry the instructions that give you some of your characteristics. It is your genes that determine your eye colour, hair colour, whether you are tall or short. They are found on **chromosomes**.

- Chromosomes are found in the **nuclei of our cells**. So the cells hold our genetic instructions.

- Chromosomes are made up of **DNA** and protein. The genes carry instructions, which are stored in the DNA. DNA is a structure or molecule that contains all the information needed to make a new organism.

Did you know?
DNA stands for deoxyribonucleic acid.

Look at *Fig. 04.01.13 (a)* to visualise where the genes are found. *Fig. 04.01.13 (b)* shows where the genes might be found on the chromosomes, and *Fig. 04.01.13 (c)* shows a microscopic image of a chromosome.

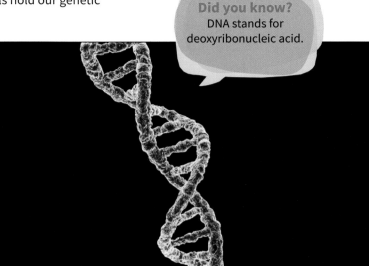

Fig. 04.01.12 The structure of DNA.

Did you know?
Recent studies estimate that we humans have approximately 20 000 genes in our bodies.

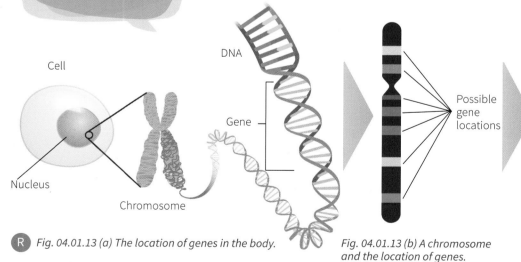

R   Fig. 04.01.13 (a) The location of genes in the body.

Fig. 04.01.13 (b) A chromosome and the location of genes.

Fig. 04.01.13 (c) A human chromosome as seen under an electron microscope.

✓ Checkpoint 4

(a) What would it mean if someone said to you that you had 'inherited your straight blonde hair from your mum'?

(b) What is a meant by a 'characteristic'? Give two examples for humans and two for plants.

(c) Where are genes located in the body?

(d) What do genes control?

(e) What are chromosomes made up of?

Investigation 04.01.02: Investigating the DNA in fruit

Equipment:

Set 1:
- two beakers
- a pestle and mortar
- a graduated cylinder
- some distilled water
- a spatula
- some ice-cold ethanol
- a water bath
- a kiwi fruit or a strawberry
- a sieve
- some washing-up liquid
- some salt
- a boiling tube
- a paper clip or cocktail stick

Set 2:
- a microscope
- a microscope slide
- a cover slip

Instructions:
1. Investigate the DNA in a kiwi or strawberry and use a microscope to view it.
2. Sketch an image of what you see.

This is a multi-stage investigation, so you need to follow the method given by your teacher.

What did you learn?
1. What is the function of the salt?
2. Why did you not heat the mixture for longer than fifteen minutes?
3. What shape are you expecting the DNA to be?
4. Why would the DNA strand you are looking for be considered delicate?

Extension:
Compare the DNA of the kiwi and the strawberry.
1. Was it easier to find the DNA in one fruit than the other?
2. Does the DNA of both fruits look the same under the microscope?

Human Reproduction

As mentioned, humans have 46 chromosomes – 23 pairs – except for the sex cells, which have 23 chromosomes only. We now know that we get our genes from our parents, but how are they passed on? *Fig 04.01.14* shows the passing on of 23 chromosomes each.

When sexual reproduction occurs, the egg and sperm **fuse** and **fertilise**. The fertilised egg has a total of 46 chromosomes. This cell is known as a **zygote**.

The zygote has a **mixture** of chromosomes, 23 pairs from mum and 23 from dad, the inherited mix.

This zygote will eventually develop into a **baby**.

With two parents, a mixture of genes from both are passed on, which is why the offspring inherits characteristics from both parents.

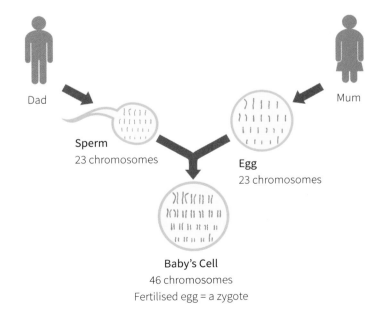

Dad

Sperm
23 chromosomes

Mum

Egg
23 chromosomes

Baby's Cell
46 chromosomes
Fertilised egg = a zygote

Fig. 04.01.14 A chromosome mix from mum and dad.

Some Inherited Characteristics

	LIP SHAPE Lips vary in shape, width, thickness and colour. There is even a pattern on your lips. But you'll need lipstick to find it! Have you the same lip shape as someone else in your family?
	EARLOBE ATTACHMENT Are your earlobes attached or unattached? Attached means they are fused to the side of your head. Unattached means that they appear to be free-hanging. Some earlobes are neither attached nor unattached but somewhere in-between!
	DIMPLES Dimples are small indentations on the cheeks, and are most visible when a person smiles.
	TONGUE ROLLING Can you roll your tongue? Try curling up the sides of your tongue to make a tube shape. Some studies argue that being able to do this is not always inherited; it can also be environmental. Evidence of this is that only 70% of identical twins share this **trait**.
	THUMB SHAPE In some people, the thumbs can be different shapes. Look at both thumbs. Is one bent back more than the other? Some people's thumbs bend right back. This is known as the 'hitchhiker's thumb'.
	INTERLOCKING FINGERS Interlock your fingers together. Which thumb is on top, left or right?
	VULCAN OR NOT VULCAN Can you spread your fingers two by two?
	FRECKLES Do you have freckles?

Table 04.01.03.

Checkpoint 5

(a) How many chromosomes are in a human body cell?

(b) Draw a diagram showing where you got your chromosomes from.

(c) Look again at *Table 04.01.03* on inherited characteristics. Did you inherit any of these characteristics from your parents, grandparents or great-grandparents? You may need to ask at home!

Asexual reproduction	Sexual reproduction
One parent – two cells produced	Two parents
Cell produced is identical to parent	Cells produced are not identical to parent
No variation in the offspring	Variation in the offspring
No fusion of gametes	Fusion of gametes (egg and sperm, or egg and pollen)
No fertilisation of cells	Fertilisation needs to happen

Table 04.01.04 Overview of the differences between asexual and sexual reproduction.

WHAT I HAVE LEARNED...

- Variation is the difference between organisms.
- Reproduction is a process where new individual cells are made.
- The two main types of reproduction are asexual and sexual.
- Asexual reproduction only involves one parent: two cells are produced and they are identical to the parent.
- Sexual reproduction involves the fusing of sex cells from parents; offspring are not genetically identical to the parent.
- A sex cell is called a gamete. Each sex cell has 23 chromosomes.
- A human cell has 46 chromosomes
- Human gametes are the egg and sperm. Plant gametes are the egg and pollen.
- 'Inherited' means the genes that are passed on from parents to their young.
- A characteristic is a distinguishing feature that allows us to tell organisms apart.
- Genes are found on chromosomes, chromosomes are found in the nucleus and the nucleus is in our cells.
- Chromosomes are made up of DNA and protein.
- During human sexual reproduction, the egg and sperm cells fuse to form a fertilised egg called a zygote.

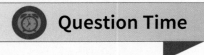

Question Time

Copy and Complete

In this unit I learned that the differences between organisms is known as _____. In animals these differences are passed on from the _____ to the baby and in plants to the young _____. Reproduction is where new _____ or individuals are made. There are two types of reproduction: _____ and _____. Asexual reproduction only needs _____ parent. Each cell is _____ to the parent. Sexual reproduction needs _____ parents, and the sex cells _____ together to produce a _____ egg. The new cell is _____ to the parents. The _____ _____ are called the gametes. The plant gametes are the egg and _____; the human gametes are the _____ and _____. The fertilised egg is called the _____. In humans, every body cell has _____ _____, except the sex cells, which have _____. They carry the genes that give us our _____. Characteristics are controlled by the _____. The chromosomes are made of DNA and protein. They are _____ from our parents and are found on _____ inside the nucleus of a cell. When sexual reproduction happens the sex cells fuse together to form _____ chromosomes and this means that there is a mix of genes. We can therefore say that our characteristics have been _____ on to us.

Questions

1. How do plants show variation?
2. Copy the flow chart and fill in the blanks.

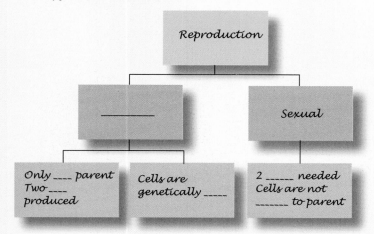

3. Raspberry and strawberry plants are able to produce many plants from one parent. What advantages does this give the plant?
4. What disadvantages, if any, would there be in plants or animals being exactly the same as the parent?
5. Sexual reproduction leads to variation among organisms. List the advantages of variation.

6. Write down three examples of both inherited and environmental characteristics of plants and animals.
7. Explain the difference between asexual and sexual reproduction. You must use all the words in the following list. The words can be used more than once.

- fertilisation • sex cells • gametes • inherit • exact copy • clone • identical • genetically different • genes

8. Which of the statements in *Table 04.01.05* are true and which are false?

Statement	True	False
Chromosomes are found on the genes		
Genes are not passed on from our parents		
The nucleus is found in cells		
Genes are found on chromosomes		
Genes are made of DNA		
There are 23 chromosomes in every cell in your body		
There are 46 pairs of chromosomes in cells		

Table 04.01.05.

9. State how many chromosomes a newborn baby would have in (i) a muscle cell; (ii) a cheek cell.
10. A survey was carried out on the different hair types in a group of thirty-five students. The students were a mix of boys and girls. The graph in *Fig. 04.01.15* shows the results of the survey.

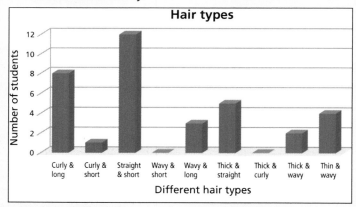

Fig. 04.01.15 Graph showing different hair types in a class.

(i) Study the bar chart and interpret or explain what the results show.
(ii) Based on your study of variation and inheritance, can you see any problems with the survey and the results?
(iii) In the information you have been given about the survey, can you suggest any errors that may have been made either in designing the survey or presenting the survey results?
(iv) What changes would you recommend if the survey were to be done again?

Inquiry

A **Present** a variation display of plants for your classroom. Observe the variations: do the leaves vary in size or shape? Do they have different numbers of leaves. Do they have flowers?

B **Create** three new Little Miss and Mr Men characters by pairing up some current characters. Decide what characteristics your new Miss or Mr will have. Remember that there will be a mix of chromosomes from each parent. (Go to *mrmen.com* to see all the characters.)

 (i) Make a list of the characteristics that they both have and that you can see.

 (ii) Draw the three new characters and list their characteristics.

 (iii) State whether each characteristic that your characters have were passed on from the Little Miss 'parent' or the Mr 'parent'.

 (iv) Name each of your characters you have created.

C **Research** what the term 'hermaphrodite' mean.

D **Choose** three inherited characteristics in your own family and trace the characteristics back as far as you can to find out who had the same ones.

E For hundreds of years scientists have been studying the differences between organisms, their habitats, how they are different, and where these differences came from. **Research** one of the scientists from each column below and write a short paragraph on their contribution to science.

Scientists [1]	Scientists [2]
A. Robert Whittaker	B. Watson & Crick
C. Gregor Mendel	D. Rosalind Franklin

F R **Research** the different lip patterns that exist. Which do you match?

Technology in Science – Cloning

Learning Outcomes

NSLO 6. Conduct research relevant to a scientific issue, evaluate different sources of information including secondary data, understanding that a source may lack detail or show bias.

NSLO 7. Organise and communicate research and investigate findings in a variety of ways fit for purpose and audience, using relevant scientific terminology and representations.

NSLO 8. Evaluate media-based arguments concerning science and technology.

NSLO 9. Research and present information on the contribution that scientists make to scientific discovery and invention, and its impact on society.

NSLO 10. Appreciate the role of science in society; its personal, social and global importance; and how society influences scientific research.

R Teacher's reference

KEYWORDS

artificial
clone
cloning
donor
ethical
harvesting
implanted
surrogate
uterus

LEARNING INTENTIONS

At the end of this unit you should:
1. Know what it means to clone.
2. Be able to list the benefits of cloning.
3. Know the advantages and disadvantages of cloning.
4. Be able to describe how new plants can be produced using cloning.
5. Be able to discuss the ethical issues surrounding cloning.

What is Cloning?

Technology in science is improving all the time. Huge advances in equipment design allow scientists to increase their knowledge, so science is advancing too. **Cloning** is an example of a scientific process. It is not a new science – it has developed over time.

Did you know?
No seeds are needed to clone plants.

Fig. 04.02.01 Cloned tomatoes, cloned lettuces and cloned plants.

- Cloning is a process that makes an individual that is a genetic copy of another.
- A **clone** is an exact genetic copy.
- Cloning is the term used to describe the **asexual reproduction** in a cell.
- It can occur **naturally** – plants can make an exact copy of themselves.
- It can also be done **artificially** by humans.

> **Cloning:** A process that makes an individual that is a genetic copy of another.

> **Clone:** An organism that is an exact genetic copy of another.

Fig. 04.02.02 Cloned animals.

Advantages and Disadvantages of Cloning

Advantages of cloning	Disadvantages of cloning
• Can produce exact copies of animals and plants	• Variation of organisms is reduced
• Can help save plants and animals from extinction	• **Ethical** issues
• Can produce copies of tissues or organs for organ transplant	• Cloned animals have a short life span
• Can bring back animals or plants from extinction	• Expensive
• Medical research	• A lot of attempts fail
• If an animal is infertile, cloning would solve the problem	• Could cause animal defects
• Food sources can be replenished	
• Helps us understand more about genetics	

Table 04.02.01 The advantages and disadvantages of cloning.

✓ Checkpoint 1

(a) In your own words, describe what cloning is.

(b) What type of reproduction occurs during cloning?

(c) List the benefits of cloning: to nature; to an individual person; to society in general.

(d) Are there any other advantages or disadvantages you would add to *Table 04.02.01*?

A Breakthrough in Science

In 1996, the world's first mammal was cloned – Dolly the sheep. How was Dolly born? By cloning an adult sheep cell. Dolly was the most famous clone in the world!

Dolly was cloned by scientists Ian Wilmut and Keith Campbell at the University of Edinburgh in Scotland. It had taken 277 attempts to clone Dolly, and she was the first mammal to be cloned from the DNA of an adult.

When scientists clone an animal, their aim is to control the reproductive process. They can select the specific genes and combination of genes that they want. They remove the nucleus (which contains the chromosomes) from one animal's egg and replace them with the nucleus from a different animal.

Fig. 04.02.03 Professor Ian Wilmut and Dolly, his cloned sheep.

How was Dolly Cloned?

Fig. 04.02.04 shows how the scientists carried out the cloning of Dolly. Since Dolly, scientists have cloned many more animals, including cows, pigs, mice and goats.

The Process of Cloning

1. The nucleus is taken out of the adult cell of the animal (A) that is going to be cloned.

2. At the same time the nucleus is removed from a donor egg cell of another animal (B) of the same type/species. (This cell is now empty.)

3. The nucleus from the original adult cell is placed into the donor's empty egg and the new egg is given an electric shock.

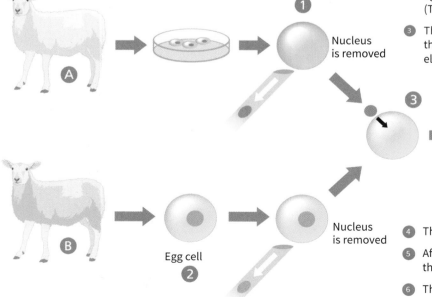

Fig. 04.02.04 How Dolly the sheep was cloned.

4. This shock starts the new cell dividing.

5. After a few days the embryo is implanted in the uterus of the surrogate mother.

6. The embryo develops and the animal is born. This is a clone, which has the exact DNA of the original adult animal.

Why do Scientists Want to Clone?

1. Cloning is an important development in medical research. It enables us to study genetic disorders or diseases of plants and animals. For example, stem cells can be cloned from someone with a disease, which can then be artificially grown and studied to help understand the disease and perhaps develop treatments.
2. **Harvesting** stem cells from animals that are close to extinction, e.g. the snow leopard, could save them from extinction. The stem cells would be banked (stored) and used in the future for cloning.
3. Human skin has been cloned for skin grafting, e.g. to treat people who have been badly burned.
4. For scientists, cloning is an important process in genetic modification.
5. Scientific research is currently being carried out on cloning farm animals, such as cattle and pigs, to produce high-quality milk or meat. It may be possible in the future for farmers to purchase and breed from these animals.

REMEMBER

In *Unit 1.1*, 'Cells and Living Things', we learned that a stem cell is a single cell that can copy itself and can then specialise into other cell types.

Cloning Plants

Cloning plants gives faster results than growing them naturally – fully grown plants are produced more quickly because we don't have to wait for seeds to germinate (begin to grow and put out shoots). If a plant grows from a seed (sexual reproduction has occurred), the plant may not be genetically identical to the parent. Cloning can also be a cheaper way to grow plants.

Cloning in plants can be carried out by:
1. Cuttings
2. Tissue culture.
You will research the tissue culture method of cloning at the end of this unit.

Cuttings

Do your parents ever take cuttings from other people's plants or shrubs? Taking a cutting is a method of cloning. You end up with an identical copy of the plant or shrub.

Gardeners and horticulturists take cuttings from a good parent plant with desirable characteristics, e.g. good fruit production, large flowers, etc. These cuttings can be planted to grow an exact copy of the parent. *Fig. 04.02.05* shows how this can be done. Sometimes hormones (hormone rooting powder) can be added to the cutting to help it grow, but this is not always needed.

Fig. 04.02.05 How a plant can be cloned.

Thinking About Cloning

Look at *Table 04.02.02*. How would you answer these questions? Think about your own opinion, but also consider the effects on society, science and the world. Are there any other ethical considerations in relation to cloning? Discuss your opinions with the class.

Thinking About Cloning	Yes	No
1. Is it ethical for humans to clone animals?		
2. Have humans a right to clone animals?		
3. If humans were to be cloned, should cloned humans have the same rights as everyone else?		
4. Should we use technology to bring back animals that are extinct, considering it is likely that human development and industry has led to their extinction?		
5. Should we clone cows that will produce more than average quantities of milk?		
6. Do you think cloning plants and animals could end world hunger?		
7. Do you think that organs for transplant should be cloned?		

Table 04.02.02 What do you think about cloning?

WHAT I HAVE LEARNED...

- Cloning is a process that makes an individual that is a genetic copy of another.
- A clone is an exact genetic copy.
- Asexual reproduction occurs during cloning.
- There are many advantages and disadvantages of cloning.
- Taking cuttings is an example of plant cloning.
- There are many ethical issues surrounding cloning.

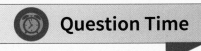
Question Time

Copy and Complete

In this unit I learned that cloning is a process that makes an individual that is a _____ copy of another. A _____ is an _____ genetic copy. In the process of cloning the type of reproduction that occurs is _____. Cloning can happen naturally or _____. Advantages of cloning include: _____ research; to help save plants and animals from _____; and to _____ _____ animals from extinction. Disadvantages of cloning include: it is _____ to do; cloned animals have a shorter _____ span; and _____ within organisms is reduced. The most famous cloned animal is _____ the sheep, who was cloned in _____. Plants can be cloned by taking _____ or by _____. Both techniques will give fast results and the plants will be genetically _____ to the parent.

Questions

1. What is a clone?
2. List five disadvantages of cloning.
3. Why might people who breed animals want to clone them?
4. Are cloned animals safe to eat?
5. Would it be cheaper to clone plants than to grow them from seed?
6. Do you think cloning Dolly the sheep was a good idea? Explain your answer in detail.
7. Do you think you should be told whether meat is cloned before you purchase it? Explain your views.
8. Choose an animal that you want to clone.
   (i) Sketch or find a picture of the animal you want to clone.
   (ii) Use the following keywords to complete a flow chart (arrows) on cloning your animal.

> • nucleus • cell • embryo • empty egg cell
> • implanted • surrogate mother

Inquiry

A **Write** a newsletter or a review for a newspaper or an article for a science magazine, entitled 'Cloning and the New Horizons in Medicine'.

B At present we are not allowed to clone humans. **Suggest** reasons why this is the case.

C (R) Cloned animals have a short life span. **Research** why this is the case.

D (R) **Research** the tissue culture method of cloning.
   (i) Describe how the technique of tissue culturing is carried out.
   (ii) Look at stories or articles that have been in the news.
   (iii) How does the technique of tissue culturing benefit us?

UNIT 4.3

Evolution and Natural Selection

Learning Outcomes

BWLO 3. Outline evolution by means of natural selection and how it explains the diversity of living things.

NSLO 6. Conduct research relevant to a scientific issue, evaluate different sources of information including secondary data, understanding that a source may lack detail or show bias.

NSLO 7. Organise and communicate research and investigate findings in a variety of ways fit for purpose and audience, using relevant scientific terminology and representations.

NSLO 9. Research and present information on the contribution that scientists make to scientific discovery and invention, and its impact on society.

(R) Teacher's reference

KEYWORDS

adapt
breed
camouflaged
compete
diversity
evolution
extinction
fossil
habitat
natural selection
organism
predator
prey
species
theory

LEARNING INTENTIONS

At the end of this unit you should:

1. Be able to describe what evolution means.
2. Know that it was Charles Darwin who proposed the theory of evolution.
3. Be able to describe some of the evidence Darwin put forward for this theory.
4. Be able to describe natural selection in your own words.
5. Understand how species have evolved over years and use examples of animals that have evolved.
6. Know that natural selection explains how evolution has occurred.
7. Know that evolution is ongoing.

Do you think that plants and animals have changed in the last 1000 years?

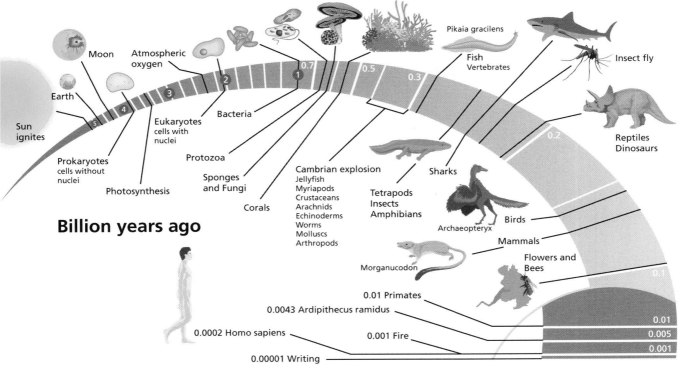

Fig. 04.03.01 The arc of evolution.

Diversity of Life

The world is made up of millions of different organisms, as explained in *Unit 4.1.* Every one of these living organisms is unique and this uniqueness is the basis of the huge variation we see in the world today. It is exciting to think that more organisms have yet to be discovered!

This huge variation is the result of **evolution**, which has been happening since life on earth began millions of years ago. Over these millions of years the conditions on earth have changed, resulting in different animals and plants surviving and evolving.

Did you know?
Scientists have identified approximately 2 million or more plants and animals that are alive today. But they estimate that millions remain to be discovered.

Animal and type	Interesting facts
New species of tuco-tuco – a rodent 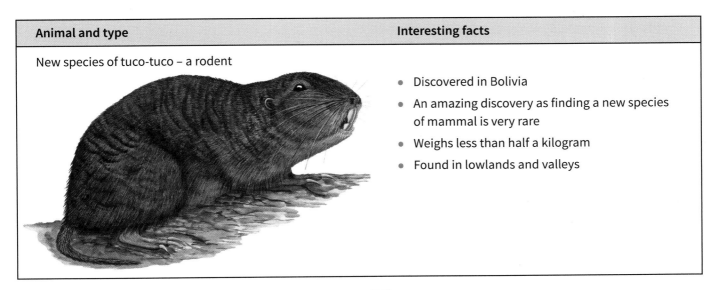	• Discovered in Bolivia • An amazing discovery as finding a new species of mammal is very rare • Weighs less than half a kilogram • Found in lowlands and valleys

Evolution

Evolution is a gradual change in an organism over a very long time. The **theory of evolution** was not immediately accepted, not even in the lifetime of some of the scientists who contributed to it, such as Charles Darwin, Alfred Russel Wallace and Jean-Baptiste Lamarck.

It is Darwin who is most recognised for his contribution to the theory of evolution. In 1859 he published a book called *On the Origin of Species*. He was the first scientist to bring together such a vast amount of evidence for the theory.

'It is not the strongest of the species that survives, nor the most intelligent, but the one most responsive to change.'

Fig. 04.03.02 Charles Darwin (1809–1882).

 **Checkpoint 1**

(a) **What does variation mean in biology?**

(b) **What has brought about the huge variation in plants and animals that we have today?**

(c) **Describe in your own words what evolution means.**

(d) **Which scientist published a book called** *On the Origin of Species*?

(e) **What concept did this book put forward?**

Ⓡ Darwin's Mechanisms of Evolution

Darwin wrote that:

- All plant and animal life shows ***variation***.
- There are ***more young produced*** than can survive (overbreeding).
- All plants and animals ***compete*** for food, living space, water, mates, etc. (a struggle for existence).
- The plant or animal that is ***better adapted*** than another is more likely to survive. This is ***natural selection*** (sometimes referred to as 'survival of the fittest').
- As **habitats** change, ***new adaptations*** will emerge over time.
- Those plants or animals that survive changes in the environment will ***pass on their genes*** to their young, which will also be better adapted.
- Those that don't survive run the risk of ***extinction***.

Note that 'fittest' does not mean those that are strongest, but rather those that are more adaptive.

Did you know?

Darwin did not coin the phrase 'survival of the fittest'. The philosopher Herbert Spencer came up with the phrase – Darwin used the term 'natural selection'. The phrase 'survival of the fittest' was added to Darwin's fifth edition of *On the Origin of Species*.

What is natural selection?	It is when an animal or plant that best adapts itself to a habitat will survive.
	When an animal moves into a new environment or habitat, the conditions in which they live change. They must adapt to living in that habitat or die – which could lead to extinction.
An example of natural selection	Darwin studied finches that lived on different Galapagos islands (see *Fig. 04.03.03*). He found that this one **species** of bird had many different shapes of beak.

✅ Checkpoint 2

Darwin carried out a lot of his studies and research on finches found on the Galapagos Islands. *Fig. 04.03.03* shows these finches, their names and their eating habits.

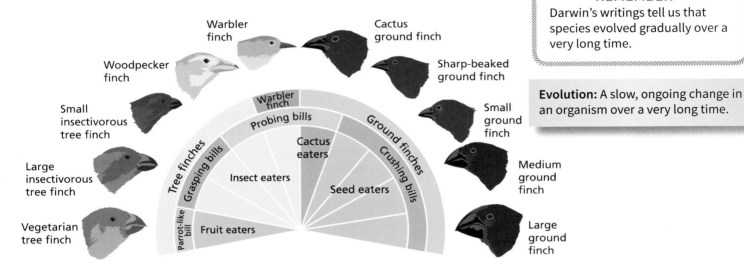

Fig. 04.03.03 Darwin's finches and their eating habits.

REMEMBER
Darwin's writings tell us that species evolved gradually over a very long time.

Evolution: A slow, ongoing change in an organism over a very long time.

(i) Discuss the shapes of the finches' beaks. Create a table of the different types of beak. Can you think of reasons why the beaks are shaped differently?

(ii) Would a finch with a short beak that ate seeds survive on an island where the only food source was insects? Give an explanation for your answer.

Characteristic: A distinguishing feature or quality, which allows us to tell organisms apart.

Natural Selection: A characteristic that an organism has, giving it a better chance of surviving; passed on genetically from generation to generation.

Fig. 04.03.04 A Galapagos tortoise.

Did you know?
The Galapagos tortoises are the product of over 3 *billion* years of evolution.

Darwin's Evidence for Evolution

Darwin backed up his theory with **fossils** and a fossil record.

Fossils are the remains of plants or animals. They show how organisms have changed over time and how some organisms have become extinct. Some fossils can give information on the past environment and how it has changed.

Darwin sent a lot of fossils from his travels back home to England so he could study them when he returned.

Fig. 04.03.05 An example of a fossil.

 **Checkpoint 3**

The evolution of the horse is visually dramatic, even if it has been happening over a period of 60 million years! *Fig. 04.03.06* shows the evolution of the horse and the changes in body size, height and the length of the fore feet. If you look closely at the pictures, the fossil evidence highlights how the horse has evolved from a small swamp-dwelling animal to what it is today.

(i)   Discuss why you think this might have happened.

(ii) What do you think might happen next to horses?

(iii) How long do you think it will take to happen?

The Theory of Evolution — Explained by Natural Selection

Plants and animals have to **adapt to survive**.
We've seen that natural selection is when the animal or plant that best adapts itself to a habitat will survive – 'survival of the fittest'. But why does this happen?

Scenario 1: Plants and animals compete with each other. Think of two animals competing for the same food. An animal with sharp claws is more likely to get the food than an animal without sharp claws.

Explanation: Sharp claws are an **advantage** to the animal – it is better adapted to win the food. Having no sharp claws is a **disadvantage** to the other animal.

Note: Only young from animals born with the genes for an advantageous characteristic will stay alive and reproduce (similarly with seeds from plants). That is why some animals and plants produce a lot of young – they are making sure that the fittest survive and that the useful genes are passed on from one generation to the next.

Animals and plants with advantages over others with whom they compete are more likely to survive and continue to **breed** or reproduce. **This is natural selection.**

Change over time	Fore feet size from fossil evidence	Body size	Height
1 million years ago		Modern horse	Height 1.6 m
10 million years ago		Pliohippus	Height 1.0 m
30 million years ago		Merychippus	Height 1.0 m
40 million years ago		Mesohippus	Height 0.6 m
60 million years ago		Eohippus	Height 0.4 m

Fig. 04.03.06 Evolution of the horse.

Natural selection

Being *adapted* to survive in a particular habitat and having advantageous characteristics can help an animal compete against another animal that has *not adapted* and has no advantageous characteristics.

This means that *predators* are more likely to prey on the animals that have not adapted. For example, an animal that is **camouflaged** will have a better chance of survival than one that is not camouflaged.

Plants and animals with *advantageous characteristics* will survive more often.

They will *breed* or reproduce.

This increases the chances of the genes with advantageous characteristics being *passed on* to their offspring.

Characteristics develop over years and years. As animals adapt to new habitats, etc., their genes are passed on. Eventually the animal will have changed so much that it becomes a *new species* – this is **evolution**.

Scenario 2: An area of woodland contains a lot of brown and white rabbits (the **prey**). Also living in the woodland are foxes (the **predator**), whose only source of food is the rabbits.

Characteristic that shows variation	The advantage	What happens?	Why?	Survival	Extinction
The fur on the rabbits – brown or white.	The brown rabbits are better camouflaged in their habitat than the white rabbits.	The foxes eat more of the white rabbits than the brown rabbits.	The white rabbits stand out more, so the fox is able to see them. The brown rabbit is able to hide in the woodland and is camouflaged.	The brown rabbits survive and reproduce. More brown rabbits are produced.	Only a few white rabbits survive and get the chance to reproduce. Fewer white rabbits are produced. White rabbits eventually die out.

Table 04.03.01 Natural selection in practice.

 Checkpoint 4

Using the information you have just read on natural selection, explain how *three* of the following evolutionary characteristics could have come about.

(i) Owls with large eyes.
(ii) A cheetah that runs very fast.
(iii) Birds with long, pointed or sharp beaks.
(iv) A giraffe's long neck.
(v) Birds that eat berries and worms.
(vi) A snake's ability to eat more than one type of animal.

Fig. 04.03.07 The nature of natural selection.

Fig. 04.03.08 Why do owls have very large eyes? Why do kingfishers have long, pointed beaks?

The Amazing Galapagos Islands

Darwin spent a lot of his time researching the unique plants and animals that lived on the sixteen remote Galapagos Islands, now a national park, marine reserve and UNESCO World Heritage Site. These islands are home to many animals and plants not seen anywhere else in the world. There is also a Charles Darwin research station where research on animals and plants still takes place today. The islands are home to animals that are extraordinarily tame and have no fear of humans, because their survival has never been threatened by humans. Birds fly beside you, lizards run in front of you, fur seals sit in your path to take a closer look at you!

Ⓡ Why was Darwin So Amazed?

It was the birds and animals Darwin found on the islands that astonished him. They really should not have been able to survive, but they did (adapting in various ways to do so, as we saw with the finches and their different shaped beaks). This is what led him to his theories on natural selection (and the later use of the phrase 'survival of the fittest'). *Fig. 04.03.09* shows some of the animals that can be found on the Galapagos Islands.

Some of the islands are inhabited, but people are not allowed to visit islands which are not, in order to preserve the habitats and protect these rare and magnificent animals.

Fig. 04.03.09 Animals of the Galapagos Islands.

Fig. 04.03.09 (cont.) Animals of the Galapagos Islands.

WHAT I HAVE LEARNED...

- Evolution is a slow, ongoing change in an organism over a very long time.
- Many scientists promoted the idea of the theory of evolution, but it was Charles Darwin who produced evidence to support the theory.
- Darwin proposed the theory of natural selection to explain the theory of evolution.
- Natural selection occurs when a characteristic that an organism has gives it a better chance of surviving, and this characteristic is passed on genetically from generation to generation.
- Darwin gathered his evidence during a five-year voyage on the HMS *Beagle* and his studies on the Galapagos Islands.
- Evolution is continuous and new organisms are being discovered all the time.

 Question Time

Copy and Complete
In this unit I learned that the world is made up of millions of different organisms. There is also a huge _____ between plants and animals. _____ is a result of this variation. It has occurred over _____ of years. There are estimated to be over ____ million different plants and animals alive today. New _____ are being discovered all the time. Charles _____ proposed the theory of _____. He explained that plants and animals are _____ and that each organism _____ with others to exist. Therefore they must _____to _____. This is where we get the phrase 'survival of the _____'. If a plant or animal adapts well to its habitat, it will _____ and not become _____. The animals that survive pass on their _____ to their young and then their young are able to _____. This is _____ selection.

Question
1. Match each keyword in *Table 04.03.02* with the correct meaning and write them in your copy. One has been done for you.

Keyword	Meaning
Characteristic	A distinguishing feature or quality that allows us to tell organisms apart
Breed	A plant or animal that shares characteristics and are able to produce young
Species	An organism changing to survive in its new habitat
Evolution	To reproduce
Environment	Evidence that can show how an organism has changed over time
Adapt	Changes in an organism that take place over a long time
Fossils	The area surrounding an organism, where it lives and how organisms interact with each other

Table 04.03.02 Match the keywords with their definitions.

2. Name the scientists who thought that evolution happened by natural selection.
3. Describe evolution in your own words.
4. Construct a mind map of evolution.
5. Write a short note on natural selection, using 'survival' as your keyword.

6. 'It is thought that sexual reproduction allows evolution to happen more so than asexual reproduction.' Can you provide an explanation for this statement?

7. What must a predator have over its prey to enable it to survive in a habitat?

8. Why do you think a polar bear would not survive for very long in the desert?

Inquiry

A **Research** how a camel survives living in the desert.

B **Project:** New Species. **Research** three new species that have been found recently. Copy *Table 04.03.03* and present your findings. Include pictures if you wish.

Type of animal/plant	Name (if known)	Picture (optional)	Country it was discovered in	An interesting fact

Table 04.03.03.

C **(R) Research** and **write** an account of one of the following scientists who were involved in developing research on evolution:
  (i)   Jean-Baptiste Lamarck
  (ii) Charles Darwin
What differences are there between Darwin's and Lamarck's ideas?
Are there any similarities between their ideas?

Hint: Be aware that some sources of information may lack detail or show bias.

D **Find out** which places in Ireland are UNESCO World Heritage Sites.

5.1 Photosynthesis

Learning Outcomes

BWLO 7. Describe respiration and **photosynthesis** as both chemical and biological processes; investigate factors that affect respiration and **photosynthesis**.

NSLO 2. Recognise questions that are appropriate for scientific investigation, pose testable hypotheses, and evaluate and compare strategies for investigating hypotheses.

NSLO 3. Design, plan and conduct investigations; explain how reliability, accuracy, precision, fairness, safety, ethics and a selection of suitable equipment have been considered.

NSLO 4. Produce and select data (qualitatively/quantitatively), critically analyse data to identify patterns and relationships, identify anomalous observations, draw and justify conclusions.

NSLO 5. Review and reflect on the skills and thinking used in carrying out investigations, and apply learning and skills to solving problems in unfamiliar contexts.

NSLO 7. Organise and communicate research and investigate findings in a variety of ways fit for purpose and audience, using relevant scientific terminology and representations.

Ⓡ Teacher's reference

KEYWORDS

absorb
biological
chemical
chlorophyll
chloroplast
energy
hypothesis
photosynthesis
process
respiration

LEARNING INTENTIONS

At the end of this unit you should:

1. Be able to describe the process of photosynthesis and why it's needed.
2. Be able to name the factors needed for, and the products of, photosynthesis.
3. Be able to explain where the substances needed for photosynthesis come from and how they enter the plant.
4. Understand and know the word equation for photosynthesis.
5. Be able to explain what happens to the products of photosynthesis.
6. Be able to explain why photosynthesis is such a critical process to the world around us and the factors that can limit photosynthesis.
7. Be able to recognise and explain links between photosynthesis and respiration.

What is Photosynthesis?

Photosynthesis is the way plants make food using **light energy**. Photosynthesis is the most important reaction on the planet. Plants need it as it provides them with food; other organisms rely on plants as their food source, either directly or indirectly. So photosynthesis is the reaction that nearly all organisms rely on.

What does the word mean? It comes from the Greek words *photo* (light) and *synthesis* (to make or put things together).

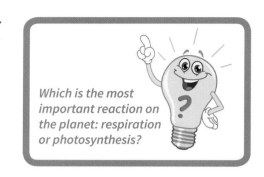

Which is the most important reaction on the planet: respiration or photosynthesis?

- It takes place in the leaves of green plants.
- It helps keep a balance of carbon dioxide and oxygen in the atmosphere.
- Plants use the food (glucose) to grow.
- It is both a **chemical** and a **biological** process.
  - ◆ It is a chemical reaction because the water and carbon dioxide that enter the plant are rearranged through reactions to form new substances.
  - ◆ It is a biological reaction because it is a process that happens in a living thing.

✔ Checkpoint 1

(a) **In pairs, look at the images (a) and (b) in *Fig. 05.01.01* and make a list of differences between the inputs and outputs in the images.**

(b) **State any similarities between the two images.**

(c) **If you were to think of one word that is involved in both, what would it be? Explain why you chose this word.**

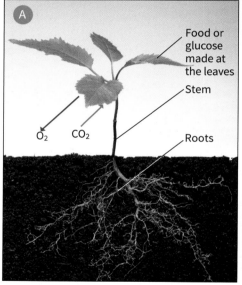

A
Food or glucose made at the leaves
Stem
O₂   CO₂
Roots

B
Oxygen
Food
Carbon dioxide
Water vapour

Fig. 05.01.01.

Factors Needed for Photosynthesis

In *Fig. 05.01.01* we can see the organs in a plant where **photosynthesis** occurs.

Four factors are needed for the chemical **process** of photosynthesis to happen:

1. Light energy
2. Chlorophyll
3. Carbon dioxide
4. Water

Fig. 05.01.02 Leaves taking in sunlight.

Where Do These Factors Come From?

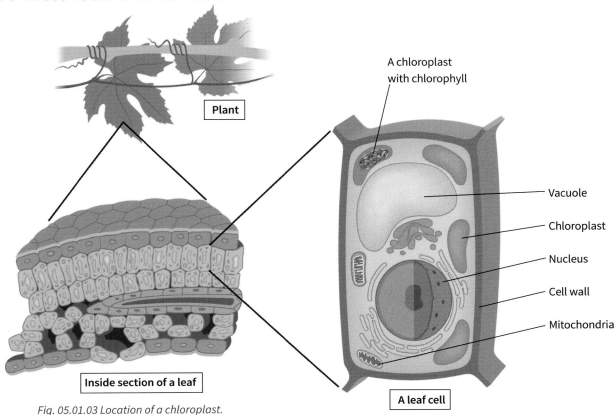

Fig. 05.01.03 Location of a chloroplast.

The leaf, stem and root are the organs of a plant that allow photosynthesis to occur.

The primary source of energy for plants is light. This provides the energy for the reaction of photosynthesis to happen. Carbon dioxide is **absorbed** from the air into the leaves. Water is absorbed by the roots from the soil and travels up the stem to the leaves. **Chlorophyll** is a green pigment found in the **chloroplast** of cells in the leaf. The chloroplast is one of the cell parts that we looked at in *Unit 1.1.* The location of the chloroplast is shown in *Fig. 05.01.03*.

Using the factors needed for photosynthesis and the products made, we can write an equation for photosynthesis. What do you notice about 'light' and 'chlorophyll'?

Note that 'light' and 'chlorophyll' are written above and below the arrow because photosynthesis has to happen in the presence of light and chlorophyll.

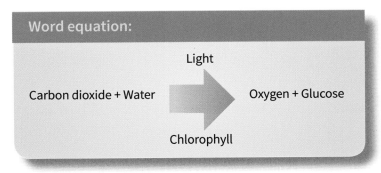

This equation can also be written as a chemical equation:

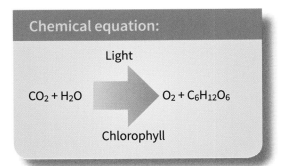

® How Does Photosynthesis Happen?

The pigment chlorophyll is a chemical that traps the light energy from the sun and converts it into chemical energy. The water and carbon dioxide that are absorbed use this energy to create reactions in the leaf that produce **oxygen** and **glucose**.

The oxygen and glucose are referred to as the **products of photosynthesis**. The oxygen is released into the atmosphere from the leaves, and the glucose is the plant's food.

Some of the carbon dioxide and water can be converted to a carbohydrate (starch). This can then be stored in the leaves, stem, or roots. For example, starch is stored in the roots of carrot and parsnip plants, the leaves of lettuce and cabbage, the leaf stalks of celery and the stems of asparagus.

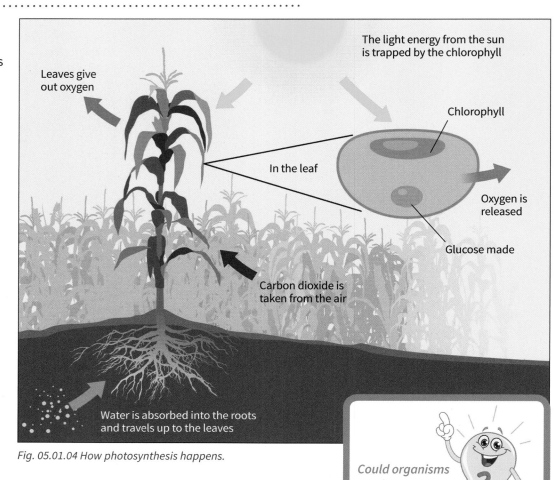

Fig. 05.01.04 How photosynthesis happens.

Could organisms survive on our planet without photosynthesis?

Fig. 05.01.05 Colonies of cyanobacteria.

Did you know?
It is not only plants that can photosynthesise. Some species of bacteria are capable of photosynthesising; they are called photosynthetic bacteria. One example is the cyanobacteria, which is blue-green in colour and approximately 2.5 billion years old!

 **Checkpoint 2**

(a) Copy *Table 05.01.01* and write beside each of the plant organs how it is involved in photosynthesis.

Plant organ	How is the organ involved in photosynthesis?
Leaf	• Light is ... • Contains ... • •
Stem	• Allows ...
Roots	• •

Table 05.01.01.

(b) Draw a diagram of a plant cell (see *Unit 1.1*) and indicate where photosynthesis occurs.

(c) *Fig. 05.01.06* shows a daffodil.
   (i) Sketch out this image and identify on your sketch where photosynthesis occurs.
   (ii) Add the words from the photosynthesis equation to the image.

(d) In your own words, explain the process of photosynthesis.

Fig. 05.01.06 Where does photosynthesis occur?

Why is Photosynthesis So Important?

Plants can make their own food, but animals (including us) cannot. We and other animals have to take food into our bodies, so we rely on plants for our food. Plants are the first step in the food chain of all animals. Animals need to release energy from food to survive. To do this they need the products from photosynthesis: the glucose (food) and oxygen. A process called **respiration** releases the energy from foods (see *Unit 5.2*). This energy allows animals to carry out daily activities, growth, repair and reproduction of cells.

Why Are Some Leaves Different Colours?

Plant leaves are different colours because they have different pigments inside them. Chlorophyll is the most important pigment of them all as it is involved in photosynthesis.

Fig. 05.01.07 Leaves are different colours due to the pigments they contain.

1. The pigment chlorophyll traps or absorbs most of the energy from the blue and reddish part of sunlight. It does not absorb the green part, so that's reflected back to our eyes and we see the leaf as green.
2. A second pigment that may be in the leaf absorbs the blue-green and blue light from the sunlight, so when the light is reflected the leaf appears yellow-orange in colour.
3. A third pigment absorbs the blue, blue-green and green light. Leaves can then appear to be red or purple to us, for example the leaves of the red oak.

All the leaves still contain the chlorophyll pigment they need for photosynthesis, but in different amounts.

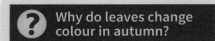

Why do leaves change colour in autumn?

As the plant is growing the leaf will have more chlorophyll so we see the leaf as green, but during the autumn when growth slows down, the chlorophyll will be less and the other pigments which have been there all along are seen. This is why we see orange, yellow or other coloured leaves in the autumn.

Investigation 05.01.01: **Revealing the different pigments in leaves**

Equipment: Some leaves from three different plants, some filter paper, a pencil, three beakers, a pair of scissors, a pestle and mortar, isopropyl alcohol, three straws, a glass rod, Sellotape or paper clip.

Instructions:
1. Cut up enough leaves to quarter-fill a beaker.
2. Use the pestle and mortar to grind the leaves into a fine pulp. Clean and dry the pestle and mortar after each use – do not mix the different pulps.
3. Cut three strips of filter paper approximately 2.5 cm wide, and long enough to hang around a straw as shown in *Fig. 05.01.08*.
4. Draw a pencil line 2–3 cm from the bottom of each filter paper as shown.
5. Set the strips of paper aside.
6. Empty the pulp into beakers, a different beaker for each sample of leaf pulp.
7. Pour the alcohol over the pulp, making sure the alcohol level is above that of the pulp. (Do not use water.)
8. Stir with a glass rod until the alcohol changes colour.
9. Taking one of your strips of filter paper, roll the end that doesn't have the pencil line on it around a straw and secure with Sellotape or a paper clip. Repeat with the other two strips.
10. Hang a strip of filter paper over each beaker, ensuring that the pencil line on the paper does not get covered with the liquid, as shown in *Fig. 05.01.08*. If your paper is too long, roll the paper around the straw again and secure with tape. (You do not want the end of the paper to get saturated.)
11. Wait approximately fifteen minutes or until you see colours move up to the top of the filter paper in each beaker.
12. Make a note of the different colours at the top of the paper and compare your results.

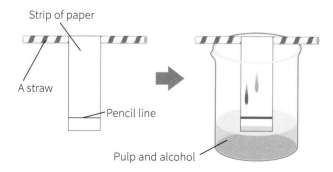

Strip of paper

A straw

Pencil line

Pulp and alcohol

Fig. 05.01.08 Leaf chromatography. For more on chromotography, see Unit 6.3.

What did you learn?
1. Do you think the leaves will have different pigment colours, or will they all be the same?
2. If the leaves were from different types of trees, would the pigment colour results be the same or different? Justify your answer with an explanation.
3. Suggest why you would not use water as a solvent. What might happen when it is added to the pulp?

Factors that can Limit Photosynthesis

You know that plants need four materials for photosynthesis to occur: sunlight, chlorophyll, carbon dioxide and water. How quickly the plant photosynthesises is affected by the amount of sunlight and carbon dioxide it can obtain. These need to be available in the right amounts for the plant to photosynthesise as quickly as it can. If they are not available, this is said to be limiting because it stops or slows down the process of photosynthesis.

Investigation 05.01.02: Showing the limiting factors in photosynthesis

Equipment: For hypotheses (i) and (ii): Some cress seeds and cotton wool, some radish seeds and soil, sunlight or a lamp, some water, a graduated cylinder, a thermometer, a ruler, a results table.
For hypothesis (iii): Some pond weed, some sodium bicarbonate, a lamp, a boiling tube, a spatula, a paper clip, a results table.
For hypothesis (iv): *Draw up an equipment list for your investigation.*

Instructions: 1. Design and carry out an investigation to test one of the following hypotheses:
　　(i)　Varying the amount of light affects the growth of plants.
　　(ii)　Varying the amount of water affects the growth of plants.
　　(iii)　Varying the level of carbon dioxide affects the growth of plants.
　　(iv)　*A hypothesis of your own relating to the factors needed for photosynthesis.*
2. Draw a conclusion from your results.
3. Compare your results with those of others in the class.

> ### *What did you learn?*
> 1. How do you think the investigation you carried out will support the hypothesis you have chosen?
> 2. How did you ensure that a fair test was maintained during your investigation?
> 3. Can you make a link between these problems of ensuring a fair test and the results you or a classmate found?

Photosynthesis and Respiration

Photosynthesis and **respiration** are both **chemical** and **biological** processes.

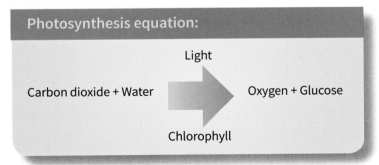

Photosynthesis equation:

Carbon dioxide + Water → (Light / Chlorophyll) Oxygen + Glucose

Respiration equation:

Glucose + Oxygen = Carbon Dioxide + Water + Energy

Can you spot any similarities and differences between the photosynthesis and respiration equations?

What is produced from photosynthesis is needed for respiration. What is produced from respiration is needed for photosynthesis. We sometimes think that the difference between them is that respiration is what animals do and photosynthesis is what plants do. This is true, but there are many more links between these two extremely important processes. Plants also respire using the oxygen and glucose they make.

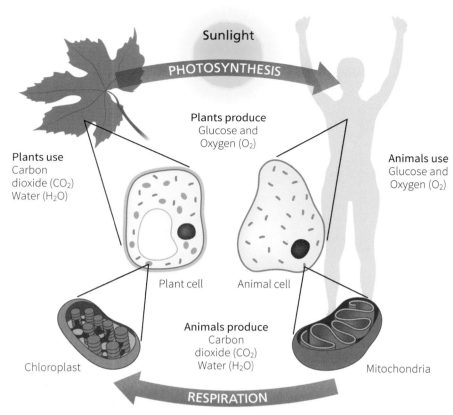

Sunlight

PHOTOSYNTHESIS

Plants produce
Glucose and
Oxygen (O_2)

Plants use
Carbon
dioxide (CO_2)
Water (H_2O)

Animals use
Glucose and
Oxygen (O_2)

Plant cell   Animal cell

Animals produce
Carbon
dioxide (CO_2)
Water (H_2O)

Chloroplast

Mitochondria

RESPIRATION

Fig. 05.01.09 Links between photosynthesis and respiration.

✓ Checkpoint 3

(a) Write out the word equations for photosynthesis and respiration. Place the chemical equation underneath each word equation.

(b) Make a list of the similarities and differences that you spotted between them.

WHAT I HAVE LEARNED...

- Light, chlorophyll, water and carbon dioxide are the materials needed for photosynthesis.
- Photosynthesis is how plants make food using light energy.
- The word equation for photosynthesis is:

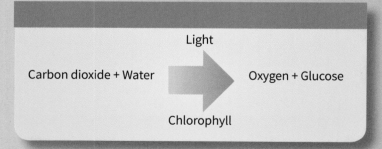

Light

Carbon dioxide + Water → Oxygen + Glucose

Chlorophyll

- Water is absorbed through the plant's roots and carbon dioxide is taken in from the atmosphere.
- The products of photosynthesis are oxygen and glucose (food): the oxygen is released into the atmosphere; the glucose can be stored in the plants and eaten by animals.
- The right amounts of the factors needed for photosynthesis allow the highest rate of photosynthesis to be achieved.
- Without photosynthesis, we would not have the oxygen needed for respiration to happen.

Question Time

Copy and Complete

In this unit I learned that photosynthesis happens in _____. It allows plants to make _____. This is food that we and other animals eat. The plant needs sunlight, chlorophyll, _____ and _____ to photosynthesise. The leaves take in carbon dioxide from the _____, the roots take up water from the _____, and the chlorophyll is found in the _____. When photosynthesis happens it produces _____ and _____. We call this food _____ or starch. We _____ in this oxygen and the plants use the food to grow or we eat the food from the plant. So we rely on plants to _____; without them we would not be able to live. Plants need the _____ amounts of carbon dioxide and light to _____ the food. Too much or too little of either means the plant will not make food as _____ as it should.

Questions

1. Name the part of the plant where photosynthesis happens.
2. Draw a diagram of a leaf as in *Fig. 05.01.10* and label the arrows with the four materials needed for photosynthesis and the two materials that are produced.

Fig. 05.01.10.

3. What pigment does the chloroplast have that allows photosynthesis to occur?
4. Sketch a graph of the results you would expect to see if a plant had reduced carbon dioxide levels over time. Use the following axes.

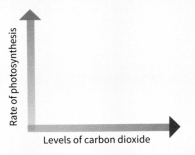

5. During the night the amount of light is low. Suggest what happens the rate of photosynthesis in a plant at night.
6. How do plants take in the essential minerals they need?
7. If you put a plant in a cupboard for two weeks and watered it regularly, would it still make food? Give a reason for your answer.

Inquiry

A **Discuss** why the process of photosynthesis is such a critical process and why the world around us would not survive without it. **Draw up** an outline for an article on this subject.

B 'Plants store energy as starch.' **Suggest** how you could prove that this statement is true.

C A product of photosynthesis is water. **Investigate** and **prove** that a plant produces water. *Hint:* Soil holds water, so you must prove that the water has come from the plant and not the soil.

D **Investigate** what colour of light is best for plants to grow in. Equipment needed: three lightbulbs (green, blue and red), a potted plant, some water.

E *Fig. 05.01.11* shows a greenhouse. Using your knowledge of the factors that can limit photosynthesis, explain or discuss how a greenhouse works and why they are so widely used around the country.

Fig. 05.01.11 Why do people use greenhouses to grow plants?

F Ⓡ **Research** the inside structure of a leaf. **Draw** the structure or **create** a model of the leaf you have drawn using plasticine. Highlight where the chlorophyll is found and how the carbon dioxide and oxygen enter and leave the leaf.

5.2 Respiration

Learning Outcomes

BWLO 7. Describe respiration and photosynthesis **as both chemical and biological processes; investigate factors that affect respiration** and photosynthesis.

NSLO 2. Recognise questions that are appropriate for scientific investigation, pose testable hypotheses and evaluate and compare strategies for investigating hypotheses.

NSLO 3. Design, plan and conduct investigations; explain how reliability, accuracy, precision, fairness, safety, ethics and a selection of suitable equipment have been considered.

NSLO 4. Produce and select data (qualitatively/ quantitatively), critically analyse data to identify patterns and relationships, identify anomalous observations, draw and justify conclusions.

NSLO 5. Review and reflect on the skills and thinking used in carrying out investigations, and apply learning and skills to solving problems in unfamiliar contexts.

NSLO 7. Organise and communicate research and investigate findings in a variety of ways fit for purpose and audience, using relevant scientific terminology and representations.

R Teacher's reference

KEYWORDS

absorbed
aerobic
anaerobic
biological
carbon dioxide
chemical
contract
energy
glucose
lactic acid
mitochondria
oxygen
products
respiration

LEARNING INTENTIONS

At the end of this unit you should:

1. Be able to identify the substances needed for respiration to take place.
2. Be able to identify the products of respiration.
3. Be able to explain where the substances needed for respiration come from.
4. Be able to recall and understand the equation for respiration.
5. Be able to explain what happens the products produced in respiration.
6. Be able to recognise the similarities and differences between photosynthesis and respiration.
7. Be able to investigate the factors that affect respiration through exercise.

What is Respiration?

- **Respiration** is the release of **energy** from food.
- It happens in every cell of all living things.
- Respiration occurs in both animals and plants.
- It takes place in the **mitochondria** of cells.
- Generally, along with the nutrients from food known as **glucose**, **oxygen** is also needed for respiration to occur.
- Respiration produces **carbon dioxide** and water vapour along with energy.
- It is both a **chemical** and a **biological** process.

How Respiration Works

A chemical reaction occurs during respiration. How does it happen?

The glucose comes from the breakdown of nutrients in the food we eat and oxygen from the air we breathe in. The glucose and oxygen are **absorbed** into the bloodstream and the blood transports it to the body cells. The glucose and oxygen are rearranged through reactions to form the **products** carbon dioxide and water.

- Glucose and oxygen get used up in the reaction.
- Carbon dioxide and water are produced as waste products.
- Energy is released and allows us to carry out activities, e.g. walking, talking, jumping, eating, sleeping. When you are hungry you eat – and you get energy from the foods you eat.
- Heat is also produced during the reaction as a **by-product**.

Respiration is a biological reaction because it is a process that happens in a living thing – an animal or plant cell.

We can represent respiration as an equation:

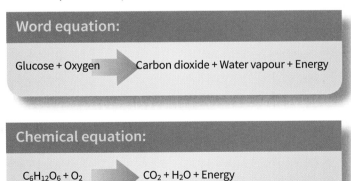

Word equation:

Glucose + Oxygen ⟶ Carbon dioxide + Water vapour + Energy

Chemical equation:

$C_6H_{12}O_6 + O_2$ ⟶ $CO_2 + H_2O$ + Energy

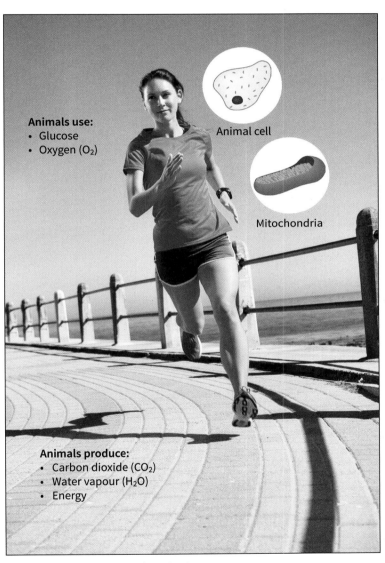

Animals use:
- Glucose
- Oxygen (O_2)

Animal cell

Mitochondria

Animals produce:
- Carbon dioxide (CO_2)
- Water vapour (H_2O)
- Energy

Fig. 05.02.01 The products of respiration.

Respiration: The controlled release of energy from food.

Checkpoint 1

(a) This 'body cell' circle represents what goes in and out of a body cell. Copy and complete the circle using all the words in the list:

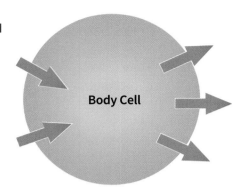

energy • water vapour • oxygen • food • carbon dioxide

(b) Make a list of the ways you think we use the energy released in respiration.

(c) You have just finished playing a game of basketball. You used more energy playing the game than you did when you were watching television, as your body systems had to work harder than normal.
  (i) Describe what happened to your circulatory system and your breathing system during and after the game.
  (ii) Explain why the events in part (i) happened.

🔍 Investigation 05.02.01: **Showing that respiration takes place**

Equipment: A handful of germinating peas, two flasks, two thermometers, some cotton wool, a beaker, a tripod, some wire gauze, some water, a pair of tongs, a sieve or filter paper, two labels.

Instructions: Design an experiment using the equipment as listed to prove that respiration occurs.

What did you learn?
1. What is the control in your investigation?
2. Why do you think a control is necessary?
3. What do you predict will be the result of the investigation?

How Energy is Used

In animals (including humans), respiration is the most important reaction in the cells.
The *energy* released is used up by:
- **The cells in the body** – they need energy to build new cells and tissues.
- **Muscles** – the energy produced by respiration allows them to **contract** and move.
- **Keeping warm** – some animals use the energy to keep them warm when they are in a cold environment.
- **Making protein** – plants use their energy to make proteins (which are needed, for example, to make enzymes).

If you want to walk, your muscles need energy to contract and move your body. If you want to run fast, the muscles need to work harder and the energy requirements needed are also higher. Therefore your cells will need more food and oxygen to release more energy.

The *carbon dioxide* that is produced during respiration is acidic. Too much carbon dioxide in the blood is dangerous, so it must be released into the atmosphere by breathing it out through the nose and mouth.

Plants use carbon dioxide during photosynthesis.

The *water vapour* is released through our nose and mouth as we breathe out.

The *heat* gets used up by our body.

Plants *lose the carbon dioxide and water vapour* that they produce during respiration through the tiny openings on their leaves – stomata – or the products are used in photosynthesis.

When can you see the water vapour that is released through our nose and mouth as we breathe out?

Anaerobic and Aerobic Respiration

Respiration can occur in two different ways, depending on whether or not oxygen is present. It will either be:

1. Anaerobic

or

2. Aerobic

Anaerobic respiration is the release of energy without oxygen. It releases a small amount of energy.

Aerobic respiration is the release of energy using oxygen. This reaction releases a lot of energy.

Our bodies can use both types. Here are two examples to help explain anaerobic and aerobic.

1. When **Usain Bolt**, currently the 100 metre World and Olympic champion, sprints the 100 m track, he does not take in oxygen. He makes energy **anaerobically**. This is because he sprints 100 m so quickly – in under 10 seconds in fact! If he runs a victory lap after the race, his muscles will now need oxygen to release energy during respiration.

2. During an 80-minute game of rugby, **Johnny Sexton**'s muscles will need high amounts of energy, so there will be a very high demand for oxygen and glucose to get to the muscles. The muscles work **aerobically** during the game. If the game goes into extra time, the muscles will start to get tired, and they can run out of glucose. The demand for oxygen and glucose is still there but it can take longer for the oxygen to reach the muscles as the muscles are tired and so have to work harder to take in the oxygen.

The Effects of Exercise on Respiration

During exercise, the muscles respire more and there is a demand for oxygen and glucose to be transported to the muscle cells more quickly than when they are not exercising or at rest. The waste product carbon dioxide must also be removed from the cells more quickly.

To do this, the body increases:

- **The heart rate:** This speeds up the flow of blood, bringing *oxygen* to the cells and removing *carbon dioxide*.
- **The breathing rate:** This increases the amount of *oxygen* taken in and the amount of *carbon dioxide* that is removed.

 Muscle Cramp
Have you ever had muscle cramp?

When you exercise, your muscles cannot always get the oxygen to the muscle cells quickly enough. So the body moves from an aerobic state to an anaerobic state. The muscles will move, but because they are respiring anaerobically they will produce **lactic acid** and only a little energy. The lactic acid builds up in your muscles and can be painful. This lactic acid build-up is what we refer to as 'muscle cramp'.

 Investigation 05.02.02: **Showing that respiration demands affect heart and breathing rates**

Instructions: Remembering that respiration releases energy from food, and that heart and breathing rates increase during exercise, supplying cells with glucose and oxygen for respiration and removing carbon dioxide, challenge yourself with the following tasks:

1. Design two investigations to see if breathing and heart rates change as the demand for respiration changes. Think about how you will change the rate of respiration. Trial your investigation on yourself or a small class group.
2. Gather your observations and results and decide how to present them.

	Respiration	Photosynthesis
Where does it happen?	In cells – in the mitochondria	In cells – in the chloroplast
What is needed?	• Glucose • Oxygen	• Carbon dioxide • Water vapour • Light and chlorophyll
What is produced?	• Carbon dioxide • Water vapour • Energy	• Oxygen • Glucose
Energy source	Chemical bonds in the glucose	Light
What happens to the energy?	Energy is released	Energy is stored (as food)
What living organisms carry it out?	All living organisms	• All plants • Some algae, some bacteria
What happens to the glucose?	Glucose is *broken down* to release energy	Glucose is *made* from carbon dioxide and water

Table 05.02.01 Similarities and differences between respiration and photosynthesis.

WHAT I HAVE LEARNED...

- The substances needed for respiration are glucose and oxygen.
- The products of respiration are carbon dioxide, water vapour, energy and heat (which is a by-product).
- Oxygen comes from the atmosphere and glucose comes from food when it is broken down by the body.
- The word equation for respiration is:

Glucose + Oxygen → Carbon dioxide + Water vapour + Energy

- Carbon dioxide and water vapour are released from the body into the atmosphere; the energy is used up when the body carries out activities.
- There are similarities and differences between the cellular reactions of photosynthesis and respiration.
- Respiration can be affected by exercise.

 ## Question Time

Copy and Complete

In this unit I learned that respiration is the _____ of _____ from foods. It happens in our body cells. The food we take into our body gets broken down and we take in _____ from the air. The food, which is called _____, and the oxygen both travel to the cells in the _____. In the cells a _____ reaction takes place and _____ is released as it happens. After the reaction the cell releases carbon dioxide and water vapour. The carbon dioxide and water vapour are released from the body when we breathe out. Plants use the _____ _____ that we release when they make food during _____. There are two types of respiration: _____ is the release of energy using oxygen; anaerobic is the release of a _____ amount of energy without using _____. In order for the body to get more oxygen to the muscles to make energy, it must breathe _____ to take in more oxygen and the heart must pump blood _____ as it transports this oxygen to the muscles.

Questions

1. Describe what happens during respiration.
2. Write out the word equation for respiration.
3. Can you explain how digested food is used by the body?
4. How do you think the glucose and oxygen needed for aerobic respiration get to all the body's cells?
5. Describe how our breathing rate changes when we exercise.
6. State what the two types of respiration are. Explain what is involved in each.
7. The equations for photosynthesis and respiration are shown below. Spend a few minutes looking at both. Make a list of any similarities and differences between them.

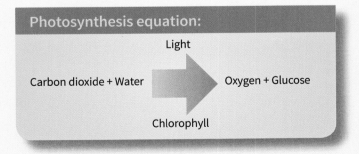

Photosynthesis equation:

Carbon dioxide + Water → Oxygen + Glucose

Light

Chlorophyll

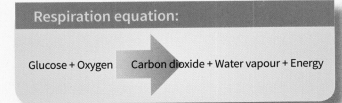

Respiration equation:

Glucose + Oxygen → Carbon dioxide + Water vapour + Energy

Inquiry

A R Three students were involved in a PE investigation on the heart's response to exercise.

Their heart rates were measured during a light exercise session lasting 20 minutes. The students do not take part in sporting activities regularly. During the session the students wore heart rate monitors. After the 20-minute session, *Table 05.02.02* was produced – this is the information from the heart rate monitors. Heart rate is measured in beats per minute (bpm).

B **Trace** the route the oxygen molecule takes after it enters the nose when breathed in, listing the route it takes.

C **Carry out** your own investigation into breathing rates in response to exercise among your classmates.
(i) Design the investigation.
(ii) Discuss the design with the class to eliminate any possible errors.

Student	BPM before start	BPM after 2 min	BPM after 4 min	BPM after 6 min	BPM after 8 min	BPM after 10 min	BPM after 12 min	BPM after 14 min	BPM after 16 min	BPM after 18 min	BPM after 20 min
A	62	62	62	84	89	110	112	112	112	112	112
B	62	75	78	79	80	84	89	100	110	113	113
C	63	74	98	98	110	115	118	120	120	118	118

Table 05.02.02 Heart rate monitor results.

Answer the following questions:
(i) Help the researchers by transferring the information from the table on to one graph.
(ii) What type of graph is the most suitable for showing this type of information? Give your reasons.
(iii) Suggest two reasons why there are differences between the students' heart rates, even though they all took part in the same level of exercise for the same amount of time.
(iv) Explain the demands that light exercise can put on the body.
(v) The researchers are looking for any anomalous or irregular results. Can you identify any? Suggest a reason for the anomaly or irregularity.
(vi) What conclusions about the effect of exercise on heart rate can you draw from the information gathered?
(vii) Why does the heart rate respond in this way?

UNIT
5.3

Habitats

Learning Outcomes

BWLO 5. Conduct a habitat study; research and investigate the adaptation, competition and interdependence of organisms within specific habitats and communities.

BWLO 8. Explain how matter and energy flow through an ecosystem.

NSLO 3. Design, plan and conduct investigations; explain how reliability, accuracy, precision, fairness, safety, ethics and a selection of suitable equipment have been considered.

NSLO 4. Produce and select data (qualitatively/ quantitatively), critically analyse data to identify patterns and relationships, identify anomalous observations, draw and justify conclusions.

NSLO 5. Review and reflect on skills and thinking used in carrying out investigations, and apply learning and skills to solving problems in unfamiliar contexts.

NSLO 7. Organise and communicate research and investigate findings in a variety of ways fit for purpose and audience, using relevant scientific terminology and representations.

R   Teacher's reference

KEYWORDS

adaptation
biosphere
camouflage
characteristic
communities
competition
consumer
ecosystem
environment
food chain
food web
habitat
interdependence
matter
population
producer
resources

LEARNING INTENTIONS

At the end of this unit you should:

1. Know what a habitat is, how they vary and how different habitats support different organisms.
2. Know that habitats can be affected by environmental factors, light, availability of water, amount of nutrients present.
3. Know what an adaptation is, give examples of adaptations and explain how they help the plant or animal survive.
4. Recognise what resources plants and animals compete for.
5. Be able to explain why at times resources are low and competition between organisms increases.
6. Be able to describe how plants and animals have to depend on each other.
7. Be able to conduct a habitat study.
8. Understand how matter and energy flow through a food chain.

Life on Earth

On planet earth, life exists everywhere: in the air, on land and in water. The surroundings and conditions that a plant or animal lives in is its **environment**. Put simply, the environment is anything outside a living thing's structure or body that influences or affects its survival. The place where a plant or animal lives is called its **habitat**.

Environmental factors determine where plants and animals live in an area on earth. The factors include:

- different temperatures
- changing availability of water
- amount of nutrients present.

The area where **communities** of plants and animals live and interact with each other and with the non-living features of the environment is called an **ecosystem**.

Ecosystems

Every plant needs to make food to survive and every animal needs food to survive. An energy flow through an ecosystem is needed for the plants and animals to survive.

So how does the energy get into and travel through the ecosystem?

Food chains and **food webs** are used to show feeding relationships in a habitat – who eats what. Energy is passed on from one organism to the next, creating a flow of energy. The transfer of **matter** from one organism to another allows this to happen.

Food Chains

Food chains (or energy chains) start with a plant or parts of a plant (leaves, seeds). They are called **producers**.

An animal in the food chain that eats something else is referred to as a **consumer**.

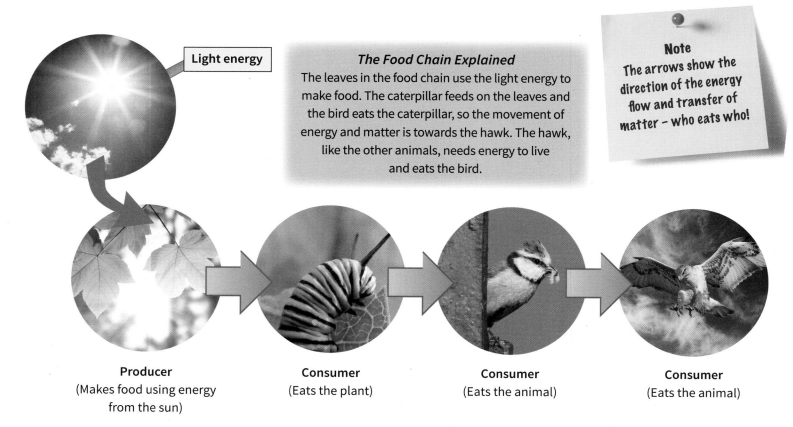

Light energy

The Food Chain Explained
The leaves in the food chain use the light energy to make food. The caterpillar feeds on the leaves and the bird eats the caterpillar, so the movement of energy and matter is towards the hawk. The hawk, like the other animals, needs energy to live and eats the bird.

Note
The arrows show the direction of the energy flow and transfer of matter – who eats who!

Producer
(Makes food using energy from the sun)

Consumer
(Eats the plant)

Consumer
(Eats the animal)

Consumer
(Eats the animal)

Food Webs

The flow of energy is not always in a straight line, such as was shown in the previous example, from leaf to caterpillar, to bird, to hawk. For this reason we use food webs, which show many interlinked food chains.

In food webs there can be more than one producer and each producer can have more than one consumer feeding off it. Food webs are therefore a truer representation of what happens in an ecosystem. Can you identify any food chains in this woodland

Did you know?
All living things need nitrogen to make protein for growth to occur.

Fig. 05.03.01 A woodland food web.

- **Food chains and food webs:** show the transfer of matter and energy from one organism to another.
- **Food webs:** many food chains interlinked together.
- **Food chains and food webs:** show the feeding relationships within an ecosystem.

✓ Checkpoint 1

(a) What organisms are producers and why are they called producers?

(b) An animal that eats an organism is referred to as a _____?

(c) If the caterpillar were to become extinct, what would happen to the number of birds in existence? Would there be an effect on the number of hawks in that food chain?

(d) Referring to the food web in *Fig. 05.03.01*, write out three separate food chains, using arrows to represent the transfer of energy and matter.

(e) Why, do you think, are food chains only four or five links long?

(f) Construct a food chain with arrows for each of these descriptions:

   (i) Grass gets eaten by a field mouse which gets eaten by a hawk.

   (ii) An owl eats a spider which ate a ladybird which fed on caterpillars which ate leaves.

(g) Place the following food chains into one food web by drawing out the links. Always begin with the producer(s) and use arrows to represent who eats what and the transfer of energy and cycle of matter.

   (i) Grass ➡ grasshopper ➡ squirrel ➡ hawk.

   (ii) Dandelion ➡ grasshopper ➡ spider ➡ field mouse ➡ hawk.

> **Producer:** A plant that brings energy into the food chain.

> **Consumer:** An organism that eats another.

Energy Loss

Not all the energy is moved along the chain or web. Why? Not all of an gets eaten and therefore some energy is not taken in. Energy is lost. H

An animal gets its energy from food and stores it, but some of the energy is lost:

- It is lost into the environment as heat (respiration).
- It is used to keep the animal warm.
- It is used up in movement.
- It is used up in digestion.

Because of these losses, animals need to eat large amounts in order to meet their energy needs.

The only amount that can be transferred to next link

Stored energy 100%

Stored energy

Wasted energy

Lost energy

Plant food is all eaten by animal = full plate = all energy transferred to next link

ℝ Habitats

> **Habitat:** A place where a plant or animal lives.

Food webs show us the feeding relationships within habitats. The plants and animals that make up the food webs will be different in different habitats.

In order for a plant or animal to survive, the habitat must meet all its needs. The habitat must provide the water, nutrients, sunlight and space for plants to grow; and the food, water and shelter needed by animals. These are referred to as the **resources** needed to survive.

> **Ecosystem:** An area where plants and animals live and interact with each other and with their environment.

Think of your local park:

It has grass, hedgerows and trees. Each of these can be labelled a habitat. Why? Because they are where plants and animals live. For example, a tree is a plant, and it will have animals living on it and feeding off it. But we can also say that the leaves and bark on a tree are habitats as they have small insects living on and in them.

But habitats do not have to be living things. For example, woodlice need a dark and damp environment to live in, so you might find them under a rock or flower pot.

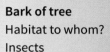

Bark of tree
Habitat to whom?
Insects

Shrubs
Habitat to whom?
Insects or small
animals such as field
mice.

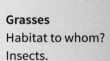

Grasses
Habitat to whom?
Insects.

Fig. 05.03.02 Different habitats in one area. Can you find any other habitats in this picture?

✓ Checkpoint 2

(a) Explain why energy is lost as it flows from one link to the next in a food web.
(b) What is a habitat?
(c) What must a habitat provide in order for a plant and an animal to survive there?
(d) If the habitat did not provide for the animals, what would they have to do?
(e) We've seen that a tree is a habitat. Name parts of the tree that could be habitats for animals.

Did you know?
Over 20% of the oxygen used on earth is produced in the Amazon rainforest, which is the site of many habitats.

Where Can We Find Habitats on Earth?

Take a look at *Fig.05.03.03*, and then *Table 05.03.01*, which gives some descriptions and examples of levels of organisation.

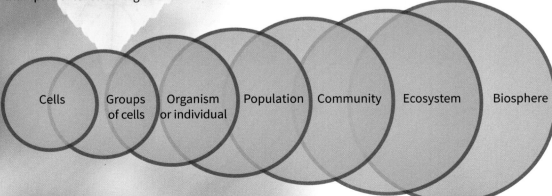

Cells | Groups of cells | Organism or individual | Population | Community | Ecosystem | Biosphere

Fig. 05.03.03 Levels of organisation.

BIOSPHERE
Part of the earth that has living things (has ecosystems)

ECOSYSTEM
The area where communities of plants and animals live and interact with each other and their environment

COMMUNITY
Groups (populations) of plants and animals that live together

POPULATION
Groups of organisms of the same species that live in an area

ORGANISM or INDIVIDUAL
A living thing, for example a plant or an animal

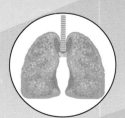

GROUPS OF CELLS
Tissues and organs

CELLS
Unit of life

Different Habitats

There are many different habitats within ecosystems around the world. You'll even find many habitats in your own locality, even in your own back garden!

- Ponds
- Lakes
- Roots of plants
- Under flowerpots and logs
- Rocks
- Hedgerows
- Woodlands
- Forest

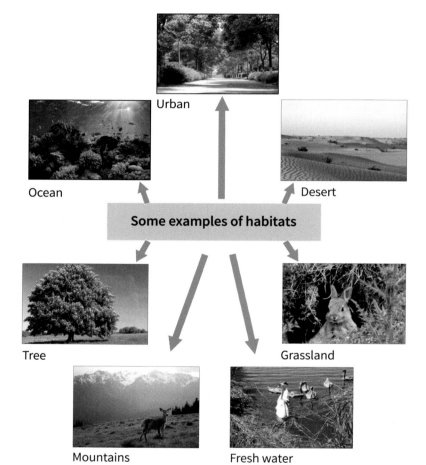

Urban

Ocean

Desert

Some examples of habitats

Tree

Grassland

Mountains

Fresh water

Fig. 05.03.04 Different habitats around the world.

Table 05.03.01 Examples of levels of organisation.

Ⓡ Adaptations to Habitats

An **adaptation** is a **characteristic** or feature that an organism has that increases its chances of survival in its environment and habitat. They help explain why some plants and animals are found in one area and not in another. For example, a lion could not survive eating only the insects in your garden.

Examples of how plants and animals can adapt are shown in *Table 05.03.02*. Can you think of any more examples?

> *Why are rabbits' eyes wide apart? Why do some plants have wide leaves? Why does a lion have sharp teeth and claws?*

Plant adaptations	Animal adaptations
• Narrow or broad leaves • Deep or shallow roots • Waxy leaves – prevent water loss • Thick fleshy leaves to store water • Broad leaves to capture the sunlight • Thorns for protection	• Migration • Body coverings: spines, thorns, scales, fur, etc. • Ability to hide • Hibernation • Wide feet/webbed feet, etc. • Wings to fly • Sensory whiskers • Large ears/small ears • **Camouflage**, e.g. stick insect

Table 05.03.02 Plant and animal adaptations.

☑ Checkpoint 3

(a) Look at the images of the different environments in *Fig. 05.03.05* and imagine yourself standing in one of them. Describe briefly what it would be like to live there.

(b) How might plants and animals be adapted to living in each particular habitat and the environment around them? Give one example of a plant and one example of an animal adaptation for each habitat.

Fig. 05.03.05 What would it be like to live in these environments?

Adaptations in a Cold Environment

Fig. 05.03.06 shows images of the Arctic poppy and a polar bear and details how they are adapted to living and surviving in a cold environment. Air temperatures are low and it is usually windy with very little rainfall. Most animals that live in cold or extreme cold conditions are warm-blooded, which means they make their own heat inside their bodies. Other animals that live in these cold conditions are penguins, whales and seals.

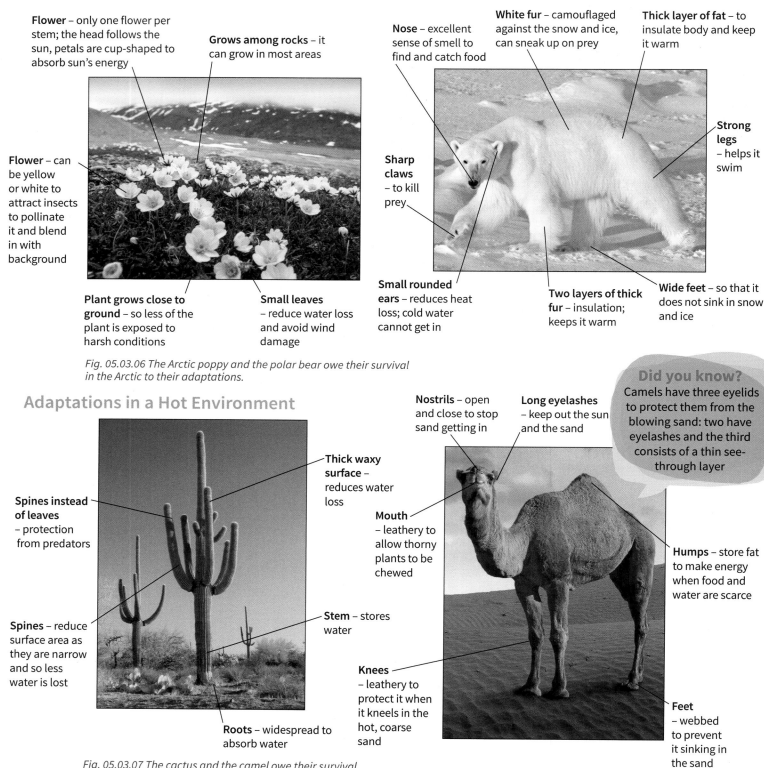

Flower – only one flower per stem; the head follows the sun, petals are cup-shaped to absorb sun's energy

Grows among rocks – it can grow in most areas

Flower – can be yellow or white to attract insects to pollinate it and blend in with background

Plant grows close to ground – so less of the plant is exposed to harsh conditions

Small leaves – reduce water loss and avoid wind damage

Nose – excellent sense of smell to find and catch food

White fur – camouflaged against the snow and ice, can sneak up on prey

Thick layer of fat – to insulate body and keep it warm

Strong legs – helps it swim

Sharp claws – to kill prey

Small rounded ears – reduces heat loss; cold water cannot get in

Two layers of thick fur – insulation; keeps it warm

Wide feet – so that it does not sink in snow and ice

Fig. 05.03.06 The Arctic poppy and the polar bear owe their survival in the Arctic to their adaptations.

Adaptations in a Hot Environment

Spines instead of leaves – protection from predators

Thick waxy surface – reduces water loss

Spines – reduce surface area as they are narrow and so less water is lost

Roots – widespread to absorb water

Nostrils – open and close to stop sand getting in

Long eyelashes – keep out the sun and the sand

Did you know?
Camels have three eyelids to protect them from the blowing sand: two have eyelashes and the third consists of a thin see-through layer

Mouth – leathery to allow thorny plants to be chewed

Stem – stores water

Knees – leathery to protect it when it kneels in the hot, coarse sand

Humps – store fat to make energy when food and water are scarce

Feet – webbed to prevent it sinking in the sand

Fig. 05.03.07 The cactus and the camel owe their survival in the desert to their adaptations.

 **Checkpoint 4**

(a) In small groups, look at the images in *Fig. 05.03.08*. Make a list of all the differences you can see between the two plants, and between the two owls.

(b) Discuss why these differences might exist and the benefits of each difference.

(c) Suggest how these differences could affect each plant's/animal's interactions in the habitat.

> **Adaptation:** A characteristic or feature of an organism that increases its chances of survival.

Fig. 05.03.08 What differences can you see between the two plants, and the two owls?

Competition within Habitats

Why do plants and animals need to adapt? To survive and avoid **competition**. Competition is when organisms such as plants and animals fight for a resource to stay alive.

Plants and animals have to compete for resources. When the resources are in short supply, competition is created between the organisms. The organisms that compete most successfully are the ones that will survive.

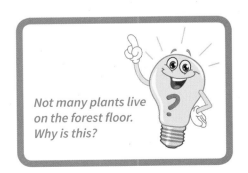

Not many plants live on the forest floor. Why is this?

- Plants complete for water, sunlight and space.

If a small plant is growing under a tree with big leaves, they will compete for sunlight. The tree will win because its leaves are larger. Can you think of another competition among plants?

- Animals compete for food (as you can see in *Fig. 05.03.09*), water, shelter and a mate so they can reproduce).

Competition: The battle for resources between organisms to ensure survival.

Fig. 05.03.09 Competition for this acorn is fierce!

Interdependence

Plants and animals in different habitats sometimes depend on each other for survival. Animals depend on plants for food and shelter. Plants depend on animals to disperse seeds so that new plants can grow. This is called **interdependence**.

Interdependence: The dependence of organisms on each other for survival.

Example	How interdependence works
 A lizard and a seal	The *lizard* needs food. It eats the flies around the seal. The *seal* has no tail to swipe away flies that sit around its eyes, so it needs the lizard to remove them.
 Bee feeding from a flower	The *bee* feeds on the nectar at the base of the petals. The *flower*'s pollen sticks to the bee and when the bee flies away the pollen is dispersed.

Table 05.03.03 Some examples of interdependence.

✓ Checkpoint 5

Look at the images in *Fig. 05.03.10*. Make a list of where interdependence might be demonstrated in each image and briefly outline how the relationship works.

Fig. 05.03.10 How does each of these relationships work?

Studying a Habitat

A range of equipment can be used to help study a habitat. *Table 05.03.04* shows some examples.

Equipment	Purpose	How to use
Soil pH meter	To measure soil pH	Place the probe in the soil and record the reading
Soil thermometer	To measure soil temperature	Place the probe in the soil and record the reading
Quadrat	To record the presence of plants within an sample area of habitat	Place or throw randomly in the area, record presence of plants, repeat ten times

Table 05.03.04 Equipment used to study a habitat.

Equipment	Purpose	How to use
Line transect	To record the presence of plants in a small area within the habitat	Set out the line and note the species that are found at each tag
Beating tray	To collect small insects	Hold the beating tray under a tree or shrub and shake the foliage or hit the branches with a stick
Sweep net	To collect insects from long grass	Sweep the net through the grass
Pooter	To collect insects	Place A in your mouth and B on the insect, then suck

Table 05.03.04 (cont.) Equipment used to study a habitat.

R A Habitat Study

Carry out a study on the plants and animals that live in a habitat of your choosing and the relationships between them.

1. Investigate the plants in the habitat by studying the distribution and quantity of the plants.
2. Investigate the animals in the habitat.
3. Research to find out if any relationships exists between the plants and the animals.
4. Create a biodiversity sheet for the plants and animals in the habitat.
5. List the non-living factors in the habitat.

WHAT I HAVE LEARNED...

- Food chains and food webs show the transfer of matter and energy from one organism to another. They also show the feeding relationships in an ecosystem.
- An ecosystem is an area where plants and animals interact with each other.
- A habitat is a place where plants and animals live. A habitat can change, which leads to the organisms in it changing too.
- A community is a group of plants and animals that live together.
- A population is a group of organisms of the same species living in an area.
- Plants and animals have to adapt to their environment to survive or they will die.
- An adaptation is a characteristic of a plant or animal that increases its chances of survival.
- Examples of adaptations in plants and animals and how these adaptations help them survive.
- Competition is when organisms fight for a resource to survive.
- Interdependence is when organisms in an area depend on each other for survival.
- How to make observations of living things in a habitat by conducting a habitat study.

Question Time

Copy and Complete

In this unit I learned that plants and animals _____ on each other to live. The relationship between plants, animals and other animals can be represented in a food chain or _____ _____. These show what eats what; the arrows tell us where the _____ is transferred. At the start of the food chain and web are the _____, which are called the producers as they produce the _____. In the chain or web an animal that eats another organism is called a _____. The place where plants and animals live within an ecosystem is called a _____. There are many habitats, for example a tree, a grassland area, a hedgerow, the desert, a forest and the sea. Each habitat has _____ plants and animals that _____ there. This is because each habitat has different _____ conditions and because of this not all plants and animals are able to live there. The organisms that do live there are _____ to survive in that area. This means that the organism has _____ that allow them to _____ in that habitat. If all the plants live in the same area they will have to _____ for water and _____. Animals will have to fight for _____, shelter and a _____ to reproduce with. If the plant or animal does not adapt to compete for these they will _____.

Questions

1. What is the source of energy in an ecosystem?
2. Explain how the source energy can then become available to an owl.
3. Describe food chains and food webs. Include all the following words and phrases:

   - producer • consumer • food chain • food web
   - energy loss • carnivore • herbivore

4. Give three examples of habitats.
5. *Fig. 05.03.11* shows a food web for a habitat: a tree. Answer the following questions relating to the web:
   (i) Name the producer for the web.
   (ii) Name three animals that are the first to eat.
   (iii) If the population of beetles decreased, what effect would this have on the population (number) of woodpeckers?
   (iv) Write out two food chains from this web.

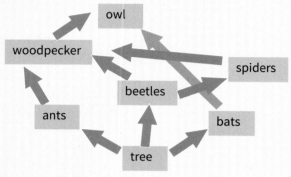

Fig. 05.03.11 Food web for a tree.

6. What does it mean to be adapted to survive?
7. Choose either a plant or an animal and describe how it is adapted to survive in a hot environment.
8. Choose either a plant or an animal and describe how it is adapted to survive in a cold environment.
9. Outline the adaptations an animal needs to survive living in the desert and in the Arctic.
10. 'Plants and animals in a habitat depend on each other.' Explain the meaning of this statement.
11. Select two out of the three organisms shown in *Fig. 05.03.12* and on an A4 sheet list the following:
    (i) The environment that the organism might live in.
    (ii) What features it has that allows it to adapt to this area.
    (iii) What resources it may have to compete for.
    (iv) Do you know of any other organism it depends on? How would you show that interdependence occurs?

Fig. 05.03.12 (a) Bladder wrack; (b) Snow leopard; (c) Snail.

Inquiry

A Food webs become unbalanced if a group of organisms within the web dies and becomes extinct. **Suggest** four reasons why an organism could become extinct.

B **Find out** about adaptations and their purpose, using the questions given in *Table 05.03.05* as prompts.

Plant adaptation questions	Animal adaptation questions
1. Why do some grassland trees in hot climates have really thick bark?	1. Why do some snakes that live in the forest have black heads and a green body?
2. What is the advantage of the dandelion having light, feathery seeds?	2. Why are some animals the same colour as their surroundings?
3. Why do ivy plants grow on structures such as walls or around poles?	3. Why do lizards have long tongues?
4. What is the advantage of some plants having deep roots in the ground?	4. Why do fish have gills?

Table 05.03.05.

C There are plans to send people to live on Mars. Knowing that we as animals need resources and depend on plants to survive, and that plants also need their resources and can depend on animals, **research** and **present** findings on how it is proposed to maintain human life on Mars.

D **Comparison of habitat studies:** Carry out a habitat study in an area at home or close to home or a park near where you live. Compare your results to those completed at school.
   (i) **Investigate** the different environmental factors present in each habitat.
   (ii) **Investigate** whether there are differences in the types of plant or animal that live there.

UNIT
5.4

Conserving the Environment

Learning Outcomes

BWLO 10. Evaluate how humans can successfully conserve ecological biodiversity and contribute to global food production; appreciate the benefits that people obtain from ecosystems.

NSLO 4. Produce and select data (qualitatively/ quantitatively), critically analyse data to identify patterns and relationships, identify anomalous observations, draw and justify conclusions.

NSLO 7. Organise and communicate research and investigate findings in a variety of ways fit for purpose and audience, using relevant scientific terminology and representations.

NSLO 10. Appreciate the role of science in society; and its personal, social and global importance; and how society influences scientific research.

(R) Teacher's reference

KEYWORDS

biodiversity
by-products
climate
conservation
ecosystem
evolve
extinction
indispensable
migration
natural resources
pollination
population
raw materials
species
sustainability

LEARNING INTENTIONS

At the end of this unit you should:

1. Understand what conservation is and the importance of conserving the environment.
2. Understand what biodiversity is and its importance to our survival.
3. Be able to explain the impact humans have on ecosystems.
4. Be able to discuss how the increase in size of the human population impacts on our environment.
5. Be able to discuss how pollution causes harm to the environment.

Conserving the Environment

Conserving the environment means looking after the earth's resources.

Ⓡ These resources are naturally present on earth – they are not made by humans. **Natural resources** include water, the air, plants and animals. We must look after these resources wisely because we benefit from them.

There are many types of **conservation** (see *Table 05.04.01*) and we should make use of all of them.

What are natural resources?

Natural resources are the **raw materials** that we get from the earth and from which we benefit. Humans cannot make natural resources but we do rely heavily on them to meet our needs and demands. Each **ecosystem** on earth provides some resources.

Conservation type	Resource looked after or managed
Biological	Living things in their habitats
Global	The atmosphere and oceans
Environmental	Non-living parts of habitats

Table 05.04.01 Types of conservation.

Think about the following:
- Are you sitting on a chair? Where did the plastic, metal or wood come from?
- Have you a copy or notebook in your bag? Where did the paper come from to make them?
- Have you a snack in your bag? What are the ingredients? Where did they come from?
- Where does the tin come from for a tin of beans?

Conservation: The wise management of natural resources.

Biodiversity

We rely on natural resources for our daily activities, so we need to protect them.

Conservation maintains diversity.

Biodiversity (*bio* means a living thing and *diversity* means difference) is all the different plants and animals that live on earth. It can also be referred to as 'species richness'.

Why is Biodiversity Important to Humans?

The more **species** of plants and animals that can exist in the world, the better it is for us and future generations. By looking after them we are identifying that they play a very important role within their habitat and in human life. What an ecosystem provides for us and the people all over the world is **indispensable** – we could not survive without it.

Human activities such as building roads and houses, deforestation (the cutting down of trees without replacing them), over-harvesting the land and feeding wild animals can lead to species becoming **extinct**. This in turn reduces biodiversity. Reducing biodiversity makes ecosystems less productive, which means that fewer natural resources are available to humans.

 Checkpoint 1

(a) **Look at this image of a polar bear. Discuss what you think has happened to its environment and what effect this will have on the polar bear.**
(b) **Do you know of any changes that are happening on earth that are causing plants and animals (including humans) to change the way they live? Suggest what factors may have caused these changes.**

Fig. 05.04.01 What has happened to this environment and in turn this polar bear?

What do Ecosystems Provide?

In other words, 'What can nature provide for us?'

Ecosystems provide:

- Oxygen, while removing carbon dioxide from the atmosphere
- Food
- Shelter
- Fresh water and water resources
- Wood
- Fuel
- Soil
- Recycling of nutrients
- Water for plants
- A contribution to **climate** stability
- Diversity of genes in the world.

 Checkpoint 2

Fig. 05.04.02 An ecosystem.

With a classmate, look at *Fig. 05.04.02*, which shows an example of a forest ecosystem. Link each point from the list above to where it is coming from in the image (e.g. oxygen – made at the leaves on the trees).

The products that an ecosystem provides leads to other useful products for humans, for example:

- Medical research
- Medical discoveries
- Economic development

How do we benefit from all of these?

The link between human health and ecosystems is often indirect, and for this reason it is not always immediately identifiable. We benefit from:

- Better medical supplies
- Recreational opportunities – walks and hikes
- Tourism
- A greater variety of foods from a greater amount of crops produced
- Farmers use the **by-products** from the crops to feed their animals
- Greater choice of plants to buy from shops and plant in our gardens
- Soil to use in gardens and pots.

What Harms Ecosystems and Reduces Biodiversity?

Did you know?
In Ireland, approximately one-third of the food we buy ends up in the bin.

Fig. 05.04.03 How humans have used an area of land. Think about the following: what had to happen for these buildings to be built here? What disruption to the environment might have been caused by building the houses? What is the effect of so many buildings in a small area?

Habitats within ecosystems change all the time – this is the nature of ecosystems. Natural occurrences do happen – rivers will burst their banks, forests will catch fire and coastlines will be destroyed in storms. However, human activity is causing change to ecosystems, harming them and reducing biodiversity.

1. Climate change

Climate change over a large or small area has an impact on plant and animal life. Most plants and animals live in habitats that have specific **climatic** conditions, such as temperature, hours of sunlight, amount of rain and when it rains, the wind and how windy it is. If a plant or animal loses its habitat, the **population** of that plant or animal will decrease. This has a knock-on effect through the entire ecosystem, which leads to the ecosystem being unable to function properly.

Climate change → Population reduced → Food chains disrupted → Energy flow reduced → Ecosystem not functioning properly

2. Extinction

As discussed in *Unit 4.3*, organisms **evolve** by adapting to a new environment, but this usually happens over a very long time. Humans are making faster changes to environments, which puts pressure on organisms to evolve and adapt over a short time span. Some organisms are not able to do this, which potentially leads to extinction. **Remember:** it's survival of the fittest.

3. Disruption to food chains

For example, pollution can kill species and deplete sources of water for plants and animals, hunting removes predators and prey.

4. Environmental pollution

We are producing more waste, whether it is industrial or everyday waste. This waste needs to be treated or destroyed. This process can lead to the air and waters becoming polluted, toxic chemical wastes getting into the water, soil and food chains.

5. Loss of land

Land is needed to build houses and businesses to meet the needs of a growing population; forests are chopped down or felled to provide us with new roads, shopping centres, houses. Hedgerows are removed to allow for greater crop production.

Climate Change

Here are some examples of what can happen because of climate change.

- The types of plants that grow in an area could change.
- Food sources for animals change – in some cases they disappear altogether.
- Supply of water for plants and animals changes.
- Life cycles of plants and animals change. Flowers bloom earlier and survive longer into autumn.
- Breeding habits of animals change.
- Birds migrate at different times of the year.
- Some animals from habitats where the temperature is getting too warm move to cooler areas.
- Some animals are wakening from hibernation earlier.
- Some plants and animals will die and some will become extinct.

Migration: Where an organism moves from living in one area to living in another.

Fig. 05.04.04 Some examples of the results of climate change. (a) Birds migrating to find a better habitat; (b) This owl's home and food sources have been destroyed by deforestation; (c) A grizzly bear waking up early from hibernation.

Environmental Pollution

Fig. 05.04.05 shows an example of environmental pollution – an oil spillage from a ship. This contaminates the waters and fish beds, sometimes closing fisheries and beaches. The habitats of plants and animals are badly damaged as a result.

Fig. 05.04.05 A ship leaking oil into the sea.

Fig. 05.04.06 What is happening in each image?

Checkpoint 3

(a) In groups, look at these four images. Suggest what you think is happening in each.

    (i) List ways in which the events shown in images a–d are impacting – both positively and negatively – on the environment.

    (ii) What are your opinions about what is shown in the pictures? Are these things that should not happen, or do they have to happen to maintain human existence?

(b) Write down a direct effect each of the following has on the plants and animals that might be living in the area.

    (i) Climate change

    (ii) Environmental pollution

    (iii) Disrupting the food chain.

Sustainability

The cost of replacing what the ecosystem provides for us would be extremely high, so it makes sense to move towards **sustainability**.

With the human population getting bigger, sustainability is more important.

- More resources are being used up.
- More land is being used.
- More waste is being produced.
- There is more pollution.

We need to be able to use the earth's natural resources to meet our current needs without harming or destroying the environment, while also leaving enough resources for future generations. We should also focus on our needs, not our wants!

We have an environmental (or ecological) responsibility to address climate change and to *reduce, reuse* and *recycle*.

Reduce ...
- our food waste
- water use
- pollution
- soil erosion

Reuse ...
- materials — don't just throw things away!

Recycle ...
- materials such as plastics, glass, paper

The Venn diagram shows that sustainability must be the heart of social, economic and environmental activity.

Sustainability
E.g. Not wasting water, not cutting trees down unnecessarily

Social
E.g. Population, recreational use of resources

Environment
E.g. Climate change, pollution

Economic
E.g. Water costs, recycling charges

Did you know?
The world's population has doubled in the last forty years. At the time of print, the estimated world population is 7.4 billion. Ireland's population is 4.6 million, and our life expectancy is increasing faster than anywhere else in Europe. The life expectancy for an Irish man is 78 years and for a woman it is 83 years.

Ecosystem: An area where plants and animals interact with each other.

Biodiversity: Different plants and animals that live on earth.

Sustainability: Using a resource to meet our needs without harming or destroying that resource for future generations.

One example of sustainability in Ireland is fish quotas.

1. Fishermen are only allowed to catch a certain number of fish. This ensures that there will be fish left to breed.
2. The mesh of fishing nets has to be big enough to allow young fish to swim through the holes. They can then grow and breed.

⊘ **Checkpoint 4**

(a) Make a list of ten ways in which you could use resources more sustainably.
(b) Join with a classmate and compare your lists. Create a 'Top 10' list between you.
(c) Look at the graph of estimated world population (*Fig. 05.04.07*). Discuss what has happened the size of the population since 1900.
  (i) Has there been a steady change? Give a reason for your answer.
  (ii) What effect will this change have on the resources we currently use?
  (iii) Thinking of the needs of future generations, what do we need to do now to make sure that they have adequate resources to survive?

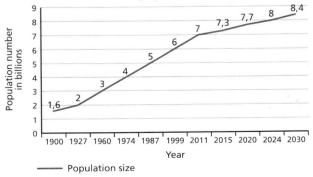

Estimated world population change since 1990.

Fig. 05.04.07 Estimated world population change since 1990.

Conserving the Environment on a World Stage

The mission of the World Wide Fund for Nature (WWF) is to prevent the planet's natural environment being ruined and to build a future in which humans live together with nature. It focuses on the diversity of life on Earth and the environments in which animals live, and tries to reduce human impact on these environments. It aims to achieve this by:

- Conserving the world's biological diversity
- Ensuring that the use of renewable natural resources is sustainable
- Promoting the reduction of pollution and wasteful consumption.

There are six main areas the WWF believes must be addressed urgently:

1. **Carbon, energy and climate:** We should reduce carbon dioxide emissions, use more renewable energy sources, reduce the impact of forest loss and have a global policy on climate change.

2. **Sustainable cities:** How cities can become more sustainable.

3. **Farming:** How to produce and process food, fibre, grazing, aquaculture and biofuels more sustainably.

4. **Fishing:** The problem of over-fishing, illegal and unregulated fishing.

5. **Forestry:** The destruction of forests for timber, paper, pulp and fuel wood.

6. **Water:** Dams, irrigation and drinking supplies – a focus on improving the way water is managed.

The WWFs' overall aim is for everyone to live within the earth's capacity to withstand people and nature, and for everyone to have rightful access to, and use of, natural resources.

(*Source:* http://wwf.panda.org/what_we_do/footprint/)

What is Ireland's Contribution to Positive Environmental Change?

The NPWS

Improving biodiversity in Ireland is the responsibility of the National Parks and Wildlife Service (NPWS), which is part of the Heritage Division of the Department of Arts, Heritage and the Gaeltacht.

The NPWS says that Ireland is home to twenty-eight species of land mammal, over 400 species of birds, more than 4000 plant species and over 12 000 species of insect. It also says that if all these species are to survive, there must be enough suitable areas for them.

R Coillte

Coillte is an Irish commercial company that manages areas of forestry around the country. Coillte's aim is to manage natural resources for everyone's benefit.

It manages forests and lands in a way that both makes a profit and provides environmental and social benefits. It helps preserve biodiversity and conserve habitats, and provides recreational opportunities for the public.

The role of the NPWS is to:

- Protect a range of ecosystems and maintain and enhance populations of flora and fauna (plants and animals) in Ireland.
- Advise on the protection of natural heritage areas.
- Make sure that national and EU legislation and policies are carried out.
- Manage, maintain and develop state-owned national parks and nature reserves.

Bees, Biodiversity and Food Production

We get our food from a variety of plants. In order for plants to produce our food, they need to grow, and they need animals to help them. When **pollination** happens in a plant, new seedlings and more fruit are produced. Pollination is the transfer of pollen from one plant to another.

In Ireland the native Irish brown bee makes honey but their most important job is to pollinate plants. If the population of bees is low, there is less plant pollination, and if there is less pollination there are fewer new seedlings and fruit. All this has a direct effect on our economy and ability to grow food and in turn our economy. Pollination is a good example of interdependence.

Bees are so important to food production that fruit farmers import bees to increase their supply of fruit. Think of the blossom on an apple tree. The bee lands on the flower and the pollen dust from the flower sticks to the bee's body. The bee flies to another flower, where the pollen falls off. This allows the plant to make seeds and – eventually – fruit. So the more pollination that occurs, the more apples are produced.

Without bees there would be no pollination, no seedlings and no fruit.

The pesticides we use to protect our shrubs or lawns are the biggest killers of bees.

Did you know?
The native Irish brown bee only lives for three weeks!

Did you know?
Without bees, the human race would only survive for about seven years – a scary thought.

Checkpoint 5

Produce a comic strip explaining how bees are involved in our food production. At the end of the strip, show what would happen if there were no bees in the world.

WHAT I HAVE LEARNED...

- Conservation is the wise management of natural resources.
- We would have no natural resources if we did not conserve the environment.
- Plants, animals, wind, coal, oil and minerals are examples of natural resources. Humans benefit greatly from these resources.
- Biodiversity is the different plants and animals that live on earth.
- An ecosystem is an area where plants and animals interact with each other.
- Humans can have a negative impact on ecosystems by polluting, hunting, deforestation and using pesticides.
- Sustainability is the use of a resource to meet our needs but without harming or destroying it so that it is available for future generations.
- The growth of the human population impacts negatively on our environment.

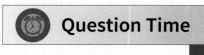

Question Time

Copy and Complete

In this unit I learned that conservation is the wise management of _____ resources. Some examples of these resources are plants, animals, air, _____ and coal. We get a lot of _____ from these resources, so it is _____ to look after them. If we don't they will be _____. We would have no plants or animals to eat, coal to burn, or _____ water to _____. By looking after our resources we are making sure that plants and animals are able to _____ where they _____. Where a plant or an animal lives is called a _____. Habitats are within a bigger area called an _____. Ecosystems provide us with, for example, oxygen, _____, shelter and _____. Plants can be used in _____ research and to help make different medicines. Humans are _____ the places where plants and animals live. We are using the trees to make things, we are _____ roads and houses, dumping waste and causing _____. We need to stop or reduce what we are doing for plants and animals to_____.

Questions

1. Explain the term 'conservation'.
2. Describe what causes the extinction of a plant or an animal.
3. What does living sustainably mean?
4. Climate change is a natural process, but the factors that trigger it are not natural. Suggest what these factors might be.
5. When humans destroy or reduce the size of habitats within an ecosystem, what are the knock-on effects for other animals in the habitat or ecosystem?
6. In relation to atmospheric gases, what is the result of deforestation?
7. Ireland is making positive moves towards environmental change. Outline the one you think is most important and explain how it is having a positive effect.
8. Some animals are kept in national parks which have fences around their perimeter. Should these fences be removed and the animals set free? Suggest the advantages and disadvantages of doing this.
9. Three-quarters of the world's biggest carnivores (e.g. lions, leopards and bears) are in decline. Suggest at least two reasons why this is happening.
10. Some countries, for example Australia, do not allow people to bring plants and seeds into their country. They are destroyed at the airport. Suggest at least three things this prevents happening.

Inquiry

A   You are a conservationist. You have been asked to raise awareness about the need to conserve a local habitat near your school. In your awareness campaign you must:
   (i)   **Inform** people how they are destroying the local habitat.
   (ii) Give them **suggestions** as to how they can reduce this destruction.

   Your campaign can use a poster, a newspaper article, a pamphlet, an IT presentation, or whatever method you think suitable.

B   **Food production project.** Choose one of the following projects.
   (i) You are the manager of a fast food outlet. You must decide where to source the beef and chicken to make the burgers you sell.
      a. **Describe** the decisions you have to make.
      b. **Think** about the following points. Will you source your meat from an organic farm? Will this increase costs? Do the costs outweigh the benefits? Do you investigate how the animals are reared? Have they enough space? What are they fed on?
   (ii) You are a farmer growing wheat to sell to a large bakery firm.
      a. **Describe** how you would control the growth of the wheat.
      b. **Think** about the following points. What weather conditions are needed? What pests could affect growth? How will you deal with these pests? Could pollution affect your crop? When should you harvest? Do you need any special equipment?

C   Bees are vital to biodiversity. **Research** and **present** a talk or article for your local conservation group on 'The importance of bees in human nutrition'. Include an explanation of what would happen to our food sources if the bee population declined.

D   Along with the tiger, polar bears and penguins are two animals whose habitats are becoming extinct. **Research** either the polar bear or the Antarctic penguin to find out what is happening to their habitats.

6.1

Solids, Liquids and Gases

Learning Outcomes

CWLO 1. Investigate whether mass is unchanged **when chemical and physical changes take place.**

CWLO 2. Develop and use models to describe the particle theory; demonstrate how they provide a simple way to account for the **conservation of mass,** changes of state, **physical change, chemical change**, mixtures and their separation.

CWLO 4. Classify substances as elements, compounds, mixtures, metals, non-metals, **solids, liquids, gases** and solutions.

CWLO 6. Investigate the properties of different materials including **solubilities,** conductivity, **melting points and boiling points.**

NSLO 3. Design, plan and conduct investigations; explain how **reliability, accuracy, precision, fairness, safety**, ethics and a selection of suitable equipment **have been considered.**

NSLO 4. Produce data (qualitatively/quantitatively), critically analyse data to identify patterns and relationships, identify anomalous observations, draw and justify conclusions.

NSLO 10. Appreciate the role of science in society and its **personal, social and global importance.**

BWLO 4. Describe the structure, function and **interactions of the** organs of the human digestive, **circulatory and respiratory systems.**

PWLO 6. Explain energy conservation and analyse natural processes in terms of **energy changes** and dissipation.

R Teacher's reference

KEYWORDS

boiling
Brownian Motion
chemical change
compressed
condensation
evaporation
flow
freezing
gases
Law of Conservation
 of Mass
liquids
mass
matter
particles
physical change
plasma
properties
solid
states of matter

LEARNING INTENTIONS

At the end of this unit you should:

1. Be able to explain why scientists classify matter into different states.
2. Be able to describe the differences between solids, liquids, gases and plasma (the states of matter).
3. Know the differences between physical changes and chemical changes.
4. Be able to explain the changes involved in freezing, boiling, melting, evaporation and condensation.

Matter and Mass

All substances and all states of substances contain **matter** and have a **mass** that can be measured. Substances are made up of small pieces of matter called **particles**. (We will study a few different types of particles in *Unit 6.4* and *Unit 7.1*.)

Icicles over frozen lake

Arctic snowscape

Water being poured

Fog over Ha'penny Bridge, River Liffey

Cloudscape in upper atmosphere

Steam from iron

Fig. 06.01.01.

Matter: Anything that takes up space and has mass.

Mass: The amount of matter in a a substance, given in grams (g) or kilograms (kg).

Particle: An extremely small piece of matter.

Fig. 06.01.01 shows different images of one substance. What is the name of this substance? When this substance changes from one state to another, is any of the substance lost?

Ⓡ Chemical and Physical Changes

We are aware from the changing weather we experience that the substance pictured above can come in different forms and can have different textures. While you can make an igloo out of this substance in the Arctic, you can't make an igloo out of it when it comes out of a kettle. You can also swim in one state of this substance but not in the others. Importantly, you can easily convert this substance from one state into another and back again.

If a substance changes but does not become a new substance, this is called a **physical change**. If the substance becomes a new substance each time it changes, this is called a **chemical change**.

Physical Change: When a substance changes its state, texture, strength or colour, but does not form a new substance.

Chemical Change: When two or more substances combine to form a new substance.

Demonstration 06.01.01 – **Making a cloud in a bottle**

Instructions: Using a small amount of water, a 2-litre bottle and a match, your teacher will show you how a cloud in a bottle can be made to appear and disappear.

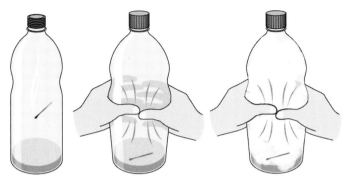

Fig. 06.01.02 The stages of making a cloud in a bottle.

> **What did you learn?**
> 1. Were the substances that made up the cloud destroyed each time the cloud disappeared?
> 2. Were the substances that made up the cloud created each time the cloud appeared?

✔ Checkpoint 1

Copy and complete *Table 06.01.01* by placing a tick to show whether you think it is a physical or a chemical change.

Change	Physical	Chemical
The smell of vinegar from chips		
Stirring sugar into coffee		
The fragrance from a scented candle		
The smoke from a burning match		
The bursting of a beach ball left in the sun		
The creation of sawdust from sanding a piece of wood		
Rust on an iron fence		
Bleaching hair to change its colour		
The drying out of a puddle of water		
Dissolving jelly granules to make a dessert		
A fizzy drink going flat		
Rain falling from a cloud		

Table 06.01.01 Substance changes – are they physical or chemical?

Law of Conservation of Mass

Since ancient times it has been believed and understood that 'nothing can come from nothing', meaning that new substances can only be created from other substances – even if you cannot see them. So, matter can be neither created nor destroyed. Rather, matter changes from one state to another. This is called the **Law of Conservation of Mass**.

To measure the change that takes place, we find the mass of a substance before and after a change has happened.

> **Law of Conservation of Mass:** Matter can be neither created nor destroyed but is rather converted from one form to another.

Investigation 06.01.01: Finding the physical and chemical changes when steel wool is burned

Instructions: Using the equipment as shown in the diagram, burn a piece of steel wool.

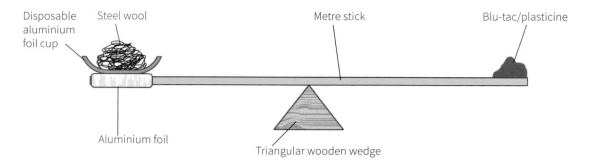

What did you learn?

1. You might think that you cannot burn steel with a standard flame. How is it possible to burn steel wool?
2. To make the steel wool burn, how do you need to arrange it in the foil cup?
3. How much steel wool should you use? Can you use too much or too little?
4. Could you conduct this experiment without using aluminium foil or the foil cup?
5. When burning any substance, safety precautions need to be taken. What precautions are needed for this particular investigation?
6. When the steel wool was burned, what **physical** change took place? Give a reason for your answer.
7. When the steel wool was burned, what **chemical** change took place? Give a reason for your answer.
8. Do the results of this investigation agree with the Law of Conservation of Mass? Justify your answer.

States of Matter

There are **four states of matter** that you meet in the laboratory and in everyday life: **solids**, **liquids**, **gases** and **plasma**. The most important difference between each state is how closely arranged the particles are in each substance, which means each state has different **properties**. Here, we will be studying solids, liquids and gases.

Property: The particular features of a substance or an object that make it similar or different to other substances or objects.

Solid: A substance that has a definite shape and volume; cannot be compressed, cannot **flow**.

Liquid: A substance that does not have a definite shape, has a definite volume; can be compressed and can flow.

Gas: A substance that does not have a definite shape or volume; can be compressed and can flow.

Plasma: A substance that does not have a definite shape or volume; can be compressed and can flow; also conducts electricity.

State of Matter	Properties	Arrangement of Particles	
Solid	Definite mass Definite volume Definite shape Cannot be compressed Cannot flow		Particles arranged in a regular pattern, packed closely together. They vibrate slightly.
Liquid	Definite mass Definite volume No definite shape Can be compressed slightly Can flow		Particles not arranged in any pattern, packed closely together. They collide and glide across each other.
Gas (Vapour)	Definite mass No definite volume No definite shape Can be compressed Can flow		Particles not arranged in any pattern, randomly colliding and causing each other to move in other directions.
Plasma	Definite mass No definite volume No definite shape Can be compressed Can flow Conduct electricity		Arranged the same as a gas but can conduct electricity and create magnetic fields.

Table 06.01.02 The properties of the four states of matter and the arrangements of their particles.

CHEMISTRY

Changing States

Substances change state when they are heated or cooled. When heated, particles in a substance gain energy, so they move more, eventually moving apart. So heating a solid causes it to melt and become a liquid. If you continue heating the liquid, it begins to boil: the particles gain more energy, moving even further apart, and eventually the substance becomes a gas. The opposite happens when you cool a gas. As the gas cools it condenses and becomes a liquid. If that liquid continues to cool, it freezes and becomes a solid.

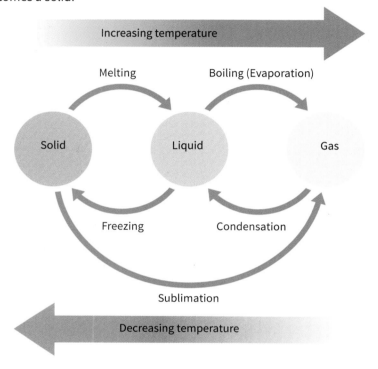

Melting: The change of state from solid to liquid, which happens at the melting point temperature (m.p.).

Boiling/Evaporation: The change of state from liquid to gas, which happens at the boiling point temperature (b.p.).

Condensation: The change of state from gas to liquid.

Freezing: The change of state from liquid to solid.

Demonstration 06.01.02 – The three-in-one states of matter

Instructions: Your teacher will put 4–5 cm depth of hot water into a jam jar, and then sit a zip-lock bag of ice in the neck of the jar.

Zip lock bag of ice cubes

Jam jar

4–5 cm depth of hot water

What did you learn?

1. There are three states of matter present in this demonstration. Explain how this is true.
2. Did any chemical or physical changes take place during the demonstration? Justify your answer.

✅ Checkpoint 2

(a) Using simple diagrams, explain how a bar of chocolate left on a hot windowsill will melt.

(b) Ice-cubes were added to a glass of orange cordial. After ten minutes, the ice-cubes had disappeared, a fog had appeared on the outside of the glass and the drink tasted watered-down. Explain how this happened.

Compression

When particles in a substance are squeezed together, they are said to be **compressed**. This is impossible to do with a solid, and very difficult to do with a liquid because their particles are already so close together. In a gas or plasma the particles are spaced far apart and are moving, and so can be compressed. Because they are moving, they have what is called **kinetic energy**. That energy gets converted to heat when the particles are compressed. This is why the tip of a bicycle pump feels hot after use – gas particles have been squeezed together inside the tyre and the bicycle pump.

Check to see if this is true by trying it out with a disposable syringe.

Compression: Forcing the particles of a substance closer together and reducing the amount of space they take up.

Kinetic Energy: Energy possessed by a body because of its motion.

CHEMISTRY

🔍 Investigation 06.01.02: **Testing the compression of solids, liquids and gases**

Instructions: Using a disposable syringe, water, a marshmallow and the air in the room, can you suggest how you could show the compression of a solid, a liquid and a gas. You may need to add other equipment to this list.

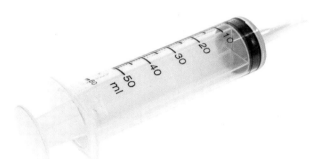

What did you learn?
1. Explain whether the changes you see are physical or chemical, and why the changes happen.
2. How might you measure these changes?
3. Can you explain what might happen if you put a piece of marshmallow into a sealed syringe and pushed the plunger down? What might happen if you drew the plunger out?

Diffusion

Because the particles of a gas, a liquid and a plasma are always moving, they will always tend to spread out. This means that they will spread out evenly into whatever space or container they are in, even without stirring. If a solid is dissolved into a liquid, it **diffuses** through the liquid until there is an even spread of solid particles through the liquid.

Diffusion: The movement of particles in a liquid or gas until the particles are evenly spread throughout the liquid or gas.

Fig. 06.01.03 Diffusion of potassium permanganate in water shown in sequence of increasing diffusion.

🔍 Investigation 06.01.03: **Looking at diffusion in a liquid**

Instructions: Using household items, design an investigation to show diffusion in a liquid.

What did you learn?

1. Do your observations prove that diffusion happens? Justify your answer.
2. Suggest factors that could speed up or slow down the diffusion in your investigation. Explain your answer.
3. Explain how you could test one of these factors in a fair investigation.

> **Did you know?**
> The air we breathe in has a higher amount of oxygen than the air we breathe out. The blood around our lungs is low in oxygen. Oxygen inside our lungs diffuses through the lungs into the blood to increase the amount of oxygen in our blood. Our heart then pumps this blood around our body. (See *Unit 3.3* and *Unit 3.4* for more on this.)

Demonstration 06.01.03 – **Observing gas diffusion in a tube**

Instructions: Your teacher will soak two pieces of cotton wool in two different chemicals, and place them at opposite ends of a sealed tube, as per the diagram. Observe carefully what happens.

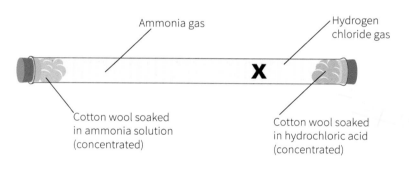

Ammonia gas

Hydrogen chloride gas

X

Cotton wool soaked in ammonia solution (concentrated)

Cotton wool soaked in hydrochloric acid (concentrated)

What did you learn?

1. What change do you observe happening at position X?
2. What has happened to the substances soaked onto the cotton wool that allows this change to happen?
3. Justify whether you think this was a chemical or physical change.
4. Suggest a reason why the change you observe does not happen in the middle of the tube.

✓ Checkpoint 3

(a) Name three examples of diffusion in everyday life.
(b) Are all the statements below about diffusion? Decide which are and which are not.

- Spreading butter evenly on a slice of bread.
- Tea spreading through hot water when making a cup of tea.
- Adding orange squash to water.
- The smell of scented candles
- Cigarette smoke filling a room.
- Slurry spreading on crops.
- Food particles passing from a mother to a baby in the womb.
- Breathing in anaesthetic gases just before an operation.

WHAT I HAVE LEARNED...

- A physical change does not cause a new substance to form.
- A chemical change causes a new substance to form.
- How to draw the arrangement of particles in the states of matter.
- What makes solids, liquids, gases and plasmas different to each other.
- In solids, particles are arranged in a tight regular pattern.
- In liquids, particles bump and glide over each other.
- In gases, particles collide with each other, changing direction constantly, and have no arrangement.
- Solids do not flow.
- Liquids and gases flow.
- Liquids, gases and plasmas take the shape of the container they are in.
- Liquids, gases and plasmas can be compressed, but only plasmas can conduct electricity.
- Increasing or decreasing the temperature of a substance causes it to change state.
- The melting point (m.p.) is the temperature at which a substance changes from solid to liquid.
- The boiling point (b.p.) is the temperature at which a substance changes from liquid to gas.
- The differences between freezing, melting, boiling, evaporation and condensation.
- Particles in a liquid or gas spread out evenly throughout the container (diffusion).

Question Time

Copy and Complete

In this unit I learned that substances can be classified into _____ of _____. In gases the particles _____ and change direction all the time. Because the particles move so much they _____ the _____ that the gas is in. The particles in liquids _____ over each other. Liquids take the _____ of the container they are in. _____ cannot flow because the particles in them are packed _____. Because the particles in gases and solids are not as close together they can be _____. When one substance spreads evenly through another this is called _____. I also learned that in a _____ change no new _____ is created. _____ is when substances change state from gas to liquid and _____ is when they change from liquid to solid. When the temperature increases the reverse changes of state are called _____/_____ and _____.

Questions

1. Fig. 06.01.04 shows the three states of matter. Identify which beaker, X, Y or Z, shows the arrangement of particles in a liquid and which shows the arrangement of particles in a gas.

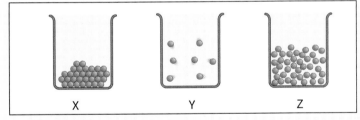

Fig. 06.01.04.

2. Fig. 06.01.05 shows the arrangement of particles in two states of matter as they are heated. Which diagram, P or Q, shows melting and which shows boiling?

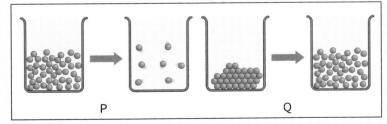

Fig. 06.01.05.

3. Name a state of matter that has no fixed shape.
4. Name a state of matter that has no fixed volume.

CHEMISTRY

5. Gas cylinders and deodorants are stored away from sources of heat to prevent them from exploding, even if the gas inside the cylinder is not flammable. Do you think this is a sensible precaution? Justify your answer.

6. State one physical change and one chemical change that takes place in the demonstration shown in *Fig. 06.01.06*. What evidence would you pick to show that a chemical change has happened?

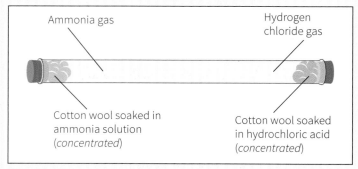

Ammonia gas

Hydrogen chloride gas

Cotton wool soaked in ammonia solution (*concentrated*)

Cotton wool soaked in hydrochloric acid (*concentrated*)

Fig. 06.01.06.

7. When the windows of a car get fogged up on a cold morning, gas has changed to liquid. What word would you use to summarise this change of state? Can you think of reasons why this change happens? Suggest a source for the gas and a useful property of the gas.

Inquiry

A When a liquid changes state to a gas, this is called evaporation. Boiling water to make a cup of coffee is an example of this. The boiling temperature of water is 100°C. **Suggest** why a puddle of water evaporates at 12°C, even if it's not a very sunny day.

B **Research** the use of plasma outside the laboratory and **create** a poster showing how it is either useful or a nuisance in everyday life. Use your poster to also **explain** the difference between plasma and the three other states of matter.

C Botanist Robert Brown discovered jittery movement of particles in water when he was examining pollen grains under a microscope. Scientists eventually realised that the random movement of the particles happened as they continually bounced off each other. This is now known as **Brownian Motion**. Do you think that Brownian Motion has any effect on diffusion? What **evidence** can you use to **explain** your answer?

Solutions and Crystallisation

CHEMISTRY

Learning Outcomes

CWLO 2. Develop and use models to describe the particle theory; demonstrate how they provide a simple way to account for the conservation of mass, changes of state, physical change, chemical change, **mixtures and their separation.**

CWLO 4. Classify substances as elements, compounds, mixtures, metals, non-metals, solids, liquids, gases and **solutions.**

CWLO 6. Investigate the properties of different materials including **solubilities,** conductivity, melting points and boiling points.

NSLO 3. Design, plan and conduct investigations; explain how reliability, accuracy, precision, fairness, safety, ethics and a selection of suitable equipment have been considered.

NSLO 4. Produce data (qualitatively/quantitatively), **critically analyse data to identify patterns and relationships,** identify anomalous observations, draw and justify conclusions.

NSLO 10. Appreciate the role of science in society and its **personal, social and global importance.**

BWLO 6. Evaluate how human health is affected by inherited factors and environmental factors including **nutrition,** lifestyle choices; examine the role of micro-organisms to human health.

(R) Teacher's reference

KEYWORDS

concentrated
concentration
crystallisation
dilute
dissolve
insoluble
saturated
solubility
solubility curve
soluble
solute
solution
solvent
suspension
universal solvent

LEARNING INTENTIONS

At the end of this unit you should:
1. Be able to explain the terms solution, solvent and solute.
2. Know the differences between dilute, concentrated and saturated solutions.
3. Be able to measure the solubility of a substance by investigation, and draw and explain a solubility curve.
4. Know how crystallisation from a saturated solution happens.
5. Know examples of crystals, their uses and how crystals are created in industry.

Investigation 06.02.01: **How well do substances dissolve?**

Instructions: Your teacher will give you samples of a variety of substances, spatulas and some beakers. Test each substance to see how it dissolves in the liquids.

> **What did you learn?**
> 1. Did each substance dissolve in the same way? Do your observations back this up?
> 2. Can you show that you carried out a fair test? Justify your answer.
> 3. List the substances in order of how well they dissolved. How did you decide this list?

Water: The Universal Solvent

Solution: A mixture in which a solute has been dissolved into a solvent.

Solvent: The liquid into which the solute is dissolved.

Solute: The substance that is dissolved into the solvent.

Concentration: The mass or volume of solute dissolved in a solvent.

Water is known as the **universal solvent** because of its ability to form solutions with many solutes at many different temperatures. This ability to form solutions is incredibly important to all life on our planet.

The most plentiful solution on the planet is seawater, covering 70% of the earth's surface and home to 50% of all known species. Because seawater has been a stable solution, with its temperature and salt content having remained constant for thousands of years, it provides a stable environment for many organisms. However, global warming is causing sea temperatures to change, and the **concentration** of substances dissolved in the oceans has changed and continues to change rapidly.

Organisms cannot survive without water's dissolving ability, as many basic chemical reactions happen in the liquid parts of animals and plants. The human brain is 70% water, our lungs are 90% water and our blood is more than 80% water; overall our body is 65% water (approximate figures).

Urine is one of the solutions that is formed in the body. Waste salts and urea are dissolved into water in the kidneys, forming urine, which is then stored in the bladder. Here, urea is known as the **solute**, water is known as the **solvent** and the mixture of the two as the **solution**.

> R Concentration is often measured as mass per volume. So 96 g of sugar dissolved in a litre of water would be written as:
> $$96 \text{ g} / 1000 \text{ cm}^3$$
> because 1 litre = 1000 cm³

Fig. 06.02.01 As soldiers often work in very stressful conditions for long periods of time without access to proper supplies of food and water, having a simple way to check the water level in their body is important. This chart was provided by the US Army to its soldiers to ensure they could monitor their hydration levels.

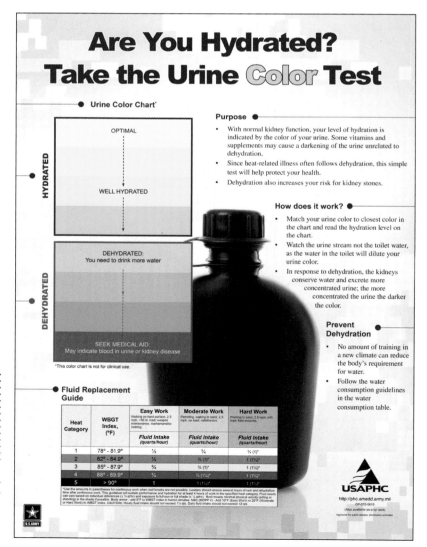

Examination of urine colour can be used to identify water levels in the body. The colour shows the strength of the solution. If the urine is pale in colour, then the solution is **dilute** and has a low concentration of urea/a high concentration of water. But if the urine is dark in colour, the solution is **concentrated** because it contains a high amount of urea/a low amount of water. This can happen if a person:

- has not taken enough of their recommended daily amount of water
- has lost water though an activity
- has consumed strong food or drink that needs to be diluted by the body, so less water is available to dissolve urea.

> **Dilute:** A solution that has a small amount of solute and a large amount of solvent.

> **Concentrated:** A solution that has a large amount of solute dissolved into a small amount of solvent.

⊘ Checkpoint 1

(a) *Fig. 06.02.02* shows a selection of cordial drinks. Each is in 'concentrated' form. What does this mean?

(b) Can you drink cordial directly from the bottle? Why?

(c) *Table 06.02.01* gives a list of solutions. Copy and complete this table, writing into the boxes the substances you think are the solute and solvent in each solution.

Solution	Solute	Solvent
soapy water		
cup of coffee		
milkshake		
seawater		
swimming pool water		
mineral water		
tap water		
blood plasma		

Table 06.02.01 List of solutions. What is the solute and the solvent in each?

Solubility

Solubility is the ability of a solute to **dissolve** in a solvent. But just because sugar is **soluble** (can dissolve) in hot water, this does not mean it will dissolve in cold water. In fact, sugar will fall to the bottom of a container of cold water. When a solute cannot dissolve in a solvent it is **insoluble**. When clay is mixed with water it does not dissolve and the particles take a very long time to settle. This is called a **suspension**.

> **Solubility:** The mass or volume of solute dissolved in a solvent.

> **Soluble:** A solute that can dissolve in a solvent.

> **Insoluble:** A solute that cannot dissolve in a solvent.

> **Suspension:** A mixture where insoluble solids will sink to the bottom of the solvent if left still.

Solubility can also be measured as grams of solute per hundred grams of solvent. If 42 g of sugar is mixed into 100 g of water, the unit is 42 g/100 g of water.

Fig. 06.02.03 A clay suspension.

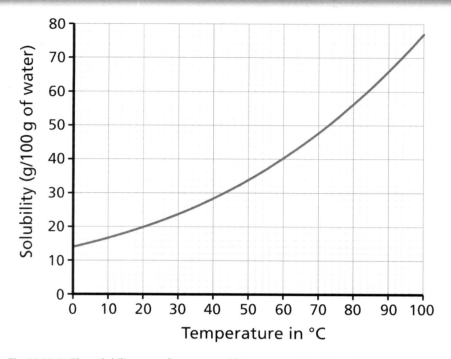

Fig. 06.02.04 The solubility curve for copper sulfate in water being heated.

Fig. 06.02.04 shows the **solubility curve** for copper sulfate in water as the water is heated. When the water can hold no more copper sulfate at a particular temperature, then that solution is said to be **saturated** at that temperature. For solids, increased temperature normally increases solubility. For gases, however, increased temperature decreases solubility.

Crystals

Crystals are substances that form regular shapes as a solid. They can be made by cooling down a hot saturated solution, or slowly evaporating the solvent.

Fig. 06.02.05 The Cave of the Crystals, Mexico.

Sodium chloride is a white crystal used to give additional taste to food. Each sodium atom is surrounded by chlorine atoms, above, below and on four sides. This pattern repeats itself throughout the sodium chloride. Many crystals have a similar arrangement of atoms, which explains their regular shape. This is called a lattice arrangement (Fig. 06.02.06).

What temperature does the water in fish tanks need to be? What gas is constantly passed through the water in a fish tank?

 **Checkpoint 2**

Use the graph in *Fig. 06.02.04* to answer the following questions:
(a) Estimate the solubility of copper sulfate crystals at 70°C.
(b) At what temperature was the solubility of the copper sulfate 30 g/100 g of water?

Saturated: A solution that has the maximum amount of solute dissolved into the solvent at a given temperature.

Did you know?
The Cave of the Crystals (*Fig. 06.02.05*) is a cave 300 metres below the surface of the earth in Naica, Mexico. The cave remained filled with a saturated solution of minerals for 500 000 years, constantly heated by a magma chamber below the cave until the solvent dried out. The largest crystal in the cave is estimated to have a mass of 56 tonnes: that's equivalent to 56 000 bags of sugar!

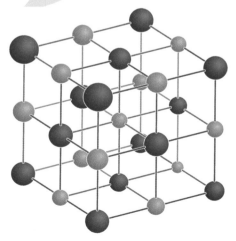

Fig. 06.02.06 Diagram of table salt crystal lattice.

The huge Naica crystals took 500 000 years to form. If a person was trying to copy what happened in the Cave of the Crystals in a lab, what advice would you give them so that they could grow the largest crystals possible?

R Did you know?

Copper sulfate is part of two of the chemicals used in food tests. Benedict's reagent is used to test simple sugars, changing colour from blue to brick red. Biuret reagent changes from blue to deep lilac when testing for proteins. It is also used to test for anaemia, as healthy blood sinks in copper sulfate.

🔍 Investigation 06.02.02: **Growing crystals of copper sulfate (or aluminium sulfate)**

Instructions: Using either copper sulfate or aluminium sulfate, create a concentrated solution. Cool the saturated solution and allow crystals to form.

What did you learn?

1. How will you know that the solution is concentrated?
2. How can you cool the solution? Pick a method of cooling and give reasons why you picked that method.
3. Compare your cooling method to the cooling method used by another investigator. Which method is better? Why?
4. Should you only ever use one method of cooling in order to make crystals? Why?

Fig. 06.02.07 (a) Copper crystals.

Fig. 06.02.07 (b) Alum crystals.

Fig. 06.02.08 Recrystallisation of ibuprofen.

Industrial Crystallisation

Investigation 06.02.02 showed us that the cooling temperature affects the size of crystals, as can the concentration. In industry, crystals are formed by cooling either slowly or quickly depending on the size crystal needed, or by evaporation of the solvent.

Evaporation of the solvent creates very pure crystals as the atoms must fit correctly into the crystal lattice. This therefore prevents impurities from affecting the substance formed. Evaporation is used in drug production such as ibuprofen (*Fig. 06.02.08*), where the drug is dissolved in hydrochloric acid. This acid is then slowly evaporated to produce pure ibuprofen, which can then be made into tablets.

WHAT I HAVE LEARNED...

- What a solution, solvent and solute are.
- The differences between dilute, concentrated and saturated solutions.
- To measure the solubility of a substance by experiment, and draw and explain a solubility curve.
- That the atoms in crystals form very regular patterns called lattices.
- How **crystallisation** from a saturated solution happens.
- How to make a saturated solution.
- How to form crystals using several methods of cooling.
- Examples of crystals, their uses and how crystals are created in industry.

Question Time

Copy and Complete
In this unit I learned that a _____ can be made by _____ a _____ into a _____. A strong solution can be called a _____ solution and a weak solution is called a _____ solution. _____ solutions have the maximum amount of _____ that is possible at a _____ _____. The solubility of a solid _____ as _____ increases. The solubility of a _____ decreases with the increase of temperature. Crystals are formed when _____ solutions are _____.

Questions
1. Can you list four substances that are insoluble in water?
2. *Fig. 06.02.09* shows three solutions of copper sulfate. Decide which diagram, A, B or C, is the **dilute** solution. Also decide which diagram is the **saturated** solution.

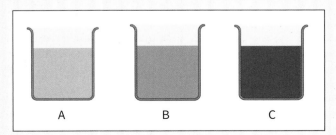

Fig. 06.02.09 Three solutions of copper sulfate.

3. Starting with a dilute solution, explain how to make it more concentrated.
4. What is the difference between a suspension and a saturated solution?
5. If you needed to create a powder from a saturated solution, how would you cool the solution?
6. List three examples of suspensions in everyday life.
7. A student investigated the effect of temperature on the solubility of the salt ammonium chloride in water. She determined the maximum mass, in grams, of the salt that would dissolve in 100 g of water at various temperatures. The data from this experiment is given in *Table 06.02.02*.

Solubility (g/100 g of water)	29	37	46	55	66	77
Temperature (0°C)	0	20	40	60	80	100

Table 06.02.02.

(i) (R) Present the information in this table as a solubility graph.
(ii) Use the graph to estimate the solubility of ammonium chloride at 70°C.
(iii) What conclusion about the solubility of ammonium chloride can be drawn from analysis of the graph?

8. An investigation of the solubility of carbon dioxide in water gathered the following results:

Solubility of CO_2 (g of CO_2 per kg of water)	3.4	2.5	1.7	14	1.0	0.8	0.6
Temperature (0°C)	0	10	20	30	40	50	60

Table 06.02.03.

(i) (R) Plot this data as a graph.
(ii) Usually the solubility of a solid increases with increasing temperature. The solubility of a gas decreases as the temperature increases. Suggest a reason why this decrease happens.
(iii) From the graph, estimate the temperature at which the solubility of CO_2 is 2 g per kg of water.

Inquiry

A   How would you **conduct** a fair test to compare an insoluble against a soluble substance?

B   *Fig. 06.02.10* shows the cordial drink lemon barley water. At one time it was popular as a home remedy to 'flush the system' by causing you to urinate more often. Can you **explain** why this drink can have both a positive and negative affect on a person's health?

Fig. 06.02.10 *Lemon barley water.*

C   Many indigestion remedies, medicines and vitamin supplements are effervescent, which means they fizz when dropped into water at room temperature. To make sure that the tablet fully dissolves, **what** do the manufacturers need to know about the solute? How do the gas bubbles help the solute dissolve?

D   When Arctic and Antarctic icebergs melt and break away, a lot of freshwater is released into the ocean. Freshwater contains almost no salt compared to ocean saltwater. What **effects** on the ocean environment do you think this might have? **Show** your information on a poster.

CHEMISTRY

Separating Mixtures

Learning Outcomes

CWLO 1. Investigate whether mass is unchanged when chemical and physical changes take place.

CWLO 2. Develop and use models to describe the particle theory; demonstrate how they provide a simple way to account for the conservation of mass, changes of state, **physical change**, chemical change, mixtures and their separation.

CWLO 4. Classify substances as elements, compounds, **mixtures**, metals, non-metals, **solids, liquids, gases and solutions**.

CWLO 6. Investigate the properties of different materials including solubility, conductivity, melting points and **boiling points**.

NSLO 3. Design, plan and conduct investigations; explain how **reliability**, accuracy, precision, **fairness**, safety, ethics and a selection of **suitable equipment** have been considered.

NSLO 4. Produce data (qualitatively/quantitatively), critically analyse data to identify patterns and relationships, identify anomalous observations, **draw and justify conclusions**.

NSLO 10. Appreciate the role of science in society and its **personal, social and global importance**.

R Teacher's reference

KEYWORDS

adsorption
boiling point
capillary action
chromatography
chromatography
 paper
distillate
distillation
evaporation
filter
filter funnel
filter paper
filtrate
filtration
flocculation
impure
insoluble
Liebig condenser
miscible
permeable
pure
residue
sedimentation
separation techniques
settling
sieve

LEARNING INTENTIONS

At the end of this unit you should:

1. Be able to explain how to separate the components of mixtures.
2. Know how to separate an insoluble solute from a solvent, by several different methods.
3. Know how to separate a soluble solute from a solvent, by several different methods.
4. Be able to separate two miscible liquids.
5. Understand the importance of a variety of separation techniques, in science and industry.

Ⓡ Why Separate Mixtures?

In this unit we are looking at a variety of **separation techniques** that can be used to separate the components of mixtures.

Fig. 06.03.01 shows the components of one of the most important mixtures we use: unpolluted air. Scientists calculated the percentages of each component from a **pure** sample of air.

Mixture: Two or more substances mingled together but not chemically combined.

Pure: When a substance or mixture is not contaminated or polluted by an unwanted substance.

Impure: When a substance or mixture has been contaminated or polluted by another unwanted substance.

CHEMISTRY

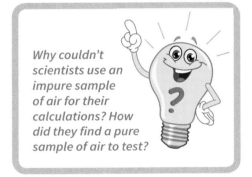

All other gases 0.04%	
Carbon dioxide (CO₂)	0.035%
Neon (Ne)	0.0018%
Helium (He)	0.00052%
Methane (CH₄)	0.00014%
Krypton (Kr)	0.00010%
Nitrous oxide (N₂O)	0.00005%
Hydrogen (H₂)	0.00005%
Ozone (O₃)	0.000007%
Water vapour (H₂O)	0–4%

Argon (Ar) 0.93%

Oxygen (O₂) 20.95%

Nitrogen (N₂) 78.08%

Fig. 06.03.01 Pure air is a mixture of gases that are present in their normal amounts. Other gases or particles that become part of the mixture, or increase the normal amounts of the gases, make the mixture impure. They are normally called pollutants.

Why couldn't scientists use an impure sample of air for their calculations? How did they find a pure sample of air to test?

⊘ Checkpoint 1

(a) *Table 06.03.01* lists a variety of mixtures. Copy and complete the table by placing a tick to show whether you think the mixture is pure or impure.

(b) Can you think of two additional mixtures you use in your daily life?

Mixture	Pure	
Impure		
Mineral water		
Tap water		
Sewer water		
Fizzy cola		
Concrete		
Iron ore		
Acid rain		
Clouds		
Smoke from a fire		

Table 06.03.01.

How Do We Separate Mixtures?

Components in mixtures can be separated by:
- Particle size of the components
- Mass of the components
- Boiling point of the solute or solvent
- Attraction to other substances
- Magnetism.

Depending on the mixture and its components, you, as a scientist, will decide the best technique to use to separate the components.

If you place a tea-bag in a container of water, what happens to the tea particles inside the tea-bag.

Separation by Particle Size

The easiest way to separate a mixture of solids that has different particle sizes is to pass it through a grid that has holes that only allow the smallest particles to fall through. The device that does this is called a **sieve**, or a **filter**.

Fig. 06.03.02 The photographs show a hand sieve that is used by gardeners to separate different types of clay (left) and a mechanical sieve used on road construction to sort different sizes of gravel (right).

When we want to separate an **insoluble** solid from a liquid (the solvent), we most often use a filter. This process is called **filtration**. The liquid that passes through the filter and is collected is called the **filtrate**. The insoluble solid that gets trapped in the filter is called the **residue**. Residue builds up in the filter, which means it has to be removed and cleaned or replaced.

Filtration: Separation of an insoluble solid from a liquid or gas.

A very good material to use as a filter is paper. Paper is made from wood, which contains air pockets. When processed to make paper, small holes or pores are present in the paper that allow water through.

Filtrate: The liquid that is collected after passing through the filter.

Residue: The insoluble solid left in the filter after filtration.

Solids

Paper

Water

Fig. 06.03.03 Water particles passing through the natural holes that are present in paper.

Car engines and air conditioning units have filters which have to be replaced regularly. What home appliances also have filters that need replacing?

🔍 Investigation 06.03.01: Testing how to filter a mixture

Equipment: A **filter funnel**, some paper, a soil–water mixture and some beakers.
Instructions: Using the equipment as listed, decide how you would set up an investigation to test filtering.

What did you learn?
1. A filter funnel is not an important piece of equipment in this investigation. Do you agree or disagree? Justify your answer.
2. Are all types of paper the same? Suggest how you might prove this.

CHEMISTRY

Investigation 06.03.02: Testing the best way to filter an insoluble solid

Method 1

① Fold here

② Then fold here

③ Pull this single flap away from the other three

④ This forms a cone

3 sheets   1 sheet

Method 2

① ② ③ ④ ⑤ ⑥

Equipment: A conical flask, a filter funnel, some **filter paper**, a 200 cm³ clay–water mixture, 2 x 100 cm³ beakers, a spatula, a clamp, a retort stand and a stop-watch.

Instructions: Using circular filter paper, test two ways of folding the paper using the instructions as shown and use both to test filtration.

What did you learn?
1. How did you set up the equipment for this investigation? Justify your answer.
2. You used additional equipment in this investigation compared to *Investigation 06.03.01*. Did the extra equipment in this investigation improve how you carried it out? Explain your answer.
3. Was there a difference between how the two filters worked? How can you prove this?

Permeable Membranes

Animal cells need to be able to allow substances to pass in and out. Nutrients need to be absorbed and wastes released. Openings in the cell membrane which allow this are called pores. However, these pores are not open all the time, and can change size depending on the particle attempting to enter or leave. This means that the movement of substances into and out of the cell is controlled by a **selectively permeable** membrane.

Gore-tex is a selectively permeable membrane used in clothing that allows sweat to pass out of the clothing but prevents rain from entering. The water in rain forms large droplets of water particles that can't fit through the pores of Gore-tex.

Permeable: Having pores that allow gases or liquids to pass through a membrane.

Fig. 06.03.04 Gore-tex is used for hiking and mountaineering clothes and footwear. The 14 million pores in every mm² of Gore-tex allow it to release sweat but stay waterproof.

Demonstration 06.03.01 – Showing selective permeability

Instructions: Your teacher will carry out this demonstration using two different solutions. Observe what happens during the demonstration.

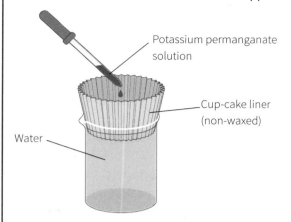

Potassium permanganate solution

Cup-cake liner (non-waxed)

Water

Did you know?
Drinks that have caffeine as an ingredient have a temporary diuretic effect on the kidneys. The kidneys become more permeable to water and so create more urine, filling the bladder more quickly.

What did you learn?
1. Non-waxed cup-cake liners must be used for this investigation – why?
2. Repeat this demonstration at home using either ink or food dye. Are the results different from the first version of this demonstration? Explain your answer.

Separation by Particle Mass

In a mixture of an insoluble solid and a liquid, like the clay–water mixture from *Investigation 06.03.02*, the mass of the solid is often big enough that the solid will sink to the bottom of the container if it is left and not shaken or stirred. This is called **settling** or **sedimentation**.

Settling is used in water treatment to remove solids floating in the water. Untreated water is poured into giant settling tanks and insoluble solids are allowed to settle onto the bottom of the tanks. To speed up the settling, aluminium sulfate is often added to the water. This causes the solids to clump together, forming heavier masses so they sink quicker. This process is called **flocculation**.

Settling: Allowing undissolved solids in a solution to sink to the bottom of a container.

Flocculation: Using chemicals to cause solids to clump together and sink.

Fig. 06.03.05 Stages of flocculation.

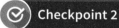 **Checkpoint 2**

(a) **Fish absorb oxygen directly from the water they swim in, but how can they do this without absorbing lots of water and becoming bloated?**
(b) **The top surface of a plant leaf has a waxy coating to help it survive in changeable weather. How do you think this waxy coat helps plants?**

Distillation: The process in which a liquid is boiled and its vapour is condensed and collected.

Evaporation: The changing of a liquid to a gas when the surface of the liquid is heated.

Separation by Heat

Temperature can be used to separate a dissolved solid from a solution in two ways: by **distillation** and **evaporation**. *Table 06.03.02* shows the similarities and differences between these two ways of separating a dissolved solid from a solution.

Distillation can also be used to separate two **miscible** liquids, which have different **boiling points**. Liquids that can mix together can be separated easily if their boiling points are not the same.

Puddles left by a rain-shower dry out by evaporation. The heat of the sun warms the surface of the puddles, causing some particles to change state to a gas. This happens over a period of hours. When this happens on a beach, rings of salt are the **residue**.

In countries where drinking water has to be extracted from seawater, evaporation is used to remove sea salt, leaving behind the **distillated** water.

Miscible: How two liquids mix evenly with each other.

Distillate: The liquid that has been condensed from a vapour and is collected from the condenser.

Residue: The solute that is left after a solvent has been removed from a solution by distillation or evaporation.

Distillation	Evaporation
Needs a lot of heat energy	Needs a little heat energy
All solvent particles are heated	Only solvent particles near the surface are heated
Vapour is collected and condensed	Vapour is not collected or condensed
Dissolved solid remains (residue)	Dissolved solid remains (residue)
The residue is the solute	The residue is the solute

Table 06.03.02 Similarities and differences between two ways of separating a dissolved solid from a solution.

CHEMISTRY

🔍 Investigation 06.03.03: **Comparing methods of evaporation**

Equipment: A Bunsen burner or hotplate, 100 cm³ salt water (or copper sulfate) solution, a tripod, a wire gauze, 1 x 500 ml beaker and an evaporating dish.

Instructions: Using the same solution for both, test the two evaporation methods shown in the diagram.

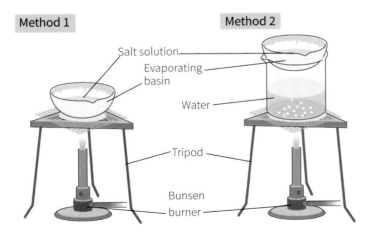

Method 1 | Method 2

Salt solution
Evaporating basin
Water
Tripod
Bunsen burner

What did you learn?

1. Which method would you prefer to use? Explain why.
2. What safety precautions did you need to take for these methods? Justify why one method is safer than the other.
3. Can you think of another method of evaporation? List the advantages and disadvantages of this method.

Investigation 06.03.04: **Separating miscible liquids**

Equipment: A **Liebig condenser**, quick-fit connections, a round-bottomed flask, a beaker, a Bunsen burner or hotplate, a tripod, some wire gauze and a 100 cm³ alcohol–water mixture.

Instructions: Set up the equipment as shown and use it to separate a mixture of water and alcohol.

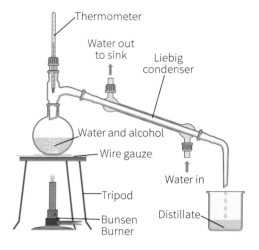

What did you learn?

1. What other piece of equipment do you need in order to set up the distillation?
2. Why does the outer tube of the Liebig condenser need water flowing through it?
3. Can you suggest why the flow of water should only be set up as in the diagram?
4. How did you know when to stop heating the mixture? Explain how this is a reliable way to decide when to stop.
5. Was the distillate pure alcohol? Give reasons for your answer.

 Checkpoint 3

(a) What is the function of the Liebig condenser?

(b) Is it possible to use the Liebig condenser without water running through it? Explain why.

(c) Do you agree that a Liebig condenser should not be used to separate a dissolved solid from a solvent? Why?

Did you know?
Animals, especially horses, played an important part in World War I, so gas masks were developed for them as well as for soldiers.

Separation by Attraction to Other Substances

Adsorption happens when a substance is attracted to the surface of a filter material and cannot pass through the filter. World War I gas masks used activated charcoal as a filter as it adsorbed the poisonous gases. Activated charcoal is also used to 'pump stomachs' after a poisoning or overdose so that the drug or poison can be quickly removed from the body before it causes further damage.

Capillarity is the ability of a liquid to travel up a narrow tube. One of the reasons this happens is that the water particles are attracted to the particles the tube is made up of, as well as to each other. **Capillary action** is one of the ways that water travels up through a plant from its roots. It is also an important part of a separation technique called **chromatography**.

Adsorption: The attraction of a substance to the surface layer of another substance.

Capillary Action: The process of water particles sticking to each other and to the walls of narrow tubes, which causes water to rise in the tubes.

CHEMISTRY

Chromatography separates substances that are present in very small amounts in a solution. The substances separate out along the length of the **chromatography paper**, and can be seen by their different colours. The name 'chromatography' comes from the Greek words *chroma* meaning colours and *graphy* meaning image-making.

The substances are carried up through natural tubes of the chromatography paper by capillary action as the solvent rises up through the paper. How far they are carried depends on several factors, the two most important of which are:

● How well the substance dissolves in the solvent and is attracted to the solvent particles.
● How strongly the substance adsorbs to the chromatography paper.

This means that substances that are more attracted to the solvent will move further up as they are less attracted to the chromatography paper.

Chromatography with paper can be done using three methods:

● Hanging Strip method
● Hanging Wick method
● Paper Tube method.

Demonstration 06.03.02 – **Testing capillary action**

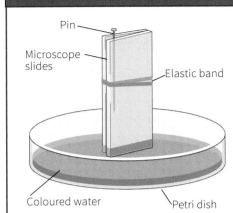

Pin
Microscope slides
Elastic band
Coloured water
Petri dish

Fig. 06.03.06 A pin is placed between two glass slides and a rubber band is used to hold them tightly together. The end of the slides is then placed into some coloured water.

Chromotography: The separation of dissolved substances in a solution by their attraction to the solvent.

Investigation 06.03.05: **Comparing chromatography methods**

Equipment: Pick your equipment based on the two methods you choose from the diagrams below. The equipment is different for each method but you will use chromatography paper and distilled water for each.

Instructions: Investigate two paper chromatography methods.

Method 1: Hanging Strip

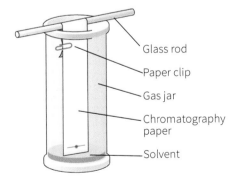

Glass rod
Paper clip
Gas jar
Chromatography paper
Solvent

Method 2: Hanging Wick

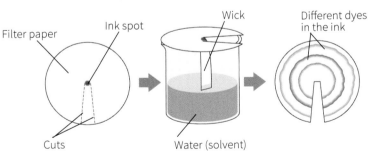

Filter paper
Ink spot
Wick
Different dyes in the ink
Cuts
Water (solvent)

Method 3: Paper Tube

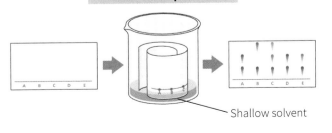

Shallow solvent

What did you learn?

1. Explain why you should use only chromatography paper and not another type of paper in this investigation.
2. Is it possible to use tap water rather than distilled water for this investigation? Justify your answer.
3. In two of the methods, why is it important that the line on the chromatography paper is in pencil?
4. Choose two particular methods to investigate. Outline your reasons for not choosing the third method.

Separation by Magnetism

Substances can also be separated by their magnetic properties. This technique is used in the recycling and iron mining industries.

In recycling it is used to separate steel or iron objects from other rubbish to avoid having to sort by hand.

The iron industry uses magnetic sorting as one of its stages to separate iron from iron ore. Most metals are found in impure ores, such as iron pyrite, also known as 'Fool's Gold'. The iron ore is first crushed into smaller stones and placed on a conveyer belt. The stones containing iron are attracted to a magnetic conveyer belt above, so are carried further before being dropped down a separate chute. Waste crushed rock can be used as gravel for construction.

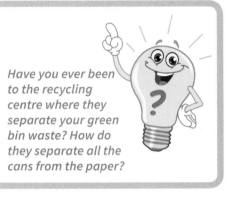

Have you ever been to the recycling centre where they separate your green bin waste? How do they separate all the cans from the paper?

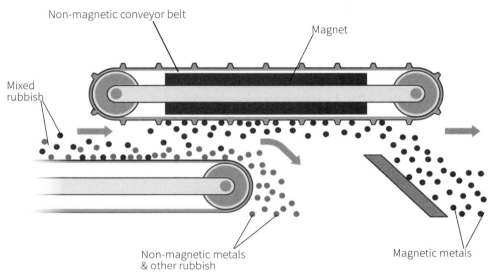

Non-magnetic conveyor belt

Magnet

Mixed rubbish

Non-magnetic metals & other rubbish

Magnetic metals

Fig. 06.03.07 The bottom conveyor belt carries mixed batches of rubbish to the magnetic conveyor belt. The magnetic conveyor belt sits above the mixed rubbish. Rubbish passes under it, sticking to the belt. When the belt moves beyond the magnets the magnetic metals fall off the belt and into a separate chute. Non-magnetic rubbish simply falls off the end of the bottom conveyor belt into another chute.

WHAT I HAVE LEARNED...

- How to separate the components of various mixtures.
- How to separate an insoluble solute from a solvent by filtration.
- How to separate two miscible liquids by distillation.
- How to separate a soluble solute from a solvent by evaporation, distillation and chromatography.
- How to choose the most suitable method for a separation technique based on scientific data and reasoning.
- The importance of a variety of separation techniques in science and industry.

Question Time

Copy and Complete

In this unit I learned that a solution can be separated into the _____ and _____ by a number of different methods. Insoluble solids can be separated by _____ or _____. Soluble solids can be separated by_____or _____. The residue is the name of the solid left behind after _____ and _____ /_____. The distillate is the liquid collected at the end of _____. _____ is the process by which puddles on beaches dry out leaving salt rings. Two _____ liquids can be separated by _____. The liquid with the lower _____ _____is changed to a vapour first. Dissolved solids can be separated from a solution by how attracted they are to the solvent; this is called _____.

Questions

1. Name the separation technique shown in *Fig. 06.03.08*.

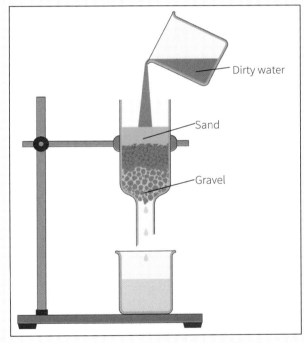

Fig. 06.03.08 *What separation technique is this?*

(i) When performing this technique in the lab, what can the sand and gravel be replaced with?

(ii) What is the general name for the substance that passes through the sand and gravel?

(iii) What is the general name for the substance that cannot pass through the sand and gravel?

(iv) Explain why this substance cannot pass through.

2. *Fig. 06.03.09* shows a separation apparatus. Copy and complete *Table 06.03.03* by correctly matching the labels A–F in the diagram with words/phrases in the table.

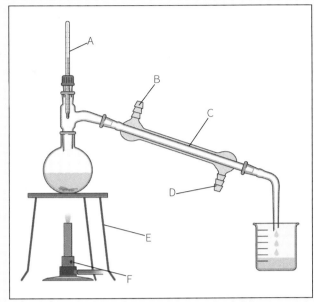

Fig. 06.03.09.

	Bunsen burner
	Cold water in
	Condenser
	Thermometer
	Tripod stand
	Water out to sink

Table 06.03.03.

(i) What is the name given to the separation technique shown in *Fig. 06.03.09*?

(ii) What is the purpose of water flowing in and out of C?

(iii) Why is it safer to have water flowing into D rather than B?

(iv) An alcohol and water mixture can be separated by this apparatus. Which of the two liquids is collected in the beaker?

(v) What is the general name given to a liquid collected in this type of separation?

(vi) What property of the liquids allows them to be separated in this way?

(vii) Why is it better not to use this equipment to separate salt from seawater?

Fig. 06.03.10 Paper chromatography.

3. Paper chromatography was used to find the composition of blue ink in a pen. The same liquid, paper and pen were used in each of the three experiments shown in *Fig. 06.03.10*. They were started at different times, C first (the beaker on the right), then B (centre) and finally A (left).
   (i) Why is the ink dot above the level of the liquid in the beakers?
   (ii) What caused the dots of ink on papers B and C to spread upwards?
   (iii) Why were colours, other than blue, seen in B and C as the ink moved up the paper?
4. *Fig. 06.03.11* shows a method for purifying unclean water using simple equipment. What separation process does this set-up use? Why is it important to place a stone or weight in the centre of the plastic?

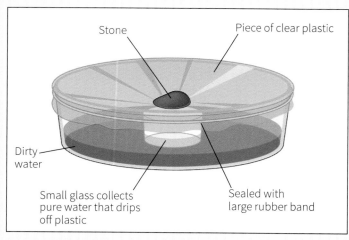

Fig. 06.03.11 DIY water purification system.

5. *Fig. 06.03.12* shows a laboratory set-up for desalination. Is this separation process evaporation or distillation? Explain. What is the purpose of the wet towel? Name an alternative piece of equipment that you can use instead of a wet towel.

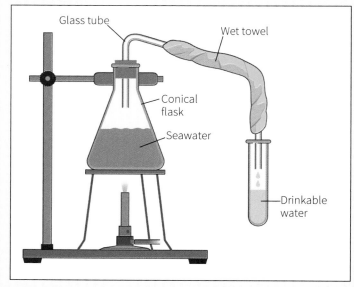

Fig. 06.03.12 Laboratory desalination set-up.

6. A 330 ml can of Coca-Cola contains the equivalent of twenty-three sachets of sugar. If each sachet holds 2.5 g of sugar, how many grams of sugar is there in a can? What separation method can be used to prove this?

Inquiry

A Decanting is another separation technique. **Explain** the disadvantages and advantages of using this method.

B A hand-cranked centrifuge can be used to separate the solids in a suspension that has been placed in a test tube. Blood components can be separated this way. **Research** and **explain** how a centrifuge works.

C Pick two mixtures that you have not already investigated, at least one of which must be a mixture from your everyday life. Based on what you think the mixtures contain, **choose** how you would separate them, and carry out the separations.

D Kidney dialysis is used by patients whose kidneys cannot filter wastes from their blood correctly. **Design** a presentation/poster that explains how dialysis machines work. Include a labelled diagram.

6.4

Elements, Mixtures and Compounds

Learning Outcomes

CWLO 1. Investigate whether mass is unchanged when chemical and physical changes take place.

CWLO 2. Develop and use models to describe the particle theory; demonstrate how they provide a simple way to account for the conservation of mass, changes of state, **physical change, chemical change, mixtures and their separation.**

CWLO 4. Classify substances as elements, compounds, mixtures, metals, non-metals, solids, liquids, gases and solutions.

NSLO 1. Appreciate how scientists work and **how scientific ideas are modified over time.**

NSLO 4. Produce data (qualitatively/quantitatively), **critically analyse data to identify patterns and relationships,** identify anomalous observations, **draw and justify conclusions.**

NSLO 7. Organise and communicate research and investigative findings in a variety of ways **fit for purpose and audience, using relevant scientific terminology and representations.**

NSLO 9. Research and present information on **the contribution that scientists make to scientific discovery and invention,** and its impact on society.

NSLO 10. Appreciate the role of science in society and its **personal, social and global importance.**

PWLO 3. Investigate patterns and **relationships between physical observables.**

R Teacher's reference

KEYWORDS

atom
ball and stick model
colloid
compound
decanting
detergent
element
emulsion
matter
mixture
molecule
Periodic Table of
  the Elements
solutions
suspension
symbol

LEARNING INTENTIONS

At the end of this unit you should:

1. Be able to explain the differences between an element and a compound.
2. Be able to explain the differences between an atom and a molecule.
3. Know that there are different types of mixtures and be able to explain their differences.
4. Know that an emulsion is a type of colloid, as well as the uses of some emulsions in daily life and industry.
5. Know what a detergent is and how it is important in daily activities, as well as its environmental effects.

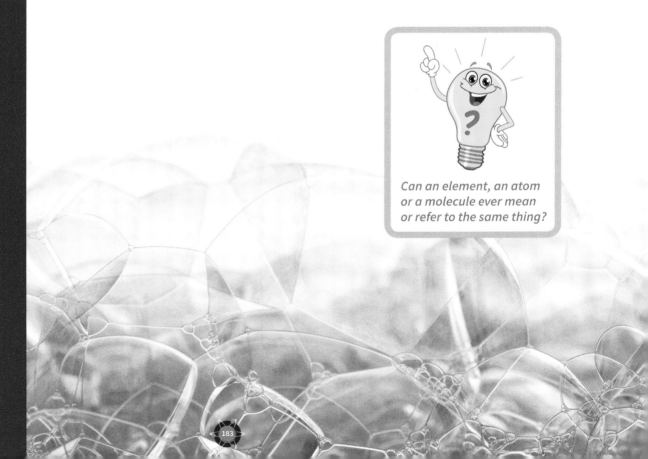

Can an element, an atom or a molecule ever mean or refer to the same thing?

What is an Atom?

'*An atom is a body which cannot be cut in two.*'

James Clerk Maxwell, *Nature* (September, 1873)

When scientist James Clerk Maxwell wrote this in the famous science journal *Nature* in 1873, philosophers and scientists had been arguing for almost 2500 years about the make-up of **matter**. All agreed that every substance was made up of matter – now they just needed to figure out *what matter was made of*.

One concept that had been agreed on for a long time was the idea of the **elements**. These were basic substances that, when combined in the correct amounts, could form any substance known. In the beginning, Aristotle and others believed that earth, water, air, fire and aether were the only five elements.

Over time it was realised that these five elements alone were not enough to explain the huge variety of substances that were being discovered; but the concept of an **atom** could. Atoms were the smallest possible particle of an element that could still behave like the element. We will explore atoms further in the next unit.

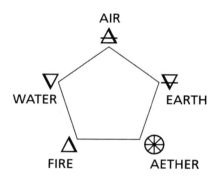

Fig. 06.04.02 The Ancient Greek symbols used for the five elements.

Fig. 06.04.01 James Clerk Maxwell (1831–79).

Matter: Anything that takes up space and has mass.

Element: A substance made up of only one type of atom.

Atom: The smallest particle of an element that has the properties of that element.

Names and Symbols

Over time the names, letter **symbols** and important basic information about each of the known elements have been collected into a table called the **Periodic Table of the Elements**. (You will learn more about this in *Unit 7.1* and *Unit 7.2*.)

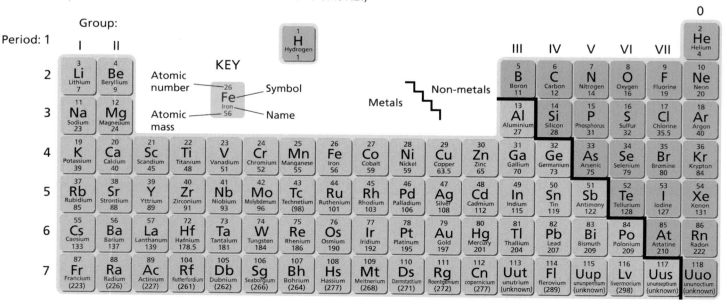

Fig. 06.04.03 The periodic table lists all the known natural elements in order of mass, starting with the lightest element. Elements that have similar properties are grouped in columns. Elements coloured blue are metals, and elements coloured green are non-metals.

(R) The original versions of the periodic table had different shapes representing the symbols for each element. So for each new element discovered, a new symbol had to be created. Not only that, different scientists used different sets of symbols. To avoid confusion and allow symbols for new elements to be created easily, it was agreed that letter symbols based on the element name would instead be used.

Did you know?
The International Union of Pure and Applied Chemistry (IUPAC) decides on new names, and one naming rule prevents new elements being named after living persons. This is to prevent arguments about who the element should be named after, as often large teams of people are working on discovering new elements.

A simple system is used to give each element its symbol

- Each symbol has only either one or two letters.
- The first letter of the name is capitalised.
- If another element has the same first letter, another letter from the name is used, and it is always written as a small letter, e.g. Germanium (*Ge*) and Gallium (*Ga*).
- Some symbols are based on traditional names or old Latin or Greek names.

Elements continue to be discovered. The names of newly discovered elements tend to be versions of the place where they are discovered or named after a deceased scientist who discovered the element or with a link to the element.

Element	Symbol
hydrogen	H
carbon	C
oxygen	O
sodium (natrum)	Na
aluminium	Al
chlorine	Cl
iron (ferrum)	Fe
copper (kupros)	Cu
krypton	Kr
silver (argentium)	Ag
tungsten (wolfram)	W
mercury (hydrargyrum)	Hg
radon	Rn
radium	Ra

Table 06.04.01 Some of the elements and their symbols. Why do you think some elements have kept the symbols from their old name (in brackets in this table, e.g. sodium/natrum: Na)?

✓ Checkpoint 1

(a) Copy and complete *Table 06.04.02* by writing the missing symbol beside each name.
(b) There are three extra symbols in the list. What are the name of these elements?

Name	Symbol
chlorine	
chromium	
cobalt	
lead	
manganese	
magnesium	
polonium	
silicon	
tin	
zinc	
zirconium	

Table 06.04.02.

List of Symbols:

Cr	V	Po	Si	Sn	Zn	Zr

Nb	Co	Cl	Mn	Mg	Pb	Os

Did you know?
A mine in Ytterby – a small town in Southern Sweden – has been the source for the discovery of nine separate elements, between 1794 and 1911. Most of the names given to those elements were versions of either the words 'Ytterby' or 'Scandinavia', for example Yttrium and Scandium.

Demonstration 06.04.01 – Testing sodium and sodium chloride properties

Instructions: Your teacher will show you samples of sodium and sodium chloride, and will place both in water. Record what you see happening in a table of observations.

What did you learn?

1. Which one of these substances is an element? Justify your answer.
2. Why can your teacher not safely demonstrate chlorine in the school laboratory? (*Hint:* See *Unit 6.3*.)

Molecules and Compounds

'*A molecule is the smallest portion of a particular substance.*'

James Clerk Maxwell, *Nature* (September, 1873)

Eventually, scientists began to realise that they needed some way of explaining how elements could combine together in different amounts to form new substances. This led to the idea of the **molecule**. This idea meant that two or more atoms of different elements, or even the same element, could chemically combine to form a molecule.

The molecule would be the smallest particle of a new substance that still had the properties of that substance. Because the new substance was made up of the atoms of two or more elements, it could be called a **compound**.

Étienne François Geoffroy was one of the first scientists to try and show how substances combined in different ways when he created what he called his 'Affinity Table' in 1718.

As scientists gained more knowledge about elements and how they reacted and combined with each other, they realised that they had to come up with an easy-to-understand system to show the reaction and combination. August Wilhelm von Hofmann suggested the '**ball and stick model**'. In this model each element would have its own colour and be drawn as a ball with sticks to show how each element was combined in a molecule.

Fig. 06.04.04 *Étienne François Geoffroy (1672–1731).*

> **Molecule:** Composed of two or more atoms chemically combined.

> **Compound:** Composed of two or more different elements chemically combined.

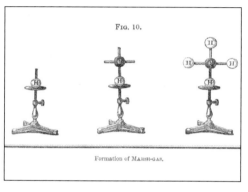

Fig. 06.04.05 *August Wilhelm von Hofmann's original ball and stick model of methane gas.*

Name	Ball and Stick Model	Chemical Formula
water		H_2O
oxygen		O_2
hydrogen		H_2
carbon dioxide		CO_2
methane		CH_4

Table 06.04.04 *Some of the elements and their models and chemical formulas. Did you notice that the modern ball and stick model for methane is different to the one suggested by Von Hofmann (Fig. 06.04.05)?*

	Element	Colour
	hydrogen	white
	carbon	black
	nitrogen	blue
	oxygen	red
	phosphorous	orange
	sulfur	yellow
	chlorine	green
	sodium	violet (purple)

Table 06.04.03 *Ball colours for some elements.*

 **Checkpoint 2**

R Using the colour code for different elements, can you draw or make the ball and stick models of these three molecules:

- **sodium chloride – NaCl**
- **ammonia – NH$_3$**
- **carbon tetrachloride – CCl$_4$**

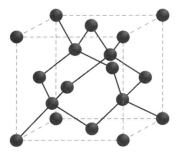 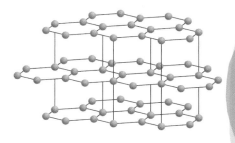

Fig. 06.04.06 Diagrams of diamond arrangement (left) and graphite arrangement.

The Differences Between Mixtures and Compounds

A **mixture** of iron and sulfur and a compound of iron and sulfur are each made up of the same elements but are different substances because in mixtures elements are mingled but not chemically combined.

Mixture: Made of two or more substances mingled together but not chemically combined.

 **Checkpoint 3**

Lay out a table in your copy which lists mixtures and compounds.

CHEMISTRY

Demonstration 06.04.02 – Sulfur and iron: mixture and compound

Instructions: Your teacher will show you test tubes of sulfur, iron and iron sulfur mix, and will test them with a magnet. The iron sulfur mix will then be heated and allowed to cool. Lay out an observations table in your copy. Fill in what you see happening as the demonstration occurs.

> *What did you learn?*
> 1. Is the iron sulfur mixture a different substance to the iron sulfur compound? Suggest more than one reason for your answer.
> 2. Explain whether or not these results agree with the Law of Conservation of Mass.

Investigation 06.04.01: Is it a compound or a mixture?

Instructions: Using a mortar and pestle, 50 g of iron-fortified breakfast cereal, a zip-lock bag and a neodymium magnet, investigate whether the iron in the breakfast cereal is part of a compound or mixture.

> *What did you learn?*
> 1. What evidence can you use to decide whether the iron in the breakfast cereal is part of a compound or a mixture? How do your observations help you make your decision?
> 2. Why was it important to slosh the breakfast cereal about in the bag with water?

 **Checkpoint 4**

Rewrite *Table 06.04.05.* Complete it using your own knowledge and with the help of your fellow students and your teacher.

Mixture	Compound
Made up of two or more different substances (or molecules)	
	Elements that make it up are in fixed portions (ratio)
	Difficult to separate elements
Properties of a mixture are similar to the substances that make it up	
Very little or no heat change	
	Elements often change state

Table 06.04.05.

Solutions, Suspensions and Colloids

You already know that **solutions** are mixtures that normally involve a solid dissolved in a liquid. You have also learned how to separate a number of different mixtures (*Unit 6.3*).

Another method that can be used is **decanting**. This allows insoluble solids in a liquid to settle at the bottom. A mixture like this is called a **suspension**. Muddy water from a river which settles and becomes clear is an example of this.

Ⓡ But what about insoluble solids that are so small that they are too light to sink to the bottom? Mixtures like this are called **colloids**. The insoluble particles spread evenly through the mixture. A simple test to tell the difference between a solution or suspension and a colloid is to shine a light through it. If the light shines through, it is a solution, or a suspension that has settled. In a colloid the particles cause the light to scatter so the beam does not pass through it.

Many mixtures we use in our daily lives are **emulsions**. An emulsion is made when a liquid–liquid colloid happens: two liquids which will not mix but one spreads evenly through another in very small droplets, e.g. mayonnaise.

Suspension: A mixture where insoluble solids will sink to the bottom of the solvent if left still.

Colloid: A mixture in which insoluble particles spread evenly through a mixture and will cause a light beam to scatter.

Emulsion: A mixture in which two liquids do not mix but one spreads evenly through the other in droplets.

Colloid	Type	Examples
Liquid emulsion	liquid in liquid	*Mayonnaise, milk, ice-cream*
Solid emulsion	liquid in solid	*Cheese, butter, hand cream, bitumen*
Liquid aerosol	liquid in gas	*Air freshener sprays, mist, clouds*
Gel	solid in gas	*Most paints, blood, toothpaste, jelly, mud*
Foam	gas in liquid	*Whipped cream, beer, froth, soap suds*
Solid foam	gas in solid	*Marshmallows, pavlova, polystyrene*

Table 06.04.06 Examples of colloids involving all three states of matter.

R Bartenders know this colloid effect as the 'ouzo effect' (ouzo being an alcoholic drink), because when water is added to alcohol drinks made from aniseed it causes the drink to go cloudy.

Fig. 06.04.07 Before, during and after water has been added to create the ouzo effect.

R The real importance of emulsions is in the food, cosmetic, medicine and paint industries. Emulsions or emulsifiers in foods keep them fresher for longer, and so increase their shelf life. In cosmetics and medicine they allow creams to be applied to the skin without leaving too much oil on the skin's surface. Emulsion paints were an important development because most colours or pigments used in paints are oil-based and oils normally only mix well in solvents like alcohol. However, alcohol solvents are very flammable and their odour can cause breathing difficulties. Emulsion paints were developed as a solution to these problems.

Detergents

Detergents are substances that cause oils to spread evenly in other liquids such as water. This is why many washing powders have detergents in them. Most difficult stains are oil-based, so the detergents cause the substances in the stains to mix with water and wash off the clothes.

A range of cleaning chemicals that doesn't contain detergents but does the same job have been developed because waste water from washing machines, sinks and showers can damage river and sea life. Detergents have been used to treat oil spills at sea by breaking up the oil, but their chemicals can interfere with and damage sea life, and so are now avoided.

Fig. 06.04.08 A tin of emulsion decorating paint.

Detergent: A substance that causes oil to spread evenly in water-based solutions.

🔍 Investigation 06.04.02: **Can water and oil mix?**

Equipment: Test tube rack, two test tubes, water, washing-up liquid, cooking oil.

Instructions: Using the equipment as listed, design an investigation to test whether water and oil can mix.

What did you learn?

1. How can you make sure you are carrying out a fair test?
2. If the oil you used was mixed with other liquids, would you get the same results? Justify your answer.
3. Was there a colloid in this investigation? How can you prove your answer?

CHEMISTRY

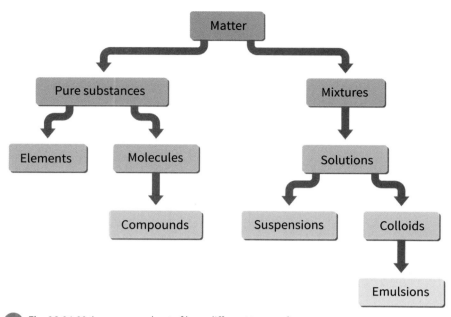

Fig. 06.04.09 A summary chart of how different types of substances are linked.

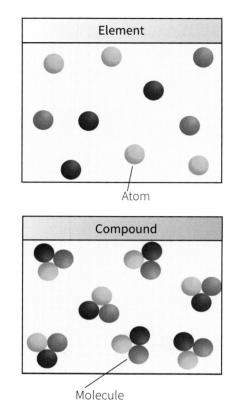

Fig. 06.04.10 A diagram summary of the differences between atoms, elements, molecules and compounds.

WHAT I HAVE LEARNED...

- The differences between an element and a compound.
- The differences between an atom and a molecule.
- The differences between a mixture and a compound.
- That there are different types of mixtures and how to explain their differences.
- How to draw ball or make ball and stick models of H_2, O_2, H_2O, CO_2, CH_4, CCl_4, NaCl, NH_3.
- That an emulsion is a type of colloid, and the uses of some emulsions in daily life and industry.
- What a detergent is, its use in daily activities, and its environmental effects.
- Examples of simple emulsions.
- How to test for a colloid.

Question Time

Copy and Complete

In this unit I learned that an _____ is made up of one type of _____. A _____ is made up of two or more _____ chemically combined. A compound is made up of two or more _____ _____ chemically combined. Two or more substances _____ together but not _____ _____ is called a mixture. Particles sink to the bottom if it is a _____ type of mixture. If insoluble solute particles are spread evenly through the solvent it is called a _____ type of mixture.

Questions

1. Write down the correct symbols from the periodic table for these elements:

   - Chlorine
   - Lead
   - Oxygen
   - Molybdenum
   - Thallium
   - Helium

   Which of these elements are gases? Which of these normally exist as pure molecules?

2. Marie Curie showed the existence of the <u>element</u> radium and she produced 0.1 g of the <u>compound</u> radium chloride in 1902 by processing tonnes of pitchblende ore, obtained from mines in Bohemia.
   Explain the underlined terms.

Fig. 06.04.11 Marie Curie (1867–1934).

3. Robert Boyle introduced the word 'element' into the language of chemistry. Copy and complete *Table 06.04.07*, identifying each of the substances listed by ticking the box for element, mixture or compound.

Substance	Element	Mixture	Compound
carbon dioxide			✔
aluminium			
water			
krypton			
fizzy cola			
blood			
ice-cream			
mayonnaise			
air			
smog			
sugar			
tears			

Table 06.04.07.

4. R The apparatus shown in *Fig. 06.04.12* was used to strongly heat 2.4 g of magnesium in a crucible. The lid of the crucible was left slightly off during the heating. A white powder with a mass of 4.0 g was produced.
   (i) Identify the compound in this experiment.
   (ii) List two ways in which it is different to the element used in the experiment.
   (iii) Name the mixture that was present in the experiment.

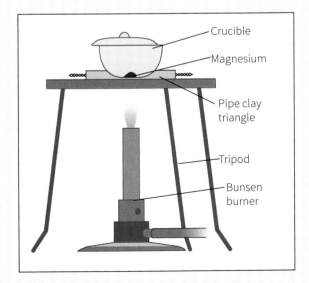

Fig. 06.04.12 Heating magnesium in a crucible.

5. Copy and complete *Table 06.04.08*. Decide which substances are colloids by ticking the True or False box for each substance.

Substance	True	False
whipped cream		
concrete		
engine oil		
muddy water		
coloured glass		
paper		

Table 06.04.08.

6. Pumice is a type of rock formed when volcanoes erupt. Why can pumice be classified as a colloid?

Inquiry

A *Fig. 06.04.13* shows gallium metal in the palm of a person's hand. When first placed in the person's hand the gallium was solid, but then it changed. What type of change is this? Has a compound or mixture been formed? **Explain**.

Fig. 06.04.13 Gallium melting in the hand.

B Iron is an element that is an essential part of our diet as it plays a very important role in transporting oxygen around our body. Lack of iron in the diet is called anaemia. **Research** the symptoms of anaemia.

C In the days before iron could be safely given as a tablet or injection, doctors advised patients to consume food and drink rich in iron. In the past in Ireland, Guinness was thought to be a source of iron and was often prescribed by doctors to patients with low iron levels. It was also given to blood donors after they had donated. Can you **suggest** some reasons why Guinness is no longer recommended in this way by doctors or blood donation clinics?

Fig. 06.04.14 Guinness advertisement with its famous slogan.

D Sudocrem was created by Dublin pharmacist Thomas Smith in 1931. Is it a solution, a suspension, a colloid or an emulsion? **Suggest** why Sudocrem is a good product for its recommended uses. **Summarise** your information in a poster.

Fig. 06.04.15 Sudocrem – an Irish invention!

7.1

The Atom

Learning Outcomes

CWLO 3. Describe and model the structure of the atom in terms of the nucleus, protons, neutrons and electrons; compare mass and charge of protons, neutrons and electrons.

NSLO 1. Appreciate how scientists work and **how scientific ideas are modified over time.**

NSLO 10. Appreciate the role of science in society **and its** personal, social and **global importance.**

PWLO 3. Investigate patterns and relationships between physical observables.

R Teacher's reference

KEYWORDS

atom
atomic number
Billiard Ball Model
Bohr Orbital Model
charge
dalton
electron
electronic
 configuration
element
energy level
isotopes
mass number
matter
negative charge
neutral
neutron
nucleus
orbit
Planetary Model
Plum Pudding Model
proton
shell
sub-atomic particles

LEARNING INTENTIONS

At the end of this unit you should:

1. Be able to describe the parts that make up an atom and where they are inside an atom.
2. Know the charges for the different parts of the atom.
3. Know the scientific definition of an atom.
4. Know the difference between atomic mass and atomic number.
5. Read the information for any element from the periodic table and describe it.
6. Draw the Bohr models showing the structure of the first twenty elements from the periodic table.

Are the atoms of each element different?

Why an Atom?

In Ancient Greece, science was conducted by men called philosophers who carried out 'thought experiments'. Some believed that all **matter** was made up of particles which could not be divided. They called these particles **atoms**, from the Greek word *atomos*, meaning indivisible. Others, however, believed that everything was made up of different combinations of five **elements** (which we came across in the previous unit): earth (solid), water (liquid), air (gas), fire (heat) and aether (an invisible substance that filled empty space).

This idea of the five elements was to last for 2000 years. In 1803, English school teacher John Dalton came up with a theory that changed the scientific meaning of the word 'element'. He suggested that not only were atoms the smallest possible particles, but that each element contained only one type of atom. Dalton's explanation become known as the **Billiard Ball Model**.

This was an incredible suggestion. If true, it meant that every atom in a particular element was identical but different from the atoms in other elements; and the way the elements reacted to each other and the environment was special to that element.

It took another 130 years of experiments to figure it out completely, but at least now scientists had a good definition of what an atom was, one that was supported by experimental results.

> **Matter:** Anything that takes up space and has mass.

> **Atom:** The smallest particle of an element that has the properties of that element.

> **Element:** A substance made up of only one type of atom.

| Aristotle 384BCE–322BCE | John Dalton 1766–1844 | J.J. Thomson 1856–1940 | Ernest Rutherford 1871–1937 | Niels Bohr 1885–1962 |

Fig. 07.01.01 Scientists involved in the changing ideas of what an atom was.

Sub-Atomic Particles

The next discovery was that atoms *did* contain smaller parts, called **sub-atomic particles**. Three types of sub-atomic particles were discovered: **protons**, **neutrons** and **electrons**. Sub-atomic particles don't have the properties of atoms, but the amount of each type does decide which element an atom belongs to.

In 1897, English physicist J.J. Thomson was able to show that there were particles that had **negative charge**. He suggested that large positive mass (which was a solid sphere) was studded on the outside with these negative charge particles. He also suggested that how these negative charge sub-atomic particles were arranged was important. This became known as the **Plum Pudding Model**, and these negative charge particles were named electrons.

> **Sub-Atomic Particles:** Particles that are smaller than an atom; different amounts of each type make up an atom.

> **Charge:** The number showing how positive or negative a particle is.

> **Electrons:** A sub-atomic particle that has a negative charge of -1 and a mass of $\frac{1}{1840}$ dalton.

In 1911, Thomson's friend and former student Ernest Rutherford was to prove him partly wrong. Rutherford fired positive particles at very thin gold foil. Most passed straight through, but some bounced almost straight back, while others deflected at angles. If J.J. Thomson's Plum Pudding Model had been correct, all the particles should have passed straight through.

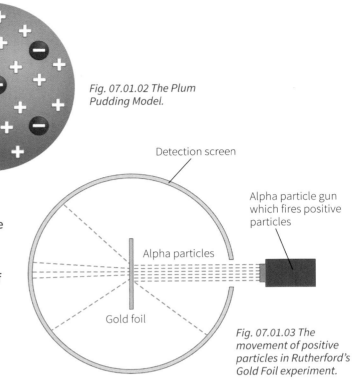

Fig. 07.01.02 The Plum Pudding Model.

Rutherford came up with several conclusions:
- Atoms were mostly empty space.
- There was a large mass in the centre which caused some positive particles to bounce almost straight back.
- Some particles passed through but at an angle because positive particles in the atom repelled them and pushed them slightly off course.

Rutherford's conclusions became known as the **Planetary Model** as it showed that electrons orbited the **nucleus** (made up of the protons and neutrons) like the planets move around the Sun.

Detection screen

Alpha particle gun which fires positive particles

Alpha particles

Gold foil

Fig. 07.01.03 The movement of positive particles in Rutherford's Gold Foil experiment.

CHEMISTRY

Investigation 07.01.01: Checking Rutherford's conclusions

Equipment: Hula hoop, string, table tennis ball, retort stand, brown rice, drinking straw.

Instructions:
1. Set up the equipment as shown so the table tennis ball is in the centre of the hula hoop.
2. Using the drinking straw, fire at least thirty single rice grains through the hula hoop.
3. Count the number of grains that pass through, are deflected, or bounce right back.

Hula hoop
Table tennis ball
Thread

What did you learn?
Can you explain why your results agree/disagree with Rutherford's conclusions from the Gold Foil Experiment?

Rutherford named these new sub-atomic particles protons as they had positive charge. Because an atom has equal numbers of electrons (negative charge) and protons (positive charge), they are **neutral** overall.

To make sense of measurements from a number of experiments, Rutherford also suggested the existence of a type of sub-atomic particle that had no charge, but had the same mass as a proton. These were called neutrons. Experiments also showed that the protons and neutrons were in the centre of the atom, called the nucleus.

(R) The mass of a proton is 1/12th the mass of ^{12}C (carbon-12) which is 0.0000000000 00000000166053892 kg! For convenience it is easier to call this unit one '**dalton**' (Da), named after John Dalton.

Protons: A sub-atomic particle that has a positive charge of +1 and a mass of one dalton.

Neutrons: A sub-atomic particle that has no charge, and a mass of one dalton.

For atoms to be atoms, and not to be changing constantly, they need to be stable. This means that the total amount of positive charges must be equal to the total amount of negative charges – they must balance. So if you know how many protons an atom has, you also know how many electrons it has. This is called the **atomic number**. It was proven in an experiment by English physicist Henry Moseley in 1913.

In 1932, another English physicist, James Chadwick, used polonium, beryllium and paraffin wax to carry out a number of delicate radiation experiments. These experiments were the final proof on top of Rutherford's work that neutrons existed, that they had no charge, and that along with protons they made up the rest of the nucleus.

Comparing the Sub-Atomic Particles

By this time scientists had calculated the mass of all three sub-atomic particles. Protons and neutrons had the same mass, but electrons were almost 2000 times less than protons or neutrons. Because of this, in most calculations the mass of the electrons was ignored.

The combined mass of the protons and neutrons is very important, because it is different for the atoms of each element. This is called the **mass number**. It is one of the ways to tell the difference between the atoms of each element.

Sub-Atomic Particle	Mass	Charge	Location
electron	$\frac{1}{1840}$ dalton	−1	orbiting the nucleus
proton	1 dalton	+1	nucleus
neutron	1 dalton	0	nucleus

Table 07.01.01 Properties of the sub-atomic particles.

How Many Neutrons are there in an Atom?

Once scientists became sure about what the atomic number and mass number meant exactly, they could use these to find one other important piece of information – the number of neutrons in an atom. It turned out to be a simple calculation: subtract one from the other.

Number of neutrons in beryllium

= 9 – 4 = 5 **neutrons**

So Beryllium (Be) has 4 electrons, 4 protons and 5 neutrons.

4
Be
Beryllium
9

Nucleus: The central part of an atom that contains the protons and neutrons.

Atomic Number: The number of protons in an atom of an element.

Mass Number: The total number of protons and neutrons in one atom of that element.

Checkpoint 1

(a) What information about an atom does the mass number give?

(b) How is an atom different to a sub-atomic particle?

Note
Number of neutrons in an atom =
Mass number – Atomic number

Checkpoint 2

Use the periodic table on page 184 to help you find the element name for each of the elements in *Table 07.01.02*. Then complete the rest of the table, filling in the number of protons and electrons and calculating the number of neutrons each element has.

What difference do you notice between each type of atom? What do you notice about the number of protons and electrons in each atom?

Element	Element name	Atomic number	Number of protons	Number of electrons	Mass number	Number of neutrons
$^{1}_{1}$H		1			1	
$^{2}_{4}$He		2			4	
$^{3}_{7}$Li		3			7	
$^{4}_{9}$Be		4			9	
$^{5}_{11}$B		5			11	
$^{6}_{12}$C		6			12	
$^{7}_{14}$N		7			14	
$^{8}_{16}$O		8			16	
$^{9}_{19}$F		9			19	
$^{10}_{20}$Ne		10			20	
$^{11}_{23}$Na		11			23	
$^{12}_{24}$Mg		12			24	
$^{13}_{27}$Al		13			27	
$^{14}_{28}$Si		14			28	
$^{15}_{31}$P		15			31	
$^{16}_{32}$S		16			32	
$^{17}_{35}$Cl		17			35	
$^{18}_{40}$Ar		18			40	
$^{19}_{39}$K		19			39	
$^{20}_{40}$Ca		20			40	

Table 07.01.02.

CHEMISTRY

ℝ What About Electrons?

Scientists were certain that the protons and neutrons sat as a solid mass in the centre of the atom (the nucleus), but where did the negative sub-atomic particles – the electrons – fit?

Both J.J. Thomson and Ernest Rutherford had made suggestions about how electrons were arranged inside an atom, but it was Danish physicist Niels Bohr who came up with an explanation that made the best sense of what scientists knew. He suggested that electrons moved around the nucleus in **energy levels**, which he called **orbits** (or **shells**). This was called the **Bohr Orbital Model**.

The number of electrons each atom of each element had, and how they filled each shell, was very specific. This was called the **electronic configuration** and can be shown as a diagram (*Fig. 07.01.05*) or as a list, e.g. Al (Aluminium) is (2, 8, 3).

The first shell holds up to 2 electrons

Nucleus

13p 14n

The second shell holds up to 8 electrons

The third shell holds up to 3 electrons

Fig. 07.01.04 The Bohr Orbital Model for aluminium.

Shell (Orbit): An energy level in which electrons move around the nucleus.

Electronic Configuration: The arrangement of electrons in the shells around an atom.

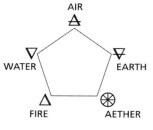

AIR

WATER   EARTH

FIRE   AETHER

The Five Elements of the Ancient Greeks

Dalton's Billiard Ball Model

J. J. Thomson's Plum Pudding Model

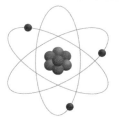

Rutherford's Planetary Model

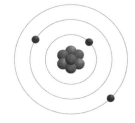

Bohr's Orbital Model

Fig. 07.01.05 The changing concepts of the basic particles of all matter.

The Octet Rule

The Octet Rule means that atoms arrange themselves so that they have eight electrons in their outer shell, and are therefore stable and unlikely to react. If an atom cannot get eight outer electrons, the next most stable number of electrons is two. Atoms react with other atoms so that they can have a stable number of electrons in their outer shell.

All this information allowed scientists to create rules for how atoms reacted. These rules eventually led to the point where new medicines could be successfully designed by computer without trying thousands of combinations of atoms in the laboratory to find the right one.

Did you know?
Robert Bunsen invented the Bunsen burner because he wanted to get a steady and hot gas flame so that he could experiment on elements. What he didn't know was that by heating the atoms of the element he was causing electrons to move between energy levels. They gave off energy as light when they did this – the colour was different for each element. This became known as the flame test.

4
Be
Beryllium
9

4p 5n

(2, 2)

13
Al
Aluminium
27

13p 14n

(2, 8, 3)

Fig. 07.01.06 Bohr diagrams for beryllium and aluminium. They show the electronic configuration for these atoms.

CHEMISTRY

R How to Draw the Electronic Configuration of Aluminium (Al)

1: Check the atomic number of the element of aluminium to find out how many protons and electrons there are.

2: For aluminium there are 13 electrons: 2 in shell one, 8 in shell two. That leaves 3 for shell three, so that equals: 2, 8, 3 (the electronic configuration). There are also 13 protons in the nucleus.

3: Subtract the atomic number from the mass number to give you the number of neutrons in the atom. For aluminium: $27 - 13 = 14$ neutrons in the nucleus.

4: Fill in the empty nucleus and shells by drawing four circles around each other. Fill each circle step by step.

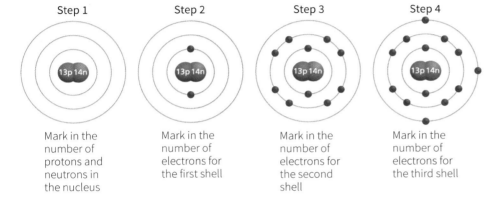

Step 1	Step 2	Step 3	Step 4
Mark in the number of protons and neutrons in the nucleus	Mark in the number of electrons for the first shell	Mark in the number of electrons for the second shell	Mark in the number of electrons for the third shell

✓ Checkpoint 3

(a) Draw and write out the electronic configuration for fluorine (F) and argon (Ar).

(b) Argon is a gas used to put out fires without causing further damage. It is also used to fill sealed packets of food to keep them fresh. Compare the outer shell of the two diagrams you have drawn. Why do you think argon can and fluorine cannot be used for both of these jobs?

Isotopes

When scientists calculated the mass of a carbon atom, it could be heavier or lighter depending on where in the world the carbon came from. But why? If all the atoms of an element are identical, then the calculation should always work out the same, no matter where the carbon was mined. The discovery of **isotopes** answered this question.

In 1913, Frederick Soddy, an English radiochemist, came up with the answer to explain why scientists were finding atoms from the same elements that had the same number of protons but different numbers of neutrons.

> **Isotopes:** Atoms of the same element which have the same number of protons but different numbers of neutrons.

It turns out that carbon has two isotopes. Most carbon is ^{12}C ('carbon-12'), with a mixture of ^{13}C and ^{14}C. Carbon-12 has 6 electrons, 6 protons and 6 neutrons, but carbon-13 has 6 electrons, 6 protons and 7 neutrons. This means that carbon-13 has an extra neutron, and explains why its mass number is one greater than carbon-12. Carbon-14 has two extra neutrons compared to carbon-12. How much of each depends on where the carbon is mined, so the exact mixture of isotopes can give information about the specific mining location of an element.

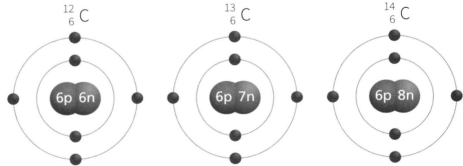

Fig. 07.01.07 Comparative Bohr diagrams of carbon-12, carbon-13 and carbon-14.

Carbon-14 is also useful in dating ancient objects containing carbon because it breaks down into carbon-13 and carbon-12 at a steady amount over time, which can be measured. So any object which contains carbon, such as cloth, wooden tools or pottery, can be dated to within ten years. This is called radiocarbon dating and is often used by archaeologists to date objects which don't have dates marked on them, as coins do.

The most famous item to be dated like this is the Shroud of Turin. This is a burial shroud that is believed to have been used to wrap the body of Jesus Christ for burial over 2000 years ago because the image of a crucified man can be seen on it. There is no reasonable scientific explanation for how this image was made, but radiocarbon dating has shown that the shroud was made in the early 1200s, suggesting that it may be a fake. (However, further to this, there has been controversy about how the testing of the cloth was done.)

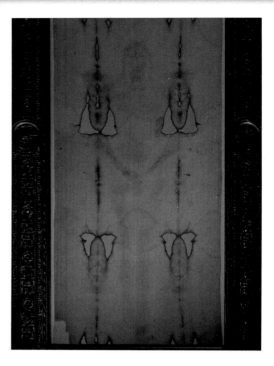

Fig. 07.01.08 Front view of the Shroud of Turin. A fire in the French chapel holding the relic in 1532 caused the four scorch marks that can be seen around the imprint of the body.

WHAT I HAVE LEARNED...

- The smallest particle of an element is an atom.
- All the atoms in an element are identical.
- Atoms are made up of electrons, protons and neutrons.
- Electrons move around the nucleus of an atom in energy levels called orbits (or shells).
- Protons and neutrons make up the centre of the atom, called the nucleus.
- Protons and neutrons both have a mass of one dalton and electrons have a mass of $\frac{1}{1840}$ dalton.
- Electrons have a charge of -1, protons have a charge of +1, and neutrons are neutral so have a charge of 0.
- The atomic number is the number of protons in an atom.
- The number of electrons in an atom is equal to the number of protons.
- The number of neutrons in an atom can be found by subtracting the atomic number from the mass number.
- How to draw the arrangement of electrons in an atom (electronic configuration/the Bohr Model).
- Isotopes are atoms of the same element which have the same number of protons but different numbers of neutrons.

Bohr's Orbital Model

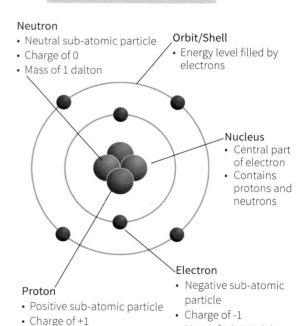

Neutron
- Neutral sub-atomic particle
- Charge of 0
- Mass of 1 dalton

Orbit/Shell
- Energy level filled by electrons

Nucleus
- Central part of electron
- Contains protons and neutrons

Electron
- Negative sub-atomic particle
- Charge of -1
- Mass of 1/1840 dalton

Proton
- Positive sub-atomic particle
- Charge of +1
- Mass of 1 dalton

Fig. 07.01.09 A Bohr Orbital Model showing the parts of an atom.

Question Time

Copy and Complete

In this unit I learned that there are three types of __ - _____ particles. Different _____ of each type make up an atom. The _____ has a charge of -1, a _____ has a charge of +1 and the _____ has no charge. Both the _____ and the _____ are located in the centre of the atom, which is called the _____. The atomic number of an atom tells you how many _____ are in that atom. The _____ number of an atom tells you how many protons and _____ are in that atom. Each atom is neutral because each _____ charge cancels each_____charge. This is because there are equal numbers of_____ and _____ in each stable atom. Isotopes are atoms of the _____ element that have the same number of protons but _____ number of _____ .

Questions

1. Where in an atom would you find:
    (i) an electron?
    (ii) a proton?
    (iii) a neutron?

2. *Fig. 07.01.10* shows an element from the periodic table. Using the information in the diagram and the periodic table on page 184, find:
    (i)   the name of this element
    (ii) how many electrons this element has
    (iii) how many protons this element has.

Fig. 07.01.10 An element from the periodic table.

3. Using the answer bank provided, copy and complete *Table 07.01.03*. Some answers may be used more than once.

Answer bank			
• 0	• Proton	• Positive	• Negative
• 1	• Electron	• Neutron	

Name of Sub-atomic Particle	Charge	Location	Mass (dalton)
		Nucleus	
		Orbit	
		Nucleus	

Table 07.01.03.

4. Niels Bohr received the Nobel Prize for Physics in 1922 for his model of the electronic structure of the atom. Potassium has an atomic number of 19. Give the arrangement of the electrons in an atom of potassium in the way that Bohr suggested.

Fig. 07.01.11 Niels Bohr commemorative stamp.

5. Chlorine's atomic number is 17. Chlorine's atomic mass is 35.5. If all chlorine atoms had 17 neutrons, its atomic mass would be about 34.00. If all chlorine atoms had 18 neutrons, its atomic mass would be about 36.00. Explain why the atomic mass of chlorine is between 34 and 36.

Inquiry

A   Americium-241 is a radioactive isotope of uranium used in smoke detectors, but in such small amounts as to be harmless. **Design** a poster that explains how americium-241 is used in a smoke alarm.

B   **Create** a model that shows how the electrons in an atom are arranged. You may choose from element 11 to element 20.

C   **Research** the work of one of the following scientists and **create** a poster or presentation on them: Aristotle, Dalton, Thomson, Rutherford or Bohr.

CHEMISTRY

The Periodic Table

Learning Outcomes

CWLO 3. Describe and model the structure of the atom in terms of the nucleus, protons, neutrons and electrons; compare **mass** and charge of protons, neutrons and electrons.

CWLO 4. Classify substances as elements, compounds, mixtures, **metals, non-metals,** solids, **liquids, gases** and solutions.

NSLO 1. Appreciate how scientists work and **how scientific ideas are modified over time.**

NSLO 4. Produce data (qualitatively/quantitatively), critically analyse data to **identify patterns and relationships,** identify anomalous observations, **draw and justify conclusions.**

NSLO 10. Appreciate the role of science in society and its personal, social and global importance.

PWLO 3. Investigate patterns and relationships between physical observables.

(R) Teacher's reference

KEYWORDS

alkali metals	noble gases
atom	octave
atomic number	period
electron	properties
element	proton
groups	shell
halogens	valency
Law of Octaves	
Law of Triads	
mass number	
matter	

LEARNING INTENTIONS

At the end of this unit you should:

1. Be able to use the periodic table to find the atomic number and atomic mass of any element.
2. Know the different groups of elements in the periodic table.
3. Know why elements are in groups and periods.
4. Know how to investigate/explain the differences between different groups of elements.

Why do scientists often put information in tables rather than lists?

Organising the Elements

For thousands of years scientists have tried to organise the information about elements in a variety of tables using symbols. As mentioned earlier, the Ancient Greeks originally thought that all **matter** was made up of only **five elements** (*Fig. 07.02.01*). However, as time went on and more elements were discovered, as well as agreement being reached on the idea of the **atom**, there was a need to have a system for how the information was written down.

One of the earliest modern attempts, in 1808, was by **John Dalton**, who not only listed the elements with symbols but also tried to create a way of showing how various elements combined.

However, the idea that a table of the elements should do more than just list the known elements was boosted in 1829 by German chemist **Johann Döbereiner** when he noticed a pattern in some of the elements. He saw that when certain elements were grouped according to similar **properties**, they formed groups of three. The mass of the middle element in each group of three was almost exactly halfway between the first and third element masses. He called this the **Law of Triads**. This Law of Triads didn't work for all elements as not all the elements had been discovered yet, but Döbereiner had made an important step by showing that elements could be grouped by similar properties.

The next person to suggest a pattern was English chemist **John Newlands**. When elements were listed according to their mass, there was 'periodicity'. This means that a repeating pattern could be seen. Newlands called this the **Law of Octaves** because it repeated every eighth element, similar to how notes in a musical scale do.

But Newlands was ridiculed, and his ideas were not taken seriously. He made the mistake of naming a serious scientific idea after a 'creative' musical idea, which didn't please scientists. His more serious mistake was not to leave gaps in his table. Not all elements had been discovered, so rather than leaving gaps for unknown elements, he forced known elements into position. Newlands' idea wasn't completely wrong, but it was ahead of its time: not enough elements were known to show that his idea had some use.

Five years later, Russian chemist **Dmitri Mendeleev** came up with a table that sorted the issue of unknown elements. He left gaps in his table and predicted what element should fill each gap based on elements on either side of it. When gallium (Ga), scandium (Sc) and germanium (Ge) were discovered, they fitted the predictions Mendeleev had given.

Matter: Anything that takes up space and has mass.

Atom: The smallest particle of an element that has the properties of that element.

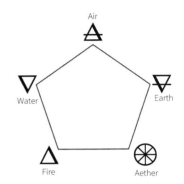

Fig. 07.02.01 The Ancient Greek system of the five elements.

Fig. 07.02.02 An octave from a musical scale. The pattern of notes repeats every eight notes.

CHEMISTRY

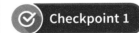 **Checkpoint 1**

(a) What was scientifically useful about Döbereiner's ideas?

(b) Why was Mendeleev's periodic table better than Newlands'?

Fig. 07.02.03 Mendeleev's 1871 revised periodic table. Dashes represent elements unknown in 1871.

Reihen	Gruppo I. — R^2O	Gruppo II. — RO	Gruppo III. — R^2O^3	Gruppo IV. RH^4 RO^4	Gruppo V. RH^3 R^2O^5	Gruppo VI. RH^2 RO^3	Gruppo VII. RH R^2O^7	Gruppo VIII. — RO^4
1	H = 1							
2	Li = 7	Be = 9,4	B = 11	C = 12	N = 14	O = 16	F = 19	
3	Na = 28	Mg = 24	Al =27,8	Si = 28	P = 31	S = 32	Cl = 35,5	
4	K = 39	Ca = 40	—— = 44	Ti = 48	V = 51	Cr = 52	Mn = 55	Fe = 56, Co = 59, Ni = 59, Cu = 63.
5	(Cu = 63)	Zn = 65	—— = 68	—— = 72	As = 75	So = 78	Br = 80	
6	Rb = 85	Sr = 87	?Yt = 88	Zr = 90	Nb = 94	Mo = 96	—— = 100	Ru = 104, Rh = 104, Pd = 106, Ag = 108.
7	(Ag = 108)	Cd = 112	In = 113	Sn = 118	Sb = 122	Te = 125	J = 127	
8	Cs = 133	Ba = 187	?Di = 138	?Co = 140	—	—	—	— — — —
9	(—)		—	—				
10	—	—	?Er = 178	?La = 180	Ta = 182	W = 184	—	Os = 195, Ir = 197, Pt = 198, Au = 199.
11	(Au = 198)	Hg = 200	Tl = 204	Pb = 207	Bi = 208	—	—	
12	—	—	—	Th = 231	—	U = 240	—	— — — —

Timeline of the Periodic Table

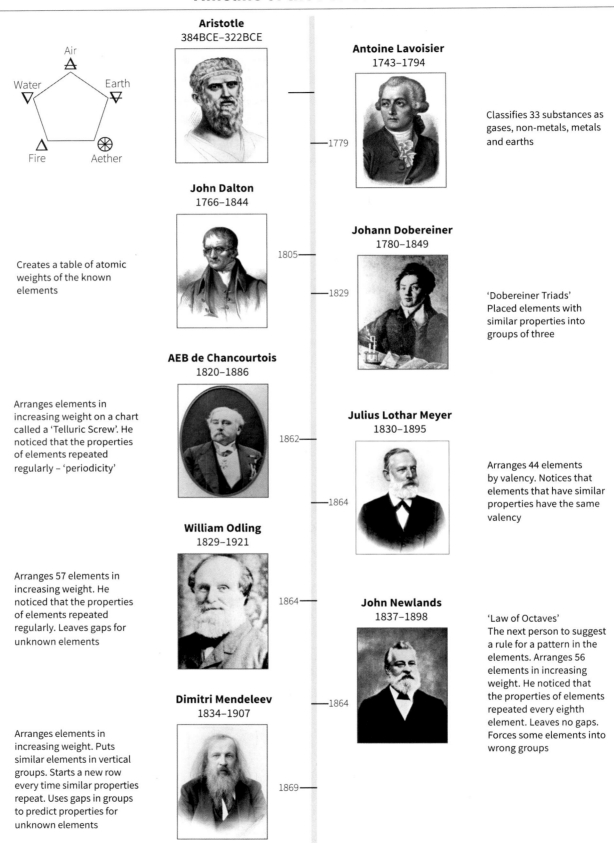

Aristotle
384BCE–322BCE

Air △

Water ▽   Earth ▽

Fire △   Aether ⊕

Antoine Lavoisier
1743–1794

1779

Classifies 33 substances as gases, non-metals, metals and earths

John Dalton
1766–1844

Creates a table of atomic weights of the known elements

1805

Johann Dobereiner
1780–1849

1829

'Dobereiner Triads' Placed elements with similar properties into groups of three

AEB de Chancourtois
1820–1886

Arranges elements in increasing weight on a chart called a 'Telluric Screw'. He noticed that the properties of elements repeated regularly – 'periodicity'

1862

Julius Lothar Meyer
1830–1895

1864

Arranges 44 elements by valency. Notices that elements that have similar properties have the same valency

William Odling
1829–1921

Arranges 57 elements in increasing weight. He noticed that the properties of elements repeated regularly. Leaves gaps for unknown elements

1864

John Newlands
1837–1898

1864

'Law of Octaves' The next person to suggest a rule for a pattern in the elements. Arranges 56 elements in increasing weight. He noticed that the properties of elements repeated every eighth element. Leaves no gaps. Forces some elements into wrong groups

Dimitri Mendeleev
1834–1907

Arranges elements in increasing weight. Puts similar elements in vertical groups. Starts a new row every time similar properties repeat. Uses gaps in groups to predict properties for unknown elements

1869

Modern Periodic Table

The Modern Periodic Table

In the modern periodic table, elements are arranged in order of atomic mass, starting with hydrogen. Each element is placed in a box with its symbol, full name, **atomic number** and **mass number**.

Each column is called a **group** and is made up of elements that have similar reactions and properties. Each row is called a **period**. Every time a pattern begins to repeat, a new period is started. All the elements in a period have the same number of **shells**.

As new elements have been discovered, gaps have been filled and elements grouped. Each group is numbered from 1–8. Group 8 is also called Group 0. Some groups also have traditional names.

Ⓡ Parts of the periodic table are often colour-coded to highlight different types of elements.

Hydrogen is normally placed on its own as it only has one **electron** and one **proton**, is a gas, and does not react in a way similar to the groups in the periodic table. Because it is very reactive and has only one electron in its outer shell, it is placed on top of Group 1 in some versions.

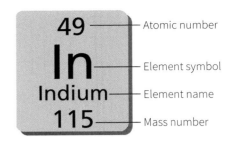

Fig. 07.02.04 The element indium from the periodic table.

Group: A column of elements in the periodic table that have similar properties.

Period: A row of elements in the periodic table that have the same number of shells.

CHEMISTRY

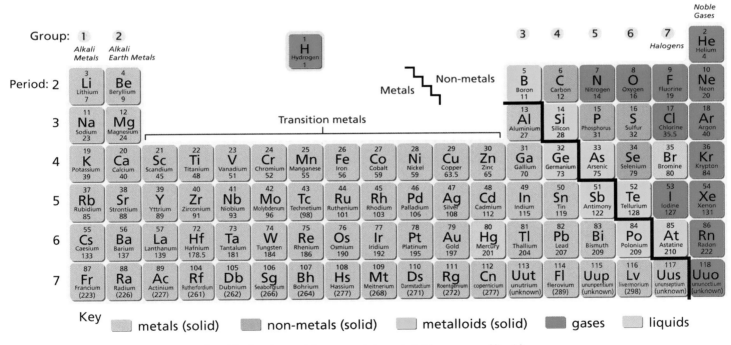

Fig. 07.02.05 Modern periodic table showing metals, non-metals, metalloids, gases and liquids. Metalloids are elements that have some of the properties of metals and non-metals.

The Octet Rule and Group Numbers

John Newlands' periodic table suggestion hadn't been fully correct, but he was right to consider eight as a special number when dealing with atoms. Scientists eventually worked out that atoms prefer to have eight electrons in their outer shell (or energy level). This is particularly true for the first twenty elements (see *Unit 7.1*).

Nowadays, Newlands' Law of Octaves is known as the Octet Rule. The Octet Rule means that atoms arrange themselves so that they have eight electrons in their outer shell, which makes them stable and unlikely to react. If an atom cannot get eight outer electrons, the next most stable number of electrons is two. How reactive an atom is with another atom depends on which of them needs to gain or lose electrons to get a stable number of electrons in its outer shell.

It turns out that the number of electrons an atom needs to lose or gain is the same as the group number. So elements in Group 1 have one electron in their outer shell. If they lose it, the next shell is full, so the atom then becomes stable.

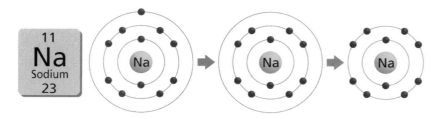

Fig. 07.02.06 Sodium (Na) is an element from Group 1. When it loses its outer electron, the next shell then becomes the outer shell. Now the element becomes stable. It is easier for sodium to lose one electron than to gain seven to get a full outer shell.

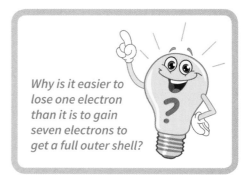

Why is it easier to lose one electron than it is to gain seven electrons to get a full outer shell?

Demonstration 07.02.01 – **Comparing Group 1 elements**

Instructions: Your teacher will show how lithium, sodium and potassium react with water. Draw up a table of your observations.

> **What did you learn?**
> Was there any pattern to how the elements did or didn't react?

🔍 Investigation 07.02.01: **Comparing Group 2 elements**

Equipment: Test tube rack, two test tubes, calcium granules, magnesium strip, water, dilute hydrochloric acid.

Instructions: Design an experiment to compare the two elements of calcium and magnesium.

> **What did you learn?**
> 1. How much of each metal will you use?
> 2. How much water/dilute hydrochloric acid will you use?
> 3. Was there any pattern to how the elements did or didn't react?
> 4. How does this compare to the Group 1 elements?
> 5. Could you test Group 1 elements with dilute hydrochloric acid? Justify your answer.

✓ Checkpoint 2

(a) Draw the same type of diagram as *Fig. 07.02.06* for both lithium and beryllium.

(b) If all the elements in a group react in the same way, can you predict how Group 1 elements react compared to Group 2 elements?

✓ Checkpoint 3

(a) Which group does the element thallium belong to? How many electrons will it lose or gain to become stable?

(b) Which group does the element xenon belong to? How many electrons will it lose or gain to become stable?

(c) If both were used as gases to fill balloons, which would be the safer gas and why?

CHEMISTRY

Group Numbers and Reactions

Group Number	1	2	7	8
Name	Alkali Metals	Alkaline Earth Metals	Halogens	Noble Gases
Number of Electrons in Outer Shell	1	2	7	8
State of Matter	solid	solid	gas/liquid	gas
General Reaction	react very vigorously	moderately reactive	very reactive	generally unreactive

Table 07.02.01 Comparing the reactions of different groups in the periodic table.

Table 07.02.01 summarises the reactions of some of the groups in the periodic table. How reactive each group of elements is depends on how many electrons there are in the outer shell of the elements. A full outer shell means that an atom is stable and will not react easily with other atoms.

Alkali Metals (Group 1) have only one electron in their outer shell. This means that they need another seven electrons to fill their outer shell. In contrast, the **Halogens** (Group 7) have seven electrons in their outer shell so only need one electron to make a full outer shell. This means that the Halogens are very good at removing electrons from other atoms. They are often used in the chemical industry to do this in order to make reactions happen more quickly.

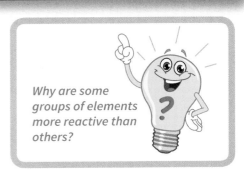

Why are some groups of elements more reactive than others?

The **Noble Gases** (Group 8) are very unreactive because they have a full outer shell. They are all gases that are not flammable, like argon. The food industry pumps argon into sealed packets to displace oxygen (which would otherwise allow micro-organisms to grow on the food and spoil it). This gives foods such as packets of sliced meat a longer shelf life. The funny smell you might get when you open a packet is very often just the argon escaping.

When the Octet Rule is applied across the periodic table, the atoms of elements in the groups have a pattern in how they lose or gain electrons. But when an atom cannot gain or lose an electron, it will share electrons with one or more atoms to get a full outer shell. The loss, gain or sharing of electrons is called an atom's **valency**. We will study this in Unit 7.3.

Valency: The number of electrons an atom must lose, gain or share to form a stable outer shell and chemically combine with other atoms.

Group	Valency	Lose	Gain	Share
Group 1	1	✔		✔
Group 2	2	✔		✔
Group 3	3	✔		✔
Group 4	4			✔
Group 5	3		✔	✔
Group 6	2		✔	✔
Group 7	1		✔	✔
Group 8	0			✔

Table 07.02.02 Table of valencies for the periodic table excluding the Transition Elements.

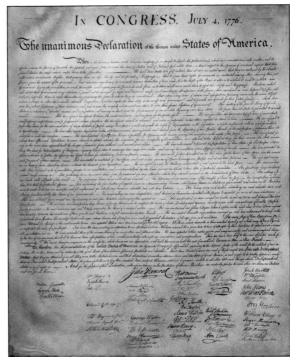

Fig. 07.02.07 The US Declaration of Independence is stored in an argon-filled sealed container to prevent it from decaying.

 Checkpoint 4

Argon is used by the computer industry in 'clean rooms' as a fire extinguishing gas. Why would argon gas rather than liquid or powder extinguishers be suitable for this purpose?

WHAT I HAVE LEARNED...

- How to use the periodic table to find the atomic number and atomic mass of any element.
- The different groups of elements in the periodic table.
- Why element are in groups and periods.
- How to investigate/explain the properties of different groups of elements.
- Why each group has a different valency.
- Some uses for the Noble Gases in industry.

Question Time

Copy and Complete

In this unit I learned that the rows in a periodic table are called _____ and the columns are called _____. Elements that react in a similar way go into _____. Alkali metals have only _____ electron in their outer_____/_____. Alkaline earth metals have_____ electrons in their outer shell. Noble Gases are very _____/_____ because they have _____ electrons in their outer shell. Atoms can _____ or gain or _____ electrons to become stable.

Questions

1. *Fig. 07.02.08* shows a blank periodic table, with five elements labelled A to E.
   (i)   Name each of the elements A to E.
   (ii) Which element has an atomic number of 29?
   (iii) Which element has an atomic mass of 28?
   (iv) Which group do elements A and B belong to?
   (v)   Give one difference between element B and element E.
   (vi) Why is element E more common in Ireland than in other countries?

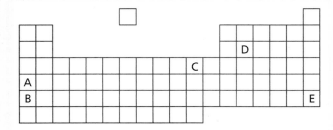

Fig. 07.02.08.

2. Döbereiner's Triads were not completely correct, but how did he help scientists understand more about the elements?

3. Why should Group 1 metals be stored in oil?
4. If you know the atomic number of an element in the periodic table, do you also know the number of neutrons in any atom of that element? Explain.
5. If you know that an atom has eight electrons on the second energy level and two electrons on the third energy level, explain how you know that this atom must be from the element magnesium.
6. Read the following statement and decide whether it is true or false, giving reasons for your answer: 'If an atom has a low valency, it is always very reactive.'
7. Neon is a gas used in electric lighting. Why is it suitable for this?

Inquiry

A On Thursday, 6 May 1937, the *Hindenburg* airship exploded as it was coming in to land in Lakehurst, New Jersey, after crossing the Atlantic from Germany. After this disaster, airships used helium gas rather than hydrogen. Can you give a reason **why** hydrogen was a good choice for an airship gas at the time of the *Hindenburg* disaster? **Explain** why helium is a better choice. **Why** do airships need to have so much gas to work?

B Rubidium, caesium and francium are stored in containers which are then topped up with argon to prevent premature explosions. Why is argon suitable to use? **Explain** why argon is used rather than other elements from the same group.

C Julius Lothar Meyer came up with a periodic table several years before Mendeleev, which was laid out in the same way. But Meyer published his ideas after Mendeleev and Mendeleev got the credit for the modern periodic table. Imagine you are on the committee deciding who gets the Nobel Prize for chemistry. **Create** a poster which gives the reasons why the prize should be shared between both these scientists.

7.3

Valency and Reactions

Learning Outcomes

CWLO 2. Develop and **use models to** describe the particle theory; **demonstrate how they provide a simple way to account for** the conservation of mass, changes of state, physical change, **chemical change**, mixtures and their separation.

CWLO 4. Classify substances as elements, compounds, mixtures, metals, non-metals, solids, liquids, gases and solutions.

CWLO 5. Use the periodic table to **predict the ratio of atoms in the compounds of two elements.**

CWLO 9. Consider chemical reactions in terms of energy, using the terms exothermic, endothermic and activation energy, and use simple energy profile diagrams to illustrate energy changes.

PWLO 3. Investigate patterns and relationships between physical observables.

(R) Teacher's reference

KEYWORDS

activation energy
bond
catalyst
charge
chemical reaction
combustion
compound
covalent bond
electron pair
endothermic
energy profile
enzyme
exothermic
ion
ionic bond
molecular formula
molecules
valency

LEARNING INTENTIONS

At the end of this unit you should:

1. Be able to use the valencies of elements from the periodic table to predict how they combine with other elements.
2. Form a chemical formula for a substance based on valency.
3. Explain the difference between ionic and covalent bonds.
4. Explain the differences between exothermic and endothermic reactions by using a diagram.

Valency

To predict how atoms of different elements might chemically combine, we need to know their **valencies**. Each time we chemically combine atoms, we form a chemical **bond**. The bonding of atoms to form **molecules** happens during a **chemical reaction**.

To be able to describe a chemical reaction, we must know how many of each atom is needed to form the reacting substances. By matching the valencies of the atoms correctly, we can predict the exact number of atoms for each element in a molecule.

We already know that atoms always try to become stable by losing, gaining or sharing electrons to get a full outer shell. They do this when forming bonds with other atoms. Some small molecules also lose or gain electrons to allow them to bond with other atoms or small molecules. When atoms or small molecules lose or gain electrons like this, they are called **ions**.

The **charge** on an ion tells you how many electrons it will lose, gain or share to bond with another ion. A positive charge means that an ion needs to gain electrons. A negative charge means that an ion needs to lose electrons. To form a stable molecule the negative charges must cancel the positive charges.

The **molecular formula** of any **compound** shows what elements are in one molecule of the substance and how many atoms of each element are in one molecule of the compound.

Valency: The number of electrons an atom must lose, gain or share to form a stable outer shell and chemically combine with other atoms.

Molecule: Composed of two or more atoms chemically combined.

Chemical Reaction: The creation of one or more new substances from atoms or molecules.

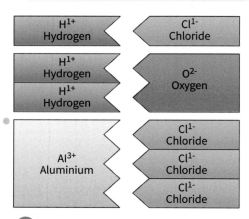

R Fig. 07.03.01 This jigsaw diagram shows how positive and negative charges balance in different molecules.

Ion: An atom or small molecule that has lost or gained electrons to become charged.

Charge: The number showing how positive or negative a particle is.

Molecular Formula: The number of atoms of each element in one molecule of a compound.

Compound: Composed of two or more different elements chemically combined.

Ion	Symbol	Valency	Charge on Ion	Ion
ammonium	NH_4	1	1+	NH_4^{1+}
hydrogen	H	1	1+	H^{1+}
potassium	K	1	1+	K^{1+}
silver	Ag	1	1+	Ag^{1+}
sodium	Na	1	1+	Na^{1+}
calcium	Ca	2	2+	Ca^{2+}
copper	Cu	2	2+	Cu^{2+}
iron	Fe	2 or 3	2+ or 3+	Fe^{2+} or Fe^{3+}
lead	Pb	2	2+	Pb^{2+}
magnesium	Mg	2	2+	Mg^{2+}
zinc	Zn	2	2+	Zn^{2+}
aluminium	Al	3	3+	Al^{3+}
bromide	Br	1	1-	Br^{1-}
chloride	Cl	1	1-	Cl^{1-}
hydrogen carbonate	HCO_3	1	1-	HCO_3^{1-}
hydroxide	OH	1	1-	OH^{1-}
iodide	I	1	1-	I^{1-}
nitrate	NO_3	1	1-	NO_3^{1-}
carbonate	CO_3	2	2-	CO_3^{2-}
oxide	O	2	2-	O^{2-}
sulfate	SO_4	2	2-	SO_4^{2-}
sulfide	S	2	2-	S^{2-}
phosphate	PO_4	3	3-	PO_4^{2-}

R Table 07.03.01 This table of common ions shows the atom or small molecule, its valency and its charge as an ion.

R Ionic and Covalent Bonds

When atoms lose or gain electrons to form a stable bond, this is called an **ionic bond**. In this type of bond, positive ions are attracted to negative ions. The reactions we have looked at so far have all been ionic bond reactions.

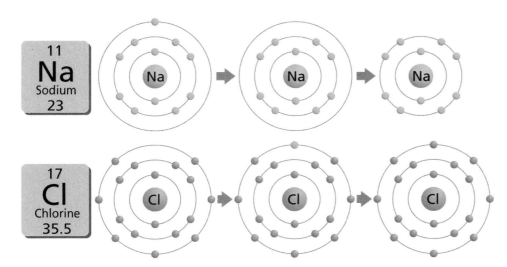

Fig. 07.03.02 Sodium losing one electron to chlorine.

Fig. 07.03.02 shows which element loses an electron and which gains an electron, but it is easier to write:

sodium + chlorine → sodium chloride

$Na^{1+} + Cl^{1-} \rightarrow NaCl$

When magnesium and oxygen bond, magnesium loses two electrons and oxygen gains two electrons. They form magnesium oxide. We write:

magnesium + oxygen → magnesium oxide

$Mg^{2+} + O^{2-} \rightarrow MgO$

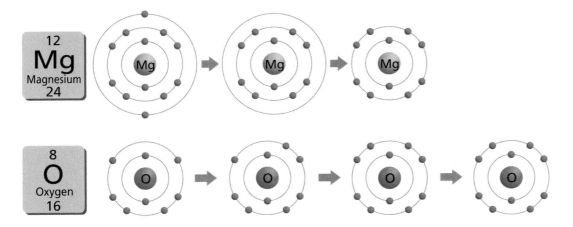

Fig. 07.03.03 Magnesium losing two electrons to oxygen.

But not all chemical reactions cause electrons to be lost or gained. In some chemical reactions, a **covalent bond** is formed when atoms share electrons.

✓ Checkpoint 1

(a) **Draw jigsaw diagrams for the following molecules:**
   (i) **silver chloride**
   (ii) **potassium oxide**
   (iii) **copper sulfate**
   (iv) **sodium nitrate.**
(b) **Using your jigsaw diagrams, write down the molecular formula for these four molecules.**

Ionic Bond: The force of attraction of oppositely charged ions.

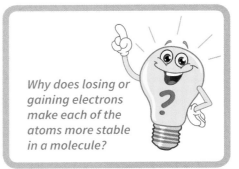

Why does losing or gaining electrons make each of the atoms more stable in a molecule?

Covalent Bond: The sharing of pairs of electrons between ions to form stable outer shells.

CHEMISTRY

When two atoms form a covalent bond, the atoms are drawn so that they overlap. The shared electrons are placed in the overlap. Shared electrons form **electron pairs** and each electron pair is a bond. This means that there can be single, double and triple bonds.

In a covalent bond diagram, electrons from one molecule are marked as dots and the electrons from the other molecule are marked as crosses.

A simple scientific rule is that 'like charges repel and unlike charges attract'. This mean that electrons repel each other but are attracted to protons. Therefore, electrons in a bond push away from each other and from the other electrons in the atoms. This is why atoms in some molecules do not link up in a straight line.

This also explains why the water molecule has a V-shape. This shape is the furthest the bonding electrons can get from each other and the other electrons in oxygen without breaking the bond. Methane has a tetrahedron shape for the same reasons. This shape is the furthest the bonding electrons can get from each other and the other electrons in carbon.

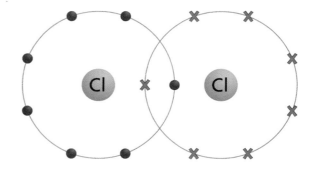

Fig. 07.03.04 When chlorine forms a molecule with itself, it makes a covalent bond. Two electrons are shared in the over-lap so a single bond is formed.

NAME	BALL & STICK MODEL	COVALENT BOND
Hydrogen		
Oxygen		
Nitrogen		
Water		Electron pair
Methane		

Table 07.03.02 Examples of covalent bonds.

✓ **Checkpoint 2**

(a) Draw a diagram of the covalent bonding in fluorine F_2 (single bond).

(b) Draw a diagram of the covalent bonding in carbon dioxide CO_2 (double bond).

(c) Draw a diagram of the covalent bonding in PCl_3 (phosphorus pentachloride).

Activation Energy

If electrons are to be lost, gained or shared in a chemical reaction, then energy is needed for this to happen. The minimum amount of energy needed to get a chemical reaction to begin is called the **activation energy**.

Friction energy is created when a match is struck against the rough side of a matchbox. This energy is enough to start a chemical reaction between the chemicals in the match-head and oxygen in the atmosphere. The chemicals burn in a type of reaction called **combustion**.

A chemical reaction that releases energy is called an **exothermic** reaction. In most cases, the energy release is in the form of heat energy – the temperature increases. The opposite of this happens when a reaction takes in heat energy. This is called an **endothermic** reaction.

Nitroglycerin is a liquid that needs only a small amount of energy for it to combust rapidly. Rapid combustion normally causes explosions as the heat released from such a reaction causes combustion gases to expand at extreme speeds.

Fig. 07.03.05 Friction providing the activation energy for a reaction.

Activation Energy: The minimum amount of energy that has to be added to the reactant energy to get the reaction started (E_{act}).

Combustion: The chemical reaction between any substance and a gas that releases energy.

Exothermic: A chemical reaction in which energy is released into the surroundings.

Endothermic: A chemical reaction in which energy is absorbed from the surroundings.

Demonstration 07.03.01 – Creating a fireball

Instructions: Your teacher will show the rapid combustion of coffee whitener using the equipment as shown in the diagram.

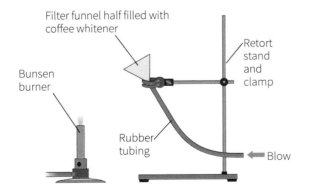

Filter funnel half filled with coffee whitener

Bunsen burner

Rubber tubing

Retort stand and clamp

Blow

Did you know?
Nitroglycerin is so sensitive that shaking it is enough to cause an explosion. Interestingly, in dilute solution it is given as a medicine for angina (chest pain).

What did you learn?

1. Why does the coffee whitener burn rapidly when blown into the air but not when in a pile of powder?
2. What other gas, besides the Bunsen gas, aids the combustion in this investigation?

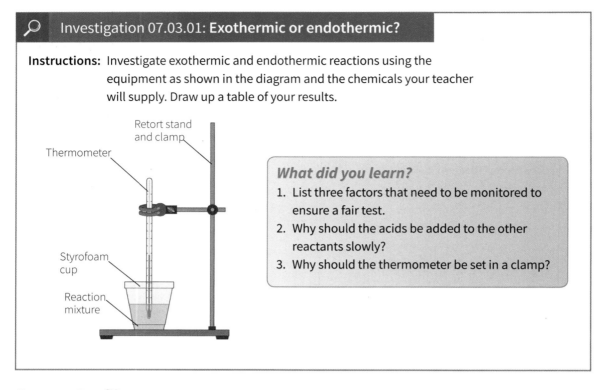

Investigation 07.03.01: Exothermic or endothermic?

Instructions: Investigate exothermic and endothermic reactions using the equipment as shown in the diagram and the chemicals your teacher will supply. Draw up a table of your results.

Retort stand and clamp

Thermometer

Styrofoam cup

Reaction mixture

What did you learn?

1. List three factors that need to be monitored to ensure a fair test.
2. Why should the acids be added to the other reactants slowly?
3. Why should the thermometer be set in a clamp?

Energy Profiles

A diagram which shows the energy changes in a reaction is called an **energy profile**. The starting energy is the energy of the reactants. This increases until the reaction begins and then drops back down to the energy of the products at the end of the reaction. The difference between the energy of the reactants and the energy needed to start the reaction is called the activation energy. It has the symbol E_{act}.

If the energy of the reactants (starting substances) is higher than the products (finishing substances), then it is an exothermic reaction. The extra energy in the reaction has to be released, very often as heat or light.

Energy Profile: A diagram showing the changes in energy levels in a reaction.

ENERGY PROFILES

S = start time of reaction   F = finish time of reaction

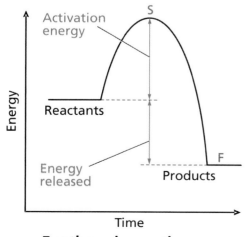

Exothermic reaction

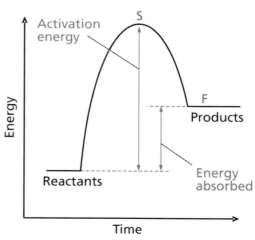

Endothermic reaction

 Fig. 07.03.06 Example of an energy profile.

The energy levels in the chemical bonds of match-head chemicals, nitroglycerin and coffee whitener are all higher than in the products of their combustion reactions. That is why they give out so much heat energy when they burn.

When the energy of the reactant is lower than the energy of the products, then more energy has to be absorbed into the reaction. This is an endothermic reaction.

For many reactions, the activation energy (E_{act}) is supplied by heating the reaction mixture. But energy can also come from sunlight, shaking the reaction mixture, and lightning.

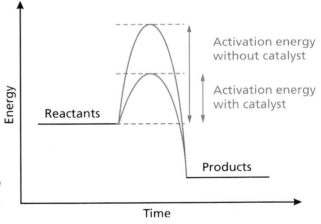

Fig. 07.03.07 Lightning provides the energy for nitrogen in the atmosphere to be converted into ammonia.

Catalysts

Inside living things, it isn't possible for energy to be added in these ways, so being able to reduce the activation energy is useful. In the chemical industry, being able to reduce E_{act} also saves money and time and increases safety in producing chemicals and medicines. Substances that reduce the E_{act} are called **catalysts**. Catalysts in laboratory reactions cannot be used in organisms because they would be poisonous, so biological catalysts are needed. These are protein catalysts and are called **enzymes**. This means that enzymes can be created from the nutrients taken in by the organism.

Importantly, it means that chemical reactions can happen in living things at low temperatures, which won't damage the organism.

Catalyst: A substance that speeds up a reaction by reducing the activation energy, but is not used up.

Enzymes: Protein catalysts used by organisms to speed up biochemical reactions.

Catalase

Hydrogen peroxide (H_2O_2) is a waste product produced by many organisms that needs to be broken down to prevent damage to cells. In the laboratory, manganese dioxide (MnO_2) can be used to break down the hydrogen peroxide into water (H_2O) and oxygen (O_2). But manganese dioxide is poisonous to organisms. (You will study this reaction more in *Unit 9.1*.) An enzyme called catalase breaks down the hydrogen peroxide safely so that the body is not damaged. The products of the reaction can then be used by the organism. (Enzymes are also studied in *Unit 2.1*.)

Fig. 07.03.08 Energy profile showing activation energy with a catalyst.

Energy

Activation energy without catalyst

Activation energy with catalyst

Reactants

Products

Time

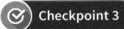
Checkpoint 3

(R) It is difficult to measure the change in heat energy directly during an investigation. Temperature changes are used to indicate heat energy increases and decreases. At the start of one investigation, the temperature of the reactants was -32°C; at the end of the investigation the temperature of the products was -21°C. Draw the energy profile diagram that suits this reaction.

CHEMISTRY

Investigation 07.03.02: **Testing the action of protein catalysts**

Instructions: Using the equipment as shown in the diagram, carry out an investigation using at least three different sources of catalase.

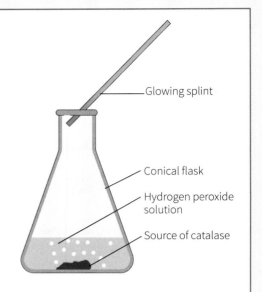

Glowing splint

Conical flask

Hydrogen peroxide solution

Source of catalase

What did you learn?

1. What factors should you control to make sure that this is a fair test?
2. Can you explain why a glowing splint is needed for this investigation?
3. What conclusion can you make about the sources of catalase based on your observations?
4. Does it matter which animal the liver comes from? How could you prove this?

WHAT I HAVE LEARNED...

- How to use the valencies of elements from the periodic table to predict how they combine with other elements.
- How to form a chemical formula for a substance based on valency.
- The difference between ionic and covalent bonds.
- How to draw the covalent bonds in simple molecules.
- The differences between exothermic and endothermic reactions.
- How to draw an energy profile for an exothermic or endothermic reaction.
- How to draw an energy profile for a reaction when a catalyst is used.

 # Question Time

Copy and Complete

In this unit I learned that _____ is the number of electrons an atom can lose, gain or _____ to form a bond. The creation of one or more new _____ from atoms or molecules is called a chemical _____. An _____ is an atom or small _____ of atoms that has lost or _____ electrons to become charged. The _____ is the number showing how _____ or negative an _____ is. A chemical _____ is a set of _____ and _____ used to explain the parts of a chemical compound. When atoms lose or gain electrons to form a bond it is called an _____ bond. When atoms share electrons to form a bond it is called a _____ bond. The minimum amount of energy needed for a chemical reaction to happen is called the _____ energy. A chemical reaction that releases energy is called an _____ reaction. A chemical reaction that absorbs energy is called an _____ reaction. _____ happens in a reaction between oxygen and another substance that releases energy. A _____ is a substance that _____ _____ a reaction without being used up.

Questions

1. Using the valencies as listed in *Table 07.03.01*, find the chemical formula for each of the following:
   (i)   potassium chloride
   (ii) calcium oxide
   (iii) lithium oxide
   (iv) barium oxide
   (v)   calcium hydroxide
   (vi) manganese dioxide.

2. Draw a diagram or make a model of the covalent bonding in:
   (i)   carbon tetrachloride CCl_4 (single bond)
   (ii) carbon disulfide CS_2 (double bond).

3. Each of the reactions below is matched with a reaction type. State whether the statements are True or False.
   (i)   Petrol and oxygen combining in a car engine is an <u>endothermic</u> reaction.
   (ii) Burning coal is an <u>exothermic</u> reaction.
   (iii) Sodium hydroxide and hydrochloric acid is an <u>endothermic</u> reaction.
   (iv) Sodium hydrogen carbonate and citric acid is an <u>exothermic</u> reaction.
   (v)   Copper sulfate and magnesium powder is an exothermic reaction.
   (vi) Sulfuric acid and magnesium ribbon is an exothermic reaction.

4. Complete the energy profile in *Fig. 07.03.09* stating whether it is an exothermic or endothermic reaction. Suggest a reaction not already mentioned that would have this energy profile.

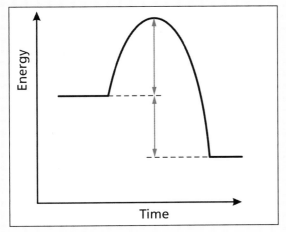

Fig. 07.03.09 Unlabelled energy profile.

5. Explain, using a sketch, how the energy profile for a reaction using a catalyst would be different.

Inquiry

A Why are workers in flour mills, mines and joineries not allowed to use naked flames or smoke? **Justify** your answer with evidence you have found during **research**.

Fig. 07.03.10 A bucket elevator dust explosion.

B Increasing the pressure inside the reaction container can change the activation energy. **Explain** how this can happen.

CHEMISTRY

Acids and Bases

Learning Outcomes

CWLO 4. Classify substances as elements, compounds, **mixtures, metals,** non-metals, solids, liquids, gases and solutions.

CWLO 8. Investigate reactions between acids and bases; use indicators and pH scale.

NSLO 10. Appreciate the role of science in society and its personal, social and global importance.

PWLO 3. Investigate patterns and relationships between physical observables.

R Teacher's reference

KEYWORDS

acid
alkali
base
concentration
indicator
ion
litmus
neutral
neutralisation
pH scale
strength
titration
universal indicator

LEARNING INTENTIONS

At the end of this unit you should:

1. Be able to explain the difference between an acid, a base and an alkali.
2. Be able to test for acids and bases using litmus indicators.
3. Be able to use the pH scale to classify the acid and base strength of substances.
4. Be able to test the pH of a variety of substances.
5. Be able to explain the difference between the strength and the concentration of acids and bases.
6. Be able to titrate an acid against a base to find the point of neutralisation.
7. Understand the importance of acids and bases in nature.

What acid can be used to both flavour food and clean glass?

What are Acids and Bases?

The word **acid** comes from the Latin for 'sour-tasting', as taste was the first test used to identify them. The Greeks also identified acids as sour substances, and they knew how to make a **base** by using ashes from a fire, but they didn't know why bases could cancel the effects of acids.

Litmus is used to indicate whether a solution is acid or base. Litmus is a chemical dye made from a type of fungus called lichen, and can come in paper strips or as a liquid. When a blue litmus paper strip is dipped in an acid substance, the paper will turn red. When red litmus paper is dipped in a base substance, it will turn blue. A **neutral** substance won't change the colour of litmus paper at all.

All acids can be dissolved in water, but not all bases can. A base that can dissolve in water is called an **alkali**. 'Alkali' comes from the Arabic word for 'roasting'.

Any substance that changes colour depending on whether it is in contact with an acid or base is called an **indicator**.

While litmus indicators can only show whether a substance is acid or base, **universal indicators** change colour depending on whether a substance is acid or base *and* how strong it is.

> **Acid:** A substance that turns blue litmus red.

> **Base:** A substance that turns red litmus blue.

> **Neutral:** A substance that does not change the colour of red or blue litmus.

Fig.08.01.01 The dye from lichens such as Parmelia sulcata *is used to test for acids and bases.*

CHEMISTRY

> **Alkali:** A base that can dissolve in water.

> **Indicator:** A chemical that changes colour showing whether a substance is acid or base.

> **Universal Indicator:** A substance that changes colour depending on the strength of an acid or base.

Acid solution   Base solution   Neutral solution

Ⓡ Both litmus and universal indicators are liquids that can be dried onto paper, so paper strips can be dipped into substances without interfering with the substance being tested.

Fig. 08.01.02 The colour changes of litmus paper in acid, base and neutral solutions.

(✓) **Checkpoint 1**

Table 08.01.01 shows the results of five substances that were tested with blue and red litmus strips. Based on the results, decide whether each substance is acid or base.

Substance	Red Litmus	Blue Litmus	Acid or Base?
tea	no change	red	
tap water	blue	no change	
distilled water	no change	no change	
soap	blue	no change	
petrol	no change	red	

Table 08.01.01.

How Do We Know the Strength of Acids and Bases?

French scientist Antoine Lavoisier came up with the name 'oxygen', from the Greek words for 'sharp' and 'producer'. He believed that acids were made of substances containing oxygen. Lavoisier was right to think that there was a key element common to all acids that made them acidic, but wrong to think that oxygen was that key element.

In fact, it is the hydrogen **ion** that is the key element (written an H^+). When electrons are removed or added to any atom, it becomes an ion (see *Unit 7.1*). Swedish scientist Svante Arrhenius was able to show that hydrogen was the key element.

Arrhenius found that when acid was dissolved into a solvent it was good at breaking up into hydrogen ions (H^+). The more hydrogen ions it released, the stronger an acid it was. When a base dissolved, it broke up releasing hydroxide ions (OH^-). Strong bases release more hydroxides than weak bases.

H^+ ions are formed when a hydrogen atom loses an electron. OH^- ions form when one of the hydrogens in a water molecule is broken off, leaving one electron behind.

Ion: An atom or small molecule that has lost or gained electrons to become charged.

R Fig. 08.01.04 From left to right, the diagrams show that acids have mostly H^+ ions, neutral substances have an equal number of H^+ and OH^-, and bases have mostly OH^- ions.

Fig. 08.01.03 Svante Arrhenius (1859–1927) not only gave an explanation of what acids and bases were, but created the idea of activation energy (E_{act}). He also helped to set up the Nobel Prizes.

The 'pH' in **pH scale** stands for 'power of Hydrogen'. Acids have a lot of H^+ ions, bases have very few, and neutral substances have an equal amount of H^+ and OH^- ions. This means that the pH scale can be used to measure the **strength** of an acid or base. On this scale, a substance that measures from 0–7 is an acid, 7 is neutral, and 7–14 is a base.

✓ Checkpoint 2

(a) Copy and complete *Table 08.01.02*, which shows the pH of various substances in the body. The pH of each substance can vary. The listed pH is the lowest pH for that substance under normal circumstances. Decide whether the substances are acid, base or neutral by ticking (✓) the appropriate box. In the 'Strength' box, note whether you think they are strong or weak.

(b) Urine and sweat have a similar pH. Based on this fact, what conclusions can you make about these two substances? Explain your answer.

Substance	pH	Acid	Base	Neutral	Strength
urine	4.6				
sweat	4.5				
tears	6.5				
blood	7.35				
stomach acid	1.5				
faeces	7.0				

Table 08.01.02.

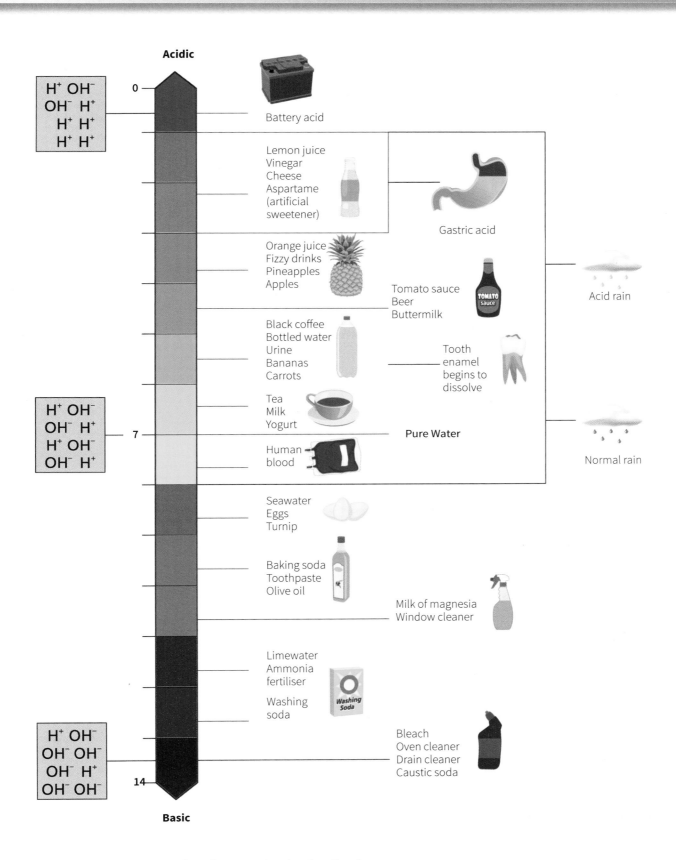

Acidic

| H⁺ OH⁻ |
| OH⁻ H⁺ |
| H⁺ H⁺ |
| H⁺ H⁺ |

0 — Battery acid

Lemon juice
Vinegar
Cheese
Aspartame
(artificial
sweetener)

Gastric acid

Orange juice
Fizzy drinks
Pineapples
Apples

Tomato sauce
Beer
Buttermilk

Acid rain

Black coffee
Bottled water
Urine
Bananas
Carrots

Tooth
enamel
begins to
dissolve

| H⁺ OH⁻ |
| OH⁻ H⁺ |
| H⁺ OH⁻ |
| OH⁻ H⁺ |

Tea
Milk
Yogurt

7 — Pure Water

Human
blood

Normal rain

Seawater
Eggs
Turnip

Baking soda
Toothpaste
Olive oil

Milk of magnesia
Window cleaner

Limewater
Ammonia
fertiliser

Washing
soda

| H⁺ OH⁻ |
| OH⁻ OH⁻ |
| OH⁻ H⁺ |
| OH⁻ OH⁻ |

Bleach
Oven cleaner
Drain cleaner
Caustic soda

14 —

Basic

Fig.08.01.05 Everyday substances placed on the pH scale.

Investigation 08.01.01:
Testing the pH of a variety of substances

Instructions:
Your teacher will provide you with a variety of test substances, universal indicator paper and a selection of simple lab equipment. Design an investigation to work out the pH of each sample.

What did you learn?
1. How can you carry out this investigation as a fair test?
2. Is it possible to get a false result in this investigation? Explain how you know your results are correct.

Investigation 08.01.02: **Testing the difference between the strength and concentration of an acid**

Equipment: Normal vinegar, 75% vinegar, 50% vinegar, 25% vinegar, baking powder, 0.1 M ethanoic acid, 0.1 M hydrochloric acid, 0.1 M sulfuric acid, and universal indicator paper.

Instructions: Design an investigation to compare different **concentrations** of the same acid by reacting baking powder with the four vinegar solutions. Using the same method, compare three different acids which are all the same concentration.

What did you learn?
1. How can you make sure that you are carrying out a fair test?
2. Is vinegar an acid? Justify your answer.
3. What substance, other than baking powder, can you use to compare the vinegar solutions? Does the pattern from testing with this substance match with how the vinegar reacts with baking powder? Explain your answer.
4. Suggest a reason(s) for any patterns of reaction you observe in the three other acids.
5. In your opinion, which had a greater effect on the reaction: acid concentration or acid strength? What evidence do you have to support your opinion?

Neutralisation

Acids and bases are chemical opposites, so what happen when they are reacted together? The reaction of an acid and a base creates a salt and water. This type of reaction is called a **neutralisation** reaction.

> **Neutralisation:** The reaction of an acid and a base to form a salt and water.

Demonstration 08.01.01 – **Neutralisation cloud in a tube**

Instructions: In this demonstration, using a sealed tube your teacher will allow the fumes from a strong acid and a base to combine.

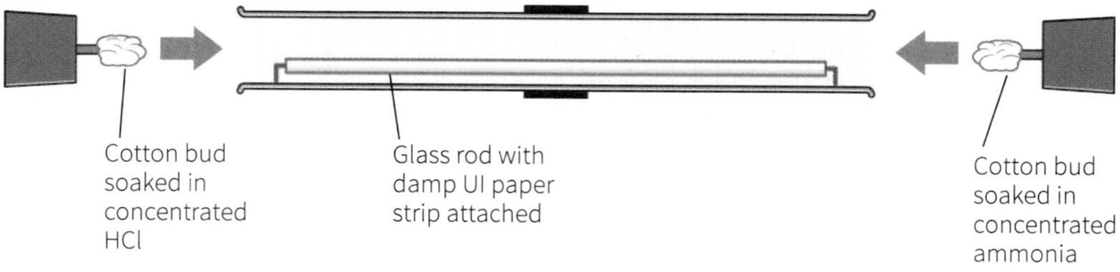

Cotton bud soaked in concentrated HCl

Glass rod with damp UI paper strip attached

Cotton bud soaked in concentrated ammonia

Fig. 08.01.06 Acid–base diffusion cloud chamber.

Neutralisation Reaction

| acid | + | base | → | salt | + water |

hydrochloric acid + sodium hydroxide → sodium chloride + water

$$HCl + NaOH \rightarrow NaCl + H_2O$$

If a base that contains carbonate (CO_3) is used, carbon dioxide is also produced. If a strong acid is used, the carbon dioxide is made rapidly. Soda-acid fire extinguishers use this idea. When the plunger is pressed, it cracks a container of acid which reacts with sodium bicarbonate. This creates a large amount of gas very quickly. The force of the gas inside the container forces out the water through the hose, giving a strong jet of water that can be aimed at a fire.

Neutralisation Reaction with Carbonate

| acid | + | carbonate | → | salt | + water + carbon dioxide |

hydrochloric acid + sodium bicarbonate → sodium chloride + water + carbon dioxide

$$HCl + NaHCO_3 \rightarrow NaCl + H_2O + CO_2$$

Fig. 08.01.07 Soda-acid fire extinguisher.

Titration

Titration is a way of finding out how much acid is needed to neutralise a base. When doing a titration, the acid is always added to the base. If the base was added to the acid, an unsafe vigorous reaction would occur as acids contain high amounts of reactive hydrogen ions. So it is safer to add an acid to a base.

 **Checkpoint 3**

Create a table which summarises the similarities and differences between neutralisation by a base and neutralisation by carbonate.

🔍 Investigation 08.01.03: **Titration**

Instructions: Using the equipment and chemicals shown in the diagram, design an investigation to titrate an acid against a base. Record the number of drops needed for titration in a results table. Give an estimate of pH based on the colour you record.

	Initial	Trial 1	Trial 2	Trial 3
Drops of hydrochloric acid				
Colour and shade				
pH estimate				

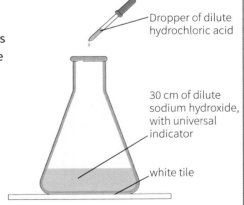

What did you learn?

1. What colour indicates that neutralisation has taken place?
2. Why should you swirl the flask gently during the reaction?
3. Explain why a conical flask is a better container to use for this investigation than a beaker.

4. The white tile helps prevent acid or base being spilled onto the lab bench, but this is not the reason it is used here. Can you think of a reason why it is used in this experiment?
5. State the advantages and disadvantages of using this method for a titration. Suggest changes that could be made to improve this method.

CHEMISTRY

Acids and Bases in Nature

Fig. 08.01.08 Whether a soil is acidic, neutral or basic affects plant growth. In hydrangea plants this is best seen in the colour of the petals. Blue hydrangeas indicate a soil with pH less than 6; purple hydrangeas indicate a soil with pH 6–7; pink hydrangeas indicate a soil with pH greater than 7.

The pH of soils is an important growth factor for plants as it can help or hinder a plant from absorbing the correct nutrients. Most plants prefer either acidic or alkaline soil conditions. This is why farmers add lime to soil to make it less acidic, or sulfur to make it more acidic.

A combination of decaying plants and animals and acid rain normally means that most soils are slightly acidic. Acid rain also removes bases from the soil by reacting with them in neutralisation reactions.

In the human body the lining of the stomach produces hydrochloric acid, which helps in the breakdown of food by dissolving it. The acid is also strong enough to kill any bacteria present in food. The lining of the intestines are sensitive to acid so pancreatic juice and bile help reduce the pH of the stomach contents as they enter the small intestine.

Fig. 08.01.09 A farmer liming land before planting to increase the soil pH to make it suitable for the next crop. Liming lowers the acidity level of land.

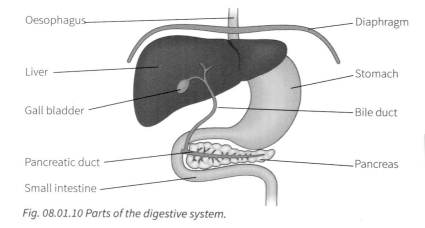

Oesophagus

Diaphragm

Liver

Stomach

Gall bladder

Bile duct

Pancreatic duct

Pancreas

Small intestine

Fig. 08.01.10 Parts of the digestive system.

Both these basic substances also play a part in breaking down fats and oils. Bile is produced by the liver and stored in the gall bladder. The pancreas releases pancreatic juice, which is a combination of enzymes and sodium bicarbonate.

Note
In most circumstances acids play an active part in the life of organisms, and bases are used either to neutralise or reduce acidic effects

Investigation 08.01.04: **Testing soil pH**

Instructions:
1. Split a sample of soil between two petri dishes.
2. Add enough deionised water to one dish to make a soil and water paste.
3. Using the squeeze bottle, add a coat of baking powder to the paste and record your observations.
4. Using the squeeze bottle, add enough vinegar to the sample in the other dish to cover the soil and record your observations.

What did you learn?
1. Which of the test chemicals is an acid and which is a base?
2. What type of acid–base reaction can happen in this investigation?
3. Can you state whether the soil is acid or base? Justify your answer.
4. Using a clean sample of soil and some deionised water, mix another paste and test with universal indicator. Explain how this compares to your previous results.

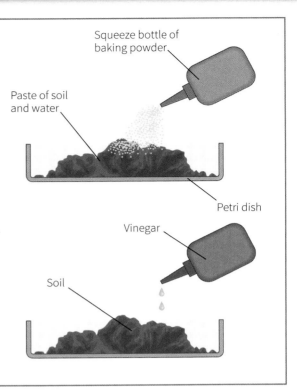

Acid Rain

Acid rain happens when gases created by the burning of fossil fuels mixes with the moisture droplets in clouds, forming weak acids (see *Unit 9.1*). Carbon dioxide forms carbonic acid, which is a weak acid. This form of acid rain occurs even in unpolluted rain, as carbon dioxide is in the atmosphere naturally from plant and animal respiration.

Nitrogen dioxide (NO_2) is created by burning fuels in vehicle engines, and nitrogen oxide (NO) is created by lightning reacting with oxygen and nitrogen in the atmosphere. Together these gases are known as NO_x. When mixed with rain droplets, they form nitric acid.

Gases carried by the wind

Acidic gases (sulfur dioxide and nitrogen oxides) released into atmosphere

Gases dissolve in rainwater to form acid rain

Acid rain kills plantlife, pollutes rivers and streams, and erodes stonework

Fig. 08.01.11 The cycle of acid rain.

CHEMISTRY

Sulfur dioxide (SO_2) is released during volcano eruptions but is also created by burning fuels in vehicle engines. Most of the NO_x and SO_2 in the atmosphere is man-made pollution. When mixed with rain droplets, it forms sulfuric acid. Both sulfuric acid and nitric acid are strong acids.

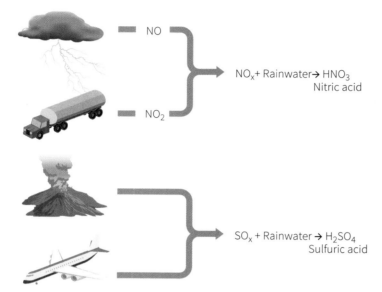

$$NO_x + \text{Rainwater} \rightarrow HNO_3$$
Nitric acid

$$SO_x + \text{Rainwater} \rightarrow H_2SO_4$$
Sulfuric acid

Fig. 08.01.13 How NO_x and sulfur dioxide emissions form acid rain.

Fig. 08.01.12 Damage to stonework on a church.

Acid Rain

carbon dioxide + water → carbonic acid

$$CO_2 \quad + \quad H_2O \rightarrow \quad H_2CO_3$$

Nitrogen dioxide + water → nitric acid + nitrogen oxide

$$NO_2 \quad + \quad H_2O \rightarrow \quad HNO_3 \quad + NO$$

Sulfur dioxide + water → sulfuric acid

$$SO_2 \quad + \quad H_2O \rightarrow \quad H_2SO_4$$

WHAT I HAVE LEARNED...

- A base is a substance that turns blue litmus red.
- An acid is a substance that turns red litmus blue.
- The pH scale measures the strength of acids and bases.
- Acids have pH 0–7.
- Neutral substances have a pH 7.
- Bases have pH 7–14.
- How to investigate whether a substance is an acid or a base.
- How to investigate the pH of various substances.
- Common substances that are acids and bases.
- How to investigate the volume of acid needed to neutralise a base.
- The type of products created in a neutralisation reaction.
- How to test soil for pH.
- The role of air pollution in forming acid rain.

Demonstration 08.01.02 – **The acidity of carbon dioxide**

Instructions: In this demonstration your teacher will place a small amount of marble chips in a test tube and add hydrochloric acid. The gas produced is allowed to pass through a tube into a solution of universal indicator.

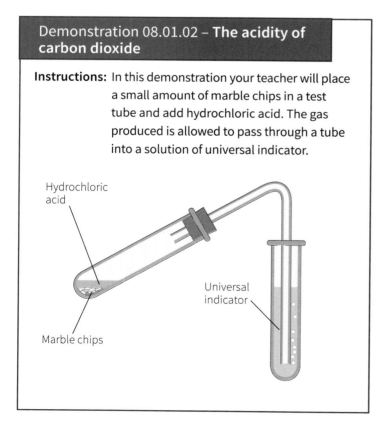

Hydrochloric acid

Universal indicator

Marble chips

Question Time

Copy and Complete

In this unit I learned that an _____ is a substance that turns _____ litmus red and a _____ is a substance that turns _____ litmus _____. A substance that does not change the_____ of blue or _____ litmus is _____. An _____ is a base that can dissolve in _____. The _____ scale measures the _____ of an acid or base on a scale from _____. _____ indicator is a substance that changes colour depending on the _____ of an acid or base. The reaction of an acid and a base to form a _____and _____ is known as a _____ reaction.

Questions

1. *Table 08.01.04* is a list of substances with a pH less than 7 or a pH greater than 7. *Fig. 08.01.14* shows the position of each substance on the pH scale. Copy and complete *Table 08.01.03*, matching each letter to the correct substance.

Substance	Letter
orange juice	
acid rain water	
toothpaste	
raw egg	
milk	
vinegar	
sour milk	
milk of magnesia	
cola	
washing soda	

Table 08.01.03.

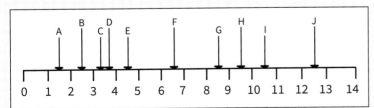

Fig. 08.01.14 Match the substances in Table 08.01.03 *with their position on the scale.*

2. You have been asked to investigate a selection of foods and drinks. You are allowed to test the foods and drinks using blue and red litmus paper, or universal litmus paper, or universal indicator. Only one type of indicator can be used. Which would you pick and why?

3. If you reacted sodium hydroxide and hydrochloric acid so that they were neutralised, what common mixture would you create? Would it be safe to drink?

4. Indigestion remedies contain calcium carbonate or magnesium carbonate. Why are these substances useful in settling an upset stomach?

Fig. 08.01.15 Dissolving indigestion tablet – a remedy for stomach ache.

5. The acid strength of faeces is pH 7.0. If the pH of a faeces sample is lower than this, what might it indicate? What damage to the body can be caused by a higher pH?

Inquiry

A 'An apple a day keeps the doctor away!' **Create** a poster/presentation that investigates the truth of this saying. In particular, **research** the role malic acid may have in maintaining good health.

B **Design** a poster/presentation explaining how a burette can be used to accurately measure the acid used in a titration.

C 'Fruit juices are bad for you.' Use your knowledge of acids and bases to create arguments for and against this statement. **Debate** this topic against an opposing team.

CHEMISTRY

UNIT
8.2

Metals and Non-Metals

Learning Outcomes

CWLO 4. Classify substances as elements, compounds, mixtures, **metals, non-metals**, solids, liquids, gases and solutions.

CWLO 6. Investigate the properties of different materials including solubilities, conductivity, melting points and boiling points.

CWLO 8. Investigate reactions between acids and bases; **use indicators** and pH scale.

NSLO 2. Recognise questions that are appropriate for scientific investigation, **pose testable hypotheses, and evaluate and compare strategies for investigating hypotheses.**

NSLO 4. Produce data (qualitatively/quantitatively), **critically analyse data to identify patterns and relationships**, identify anomalous observations, **draw and justify conclusions.**

PWLO 3. Investigate patterns and relationships between physical observables.

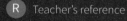 Teacher's reference

KEYWORDS

- alloys
- brittle
- conductivity
- corrosion
- ductile
- flame test
- lustre
- malleable
- metalloids
- metals
- non-metals
- reactivity series
- rust
- sonorous

LEARNING INTENTIONS

At the end of this unit you should:

1. Be able to describe the properties of metals and non-metals.
2. Be able to explain the differences between metals, non-metals and metalloids.
3. Be able to investigate and classify the reactivity series of a selection of metals.
4. Be able to investigate the conditions needed for rusting and to prevent rusting.
5. Be able to describe alloys and their uses.

How do you know that a substance is a metal? What list of words would you use to tell the differences between metals and other substances?

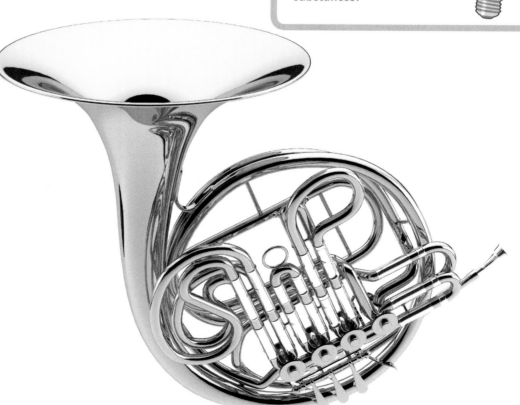

What are Metals?

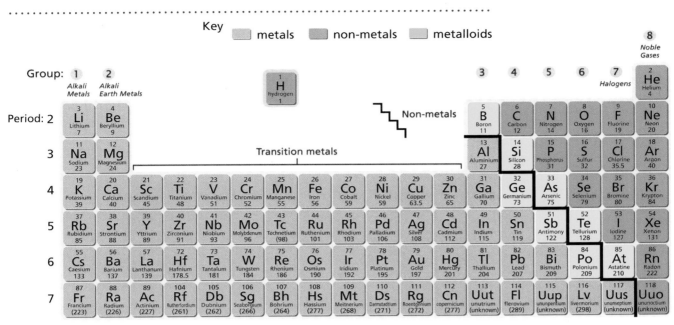

Fig. 08.02.01 Modern periodic table showing metals, non-metals and metalloids.

Colour-coding the periodic table can show us which elements are **metals**, **non-metals** and **metalloids**, but doesn't tell us why. The best way to know a metal from a non-metal is by their properties.

> ### Knowing a Metal
> - **lustre** – the shininess of a substance
> - hardness
> - heat conduction
> - electrical conduction
> - **malleable** – can be beaten into shape
> - **ductile** – can be stretched into a thin wire without snapping
> - **brittle** – break, snap or tear easily
> - **sonorous** – can make a clear ringing sound when hit.

Metalloids have properties that are in between metals and non-metals.

Property	Metal	Metalloid	Non-Metals
State of Matter	mostly solid	solid	mostly gases
Shiny (Lustre)	shiny	shiny	non-shiny
Hardness (Density)	high	intermediate	low
Heat Conduction	high	intermediate	low
Melting Point	high	intermediate	low
Electrical Conduction	good	intermediate to good	poor
Malleable	malleable	brittle	brittle when solid
Ductile	ductile	non-ductile	non-ductile
Sonorous	sonorous	non-sonorous	non-sonorous
Outer Shell Electrons	easily lost	depends on group	gains or shares
Bonds	mostly ionic	ionic or covalent	many covalent
Oxides	basic	weakly acidic	acidic
Oxide State of Matter	solid	solid	solid, liquid or gas

Ⓡ *Table 08.02.01 Comparing the properties of metals, metalloids and non-metals.*

CHEMISTRY

Before scientists understood the atomic make-up of the various elements, one of the few ways to tell the difference between metals was by doing **flame tests**. In these tests, a small sample of the metal was dissolved in alcohol and burned in a gas flame. The flame changed colour depending on which metal element was being burned.

But scientists had difficulty distinguishing between the different metals. As the gas didn't always burn properly, it could be difficult to figure out the true flame colour of the metal. This lead to Robert Bunsen designing the Bunsen burner. It allowed air to enter at the bottom of the chimney so that the air–gas mixture would burn cleanly and the colour of the metal could be seen easily in the flame.

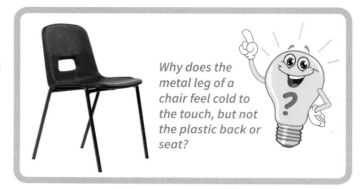

Why does the metal leg of a chair feel cold to the touch, but not the plastic back or seat?

Did you know?
Small amounts of various metals are added to fireworks to give them specific colours.

Demonstration 08.02.01 – **Elemental flames**

Instructions: Your teacher will spray six solutions of metal salts in alcohol through a Bunsen flame so you can see the colour of each metal. The solutions are labelled A–F. Draw up a results table that matches each solution with the correct element, based on flame colour.

> #### What did you learn?
> 1. Why are alcohol solutions used?
> 2. Is the distance between the spray bottle and the Bunsen flame important? How would you prove this?
> 3. Flame tests are no longer used to identify elements. Based on this demonstration, can you think of two reasons why this is so?

Alkali Oxides

When alkali metals react with water they form oxides, which dissolve into the water. Oxides form when the alkali metals chemically combine with oxygen.

$$\text{lithium} + \text{oxygen} \rightarrow \text{lithium oxide}$$
$$\text{Li} + \text{O}_2 \rightarrow \text{Li}_2\text{O}$$

The water can then be tested using red litmus paper and blue litmus paper.

REMEMBER
Red litmus turns blue if a substance is a base. Blue litmus turns red if a substance is an acid.

Demonstration 08.02.02 – **Testing Group 1 elements**

Instructions: Group 1 elements are very reactive so your teacher will only use small amounts of each element to test them. Draw up an observations table that shows the colour change of blue and red litmus when dipped in the water for each metal.

> #### What did you learn?
> 1. What conclusion can you make about all the Group 1 elements? Give reasons for you answer.
> 2. What other properties of Group 1 elements did you notice? Are they similar to other metals? Explain your answer.
> 3. Can you explain why these elements are stored under oil?

🔍 Investigation 08.02.01: **Testing the electrical conductivity of metals and non-metals**

Equipment: 6V battery, 3 wires, 2 crocodile clips, small bulb (or LED), variety of test substances – including three of the solutions used in the flame test.

Instructions: Using the equipment as listed, design an investigation to test the electrical **conductivity** of a range of substances. Construct a table to record whether each substance was a metal, metalloid or non-metal.

> *What did you learn?*
> 1. What other evidence can you use to back up your decisions about whether each material is a metal, non-metal or metalloid?
> 2. Did any of the test materials that you know to be metals not conduct electricity? Can you explain why?
> 3. This investigation uses electrical conductivity to classify the test materials. If you were given rods of copper, steel, glass and carbon, how would you use heat conductivity to classify each of these materials? How would you make sure it was a fair test?
> 4. Was this electrical conduction investigation a fair test? Justify your answer.

Metalloids

As we have established, metalloids have properties that are in between metals and non-metals. Metalloid chemistry can be complex, but many metalloids are used in everyday objects and in industry. For example, metalloids have been used as fire retardants. For hundreds of years, cloths have been soaked in borax (a boron oxide) to reduce their flammability. Silicon and germanium are common in the electronic industry as electrical semi-conductors. Many oxides of the metalloids are used to make different types of glass and glass fibre for fibre optic cables. Oxides of silicon are used to make a variety of materials, including ceramics, which have been used in brake discs on cars and heat shield tiles for NASA's Space Shuttle. In both cases, the ability of the ceramic to cope with high temperatures caused by friction makes them useful.

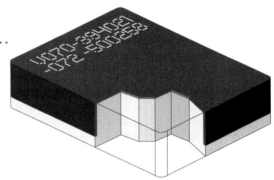

Fig. 08.02.02 The heat shield tile of the Space Shuttle has a black outer layer made of borosilicate and a foam-like inner layer made of silica fibres.

Mercury

Mercury (Hg) is an extremely useful exception amongst the metals. It is a liquid at room temperature and has a high density (for more on density, see *Unit 13.1*). This means that it expands at a very steady rate when it is heated, unlike some materials that expand by different amounts for each degree in temperature change. Because mercury expands at a steady rate, putting it in a narrow tube means that we can use it to measure temperatures accurately with a thermometer.

Fig. 08.02.03 Mercury has a high density so many substances can float in it. While you can easily lift a 1 kg bag of sugar, the same size container of mercury would have a mass of almost 14 kg!

Copper

Copper (Cu) is one of the most widely used metals in modern life. It is lightweight and malleable but also hard-wearing and does not corrode easily. It is also one of the best electrical conductors available.

Because it is lightweight, malleable and resists **corrosion**, it is an excellent material for pipework as it can be easily bent into curves and be joined using solder and brass fittings. Unless otherwise damaged, copper water pipes don't corrode. As the copper pipes connect to the street network, electricians often earth electrical systems to them.

A very ductile metal, copper can be stretched into thin wires, allowing high conduction electrical wires to be made. It is also a good heat conductor, so copper cooking pots and pans are sometimes preferred because they heat quickly and stay at a high temperature.

Copper is also a good roofing material as it can be beaten into complex shapes and can withstand the weather as it forms its own protective coat called verdigris. The green roofing on many older buildings is copper that has weathered.

Fig. 08.02.04 The Statue of Liberty, completed in 1886, is the largest copper statue in the world. It has turned green over the years and its copper skin has allowed it to survive powerful lightning strikes.

Alloys

Alloys are mixtures of two or more metals, or a metal and non-metal that have a mixture of properties that make the metal more useful.

Iron corrodes easily and is a heavy but not very strong metal. However, when it is mixed with carbon it forms steel, which is not only stronger but more flexible. Until steel could be made in large quantities, high quality cast iron was often used for bridges. But because of the flexing of bridges in high winds and under the weight of trains, it was used less and less. Brittle cast iron was one major factor that lead to the Tay Bridge disaster.

> **Alloy:** A mixture of two or more metals.

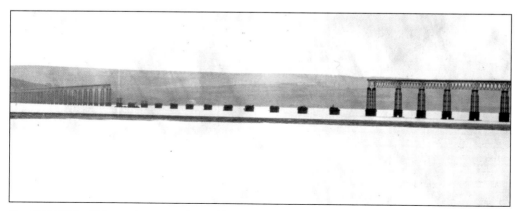

Fig. 08.02.05 On 28 December 1879, the middle section of the Tay Bridge, which spanned the River Tay in Scotland, collapsed during a violent storm as a train passed over it. Seventy-five people – passengers and crew – lost their lives. As a result of this disaster, the quality and types of metals and how they were used in bridge construction became an important part of training for engineers.

Alloy	Mixture	Useful Properties	Examples	Uses
Steel	Iron and carbon	Strong but can flex under strain		Steel beams (bridges and buildings) Car bodies Aircraft frames Tools
Stainless steel	Iron, carbon and chromium	Strong and resistant to corrosion		Kitchen fittings Kitchen utensils Surgical equipment
Solder	Lead and tin	Low melting point, soft		Metal welds
Brass	Copper and zinc	High melting point, can be hammered into thin sheets and various shapes, resist corrosion		Musical instruments Ornaments Bearings in machines
Bronze	Copper and tin	High melting point, strong and hard wearing, sonorous, resist corrosion		Ship propellers Statues Water valves Church bells
Niobium alloy	Niobium Hafnium Titanium	Can cope with extreme temperatures and stress		Jet engine blades Space rocket nozzles
Titanium alloys	Titanium Aluminium Niobium Zirconium Vanadium	High strength, light weight compared to steel, biocompatible (non-toxic)		Hip replacements Submarine hulls Golf clubs Spectacle frames Surgical instruments

Table 08.02.02 Examples of alloys in everyday use.

CHEMISTRY

⊘ Checkpoint 1

(a) The members of a church wish to buy a new bell for their bell tower. When positioned, the bell will sit partly exposed to the elements. The committee in charge of buying the bell have been given the choice of three metals: cast iron, steel or bronze. Which metal would you recommend they choose and why?

(b) Find pictures of objects which are made of each of these three alloys (cast iron, steel and bronze), and not already given in *Table 08.02.02*.

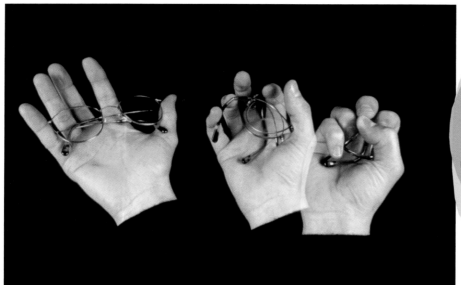

Corrosion: The undesired process of a metal combining with oxygen to form its oxide.

Corrosion

Metals react with their surroundings and, if used as containers, sometimes with the substances they hold. This unwanted chemical breakdown of the metal is called corrosion. Most corrosion damage is caused by reaction with oxygen and water.

Over time, corrosion will weaken a metal and can make it unsafe to use. Metals that contain iron are the most used types of metals, so iron corrosion is an important factor to consider in their use. Iron-containing metals are normally treated to prevent as much corrosion as possible. Corrosion of metals that have iron in them is called **rusting**.

Corrosion can be prevented by placing a protective coating over the metal. Oil, paint and rubber act as protective coats. Other metals such as zinc and chrome, which do not corrode, can be added to the surface of a metal to protect it. This process is called electroplating.

Rusting: The process of iron combining with oxygen to form iron oxide.

R Did you know?
Mercury was used by secret agents and French Resistance fighters in World War II to sabotage German fighter planes. Mercury corrodes aluminium, causing it to become brittle and snap easily. As aircraft parts are mainly made out of aluminium, the mercury damaged the aircraft, resulting in fighter aircraft crashing shortly after take-off or failing during flight.

Checkpoint 2

(a) Inspect metals in your surroundings (at home or in school) for corrosion. Note if the metals have corrosion and the exact environment they are in. Are there any patterns to the corrosion?

(b) Can you suggest why bridges on motorways are made mostly from concrete rather than steel? Give more than one reason for your answer.

(c) Name the element that is used to protect other metals in the galvanising process.

(d) Each of the photographs in *Table 08.02.03* show metal that has been protected. How was each object protected? Rewrite *Table 08.02.04* into your copy and fill it in.

Fig. 08.02.06 A WWII German Me109 fighter plane.

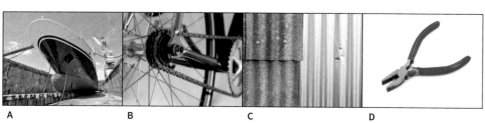

A   B   C   D

Table 08.02.03.

Protected object	Protected by ...
A	
B	
C	
D	

Table 08.02.04.

(e) Garden Furniture Ltd. have asked you to advise them on the best ways to prevent their steel garden gates from rusting. What would you suggest?

CHEMISTRY

Investigation 08.02.02: **Finding out what causes rusting**

Instructions: Using the equipment as shown, carry out an investigation to test the factors causing rusting. Before you begin this experiment, find out what calcium chloride can be used for, and also what are the chemical differences between boiled and unboiled water.

What did you learn?

1. How long is needed to complete your investigation?
2. Is there evidence of different amounts of rusting on each nail? Explain.
3. What is different about the set-up in test tubes A and B? Is there a chemical difference?
4. Cotton wool is used in test tube D. What else could be used that might be better than cotton wool?
5. If an iron nail covered in cooking oil or petroleum jelly was used in test tube E, would the result be the same? Why?
6. Based on your results, how would you protect iron nails from rusting? Could this method be used with other metals?

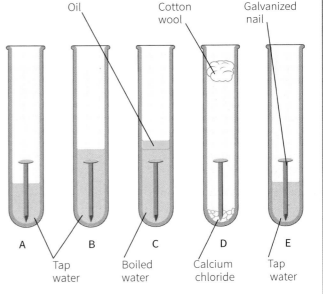

Oil Cotton wool Galvanized nail

A — Tap water
B — Boiled water
C —
D — Calcium chloride
E — Tap water

Reactivity

You have seen how the alkali metals become more reactive as you go down Group 1 of the periodic table. Is it possible that all metals have different reactivities? Do they react with each other? On their own these questions seem interesting, but are they important?

To answer these questions, scientists created the **reactivity series**. This list puts metals in order of how reactive they are. It also shows how one metal can displace another. When a metal displaces another in a reaction, it 'pushes' a lower metal out of a compound, often causing a colour change.

Reactivity Series: An ordered list of metal reactivities with water, acid and other metals.

Investigation 08.02.03: Reactivity series (Part A)

Equipment: Four test tubes, calcium granules, magnesium powder, zinc powder, copper powder, iron powder, tin powder, tap water, dilute hydrochloric acid, copper sulfate, retort stand and clamp, styrofoam cup, thermometer, beaker, test tube rack, spatula, graduated cylinder.

Instructions:
1. Place four clean test tubes into a test-tube rack.
2. Add an equal amount of tap water to each tube.
3. Using a spatula, add an equal amount of calcium granules, magnesium powder, zinc powder and copper powder to separate test tubes.
4. Record your results in a results table.
5. Clean the test tubes and add an equal amount of hydrochloric acid to each one.
6. Using a spatula, add an equal amount of calcium granules, magnesium powder, zinc powder and copper powder to separate test tubes.
7. Add the results of this part of the investigation to your results table.

Investigation 08.02.03: Reactivity series (Part B)

Instructions:
1. Place 20 cm³ of copper sulfate solution into a styrofoam cup and set up as shown.
2. Draw up a results table and record the temperature of the copper sulfate.
3. Use a spatula to add iron powder to the cup.
4. Observe any changes to the reaction mixture and record.
5. After the reaction has finished, clean the styrofoam cup and refill with 20 cm³ of copper sulfate solution.
6. Repeat the procedure for zinc, tin and magnesium.
7. Record all your observations as you work through the investigation.
8. Use your observations to decide an order of reactivity.

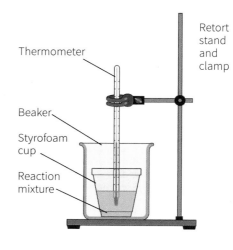

Thermometer

Retort stand and clamp

Beaker

Styrofoam cup

Reaction mixture

What did you learn?
1. Does the order of reactivities in Part A and Part B match? Why?
2. Is it scientifically sound to make an overall reactivity series based on two different methods? Why?
3. The thermometer in Part B was clamped and the styrofoam cup was placed into a beaker. This investigation can be done without either of these steps being done. Should it? Why?
4. In both Part A and Part B, the tested metals were dissolved into solution. What substance could you use to classify the products of each reaction?

WHAT I HAVE LEARNED...

- The properties of metals and non-metals.
- The differences between metals, non-metals and metalloids.
- How to investigate the reactivity series of a selection of metals with water and acid.
- How to classify the reactivity of a selection of metals fairly.
- The difference between corrosion and rusting.
- How to investigate the conditions needed for rusting.
- Several methods that prevent rusting/corrosion.
- What an alloys is, and the name and uses of some alloys.

Question Time

Copy and Complete

In this unit I learned that _____ can conduct _____ and _____ but ___-_____cannot. In the periodic table most _____ are metals. ____ _____ have a lower density than metals so tend to _____ in water. A mixture of two or more metals to form a substance with different physical _____ is called an _____. The undesired process of a metal combining with oxygen is called _____. When this process happens with iron it is called _____. The order in which metals react with water, acid and other metals is known as the _____ series.

Questions

1. Gold and silver have similar melting points at about 1000°C. This means they can be easily melted by a workshop blowtorch. What other property makes them suitable to be made into jewellery?

Fig. 08.02.07 Fabergé eggs were delicate gifts that were made of gold and other precious materials. Roughly fifty were given as Easter gifts by several Russian emperors.

2. What is an alloy and why are alloys sometimes better to use than a pure metal?

3. For each of the following, name a suitable metal, give its symbol and a reason why it is used rather than other metals:
   (a) Used in lightning conductors
   (b) Can be used in thermometers
   (c) Can be used as roofing material
   (d) Is used as a coat on iron nails to prevent rust
   (e) Is used in window frames.

4. What is the difference between corrosion and rust?

5. Tin foil is no longer made from tin but from aluminium. What property of aluminium makes it suitable for covering cooked food and being used in aluminium window frames?

Fig. 08.02.08 Tin foil – a handy material!

6. Fig. 08.02.09 shows the State limousine, which is used for ceremonial occasions by the President of Ireland. The radiator grille, headlights and bumper are made of steel which has a layer of chromium metal. Suggest two reasons why a layer of chromium has been put on these parts of the car.

Fig. 08.02.09 The State Limousine of Ireland.

7. Pick an alloy that you think would be suitable for blades in a food blender. Give reasons for your answer.

Inquiry

A Silver, gold and platinum are considered 'precious metals', so are often used in jewellery making. Are there scientific reasons for these metals being considered precious? If you were asked to decide that a newly discovered metal was precious or not, **what scientific factors** would you consider before making your decision?

B Silica is the common name given to a metalloid compound that is used to preserve products stored in shops. **Create** a poster which shows how this metalloid compound works.

C Most everyday-use thermometers are now alcohol or digital thermometers due to the toxicity of mercury. **Research** the advantages and disadvantages of using mercury thermometers and present this information as a poster.

8.3

Water

Learning Outcomes

CWLO 4. Classify substances as elements, compounds, mixtures, metals, non-metals, **solids, liquids, gases and solutions.**

CWLO 6. Investigate the properties of different materials including **solubilities,** conductivity, melting points and boiling points.

ESLO 3. Interpret data to compare the Earth with other planets and moons in the solar system, with respect to properties including mass, gravity, size and composition.

NSLO 6. Conduct research relevant to scientific issues, evaluate different sources of information, **understanding that a source may lack details or show bias.**

NSLO 8. Evaluate media-based arguments concerning science and technology.

NSLO 10. Appreciate the role of science in society and **its personal, social and global importance.**

(R) Teacher's reference

KEYWORDS

contaminated	polar
coolant	molecule
deionising	polluted
distillation	positive
Goldilocks Zone	pure
hard water	soft water
ice	solute
impure	solution
insulator	solvent
lather	specific heat
limescale	capacity
molecule	steam
negative	surface tension
non-polar	universal
molecule	solvent
osmosis	water

LEARNING INTENTIONS

At the end of this unit you should:

1. Be able to explain why water is such a useful solvent and coolant.
2. Be able to explain what a polar molecule is.
3. Be able to describe the difference between a polar and non-polar solvent by investigation.
4. Be able to demonstrate and explain that water has surface tension.
5. Be able to explain why water has two different densities.
6. Be able to show water transport by osmosis and predict the effect of osmosis by investigating a number of substances.
7. Be able to explain what hard water is as well as its advantages and its disadvantages.
8. Be able to test for water hardness and rank the hardness in a water sample.

Is it accurate to call water the 'universal solvent'?

The Search for Life

On Earth, where there is **water**, there is life. Water is known as the **universal solvent** because it can form many **solutions** from a wide variety of **solutes**. In fact, water dissolves more substances than any other liquid. This unique dissolving ability makes water an excellent transporter of many substances. It means that water, as it moves around our planet as seas, oceans, clouds, rain and snow, also carries many other dissolved substances. In our daily life the water in our food and drink allows us to absorb nutrients more easily. The water in our bodies allows us to dissolve the food we consume and carry its nutrients around our bodies to the cells.

Because water is so important to life on Earth and such a useful **solvent**, its existence on other planets may indicate life; Mars rovers have been scanning the planet of Mars to determine whether water, and so life, ever existed on the planet.

Fig. 08.03.01 An artist's impression of the Mars Rover Spirit in action on Mars.

The space-based telescope Kepler searches for planets in the '**Goldilocks Zone**' around stars similar to our sun. This 'just right' zone is the distance a planet needs to be from a star to have enough liquid water to sustain life: too close and the planet will be too warm to have liquid water; too far and its water will be locked up as **ice**.

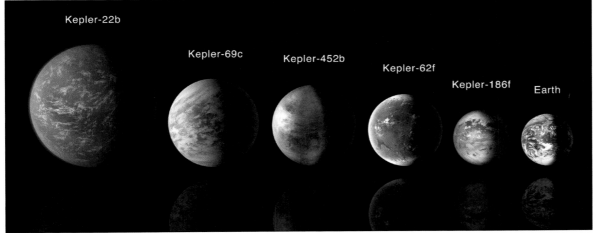

Fig. 08.03.02 An artist's impression of the 'Goldilocks Zone' planets discovered by the Kepler space telescope, compared to Earth.

🔍 Investigation 08.03.01: **Testing the universal solvent**

Instructions: Devise an investigation to test whether water deserves to be called the universal solvent.

What did you learn?

1. How many substances do you need to test for your results to be valid?
2. What should you do to make sure that this is a fair comparison of all the substances?
3. How would you carry out this test at home as a fair comparison?
4. What substances might you use?
5. Based on your testing at home and in school, do you think it is still a reasonable idea to call water the 'universal solvent'?

Water the Insulator

Water is a poor conductor of heat energy, so that means it is a good **insulator**. Most insulating materials are not only poor at conducting heat energy, but cannot absorb heat energy either. Water can.

Like all liquids, the heat energy absorbed by water **molecules** causes them to move further and further apart until a gas is formed. But unlike many other liquids, water needs much more energy for the molecules to move apart.

The amount of heat energy that 1 kg of a substance can absorb before it increases its temperature by 1°C is called the **specific heat capacity**. The specific heat capacity for water is very high compared to molecules of a similar size and mass (see *Unit 11.2*). This is why it takes water so long to boil.

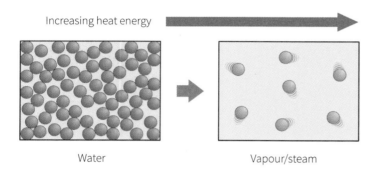

Increasing heat energy

Water   Vapour/steam

Fig. 08.03.03 Water molecules gain energy, moving further apart until they change state from liquid to gas.

Heated water absorbs a lot of heat energy in order to have enough energy to change from liquid to gas. This makes it a good **coolant**. Coolants are substances that are good at absorbing heat energy so they can be used to stop systems from overheating. This is the reason water is used to cool vehicle engines and nuclear power stations.

Once heated, water takes a long time to release the energy it has absorbed; this quality makes it useful in biological or mechanical systems to keep temperatures from changing too much. For both of these reasons water is also used in heating systems.

🔍 **Investigation 08.03.02: The cooling rate of water**

Instructions: Design an investigation to boil three different volumes of water and, over a fixed period of time, measure the temperature changes of each water sample.

What did you learn?
1. How can you make sure that this is a fair test?
2. Based on your results, do you agree that water is a good coolant?
3. Can you display your results in a way that is more convincing?
4. Can you see any other patterns in your results? Explain.

 Checkpoint 1

(a) Water can be found all over the world. Can you list and explain two disadvantages of water being an excellent solvent?

(b) Teagasc – a government agency that advises farmers on agriculture science – recommends that farmers spread slurry on a damp day. Why?

> **Insulator:** A substance which does not easily allow the passage of heat (or sound).

> **Specific Heat Capacity:** The heat energy needed to increase the temperature of 1 kg of a substance by 1°C.

Fig. 08.03.04 Steam from an overheated car radiator.

> **Coolant:** A liquid or gas that is used to remove heat from something.

 **Checkpoint 2**

(a) Check the kW h rating of five electrical devices in your home. Does the physical size of the device or whether it heats water decide the kW h rating of the electrical device?

(b) List and explain two disadvantages and two advantages of using water as a coolant.

Water the Molecule

It makes sense to think that a bigger molecule needs more energy to change state from liquid to gas. For example, ethanol (C_2H_5OH) is a bigger molecule than water (H_2O) but it changes state at a much lower level of energy than water. So molecule size is not the reason for water needing such high amounts of energy to change state. What is?

In the water molecule, most of the electrons are around the oxygen atom, so it is the more **negative** end of the molecule. Because there are so few electrons at the hydrogen ends of the molecule they are less negative. This means that the hydrogen ends are **positive** compared to the oxygen. Water is a **polar molecule** because it has negative ($\delta-$) and positive ends ($\delta+$). The symbol for the Greek letter *delta* (δ) is used indicate the polarity in molecules.

Fig. 08.03.07 An energy rating label.

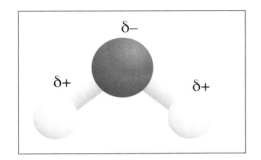

Fig. 08.03.05 The arrangement of the oxygen atom and two hydrogen atoms in a water molecule. This shape means that the molecule has a negative end and two positive ends.

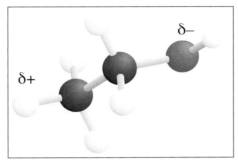

Fig. 08.03.06 The arrangement of carbon, hydrogen and oxygen in ethanol.

The positive and negative ends of the water molecules attract each other. This force of attraction between two water molecules is very weak. However, because a water molecule is so small, a huge number of these attractions happen in water in a very small space. These attractions can only be broken if enough energy is added to the water. This is why water can absorb so much energy before converting to vapour or **steam**.

The positive and negative ends also allow water to become attracted to the positive and negative ends of molecules in other substances. When this happens, the substance dissolves better. This explains why water is such a good solvent of so many substances. Substances that do not have either positive or negative ends do not dissolve easily in water. These are **non-polar molecules**.

> **Polar Molecule:** A molecule which has a negative and positive end because electrons tend to sit at one end of a molecule.

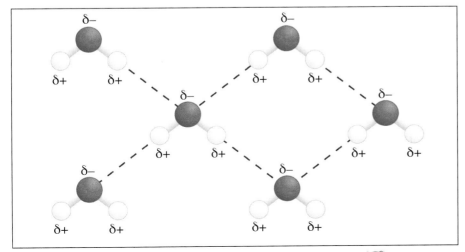

Fig. 08.03.08 Attraction between the positive and negative ends of water molecules.

✓ Checkpoint 3

(a) Ethanol is also a very good solvent. Can you explain why?

(b) Name a household liquid that does not dissolve in water. Based on the fact that this substance does not dissolve in water, what can you say about its molecules?

CHEMISTRY

Walking on Water

Water can also form a layer that small insects can walk across. This property is called **surface tension**. This surface tension happens because of the attraction of water molecules to each other and their lack of attraction to the molecules in the air.

> **Surface Tension:** A layer formed on the surface of a liquid by the force of attraction between the molecules in that liquid.

🔍 Investigation 08.03.03: **Testing surface tension**

Equipment: Three wide-neck containers or bowls, three powders, washing-up liquid.

Instructions:
1. Place some water into the container/bowl.
2. Gently sprinkle one of the powders over the water surface.
3. Dip one finger gently into the water and remove.
4. Rub a small amount of washing-up liquid onto your finger and dip your finger in again.
5. Repeat with the other two powders.

What did you learn?
1. How can you ensure that this is a fair test?
2. Compare your observations for each powder. What patterns do you see?
3. Can surface tension alone explain your results? Justify you answer.

Fig. 08.03.09 Pond skaters, also known as water striders, can walk on the surface of water.

Water Floating on Water

Water has another unusual property. As it cools, it expands. As a substance cools it loses heat energy, which means that the particles in the substance have less energy to move about. As the particles slow down, the substance changes state from gas to liquid, and if cooled enough it changes from liquid to solid (see *Unit 6.1*).

As water is cooled it follows the normal pattern of contraction until it hits 4°C. It then begins to expand, forming crystals, and is fully frozen at 0°C. Ice is the solid state of water that floats on water rather than sinking. Again this marks water out as a unique substance, as solid states of a substance normally sink in the liquid state of that substance.

Fig. 08.03.10 An iceberg is made of compacted snow and ice – the solid state of water.

🔍 Investigation 08.03.04: **Expansion and sinking**

Instructions: Using ice-cube trays, devise an investigation to compare water ice-cubes and cooking oil 'ice-cubes'.

What did you learn?
1. How could you compare the density of these two types of 'ice-cubes' without calculating the exact figures? (See *Unit 13.1* for more on density.)
2. What do you need to do to ensure that this is a fair test?
3. Did both 'ice-cubes' behave in the same way? Explain the differences you observed. What evidence do you have for this?

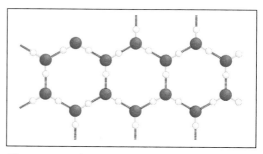

Fig. 08.03.11 When water cools, the force of attraction between the positive and negative ends of the water molecules changes. The molecules form a hexagonal crystal. This takes up more space than the attraction arrangement in the liquid state, so water expands as it becomes solid.

Osmosis

A semi-permeable membrane is a barrier that allows some substances to pass through it but not others. This is important for organisms. It means they can absorb substances through the outer layer of their cells without losing what is already in their cells. It also allows them to get rid of wastes in their cells.

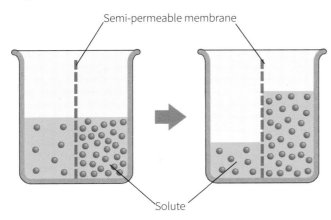

Semi-permeable membrane

Solute

Fig. 08.03.12 The semi-permeable membrane allows water molecules to pass through it but not the larger solute molecules. The water stops moving when the concentration of solute is the same on both sides of the membrane.

(R) **Osmosis** is the way in which water moves from place to place through a semi-permeable membrane. For this to happen, the water needs to move from low solute concentration to high solute concentration. The water keeps moving until the two concentrations are equal.

The holes in the membrane (pores) are large enough to allow water molecules through, but too small to allow the solute molecules through.

 Checkpoint 4

(a) Salt can be used to kill slugs. How does sprinkling salt on a slug kill it?

(b) Explain how osmosis causes the skin on our fingers to wrinkle if they are left in water too long.

> **Osmosis:** The movement of water from low solute concentration to high solute concentration through a semi-permeable membrane.

CHEMISTRY

 Investigation 08.03.05: Osmosis

Instructions: Using a food sample (a fruit, a vegetable or a jelly sweet), design an investigation to show osmosis. Test your food sample against distilled water, sugar solution and salt solution.

What did you learn?
1. How can you ensure that your results are valid?
2. What conclusion can you make about the sugar or salt content of your food sample? Justify your answer.
3. Would this conclusion be the same for all fruits, vegetables, or jelly sweets? Explain.

Hard Water

Because water is such a good solvent, even when it comes from natural sources it is **impure**. **Pure** water is pure because it is treated to remove anything that could contaminate it.

When water is **contaminated** it is no longer pure, but is not unsafe to drink unless the amount of substance rises above a safe dose. Spring water is an impure type of water that is safe to drink. Spring water often contains beneficial minerals depending on its source.

Polluted water contains substances that are harmful to organisms. Fish kills happen in rivers because of the leakage of chemicals from factories, mines or farms.

Hard water is an impure type of water, but it is not harmful to drink as it is not a polluted type of water. In fact, hard water is used in brewing and distilling to add taste to beer and whiskey. Many old distilleries were located next to a local spring which helped to give each whiskey its own particular taste. Hard water contains calcium so it is also a source of calcium for the body. Most bottled spring waters are from hard water sources as pure water has no taste.

Hard water, however, leads to a build-up of **limescale** in appliances (such as on the heating elements in kettles and in the pipes in washing machines). Also, hard water is a poor agent in creating soap bubbles for washing – it does not form a **lather** easily. You might live in an area supplied with hard water, in which case you might notice that your towels or clothes are often 'hard' when they dry, or you might see a soap scum on the surface of water.

Fig. 08.03.13 A fish kill caused by pollution.

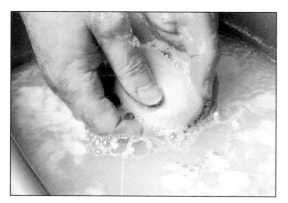
Fig. 08.03.14 Hard water does not create good soap bubbles!

Fig. 08.03.15 Limescale build-up on the element in a kettle.

Hard Water: Water that does not form a lather easily with soap.

Soft Water: Water that forms a lather easily with soap.

Did you know?
Boiling vinegar in kettles is a traditional way of removing the limescale. Modern remedies are often sold in the form of sprays or tablets.

Fig. 08.03.16 Limescale remover.

Hardness in water is caused by calcium ions (Ca^+) and magnesium ions (Mg^{2+}). As much of the rock and stone in Ireland is limestone or contains calcium compounds, many natural water sources produce hard water. The water passes through the rocks and soils as it moves to the surface or runs off mountains.

Hard water can be converted to **soft water** by boiling, **distillation**, **deionising** and ion exchange. When boiled, the ions fall to the bottom of the container, resulting in limescale build-up.

 **Checkpoint 5**

(a) Decide which of these statements are True or False:

(i) Hard water is useful for washing clothes.	(v) It is safe
(ii) Soft water is useless when washing clothes.	(vi) Unpolluted water is normally safe to drink.
(iii) It is safe to wash clothes with impure water.	(vii) Deionised and distilled water are the same.
(iv) It is always safe to prepare food with contaminated water.	(viii) Mineral water is always better for washing clothes.
	(ix) Soft water gives beer a better taste.

(b) Name two household appliances that heat water in a similar way to kettles. Why should you not use vinegar to get rid of limescale in these devices?

CHEMISTRY

Investigation 08.03.06: **Comparing water from different sources**

Instructions: Design an investigation that compares samples of water hardness from at least three different sources.

> ### *What did you learn?*
> 1. Does the type of soap you use to test for hardness affect your results?
> 2. Describe how this investigation can be set up as a fair test.
> 3. What change in your investigation results could you expect if you boiled your water samples and tested them again for hardness. Justify your answer.

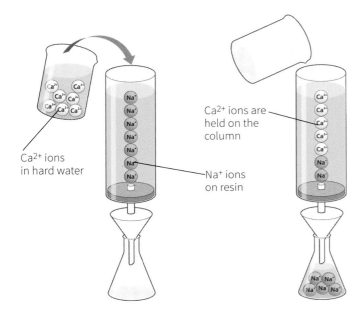

Fig. 08.03.17 An ion exchanger removes Ca+ ions and replaces them with Na+ ions which do not cause hardness. Water is poured in at the top and passes through a resin which absorbs the Ca+ and releases the Na+. Deionisers also use a column of resin to completely remove all ions, not just replace them.

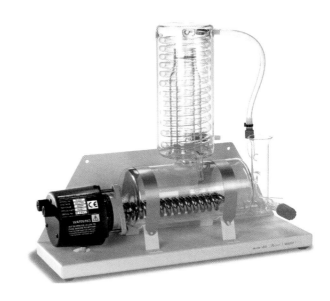

Fig. 08.03.18 This is a water still. It works in a similar way to a Liebig condenser except it is designed to separate pure water from impure water. Tap water is boiled in a chamber and the steam rises up through a cooling tower where it condenses and is then collected. This is the best way to purify water in the lab as only the water is vapourised and not any of the substances that may be dissolved in it. It also works more consistently than deionisers and ion exchangers. A similar device is used to 'purify' whiskey and other spirit drinks.

Distillation is the best method to purify water, but the process of distillation requires a lot of energy so is only used in situations where the water has to be very pure. Delicate chemical experiments and water used to top up car batteries are two examples. Drugs are often dissolved in distilled water so that there are no contaminants that could affect how the drug may work.

WHAT I HAVE LEARNED...

- Water is important to organisms and may be a sign of life on other planets.
- The properties of water.
- Water is a polar molecule because it has positive and negative ends.
- Water is a good solvent because its polar molecules cause other polar substances to dissolve.
- How to show the differences between a polar and non-polar solvent by investigation.
- Why the high specific heat capacity of water makes it a good coolant.
- How to demonstrate and explain that water has surface tension.
- How to show that water has two different densities.
- How to show water transportation by osmosis.
- What hard water is, its advantages and its disadvantages.
- To test for water hardness and rank the hardness in a water sample.

Question Time

Copy and Complete

In this unit I learned that water is a _____ molecule. This means that it has a _____ end and a _____ end. Because water has _____ and _____ ends they _____ each other which makes it difficult to get water to _____ its _____ of matter. A lot of _____ is needed to do this so this makes water a good _____. Water is also called the _____ solvent because it can _____ many _____. _____ tension is a layer on the surface of a liquid caused by the force of _____ between the _____ in that liquid. Osmosis is the _____ of water from _____ solute concentration to _____ solute concentration. Pure water is made up of only _____ molecules. Water that forms a _____ easily with soap is _____ water. Water that does not form a _____ easily with soap is _____ water.

Questions

1. List and explain three properties of water.
2. (R) A science student investigated the solubility of two common substances – sugar and salt – in water for a range of temperatures. The data for sugar are given in *Table 08.03.01*. Salt maintained a constant solubility of 40 g/100 g of water for the temperature range investigated, 0°C to 100°C.

Sugar (g/100 g of water)	175	200	240	290	370	480
Temperature (°C)	0	20	40	60	80	100

Table 08.03.01.

   (i) Draw a graph of the effect of temperature on the solubility of sugar.
   (ii) Use the graph to estimate the increase in the solubility of sugar if the temperature of the solution is raised from 50°C to 70°C.
   (iii) Using the same grid, draw a graph of the effect of temperature on the solubility of salt.
   (iv) If water is a very good solvent of a wide variety of substances, why does heat energy increase the solubility of substances in water?
   (v) Why is the increase in temperature not changing the solubility of salt in this experiment?

3. *Fig. 08.03.19* shows a simple device used to keep people warm in bed. What is the name of this device? Why is water a good substance to use to fill this device?

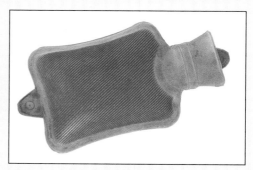

Fig. 08.03.19 A heating device to keep you warm in bed.

4. Describe, with the aid of a diagram, why ice floats on water.
5. As well as keeping our body at a steady temperature, name two other reasons why water is necessary for our bodies to work properly.

6. Water had been flowing through the pipe shown in *Fig. 08.03.20* for some time. The pipe originally had no internal deposit. Give a possible reason for the formation of the deposit. What do you think the deposit is?

Fig. 08.03.20 What has caused the internal deposit in this pipe?

7. Water hardness is a common problem.
   (i) Describe a test that distinguishes between hard and soft water.
   (ii) Name a compound that causes hardness when it dissolves in water.
   (iii) Examine the diagram in *Fig. 08.03.21*. Would you expect the water from the column of resin to be hard or soft? Justify your answer.
   (iv) How could you test the water to confirm this answer? What result would you expect?

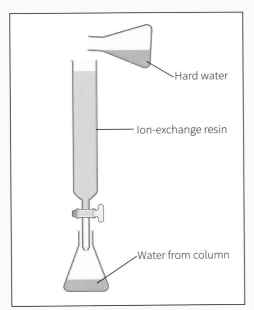

Hard water

Ion-exchange resin

Water from column

Fig. 08.03.21 Hard water being passed through an ion-exchange resin.

8. Both vinegar and lemon juice are traditional limescale removers. Explain why these two liquids are suitable for removing limescale. Based on your conclusions about these traditional remedies, what type of substance do you believe modern limescale removers contain?

Inquiry

A **Design** a poster/presentation explaining the treatment of water to make it suitable for drinking. You must include and explain each of the following in your poster/presentation:
   (i) Screening
   (ii) Settling
   (iii) Flocculation
   (iv) Filtration
   (v) Desalination
   (vi) Chlorination
   (vii) Fluoridation.

B The Mpemba Effect shows that hot water can freeze faster than cold water. Scientists do not yet have an explanation for this. **Describe** two theories that explain the Mpemba Effect and **decide** which theory you think is more likely to be correct.

C **Design** an investigation to see how the temperature of water affects its ability to act as a solvent.

D A plastic bottle placed in direct sunlight can be used to purify urine to make drinkable water in emergency situations. **Research** how this is possible.

CHEMISTRY

Learning Outcomes

CWLO 4. Classify substances as elements, compounds, mixtures, metals, non-metals, solids, liquids, gases and solutions.

CWLO 7. Investigate the effect of a number of variables on the rate of reactions including the productions of common gases and biochemical reactions.

CWLO 8. Investigate reactions between acids and bases; **use indicators and pH scale.**

NSLO 1. Appreciate how scientists work and **how scientific ideas are modified over time.**

NSLO 3. Design, plan and conduct investigations; explain how reliability, accuracy, precision, **fairness, safety**, ethics and a **selection of suitable equipment have been considered.**

NSLO 4. Produce data (qualitatively/quantitatively), critically **analyse data** to identify patterns and relationships, identify anomalous observations, **draw and justify conclusions.**

BWLO 7. Describe respiration and photosynthesis as both chemical and biological **processes**; investigate factors that affect respiration and photosynthesis.

R Teacher's reference

KEYWORDS

activation energy
aerobic respiration
anaerobic respiration
atmosphere
characteristic test
combustion
downward displacement
exothermic
fire triangle
fuel
Law of Conservation
  of Mass
Phlogiston Theory
photosynthesis
respiration
upward displacement

LEARNING INTENTIONS

At the end of this unit you should:

1. Be able to produce gases, in particular oxygen, carbon dioxide and hydrogen.
2. Be able to carry out the characteristic tests for oxygen, carbon dioxide and hydrogen gases.
3. Be able to identify some of the properties of carbon dioxide.
4. Be able to explain combustion and the fire triangle.
5. Know how to compare and contrast combustion, respiration and photosynthesis as chemical reactions.
6. Understand that the atmosphere is a mixture of gases in a number of layers.
7. Be able to test for the presence of oxygen, carbon dioxide and water vapour in the air.
8. Understand the Law of Conservation of Mass through the production and identification of a gas.
9. Understand the role of carbon dioxide in photosynthesis and extinguishing fire.

The Earth's Atmosphere

When we talk about Earth's **atmosphere**, we are talking about the layers of gases that surround the planet and that support the organisms that live on it. There are five main layers but most organisms live in the lowest layer, the troposphere. This layer contains 80% of all the gases in the atmosphere but is the thinnest layer.

The gas mixture we breathe is known as air. It is made up of over 70% nitrogen, 20% oxygen and 10% other gases. Of that mixture, there is only one gas in it that we need to use directly – oxygen. However, pure oxygen taken into your body over a long period of time would cause cell damage.

The main use of oxygen is in the process of **respiration**, which unlocks energy from nutrients. **Aerobic respiration** happens when oxygen is used. In some circumstances respiration in organisms can happen without oxygen. This is called **anaerobic respiration**. (See *Unit 5.2*.)

Aerobic Respiration: The release of energy from nutrients in organisms by chemical reaction with oxygen.

Anaerobic Respiration: The release of energy from nutrients in organisms without a chemical reaction with oxygen.

Outside of organisms, a similar chemical process is **combustion**. Combustion can only happen if oxygen is present. A **fuel** and heat energy are also needed. These factors together are called the **fire triangle**. If any one part of the fire triangle is missing, combustion cannot happen. Fire extinguishers work on the idea that removing one of these stops fire from burning.

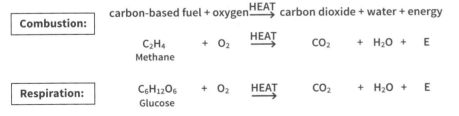

Combustion:
$$\text{carbon-based fuel} + \text{oxygen} \xrightarrow{\text{HEAT}} \text{carbon dioxide} + \text{water} + \text{energy}$$

$$C_2H_4 \quad + \quad O_2 \xrightarrow{\text{HEAT}} CO_2 \quad + \quad H_2O \quad + \quad E$$
Methane

Respiration:
$$C_6H_{12}O_6 \quad + \quad O_2 \xrightarrow{\text{HEAT}} CO_2 \quad + \quad H_2O \quad + \quad E$$
Glucose

Fig. 09.01.02 The fire triangle shows the three factors needed for combustion to happen.

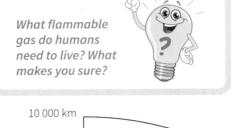

What flammable gas do humans need to live? What makes you sure?

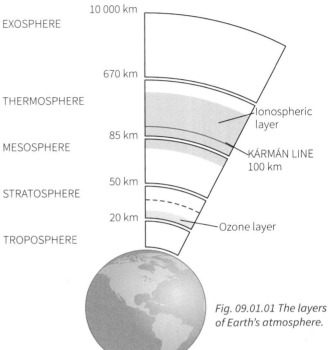

10 000 km
EXOSPHERE

670 km
THERMOSPHERE

Ionospheric layer

85 km
MESOSPHERE

KÁRMÁN LINE 100 km

50 km
STRATOSPHERE

20 km

Ozone layer

TROPOSPHERE

Fig. 09.01.01 The layers of Earth's atmosphere.

CHEMISTRY

Did you know?
Scuba divers know that the oxygen–nitrogen mix in their tanks has to be monitored carefully as the human body cannot tolerate high oxygen levels for long periods. Scuba-diving air is normally 40% oxygen. In technical cave-diving, the mix can have up to 80% oxygen.

Combustion: The release of heat energy from substances by chemical reaction with oxygen.

Fuel: A substance that releases its chemical energy as heat energy when reacted with oxygen.

Fire Triangle: The three factors that are needed for combustion: fuel, heat energy and oxygen.

For each of these reactions, the heat energy provides the **activation energy** (E_{act}). As the reactions are **exothermic**, they release more heat energy. Adding a small amount of heat energy to the reactant mixture begins a chain reaction and continues until the reactants (fuel and oxygen) run out or are removed. Removing the heat energy by cooling also stops the chain reaction.

> **Activation Energy:** The minimum amount of energy needed for a reaction to happen.

> **Exothermic:** A chemical reaction in which energy is released into the surroundings.

Fig. 09.01.03 A matchstick often provides the E_{act} at the start of a combustion reaction.

Fig. 09.01.04 Philo of Byzantium did one of the first investigations into the importance of oxygen in combustion more than 2000 years ago! He placed a burning candle surrounded by water in one container and then turned another container upside down on top of it. He believed that the burning candle sucked water into the upside-down container. Versions of this experiment are still used today to show how much of the air mixture we breathe is made of oxygen.

🔍 Investigation 09.01.01: **How much of air is oxygen?**

Instructions: Using simple lab equipment, design an investigation similar to Philo of Byzantium's experiment (*Fig. 09.01.04*) that can also measure the amount of oxygen used up.

What did you learn?

1. Can another source of flame instead of a candle be used for this investigation? Justify your answer.
2. Could the size or shape of the candle, or other pieces of equipment, make a difference to the results of your investigation?
3. Can you explain why the flame on the candle should be left lit for a few minutes before the upside-down container is placed over it?
4. How can you stop water swamping the candle as you place the upside-down container over it?
5. Can you think of a way to measure the amount of oxygen used by the flame?
6. Suggest reasons why your measurement might not be accurate and how you could improve accuracy in this investigation?
7. Other chemical reactions also use oxygen from the atmosphere. Is there a reaction you can use to get a more accurate measurement of oxygen used?
8. In your opinion, is the percentage of oxygen in air always the same? Justify your answer.

✓ Checkpoint 1

(a) Firefighters use water in most situations. Which factor in the fire triangle does using water remove?
(b) Oil-well firefighters use explosives in the 'blowout' technique to extinguish oil-well fires. This is similar to blowing out birthday candles. Which factor in the fire triangle does this remove?
(c) Which factor is the most difficult to remove from a fire? Explain your answer.

Phlogiston Theory and Oxygen

The discovery of oxygen is shared by three scientists: Carl Wilhelm Scheele (Swedish), Joseph Priestley (English) and Antoine Lavoisier (French). All three had been conducting experiments on a theory common at the time known as the **Phlogiston Theory**. This theory stated that combustion released a substance called 'phlogiston' into the air. When all the phlogiston was released, combustion stopped, while air that contained this released phlogiston could not allow combustion as it could not absorb any more of it.

Antoine Lavoisier gave the clearest explanation of why this theory was wrong. When he heated mercury in a sealed container called a retort for several days, the inside surface became covered with red particles. While this happened, the amount of air in the bell jar reduced and the water level rose. The remaining air could not support either respiration (life) or combustion.

He then heated the red powder, which converted back into mercury. As he did this, the powder gave off a gas equal in volume to that used up in heating the mercury. So the water level in the bell jar fell back to where it had started. When tested separately, this gas did support combustion.

By doing this experiment, Lavoisier had proved that this gas, which he was to name 'oxygen', not only allowed combustion to happen, but was absorbed by the reaction, not released. The Phlogiston Theory had been disproved.

All three scientists had also discovered the **characteristic test** for oxygen – combustion. Oxygen caused a dying flame to rekindle, or a flame to become stronger. Simple characteristic tests for other gases were also discovered.

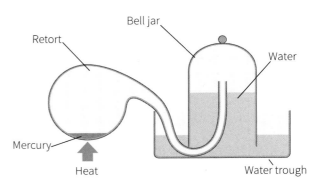

Fig. 09.01.05 A diagram of the apparatus Antoine Lavoisier used to show that the Phlogiston Theory was incorrect.

> **Characteristic Test:** A chemical test that identifies a specific substance and no other.

Gas	Test	Characteristic Result
Oxygen	Place a glowing wooden splint into gas	Splint relights
Hydrogen	Place a burning wooden splint into gas	Burns with a pop
Carbon dioxide	Pass through limewater	Turns limewater milky-white

 Table 09.01.01 Tests and characteristic results for oxygen, hydrogen and carbon dioxide.

As *Table 09.01.01* states, the characteristic test for carbon dioxide is to cause colourless limewater to change colour to milky-white.

carbon dioxide + limewater → calcium carbonate + water

$$CO_2 + Ca(OH)_2 \rightarrow CaCO_3\downarrow + H_2O$$

The true chemical name for limewater is calcium hydroxide. When carbon dioxide reacts with calcium hydroxide it forms a white solid called calcium carbonate. This causes the limewater to form a milky-white suspension.

Hydrogen is a gas that burns very well – even in small amounts – burning as it does with a 'pop'.

> ✓ **Checkpoint 2**
>
> You are given three gas jars labelled X, Y and Z. You are told that a different gas has been placed in each gas jar. The three gases are oxygen, carbon dioxide and nitrogen. You have enough limewater to test all three gases, but only two wooden splints, so you can only test two gases with these. How would you carry out an investigation to identify the three gases?

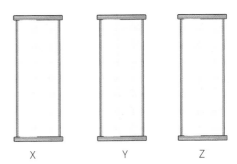

Law of Conservation of Mass

While doing experiments to disprove the Phlogiston Theory, Antoine Lavoisier also discovered the **Law of Conservation of Mass**. This law states that matter can be neither created nor destroyed during a chemical reaction but converted from one form to another.

It can be shown easily by finding the mass of all of the reactants before the reaction begins. At the end of the reaction, the total mass of any remaining reactants and products should be the same as the mass of reactant at the beginning of the experiment.

> **Law of Conservation of Mass:** Matter can be neither created nor destroyed but rather converted from one form to another.

🔍 Investigation 09.01.02: Confirming the Law of Conservation of Mass

Instructions: Using the equipment in the diagram, create a set of instructions for carrying out this investigation, and then carry out the investigation.

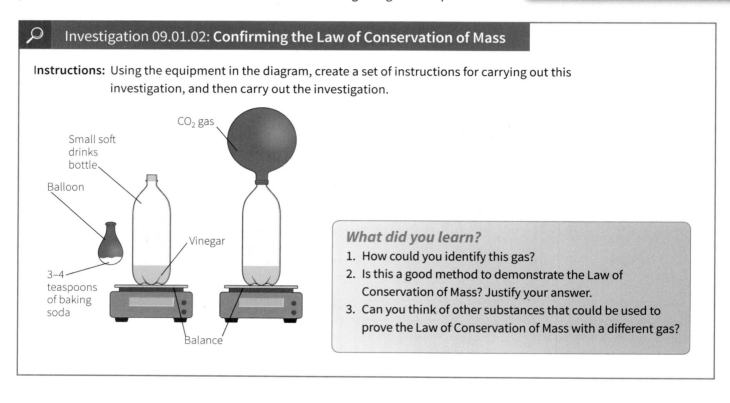

Labels: CO_2 gas; Small soft drinks bottle; Balloon; 3–4 teaspoons of baking soda; Vinegar; Balance

What did you learn?
1. How could you identify this gas?
2. Is this a good method to demonstrate the Law of Conservation of Mass? Justify your answer.
3. Can you think of other substances that could be used to prove the Law of Conservation of Mass with a different gas?

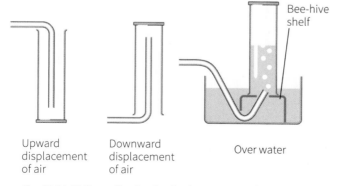

Upward displacement of air

Downward displacement of air

Over water

Bee-hive shelf

Fig. 09.01.06 Gas collection by displacement methods.

Producing Gases

To test any gas, we must know how to produce and collect a sample of that gas. Gases produced in the laboratory are collected by displacement. **Upward displacement** works for gases that are heavier than air so will sink into the gas jar and push the air up and out. **Downward displacement** works for gases that are lighter than air so float upwards, filling the top of the glass jar and pushing the air out of the bottom of it. Upward displacement over water is for gases that are lighter than air but do not dissolve well in water.

Investigation 09.01.03: Identifying the properties of three unknown gases

Instructions: Your teacher will show you how to set up the equipment for each of the three gases and how to use chemicals A–F safely. The set-up and equipment needed for each gas is slightly different due to the properties of each gas. Rewrite and complete the gas identification table (*Table 09.01.02*) below, placing a tick as appropriate and naming the gas at the end.

Method 1

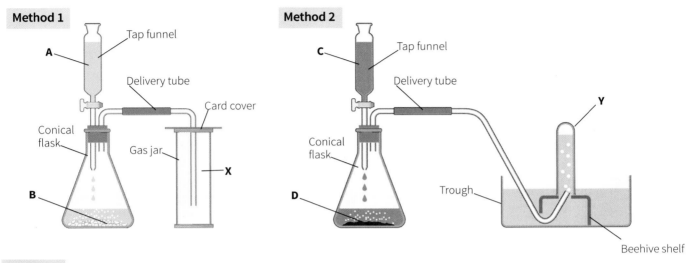

Method 2

Method 3

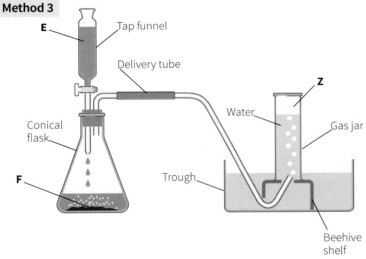

Gas	X	Y	Z
Heavier than air			
Lighter than air			
Has an odour			
Has a colour			
Glowing splint relights			
Lighted splint extinguished			
Burns with a pop			
Limewater turns milky			
Name of gas			

Table 09.01.02.

What did you learn?

1. How can you prove which gas is heavier than air?
2. Should you rely on the first sample of each gas that you collect? Explain your answer.
3. Does solid F get used up? Why do you think this happens?

 **Checkpoint 3**

(a) **Using the information above and the information given to you by your teacher, write a word equation for each gas production reaction:**

Gas X reaction: liquid A + solid B → salt + water + gas X

Gas Y reaction: liquid C + solid D → salt + gas Y

Gas Z reaction: liquid E $\xrightarrow{\text{solid F}}$ water + gas Z

(b) **When you have completed the word equations, write the chemical equations using the chemical formula for each substance.**

Air as a Mixture

Air is a mixture of gases. We have the ability to test for three of these gases easily in the school laboratory: oxygen, carbon dioxide and water vapour. We can do this because there is a characteristic test for each of these gases.

As we have noted, the presence of oxygen in air is proven by its ability to support combustion. Carbon dioxide can be bubbled through lime-water, which will turn from clear to milky-white. (Carbon dioxide is the only gas that does this to limewater.)

Test compound	Colour	Colour in presence of water
cobalt chloride ($CoCl_2$)	blue	pink
anhydrous copper sulfate ($CuSO_4$)	white	blue

Table 09.01.03.

Water causes two chemicals to change colour when it is in liquid form, not vapour. So to detect the water vapour in air we need to change its state from a gas to a liquid.

Like a dry sponge, dry air can absorb a lot of water as a vapour. The amount of water vapour in the air is referred to as 'humidity'. Humidity increases as temperature increases because warm air can hold more water vapour.

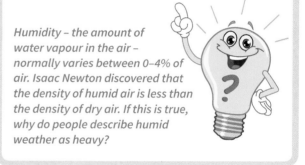

Humidity – the amount of water vapour in the air – normally varies between 0–4% of air. Isaac Newton discovered that the density of humid air is less than the density of dry air. If this is true, why do people describe humid weather as heavy?

Tropical rainforests are humid because they grow where there is constant sunlight in the daytime and high rainfall. This combination of weather and environment makes ideal conditions for high humidity. In Ireland, an example of this happens when there is a heavy sun-shower during the summer. The high temperature dries out the air, but a short, heavy rainfall provides the water to make the air temporarily humid. Depending on other weather conditions, the humidity may last longer.

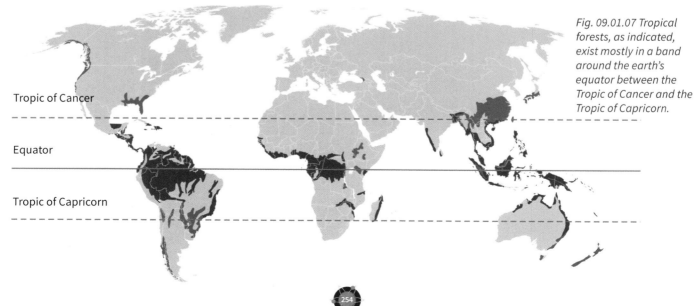

Tropic of Cancer

Equator

Tropic of Capricorn

Fig. 09.01.07 Tropical forests, as indicated, exist mostly in a band around the earth's equator between the Tropic of Cancer and the Tropic of Capricorn.

Water is a good absorber of heat energy, so humidity can help maintain temperatures in rainforests. Water vapour in the atmosphere also helps to maintain steady global temperatures. (Our body uses water in a similar way.)

Carbon dioxide is a good insulator and helps to maintain temperatures. Both carbon dioxide and water vapour play an important part in controlling the atmosphere's temperature levels. A certain amount of each gas is always needed to maintain steady global temperatures, but too much of either could increase global temperatures to a point that life on our planet is affected (see *Unit 9.3*).

Fig. 09.01.08 Isaac Newton (1642–1727) wrote about the density of humid air compared to dry air in his book Optiks.

⊘ Checkpoint 4

Using your knowledge of gases, and tests for them, design an investigation that can test for the carbon dioxide present in air and another that can convert water vapour into water to test with anhydrous copper sulfate. Give reasons for the methods you chose.

 Investigation 09.01.04: Testing for carbon dioxide and water vapour in air

Instructions: Using the investigation design you came up with in Checkpoint 4, test for carbon dioxide and water vapour in air. Before you begin, check with your teacher for available equipment and adjust your method if necessary. Also check for safety issues before you begin your investigation.

What did you learn?
1. If you repeat the investigations again, will you get the same results? Justify your answer.
2. Can you think of how to combine these two tests into one equipment set-up?

Fig. 09.01.09 A bus conductor guides his bus during the four-day Great Smog of London in 1952. Smog is a mixture of fog and air pollution particles. The Great Smog was caused by cold, foggy weather and the burning of coal in homes and factories. Four thousand people died in five days as a direct result of the effects of this smog.

Carbon Dioxide

Every time you burn something, carbon dioxide is produced. It causes major problems in the environment including smog, acid rain and increased greenhouse effects (see *Unit 9.3*).

Calcium carbonate is the main chemical in limestone, marble and chalk. It is also, along with sodium carbonate and sodium hydrogen carbonate, an important ingredient in antacid remedies, vitamin tablets and baking powder. When calcium carbonate, e.g. in limestone, reacts with acid rain, it gives off carbon dioxide gas (see *Unit 8.1*). This causes the stone to change colour and eventually crumble.

Fig. 09.01.10 Acid rain can cause extensive damage to forests.

Fig. 09.01.11 The Taj Mahal was built using brilliant white marble stone. This stone has become discoloured in recent years due to acid rain.

Carbon dioxide also slightly dissolves in water to form a weak acid called carbonic acid. This is one of the acids that makes up acid rain. Carbon dioxide in smoke mixes with water droplets in clouds.

carbon dioxide + water → carbonic acid + carbon dioxide + water

$$CO_2 + H_2O \rightarrow HCO_3 + CO_2\uparrow + H_2O$$

Most of the carbon dioxide in liquids or drinks does not stay dissolved so is released as bubbles. If this happens in a sealed container, the gas bubbles are forced to dissolve by the pressure of the gas building up inside the container. When the container is opened it fizzes because the pressure has suddenly dropped. This happens when a fizzy drink is first opened or poured into a glass because carbon dioxide has been bubbled through them to add fizz.

🔍 Investigation 09.01.05: **Investigating carbonic acid**

Instructions: Using limewater, universal indicator and the equipment in the diagram, design an investigation to test the gas given off by a soluble vitamin or antacid tablet.

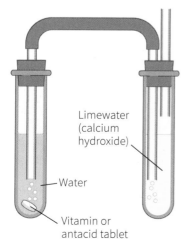

Limewater (calcium hydroxide)

Water

Vitamin or antacid tablet

What did you learn?

1. Is using a vitamin tablet (or antacid tablet) a useful way to produce carbon dioxide gas? Justify your answer.
2. What does the second part of the experiment tell you about carbon dioxide?
3. Would using deionised water instead of tap water to dissolve the tablet make a difference to the reaction?
4. Can you name another solid and liquid that could be used to produce carbon dioxide?

Fig. 09.01.12 A fire extinguisher that uses carbon dioxide.

Carbon dioxide is used to extinguish fires. To be useful as a fire extinguisher it must remove one of the three parts of the fire triangle. It does not replace the fuel as it cannot burn. And as it is a good insulator, it doesn't reduce the heat energy. So it must replace the oxygen. How does it do this?

Demonstration 09.01.01 – Quenching a candle flame

Instructions: Using the equipment as shown in the diagram, your teacher will demonstrate carbon dioxide being used to quench (extinguish) a flame.

What did you learn?
1. If the reaction mixture started producing carbon dioxide almost immediately, why did it take so long for the flame to die out?
2. If the reaction was producing oxygen, what would happen, and would it happen faster than if carbon dioxide was being produced? Justify your answer.

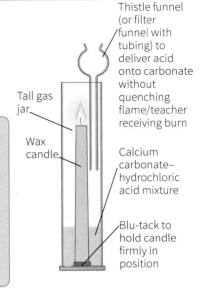

Thistle funnel (or filter funnel with tubing) to deliver acid onto carbonate without quenching flame/teacher receiving burn

Tall gas jar

Wax candle

Calcium carbonate–hydrochloric acid mixture

Blu-tack to hold candle firmly in position

 Investigation 09.01.06: **Testing cabon dioxide as a fire extinguisher**

Instructions: Using simple equipment, including a vitamin tablet (or antacid tablet), tap water and a tea-light candle, design a test to show how effective carbon dioxide is as a fire extinguisher.

What did you learn?
1. Suggest the factors that could affect how well carbon dioxide works as a fire extinguisher.
2. What steps would you need to take to ensure that this was a fair test?
3. Would you recommend your design to a fire extinguisher company? Explain your answer.

Photosynthesis

Carbon dioxide plays an important part in the life of plants and phytoplankton (microscopic marine organisms). These organisms absorb carbon dioxide, water and sunlight energy to create their own food.

The levels of water and carbon dioxide in greenhouses are kept artificially high in order to increase plant growth. All these organisms contain a green pigment called chlorophyll that absorbs sunlight energy, which provides the activation energy (E_{act}) for the reaction. **Photosynthesis** is the reverse chemical reaction of respiration.

| **Photosynthesis:** | carbon dioxide + water $\xrightarrow{\text{CHLOROPHYLL}}$ glucose + oxygen |
| | $CO_2 \quad + \quad H_2O \xrightarrow{\text{CHLOROPHYLL}} C_6H_{12}O_6 + \quad O_2$ |

| **Respiration:** | $C_6H_{12}O_6 + O_2 \xrightarrow{\text{HEAT}} CO_2 + H_2O + E$ |
| | GLUCOSE |

Glucose produced by plants can be converted into cellulose, which gives strength to plant structure. Photosynthesis absorbs much carbon dioxide, so plants are often called 'carbon sinks', as they store carbon within themselves as glucose and cellulose.

WHAT I HAVE LEARNED...

- The differences and similarities between respiration, combustion and photosynthesis as chemical reactions.
- How to produce oxygen, carbon dioxide and hydrogen by upward and downward displacement.
- How to carry out the characteristic tests for oxygen, carbon dioxide and hydrogen gases.
- The differences and similarities between the properties of oxygen, carbon dioxide and hydrogen gases.
- How to explain combustion and the fire triangle.
- How to compare and contrast combustion, respiration and photosynthesis as chemical reactions.
- An understanding that the atmosphere is a mixture of gases in a number of layers.
- To show the Law of Conservation of Mass through the production and identification of a gas.
- An understanding of the role of carbon dioxide in photosynthesis and extinguishing fire.

Question Time

Copy and Complete

In this unit I learned that _____ respiration is the release of _____ from _____ in organisms by chemical reaction with oxygen. When heat energy is released from other chemicals by reacting with oxygen this is called _____. Oxygen is produced by reacting _____ _____and_____ _____. The black powder used in this reaction is a _____ so does not get _____ _____. Oxygen causes a _____ splint to _____. One part of the fire _____ is oxygen; the other parts are _____ and _____. _____ burns with a pop when a _____ splint is placed in it. This gas is produced when _____ metal is reacted with _____ acid. A lighted splint is _____ when placed in _____ _____ gas. _____ acid and calcium _____ react to give this gas. Marble, _____/_____ and _____ powder all contain calcium _____. Carbon dioxide can be used for fire extinguishers, _____ _____ and _____ _____. This gas is absorbed by plants during photosynthesis to make _____ for the plants.

Questions

1. Complete the word equations below by writing a suitable 'fuel' for each one:

   Respiration: _____+ oxygen —HEAT→ carbon dioxide + water + energy

   Combustion: _____+ oxygen —HEAT→ carbon dioxide + water + energy

2. The gas produced in the reaction detailed in *Fig. 09.01.13* turns limewater milky-white. Name the gas. Name two household products that can react to form this gas.

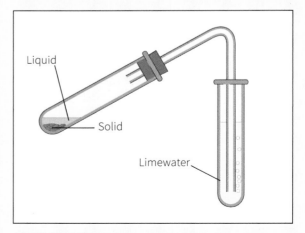

Fig. 09.01.13 Limewater experiment.

3. *Fig. 09.01.14* shows the set-up for producing a gas. Copy and complete *Table 09.01.04* by placing the correct letter A–K in the box next to the label.

Letter	Label
	hydrogen peroxide
	beehive-shelf
	oxygen
	delivery tube
	tap funnel
	manganese dioxide
	gas jar
	conical flask
	trough
	water

Table 09.01.04.

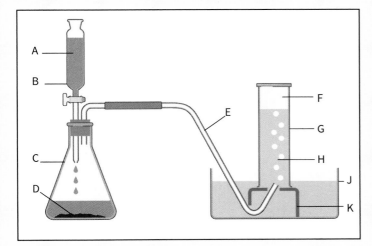

Fig. 09.01.14.

4. *Fig. 09.01.15* shows the apparatus used to prepare and collect carbon dioxide gas in the laboratory. Below it is a list of substances that can be used to produce gases.

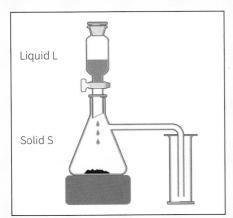

Fig. 09.01.15.

- Hydrogen peroxide   • Hydrochloric acid
- Marble chips   • Manganese dioxide

(i)   Liquid L is used to prepare carbon dioxide. Which substance in the list is liquid L?

(ii)   Solid S is used to prepare carbon dioxide. Which substance in the list is liquid S?

(iii)   What would a student observe when liquid L is allowed to drop onto solid S?

(iv)   Name the liquid which turns milky-white when carbon dioxide is bubbled through it.

(v)   State one use for carbon dioxide in everyday life.

5. *Fig. 09.01.16* show carbon dioxide being produced in order to extinguish a candle flame. Which version, A or B, will work most effectively? Explain your answer. If oxygen gas was being produced instead of carbon dioxide, would a glowing candle wick in set-up A or B relight? Justify your answer.

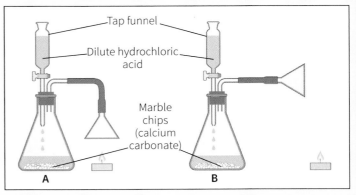

Fig. 09.01.16 Comparative methods A and B for carbon dioxide production to extinguish a candle flame.

Inquiry

A   **Create** a poster/presentation which shows how the 'blowout' method was used by Red Adair to extinguish the 'Devil's Cigarette Lighter' – a 140 m pillar of fire from an oil well in 1962.

B   **Investigate** how concentration of HCl in the production of CO_2 affects the rate or volume of CO_2 produced. **Suggest** other factors that may also have the same effect.

C   **Design** a simple demonstration which proves that water vapour is one of the components of air.

9.2

Fuels

Learning Outcomes

CWLO 4. Classify substances as elements, **compounds, mixtures,** metals, non-metals, **solids, liquids, gases and solutions.**

CWLO 9. Consider chemical reactions in terms of energy, using the terms exothermic, endothermic and activation energy, and use simple energy profile diagrams to illustrate energy changes.

CWLO 10. Evaluate how humans contribute to sustainability through the extraction, use, disposal and recycling of materials.

ESLO 6. Research different energy sources; **formulate and communicate an informed view of ways that current and future energy needs on Earth can be met.**

NSLO 3. Design, plan **and conduct investigations;** explain how reliability, accuracy, precision, fairness, safety, ethics and selection of suitable equipment have been considered.

NSLO 6. Conduct research relevant to scientific issues, **evaluate different sources of information,** understanding that a source may lack details or show bias.

NSLO 8. Evaluate media-based arguments concerning science and technology.

R Teacher's reference

KEYWORDS

aerobic respiration
chemical energy
coal
combustion
crude oil
fire triangle
fossil fuel
fracking
fuel
hydrocarbons
methane
natural gas
oil
thrust
turf

LEARNING INTENTIONS

At the end of this unit you should:

1. Be able to explain the difference between a fuel and a fossil fuel.
2. Be able to describe how different fossil fuels are formed.
3. Be able to test and identify the product of combustion.
4. Be able to test and compare a selection of fuels.
5. Understand that crude oil is a mixture.
6. Understand the differences between fossil fuels and hydrogen fuels cells.
7. Be able to explain that the burning of fuels can be used to create thrust.

Fuel

Combustion is a chemical reaction that releases heat energy. Combustion can only happen if a **fuel**, heat energy and oxygen are present. These three factors together are called the **fire triangle**. If any one part of the fire triangle is missing, combustion cannot happen. Fire extinguishers work on the idea that removing one of these stops the fire from burning.

Fig. 09.02.02 The three parts of the fire triangle.

Combustion: The release of heat energy from substances by chemical reaction with oxygen.

Aerobic respiration is another type of chemical reaction in which oxygen combines with a substance to release energy. This released energy is easily converted to heat energy. This means that a chemical reaction that releases energy can happen within an organism without damaging that organism.

For both types of reaction, carbon-based compounds react with the oxygen to release the energy. Carbon compounds are useful for this because they can store large amounts of **chemical energy**. Chemical energy is the energy stored within a compound that can be released during a chemical reaction. Very often this energy is released as heat or light energy.

A substance that can be combusted (burned) and which releases heat energy when burned is called a fuel. Fuels can release energy in other ways but are useful because most of their chemical energy is released as heat energy when they react with oxygen.

Are the foods we eat fuel?

Fig. 09.02.01 A type of fuel?

CHEMISTRY

Aerobic Respiration: The release of energy from nutrients in organisms by chemical reaction with oxygen.

Chemical Energy: The stored energy in chemicals that can be released in reactions.

Fuel: A substance that releases chemical energy as heat energy when reacted with oxygen.

✅ Checkpoint 1

(a) Below are the chemical equations for a combustion reaction and a respiration reaction. Complete these reactions by filling in the blanks.

Combustion: _____ + O_2 $\xrightarrow{\text{HEAT}}$ _____ + H_2O + _____

Respiration: _____ + O_2 $\xrightarrow{\text{HEAT}}$ _____ + H_2O + _____

(b) All three parts of the fire triangle must be present for a combustion reaction to happen. Which part of the fire triangle is missing from the combustion reaction above?

Fossil Fuel

In Ireland, **turf** and **coal** were the most common **fossil fuels** used to heat homes and cook food. Nowadays electricity and gas have taken over these tasks in the home, with turf and coal now used mainly for open fireplaces and stoves to warm and decorate individual rooms. However, we still use a lot of fossil fuels, as gas is a fossil fuel and electricity is generated by burning coal, **oil**, gas and peat.

Fig. 09.02.03 Turf briquettes, coal and petroleum (petrol) are common fossil fuels.

Fig. 09.02.04 In times past, campfires arranged with a spit or grill were a good way to heat and cook when on the move during cattle herding. However, much of the energy released by the fuel was lost in the open surroundings.

Fossil fuels come from the remains of dead plants and animals that are converted over long periods of time into a variety of substances that can be used as fuels. These fuels are removed from the earth by either mining or drilling, a process known as 'extraction'.

Fossil Fuel: A fuel based on animal and plant remains that is extracted from the earth.

How oil, petroleum and natural gas were formed

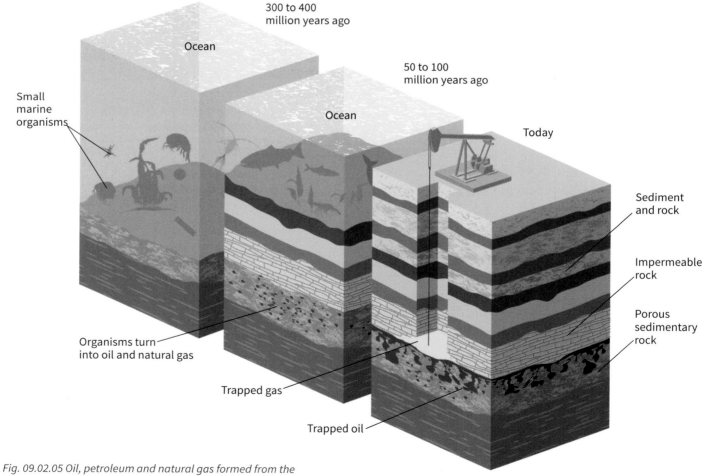

300 to 400 million years ago

Ocean

50 to 100 million years ago

Ocean

Today

Small marine organisms

Sediment and rock

Impermeable rock

Porous sedimentary rock

Organisms turn into oil and natural gas

Trapped gas

Trapped oil

Fig. 09.02.05 Oil, petroleum and natural gas formed from the remains of marine plants and animals. Over time the pressure from layers of sediment and rock above them and heat from the earth's core converted the remains into fossil fuels.

How coal and turf were formed

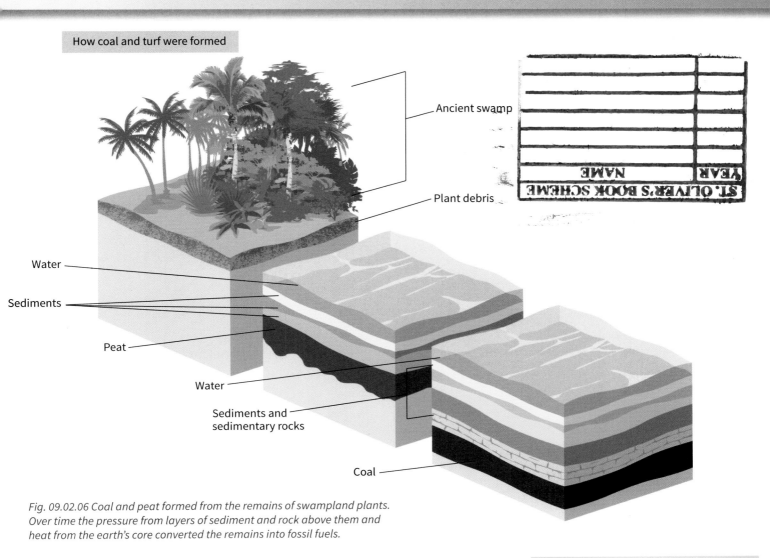

Fig. 09.02.06 Coal and peat formed from the remains of swampland plants. Over time the pressure from layers of sediment and rock above them and heat from the earth's core converted the remains into fossil fuels.

CHEMISTRY

It is important to remember that we use many fuels in different circumstances but not all of these fuels are fossil fuels. All fuels contain hydrogen and carbon atoms and many contain small amounts of other atoms as well. Compounds that contain only hydrogen and carbon atoms are called **hydrocarbons**.

Hydrocarbons: Compounds that are made only of hydrogen and carbon atoms.

Investigation 09.02.01: **Chemical identification of combustion products**

Instructions: Using simple equipment, design an experiment that can chemically test two of the products of combustion.

What did you learn?
1. What products of a combustion reaction can be identified by simple tests?
2. How are the samples of the combustion products captured in the first place? Can you think of a better way to capture them?
3. Is this method suitable to test a range of different combustion reactions? How do you know this?

Checkpoint 2

(a) Coal has been mined and peat harvested for centuries in Ireland. Oil and gas have never been discovered on this island except in small pockets. Based on the plant and animal origins of fossil fuels, what can you say about the surface terrain of Ireland in ancient times?

(b) Fossils fuels can be solids, liquids or gases. Which state of matter do you think releases more energy? Justify your answer.

Demonstration 09.02.01 – **Faraday's candles**

Instructions: Your teacher will show a demonstration from a famous lecture in 1860 by Michael Faraday called 'The Natural History of the Candle'. Here, two candles and a lighter are used.

What did you learn?
1. If you were to repeat this demonstration, what steps (actions) would you take to make it a successful demonstration?
2. Can you put together a scientific explanation for how a flame can transfer from one candle to another?
3. Why might this be important in coal mines, saw mills and flour mills?

Did you know?
Paraffin oil rises up through the wick of an oil lamp in the same way that water rises up the xylem of a plant.

Investigation 09.02.02: **Comparing the energy content of three fuels**

Instructions: Using simple equipment, design a fair experiment to compare the energy content of paraffin wax, methanol and propanol (propan-1-ol).

What did you learn?
1. How can you make sure that you are comparing each fuel fairly?
2. Is there another way of comparing these fuels using similar equipment?
3. Which of these fuels are fossil fuels?
4. Is there a simple way to tell the difference between a fossil fuel and another fuel?
5. What do fossil fuels and other fuels have in common?

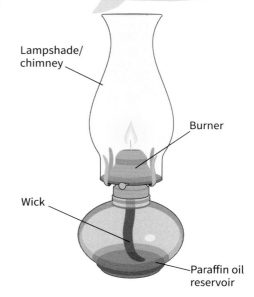

Lampshade/chimney

Burner

Wick

Paraffin oil reservoir

Fig. 09.02.07 A paraffin oil lamp.

✓ Checkpoint 3

(a) *Table 09.02.01* shows four fuels. Match the correct fuel to each device.

(b) Does the number of carbon atoms in a fuel have any effect on how that fuel burns? Reflect on the results of your investigations.

Fuels	Methane CH_4	Ethane C_2H_6	Propane C_3H_8	Butane C_4H_{10}
Devices				

Table 09.02.01.

Fossil Fuel Extraction

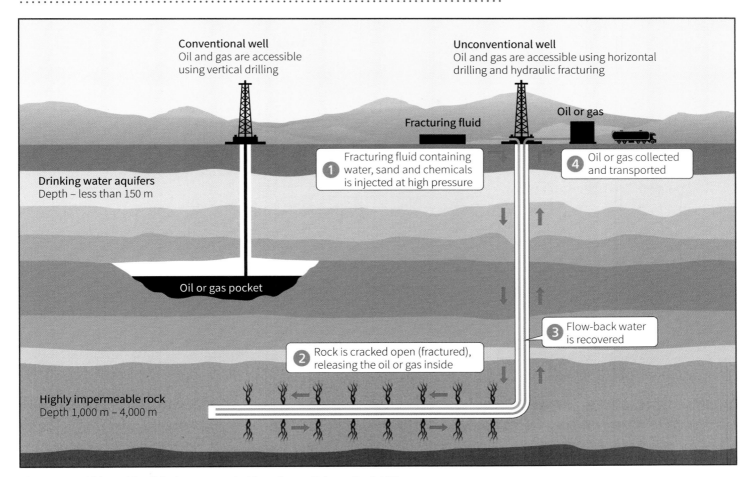

Fig. 09.02.08 Oil-based fossil fuels are extracted from the earth by vertical drilling and by hydraulic fracturing – 'fracking'.

Fossil fuels are extracted in a variety of ways:

- Mining for coal, coke, anthracite
- Strip harvesting for turf (peat)
- Vertical drilling for **crude oil** and **natural gas** (**methane**) in pockets
- Hydraulic fracturing (**fracking**) for natural gas and crude oil in shale rock.

Oil-based fossil fuels come from crude oil, which is a mixture of oil and natural gas and is formed from the remains of dead plants and animals. Petroleum, diesel and lubrication oils are all separated from crude oil by fractional distillation. Each different oil product boils off at a different temperature. Lighter oils are boiled off first as they have lower boiling temperatures.

Another method of extraction is hydraulic fracturing (fracking). A hole is drilled down into a shale layer of rock and then sideways. A high-pressure water and sand mixture is forced down this drill hole, which causes cracks in the shale rock. As the water is pumped out of the drill hole, natural gas seeps through the cracks in the shale. Oil can also be found this way. A second hole can be used to let waste water drain down into the shale rock and fill any pocket left by the extraction of the gas or oil.

All fossil fuels release large amounts of carbon dioxide into the atmosphere, but how they are extracted can also impact the environment in negative ways.

 **Checkpoint 4**

(a) List and describe two environmental impacts from oil and gas extraction.

(b) Peat is extracted on a very large scale in both Ireland and large parts of Russia. What effect do you think peat extraction may have on the environment?

(c) Coal was a very common fossil fuel in Ireland for most of the last two centuries. Why is it no longer used so much?

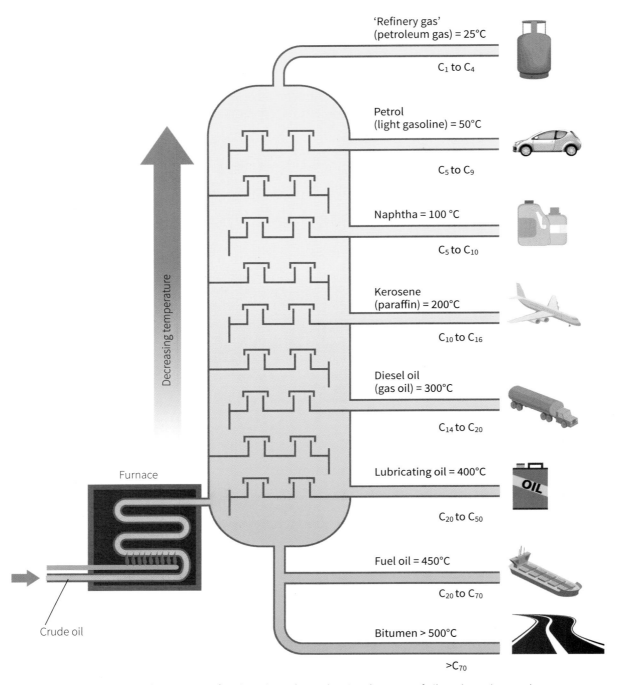

'Refinery gas'
(petroleum gas) = 25°C

C_1 to C_4

Petrol
(light gasoline) = 50°C

C_5 to C_9

Naphtha = 100 °C

C_5 to C_{10}

Kerosene
(paraffin) = 200°C

C_{10} to C_{16}

Diesel oil
(gas oil) = 300°C

C_{14} to C_{20}

Lubricating oil = 400°C

C_{20} to C_{50}

Fuel oil = 450°C

C_{20} to C_{70}

Bitumen > 500°C

$>C_{70}$

Decreasing temperature

Furnace

Crude oil

Fig. 09.02.09 A fractionating column showing the range of oil products that can be extracted from crude oil.

Fig. 09.02.10 A fossil of a trilobite (an extinct marine creature) found in the Burgess Shale rock formation in British Columbia, Canada. The Burgess Shale Formation is a famous source of fossils amongst palaeontologists and a possible source of oil in the future.

Fossil Fuel Burners

Different types of fossil fuel burners allow fossil fuels to be used for more than just heating and cooking. Oxy-acetylene blow torches are used to weld metal together and to cut it. The amounts of oxygen and acetylene fuel in the combustion mixture decide how hot the flame will be. The flame is normally ignited using a flint striker. In order for a steady flame to be produced, the flow of each gas has to be controlled or regulated. Regulating the flow of gases in a combustion mixture is an important way to control the flame temperature.

acetylene (ethyne) + oxygen → carbon dioxide + water

$$2C_2H_2 \quad + \quad 5O_2 \rightarrow \quad 4CO_2 \quad + 2H_2O$$

When Robert Bunsen redesigned the laboratory burners his students were using, he made one important change. He added in a regulator collar. This meant that oxygen combined with the fuel in the chimney before it reached the top. When sparked at the top, a strong, steady flame would be produced. With this design Bunsen was controlling two parts of the fire triangle: the amount of fuel and the amount of oxygen. By doing this he was able to control the temperature of the flame.

Carburettors do a similar job for petrol engines. They help control the air–fuel mix so that the minimum amount of fuel is used each time the engine starts up. Too much fuel in the mix 'floods' the engine and ignition does not happen easily. The spark plugs provide the activation energy for the reaction (see *Unit 7.3*).

This gas mixture releases a lot of energy as it combusts, causing a gas ball to expand, pushing on the pistons of the engine. These are connected to the wheels by a crankshaft and gears. The force of this expanding gas ball turns the wheels of the vehicle. Waste gases pass out through the exhaust. This can happen thousands of times per minute when an engine is running.

Engineers call this a 'controlled burn', but in effect it is a gas explosion inside a strong metal block!

In a rocket engine, all the expanding gases are forced through a nozzle so that the force of the gases hitting the ground underneath the rocket pushes the rocket upwards. This force is called **thrust**.

Thrust: The force created by rocket engine exhaust gases.

CHEMISTRY

Demonstration 09.02.02 – Burning ice

Instructions: Your teacher will set a bowl of ice on fire. How is it possible that if ice is made from water, it can burn and be used as fuel?

Fig. 09.02.11 Burning ice.

Fig. 09.02.12 A construction worker using an Oxy-acetylene blowtorch.

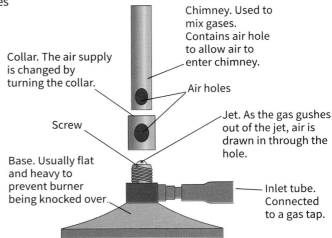

Chimney. Used to mix gases. Contains air hole to allow air to enter chimney.

Collar. The air supply is changed by turning the collar.

Air holes

Screw

Jet. As the gas gushes out of the jet, air is drawn in through the hole.

Base. Usually flat and heavy to prevent burner being knocked over.

Inlet tube. Connected to a gas tap.

Fig. 09.02.13 The parts of a Bunsen burner.

Demonstration 09.02.03 – **Mentos reaction**

Instructions: Your teacher will show you how a Mentos sweet and diet cola react together.

Diet cola and Mentos

Mentos dropped into diet cola

Explosion of diet cola

What did you learn?

1. Based on your observations, do you think that a DIY rocket could be made from this equipment? Explain.
2. How could you make sure that the rocket moves upwards, without causing damage or injury?

Rocket Fuel

Fig. 09.02.14 The main engine of the Space Shuttle burns hydrogen, which has a colourless flame but releases enormous amounts of energy when burned.

Rocket fuel needs to be extremely efficient for two main reasons. Liquid fuels are heavy to carry, and spacecraft don't have regular fuels stops on their journey! Hydrogen is perfect for this job as it can be pressurised and stored as a liquid and needs little activation energy.

But this is also a problem. Because hydrogen is so reactive, it can be dangerous and has to be cooled to be stored safely. So far, only rocket systems use hydrogen as a fuel for their engines.

hydrogen + oxygen → water

$$2H_2 \quad + \quad O_2 \quad \rightarrow \quad 2H_2O$$

Hydrogen fuel has one huge advantage over all other fuels: when burned it does not produce carbon dioxide or other possible pollutants; water is the only product of this reaction. This is called a 'clean burn' reaction. If the storage and reaction of hydrogen with oxygen can be miniaturised safely, then it may be possible to use hydrogen as a 'clean burn' fuel for internal combustion engines.

Hydrogen Fuel Cell

Demonstration 09.02.04 – **Electrohydrolysis**

Instructions: Your teacher will show how Hofmann's Voltameter can be used to split water into hydrogen and oxygen. This is called electrohydrolysis. Hydrogen fuel cells reverse this idea.

What did you learn?

1. Explain why this experiment won't work unless the water is acidified.
2. How is it possible to tell the difference between the two gases produced by this method?
3. Do the amounts of each gas tell us anything about water?

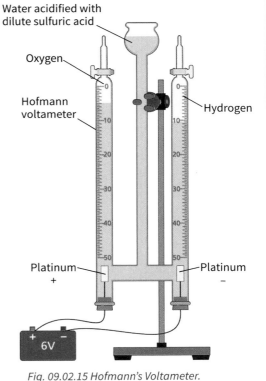

Fig. 09.02.15 Hofmann's Voltameter.

CHEMISTRY

The first effective hydrogen cell was invented in 1959 by Thomas Bacon and a few years later was adapted by NASA to use in the Space Program. Hydrogen fuel cells have been used by NASA on a range of spacecraft to generate electrical power. They are also a water source for crew so little water needs to be carried by the spacecraft.

Fig. 09.02.16 Toyota recently launched the Mirai, a car that uses hydrogen fuel cells to power it.

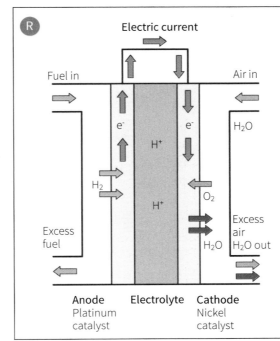

Hydrogen gas is passed through a platinum catalyst which splits it into H^+ ions and electrons (e^-).

The electrolyte allows the ions to pass through, but blocks the electrons. The electrons flow around a circuit to the cathode.

The cathode is a nickel catalyst which causes the electrons to re-combine with the H^+ ions and oxygen from air, forming water.

The combination of two catalyst reactions in a circuit allows electricity to be generated efficiently and produces water.

Table 09.02.02 How a hydrogen fuel cell works.

Checkpoint 5

(a) Why is burning hydrogen environmentally friendly?

(b) Explain why hydrogen fuel cells could be dangerous. Is this a realistic danger?

(c) Could using hydrogen fuel cells be harmful to the environment?

(d) Compare the advantages and disadvantages of fossil fuels and hydrogen.

(e) Why does the Space Shuttle use hydrogen rather than a fossil fuel?

WHAT I HAVE LEARNED...

- The difference between a fuel and a fossil fuel.
- How different fossil fuels are formed.
- To test and identify the product of combustion.
- To test and compare a selection of fuels.
- That crude oil is a mixture.
- How to split water into hydrogen and oxygen.
- The differences between fossil fuels and hydrogen fuels cells.

Question Time

Copy and Complete

In this unit I learned that combustion is the release of heat energy from _____/_____ by chemical reaction with oxygen. The stored _____ in chemicals that can be released in reactions is called _____ energy. A substance that releases its _____/_____ energy as _____ energy when reacted with oxygen is called a _____. Fuels based on animal and plant remains that are extracted from the earth are called _____ fuels. _____ are compounds that are made only of _____ and _____ atoms. A _____ fuel cell converts _____ and _____ into water and generates _____. The force created by rocket engine _____ gases is called _____.

Questions

1. 'Food and drinks are fuel.' True or false? Explain your answer.

2. The experiment shown in *Fig. 09.02.17* was carried out to investigate the products of the combustion of a hydrocarbon wax produced from the fossil fuel oil. In the experiment the products of the combustion were drawn through the apparatus by the vacuum pump.

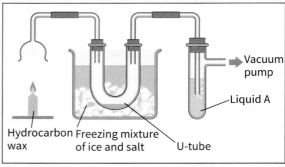
Fig. 09.02.17 Products of combustion set-up.

(i) A colourless liquid formed at the bottom of the U-tube after a while. What do you think the liquid that formed in the U-tube was? Give a test that could be used to confirm your identification.

(ii) What would you expect the pH of this liquid to be? Explain.

(iii) Why was the U-tube placed in a freezing mixture of salt and ice?

(iv) Identify Liquid A.

3. Name a fossil fuel other than oil.

4. Why would the engine of a car not work properly if the air intake was blocked?

5. Flint strikers ignite oxy-acetylene torches and spark plugs ignite petrol in car engines. Which part of the fire triangle do both of these provide?

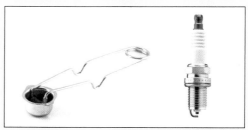
Fig. 09.02.18 A flint striker and a spark plug.

Inquiry

A **Design** a fair investigation to find the energy content of three foods by burning food samples.

B **Research** the arguments for and against fracking to extract oil and **design** a poster showing your research.

C The combustion of fuel in an internal combustion engine is a 'controlled burn'. Does that mean that explosives like TNT (dynamite) are simply extremely fast-burning fuels? **List** arguments for and against this idea.

9.3

Atmospheric Pollution

Learning Outcomes

CWLO 10. Evaluate how humans contribute to sustainability through the extraction, **use, disposal** and recycling of materials.

ESLO 7. Illustrate how the Earth processes and human factors influence the Earth's climate, **evaluate effects of climate change and initiative that attempt to address those effects.**

NSLO 6. Conduct research relevant to scientific issues, evaluate different sources of information, understanding that a source may lack details or show bias.

NSLO 8. Evaluate media-based arguments concerning science and technology.

PWLO 3. Research and discuss the ethical and sustainability issues that arise from our generation and consumption of electricity.

R Teacher's reference

KEYWORDS

acid rain
aerosols
anthropogenic gases
atmosphere
atmospheric pollution
Carbon Cycle
chloro-flouro-carbons
climate
climate engineering
Enhanced Greenhouse
  Effect
fossil fuels
Global Carbon Budget
Global Warming
  Potential (GWP)
Greenhouse Effect
greenhouse gas
Keeling curve
methane
ozone layer
pollution
water cycle
water vapour
weather

LEARNING INTENTIONS

At the end of this unit you should:
1. Be able to explain the difference between weather and climate.
2. Be able to describe the Carbon Cycle and the Water Cycle.
3. Be able to describe the importance of the Greenhouse Effect.
4. Be able to demonstrate the Greenhouse Effect using a simple model.
5. Be able to describe the main greenhouse gases and their effects on the environment.
6. Be able to specify the differences between the Greenhouse Effect and the Enhanced Greenhouse Effect.
7. Understand the importance of the ozone layer.
8. Be able to explain how acid rain is formed and understand its effects on the environment.
9. Understand the causes of global climate change and possible ways to reduce large changes to the climate.

Is there a difference between weather and climate? Explain.

Pollution

Most of us know what **pollution** is. We experience it every day: fumes from vehicle engines, litter on our streets, effluent leaking into our rivers and streams. Vehicle fumes damage our lungs. Litter is not only an eyesore, whether it be on the streets, in hedgerows or in rivers or seas, but also a choking hazard to animals, birds and marine life. Effluent leaks are often poisonous to fish. There are many different examples of pollution, and all of these examples – whether they are solids, liquids or gases – have one effect in common: they cause harm to organisms.

> **Pollution:** The addition of substances to the environment that are harmful to organisms.

When pollution happens in the **atmosphere** it is called **atmospheric pollution**. In this unit we will be looking at how atmospheric pollution is caused and some of its effects.

> **Atmosphere:** The gas layers surrounding the surface of a planet.

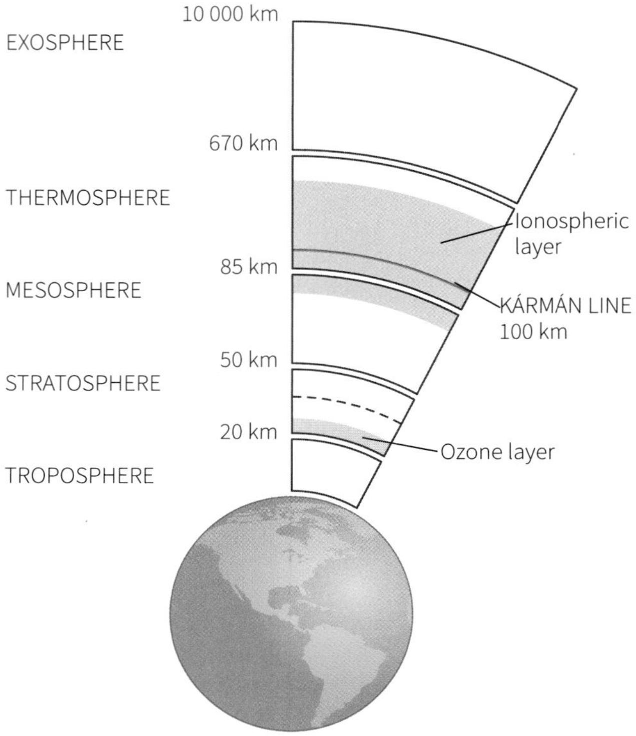

EXOSPHERE

10 000 km

670 km

THERMOSPHERE

Ionospheric layer

85 km

KÁRMÁN LINE 100 km

MESOSPHERE

50 km

STRATOSPHERE

20 km

Ozone layer

TROPOSPHERE

Fig. 09.03.01 The layers of Earth's atmosphere.

The Carbon Cycle

Fig. 09.03.02 The Carbon Cycle shows how carbon is recycled through combustion, respiration and photosynthesis reactions in nature. **1** Burning fossil fuels and cement production **2** Respiration of plants and animals **3** Plant and animal decay, crop burning **4** Build-up of carbon dioxide in the atmosphere **5** Photosynthesis by plants **6** Carbon stored in plant organic matter and soil (sink) **7** Ocean carbon dioxide exchange (sink) **8** Photosynthesis by phytoplankton which are eaten by marine organisms (sink) **9** Dead marine organisms sink to seabed (sink) **10** Rock formation over centuries fossilises bones of marine organisms and converts organic matter to coal, oil and gas (sink).

Checkpoint 1

(a) Write one sentence that explains what weather is.

(b) Write one sentence that explains what climate is.

(c) Is there a difference between 'air pollution' and 'atmospheric pollution'? Justify your answer.

(d) There are other types of pollution besides atmospheric pollution. List three other types and give an example of each.

> **Weather:** Short-term changes to the atmosphere over a specific area.

> **Climate:** Long-term patterns in changes to the atmosphere.

The **Carbon Cycle** is the natural system of carbon recycling that happens on the earth due to combustion, respiration and photosynthesis reactions. The cycle works to keep a balance between the gases present in the earth's atmosphere.

In this cycle, carbon sinks are used to store carbon so that there is never too much carbon released into the atmosphere or oceans at once. Since the beginning of the Industrial Revolution in the late seventeenth century, humans have been burning carbon sinks such as trees and **fossil fuels**. This has released carbon dioxide into the atmosphere at a rate faster than the planet can naturally cope with.

This imbalance in the Carbon Cycle is beginning to have effects on our **climate** and may cause permanent damage to the planet and the ability of organisms to survive.

Checkpoint 2

Similar to the Carbon Cycle, the Water Cycle is the natural system that keeps the balance of water in the oceans, lakes, rivers and atmosphere. Draw an A4 poster of the Water Cycle based on your research.

The Greenhouse Effect

Irishman John Tyndall was the first to prove by an experiment in 1869 that the Greenhouse Effect existed. A number of scientists had suggested the idea, and inventor of the telephone, Alexander Graham Bell, came up with the phrase '**The Greenhouse Effect**', but it was Tyndall who showed that gases could absorb energy from the sun and act as insulators, trapping heat energy beneath a blanket of gas. It was called the Greenhouse Effect because gases can act like the glass of a greenhouse, which prevents heat energy from escaping but allows sunlight energy (UV radiation) to pass through it.

Demonstration 09.03.01 – **The Greenhouse Effect**

Instructions: Using two thermometers and a glass bowl, your teacher will demonstrate the Greenhouse Effect. Note the temperature in each thermometer every minute for fifteen minutes.

CHEMISTRY

John Tyndall (1820–93)

Svante Arrhenius (1859–1927)

Charles David Keeling (1920–2005)

Joe Farman (1930–2013), Brian G. Gardiner and Jon Shanklin

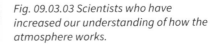

Fig. 09.03.03 Scientists who have increased our understanding of how the atmosphere works.

If you think of our planet as a type of greenhouse, the gases in our atmosphere act like the glass of a greenhouse acts. The atmosphere allows UV radiation to pass through. This sunlight (solar) energy heats the earth. Unused energy is emitted into the atmosphere as infrared radiation (heat energy). Gases in the atmosphere absorb this heat energy and reflect some of it back to the surface.

This allows Earth to maintain a steady overall mean temperature across the planet, and means that H_2O can exist as a gas, liquid and solid, which supports a wide variety of life on Earth.

If the Greenhouse Effect became stronger than normal it would eventually decrease the amount of water available and would disrupt the **Water Cycle** of the planet, affecting much of the plant and animal life. When this happens it is called the 'runaway Greenhouse Effect'. A situation like this may have happened on Mars in the ancient past.

The **Enhanced Greenhouse Effect** is when the amount of gases added to an atmosphere rises above the normal levels expected in the life of a planet. If it continues to increase it can lead to a runaway Greenhouse Effect. It is the Enhanced Greenhouse Effect that scientists are currently worried about.

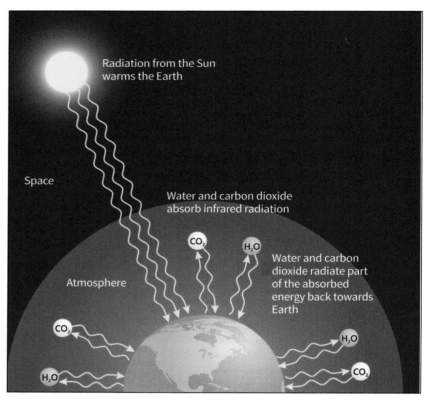

Fig. 09.03.04 The planet scale version of the Greenhouse Effect.

Greenhouse Gases

Demonstration 09.03.02 – The effect of a greenhouse gas

Instructions: Using two thermometers, two glass bowls and Alka Seltzer tablets, your teacher will demonstrate the effect of a **greenhouse gas**. Note the temperature in each thermometer every minute for fifteen minutes. Compare the results with the previous demonstration.

What did you learn?

1. Why are Alka Seltzer tablets used in this demonstration?
2. Does this demonstration show the effect of a greenhouse gas?
3. Explain how this demonstration shows the Enhanced Greenhouse Effect.

✓ **Checkpoint 3**

(a) Using the glass bowl model demonstrated by your teacher, draw an A4 poster explaining the Greenhouse Effect.

(b) Carbon dioxide is added to the atmosphere of greenhouses by professional growers. List two or more reasons why this is done.

(c) Why is the Greenhouse Effect necessary for life on Earth?

(d) The Enhanced Greenhouse Effect will cause Earth's climate to change. Research three changes that could happen and how they will affect the environment.

How powerful each greenhouse gas is depends on how well it can absorb heat energy and how long it lasts in the atmosphere before breaking down. Water is the most powerful greenhouse gas as so much of it is in the atmosphere. But **water vapour** is constantly cooling and falling back to Earth as part of the water cycle. This means that water vapour does not increase the overall temperature of the planet but helps to maintain a steady global temperature. The water in our sweat acts in the same way. It evaporates from our skin when we sweat, taking heat energy from our bodies and so cooling us down.

It is the levels of the other greenhouse gases that can cause environmental damage that scientists are monitoring. Because each gas absorbs heat energy differently and breaks down at different rates, scientists have calculated the **Global Warming Potential** (GWP) of each gas. A molecule of carbon dioxide breaks down after one year in the atmosphere and has a heat energy absorption of 1 GWP. The other gases get a GWP rating compared to carbon dioxide. Except for carbon, the GWP number does not tell you how long it lasts, it only tells you how powerful the other gases are compered to carbon dioxide.

Carbon dioxide is made naturally by all organisms during respiration, so is always present, even in unpolluted air. But most of the carbon dioxide currently in our atmosphere comes from burning fossil fuels or other chemical reactions that release carbon dioxide.

Greenhouse gas	Formula
Water vapour	H_2O
Carbon dioxide	CO_2
Methane	CH_4
Nitrous oxide	N_2O
Ozone	O_3
CFCs	Coolant chemicals that contain fluorine or chlorine

Table 09.03.01 The main greenhouse gases at work in the earth's atmosphere.

Greenhouse gas	Source	GWP
Carbon dioxide CO_2	Burning fossil fuels, respiration	1
Methane CH_4	Decay of plants and animals, digestion	34
Nitrous oxide N_2O	Burning of fossil fuels	298
HFC-134a	CFC coolant	1550
CFC-11	CFC coolant	5350

Table 09.03.02 The Global Warming Power (GWP) of some of the greenhouse gases.

Methane is produced when plant and animal remains decay, which is why it is often found in oil deposits and why landfill sites have pipes to release gas pressure after they are back-filled. It is also produced in enormous amounts by cattle as they digest grass and hay.

Nitrous oxide is produced whenever a fossil fuel is burned in air. Nitrogen from the atmosphere is combined with oxygen during combustion. It is also added to engines to make the combustion happen at a higher temperature.

Chloro-flouro-carbons (CFCs) are a group of carbon compounds that contain fluorine or chlorine but are very useful as coolants because they can absorb a lot of heat energy. Freon was the first CFC and it was used as a coolant for fridges and freezers. CFCs are banned in most circumstances and are being phased out except for a small number of specialist uses. They are responsible for damage to the **ozone layer** and are very strong greenhouse gases, so have a double effect on the atmosphere.

The Ozone Layer

Ozone is an oxygen compound made up of three oxygen atoms with the formula O_3. Natural ozone acts as a protective barrier 20 km above the earth's surface. John Tyndall calculated that the ozone layer absorbs 80% of the UV radiation from the sun. This protects the planet from overheating. Too much UV radiation can cause surface cancers in organisms.

In 1983, Joe Farman, Brian G. Gardiner, and Jon Shanklin discovered that there was a hole in the ozone layer above Antarctica. Initially they were not believed as the results from their weather balloon contradicted almost twenty years of satellite data. Unfortunately it turned out that they were correct. A computer programme had eliminated important readings as anomalies until scientists re-checked the satellite data.

As a result of their discovery, CFCs were quickly banned. Within a few years the hole in the ozone had reduced significantly, but it has still not completely closed and is today still monitored carefully.

 Checkpoint 4

(a) **Is it correct to say that carbon dioxide (CO_2) is the most important greenhouse gas? Explain.**

(b) **Why are greenhouse gases a global problem now but not in the past?**

(c) **If the hole in the ozone layer over the Antarctic had gotten bigger it would have increased the Enhanced Greenhouse Effect significantly. Explain how this is true.**

Anthropogenic Gases

While a certain amount of greenhouse gases are necessary for life on Earth, too much of any or all could have enormously damaging effects on plant and animal life across the planet. Because of the potential for damage to the planet, man-made gases are monitored very carefully. Greenhouse gases, which are man-made or released into the atmosphere because of human activity, are called **anthropogenic gases**.

Anthropogenic Gases: Man-made or caused by human activity.

In 1988 the Intergovernmental Panel on Climate Change (IPCC) was set up by the United Nations to monitor anthropogenic gases in the atmosphere, investigate their causes and suggest ways to reduce their harmful effects.

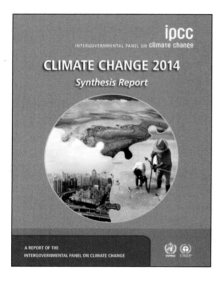 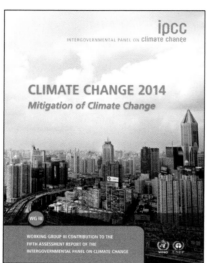 

Fig. 09.03.05 Assessment reports from the IPCC.

R Carbon dioxide (CO_2) has the lowest GWP but it is the most important of the man-made greenhouse gases as it is the most prevalent one in the atmosphere. Scientists have tracked the increasing levels of carbon dioxide back 800 000 years on a graph known as the **Keeling curve**. On this graph, CO_2 emissions show a spike at the start of the Industrial Revolution, when there was an increased use of fossil fuels to meet increased energy needs (*Fig. 09.03.08*). The Keeling curve is named after Charles David Keeling, who started monitoring CO_2 in the atmosphere at the Mauna Loa Observatory, Hawaii, in 1958.

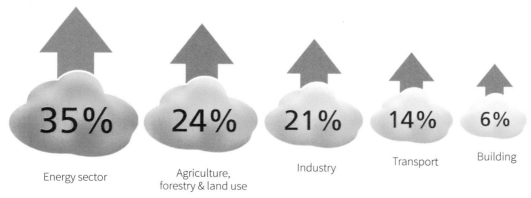

35%	24%	21%	14%	6%
Energy sector	Agriculture, forestry & land use	Industry	Transport	Building

Fig. 09.03.06 The IPCC estimate of anthropogenic greenhouse gases contributed by each sector of industry.

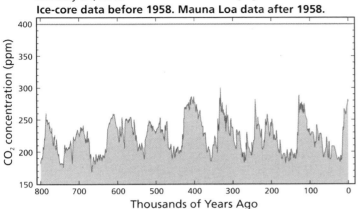

Latest CO₂ reading
January 24, 2015
400.01 ppm
Ice-core data before 1958. Mauna Loa data after 1958.

Fig. 09.03.07 Based on ice-core and rock samples, and weather station readings, this is the Keeling curve of CO₂ in the atmosphere over 800 000 years. Humans have existed for approximately 1.5 million years.

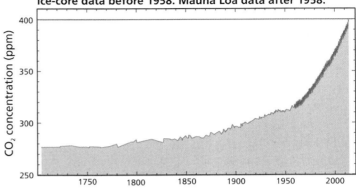

Latest CO₂ reading
January 24, 2015
400.01 ppm
Ice-core data before 1958. Mauna Loa data after 1958.

Fig. 09.03.08 The Keeling curve of CO₂ in the atmosphere since the beginning of the Industrial Revolution. This is the famous 'Hockey Stick graph'.

CHEMISTRY

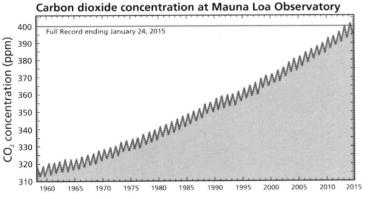

Latest CO₂ reading
January 24, 2015
400.01 ppm
Carbon dioxide concentration at Mauna Loa Observatory

Full Record ending January 24, 2015

Fig. 09.03.09 The Keeling curve of CO₂ in the atmosphere since 1958, taken daily at Mauna Loa Observatory. The CO₂ concentration has repeatedly peaked at 400 ppm (parts per million) or above since June 2014. Scientists believe that persistent readings above 400 ppm could indicate a global temperature rise of more than 2°C.

✓ Checkpoint 5

(a) Check the three Keeling curves. Can you see evidence of cool periods (mini-Ice Ages)? Explain.

(b) Why is the 'Hockey Stick graph' strong proof that CO₂ causes the Enhanced Greenhouse Effect?

(c) One of the Keeling curves shows summer and winter readings. Which curve is it and why does it have that shape?

Global Carbon Budget

The IPCC measures the amount of carbon dioxide in the atmosphere in gigatonnes (Gt). A gigatonne is 1 000 000 000 tonnes. It has been estimated that our planet can cope with a maximum of 2900GtCO₂ if we are to limit the global temperature rise to 2°C. But this can only happen if fossil fuels are reduced and eventually eliminated by the year 2100. Of the amount available to us, 1900GtCO₂ has already been used. The amount left is called the **Global Carbon Budget**.

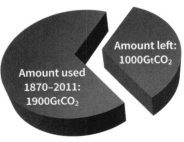

Total Carbon budget: 2900GtCO₂

Amount left: 1000GtCO₂

Amount used 1870–2011: 1900GtCO₂

Fig. 09.03.10 The Global Carbon Budget for a 2°C global temperature rise.

A 2°C temperature rise does not seem very big; in fact, humans would be unable to sense such a small change. So how can a 2°C change be such a problem?

Our planet can cope with major temperature changes over short periods, even periods of a few years, because the planet can use the water cycle and carbon cycle to control temperatures and greenhouses gases over time. But persistently high amounts of greenhouse gases, especially carbon dioxide, do not allow the planet to recover. This is why carbon dioxide levels need to be controlled and reduced. Temperature changes like this cause global warming and climate change as they affect long-term weather patterns.

A permanent 2°C change throughout the planet could cause:

- Some parts of the oceans to become toxic because they have absorbed too much CO_2
- More frequent and longer heat waves, increasing the danger of fatality as well as environmental damage (e.g. forest fires)
- Increased drought
- The melting of large amounts of ice in the Arctic and Antarctic
- Threat of extinction of two-thirds of all species
- Crop failure and therefore food shortages.

Even if massive cuts in fossil fuel use are made immediately, it will take several centuries for CO_2 levels to fall. Cutting emissions stops more CO_2 being added to the atmosphere but does not remove it.

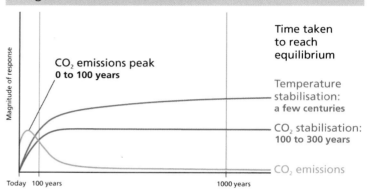

Fig. 09.03.11 CO_2 levels will slowly fall after fossil fuel emissions stop.

Climate Engineering

Other than decreasing fossil fuel use and increasing renewable energy generation, large and deliberate changes to the earth's atmosphere – **climate engineering** – have been suggested. Climate engineering involves two main ideas to reduce the Enhanced Greenhouse Effect:

- Removing CO_2 from the atmosphere
- Reflecting sunlight energy.

CO_2 removal methods	Sunlight reflection methods
Increased forestation	Spray seed clouds with sea spray from misters
Artificial trees to absorb CO_2 from the atmosphere	Spray seed clouds with sulfates from volcanoes, aircraft and balloons
Industrial scrubbers to capture CO_2 from smoke stacks	Place mirrors outside the atmosphere
Genetically modify plants to have deeper roots so that they use up more CO_2 and can access deep water	Cover building roofs, roadways and deserts with bright material
Capture CO_2 and pump it into empty oil and gas reservoirs or deep into the oceans	Genetically engineer plants to be brighter

Table 09.03.03 Climate engineering methods.

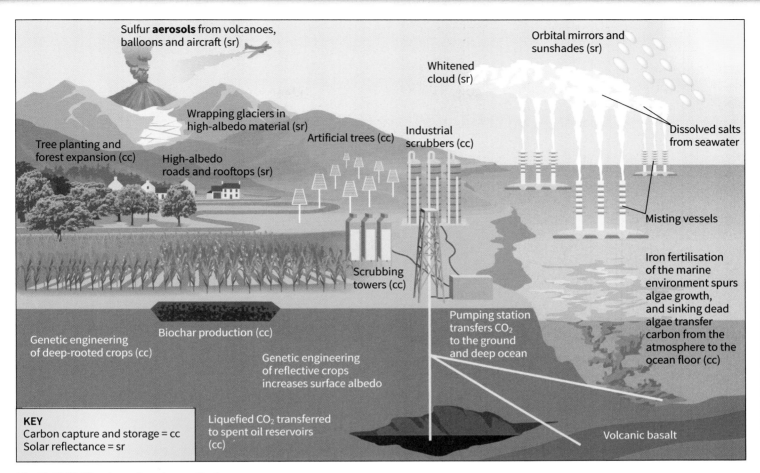

Fig. 09.03.12 Climate engineering methods.

When Mount Pinatubo in the Philippines erupted in 1991, the ash cloud that formed took two years to fall from the atmosphere and caused a 0.6°C drop in mean global temperature for those two years. This is because the ash cloud reflected much solar energy. So artificially creating clouds to reflect sunlight seems like an attractive option in combating global warming, but doing this has a short-term effect and does nothing to remove excess greenhouse gases in the atmosphere.

> ✅ **Checkpoint 6**

List two advantages and two disadvantages of using climate engineering to reduce the Enhanced Greenhouse Effect.

Acid Rain

. . . .

Carbon dioxide (CO_2) occurs in unpolluted air as a product of respiration by plants and animals and from the decay of plants and animals. Combustion of fossil fuels has increased the amount of CO_2 in the atmosphere, which can combine with water vapour to form a weak acid called carbonic acid.

carbon dioxide + water → carbonic acid

$$CO_2 + H_2O \rightarrow H_2CO_3$$

The most destructive types of **acid rain** happen when nitrogen and sulfur gases combine with water vapour. Because they are strong acids, even a dilute solution can cause damage. These acids dissolve stone and cement, and corrode metals. They also wash nutrients out of soils, causing them to become acidic. This can kill plants and even fish. For example, acid rain run-off from mountains surrounding fjords in Norway has caused large fish kills. Forests on the slopes of the fjords have also been damaged.

> **Aerosol:** A suspension of liquid or solid particles in a gas.

> **Acid rain:** A mixture of rain water and pollutants that forms an acid.

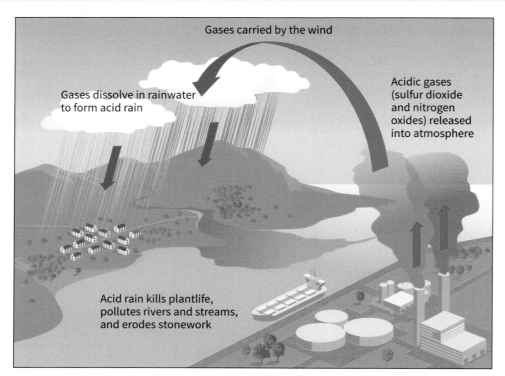

Fig. 09.03.14 Damage to stonework on a church.

Fig. 09.03.13 The Acid Rain Cycle.

Fig. 09.03.15 Pollution clouds forming over an oil refinery on Curacao in the Caribbean.

Fig. 09.03.16 A 'dirty thunderstorm' at the Eyjafjallajökull eruption, Iceland, 17 April 2010.

Nitrogen dioxide (NO_2) is created by burning fuels in vehicle engines, and nitrogen oxide (NO) is created by lightning reacting with oxygen and nitrogen in the atmosphere. Together these gases are known as NO_x. When mixed with rain droplets they form nitric acid.

Nitrogen dioxide + water → nitric acid + nitrogen oxide

$$NO_2 \quad + H_2O \quad \rightarrow \quad HNO_3 \quad + \quad NO$$

Sulfur dioxide (SO_2) is released during volcano eruptions but is also created by burning fuels in vehicle engines. Most of the NO_x and SO_2 in the atmosphere is man-made pollution. When mixed with rain droplets it forms sulfuric acid. Both of these are strong acids.

Sulfur dioxde + water → sulfuric acid

$$SO_2 \quad + H_2O \quad \rightarrow \quad H_2SO_4$$

Catalytic converters reduce the amount of NO_2 from vehicle exhausts, but the best way to reduce all three gases from being converted into acid rain is to reduce the burning of fossil fuels.

Volcanoes are the only combined natural source of SO_2 and NO in the atmosphere. When they erupt, volcanoes throw out large amounts of dust and sulfur gases. The dust can cause 'dirty thunderstorms', creating lightning which produced the NO.

Investigation 09.03.01: Testing and comparing acid rain

Instructions: Compare a sample of vinegar, rainwater and water from three other sources by placing a stick of white chalk into each sample.

What did you learn?

1. Why can sticks of chalk be used to test for acid rain?
2. How can you ensure that this is a fair test?
3. Why should the chalk be white?
4. Can you suggest another substance that can be used for this comparison? Is this substance better than chalk sticks? Justify your answer.

WHAT I HAVE LEARNED...

- The difference between weather and climate.
- How the Carbon Cycle and Water Cycle help maintain a stable atmosphere.
- The importance of the Greenhouse Effect.
- How to show the Greenhouse Effect using simple equipment.
- The main greenhouse gases and their effects on the environment.
- To specify the differences between the Greenhouse Effect and the Enhanced Greenhouse Effect.
- How to show the Enhanced Greenhouse Effect using a simple model.
- The importance of the ozone layer and how the hole in the ozone layer causes climate change.
- How acid rain is formed and its effects on the environment.
- How to test for acid rain in rainwater and compare it with other water sources.
- That the Keeling curves show proof of climate change.
- The causes of global climate change and possible ways to reduce large changes to the climate.

Question Time

Copy and Complete

In this unit I learned that weather is about _____ - _____ changes to the atmosphere. Climate is about _____ - _____ changes to the atmosphere. The _____ Cycle is the natural system of carbon recycling that happens on Earth due to combustion, respiration and _____ reactions. The _____ Cycle is the natural system that keeps the balance of water in the oceans, lakes and rivers and _____. The _____ layer protects the earth from too much __-_____/_____ radiation. The _____ Effect is the _____ effect of _____ in the atmosphere that keep Earth_____. The Enhanced_____ Effect means that _____ _____ gases have been added to the atmosphere. Something which is man-made or caused by human activity is _____. Deliberate and _____-scale changes to the atmosphere to _____ the effects of climate change is called __-_____. _____ rain is formed from _____ and combustion fumes and causes the _____ of metals and stonework.

Questions

1. True or False: The Greenhouse Effect is not necessary for life on Earth. Why?
2. What natural system controls carbon dioxide in our atmosphere? Why do scientists believe that it is out of balance?
3. True or False: Global warming causes climate change. Justify your answer.
4. Create a table listing five changes to the earth's climate and how they might affect the environment
5. CFC compounds have two major effects on the environment. What are these effects and why are they important to life on Earth?
6. (R) An experiment was performed to investigate the effect of temperature on the solubility of carbon dioxide in water. The data obtained from this experiment is given in *Table 09.03.04*.

Solubility of CO_2 (g of CO_2 per kg of water)	3.4	2.5	1.7	1.4	1.0	0.8	0.6
Temperature (°C)	0.0	10.0	20.0	30.0	40.0	50.0	60.0

Table 09.03.04.

(i) Draw a graph of solubility against temperature using the data from *Table 09.03.04*. A smooth curve is required.

CHEMISTRY

(ii)   From the graph, estimate the temperature at which the solubility of CO_2 is 2 g per kg of water.

(iii) Usually the solubility of a solid increases with increasing temperature. The solubility of a gas decreases as the temperature increases. Suggest a reason why this decrease happens.

(iv) Oceans are becoming more acidic as CO_2 from the atmosphere dissolves in it. How might this affect marine life?

(v)   If global warming continues and ocean temperatures continue to rise, CO_2 will stop dissolving into the oceans. Does this mean that if we allow the oceans to continue heating we will solve the ocean acidification problem? Give reasons for your answer.

7. The bar chart in *Fig. 09.03.17* shows data collected by Charles David Keeling in ten-year gaps. Your friends believe that climate change is temporary and won't have a permanent effect on the planet. Use the information in the bar chart to write a paragraph to convince them that climate change could have serious, long-term effects on the planet.

Inquiry

A   Climate change sceptics believe that the 'Little Ice Age' shows that the current higher level of the Greenhouse Effect is temporary. **How** does the evidence of the Little Ice Age support this idea? Do you agree with this notion? Justify your answer.

B   Cement production is a major part of the carbon footprint of Ireland. **What** is a carbon footprint? Why does Ireland need to monitor its cement production? What is your carbon footprint? **Explain** why you think carbon footprints might not be a good way to make people aware of their role in climate change.

C   Climate scientists are worried that the changes in the Arctic ice sheet could have global consequences. **Design** a poster to explain why scientists are worried by this.

Changes in CO_2 levels in 10-year periods

Fig. 09.03.17 Changes in CO_2 levels in ten-year periods.

Measuring Physical Quantities

Learning Outcomes

PWLO 1. Select and use appropriate measuring instruments.

PWLO 2. Identify and measure length, time, area and volume.

NSLO 2. Recognise questions that are appropriate for scientific investigation, pose testable hypotheses, and evaluate and compare strategies for investigating hypotheses.

NSLO 3. Design, plan and conduct investigations; explain how reliability, accuracy, precision, fairness, safety, ethics and a selection of suitable equipment have been considered.

R Teacher's reference

KEYWORDS

area
density
error
force
length
mass
measurement
metre stick
opisometer
physical
 quantity
quantified
SI units
temperature
thermometer
time
trundle wheel
Vernier
 callipers
volume

LEARNING INTENTIONS

At the end of this unit you should:

1. Be able to measure length, mass, time and temperature.
2. Be able to perform simple calculations based on measurements.
3. Understand that units of measurement follow the SI system.
4. Know the standard units for different physical quantities.

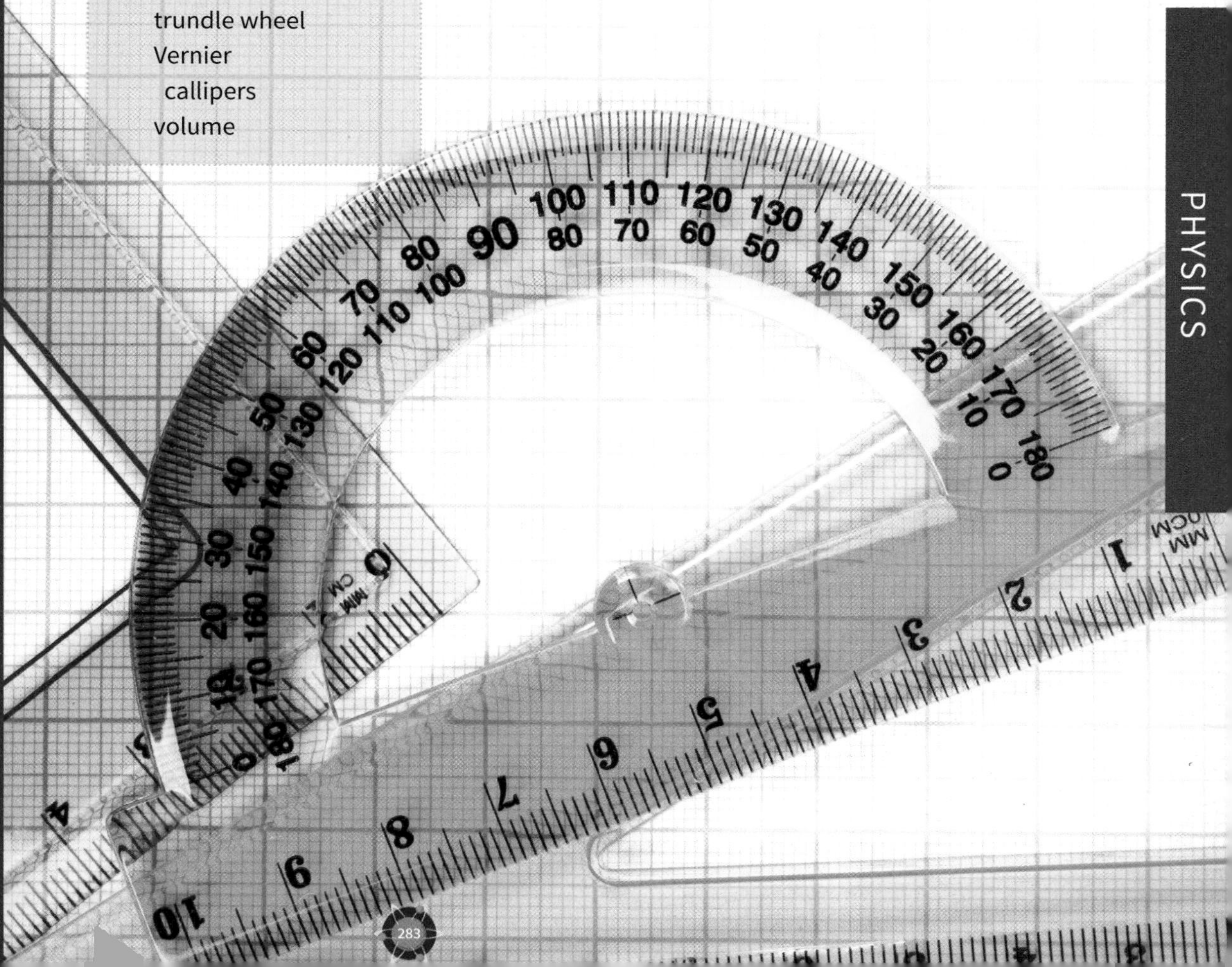

PHYSICS

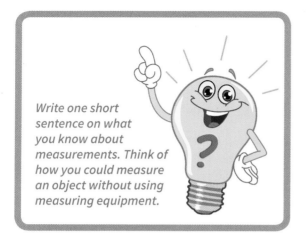

Write one short sentence on what you know about measurements. Think of how you could measure an object without using measuring equipment.

Did you know?
In ancient Egypt, humans used their forearms, hands and fingers to measure objects. So instead of saying Ahmed was '6 foot tall', they probably would have said that Ahmed was '4 and a half forearms'. The problem with this was that these units of measurement were different wherever you went, as everyone's forearms, hands and fingers were different lengths!
It wasn't until the French Revolution in 1790 that the term 'metre' first came into use. In France, it was estimated that there were up to a quarter of a million different units in use, and only a few of them were standard across all of France. This meant that in some provinces you would get more money for selling your land because of a wide difference in how big an acre was. This added to the already growing tension in France. The metre was therefore brought into use and was calculated as one ten-millionth the distance from the North Pole to the equator.

NAME	EGYPTIAN NAME	EQUIVALENT EGYPTIAN VALUES	APPROX. METRIC EQUIVALENT
Finger	djeba	1 finger = 1/4 palm	1.875 cm
Palm	shesep	1 palm = 4 fingers	7.5 cm
Hand	drt	1 hand = 5 fingers	9.38 cm
Fist	3mm	1 fist = 6 fingers	11.25 cm
Span (small)	pedj-sheser	1 small span = 3 palms = 12 fingers	22.5 cm
Span (large)	pedj-aa	1 large span = 3.5 palms = 14 fingers	26.25 cm
Djeser	djeser	1 djeser = 4 palms = 16 fingers = 1 ft	30 cm
Remen	remen	1 remen = 5 palms = 20 fingers	37.5 cm
Short cubit	meh nedjes	1 short cubit = 6 palms = 24 fingers	45 cm
Royal cubit	meh niswt	1 royal cubit = 7 palms = 28 fingers	52.5 cm
Pole	nbiw	1 nbiw = 6 hands = 8 palms = 32 fingers	60 cm
Rod of cord	khet	1 rod of cord = 100 cubits	52.5 m
River measure	iteru	1 iteru = 20 000 cubits	10.5 km

Fig. 10.01.01 The Ancient Egyptian system of measurement. Notice how they used physical units such as their finger and palm to measure objects.

Do you know of anything that is still measured in hands?

Investigation 10.01.01: Basic measurements

Equipment: A ruler, a desk and your hand.

Instructions: In pairs, measure the length of your desk. One person uses their hand, the other uses a ruler. Write down your measurements. Now swap around so that the person who used the ruler now uses their hand.

What did you learn?

1. Was there any difference between your measurements?
2. Compare your hand measurement with the others in the class.
3. Which graph would you use to represent this data?

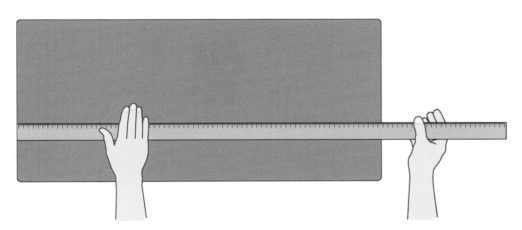

Physical Quantities

To learn about measurement, the first thing we need to do is understand the term **physical quantity**. This is the scientific term for a measurable characteristic, for example **length**, **time** and **temperature**. Can you think of other physical quantities? Can you think of anything that is not a physical quantity (something that cannot be measured)?

Another important word that you will come across is **quantified**. This is the scientific word for saying an object has been measured. You use quantification in your everyday life:

- He stole <u>all</u> of my lunch money.
- I only watched <u>half</u> of the match last night.
- <u>Sixteen</u>? He bought sixteen bottles of coke?
- I only attempted <u>part A</u> of last night's homework.

All of the underlined terms represent quantification. In the above examples, the person is giving specific quantities of the objects in question, i.e. lunch money, the match, coke, homework.

With this new knowledge we can begin looking at **measurement**.

> **Physical Quantity:** The scientific term for a measurable characteristic, for example length, time and temperature.

> **Quantified:** The scientific word for saying an object has been measured.

PHYSICS

✓ Checkpoint 1

(a) What is a physical quantity? Name five.
(b) Write sentences to quantify the following items: bread, water, cereal, toast.

Measurement

What is **measurement**? Why is it important? How do I measure an object? These seem like simple questions. However, in science, these questions are the foundation of our subject. To measure something is to give a numerical value (a number) to a physical quantity (e.g. height):

John is six feet tall. Jack is 186 centimetres tall. Mary is 1.5 metres tall.

Notice how there are three different units of measurement given for the same physical quantity, i.e. **length** (height). Which one is right? Or are they all right?

> **Measurement:** Giving a numerical value to a physical quantity.

SI Units

In science we need to make sure that all measurements are given in the same units. For this, scientists created the *Système International d'Unités,* or International System of Units (**SI Units**). This system is an updated version of the metric system, one of two main systems for measuring distance and weight (the other being the imperial system). These SI units are the standard units of measurements for specific physical quantities. Below is a table containing all the SI units.

Physical Quantity	Name of SI Unit	Symbol	Other commonly used units	Conversion
length (l or s)	metre	m	kilometre (km), centimetre (cm), millimetre (mm), micrometre (μm)	1 cm = 10 mm 1 m = 100 cm 1 km = 1000 m
time (t)	second	s	minute (min), hour (h); note that you may also be given days and years	1 day = 86 400 s
mass* (m)	kilogram	kg	gram (g)	1 kg = 1000 g
current* (I)	ampere	A		
temperature* (T)	kelvin	K	For your course you will deal mostly with Celsius (°C)	0 K = −273°C
area (A)	square metre	m²	centimetres squared (cm²) kilometres squared (km²)	
volume (V)	cubic metre	m³	litre (L), cubic centimetre (cm³)	1 L = 1000 cm³
speed* (v or u)	metre per second	m/s	centimetres per second (cm/s) kilometres per hour (km/h)	
density (ρ)	kilogram per cubic metre	kg/m³	g/cm³	1 kg/m³ = 0.0001 g/cm³
force* (F)	newton	N	kilograms metres per second squared (kg m/s²)	
pressure* (P or p)	pascal	Pa	N/m²	
velocity* (v or u)	metre per second	m/s	centimetres per second (cm/s) kilometres per hour (km/h)	
acceleration* (a)	metre per second squared	m/s² or m/s/s		
potential difference* (V)	voltage	V	joule per coulomb (J/C)	
resistance* (R)	ohm	Ω		
electrical power*	watt	W	kilowatt (kW)	

Table 10.01.01 The SI system of measurement (*we will learn about these in later chapters).

Checkpoint 2

(a) Define measurement and give two examples.

(b) Why were SI units created? Do you think they are a good idea? Why?

(c) Choose four SI units. Name them, name their units of measurement and list at least one alternative measurement for each of them.

(d) Thinking back to John, Jack and Mary, which expression of their height is correct?

Measuring Length

There are many instruments you can use for measuring length. How many can you name?

The most commonly used are a ruler (15 cm or 30 cm) and a **metre stick** (1 m) for straight lines, an **opisometer** (cm) and **trundle wheel** (m) for curved lines, and a **Vernier callipers** for measuring the thickness of objects (usually mm or cm).

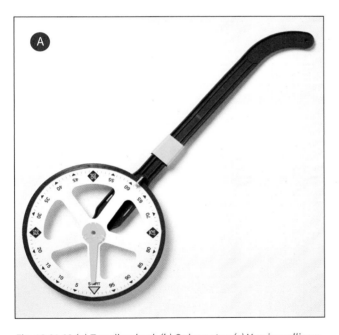

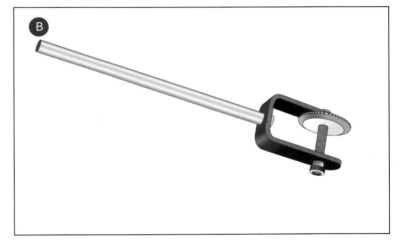

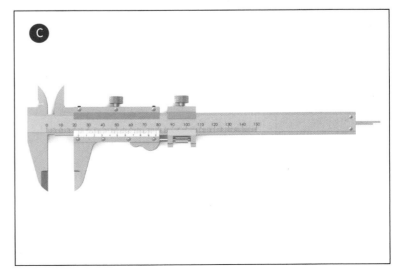

Fig. 10.01.02 (a) Trundle wheel; (b) Opisometer; (c) Vernier callipers.

PHYSICS

Investigation 10.01.02: **Selecting appropriate measuring tools**

Equipment: An opisometer, a trundle wheel, a ruler, a metre stick and a Vernier callipers.

Instructions: Copy and complete *Table 10.01.02* below (you can add your own objects to measure). Measure each of the objects using the available measuring instruments in your lab and select the unit of measurement. Select the tool you believe to be the best for measuring each object.

What to measure	Instrument to use	Unit of measurement
Length of a pencil		
Length of a book		
Thickness of a strand of hair		
The distance of a river on a map		
The distance between your house and the school		
Another object to measure		
Another object to measure		

Table 10.01.02.

What did you learn?

1. When considering which instruments to use, remember that the question asks you to choose 'the best' for measuring each object/distance. There are two factors we must consider: 'ease of use' and 'error'. These might be considered good reasons not to use a 15 cm ruler to measure a long distance.
2. Can you think of an item to measure in which two or more of the measuring tools mentioned in *Table 10.01.02* might be appropriate?

Error

When we measure something it is always possible we will make slight mistakes. These mistakes are called **errors**.

Consider having to measure someone with a measuring tape and then with a ruler. Which would lead to less error?

Error: How far off the correct value you are.

Checkpoint 3

Copy and complete *Table 10.01.03*. Change your chosen instrument from *Investigation 10.01.02* if you feel another one could reduce the error in your measurement. Determine which instrument you think would have the highest error for the stated measurement.

What to measure	Instrument to use	Instrument with highest error
Length of a pencil		
Length of a book		
Thickness of a strand of hair		
The distance of a river on a map		
The distance between your house and the school		

Table 10.01.03.

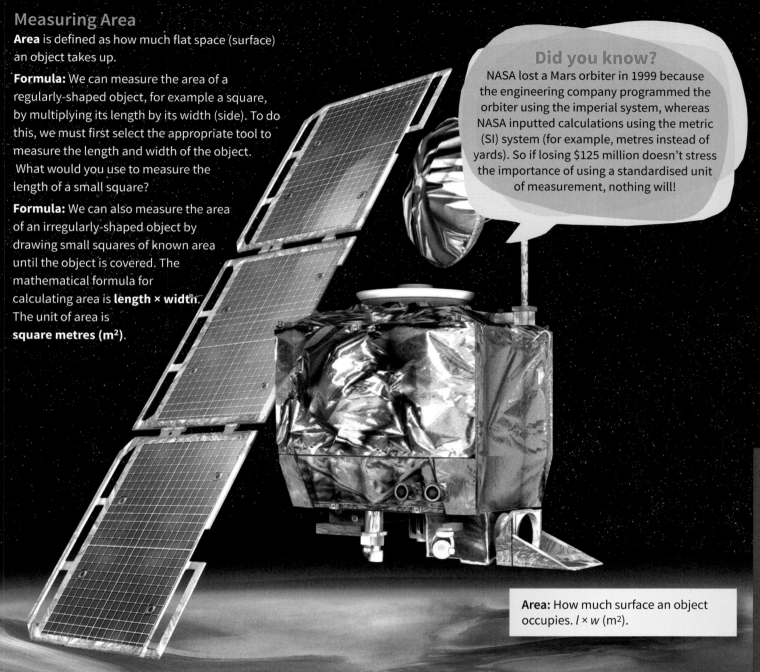

Measuring Area

Area is defined as how much flat space (surface) an object takes up.

Formula: We can measure the area of a regularly-shaped object, for example a square, by multiplying its length by its width (side). To do this, we must first select the appropriate tool to measure the length and width of the object. What would you use to measure the length of a small square?

Formula: We can also measure the area of an irregularly-shaped object by drawing small squares of known area until the object is covered. The mathematical formula for calculating area is **length × width**. The unit of area is **square metres (m²)**.

Did you know?

NASA lost a Mars orbiter in 1999 because the engineering company programmed the orbiter using the imperial system, whereas NASA inputted calculations using the metric (SI) system (for example, metres instead of yards). So if losing $125 million doesn't stress the importance of using a standardised unit of measurement, nothing will!

Area: How much surface an object occupies. $l \times w$ (m²).

PHYSICS

Fig. 10.01.03 A Mars Climate Orbiter. Losing one of these will set you back a few million dollars.

Investigation 10.01.03: **Measuring the area of your hand**

Equipment: Your hand, a pencil, some graph paper and a ruler.

Instructions: Using the equipment as listed, design an investigation to calculate the area of your hand.

What did you learn?

1. Compare the area of your hand to the person beside you. Is it the same, bigger or smaller?
2. Create a table of the hand sizes in your class.

Measuring Volume

If we want to measure the **volume** of a regularly-shaped object, e.g. a sugar cube, we simply multiply **length x width x height**. The unit of volume is **cubic metres (m³)**.

But what happens if an object is irregularly shaped?

Volume: How much space an object takes up. *l* x *w* x *h* (m³).

 Investigation 10.01.04: **Measuring the volume of an irregularly-shaped object**

Equipment: A graduated cylinder, an irregularly-shaped object, an overflow can and a beaker.

Instructions: Using the equipment as listed, design an investigation to find the volume of an irregularly-shaped object.

What did you learn?

1. Could this method be used to find the volume of a regularly-shaped object?
2. Suggest one change you would have to make if your irregularly-shaped object did not fit into the overflow can.

⊘ **Checkpoint 4**

(a) Calculate the area of an item in your schoolbag.
(b) Calculate the volume of an item in your schoolbag.

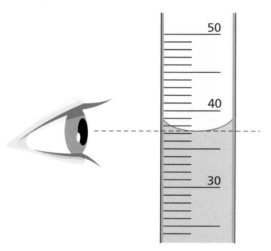

Fig. 10.01.04 Reading the meniscus. It is important when noting the volume of a liquid to read from the bottom of the semi-circular dip in the liquid, known as the meniscus. To do this accurately, you must get down to eye level with the liquid.

Did you know?

Archimedes, an ancient Greek philosopher, was tasked by King Hiero II of Syracuse to determine if a crown he had commissioned was made of pure gold. Suspecting it had been made out of a mixture of gold and silver, the king asked Archimedes to confirm this suspicion without destroying the crown.
One day when climbing into his bath, Archimedes noticed that the water level rose as he got into it. Suddenly it became clear how he could measure the gold without destroying the crown. Archimedes used a system of pulleys which allowed him to measure the displacement of water (amount of water 'pushed out') and the mass of the crown to figure out if it was fake. Legend has it that Archimedes was so excited about this discovery that he ran down the street naked shouting 'Eureka'!

Fig. 10.01.05 A Eureka moment!

Force, density and temperature will be dealt with in detail elsewhere, but we will look at them briefly now.

Measuring Force

To measure **force** we use a spring balance, as shown in *Fig. 10.01.06*.

When a force is applied to the spring balance, the spring inside extends and gives a reading. You should keep in mind that the spring balance measure is newtons (N) because it is measuring weight/force/gravity and not mass (kg).

Calculating Density

Formula: To calculate the **density** of an object, you must find the **mass** and volume of that object. This is found by first getting the mass of the object on a balance. The object is then placed in an overflow can, and the volume of liquid that overflows is measured. The unit of density is kilogram per cubic metre (kg/m³). Use this formula to calculate density:

Density = mass/volume (kg/m³)

15.6 g

Fig. 10.01.07 (a) First, measure the mass of the object.

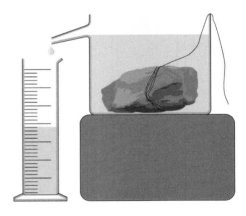

Fig. 10.01.07 (b) Second we need to find the volume of the object, just like we did in Investigation 10.01.04.

Fig. 10.01.06 The spring in the balance is extended when an object is hung from the hook.

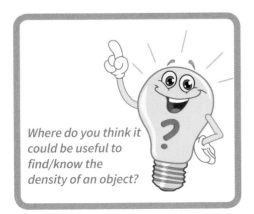

Where do you think it could be useful to find/know the density of an object?

PHYSICS

Investigation 10.01.05: **The diet cola challenge**

Equipment: A container filled with water, a can of regular cola, a can of diet cola, and some masking tape.

Instructions: Cover the outside of two cans of cola – one regular, one diet – with masking tape so that the labels are covered and one cannot be distinguished from the other. Fill up a container with water and place the cans in the water.

What did you learn?
1. How do you know which can is diet and which can is regular? Explain your answer.
2. Is this a fair test?
3. Does the amount of masking tape used change the density of the can?

Measuring Temperature

Temperature is measured with a **thermometer**. The two most common ones you will use are the digital thermometer and the alcohol thermometer.

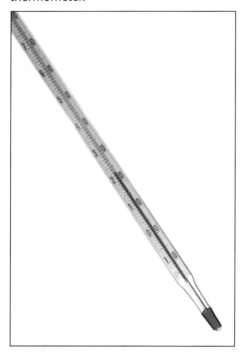

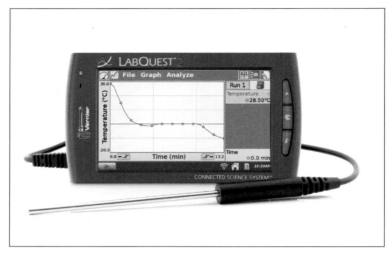

Fig. 10.01.08 A digital thermometer (above) and an alcohol thermometer (left).

Why is a digital thermometer more definite than an alcohol thermometer?

How to read a thermometer

Digital

Place the thermometer into the object you are measuring and the display will give you the reading.

Alcohol

Place the thermometer into the object and allow the liquid in the thermometer to rise. You can then read off the scale on the thermometer. (You will learn more about alcohol thermometers in *Unit 11.2*).

🔍 **Investigation 10.01.06: How to measure objects using a thermometer**

Equipment: Five beakers containing:
    (i) Water from a cold tap
    (ii) Water from a hot tap
    (iii) Boiling water from a kettle
    (iv) Tea with milk
    (v) Water from the fridge.

Instructions: Using the equipment as listed, design an investigation to compare the temperatures of different liquids.

What did you learn?

1. Using the results from your investigation, represent your data in a table and place them in order of hottest to coldest.
2. What effect (if any) does milk have when added to boiling water from a kettle.
3. What precautions did you take to ensure your measurements were correct in each instance?
4. Write one safety precaution you must take when performing this investigation.

°C

Important!
When heating a liquid, it is vital you stir the liquid around. Otherwise you will get 'hot spots' and the liquid will not rise in temperature evenly. This will lead to errors in readings.

Fig. 10.01.09 An alcohol thermometer reading 20°C.

 **Checkpoint 5**

(a) What apparatus would you use to measure force?

(b) Which two actions are you required to perform to calculate the density of an object?

(c) Name two occasions when it would be useful to use a digital thermometer.

WHAT I HAVE LEARNED...

- A physical quantity is a scientific term for a measurable characteristic.
- When an object is measured we say it has been quantified.
- Measurement is giving a numerical value to a physical quantity.
- SI units are our standard units of measurement.
- There can be error in measurement.
- The importance of carefully selecting the appropriate measuring tool for each measurement.
- To accurately measure various objects using a variety of instruments.
- To be aware of the standard units in each physical quantity.

 ## Question Time

Copy and Complete

In this unit I learned that the scientific term for a _____ characteristic is _____ _____. Examples of these include time, _____ and _____. In order to ensure everyone used the same units for measurements, the *Système International d'Unités*, or __ _____ , were developed. Length is measured in _____, the symbol of which is m. However, length can also be measured in smaller units called _____ (cm), and also millimetres (__). ____ is measured in seconds (_). Mass is measured in _____ and its symbol is __. I also learned that area is how much flat space an object _____. Also, _____ is the amount of space an object takes up.

Questions

1. Define a physical quantity.
2. Define measurement.
3. Explain what 'quantified' means.
4. Compose five sentences in which a physical quantity is quantified, for example: 'He stole <u>all</u> of my lunch money.'

5. Copy and complete *Table 10.01.04*, selecting an appropriate measuring tool for each task.

Objective	Tool
Measure the height of a student in class	
Measure the length of someone's stride	
Measure the distance from your school to your home	

Table 10.01.04.

Inquiry

A **Suggest** three methods for calculating the area of this book. Name the tools you would use and why you would use them. Then **decide** which method was the most accurate and which was the fastest. Which method gave the closest result in the fastest time?

B When buying shoes, you must consider your shoe size in your purchase. **Explain** how shoe size is determined. Do you think this generalisation is accurate for all types of feet and shoes? Can you **recommend** an alternative way to measure shoe size?

C Ask your parents and/or grandparents what units they used for measurement when they were in school. **Write** a brief paragraph about these units, including their use today (if they are still used) and try to convert them into SI units.

D **Design** a poster/presentation about the life and times of Archimedes and his contributions to science and society today.

E **Research** how very small distances (atomic diameter) and very large distances (distance to the moon) are measured.

PHYSICS

10.2 Motion

Learning Outcomes

PWLO 1. Select and use appropriate measuring tools.
PWLO 2. Identify and measure/ calculate length, time, speed and acceleration.
NSLO 2. Recognise questions that are appropriate for scientific investigation, pose testable hypotheses, and evaluate and compare strategies for investigating hypotheses.
NSLO 3. Design, plan and conduct investigations; explain how reliability, accuracy, precision, fairness, safety, ethics **and a selection of suitable equipment have been considered.**
NSLO 4. Produce and select data (qualitatively/ quantitatively), critically analyse data to identify patterns and relationships, identify anomalous observations, **draw and justify conclusions.**
NSLO 5. Review and reflect on the skills and thinking used in carrying out investigations, and apply learning and skills to solving problems in unfamiliar contexts.

R Teacher's reference

KEYWORDS

acceleration
distance
distance–time graph
rate of change
speed
time
velocity
velocity–time graph

LEARNING INTENTIONS

At the end of this unit you should:

1. Be able to state the relationship between speed, velocity and acceleration.
2. Be able to draw and interpret distance–time graphs.
3. Be able to draw and interpret velocity–time graphs.
4. Be able to calculate the speed, velocity and acceleration of objects.

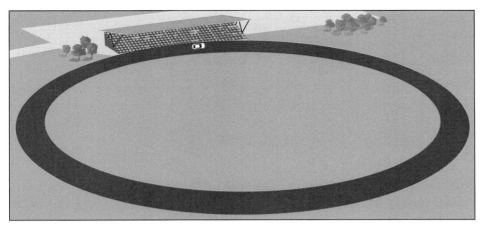

Fig. 10.02.01 Is this car changing its speed, its velocity or its acceleration?

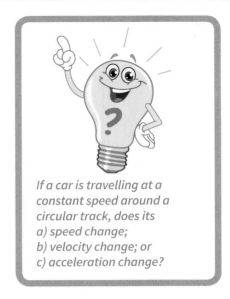

If a car is travelling at a constant speed around a circular track, does its
a) speed change;
b) velocity change; or
c) acceleration change?

In this unit you will be required to change between different SI units. You will find some questions where metres (m) need to change to kilometres (km), and instead of metres per second (m/s) for speed, you'll see kilometres per hour (km/h). You will also have to convert **time** from minutes (min) and hours (h) into seconds (s). *Table 10.02.01* will help you with these conversions.

Given unit	SI unit	Conversion	Mathematical
kilometre (km)	metre (m)	Multiply kilometres by 1000 to give m	km × 1000 = m
minute (min)	second (s)	Multiply minutes by 60 to give seconds	min × 60 = s
hour (h)	second (s)	Multiply hours by 60 to give minutes, then multiply by 60 again to give seconds	h × 60 × 60 = s
kilometre per hour (km/h)	metre per second (m/s)	Multiply km/h by 1000, then divide this answer by 60 × 60	km/h × 1000/(60 × 60)

Table 10.02.01 SI unit conversion table. It is worth noting that 'kilo' before anything means it is in thousands.

Speed, Distance and Time

You probably think you know what **speed**, **distance** and **time** are. However, in science there is a formal definition for speed. Note how the formal definition differs from your understanding of the word.

> **Speed:** The distance an object travels in one unit of time. It can also be described as the **rate of change** of distance with respect to time. Unit: metre per second (m/s).

Distance and time can also be defined, and you might be surprised (or not!) by their formal definitions.

> **Distance:** The length of space between two points. Unit: metre (m).

> **Time:** A universal unit of measurement through which we measure events in the past, present and future. Unit: second (s).

PHYSICS

R **Formula:** Speed is calculated by dividing time by distance. An easy way to remember the formula is by using the **Dad's Silly Triangle** rule. The unit of distance is the metre (m). The unit of time is the second (s). So if we wish to calculate speed we use:

$$\text{Speed} = \frac{\text{Distance}}{\text{Time}} = \frac{\text{metres}}{\text{seconds}} = \text{m/s}$$

Fig. 10.02.02 Dad's Silly Triangle.

This handy formula can be used to calculate the average speed of a sprinter. It is average speed because we cannot assume the sprinter is always running at the same speed throughout the race. Why can we not assume this? Let us look at the fastest man in the world (for the time being!), Usain Bolt.
Formula: Bolt holds the world record for the 100 m sprint. He completed it in a time of 9.58 s. So to calculate his speed we use the following formula:

$$\text{Speed} = \frac{\text{Distance}}{\text{Time}} = \frac{100 \text{ m}}{9.58 \text{ s}} = 10.44 \text{ m/s}$$

This means that on average he ran 10.44 metres every second. We can compare that result to this author's personal best, who has run 100 m in 11.2 seconds. So let's calculate the average speed:

$$\text{Speed} = \frac{\text{Distance}}{\text{Time}} = \frac{100 \text{ m}}{11.2 \text{ s}} = 8.93 \text{ m/s}$$

This means that, on average and at his best, this author ran 8.93 metres every second ... and is not going to challenge Usain Bolt any time soon.

You can find your own average speed over 100 m by asking a friend to time you sprinting over the distance with a stopwatch.

🔍 **Investigation 10.02.01: To calculate the average speed of three wind-up toys**

Equipment: Three wind-up toys, a long, smooth surface and a stopwatch.
Instructions: Calculate the average speed of three wind-up toys.

> *What did you learn?*
> 1. How would you make sure this was a fair test?
> 2. Write a report on your experiment.
> 3. Which toy was the fastest? Can you explain why?

✓ **Checkpoint 1**

(a) What is the formula for calculating distance?
(b) In what units are speed, distance and time measured?
(c) Would it be a fair test to run 10 m to calculate your average speed for 100 m? Why/why not?
(d) Calculate the speed of a person walking 100 m in 60 s.
(e) Calculate the speed of a person running 200 m in 24 s.
(f) How long does it take a car to travel 7 km at a speed of 14 m/s?
(g) How far will a person walk in 1 hour if they walk at a speed of 1.5 m/s?
(h) Calculate the speed of a car travelling 2 km in 45 seconds.
(i) Calculate the speed of a car travelling 10 km in 15 minutes.
(j) How long does it take a truck to travel 15 km if it has a speed of 80 km/h?
(k) How far can a person get if they run at a speed of 8 m/s for 1 h and 10 min?
(l) Compare the speed of the cars in (h) and (i).

Velocity

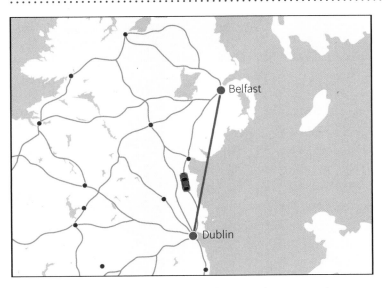

Fig. 10.02.03 *If you are asked to give the velocity, make sure you give the direction as well as the speed.*

Velocity is similar to speed, but the one key difference is that you must give the **direction** as well as the speed. This means you must state the speed at which an object, e.g. a ship, is going, as well as the direction in which it is going, e.g. north.

Formula: Calculating velocity is similar to calculating speed:

$$\text{Velocity} = \frac{\text{Distance}}{\text{Time}} = \frac{\text{metres}}{\text{seconds}} = \text{m/s}$$

You must ensure when calculating velocity that you give the direction with the SI unit. For example, if you are asked for the velocity of a car travelling from Dublin to Belfast at 26 m/s, then you must also state the direction, i.e. 26 m/s north. When asked to calculate the average velocity, it is not necessary to give the direction.

> **Velocity:** Speed in a given direction.
> Unit: metre per second (m/s).

PHYSICS

Checkpoint 2

(a) A person walks north for 190 m. They walk this distance in 24 seconds. What is their velocity?

(b) Calculate the velocity of a rollercoaster if it covers 40 m in 1.5 s.

(c) Which is faster: this rollercoaster in part (b) or a car covering 1 km in 35 s? What is the speed of this car in km/h?

(d) A car travels from Dublin to Galway – a distance of 210 km – in 2 h and 5 min. What is the velocity of the car?

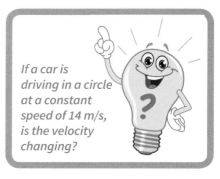
If a car is driving in a circle at a constant speed of 14 m/s, is the velocity changing?

Acceleration

Acceleration is the speeding up or slowing down of an object and indicates a change in velocity in any way (not just an object speeding up, as we commonly understand acceleration to mean). If an object is speeding up we say it is accelerating; if it is slowing down we say it is decelerating. Acceleration can also change when we change direction.

Acceleration: The change in velocity over time, or the rate of change of velocity with respect to time.

For example, a car going around a circular track changes direction as it goes around the bend. So even if the speedometer of the car reads 30 km/h, the acceleration of the car is changing due to the change in direction.

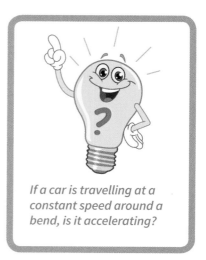
If a car is travelling at a constant speed around a bend, is it accelerating?

Formula: The unit of acceleration is metre per second squared (m/s² or m/s/s). We can represent this mathematically as follows:

$$\text{Acceleration} = \frac{\text{Final velocity} - \text{Initial velocity}}{\text{Time taken}}$$

$$\text{Acceleration} = \frac{\text{Change in velocity}}{\text{Time taken}}$$

For example:

The Bugatti Veyron can reach 0–100 km/h (27.78 m/s) in 2.5 s. To calculate the acceleration we can use the formula here:

$$\text{Acceleration} = \frac{\text{Final velocity} - \text{Initial velocity}}{\text{Time taken}} = \frac{27.78 - 0}{2.5\ s} = 11.12\ \text{m/s}^2$$

✓ Checkpoint 3

(a) Which of the following three examples involves acceleration?
  (i) A car changing its velocity from 10 m/s to 14 m/s.
  (ii) A car travelling at a constant velocity.
  (iii) A car changing its velocity from 14 m/s to 10 m/s.

(b) In *Table 10.02.02* you see a list of animals and their top speeds. These are not the speeds of these animals in nature. These are the speeds of the animals if they were the size of a human. Use the table to answer these questions.
  (i) Which animal is the fastest?
  (ii) Which animal is the slowest?
  (iii) Explain, in your own words, why you think the mouse is as fast as the cheetah, according to the table.
  (iv) Suggest one possible method for calculating the speed of the animals in their natural habitat. State how you would ensure it is a fair test.

(c) A car starting from rest accelerates to 15 m/s in 4 s. What is the acceleration of the car?

(d) A car is moving at 27 m/s when it slams on the breaks and comes to a stop 1.2 s later. What is the acceleration of the car?

Animal	Land/air/sea	Top speed
African bush elephant	Land	10.4 km/h
Cheetah	Land	160 km/h
Mouse	Land	160 km/h
Mallard	Air	210 km/h
Pigeon	Air	156 km/h
White-throated needletail (bird)	Air	805 km/h
Bottlenose dolphin	Sea	21 km/h
Swordfish	Sea	83 km/h
Great white shark	Sea	15 km/h

Table 10.02.02 The top speeds of some animals, birds and fish if they were human-sized.

Fig. 10.02.04 (a) The cheetah; (b) the white-throated needletail; (c) the swordfish. You can find out more about these animals at http://speedofanimals.com/land

PHYSICS

Reading Distance–Time Graphs

Distance–time graphs are used to plot an object's distance from a point against the time taken for the journey.

> *For example:*
> A cyclist starts from rest. The time taken to reach 10 m markers were recorded as follows:
>
> | Time (s) | 0 | 1 | 2 | 3 | 4 | 5 | 6 | 7 | 8 |
> |----------|---|----|----|----|----|----|----|----|----|
> | Distance (m) | 0 | 10 | 20 | 30 | 40 | 50 | 60 | 70 | 80 |
>
> *Table 10.02.03.*

Fig. 10.02.05 (a) shows a distance–time graph of the data in *Table 10.02.03*. A distance–time graph plots distance (y-axis) against time (x-axis). We can use this graph to get various kinds of information.

A. How long does it take the cyclist to reach the 50 m mark?
   (1) Draw a straight line from 50 m on the distance axis until it touches the straight line through the origin.
   (2) Then draw another straight line down from here until it touches the time axis. The point of contact on the time axis is how long it took.
   Answer = 5 s

B. What was the cyclist's average speed?
   (1) Pick a point on the line, say (5, 50).
   (2) Use **D**ad's **S**illy **T**riangle rule by replacing 'distance' with 50 m and 'time' with 5 s.

   $$\text{Speed} = \frac{\text{Distance}}{\text{Time}} = \frac{50 \text{ m}}{5 \text{ s}} = 10 \text{ m/s}$$

   Answer = 10 m/s

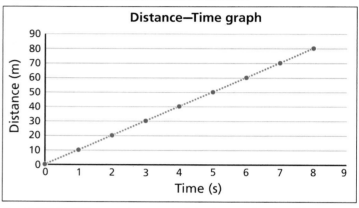

Fig. 10.02.05 (a) Distance–time graph of the data as given in Table 10.02.03.

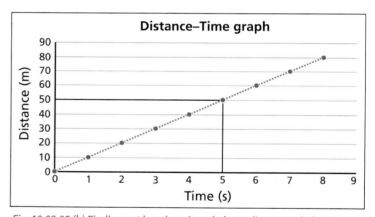

Fig. 10.02.05 (b) Finding out how long it took the cyclist to reach the 50 m mark.

 **Checkpoint 4**

Table 10.02.04 shows the distance covered by a car starting from rest to 20 s later.

Time (s)	0	2	4	6	8	10	12	14	16	18	20
Distance (m)	0	120	240	360	480	600	720	840	960	1080	1200

Table 10.02.04.

Represent the information in *Table 10.02.04* on a graph. Use the graph to answer these questions.
   (i) How far had the car travelled after 2 s?
   (ii) At what time did the car reach 60 m?
   (iii) What was the speed of the car at 8 s and 10 s? Explain your answer.
   (iv) Give the time taken for the car to reach 800 m.
   (v) Is the car accelerating? Justify your answer.

Reading Velocity–Time Graphs

Velocity–time graphs are used to plot an object's speed in a given direction (velocity) from a point against the time taken for the journey. The information we can obtain from a velocity–time graph is different to that obtained from a distance–time graph. On a velocity-time graph we can find the following information:

- Velocity at a certain time
- Acceleration

> *For example:*
> A cyclist who competes in the Tour de France wants to work on his speed at the start of the race. In order to do this he sets out markers every 10 m from the start and his coach notes the time at each marker. Starting from rest, the times taken to reach the 10 m marks were recorded as follows:
>
> | Time (s) | 0 | 1 | 2 | 3 | 4 | 5 | 6 | 7 | 8 | 9 | 10 |
> |---|---|---|---|---|---|---|---|---|---|---|---|
> | Velocity (m/s) | 0 | 10 | 20 | 30 | 40 | 50 | 60 | 70 | 80 | 90 | 100 |
>
> *Table 10.02.05.*

Fig. 10.02.06 (a) is a velocity–time graph of the data in *Table 10.02.05*. A velocity–time graph plots velocity (y-axis) against time (x-axis). We can use this graph to get various kinds of information.

A. Calculate the velocity at 6 s.
  (1) Draw a straight line from 6 s on the time axis up to the straight line through the origin.
  (2) Then draw another straight line across from here until it touches the velocity axis. The point of contact on the velocity axis is the velocity at a certain time, in this case 6 s (*Fig. 10.02.06 (b)*).
  Answer = 60 s

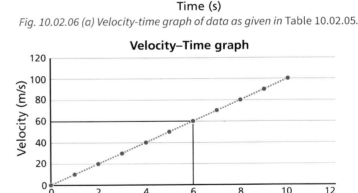

Fig. 10.02.06 (a) Velocity-time graph of data as given in Table 10.02.05.

B. Calculate the acceleration.
  (1) Remember that acceleration is the change in velocity over time taken. So if we want to find the acceleration in a velocity–time graph, we must pick two velocities, say 40 m/s and 60 m/s, and find the time taken for this change, i.e. 2 s in this case.
  (2) **Formula:** Use the acceleration formula:

$$\text{Acceleration} = \frac{\text{Change in velocity (FV} - \text{IV)}}{\text{Time taken}} = \frac{60 - 40}{2} = \frac{20}{2}$$

  Answer = 10 m/s²

Fig. 10.02.06 (b) Graph of velocity at 6 s.

 Checkpoint 5

Tracking a jogger around a field, a graph of their movement can be seen in *Fig. 10.02.07*.
Using this graph, answer these questions.
  (i) What is the velocity of the runner at 1 s?
  (ii) What is the velocity of the runner at 11 s?
  (iii) In your own words, describe the motion of the runner between 0–10 s. (*Cont. overleaf*)

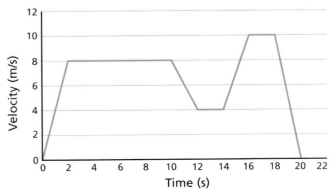

Fig. 10.02.07 Graph of a jogger's run.

PHYSICS

(iv) What do we call the motion of the runner between 2–10 s?
(v) Calculate the acceleration of the runner between 0 and 2 s.
(vi) Calculate the acceleration of the runner between 10 and 12 s.
(vii) What is the acceleration of the runner between 18 and 20 s?

Analysing Distance–Time Graphs

The shape of a distance–time graph can give us information about the object.

1. Straight line through the origin (where the two axis meet)

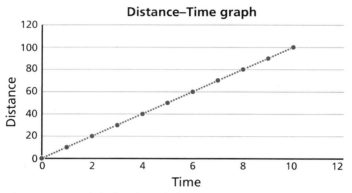

Fig. 10.02.08 Straight line through the origin.

2. Sharp declining straight line not going through the origin

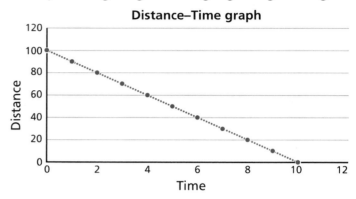

Fig. 10.02.09 Sharp declining straight line; not through the origin.

Here we see that the line goes through the origin and continues to move in an unchanging straight line. In a distance–time graph this means that the speed is constant, i.e. covering the same distance every second.

In this instance we see a declining straight line starting at 100 and going down to zero. In a distance–time graph this generally means the object is moving towards the start point. If we stand at the start of a 100 m race and the sprinters start at the finish line and run towards us, we would show this as a declining straight line.

3. Straight line going across the graph

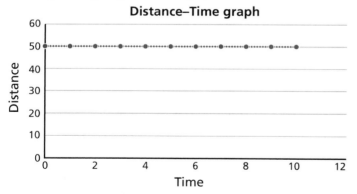

Fig. 10.02.10 Straight line across the graph.

This time we have a horizontal line that does not go up or down, it just stays stationary at the 50 m mark. In a distance–time graph this means that the object starts 50 m away from the start line and does not move over the 10 s.

 **Checkpoint 6**

Some graphs, like the one in *Fig. 10.02.11,* include all three conditions. Tell the story of this graph.

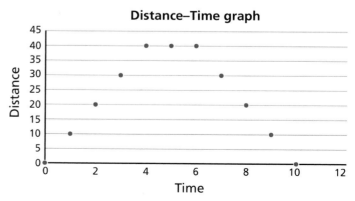

Fig. 10.02.11 All three conditions.

Analysing Velocity–Time Graphs

The shape of a velocity–time graph can also give us information about the object.

1. Straight line through the origin (where the two axis meet)

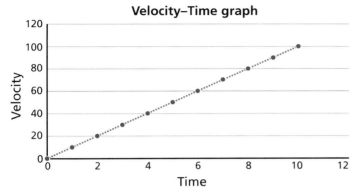

Fig. 10.02.12 Straight line through the origin.

Here we see that the line goes through the origin and continues to move in an unchanging straight line. In a velocity–time graph this means that the acceleration is constant, i.e. the car is speeding up at a constant rate.

2. Sharp declining straight line not going through the origin

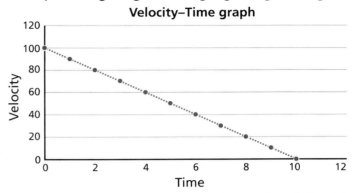

Fig. 10.02.13 Sharp declining straight line; not through the origin.

In this instance we see a declining straight line starting at 100 and going down to zero. In a velocity–time graph this means that at 0 seconds the object is moving with a velocity of 100 m/s and over the next 10 s is constantly decelerating to 0 m/s.

3. Straight line going across the graph

This time we have a straight line that does not go up or down, it just stays stationary at the 50 m mark. In a velocity–time graph this means that at 0 seconds the object was moving with a constant velocity of 50 m/s.

> It is important to remember that if there is no change in velocity (i.e. velocity is constant), then the acceleration is 0.

Formula:

Acceleration =

$$\frac{\text{Change in velocity (FV − IV)}}{\text{Time taken}} = \frac{50 - 50}{10} = \frac{0}{10} = 0 \text{ m/s}^2$$

You will have noticed that while distance–time and velocity–time graphs looks similar, the story these graphs tell is actually different.

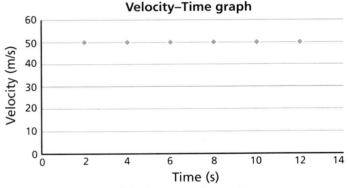

Fig. 10.02.14 Straight line across the graph.

PHYSICS

⊘ **Checkpoint 7**

You may see a graph with all three conditions involved, like the one shown in *Fig. 10.02.15*. Can you explain the motion of the object?

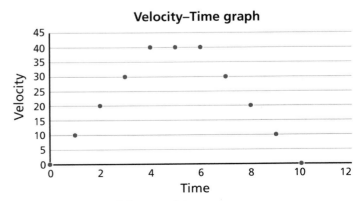

Fig. 10.02.15 All three conditions.

WHAT I HAVE LEARNED...

- The speed of an object is the distance it travels in a second, or the rate of change of distance with respect to time.
- The unit of speed is the metre per second (m/s).
- Velocity is speed in a given direction.
- The unit of velocity is the metre per second (m/s).
- Acceleration is the change in velocity divided by time, or the rate of change of velocity with respect to time.
- The unit of acceleration is the metre per second squared (m/s² or m/s/s).
- A distance–time graph plots distance (y-axis) against time (x-axis). A distance–time graph tells you:
  - How long it takes to reach a certain distance
  - How far the object has travelled after x seconds
  - Average speed
  - Velocity.
- A straight line through the origin of a distance–time graph means the object is speeding up at a constant speed.
- A straight line that decreases on a distance–time graph means the object is moving towards the starting point (think of running the 100 m backwards/the wrong way).
- A horizontal line across a distance–time graph means the object is neither speeding up nor slowing down but is stationary.
- A velocity–time graph plots velocity (y-axis) against time (x-axis). A velocity–time graph tells you:
  - Velocity at a certain time
  - Time taken to reach a certain velocity
  - Acceleration.
- A straight line through the origin of a velocity–time graph means the object is speeding up at a constant velocity.
- A straight line that decreases on a velocity–time graph means the object is slowing down at a constant velocity.
- A horizontal line across a velocity–time graph means the object is neither speeding up nor slowing down but rather staying at a constant velocity.

Question Time

Copy and Complete

In this unit I learned about _____, speed and time. I also learned the difference between speed, _____ and _____. Speed just gives us a value of how fast a car is going, whereas velocity gives us the speed and the _____. The unit of speed and velocity is _____ __ ____ (_/_). Acceleration is the _____ of _____ of velocity. The unit of acceleration is the _____ ___ ____ ____ (_/_). An alternative word for negative acceleration is _____. A distance–time graph allows me to see how far an object has travelled in a certain amount of _____. A _____ – _____ graph tells me how _____ an object is moving at a certain point in time.

Questions

1. Define speed. What is the unit of speed?
2. Define velocity. What is the unit of velocity?
3. Define acceleration. What is the unit of acceleration?
4. A ball was dropped from a balcony in a sports hall. The ball's approximate velocity was measured each second as it fell. The data collected during this experiment is given in the graph below (*Fig 10.02.16*).

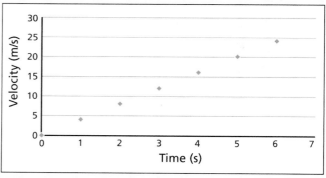

Fig. 10.02.16 Velocity–time graph of a ball dropped from a balcony in a sports hall.

   (i) What was the velocity of the ball after 3 s?
   (ii) How long did it take the ball to reach a velocity of 15 m/s?
   (iii) What was the acceleration of the ball?

5. A person decided to see how far they could walk in 10 s. The data as given in *Table 10.02.06* was recorded.

Time (s)	0	1	2	3	4	5	6	7	8	9	10
Distance (m)	0	2	4	6	8	10	12	14	16	18	20

Table 10.02.06.

   (i) Draw a graph representing the data as given in *Table 10.02.06*.
   (ii) What is the distance travelled after 4 s?
   (iii) How long did it take to travel 12 m?
   (iv) What was the walker's speed at 5 s?

(v) Comment on the shape of the graph.

(vi) What does the shape of the line tell you about the speed of the walker?

6. A cyclist cycled to work. His velocity was recorded over the first minute of the cycle at 5 s intervals. The data as given in *Table 10.02.07* was recorded.

Time (s)	0	5	10	15	20	25	30	35	40
Velocity (m/s)	0	2	5	10	12	12	12	12	0

Time (s)	45	50	55	60
Velocity (m/s)	0	5	7	10

Table 10.02.07.

(i) Draw a graph representing the data as given in *Table 10.02.07*.

(ii) What is the cyclist's velocity after 10 seconds?

(iii) At what times was the cyclist's velocity 10 m/s?

(iv) What was the cyclist's acceleration after 20 seconds?

(v) Comment on the general shape of the graph, referring to specific phases.

(vi) Give a possible explanation for the sudden drop in velocity at 40 s and 45 s.

7. A stone was dropped from the top of a cliff and the distance that it fell was measured at the intervals of time as given in *Table 10.02.08*.

Distance (m)	0	5	20	45	80	100
Time (s)	0	1	2	3	4	4.5

Table 10.02.08.

(i) Copy the grid given in *Fig. 10.02.17* (or use graph paper) and draw a graph of distance against time. A smooth curve through the plotted points is required.

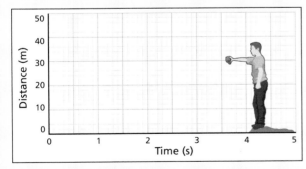

Fig. 10.02.17 Grid of a stone dropped from a cliff top.

(ii) Use the graph to find how far the stone had fallen in 3.5 s.

(iii) Calculate the average speed of the falling stone between the second and the fourth second. Give the unit with your answer.

(iv) In this experiment, is distance fallen directly proportional to time? Justify your answer.

Inquiry

A The graph in *Fig. 10.02.18* shows how the speed of a racing car varies along a flat 3 km track during its second lap.

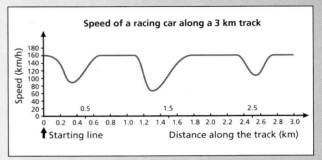

Fig. 10.02.18 The speed of a racing car varying along a flat 3 km track.

Fig. 10.02.19 shows five racing tracks. **Examine** the five tracks and **decide** which one represents the speed graph shown in *Fig. 10.02.18*?

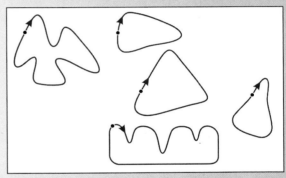

Fig. 10.02.19 Five car racing tracks.

B In a group, **design** an investigation to measure the speed, velocity and acceleration of a person, a cheetah, a car and a motorbike. You must include all background research (websites) and present your work either via PowerPoint, video or short oral presentation. Make sure to include your methodology (how you collected data), how you ensured fair testing and some reference to how you will show your results (*hint:* graphs!).

C In a group, **design** and **carry out** an experiment to investigate the speed of athletes from various sports. Use students similar to your own age. Ensure you follow the fair test procedure. **Create** a presentation detailing your results. Make sure to include your methodology (how you collected data), how you ensured fair testing and some reference to how you will show your results (*hint:* graphs again!).

PHYSICS

11.1 Energy

Learning Outcomes

PWLO 3. Investigate patterns and relationships between physical observables.

PWLO 4. Research and discuss an aspect of modern physics/technologies in terms of scientific, societal and environmental impact.

PWLO 6. Explain energy conservation and analyse natural processes in terms of energy changes and dissipation.

PWLO 7. Design, build and test a device that transforms energy from one form to another in order to perform a function; describe the energy changes and ways of improving its efficiency.

PWLO 8. Research and discuss the ethical and sustainability issues that arise from generation and consumption of electricity.

NSLO 2. Recognise questions that are appropriate for scientific investigation, pose testable hypotheses, and evaluate and compare strategies for investigating hypotheses.

NSLO 3. Design, plan and conduct investigations; explain how reliability, accuracy, precision, fairness, safety, ethics and a selection of suitable equipment have been considered.

NSLO 4. Produce and select data (qualitatively/quantitatively), critically analyse data to identify patterns and relationships, identify anomalous observations, draw and justify conclusions.

NSLO 5. Review and reflect on the skills and thinking used in carrying out investigations, and apply learning and skills to solving problems in unfamiliar contexts.

BWLO 7. Describe respiration and **photosynthesis** as both chemical and biological processes.

R Teacher's reference

KEYWORDS

biomass energy
chemical energy
electrical energy
geothermal energy
greenhouse gases
heat energy
hydro-electric energy
joule
kinetic energy
Law of Conservation of Energy
light energy
non-renewable energy
nuclear energy
nuclear fission
nuclear fusion
particles
potential energy
renewable energy
solar energy
sound energy
wave energy
wind energy

LEARNING INTENTIONS

At the end of this unit you should:

1. Be able to define energy and give the SI units that it is measured in.
2. Be able to identify different forms of energy and carry out simple investigations to show the following energy conversions:
   (a) chemical energy to electrical energy to heat energy
   (b) electrical energy to magnetic energy to kinetic energy
   (c) light energy to electrical energy to kinetic energy.
3. Know examples of energy conversion from everyday life.
4. Be able to state the principle of conservation of energy.
5. Know how to classify sources of energy as renewable or non-renewable.
6. Be able to explain why the Sun is considered our primary source of energy.
7. Be able to list the advantages and disadvantages of different energy sources, including nuclear sources of energy, as part of the solution to national energy need.

What is Energy?

'I don't have the energy to go training today.
I don't even have the energy to get out of bed!'
'So have an energy drink!'

How would you show someone what energy is? Energy is one of those concepts we all 'know', but what does it mean exactly?

Energy is the ability to move, to work, to do things, with this energy being released from food. The unit of energy is the **joule** (J).

There are many forms of energy. Let us look at the main ones you encounter in your everyday lives.

Kinetic Energy

Kinetic energy is the energy that an object has due to its movement. For example, a jogger has kinetic energy.

Potential Energy

Potential energy is the energy an object gains due to its position or state. Think of a coiled spring. When you fully press a spring down before letting it go, it has potential energy (due to its state). Similarly, when an object is held high before letting it go, it has potential energy (due to its position).

Fig. 11.01.02 This ball has great potential energy.

Energy: The ability to do work.
Measured in **joules** (J).

Fig. 11.01.01 Joggers exhibiting kinetic energy.

Fig. 11.01.03 This fire exhibits heat energy.

Heat Energy

You might wonder, how is **heat** considered as energy? It doesn't cause anything to move.
But heat can have considerable energy. We will look at heat energy in more detail in the next unit.

🔍 **Investigation 11.01.01: Can heat cause particles to move?**

Equipment: Two beakers, water, kettle, food colouring.
Instructions: Design an investigation to ascertain whether heat is a form of energy.

> ### What did you learn?
> 1. Were you able to see any visible movement in the water?
> 2. Identify possible errors in this investigation.
> 3. Can you suggest one alternate way of conducting this investigation?

Sound Energy

When you are near a very loud speaker, you can actually feel the energy of the **sound** it is emitting. This is because sound waves cause the diaphragm of the speaker to move and vibrate, causing the air molecules behind it to move and vibrate.

Fig. 11.01.04 The paint in these speakers (added for effect) demonstrates the vibration of air molecules due to the energy of the sound.

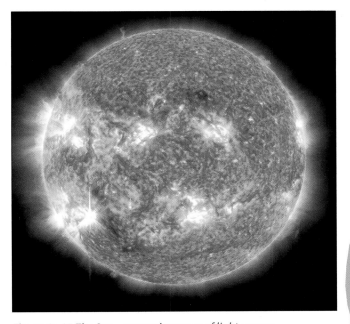

Fig. 11.01.05 The Sun – our main source of light energy.

Light Energy

Light is the only form of energy that we can indirectly see. Light is made up of packets of energy called photons. Our main source of light comes from the Sun. We will look at light in more detail in *Unit 11.3*.

Did you know?

Light can be referred to as packets of energy called photons (particles). You will also see in *Unit 11.3* that we refer to light as a wave. Believe it or not, light is thought to be both a wave and a particle. This is because it has wave-like properties and matter (particle)-like properties. This phenomena is called Wave–Particle Duality. This idea first came about when Isaac Newton and Christiaan Huygens individually developed competing theories of light. Newton said that light consisted of particles and Huygens said that it consisted of waves. It wasn't until the early twentieth century that work from scientists such as Planck, Einstein, De Broglie, Bohr and Compton led to the conclusion that light is both a wave and a particle.

Fig. 11.01.06 The Solvay Conference of 1927 on quantum mechanics contained most of the revolutionary scientists of the twentieth century, among them: Arthur Compton (middle row, fourth from right), Louis de Broglie (middle row, third from right), Niels Bohr (middle row, extreme right), Max Planck (front row, second from left, holding cap in hands) and Albert Einstein (front row, centre).

PHYSICS

Electrical Energy

Electrical energy is caused by the movement of electrically charged **particles**.

Fig. 11.01.07 Common electrical devices.

Chemical Energy

Chemical energy is the stored energy in chemicals that can be released during reactions. Examples include the food that we digest, photosynthesis in plants and forest fires.

Nuclear Energy

Nuclear energy is the release of energy by the splitting (fission) or joining (fusion) of atoms.

Conservation of Energy

We cannot create energy out of nothing. At the same time, there is no known way to destroy energy. The amount of energy in the universe remains stable. So when we use energy, we don't use it up, we simply transform it from one form into another. This is called the **Law of Conservation of Energy**.

(R) In any system (think of a ball about to be dropped from a height) all energy is conserved. This means:

Energy before = Energy after

No energy is wasted or disappears. So let us consider the ball being dropped from a height.

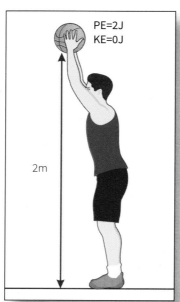
Fig. 11.01.08 (a) The ball is being held.

Fig. 11.01.08 (b) The ball has been released.

Fig. 11.01.08 (c) The ball just before it hits the ground.

1. In *Fig. 11.01.08 (a)*, we see a ball being held at a height of 2 m above the ground. We know that when something is held at a height it has **potential energy**. To calculate potential energy (PE), we multiply the **m**ass by **g**ravity by the **h**eight.

2. The ball has a PE of 2 J. When the ball is released, the potential energy slowly changes to **kinetic energy** (KE). So just when the person lets go of the ball, the potential energy is still 2 J and the kinetic energy is 0 J.

3. In *Fig. 11.01.08 (b),* the ball is mid-fall. At this stage, half of the potential energy has changed into kinetic energy, so we now have 1 J of potential energy and 1 J of kinetic energy.

4. In *Fig. 11.01.08 (c)*, we see the ball is just about to hit the ground. All of the potential energy has been converted to kinetic energy, so we have 2 J of kinetic energy and 0 J of potential energy.

Then obviously the ball will bounce and the conversion will continue again. This leads us to our definition of the Law of Conservation of Energy.

$$PE = mgh$$

Law of Conservation of Energy: Energy can neither be created nor destroyed; it can only be converted from one form to another.

 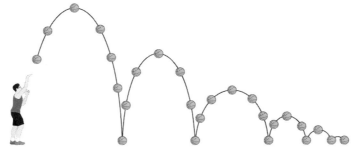

If energy is conserved, why does a ball dropped from a height of two metres not bounce back to a height of two metres?
Why does it come to a stop eventually?

Fig. 11.01.09 We can see here that with the first bounce, the ball reaches its maximum rebound height. Then, in each consecutive bounce, the ball rebounds less and less. We know energy is converted from one form to another, so why isn't the ball bouncing back to its original height?

Conservation of Energy from One Form to Another

As stated, energy cannot be created or destroyed. We now must discuss energy conversions. Look at the examples below.

1. Photosynthesis (*Unit 5.1*): light energy to chemical energy.
2. Respiration (*Unit 5.2*): chemical energy to heat energy.
3. Walking up stairs: chemical energy to kinetic energy to potential energy.

These are examples of natural energy conversion. Plants use the energy from sunlight as a source of energy for all their functions. Humans break down food using respiration. Respiration is a chemical reaction as the nutrients from food and the oxygen that enter the cells are rearranged through reactions to form carbon dioxide and water. When we walk up stairs, we use the energy gained from our food to power the climb. When we reach the top of the stairs we are at a height, so we now have potential energy.

Examples of Natural Energy Conversions

On Earth there are many examples of natural energy conversion: animal movement, waterfalls, apples falling from trees, volcanos and thunderstorms, to name a few.

PHYSICS

🔍 **Investigation 11.01.02: Converting energy into other forms**

Equipment: Solar cell, wires, battery, heating element, beaker, water, thermometer, nail, iron filings, small motor.

Instructions: Using the equipment as listed, design and carry out a series of investigations to demonstrate the following energy conversions:
  (i) Chemical energy to electrical energy to heat energy.
  (ii) Electrical energy to magnetic energy to kinetic energy.
  (iii) Light energy to electrical energy to kinetic energy.

What did you learn?
1. What issues did you face when designing and carrying out these investigations? How did you overcome these?
2. Compare your set-up to another classmate's, and discuss the differences in accuracy and reliability to your own set-up.

Fig. 11.01.10 Examples of energy conversion: the swing of a pendulum and a child on a swing.

✓ Checkpoint 1

(a) Explain the energy conversions taking place in the examples of natural energy conversions just given.

(b) Can you identify what energy conversions are taking place in *Fig. 11.01.10 (a)* and *(b)*?

(c) Name all the useful energy conversions which take place in a car.

We could write a whole book examining examples of the natural energy conversions we see in our daily lives. However, there is a very important consequence of energy usage on our planet that we must examine, an effect that we humans are directly responsible for: the effect of our daily lifestyles is causing rising temperatures. This effect is known as the Greenhouse Effect.

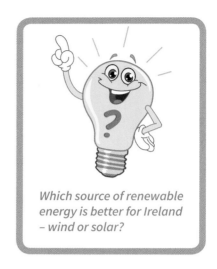

Which source of renewable energy is better for Ireland – wind or solar?

The Greenhouse Effect

It cannot be ignored that humans are the main cause of global warming on Earth. How did we cause this? Can it be reversed? Can we do anything about it? First we must look at the role **greenhouse gases** play in all this.

Greenhouse gases are man-made in nature (see *Unit 9.2*). They are produced by burning fossil fuels. So activities such as using electricity, driving a car, burning plastics, constructing buildings, all contribute to the rise in greenhouse gases.

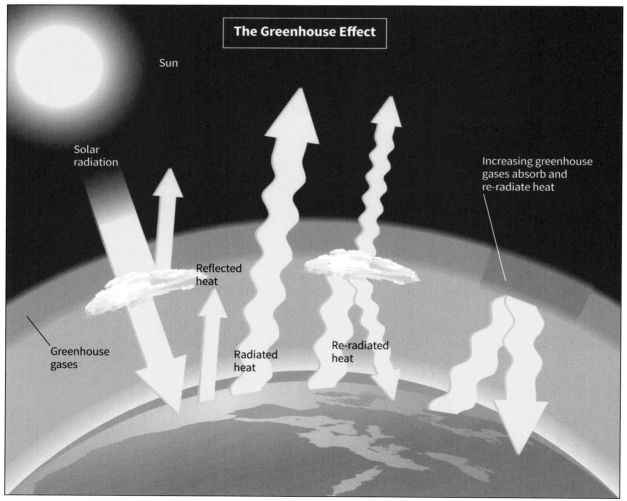

Fig. 11.01.11 The Greenhouse Effect in action.

Fossil fuels produce these harmful greenhouse gases when burned. It is currently estimated that 79% of the world's total energy is produced from burning fossil fuels. Unfortunately, fossil fuels, as the name suggests, come from fossils. This means that at some stage we will run out of this fuel. There is no way to recycle the fuel and reuse it again. This type of fuel is called **non-renewable energy**.

Non-renewable Energy: An energy that is not easily replaced/recycled/renewed.

Reducing Our Greenhouse Gases

While there is no real way to change greenhouse gases to other less harmful gases, there are ways in which we can reduce our production of these gases. By using alternative fuel sources, we can aim to reduce our overall greenhouse gas levels. There are seven alternative fuel sources, as shown in *Table 11.01.01*.

The Greenhouse Effect: The trapping of radiated heat from the sun by greenhouse gases in the earth's atmosphere.

Energy Source	Definition	Example
Solar	Energy from the radiation of the sun	Solar panels on residential roofs
Hydro-Electric	Energy harnessed from the movement of water over a wheel which turns to generate electricity	Ardnacrusha, Hoover Dam
Wind	Uses the wind to turn a wheel, which generates electricity	Wind turbines visible throughout the Irish countryside
Wave	Movement of waves pass over a floating generator, producing energy via movement	*Not commercially available yet*
Geothermal	Using the heat under the planet. As you increase depth you increase heat	Nesjavellir Geothermal Power Station, Iceland
Biomass	Using plants to produce oils and alcohols	Wood chips, vegetable oils, animal fats
Nuclear	The splitting of one or the joining of two atoms produces large amounts of energy	Sellafield Nuclear Power Station (England)

Table 11.01.01 Alternative fuel sources.

You will notice that all of the above fuel sources share something in common: they are all **renewable**! This means all of these resources can be recycled and reused.

Renewable Energy: An energy that is easily replaced/recycled/renewed.

As you can imagine, there are some benefits to using renewable energies:

- They will not run out
- They produce little to no greenhouse gases
- They are generally safe to use.

Solar Energy

The most readily available renewable energy is **solar energy**. As you may have noticed, over the last few years there has been an increase in the number of houses using solar panels. This is because the technology used to build a solar panel is fairly simple and, most importantly, cheap! The solar panel is able to convert the light energy (radiation) into electrical energy. This is achieved via the photoelectric effect. The light can free an electron from the chemical compounds that are used to make the solar panels. This free electron has energy and then moves around to generate electricity.

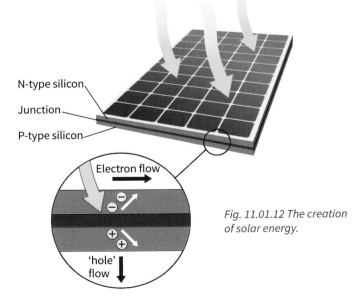

Fig. 11.01.12 The creation of solar energy.

Investigation 11.01.03: Converting energy from one form to another

Instructions: Design, build and test a device, different to what has been done in the previous investigations, which can convert energy from one form to another. Here are some pointers to help you focus your research:

- Decide what energy conversions you wish to achieve (for example: light to electrical).
- Look at what devices have been used already do this conversion (for example: solar panel).
- Find the materials list to build the device and check with your teacher if resources are available.
- Decide early on how you are going to test the efficiency of the device.

> *What did you learn?*
> 1. Think critically about whether your device was efficient or not.
> 2. If your device was not very efficient in converting the energies, state this and come up with possible solutions to these shortcomings.

Checkpoint 2

(a) What is global warming?

(b) What are greenhouse gases?

(c) How are greenhouse gases produced? Name some common sources of greenhouse gas in nature and in everyday activities.

(d) What is renewable energy?

(e) Name seven sources of renewable energy.

(f) Explain three ways we could reduce our greenhouse gas production.

Nuclear Energy: A Blessing or a Curse?

At the start of the twentieth century, scientists finally began to unravel the mystery of the atom. It was confirmed that the nucleus was made up of protons and neutrons. Unlocking the energy of the force which held the protons and neutrons together became the next major goal for scientists.

Ernest Walton

John Cockcroft

Otto Hahn

Fritz Strassmann

Fig. 11.01.13.

The first attempt to split the nucleus came jointly from Waterford physicist Ernest Walton and British physicist John Cockroft. They successfully split the nucleus of an atom by bombarding metals with fast-moving protons. When hit by a proton, the metal released energy. Then in 1938, German scientists Otto Hahn and Fritz Strassmann fired neutrons into uranium in an attempt to create an even heavier element. Much to their surprise, they discovered that instead of getting a heavier element, much lighter elements were found. These elements were half the size of uranium. For years they pondered the implications of this, until one day they realised that this reaction produced spare neutrons. These neutrons could then break up more uranium and produce a chain reaction. This chain reaction is the principle of a nuclear reaction.

There are two types of nuclear energy:

- **Fission** (in use)
- **Fusion** (being worked on).

	Definition	How it works	Uses	Waste Production
Fission	The splitting of uranium into smaller elements, producing massive amounts of energy.	Chain reactions: Uranium is split into smaller elements producing neutrons to split even more uranium.	• Energy production (Sellafield) • Nuclear weapons	• *High Level Waste:* Generally from waste products of the reaction itself. Highly radioactive waste stored in stainless steel drums lined with concrete.  *Fig. 11.01.15 Stainless steel drums storing HLW glass.* • *Intermediate Level Waste:* Generally from the metal of the reactor. Contained in stainless steel drums.  *Fig. 11.01.16 Stainless steel drum to house ILW.* • *Low Level Waste:* Generally from clothing, paper and tools that contain small amounts of radioactivity. It is placed in a metal drum and buried shallowly in a special landfill.  *Fig. 11.01.17 Barrel storing LLW.*

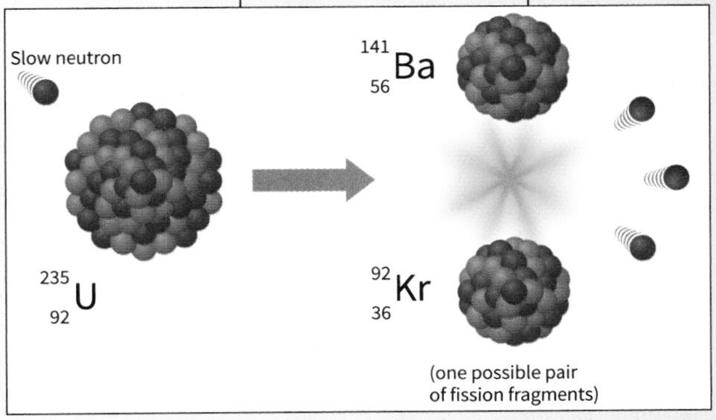

Slow neutron

$^{141}_{56}$Ba

$^{235}_{92}$U

$^{92}_{36}$Kr

(one possible pair of fission fragments)

Fig. 11.01.14 Fission in action.

Table 11.01.02 (a) Nuclear Fission.

PHYSICS

	Definition	How it works	Uses	Waste Production
Fusion	The merging of two nuclei to form heavier ones, releasing massive amounts of energy.	Two hydrogen atoms combine together under huge heat and pressure to form a new molecule (isotope): deuterium. The deuterium then combines with hydrogen to form tritium. The combining of these elements releases massive amounts of energy.	The main reactor used by the sun to produce energy (light and heat). Can be used as a source of clean power on earth.	No waste is produced.

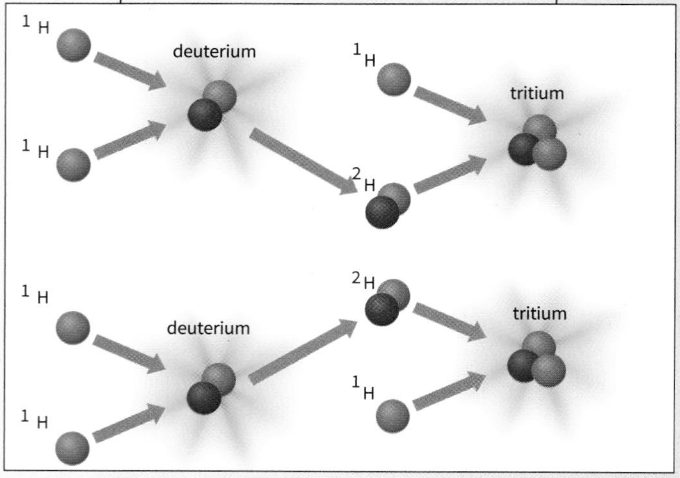

Fig. 11.01.18 The fusion of hydrogen atoms.

Table 11.01.02 (b) Nuclear Fusion.

Did you know?
The 'vapour' that you see coming out of a nuclear station is in fact steam, not nuclear waste as some people think.

Checkpoint 3

(a) What is nuclear fission?
(b) What is a chain reaction?
(c) How do you produce a chain reaction in a nuclear reactor?
(d) In groups of two, draw a table detailing the pros and cons of nuclear fission as an alternative power source. Make sure to include environmental, scientific and societal impacts.

Nuclear Fission: The splitting of uranium into smaller elements producing massive amount of energy.

Nuclear Fusion: The merging together of two nuclei to form heavier ones, releasing massive amounts of energy.

Fig. 11.01.19 Sellafield Nuclear Power Station, England.

How a Fission Reactor Works

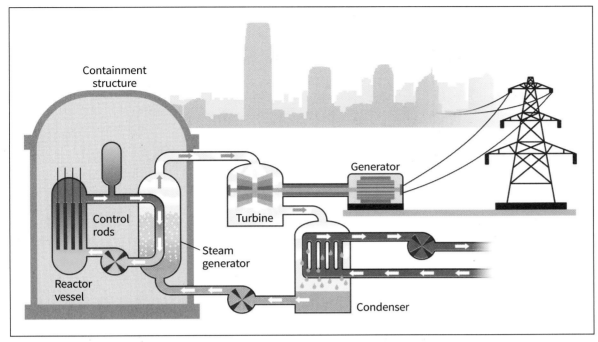

Fig. 11.01.20 The workings of a fission reactor.

As we have learned, nuclear fission works on splitting heavy elements into smaller elements, which release spare neutrons and produce massive amounts of energy. To capture this energy and use it for electricity, a nuclear reaction vessel is used (*Fig. 11.01.20*). There are three main sections to this reaction vessel.

1. Containment Structure

This containment structure houses the reactor vessel, which is where the reaction takes place. Inside the reactor vessel are control rods. These are made of carbon and are used to slow down the free neutrons so we don't get an uncontrollable chain reaction. This reactor vessel is run through a container of water which, due to the massive energy produced (in the form of heat) from the reaction, turns the water into steam.

2. Turbine and Generator

The steam from the water container is then pushed through a turbine, which spins around powering up the generator and creating electricity.

3. Condenser

The condenser is used to turn the steam back into water so that it can be reused in the water container of the containment structure again.

The Dangers of Nuclear Fission

The Atomic Bomb

Unfortunately for science, and the world, the discovery of nuclear fission came at the time of World War II. This meant that instead of trying to find ways to make fission an alternative energy source, Germany and America secured famous scientists, such as Albert Einstein and Wernher von Braun, to find ways to weaponise this discovery. On 6 August 1945, the first nuclear bomb was dropped on Hiroshima, Japan. Three days later another one was dropped on Nagasaki. It is reported that 200 000 people died in the two bombings, not all of them immediately from the blast. Some died from horrific radiation poisoning and other side effects.

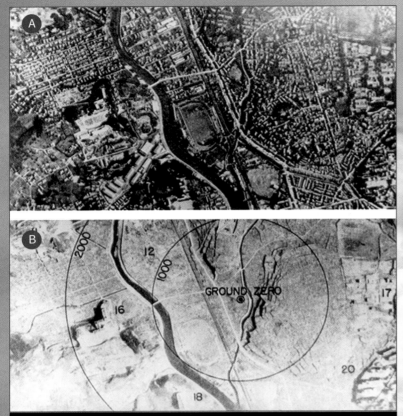

Fig. 11.01.21 (a) Nagasaki before and (b) after the bomb. The complete devastation of the city can be seen in the bottom image, showing the immense power of a nuclear bomb.

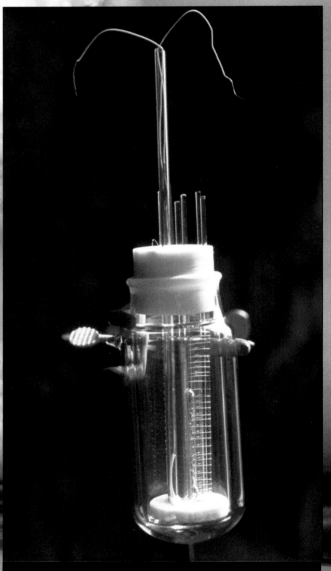

Fig. 11.01.22 Cold Fusion apparatus.

WHAT I HAVE LEARNED...

- Energy is the ability to cause something to move.
- The unit of energy is the joule (J).
- There are seven types of energy:
  - (i) Kinetic: When an object is moving
  - (ii) Potential: When an object is held at a height
  - (iii) Chemical: Energy produced from chemicals such as petrol
  - (iv) Heat: Gives energy to its surroundings, causing the temperature to increase
  - (v) Light: For example, solar panels
  - (vi) Sound: For example, speakers in a car
  - (vii) Electrical energy: For example, PlayStation, hairdryer.
- The conservation of energy states that energy is neither created nor destroyed, but rather converted from one form to another.
- Natural energy conversions include the pendulum swing of a clock or a playground swing, waves and earthquakes.
- Fission is the splitting of an atom into two smaller atoms, neutrons and massive amounts of energy.
- Fission is currently used to generate electricity in some countries.
- A chain reaction occurs when a heavy element undergoes fission to become a lighter element.
- If the chain reaction is not controlled, a nuclear disaster can occur.
- Fission generates a lot of radioactive waste which we cannot recycle.
- Fission reactors are very dangerous if not looked after properly.
- Fusion is the joining of two smaller nuclei into one heavier atom.
- Fusion occurs in our sun and in the formation of stars.
- Fusion is the cleanest, most efficient way of producing energy from nuclear reactions.
- Fusion is difficult to achieve as we need massive temperatures and pressures.

Question Time

Copy and Complete

In this unit I learned that _____ is the ability to cause something to _____. There are many forms of energy, including Heat, L_____, Kinetic, P_____, S_____, E_____ and Chemical. The Law of Conservation of _____ states that energy cannot be _____ nor _____, rather it is _____ from one form to _____. I also learned that there are two types of _____ reactions. _____ is the splitting of a heavy element into smaller elements producing _____ and _____. To split an atom of _____ you must fire a _____ at the nucleus. The production of more _____ is called a _____ reaction. In order to safely generate _____ we must make sure that the _____ are slowed down. The way we capture the _____ generated from this reaction is through boiling _____. The _____ turns to _____, which in turn spins a _____. This _____ is what we see coming out of the chimneys in a nuclear power plant. _____ is the merging of two _____ to form a new _____. _____ occurs all the time in our _____. The main fusion reaction is between _____. Two _____ atoms combine to form _____. This then combines with another _____ atom to form _____ and huge amounts of _____. Fusion is not currently possible on earth because we need to achieve high _____ and _____.

Questions

1. Write a sentence defining energy.
2. Name the type of energy involved in the following:
   (a) A ball held at a height
   (b) A ball dropped from a height
   (c) Toast popping from a toaster.
3. Describe the energy conversion involved in the following:
   (a) Dropping a ball from a height
   (b) Throwing a ball up in the air
   (c) A Jack in a Box
   (d) The boiling of a kettle.
4. Distinguish between nuclear fission and nuclear fusion.
5. Describe and write/draw the fusion reaction that commonly occurs in the sun.
6. Pick four everyday items in your home and describe the energy conversions involved in each.
7. Describe the motion of a football which is kicked directly up in the air and returns to the ground, bouncing until it reaches a complete stop. Make reference to the energy conversions taking place and suggest one reason why the ball does not bounce forever.

PHYSICS

Question Time (cont.)

8. Looking at Fig. *11.01.23*, which image shows nuclear fission and which shows nuclear fusion? Justify your answer.

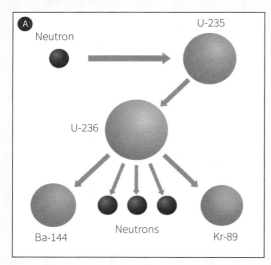

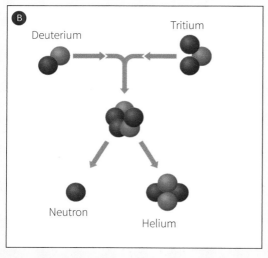

Fig. 11.01.23 Which image shows nuclear fission and which shows nuclear fusion?

9. Explain how waste from nuclear fission reactions is managed.

Inquiry

A **Research** suspension bridges. In particular, examine what natural force they must overcome and how energy is converted. How are they designed and built? Note any disasters which may have occurred involving suspension bridges.

B **Develop** a presentation detailing the difference between nuclear fission and fusion. In your presentation you should include:
   • The environmental impact of each
   • The societal impact of each
   • The advantages of each
   • The disadvantages of each
   • The current status of each.

C Your teacher will split you into teams of 4/5. Your task is to **debate** from one of these positions:
   • You are pro-nuclear fission/fusion
   • You are anti-nuclear fission/fusion.
   You must debate the following aspects:
   • Ethical issues   • Societal impact
   • Sustainability issues   • Environmental impact.

D In groups of three or four, **research** and **develop** a presentation on one of the following topics:
   • The environmental and sustainability issues involved with fission reactors
   • The Fukushima Nuclear Disaster, 2011
   • The history of the atomic bomb, beginning with the Manhattan Project
   • The impact of the bombings in Hiroshima and Nagasaki.

E **Discuss** the pros and cons of biomass as a renewable energy.

F **Design** a poster/presentation on one of the following renewable energies. **Discuss** their advantages and disadvantages compared to using coal to generate energy. Include information on environmental impact and any ethical or social issues involved:
   • Wave power   • Geothermal
   • Tidal power   • Hydroelectric
   • Solar   • Wind.

G Referring back to *Fig. 11.01.06*, **research** any three of the scientists mentioned and write one sentence on each of them.

H **Research** and **write** four sentences on the Greenhouse Effect.

I **Research** and **present** a PowerPoint presentation on a nuclear reactor disaster. Discuss how the disaster happened and what effect it had/has on the environment and general population.

11.2 Heat

Learning Outcomes

PWLO 1. Select and use appropriate measuring tools.

PWLO 3. Investigate patterns and relationships between physical observables.

NSLO 1. Appreciate how scientists work and how scientific ideas are modified over time.

NSLO 2. Recognise questions that are appropriate for scientific investigation, pose testable hypotheses, and evaluate and compare strategies for investigating hypotheses.

NSLO 3. Design, plan and conduct investigations; explain how reliability, accuracy, precision, fairness, safety, ethics and a selection of suitable equipment have been considered.

NSLO 4. Produce and select data (qualitatively/quantitatively), critically analyse data to identify patterns and relationships, identify anomalous observations, draw and justify conclusions.

NSLO 5. Review and reflect on the skills and thinking used in carrying out investigations, and apply learning and skills to solving problems in unfamiliar contexts.

NSLO 7. Organise and communicate research and investigative findings in a variety of ways fit for purpose and audience, using relevant scientific terminology and representations.

R Teacher's reference

KEYWORDS

bimetallic strip
conduction
conductor
convection
convection current
energy
expansion
heat
insulator
joules
latent heat
radiation
specific heat capacity
temperature
thermometer
vacuum

LEARNING INTENTIONS

At the end of this unit you should:

1. Be able to show that heat is a form of energy and that it can be converted into other forms of energy.
2. Be able to identify good and bad conductors of heat and compare the insulating ability of different materials.
3. Be able to describe the difference between an insulator and a conductor.
4. Know how to investigate and explain why matter expands when heated and contracts when cooled.
5. Be able to explain why water expands on freezing.
6. Be able to measure the temperature of various solids and liquids at, above and below room temperature.
7. Understand the difference between heat and temperature.
8. Know how to carry out experiments that involve changes of state from:
   - solid to liquid and liquid to solid
   - liquid to gas and gas to liquid.
9. Be able to plot a cooling curve/heating curve and use latent heat to explain the shape of the curve.

PHYSICS

What is Heat?

Heat is a form of **energy**, which means that heat energy is released from an object. The unit of heat is the **joule (J)**. When there is a fire lit in a room and you can feel the hotness of the flame, this also shows that heat can travel. Here are some other examples which show that heat travels:

- When you place a thermometer in a hot liquid, the column of alcohol rises; this is because the heat energy from the hot liquid is transferred to the alcohol molecules in the thermometer. These molecules then convert the heat energy into kinetic energy and begin to expand (move) in the column of the thermometer.
- We feel the heat energy from the sun as it can travel through the vacuum of space and down to the earth.

 **Checkpoint 1**

(a) Look at *Fig. 11.02.01*. **Can you list the objects that are giving out heat?**
(b) **Suggest a reason why you feel the heat from a fire in a room.**

When you hear the word 'heat', what other words do you think of?

Heat: A form of energy. Unit: the joule (J).

Heat Transfer

There are three ways of transferring heat:
1. Conduction
2. Convection
3. Radiation.

Conduction

Conduction can only happen in a solid. Looking at *Fig. 11.02.02*, conduction relies on the interaction of particles to pass heat through the solid. Heat energy from the Bunsen flame is transferred to the particles on the surface of the metal. This causes the particles to vibrate; they then start 'bumping' into nearby molecules, causing them to vibrate too. Eventually, the heat energy is transferred the whole way along the solid. Remember, even though the molecules vibrate, they do not move out of their original position. Remember also that particles in a solid are in a fixed position.

Fig. 11.02.01 Can you identify which objects are giving out heat?

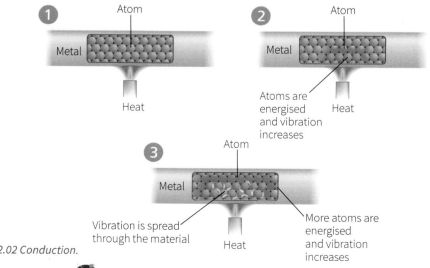

Fig. 11.02.02 Conduction.

 **Checkpoint 2**

(a) Define heat.

(b) What is the unit of heat?

(c) Complete the sentence, 'Heat is a form of _____'.

(d) Why, when we put a poker into a fire, does it not burn our hands?

🔍 Investigation 11.02.01: **Good and bad conductors**

Equipment: Wax, some metal rods, boiling water, some identical nails.

Instructions: Design an experiment which will allow you to test the conductivity of various metals.

> **What did you learn?**
> 1. Compare which metal was the best conductor and which was the worst.
> 2. How did you ensure this was a fair test?
> 3. What other substances could you have used instead of wax?

Fig. 11.02.03 Why doesn't a poker burn our hands when we hold it in the fire?

Conduction: The transfer of heat energy through a solid by the vibration of particles.

Conductor: Allows heat energy to transfer through it easily.

Insulator: Does not allow heat energy to transfer through it easily.

Not all solids will heat up at the same speed. Some metals are much better at transferring heat than others; for example, copper is used in radiator pipes as copper allows the heat energy to travel much faster than, say, lead. This property allows us to sort our solids into two types: **conductors** and **insulators**.

Fig. 11.02.04 (a) Copper is an excellent conductor of heat, which is why it is used in heating pipes in homes.

Fig. 11.02.04 (b) Polystyrene is an example of a good insulator. This is why it is used to hold hot drinks.

Convection

Convection is the transfer of heat through a liquid or gas. Similar to conduction, convection relies on the movement of liquid/gas particles to transfer the heat energy. However, unlike conduction, the particles in the liquid or gas are free to move about so there is large scale molecular movement. This means that rather than molecules vibrating on the spot, the molecules take the heat energy and move to another part of the liquid/gas (usually a colder spot). The movement of these hot molecules is called a **convection current**.

Convection: The transfer of heat through a liquid or gas.

PHYSICS

Fig. 11.02.05 Where does the steam come from?

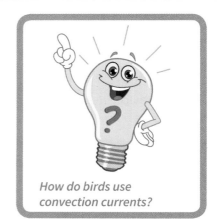

How do birds use convection currents?

✓ **Checkpoint 3**

(a) **Put your hand over a warm radiator. What do you feel?**

(b) **Where does the steam come from when a kettle of water boils?**

Demonstration 11.02.01 – Showing a convection current

Instructions: Your teacher will show you a convection current using potassium permanganate crystals. Compare the convection current you saw here with the observations you made in *Investigation 11.01.01* and comment on any similarities or differences.

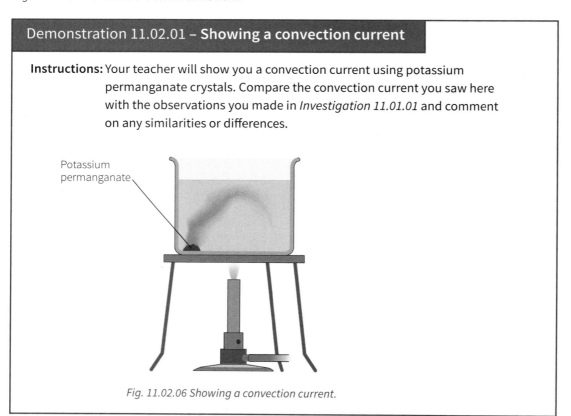

Potassium permanganate

Fig. 11.02.06 Showing a convection current.

Radiation

We mentioned before about the heat energy of the sun travelling to Earth. In space there is a **vacuum**, and therefore no particles for the heat energy to transfer to. So how can the sun's heat energy reach the earth?

The energy from the sun can travel through the vacuum by **radiation**. As we will learn in *Unit 11.3*, energy from the sun (ultraviolet, infrared and visible) can travel through a vacuum because it has the properties of an electromagnetic wave. This means that it does not need particles to transfer its energy.

Vacuum: A region of space where all atoms have been removed.

Radiation: The transfer of heat energy from a hot object without particles.

All hot objects radiate heat energy, and this radiated heat travels in all directions from the hot object. When the **temperature** of the object reaches about 1000°C, it emits heat energy in the visible regions and glows a red colour.

Just as some metals conduct heat better than others, some materials give out heat (radiate) and take in heat (absorb) better than others.

✓ Checkpoint 4

(a) How many methods of heat transfer are there? Name these methods.
(b) 'All metals are good conductors of heat.' Give your own opinion on this statement and back it up with evidence.
(c) 'If you want to heat your house, your radiators should be made of insulating material.' State your opinion on this theory and give evidence for your opinion.

Which colour clothing – black or white – would be best to wear on hot days, and which colour would be best suited for cold days?

Expansion of Solids, Liquids and Gases

Most states of matter will expand (get bigger) when heated, or contract (get smaller) when cooled.

Solids

When a solid is heated, the molecules vibrate. The hotter the solid gets, the faster the vibration. This vibration causes the particles to create more space within the metal and this in turn makes the metal expand.

🔍 Investigation 11.02.02: **The heating effect on a metal**

Equipment: Ball and ring apparatus, Bunsen burner.

Instructions: Design an experiment using the equipment as shown to investigate the effect of heat on metal.

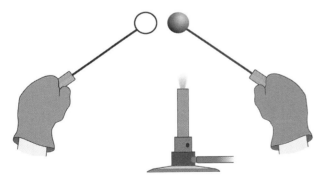

What did you learn?
1. What did you observe in your investigation?
2. What would you need to do if you wanted to repeat this investigation multiple times?
3. What safety precautions did you take when conducting this investigation?

Did you know?
On older train tracks there are gaps left between each track. This is because on hot days the metal expands. If no gaps were left, the metal of each track would push against each other and warp the track. This would cause the train to derail when passing over the affected tracks.

Fig. 11.02.07 A warped railway line.

PHYSICS

Just as all metals do not conduct heat at the same rate, all metals do not expand at the same rate. This is the basic principle of the **bimetallic strip** where two metals, usually iron and copper, are welded together. Copper will conduct heat energy faster than iron and therefore expand more. This **expansion** causes the strip to bend a certain way, depending on where the copper is placed. The bimetallic strip is placed inside heat-sensitive circuits (i.e. circuits where only certain temperature ranges are allowed). In a clothes iron, if the temperature goes over a specific value, the bimetallic strip will heat up, causing the copper to bend, and thus break the circuit, which turns off the iron.

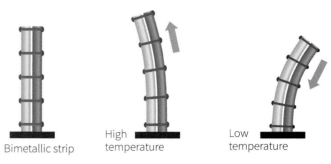

Bimetallic strip   High temperature   Low temperature

Fig. 11.02.08 Iron and copper welded together to create a bimetallic strip.

Gases and Liquids

It is no stretch of the imagination to realise that if metals expand when heated, then so too must liquids and gases. When a gas is heated it expands, and when cooled it contracts. Similarly, when a liquid is heated it expands and when cooled it contracts (though one liquid – water – does not behave in this way).

Checkpoint 5

Explain how a bimetallic strip works and name the two metals used.

Temperature

The instrument we use to measure the hotness or coldness – the temperature – of an object or substance is called a **thermometer**.

Temperature: The measure of how hot or cold an object is.

As we saw in *Unit 10.1*, there are two types of thermometers: the digital thermometer and the alcohol thermometer. Here we will look at the alcohol thermometer.

Alcohol thermometers consist of a glass tube that contains a liquid which, as the name suggests, is normally alcohol. As we know, when liquids are heated they expand and when cooled they contract. This is the basic principle of an alcohol thermometer. When the thermometer is placed in a hot object, the liquid heats up and expands. When it is placed in a cold object, the liquid cools and contracts.

Calibrating an Alcohol Thermometer

To calibrate an alcohol thermometer (mark it with a standard scale to read it), we only need two measurements: 100°C and 0°C, both of which are easy to determine. When an alcohol thermometer is made, it is placed in boiling water. This is because water boils at 100°C. A mark is made when the liquid reaches its reading for this temperature. Next, the water is placed in ice water because ice water is 0°C. This point is also marked. Then, marks are made on the thermometer at intervals of 1°C.

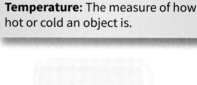

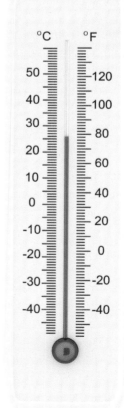

Fig. 11.02.09 An alcohol thermometer.

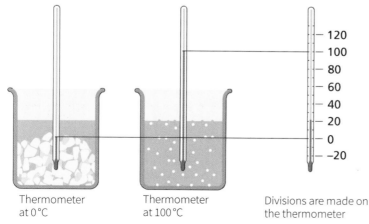

Thermometer at 0°C   Thermometer at 100°C   Divisions are made on the thermometer

Fig. 11.02.10 Calibrating a Celsius thermometer.

We need to keep in mind that heat and temperature are not the same. Remember that temperature is the measure of hot and cold but heat is a form of energy. Consider this: if we have two cups of hot water at 80°C, one half full and the other completely full, which one has the greatest heat energy? The temperature is the same in both cups, but the cup which is full of water holds the greatest heat. This is because the amount of heat energy provided depends on three factors:

1. The mass of the liquid
2. The **specific heat capacity** of the liquid
3. The temperature of the liquid.

So if we consider our two cups of hot water – one full and one half full – we can see why the full cup has more energy. Even though both have the same temperature and heat capacity (because they are both water), one cup has a greater mass and so it has more heat energy.

Specific Heat Capacity

Specific heat capacity is defined as the amount of energy needed to change the temperature of a 1 kg substance by 1°C. The higher the specific heat capacity, the better the substance is at retaining its heat. This is why we use water in our hot water bottles: water has a very high heat capacity, which means it has more heat to release. This is also why water is used in radiators. If a substance has a higher specific heat capacity, it means it will take on much more energy and therefore release more energy. In the case of seawater, the sun continuously pumps energy into the water, but never enough to heat it to boiling point. However, the water holds onto all this energy and will release it overnight.

Changes of State

We know that if we freeze water, we get ice. We also know that if we boil water, we get steam (water vapour). We refer to this as **changes in state**. As we remember from *Unit 6.1*, there are four states of matter: solid, liquid, gas and plasma. So let us look at what happens when ice is heated.

Which do you think is worse and why: getting burnt by water at 100°C or steam at 100°C?

Specific Heat Capacity: The amount of energy needed to change the temperature of a 1 kg substance by 1°C.

Latent Heat: The heat energy required to change a substance from one state to another without a change in temperature.

PHYSICS

🔍 Investigation 11.02.03: **The effects of heat on ice**

Equipment: Bunsen burner/hot plate, ice cubes, beaker, tripod, wire gauze and thermometer.

Instructions: Using the equipment as listed, design an investigation to measure the temperature of ice as you heat it to 100°C. Draw a graph of your results.

What did you learn?

1. How did you ensure this was a fair test?
2. Is your graph similar to *Fig. 11.02.11*? If so, tell the story of this graph. If not, explain the story of your graph and suggest possible reasons why your graph is different.
3. Does your graph show **latent heat**? Justify your answer.

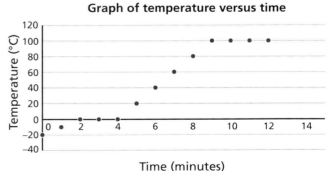

Graph of temperature versus time

Fig. 11.02.11 This graph demonstrates what happens to ice as it transitions from ice to water to steam. Can you identify where the changes in state occurred?

WHAT I HAVE LEARNED...

- Heat is a form of energy.
- Heat is measured in joules.
- Heat moves from hot to cold.
- There are three methods of heat transfer:
  1. **Conduction:** The transfer of heat through a solid via the vibration of molecules.
  2. **Convection:** The transfer of heat through a liquid via the movement of molecules in a convection current.
  3. **Radiation:** The transfer of heat through a vacuum via electromagnetic radiation.
- Conductors allow heat to pass through them easily.
- Insulators do not allow heat to pass through them easily.
- Solid, liquids and gases all expand when heated.
- Solids, liquids and gases all contract when cooled.
- Water contracts when cooled between 20°C and 4°C.
- Water expands when cooled below 4°C.
- Temperature is the measure of how hot or cold an object is.
- Heat and temperature are not the same.
- Heat stored/released depends on three factors:
  (i) Temperature
  (ii) Mass
  (iii) Heat Capacity.
- Latent heat is the heat used to change a substance from one state to another, without increasing its temperature.

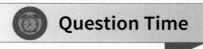

Question Time

Copy and Complete

In this unit I learned that _____ is a form of _____. There are ____ methods for heat transfer. Conduction is the transfer of heat through a _____ via the _____ of _____. _____ is transfer of heat through a liquid via the _____ of particles through a _____ current. Radiation is the transfer of heat through a _____ via _____ radiation. If an object allows heat to pass through it easily it is called a _____. If it does not allow heat to pass through it easily it is called an _____. When heated, _____, _____ and _____ all expand. Similarly when cooled, _____, _____ and _____ all contract. Temperature is the measure of how _____ or _____ a body is. I must remember that _____ is not the same as _____.

Questions

1. Explain temperature.
2. Distinguish between temperature and heat.
3. Define latent heat.
4. What are the four states of matter?
5. Using diagrams to justify your explanation, describe how much energy particles have in the three states of matter.
6. Describe how to calibrate an alcohol thermometer.
7. Latent heat changes the state of the substance without changing the temperature. Using your knowledge of bonding, can you suggest the reason why there is no increase in temperature?
8. Peter is working on repairs to an old house. He has left a bottle of water, some metal nails and a piece of timber inside the boot of his car. After the car has been out in the sun for three hours, the temperature inside the car reaches about 40°C. What happens to the objects in the car? Copy and complete *Table 11.02.01* by answering 'Yes' or 'No' for each statement, and give your reasons.

Does this happen to the object(s)?	Yes or No?
They all have the same temperature.	
After some time the water begins to boil.	
After some time the metal nails begin to glow red.	

Table 11.02.01.

9. *Table 11.02.02* shows the data collected for the cooling curve of chocolate.

Time (mins)	0	2	4	6	8	10	12	14	16	18	20	22	24	26	28	30
Temp (°C)	30	28	25	23	22	22	22	22	22	22	20	17	14	11	8	5

Table 11.02.02.

(i) Draw the cooling curve for the data contained in *Table 11.02.02*.

(ii) Which state of matter describes the chocolate when it is at 30°C?

(iii) Which state of matter describes the chocolate when it is at 10°C?

(iv) In terms of heat loss or heat gain, describe and explain what happens to the chocolate between position A and position B in *Fig. 11.02.12*. (*2014 JC HL*)

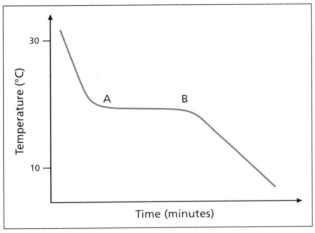

Fig. 11.02.12 The cooling curve for chocolate.

Inquiry

A **Design** an investigation to show convection currents above a radiator.

B **Design** an investigation to compare the melting points and boiling points of different substances.

C **Devise** a list of objects and **investigate** how heat energy could be transferred through them.

D **Research** U or R values and how they determine if materials are heat insulators or conductors.

E **Create** a poster on what happens to the bonds between particles during the change in state of a substance.

F **Design** an investigation to calibrate an alcohol thermometer.

G **Construct** an experiment to investigate the latent heat when boiling water.

PHYSICS

11.3 Light

Learning Outcomes

PWLO 1. Select and use appropriate measuring tools.

PWLO 3. Investigate patterns and relationships between physical observables.

NSLO 1. Appreciate how scientists work and how scientific ideas are modified over time.

NSLO 2. Recognise questions that are appropriate for scientific investigation, pose testable hypotheses, and evaluate and compare strategies for investigating hypotheses.

NSLO 3. Design, plan and conduct investigations; explain how reliability, accuracy, precision, fairness, safety, ethics and a selection of suitable equipment have been considered.

NSLO 4. Produce and select data (qualitatively/quantitatively), critically analyse data to identify patterns and relationships, identify anomalous observations, draw and justify conclusions.

NSLO 7. Organise and communicate research and investigative findings in a variety of ways fit for purpose and audience, using relevant scientific terminology and representations.

(R) Teacher's reference

KEYWORDS

concave
convex
dispersion
electromagnetic
  spectrum
gamma rays
image
infrared
luminous
medium
microwaves
non-luminous
normal
periscope
perpendicular line
prism
radio waves
ray
reflection
refraction
shadow
spectrum
ultraviolet light
visible light
wave
x-ray

LEARNING INTENTIONS

At the end of this unit you should:

1. Know that light is a form of energy and that it can be converted to other forms.
2. Be able to design an investigation demonstrating how light travels in straight lines.
3. Understand how shadows are formed.
4. Understand the difference between luminous and non-luminous objects.
5. Understand that white light is made up of different colours which can be separated by dispersion.
6. Be able to produce white light, a spectrum of light, and list the colours of the spectrum.
7. Understand the operation of a simple periscope.
8. Be able to design a simple periscope.
9. Understand reflection and refraction.
10. Be able to describe how concave and convex lenses can be used in glasses to resolve common eye disorders.
11. Be able to identify the regions on the electromagnetic spectrum and briefly describe each region.

What is Light?

We all think we know what light is. Without it, we wouldn't be able to see a thing. But did you know that light is a form of energy (see *Unit 11.1*)?

Fig. 11.03.02 Solar panels on the side of a house.

Why does a straw appear to bend when it is placed in a glass of water?

Fig. 11.03.01 Why does this straw look like it's bending?

A modern example of light as energy is the solar panel. The solar panels on houses are able to change the energy from the sun into usable home energy. There are two types of solar panel: the photovoltaic solar panel and the solar thermal panel. The photovoltaic solar panel, which can be seen in *Fig 11.03.02*, produces electricity when light is shone on it by releasing electrons to carry the electricity from the panel cells to the house. A solar thermal panel (*Fig. 11.03.03*) is used to heat up the water in your hot water tank. There is a freeze-proof liquid inside thermal solar panels which heats up when the sun shines on the panels. This heated fluid is then pumped through a coiled pipe into your hot water tank, heating up the water. The now cold fluid is pumped back up into the solar panel to be heated again. In both of these solar panels, light has been converted into either heat or electricity. So we can conclude that **light contains energy** (*see* Conservation of Energy definition, p. 310).

Sources of Light

We can group sources of light into two different categories: **luminous** and **non-luminous**. Sources that produce their own light are said to be luminous. Sources that do not give out their own light are non-luminous and we can only see them because they reflect light into our eyes.

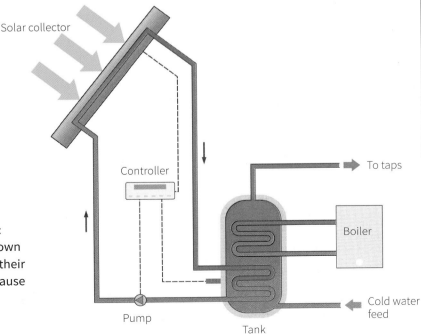

Fig. 11.03.03 Solar thermal panel.

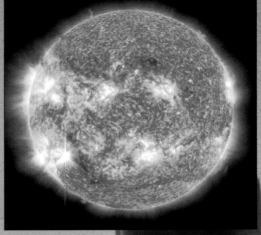

Fig. 11.03.04 A switched-on bulb and the sun are examples of luminous objects.

Luminous Object: An object that produces its own light.

Non-luminous Object: An object that does not produce its own light. It can reflect light from luminous objects.

Fig. 11.03.05 The moon is an example of a non-luminous object as it reflects the light from the sun and other stars.

⊘ **Checkpoint 1**

Can you give other examples of luminous and non-luminous objects?

🔍 Investigation 11.03.01: **How light travels**

Equipment: Lightbulb, three or more pieces of cardboard with hole in centre, Blu-tack.

Instructions: Using the equipment as listed, design an investigation to discover how light travels.

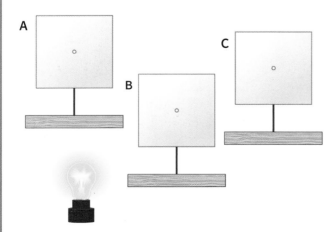

A
B
C

What did you learn?

1. How did you ensure this was a fair test? Justify your answer.
2. Does light bend around corners? Explain your answer.
3. Would your conclusion change if the holes in the cards were bigger? Why?

Shadows

As light only travels in straight lines, it gets blocked when it hits an object. The darkness where the light is blocked is referred to as a **shadow**.

> **Shadow:** The darkness behind an object when light cannot pass through it.

✓ Checkpoint 2

(a) True or false: Light is a form of energy.

(b) How can you justify that light is/is not a form of energy?

(c) Distinguish between luminous and non-luminous objects.

(d) Give the definition for a shadow.

Fig. 11.03.06 Amazing shadow puppets constructed out of wood and other materials.

Reflection of Light

We all use mirrors, but do you know how they work? When a **ray of light** strikes a mirror, it is **reflected** (bounces) off the mirror and into our eyes. This reflecting of the light allows us to see our **image** in the mirror.

> **Ray of Light:** A single beam (column) of light.

🔍 Investigation 11.03.02: **The principle of reflection**

Equipment: Mirror, light source, paper, protractor, pencil.

Instructions: Design an investigation to determine if a relationship exists between the incident ray (the ray from the light source) and the reflected ray (the ray of light that comes off the mirror) when a ray of light is shone on a mirror.

> **What did you learn?**
> 1. Does a relationship exist between the incident ray and the reflected ray? Explain your answer.
> 2. Suggest one change you would make to improve the accuracy of this investigation

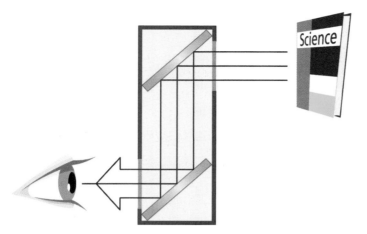

Fig. 11.03.07 Periscopes can be used to view objects over walls or tables.

The principle of reflection explains how a submarine's **periscope** works. You can build your own periscope using much of the same equipment listed in *Investigation 11.03.02*. The periscope can be built into cardboard boxes.

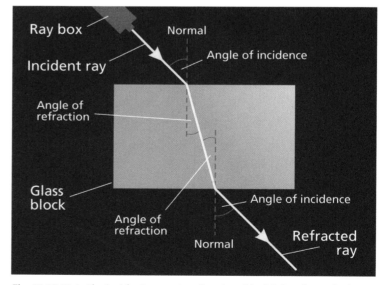

Fig. 11.03.08 Periscopes are used on submarines to look ahead either in the water or just above the surface.

Fig. 11.03.09 A soldier using a periscope attached to his gun to keep watch above the trench while he remains safely hidden.

Reflection: The bouncing of light from a surface.

Refraction: The deflection of light at the surface/interface as it passes from one medium into another.

Medium: A solid, liquid or gas which allows waves to travel through it.

Ⓡ Refraction of Light

We know light travels in a straight line. But is this true when light travels through another material, for example water? Well, it does still travel in a straight line. However, when light passes from air to water, the light changes direction at the surface/interface. This change in direction is what causes the bending of the straw, as shown in *Fig. 11.03.01*. This bending is known as **refraction** and occurs because the speed of the wave changes.

There are two rules to remember:
1. When light travels from a less dense **medium** to a denser one, the light refracts *towards the normal*.
2. When light travels from a dense medium to a less dense one, the light refracts *away from the normal*.

The **normal** is a **perpendicular line** at 90° to the incident ray. To find this line, look at where the first point of contact of the incident ray is. From here, draw a straight line up from this point of contact.

Fig. 11.03.10 As the incident ray enters the glass block it is refracted. The glass block is a denser medium, so the light refracts towards the normal. It continues to travel in a straight line until it exits the block. Since air is less dense than the glass block, the ray of light refracts away from the normal.

Investigation 11.03.03: The effect of refraction of light

Equipment: Glass block, laser, paper, protractor, pencil.

Instructions: Using the equipment listed, design an investigation into the effect of the refraction of light.

> *What did you learn?*
> 1. What was the angle of refraction as the light entered the glass block?
> 2. What was the angle of refraction as the light exited the glass block?
> 3. If possible, can you describe the relationship between the angles of refraction (entering and leaving the block)?
> 4. Conduct this investigation again using a beaker of water instead of a glass block. What do you expect to happen?

Lenses

For some people, light does not focus correctly in their eyes. This causes their vision to be 'blurry'. The structure in the eye that focuses light rays is called the lens. When light passes though the cornea, the lens focuses it onto the retina at the back of the eye, which interprets the image and sends it to our brain.

Fig. 11.03.11 shows light focusing correctly through the lens and onto the retina. The image is formed directly onto the retina and is therefore a clear one.

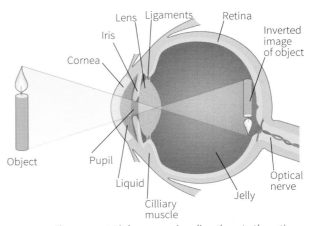

Fig. 11.03.11 Light converging directly onto the retina.

There are two common eye conditions: **long-sightedness** (you can see far away but up close is blurry) and **short-sightedness** (you can see up close but far away is blurry).

If a person is long-sighted their eyes find it difficult to focus light from close-by objects. This is because their eyes form the image beyond the retina (as seen in *Fig. 11.03.12*).

Fig. 11.03.12 How images are formed for long-sighted people.

If a person is short-sighted their eyes find it difficult to focus light from distant objects. This is because their eyes form the image before the retina (as seen in *Fig. 11.03.13*).

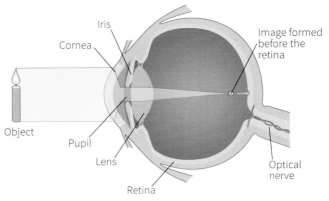

Fig. 11.03.13 How images are formed for short-sighted people.

PHYSICS

Glass lenses can be created to fix long- and short-sightedness by correcting the focus of light onto the retina. A lens is a curved piece of glass or other transparent material that works using the principle of refraction. There are two types of lens: **convex** and **concave**.

Convex Lens

A convex lens suits a long-sighted person as it converges (focuses) the light so that the image is formed back onto the retina.

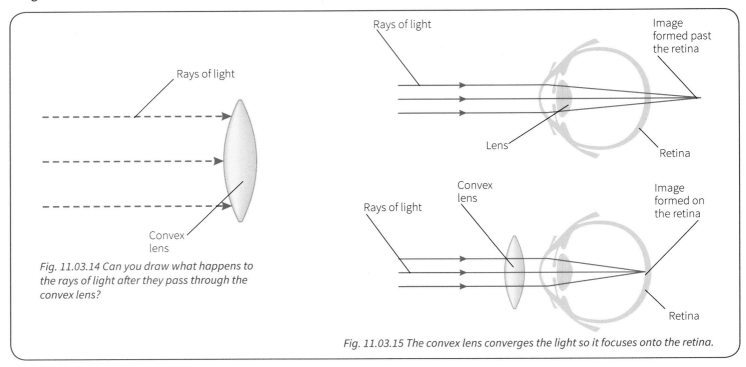

Fig. 11.03.14 Can you draw what happens to the rays of light after they pass through the convex lens?

Fig. 11.03.15 The convex lens converges the light so it focuses onto the retina.

Concave Lens

A concave lens suits a short-sighted person as it diverges (spreads) the light so that the image is formed further forward onto the retina.

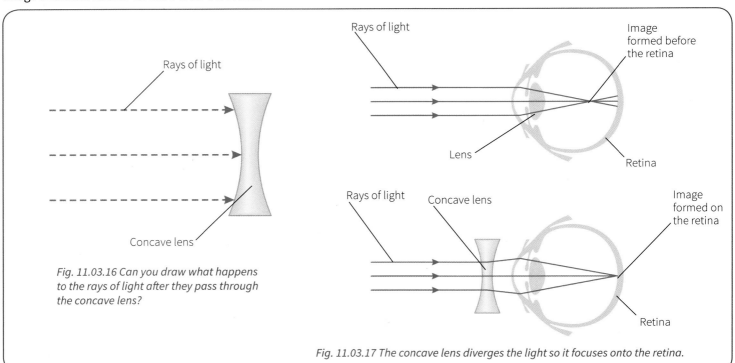

Fig. 11.03.16 Can you draw what happens to the rays of light after they pass through the concave lens?

Fig. 11.03.17 The concave lens diverges the light so it focuses onto the retina.

Checkpoint 3

(a) Give the definition of reflection.
(b) Give the definition of refraction.
(c) How are shadows formed?
(d) What is the name given to the ray coming from the light source heading towards a medium?
(e) Where can you find the reflected ray?
(f) Name the two types of lens and the eye disorders they are used to resolve.
(g) Where in the eye do we want the image to form?

Colour Spectrum

There are seven colours in the rainbow: red, orange, yellow, green, blue, indigo and violet. This little mnemonic device can help you remember them:

Richard	Red
Of	Orange
York	Yellow
Gave	Green
Battle	Blue
In	Indigo
Vain	Violet

Did you know?
When the rays of light hit your retina the image is actually upside down. Your brain receives this upside-down image and then turns it right side up. You can test this by shining a bulb with the power rating on it through a convex lens and looking for the image of the power rating on the other side ... it will be upside down!

Find a CD and hold it close to some light. What do you notice?

🔍 Investigation 11.03.04: **The dispersion of white light**

Equipment: Glass prism, ray box, paper.
Instructions: Using the equipment as listed, design an investigation to demonstrate the dispersion of white light.

> *What did you learn?*
> 1. Can you produce a spectrum every time you try to?
> 2. Using the idea of refraction, can you explain (or draw) what happens to the light as it travels through the prism?

Dispersion: The breaking up of white light into its constituent colours.

Spectrum: A band of colours produced by separation of the components of light by their different degrees of refraction according to wavelength.

When white light (from the sun or from a bulb) is sent through a **prism**, we can break it up into its constituent colours. This means that white light is made up of the seven colours of the rainbow. This phenomenon is called **dispersion** and the band of colours it forms is called a **spectrum**.

PHYSICS

Electromagnetic Spectrum

We have discussed that light is a form of energy, it travels in straight lines and it can reflect and refract. Light has one other very important property: it is a **wave**.

Light belongs to a range of waves called the **electromagnetic spectrum** (see *Fig. 11.03.18*). This spectrum consists of **radio waves**, **micro waves**, **infrared rays**, the **visible colours**, **ultraviolet rays**, **x-rays** and **gamma rays**.

In *Fig. 11.03.18* you will notice numbers at the bottom of the spectrum: these numbers represent the **wavelength** of that wave. The wavelength is the amount of space covered before a wave repeats itself, and it is typically given the symbol λ (Lambda). The wave has two main identifying points: the crest (top of wave) and the trough (bottom). So one wavelength can go from crest to crest or trough to trough.

At the right of the spectrum you can see that we have radio waves, which have a wavelength of 1×10^4 m which is 10 000 m or 10 km. This means that one radio wave will begin to repeat itself after 10 km. Not all radio waves are 10 km long – they can go all the way down to 1 m in wavelength. The shortest wavelength we have is in the gamma ray region, where the wavelength is 1×10^{-14} m; that's 0.00000000000001 m.

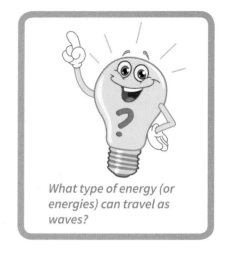

What type of energy (or energies) can travel as waves?

Wavelength: The length of a wave from crest to crest and trough to trough before it starts to repeat itself.

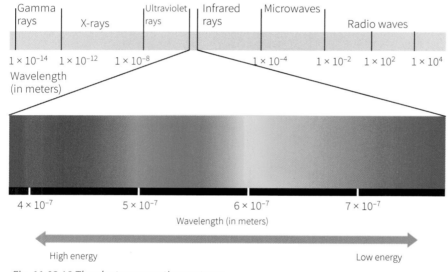

Fig. 11.03.18 The electromagnetic spectrum.

Fig.11.03.19 is a diagram of a wave. One cycle (wavelength) is from one crest (top of wave) to the next crest.

Fig. 11.03.19 Diagram of a wave showing its wavelength.

Types of Waves

Radio Wave

Radio waves are on the far right of the spectrum. These waves are massive: one wavelength (from one crest to the next) is up to 10 km long! Television and radio stations use these waves to broadcast to our TVs and radios.

Microwaves

The wavelength of microwaves is in the cm region. These are the waves that are used to heat up your food in a microwave.

Infrared Rays

The wavelength of infrared rays is too tiny to imagine. Infrared rays can be used to see heat patterns in bodies or to detect an enemy lying in the grass with an infrared gun scope.

Fig. 11.03.20 An infrared image of the heat energy in a suburban house on a cold day.

Visible Light

The visible light section of the electromagnetic spectrum contains all the waves that our eyes can detect. It is also the smallest region of the electromagnetic spectrum and its range is from 4×10^{-7} m to 7×10^{-7} m (400 nm to 700 nm).

Ultraviolet Light

As with microwaves and radio waves, our eyes cannot detect ultraviolet light. Ultraviolet waves are usually emitted by the sun.

X-rays

X-rays are very high-energy waves used to see through human tissue and inspect if bones are broken.

REMEMBER

Two key points to remember:
- As we go from right to left of the spectrum the energy of the waves increases.
- As we go from right to left of the spectrum the wavelength of the waves gets shorter.

Gamma Rays

Gamma rays are ultra-high-energy waves emitted from radio-active elements and nuclear bombs. Exposure to gamma rays for too long can lead to cell mutation (cancer) or even death. However, this effect is used in medicine (radiotherapy) to fight cancer.

One thing all electromagnetic waves have in common is that they contain energy. Ultraviolet rays emitted from the sun can burn your skin, x-rays can penetrate through organic tissue and microwaves can heat up your food by converting light energy into heat energy.

WHAT I HAVE LEARNED...

- Light is a form of energy.
- Luminous objects produce their own light.
- Non-luminous objects do not produce their own light, but can reflect the light of other objects.
- Light travels in straight lines.
- Reflection is the bouncing of light off a surface.
- Refraction is the bending of light at the surface as it passes from one medium into another.
- When passing from a less dense to a denser medium the light rays refract towards the normal.
- When passing from a dense to a less dense medium the light ray refracts away from the normal.
- A concave lens causes the light to diverge.
- Convex lenses converge the lights onto a single point.
- White light is made up of the seven colours of the rainbow. Even though there are millions of colours, we group them into seven main colours.
- Dispersion is the breaking up of white light into its constituent colours.
- Wavelength is the distance from one crest to the next crest in a wave.
- The electromagnetic spectrum is a spectrum of waves ranging from radio waves to gamma rays.
- As you go from right to left in the spectrum the energy of the waves increases.
- As you go from right to left in the spectrum the wavelength of the waves gets shorter.

PHYSICS

Question Time

Copy and Complete

In this unit I learned that _____ is a form of _____. All objects either produce their own _____ while others do not and just _____ it. Objects that produce their own light are called _____ while those that don't are called __-_____. Light travels in a _____ _____. When light bounces off a surface it is called _____. This is how we see our _____ in the _____. Reflected light obeys this simple rule: the angle of _____ is _____ ___ the angle of _____. I also learned why a pencil appears to _____ when placed in a glass of water. This is due to _____. This phenomenon occurs when light passes from one _____ into another. When light passes from a less _____ medium to a more _____ medium, the light is _____ towards the _____. When light passes from a more _____ medium to a less _____ medium, the light is _____ away from the _____. _____ lenses are prescribed to long-sighted people as they _____ the light to one spot. _____ lenses are prescribed to short-sighted people as they _____ the light out. White light is made up of seven colours: _____, _____, _____, _____, _____, _____ and _____. The splitting of white light into its _____ colours is called _____. The _____ spectrum contains the different wavelengths of light. At the right of the spectrum we have _____ waves. These waves can be as long as _____ km. One wavelength is measured from ___/___ to ___/___. As we go from right to left of the spectrum the _____ gets shorter and the _____ increases.

Questions

1. Draw a diagram explaining refraction.
2. What is the rule for reflection?
3. What is wavelength?
4. Where in the electromagnetic spectrum do you find x-rays?
5. Give an example of where you can find x-rays in your everyday life.
6. What is the angle at which the incidence ray hits the mirror?
7. What is the angle at which the reflected ray leaves the mirror?
8. Explain how, with the aid of diagrams, a straw appears to bend at the surface in water.
9. What lens would you prescribe to a long-sighted person? Explain your answer using diagrams to show the light waves with and without the lens.
10. Describe an investigation to show the dispersion of white light. Include both method and diagram.

11. Can you distinguish between the low-energy wavelengths and the high-energy wavelengths of the electromagnetic spectrum?
12. Examine *Fig. 11.03.21* and answer the following questions.

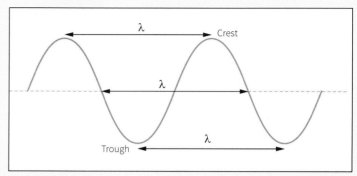

Fig. 11.03.21 Diagram of a wave showing its wavelength.

(i) Using a drawing, show what will happen if we increase the wavelength. Explain your reasoning.
(ii) Using a drawing, show what will happen if we decrease the wavelength. Explain your reasoning.

Inquiry

A In pairs, **design** and **build** a simple periscope.

B **Construct** an obstacle course where a ray of light (from a laser) will get from one end of the bench to the other. In the obstacle course you must show:
(i) reflection
(ii) refraction
(iii) that light travels in a straight line.

C **Investigate** the relationship between different angles of incidence and their matching angles of refraction for a glass block. **Analyse** the relationship by plotting a graph and commenting on any patterns you see.

D **Create** a poster/presentation about laser eye surgery and what happens to the cornea of the eye during the surgery.

E **Create** a poster/presentation about the nature of light (a wave or a stream of particles).

F **Research** how we can see more clearly under water using goggles.

G **Design** an investigation to show light energy being changed into another form of energy.

11.4

Sound and Magnetism

Learning Outcomes

PWLO 1. Select and use appropriate measuring tools.

PWLO 3. Investigate patterns and relationships between physical observables.

NSLO 2. Recognise questions that are appropriate for scientific investigation, pose testable hypotheses, and evaluate and compare strategies for investigating hypotheses.

NSLO 3. Design, plan and conduct investigations; explain how reliability, accuracy, precision, fairness, safety, ethics and a selection of suitable equipment have been considered.

NSLO 7. Organise and communicate research and investigative findings in a variety of ways fit for purpose and audience, using relevant scientific terminology and representations.

R   Teacher's reference

KEYWORDS

attract
decibels
echo
echolocation
electromagnetism
magnetic north
magnetism
north pole
repel
sonar
south pole
ultrasound
vibration

LEARNING INTENTIONS

At the end of this unit you should:

1. Be able to show that it is a form of energy and understand that it is produced by vibrating particles.
2. Be able to show that sound transmission requires a medium and that echoes are reflected sound.
3. Understand how the ear detects sound vibrations and know how very loud sounds can cause hearing damage.
4. Understand that the speed of sound is less than the speed of light.
5. Be able to carry out simple investigations to show attraction and repulsion between magnets and test a variety of materials for magnetism.
6. Be able to demonstrate that the earth has a magnetic field, and locate north and south.
7. Be able to explain how magnetism is a form of energy.

Sound

CAN ANYBODY HEAR ME?

If a tree falls in the forest, and no one is around to hear it, does it make a sound?

Sound: A form of energy caused by vibrations through mediums such as air and which can be detected by a person's ear.

Sound is generated by vibrating particles. Think of the strings on a guitar, a ruler on a desk, the clap of our hands: what happens when these objects are plucked/struck?

🔍 Investigation 11.04.01: **Generating sound using a ruler**

Equipment: Plastic ruler, desk.

Instructions: Place a plastic ruler over the edge of your desk, holding it down with the flat of your hand. With your other hand, press down on the length of the ruler hanging over the edge of your desk, and then let it go.

What did you learn?
1. What happened when you let go of the ruler?
2. Do you think the same observation would happen if you used a ruler made of a different material, such as metal, wood, 'unbreakable' rulers?
3. What happens when you increase/decrease the length of the ruler over the edge of the desk?

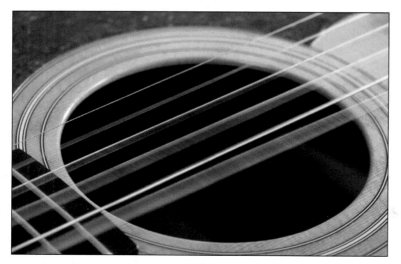

 ✓ Checkpoint 1

'Sound is a form of energy.' Do you agree or disagree with this statement? Justify your position by giving examples.

Fig. 11.04.01 Guitars generate sound through the vibration of their strings. The vibration is then amplified by either a hollow hole in the body (acoustic) or through electronic pickups (electric).

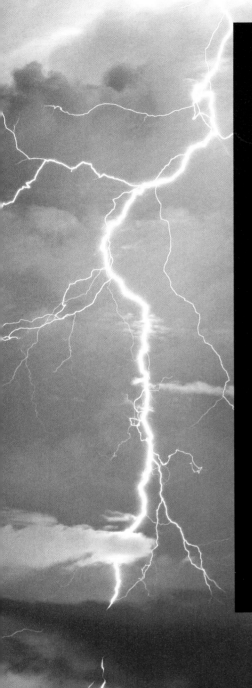

Investigation 11.04.02: **Identifying what sound needs to travel**

Equipment: Bell jar, vacuum pump, sound-producing equipment (alarm, phone, buzzer, etc.).

Instructions: Using the equipment as listed, design an investigation to determine how sound travels.

The Speed of Sound

Sound travels at different speeds depending on the medium it is in. In air the speed of sound is 340 m/s. In liquids it is 1400 m/s, and in solids it travels even faster, at a whopping 5000 m/s. However, when you compare the speed of sound to the speed of light, it is much, much slower. This is why we see lightning before we hear the thunder.

Formula: You can calculate how far away the lightning is from you by using your distance-speed-time formula from *Unit 10.2*.

$$\text{Speed} = \frac{\text{Distance}}{\text{Time}} = \frac{\text{metres}}{\text{seconds}} = \text{m/s}$$

We know that sound travels at 340 m/s. If we count the time taken in seconds between the flash of lightning and the sound of thunder, we simply calculate distance using:

distance = speed x time

✓ Checkpoint 2

(a) A boy sees lightning and counts eight seconds before he hears the thunder. How far away is the lightning?

(b) Two people are on the phone to each other. Person A sees lightning and hears the thunder instantly. Person B sees the flash of lightning but it takes thirty-two seconds before they hear the thunder. How far away is Person B from Person A?

Reflection of Sound

Much like light, sound can be reflected. You've all experienced this. If you are standing in a large empty hall and you shout, you will hear yourself. This is because the sound has reflected (bounced) off the wall. This is called an **echo**.

Reflection of sound waves is the principle behind **sonar** technology. For example, a ship will produce an **ultrasound** frequency wave which will travel towards the bottom of the ocean floor; the sound wave will reflect off the floor and return to the ship. The sonar system can then determine how deep the floor is, as well as give very good estimations as to where schools of fish and other marine animals may be.

Echo: The reflection of a sound off a surface.

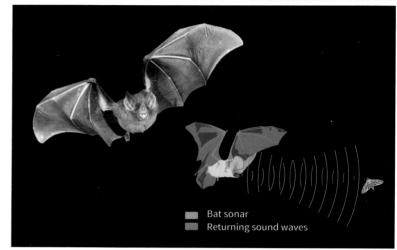

Bat sonar
Returning sound waves

*Fig. 11.04.02 Bats use **echolocation** to determine where they are in dark caves. They emit very high-pitched sounds called ultrasounds and these reflect off nearby objects. The bat can now determine how far away an object is.*

Formula: To calculate the distance from the ship to the sea bed and back, we use the following formula:

Velocity = two times the distance divided by the time taken

$$V = \frac{2d}{t}$$

But remember this is for the total distance, down and up. So you need to half the answer you get for the distance to the sea bed.

Formula: First we need to note what information we are given. We are given the speed of sound in water, which is 1500 m/s, and the total time (t) taken for the ultrasound to be heard again, which is 0.3 s. So plugging into our formula we get:

$$1500 = \frac{2d}{0.3}$$

Manipulating the formula we now get:

2d = 1500 x 0.3   2d = 450 m

But this is for the whole journey, to the sea floor and back. So we must divide by two to get the distance to the sea floor.

$$\frac{450}{2} = 225 \text{ m to the sea floor}$$

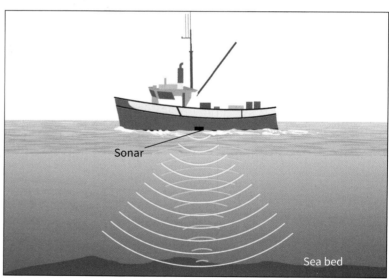

Sonar

Sea bed

Fig. 11.04.03 A ship using sonar.

 **Checkpoint 3**

(a) Bats are not the only animals that use echolocation. Can you name one other animal and one object that uses echolocation?

(b) A ship sends a pulse of ultrasound and receives an echo 0.1 of a second later. The speed of sound in water is 1500 m/s.
   (i)   What is the distance to the sea floor?
   (ii) What is the total distance the ultrasound wave travelled?
   (iii) A map of the area shows that where they are currently anchored, the sea floor is 65 m deep. By what percent is the sonar reading off?
   (iv) Suggest a reason why the map and the sonar could be giving different depths?

The Structure of the Ear

The ear consists of three section:

1. The **outer ear:** the part we can see, comprising the ear and ear canal.
2. The **middle ear:** containing three bones called ossicles. These are called the hammer, anvil and stirrup.
3. The **inner ear:** containing the cochlea.

When a sound reaches our ears the sound vibrates our eardrum. This **vibration** causes the hammer, anvil and stirrup to pass the vibrations along to the fluid in the cochlea. These vibrations are turned into an electrical signal, which are sent through the nerves to the brain.

Our Ears and How to Protect Them

Recall that sound is a form of energy. This means that at high energies, sound can actually damage our ear drum and in turn our hearing. The level of sound loudness is measured in units of **decibels** (dB). We can measure loudness of a sound using the sound level meter.

At the start of the decibel scale we have 0 dB, which we call the threshold of hearing. This is the lowest sound that human ears can hear.

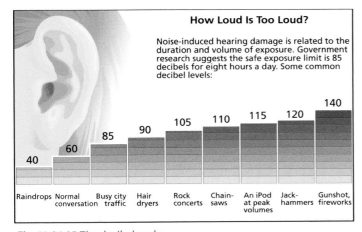

How Loud Is Too Loud?

Noise-induced hearing damage is related to the duration and volume of exposure. Government research suggests the safe exposure limit is 85 decibels for eight hours a day. Some common decibel levels:

| 40 | 60 | 85 | 90 | 105 | 110 | 115 | 120 | 140 |
| Raindrops | Normal conversation | Busy city traffic | Hair dryers | Rock concerts | Chain-saws | An iPod at peak volumes | Jack-hammers | Gunshot, fireworks |

Fig. 11.04.05 The decibel scale.

Fig. 11.04.04 Diagram of the ear.

Labels: Pinna, Semi-circular canals, Vestibular nerve, Cochlear (auditory) nerve, Eardrum, Ossicles, Cochlea, Auditory canal, Eustachian tube, Outer ear, Middle ear, Inner ear

As the sound level increases, the vibrations will cause increased damage to the human ear, and at 85 dB, long exposure will have lasting damage on a person's hearing.

At the top end of the scale we have concerts (100 dB) and airplanes taking off (120 dB). 120 dB is regarded as the pain threshold; anything above this will not only cause damage to hearing but will also cause pain. You know you've damaged your hearing when you have a ringing in your ears. If this happens, rest your ears for a day before exposing them to loud noises again, i.e. leave out the earphones!

Building sites, concerts and even airports are all examples of dangerous places for our hearing. This is why builders and airport staff on the runway are required by law to wear ear protection. Ear protection reduces the damage done to the ear drum and protects hearing.

Magnetism

You have more than likely come across a magnet in your life. They are sometimes used in children's toys and board games. But did you know that **magnetism** is a form of energy? A magnet is made up of an iron core, or cobalt, nickel and lodestone. These metals have the property of attracting other magnetic elements.

When two magnets are brought near each other they will either **attract** or **repel**. Each magnet has two ends, called poles, and are either the **north pole** or the **south pole**.

Magnetism: The force of attraction or replusion between two magnetic objects; a form of energy.

Fig. 11.04.06 Toys that include magnets as part of their design.

PHYSICS

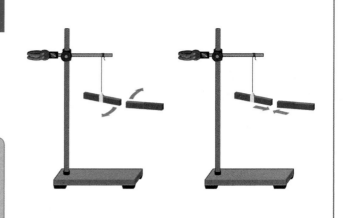

> **Investigation 11.04.03: The attraction/repulsion of north and south poles**
>
> **Equipment:** Bar magnets, retort stand, string.
> **Instructions:** Using the equipment as listed, design an investigation to demonstrate the attraction/ repulsion of the north and south pole on another magnet's north and south pole.
>
> ### What did you learn?
> 1. Why shouldn't we use a metal retort stand?
> 2. How did you determine which pole of the magnet was which?
> 3. What are the rules for attraction and repulsion?

The Earth's Magnetic Energy

If you allow two magnets to hang from two retort stands (not near each other), you will notice that both magnets line up in the same direction. In other words, the north poles of each magnet will face the same direction, as will the south poles. This is because the earth itself has a magnetic energy of its own. This is how compasses work.

It is generally believed that inside the earth there is a hot iron core. This core produces the magnetic energy via the rotation of the core. As the core rotates, current is generated, which in turn produces a magnetic field. This phenomenon is called **electromagnetism**.

You might naturally presume then that this is why the North Pole is called the North Pole, and the South Pole the South Pole. But as you will have seen from *Investigation 11.04.03*, like poles (south with south, north with north) repel each other, while opposite poles (south with north) attract each other. This means that if the North Pole contained the north pole of a magnet, a compass would always face south. In fact, the North Pole contains South Pole magnetism, which means that the north pole of a magnet is attracted to it. This is why a magnet points north, and is referred to as **magnetic north**.

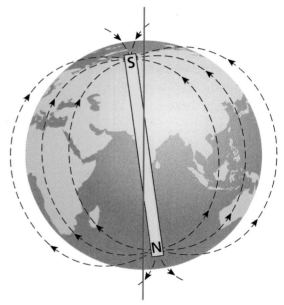

Fig. 11.04.07 The geographic north and south poles and the magnetic north and south poles of the earth.

WHAT I HAVE LEARNED...

- Sound is a form of energy.
- Sound needs a medium to pass through.
- The speed of sound in air is 340 m/s.
- Sound can be reflected.
- To calculate the distance of a reflected sound we use the formula $v = \frac{2d}{t}$.
- Light travels faster than sound.
- The loudness of a sound is measured in decibels (dB).

- Magnetism is a form of energy.
- Magnets have two poles: north and south.
- Like poles repel and opposite poles attract.
- The earth has a weak magnetic energy.
- The South Pole contains north magnetism.
- The North Pole contains south magnetism.

Question Time

Copy and Complete

In this unit I learned that _____ and _____ are forms of energy. Sound is produced by the _____ of particles. Sound can only travel where particles are present and as such it cannot travel in a _____. The _____ of sound is measured in _____. Anything under _____ is safe for our hearing. However, anything over this value could cause damage to our hearing. We know our hearing has been damaged when we can _____ _ _____ in our ears. I also learned that _____ have two _____, _____ and _____. _____ attract and _____ repel. This means that the north pole _____ another north pole but _____ a south pole. This is the principle of the _____. The earth has a North and South Pole. The North Pole contains _____ _____ magnetism.

Questions

1. Describe an experiment to verify that sound needs a medium to travel.
2. How is sound detected by our ears?
3. The 1979 science fiction film, *Alien,* used the slogan, 'In space no one can hear you scream'. With reference to the properties of sound, explain the physics of this slogan. (*2014 HL JC*)
4. What are echoes?
5. A man stood 250 m from a wall and fired a starting pistol. 1.5 s later he heard the echo of the shot. Use this data to calculate the speed of sound in air. (*2014 HL JC*)
6. At what dB should a person wear ear protection?
7. What is the dB of a normal conversation?
8. What are Earth's two poles called?
9. What magnetism does the North Pole contain?
10. Explain how the earth generates its magnetic field.
11. Explain how the earth's magnetism is used in the design of compasses.

Inquiry

A **Research** the hearing range of different species and compare them to humans.

B **Research/create a poster/make a presentation/ take part in a debate** on the long-term effects of listening to music too loudly through headphones.

C **Design** an investigation to find the best material for sound insulation.

D **Design** an investigation to show the magnetic field lines of a bar magnet.

E **Construct** a simple electromagnet.

F **Make** a model of the earth's magnetic field.

G **Research** what would happen to us if the earth's magnetic field reduces, or if it were to flip poles!

H **Design** an investigation to show magnetic energy being converted to other forms of energy.

I **Design** an investigation to show sound energy being converted to other forms of energy.

J **Research/create a poster/make a presentation** on where infrasound, ultrasound etc. are used in industry.

ALIEN

In space no one can hear you scream.

PHYSICS

Learning Outcomes

PWLO 1. Select and use appropriate measuring tools.

PWLO 2. Identify and measure/calculate mass and force.

PWLO 3. Investigate patterns and relationships between physical observables.

NSLO 2. Recognise questions that are appropriate for scientific investigation, pose testable hypotheses, and evaluate and compare strategies for investigating hypotheses.

NSLO 3. Design, plan and conduct investigations; explain how reliability, accuracy, precision, fairness, safety, ethics and a selection of suitable equipment have been considered.

NSLO 4. Produce and select data (qualitatively/ quantitatively), critically analyse data to identify patterns and relationships, identify anomalous observations, draw and justify conclusions.

(R) Teacher's reference

KEYWORDS

acceleration
direct proportion
extension
force
friction
gravity
lubrication
mass
newton
weight
weightlessness
work

LEARNING INTENTIONS

At the end of this unit you should:

1. Understand force and know that the newton (N) is the unit of force.
2. Be able to describe forces and their effects.
3. Know how to investigate examples of friction and the effect of lubrication.
4. Know how to investigate the relationship between the extension of a spring and the applied force.
5. Understand that weight is the force of gravity and that it varies with location; recall that mass in kilograms multiplied by 10 is approximately equal to weight in newtons on the surface of the earth.
6. Be able to explain and give the unit for work.

What do you think a force is?

The Force you are looking for, this is not

What is a Force?

When we think about forces we may think of pushing, pulling, etc. **Force** is anything that causes the motion of an object to change. As well as pushing and pulling, other examples of forces include **friction**, **gravity**, electric force, magnetic force and **weight**.

How did we find out what a force was? As we have already established, the Greeks were great scientists in their day. However, one thing they couldn't explain adequately was what a 'force' was. Aristotle gave a basic idea of what a force was, but could not account for forces such as friction. It wasn't until 1687 when Sir Isaac Newton published his *Principia Mathematica* that the concept of force was finally understood.

Newton developed Three Laws of Motion:

1. A body at rest will remain at rest, and a body in motion will remain in motion unless it is acted upon by an external force.
2. The force is directly proportional to the **acceleration** and **mass** of an object.
3. For every action, there is an equal and opposite reaction.

Force: Anything which causes the motion of an object to change. The unit of force is the **newton** (N).

Fig. 12.01.01 *Aristotle gave a basic idea of what a force was, while Isaac Newton established the concept of force with his Three Laws of Motion.*

Fig. 12.01.02 *This camogie player is about to cause the motion of an object to change.*

PHYSICS

Newton's First Law of Motion

Newton's First Law of Motion states:

> *A body at rest will remain at rest, and a body in motion will remain in motion unless it is acted upon by an external force.*

Newton stated that if an object is at rest (stationary/not moving) it will stay at rest, unless something external acts on it, such as a push/pull. Think of a football on the penalty spot: it will sit there all day until the player kicks it towards the net. The second part of this law states that objects in motion will stay in motion unless acted upon by an external force. If we kick a ball along the ground, we know it will not roll forever. This seems to violate Newton's law! Nothing external is acting on it, so why does it slow down and stop? This is because forces such as gravity and friction are acting on the ball. In fact, we can actually calculate the size of the forces involved, i.e. calculate the force of the ball being kicked from the penalty spot, by using Newton's second law.

Newton's Second Law of Motion

Newton's Second Law of Motion states:

> *The force is directly proportional to the acceleration and mass of an object.*

Force = Mass x Acceleration	Where F = Force; m = Mass (in kilograms); a = Acceleration (in m/s^2)

So if we know the mass of the object and the acceleration it undergoes, we can calculate the force.

We learned back in *Unit 10.2* that acceleration was the rate of change of velocity with respect to time, and we looked at examples with cars, bikes and people. But did you know that gravity, the force which pulls us towards the earth, also has an acceleration? This is called **Acceleration Due to Gravity** and has a value of roughly 10 m/s^2.

> **Acceleration Due to Gravity:** The downward force experienced on the earth. The value of gravity on the earth is approximately 10 m/s^2.

Calculations using F = ma

You will be asked to calculate force, mass or acceleration using $F = ma$

For example:

Question: A body of mass 50 kg undergoes an acceleration of 1.5 m/s^2. What is the resulting force?

Formula: In this question we are given mass (m) to be 50 kg.
We are also given acceleration (a) to be 1.5 m/s^2. Both are in SI units and so there is no need to convert.

$F = ma$
$F = 50 \text{ kg} \times 1.5 \text{ m/s}^2$
$F = 75 \text{ kg m/s}^2$
$F = 75 \text{ N}$

Note: kg m/s^2 is the alternative unit for force. 1 kg m/s^2 = 1 N.

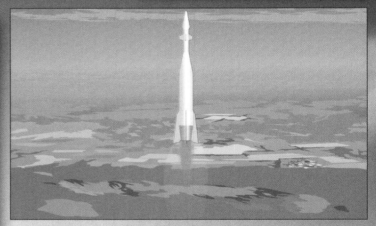

Fig. 12.01.03 *A rocket is an example of changing the mass to create force. The fuel in the rocket is burned, which generates energy. (There is even more than this at play, which we will discuss later in this unit.)*

Checkpoint 1

(a) Copy and complete *Table 12.01.01*, establishing what caused the change (mass/ acceleration), the approximate size of the force (small/large) and in what direction the force acted (up/down/left/right, etc.). Add some more examples of your own.

Scenario	What Caused the Change?	Size of Force Required	Direction of Force
Apple falling from tree	Acceleration due to gravity	Small	Downward
A person being pushed			
A car slowing down			
A rocket taking off			
Another example			
Another example			

Table 12.01.01.

(b) What does Newton's Second Law of Motion state?

(c) What is the mathematical statement of Newton's Second Law of Motion?

(d) An object of mass 10 kg is accelerated at 1 m/s². What is the resultant force?

(e) A person has a mass of 55 kg. What force would be required to accelerate this person at 15 m/s²?

(f) An apple falls from a tree under an acceleration of 9.8 m/s², and hits you on the head. What force would it exert on a person's head if the apple has a mass of 0.0125 kg?

(g) A toy car of mass 5 g gains a force of 4.5 N. What acceleration did it obtain to achieve this force?

(h) A force of 100 N is required to accelerate a boulder 0.5 m/s². Find the mass of the boulder.

Fig. 12.01.04 As discussed earlier, an external force has been applied to this ball: an example of Newtons first and second laws.

Newton's Third Law of Motion

You might already be familiar with Isaac Newton's Third Law of Motion. Newton's Third Law of Motion states:

For every action, there is an equal and opposite reaction.

Fig. 12.01.05 Newton discovering gravity. Legend has it that while sitting under an apple tree contemplating the laws of nature an apple fell and hit him on the head, thus inspiring him to develop his theory of gravity.

PHYSICS

Investigation 12.01.01: **Action and reaction forces**

Equipment: You and a classmate (though you won't be using ice skates!).

Instructions: Grab a partner and position yourselves as the figures in *Fig. 12.01.06.*

What did you learn?

1. Before carrying out the investigation, copy *Fig. 12.01.06* and draw what you think would be the force arrows.
2. Now re-enact the diagram with your partner. Do your force arrows accurately represent what happens in the investigation? If not, redraw the force arrows in a different colour pen.
3. Now get one person to push harder. What happens? Redraw the arrows again using a different colour pen, this time indicating which force was greater.

Fig. 12.01.06 Action and reaction forces.

Remember the rocket image from *Fig. 12.01.03*? As Newton's third law states, for every action there is an equal and opposite reaction. In the rocket, the fuel is burned and the exhaust fumes are forced through the engine nozzles. This downward force generates an upward force, which propels the rocket forward (*Fig. 12.01.07*)?

Investigation 12.01.02: **The forces acting on a spring balance**

Equipment: Spring balances.

Instructions: With a partner, hook together a pair of spring balances. Very gently, one of you pulls away from the other. Take a note of the readings.

What did you learn?

1. Draw a diagram of the spring balances and the relevant force arrows.
2. What do you notice about the weight in each balance?
3. Can you draw a conclusion about the relationship between the forces involved in the spring balances?

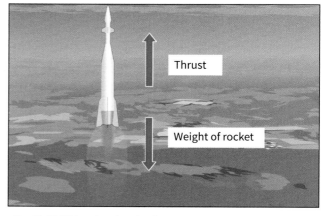

Thrust

Weight of rocket

Fig. 12.01.07 A rocket showing force.

Weight and Mass

In our everyday lives, weight and mass mean the same thing. However, in science they are like chalk and cheese!

Mass is the amount of matter in an object.

Weight is the force of gravity acting on an object.

$$w = mg$$

where w = Weight; m = Mass; g = acceleration due to gravity

Mass: The amount of matter in an object. Mass is constant for a particular object. This means it is a property of that object.

Weight: The force of gravity acting on an object. The unit of weight is the newton (N). Weight = mass x gravity.

Question:

An astronaut of mass 85 kg is on a mission to the moon. During his mission he will complete repair work on the ship before landing on the moon. Calculate his weight during the repair work.

Formula:

(i) Remember, in space there is no acceleration due to gravity, so gravity (g) is zero. Plugging this into the formula we get:

$w = mg$

$w = 85 \text{ kg} \times 0 \text{ m/s}^2$

$w = 0 \text{ N}$

(ii) We have a body of mass 85 kg and gravity 1.62 m/s^2

$w = mg$

$w = 85 \text{ kg} \times 1.62 \text{ m/s}^2$

$w = 137.7 \text{ N}$

This is the ultimate diet – I weigh nothing!
You're still massive though!

When astronauts go into space they experience **weightlessness**. This means that if the astronauts tried to stand on a weighing scales (which is not possible anyhow due to lack of gravity), the scales would read zero. However, the astronauts still retain their mass. Remember: mass is constant for an object. It is the amount of matter in the object. We can show this mathematically as follows:

$w = mg$

$w = 80 \text{ kg} \times 0 \text{ m/s}^2$

$w = 0 \text{ N}$

This explains how astronauts 'float' in space.

Checkpoint 2

(a) Copy and complete *Table 12.01.02* by calculating the weight of each astronaut on each planet.

(b) On which planet/moon do the astronauts weigh the least?

(c) Which planets/moons can the astronauts actually land on? Justify your answer with reference to your calculations.

Planet	Astronaut 1 (60 kg)	Astronaut 2 (45 kg)	Astronaut 3 (93.5 kg)
Earth (9.81 m/s^2)			
Space			
Mars (3.71 m/s^2)			
Venus (8.87 m/s^2)			
Jupiter (24.79 m/s^2)			
Saturn (10.44 m/s^2)			
Pluto (0.658 m/s^2)			
Phobos (0.0057 m/s^2)			

Table 12.01.02.

REMEMBER

Gravity always acts towards the centre of the planet, i.e. gravity is always acting down.

Friction as a Force

Friction is the force that opposes motion. One of the most common uses of friction is in the brakes in cars. A car will use rubber pads to stop the wheels turning; this causes massive amounts of friction on the wheels and will slow the car to a stop.

Rub your hands together. What do you notice? You should notice that your hands get hotter. This is one of the effects of friction. Some car manufactures will use this as a special effect on their brake disks. When a car is braking, the brake pads will glow red hot, as seen in *Fig. 12.01.08*.

Friction: The force that opposes motion.

Fig. 12.01.08 Car breaks heating up and glowing red.

Lubrication: A method of reducing friction.

In many cases we will wish to reduce the effects of friction, i.e. in the slowing down of skateboards, toy cars, etc. To do so we must use a technique called **lubrication**. Lubrication involves polishing the surface or applying oil to the surface or wheels. In doing so, we reduce the amount of friction between the objects in contact. Applying oil to wheels in a skateboard allows the wheels to move more easily, so in turn the skateboard moves faster.

A car of mass 1000 kg encounters friction on the road when it is moving. If the car is moving at a constant speed of 27.7 m/s and the force of friction is 2770 N, what is the force the engine exerts?

The Extension of a Spring

The **extension** of a spring is the difference between the natural length of the spring and the spring length when force is applied to it.

Investigation 12.01.03: **The effects of forces**

Equipment: The apparatus as shown in the diagram.

Instructions: Using the equipment as shown, design an experiment to investigate the effect of forces by hanging different objects from a spring.

What did you learn?

1. Draw a table of the force (N) and the extension caused by that force.
2. Did you notice a pattern in the data obtained?
3. Now draw a graph of the table you made.
4. Can you describe the pattern you found (if any) in your graph?
5. Is this pattern consistent with the pattern (if any) you found in your table?
6. What do you think will happen if you use a different spring for this experiment?
7. Could you use another of your class group's graphs to determine an unknown force for your spring? Why?

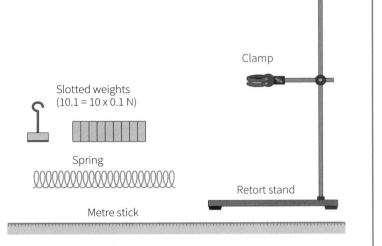

Clamp

Slotted weights
(10.1 = 10 x 0.1 N)

Spring

Retort stand

Metre stick

You should have noticed that when you place a weight on the spring it extends by a certain amount. Adding more of the same weight, you should have noticed it always extended by the same amount. This is what we call **direct proportion**, and is a key relationship. The relationship is called **Hooke's Law** and it states:

Direct Proportion: When one physical quantity changes, the other physical quantity changes at the same rate.

The extension of a spring is directly proportional to the force applied to it.

So as the force goes up, so too does the extension.

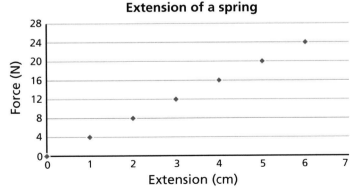

Fig. 12.01.09 *We can see that as the force increases by 4 N, the spring extends by 1 cm each time.*

ROBERT HOOKE
1635 - 1703

Fig. 12.01.10 *Robert Hooke (1635–1703), who gave his name to Hooke's Law.*

PHYSICS

Work

Work is a way of measuring how much energy is used. Work depends on two factors:

(i)   The force applied

(ii) Distance this force is applied over.

For work to happen, energy is needed to create a force. We can calculate the work done using the formula:

Work = force x distance

W = f x d

Because work requires energy it can be measured in joules as well as newton metres. Imagine you are carrying a bag of potatoes from a person's car. The car is parked 20 m away from the house and the bag of potatoes has a force of 100 N. To calculate the work done:

Work = force x distance

Work = 100 N x 20 m

Work = 2000 J

Fig. 12.01.11 Carrying potatoes is a lot of work.

WHAT I HAVE LEARNED...

- A force is something that causes an object to change its motion. This means the object can start moving, move faster, stop moving or simply change direction.
- Force is measured in newtons (N).
- **Force = mass x acceleration** (F = ma).
- Newton's Third Law of Motion: For every action (force) there is an equal and opposite reaction (force).
- Mass is the amount of matter in an object. This never changes, even if you are in space.
- Weight is the force of gravity acting on the mass of the object. If there is no gravity present, the object will float due to weightlessness, but it still has a mass!

- Weight = mass x gravity (W = mg).
- Friction is the force that opposes motion. In other words, it is the force that tries to slow objects down.
- Friction in the form of brakes slows cars down.
- To reduce friction we lubricate either the surface or the object.
- Hooke's Law states that the extension of a spring is directly proportional to the force applied to the spring.
- Work is done when a force moves an object over a certain distance.

Question Time

Copy and Complete

In this unit I learned that a _____ causes something to _____. To find force we multiply _____ and _____ _____ _____ _____. I also learned that Newton's Third Law states that for every_____ there is an equal and _____ _____. _____ is the amount of matter in a body. Mass is always constant. I also learned that _____ and _____ are not the same. _____ is the force of gravity acting on a body. This is why astronauts experience _____ in space. _____ is the force which opposes motion. There are useful examples of friction such as in car _____. However, if we want to reduce friction we use a technique called _____. I also learned a key relationship between the force applied to an elastic object and the _____ of this object. This is also known as _____ Law. Finally I learned that _____ is done when a _____ moves an object over a certain _____.

Questions

1. What is a force and what is its unit of measurement?
2. What tool is used to measure forces?
3. State Newton's Second Law of Motion.
4. What is the mathematical formula for Newton's second law?
5. State Newton's Third Law of Motion.
6. Give three examples of action/reaction pairs of forces.
7. Define friction.
8. Give five examples of where you would encounter friction.
9. Can friction be helpful? If so, give an example.
10. What is the method used for reducing friction?
11. A person has a mass of 55 kg and accelerates at 5 m/s². Calculate the force when a mass of 55 kg is accelerated at 5 m/s².
12. Calculate the work done when a 50 N rock is pushed 5 m.
13. Calculate the force of an object that produces a work of 4400 J when moved over 12 m.
14. Calculate the mass of an object which, when moved 2.5 m, produces 1200 J of work.
15. A 78 kg person is pushed with a force of 8.76 N. What is their acceleration?
16. A driver slams on his brakes, causing the brakes to undergo a force of 1200 N. If the car weighs 1000 kg, what is the deceleration (slowing down) of the car?
17. Calculate the work done when a 65 kg person runs up a flight of stairs. The flight of stairs contains fourteen steps, each at a height of 0.15 m.

18. (R) Design an experiment to investigate what the magnitude (size/extent) of the force of friction is on the following objects:
    (a) Moving a skateboard on gravel
    (b) Moving a ball along a flat surface
    (c) Moving a rubber-soled shoe across a tiled floor.

19. The equipment shown in *Fig. 12.01.12* was set up and used to investigate the relationship between the extension of a spring and the force applied to it. The data collected is presented in *Table 12.01.03*.

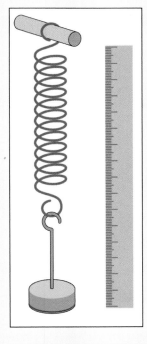

Fig. 12.01.12 Investigating the relationship between the extension of a spring and the force applied to it.

Force (N)	2	4	6	8	10
Extension (cm)	5	10	15	20	25

Table 12.01.03.

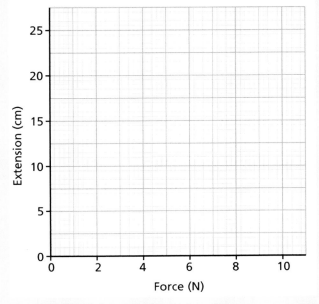

Fig. 12.01.13 Grid of extension in relation to force.

PHYSICS

(i) Use the data in *Table 12.01.03* to draw a graph of Extension (y-axis) against Force (x-axis) using the grid as shown in *Fig. 12.01.13*.

(ii) Use the graph to estimate the extension if a force of 3 N is applied to the spring.

Extension: _____ cm

(iii) What would happen if too large a force is applied to the spring? (*JC OL 2014*)

20. *Fig. 12.01.14* shows the brakes on a bicycle. When the cyclist wishes to slow down, she pulls a lever, which pushes the rubber brake pad against the rim of the wheel. Explain why the brakes might not work as well after it has been raining? (*JC HL 2014*)

Fig. 12.01.14 The brakes on a bicycle.

Inquiry

A **Design** an experiment to investigate how far equally weighed objects will slide on different surfaces. Once designed, carry out your investigation.

B Space shuttles have to withstand massive heat on re-entering Earth's orbit. **Explain** how this heat is generated on space shuttles and **research** and **present** information on how this heat is reduced, used, convert or minimised.

C When it rains, drivers are advised to slow down as their stopping distance is increased. **Research** normal stopping distance for 30 km/h, 50 km/h, 60 km/h, 80 km/h, 100 km/h and 120 km/h. **Compare** these stopping distances to the stopping distance in rain and **comment** on the effect rain has on a car's stopping power. Using the information you have been given so far in this unit, offer a **hypothesis** as to why the stopping distance is increased.

12.2 Pressure

Learning Outcomes

PWLO 1. Select and use appropriate measuring tools.
PWLO 3. Investigate patterns and relationships between physical observables.
NSLO 2. Recognise questions that are appropriate for scientific investigation, pose testable hypotheses, and evaluate and compare strategies for investigating hypotheses.
NSLO 3. Design, plan and conduct investigations; explain how reliability, accuracy, precision, fairness, safety, ethics, **and a selection of suitable equipment have been considered.**

(R) Teacher's reference

LEARNING INTENTIONS

At the end of this unit you should:
1. Understand the relationship between pressure, force and area; perform simple calculations using this relationship.
2. Be able to explain the relationship between pressure and depth for a liquid.
3. Be able to explain that air has mass and occupies space.
4. Understand that the atmosphere exerts pressure and that atmospheric pressure varies with height.
5. Be able to examine weather charts to observe variations in atmospheric pressure and relate these to weather conditions.

PHYSICS

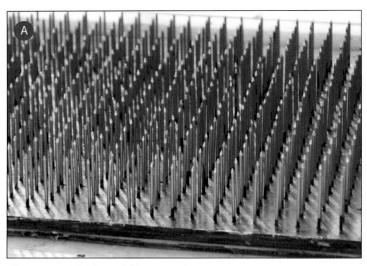

Fig. 12.02.01 Which would hurt more?

Which do you think would hurt more: lying on a bed of nails or sitting on a single nail?

What is **pressure**? Not to be confused with force, pressure is the amount of force over an area.

Imagine we have two identical thumbtacks, except one is sharp and the other is blunt (*Fig. 12.02.02*). If you apply equal force of 2 N to both of these, only one goes into the corkboard. Why, you might ask? Pressure is equal to the force divided by the area. So if we apply equal force, the only factor that changes is the area. One thumbtack is sharp and the other blunt: the sharp thumbtack has the smallest area and this creates the greatest force.

Pressure: The amount of force acting over a unit area.

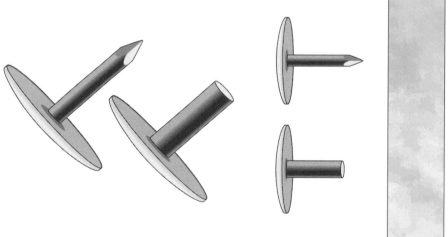
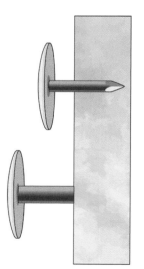

Fig. 12.02.02 Two thumbtacks – one sharp, the other blunt. When they are pushed into a corkboard, the sharp thumbtack is easily pushed through, while the blunt one is not.

Checkpoint 1

(a) Try pushing your finger against the desk. Now, using the same amounts of force, push your fist against the desk. What did you notice? Which hurt more?

(b) Which do you think exerts the greater pressure:
   (i) An elephant's foot or high heels?
   (ii) A thumbtack exerting 5 N or the same thumbtack exerting 4 N?

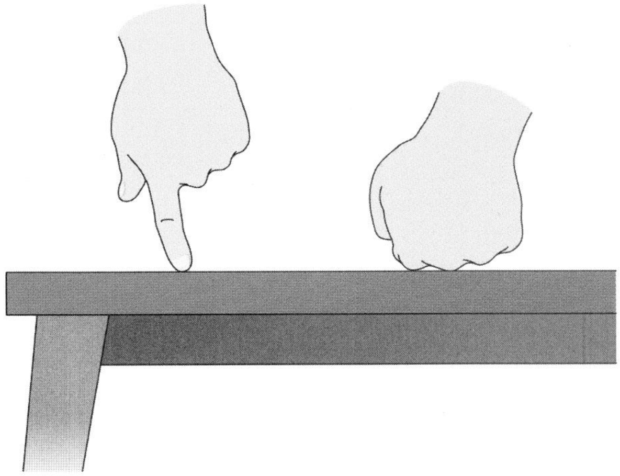

Fig. 12.02.03 Exerting a force.

Fig. 12.02.04 Which exerts the greater pressure?

Remember that pressure is the force per unit area, or mathematically:

$$\text{Pressure} = \frac{\text{Force}}{\text{Area}} \qquad P = \frac{F}{A}$$

Replacing the units we get:

$$\text{Pressure} = \frac{\text{newton}}{\text{metre}^2}$$

Another name for N/m^2 is the **pascal** (Pa) and this is the standard unit of pressure.

UNITS
Pressure = Pa (Nm^2)
Force = N
Area = m^2 (cm^2)

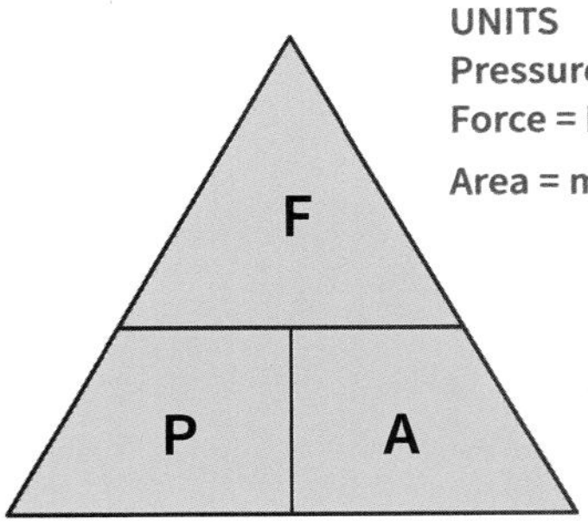

$$\text{Pressure} = \frac{\text{Force}}{\text{Area}} \qquad P = \frac{F}{A}$$

Question: Imagine we have a solid concrete rectangular block with a weight of 4000 N (*Fig. 12.02.05*). The sides measure 4 m and 5 m, with a height of 3 m.

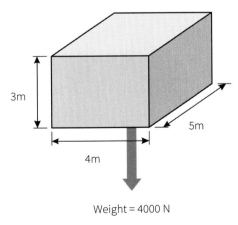

Weight = 4000 N

Fig. 12.02.05.

Formula: We want to calculate the pressure, so we first find the area under the block.
   Area = 4 m x 5 m = 20 m²

Remember: we only want the area touching the surface.
We know the force is 4000 N so now we can find pressure:

$$\text{Pressure} = \frac{\text{Force}}{\text{Area}} = \frac{2000\ N}{20m^2} = 200\ Pa\ (N/m^2)$$

Question: Now let's put this box on its side so the new area at the bottom is 3 m x 4 m with a height of 5 m. The box still weighs the same. Fill in the blanks to complete the calculation.

   Pressure = _____ /Area

   Pressure = 4000 N/ _____

   Pressure =_____ Pa

Question: Finally let's turn the block so we get a new area under the block of 3 m x 5 m. Fill in the blanks to complete the calculation.

   Pressure = _____/ _____

   Pressure = _____/ _____

   Pressure = _____ Pa

PHYSICS

Checkpoint 2

(a) What is pressure?

(b) What is the unit of pressure?

(c) Name another unit of pressure.

(d) Which exerts the greatest pressure on a road surface: a bicycle tyre or a car tyre?

Fig. 12.02.06 Which exerts the greatest pressure on a road surface?

(e) Calculate the following:

   (i) The pressure of a 50 N block with an area of 10 m².

   (ii) The pressure of a 75 N block with an area of 100 m².

   (iii) The pressure of a 100 N block with height of 1 m and sides of 2 m and 3 m.

(f) Calculate the pressure of a 200 N block with a height of 2 m, length of 3 m and depth of 5 m (*Fig. 12.02.07*).

(g) Calculate the pressure of a 450 N block with a height of 3 m, length of 5 m and depth of 2 m (*Fig. 12.02.08*).

(h) Calculate the pressure of a 1000 N block with a height of 5 m, length of 3 m and depth of 2 m (*Fig. 12.02.09*).

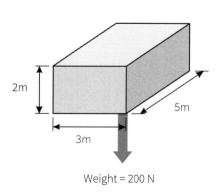

Weight = 200 N

Fig. 12.02.07.

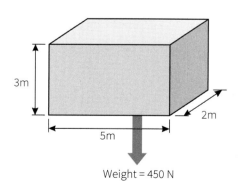

Weight = 450 N

Fig. 12.02.08.

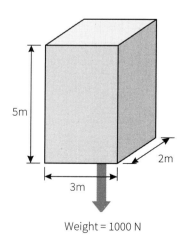

Weight = 1000 N

Fig. 12.02.09.

Pressure in a Liquid

We've already spoken about pressure in terms of solid objects. But what about pressure in liquids? Can a liquid even exert pressure? Yes, it can! Pressure in a liquid acts in all directions. Here is a quick investigation you can do to show there is pressure in a liquid.

🔍 Investigation 12.02.01: **Pressure in a liquid**

Equipment: Empty 2-litre bottle, water, pin, sink/basin.

Instructions: Fill a 2-litre bottle fully with water. Poke three holes in the bottle with a pin – one at the top, one in the middle and one at the bottom. (Do this activity over a sink or basin!)

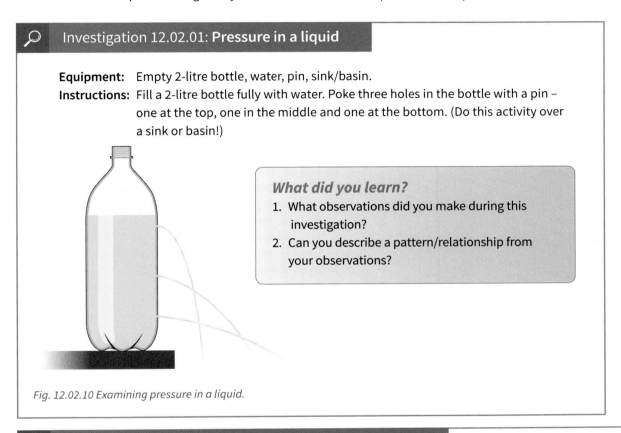

> **What did you learn?**
> 1. What observations did you make during this investigation?
> 2. Can you describe a pattern/relationship from your observations?

Fig. 12.02.10 Examining pressure in a liquid.

🔍 Investigation 12.02.02: **Horizontal pressure in a liquid**

Equipment: Empty 2-litre bottle, cap, water, pin, sink/basin.

Instructions: Using a different bottle, or covering up the holes of the first bottle, fill it up again with water, ensuring to put the cap on the top this time. Place the bottle on its side. Uncover the holes or make new ones in exactly the same place as in *Investigation 12.02.01*.

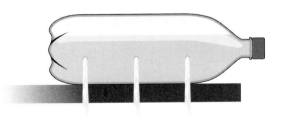

> **What did you learn?**
> 1. What observations did you make this time?
> 2. How do your observations compare to those made in *Investigation 12.02.01*?
> 3. Can you describe a pattern/relationship for the pressure horizontally in a liquid?

Fig. 12.02.11 Examining horizontal pressure in a liquid.

PHYSICS

Pressure and Temperature

 Investigation 12.02.03: **The effect of pressure**

Equipment: Gas syringe, air, your finger.

Instructions: Using the equipment as listed, design an investigation to determine the effect pressure has on:

(a) Particles in a gas

(b) Temperature of the gas.

Below is a simple diagram to help you visualise the particles in the syringe.

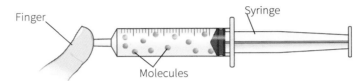

Finger

Syringe

Molecules

> **What did you learn?**
> 1. Draw a diagram of the particles when you compressed the syringe.
> 2. Hypothesise what the effect on the temperature is as a result of compressing the air in the syringe.

 Checkpoint 3

(a) Referring to *Investigation 12.02.03*, draw diagrams of what the particles would look like when the plunger was half pressed and then fully pressed.

(b) Was there a change in temperature? If yes, how do you know?

(c) From your observations, do you think that a relationship exists between pressure and temperature?

Does Air Have Mass?

We know that everything is made up of matter: humans, cars, food, water, etc. But what about air? When a container appears to have nothing in it, we say it's empty, but is it really empty? No, it is not empty – it is full of air! So we know air occupies the 'empty' space in the container, but what about mass? Does air have mass?

 Investigation 12.02.04: **Showing that air has mass**

Equipment: Two balloons, retort stand, metre stick, sticky tape, taper/wooden splint.

Instructions: Using the equipment as listed, design an investigation to show air has mass.

> **What did you learn?**
> 1. How did you ensure this was a fair test?
> 2. What precautions did you take to ensure the investigation was carried out safely?
> 3. What possible errors may have occurred during this investigation.

Weather and Atmospheric Pressure

Atmospheric pressure is the pressure (force per unit area) exerted by the weight of the air above us. In a similar way to the upright bottle, atmospheric pressure decreases the higher up we go. This means that if we climb a mountain, the atmospheric pressure is less than it is on the ground. This is because the column of air above us is less dense. This becomes a problem for people climbing some of the world's highest mountains: the air is so thin at the top that most climbers need breathing masks for sufficient air supply.

> **Atmospheric Pressure:** The force per unit area exerted by the weight of the column of air above us.

Fig. 12.02.12 This climber needs a breathing apparatus to help her continue her climb.

A similar example is divers. The deeper divers descend, the greater the pressure. This is because there is more and more water above them. This is why divers can only go down a certain distance, otherwise they risk damage to their internal organs.

The standard atmospheric pressure where we stand (at sea level) is 101 325 Pa. You might be wondering, 'If the pressure is so great, why aren't we squashed into the ground?' The reason for this is that we have gases and liquids in our own bodies. The gases inside us push out an equal amount of pressure as the air pressure outside pushes us in. If we removed the air from our bodies, we could crumble under the outer air pressure.

If you pay attention to weather forecasts, you will notice that forecasters use phrases such as 'low area of pressure' or 'high area of pressure'. What do you think these are? Generally speaking, areas of low pressure give unsettled weather, whereas high pressure gives settled weather.

Fig. 12.02.13 There is only so far divers can descend before the pressure above them becomes too great.

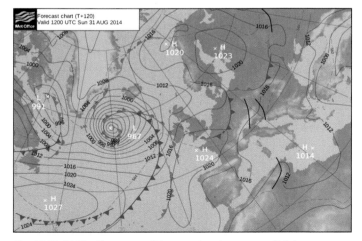

Fig. 12.02.14 Weather map of Europe showing areas of high and low pressure.

PHYSICS

Investigation 12.02.05: **Investigating the accuracy of weather forecasting**

Equipment: Access to a weather channel or news broadcast.

Instructions: Take note of the weather forecast tonight for tomorrow's weather. See if we are to have high or low pressure, then observe the weather tomorrow.

> ### *What did you learn?*
> Was the forecast accurate? Be sure to compare the forecast from at least two different sources, i.e. TV, radio, internet, and then comment on the accuracy of each source. You can also do this over a week and comment on the constancy of each source.

Measuring Atmospheric Pressure

We know that normal atmospheric pressure is 101 325 Pa, but how do we measure this? The tool we use to measure atmospheric pressure is called a **barometer**.

There are two types of barometer: a **mercury barometer** and an **aneroid barometer**.

Mercury barometers are made up of a glass tube which is 1 m in length. This tube is semi-filled with mercury and inverted (turned upside down) into a bowl of mercury. When inverted, some of the mercury will appear to leave the tube and create a vacuum (the area with no mercury) at the top of the tube. What happens is that the atmospheric pressure is pushing down on the mercury in the bowl, which in turn keeps the mercury in the tube. The height of the mercury is then measured in the tube to give a reading for atmospheric pressure. The normal atmospheric pressure is 76 cm of mercury.

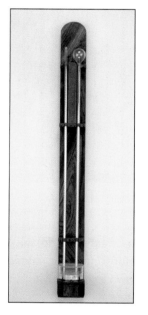
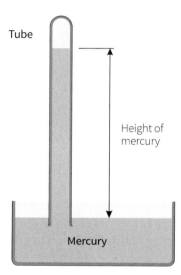

Fig. 12.02.15 Torricelli's mercury barometer (left), named after Evangelista Torricelli, who is universally credited with the invention of the barometer; and how it is constructed (right).

An aneroid barometer, which you will see more commonly in homes, uses a mechanism to measure atmospheric pressure. In an aneroid barometer a metal box, which has had most of the air removed, contains a metal plate, which moves up or down according to the atmospheric pressure. This movement causes some chains and levers to move, which in turn moves the needle on the face, which details measurements in cm and/or mm of mercury.

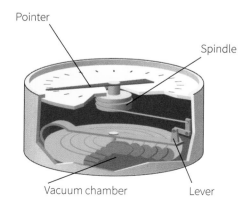

Fig.12.02.16 An aneroid barometer (left) and its internal workings (right).

WHAT I HAVE LEARNED...

- Pressure is the force per unit area.
- Pressure = Force/Area.
- Pressure is measured in Pa.
- Pressure can also be measured in N/m².
- Remember: N/m² and Pa are the same, so there is no need to convert.
- Small area equals greater pressure.
- There is pressure in a liquid.
- The pressure in a liquid increases with depth.
- Pressure in a liquid (and in air) acts equally in all directions.
- Atmospheric pressure is caused by the weight of the area above us.
- Atmospheric pressure decreases as height increases (exactly like in a liquid).
- Normal atmospheric pressure is 101 325 Pa at sea level.
- Low atmospheric pressure = less air = more clouds = bad weather.
- High atmospheric pressure = more air = fewer clouds = better weather.
- We measure atmospheric pressure using a barometer.
- Two types of barometers: mercury and aneroid.
- Mercury barometers are made from glass tubes that are semi-filled with mercury and inverted into a bowl of mercury to create a vacuum. As the atmospheric pressure increases, the height of the mercury in the tube increases and vice-versa.
- Aneroid barometers are a vacuum, with a metal plate moving up and down depending on atmospheric pressure.
- Normal atmospheric pressure on a barometer is 76 cm of mercury.

Question Time

Copy and Complete

In this unit I learned that _____ is the force per _____ ____. The unit of pressure is the _____ or the _____/___. Area is a big factor in pressure. If we exert a _____ over a small _____ the resulting pressure will be _____ than if the same force was applied over a _____ area. This is why thumbtacks and nails have sharp ends as this _____ the pressure. In a liquid, the pressure is greatest at the _____ and smallest at the ____. In general we can say the _____ in a liquid increases with _____. I also learned that atmospheric pressure is caused by the _____ of the _____ above us. This means when we have low atmospheric pressure there is _____ air above us. Low atmospheric pressure gives us _____ weather. High atmospheric pressure generally gives us _____ weather. Normal atmospheric pressure is 101 325 __.

Questions

1. Define pressure.
2. What is the unit of pressure?
3. A rectangular box of height 6 m and sides of 7 m and 8 m has a weight of 6000 N. Find the pressure it exerts.
4. Describe an investigation to show that the pressure in a liquid increases with depth.
5. What is the instrument in *Fig. 12.02.17* called?
   (i) What does this instrument measure?
   (ii) How does it measure this?

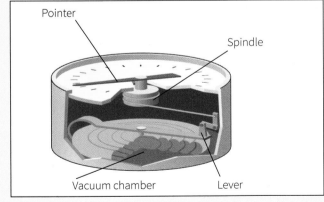

Fig. 12.02.17 What is this instrument called?

6. Water boils at 100°C at sea level. Do you think water would boil at a higher or lower temperature on Mount Everest? Give reasons to support your answer.

PHYSICS

7. A block of metal of weight 240 000 N has sides of length 2 m, 3 m and 5 m (*Fig. 12.02.18*). Calculate the maximum pressure the block can exert when it is resting on a level surface. (*2014 JC OL*)

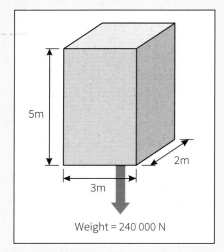

Fig. 12.02.18.

8. Felix Baumgartner set the world record for skydiving when he jumped from an altitude of 39 km above the earth. Did Felix expect the atmospheric pressure to increase or decrease as he fell to earth? What effect would atmospheric pressure have had on his safety during re-entry? Make sure to factor in friction. (*Adapted from 2014 JC HL*)

Fig. 12.02.19 Felix Baumgartner about to set a world record.

Inquiry

A **Design** an investigation to show how pressure varies with volume (temperature needs to be kept constant).

B **Research** how climbers/divers cope with decreased/increased pressure on their bodies.

C Athletes will often train at higher altitudes. **Research** why athletes do this and what benefits they get from such training.

D You have been asked to explain how an altimeter works. **Research** what an altimeter measures and **create** a PowerPoint presentation detailing how it works.

12.3

Moments – Turning Forces

PHYSICS

Learning Outcomes

WLO 3. Investigate patterns and relationships between physical observables.

SLO 2. Recognise questions that are appropriate for scientific investigation, pose testable hypotheses, and evaluate and compare strategies for investigating hypotheses.

SLO 3. Design, plan and conduct investigations; explain how reliability, accuracy, precision, fairness, safety, ethics and a selection of suitable equipment **have been considered.**

SLO 4. Produce and select data (qualitatively/quantitatively), critically analyse data to identify patterns and relationships, identify anomalous observations, **draw and justify conclusions.**

R Teacher's reference

KEYWORDS

balance
centre of gravity
equilibrium
fulcrum
lever
moment

LEARNING INTENTIONS

At the end of this unit you should:

1. Be able to find the centre of gravity of an object.
2. Be able to investigate the role of the centre of gravity in a design for stability and equilibrium.
3. Be able to investigate the law of the lever.
4. Be able to give everyday applications of levers.

Centre of Gravity

Investigation 12.03.01: **Balancing an object**

Equipment: Objects as listed in *Table 12.03.01*.

Instructions: Working in pairs and using *Table 12.03.01*, try to **balance** the objects as listed. You can balance the objects on your finger, a pen, table, etc. Once successfully balanced, note the balancing point of the objects.

Object	Balancing Point
15 cm ruler	
30 cm ruler	
A metre stick	
Your school journal	
This science book	
An A4 page	
A bottle of water	
The shape your teacher has printed off	

Table 12.03.01.

What did you learn?

1. Comment on your observations.
2. Was the centre of gravity always in the centre of the object?
3. Did you find the centre of gravity of the irregularly shaped object? If so, how?

What do you think a turning force is?

The point where the object balances is called the **centre of gravity**. For an object to balance, the upward and downward forces must be equal:

Forces up = Forces down

Balance: When the upward and downward forces are equal, the object is balanced.

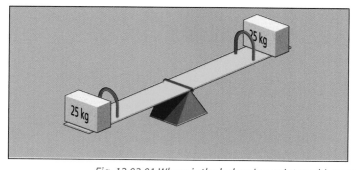
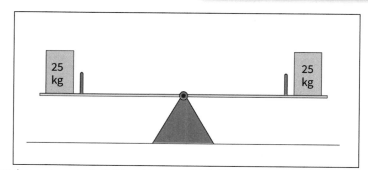

Fig. 12.03.01 Where is the balancing point on this see-saw (seen at an angle [left] and head-on [right])?

States of Equilibrium

A body is said to be in **equilibrium** when all the forces are balanced. There are three states of equilibrium: stable, unstable and neutral.

Stable: An object is said to be stable if its centre of gravity is inside the base of the object.

Unstable: An object is said to be unstable if its centre of gravity is outside the base of the object.

Neutral: An object is said to be neutral if its centre of gravity does not change.

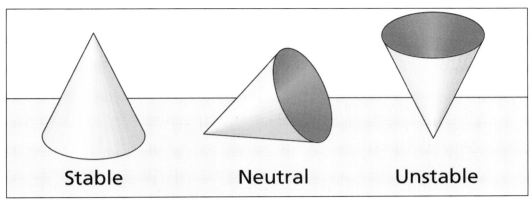

Fig. 12.03.02 Stages of equilibrium.

 **Checkpoint 1**

Draw the stable, neutral and unstable stages of equilibrium of the three objects as seen in *Fig. 12.03.03*:
   (i) **Wine glass**
   (ii) **Thumbtack**
   (iii) **Football.**

Fig. 12.03.03 Draw the stable, neutral and unstable stages of equilibrium of these three objects.

Stable Designs

It is important that designs are stable in equilibrium. Consider double decker buses. These buses must be stable, otherwise they would topple over when turning corners. How does the bus achieve its stable equilibrium?

For an object to be in stable equilibrium, it must have the following:
- A wide base
- A low centre of gravity.

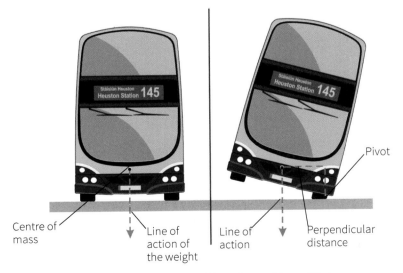

Centre of mass • Line of action of the weight • Line of action • Perpendicular distance • Pivot

Fig. 12.03.04 A double decker bus in stable and unstable equilibrium.

Fig. 12.03.05 An early tilt test of a bus in the United Kingdom.

PHYSICS

The tilt test is conducted on government vehicles such as buses (*Fig. 12.03.05*). A hydraulic table is used to test the vehicle's equilibrium. If the vehicle is to pass the test it must not tip over before reaching the specified angle of 28 degrees. Another specification is that the bus must be fully laden, i.e. full of passengers. However, in the tilt test sandbags are used instead of people.

Moment of a Force

Look at the nearest door handle – can you identify its turning point? A special name is given to the turning point of an object. It is called the **fulcrum**. A **lever** is a rigid body that rotates about the fulcrum. Can you locate the lever on the door handle?

When you open the door you put your hand on the lever and push down. The lever then rotates about the fulcrum. This rotation about the fulcrum is known as the moment of a force. Try to think of another example like this, considering it in terms of fulcrums, lever and moment of the force.

Law of the Lever

The **law of the lever** is the law that governs how see-saws, for example, work. *Fig. 12.03.07* gives other examples of objects that use the law of the lever.

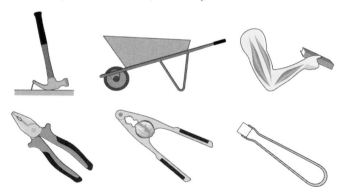

Fig. 12.03.07 Examples of levers.

> ### ✓ Checkpoint 2
>
> (a) Why are passengers not allowed stand up on the upper deck of a double decker bus (unless they are getting off)?
> (b) Which is more stable:
>   (i) A bus with its engine at the front
>   (ii) A bus with its engine under the floor
>   (iii) A bus with its engine at the back?
> (c) Why are double decker buses stable even at speed around corners?

> **Fulcrum:** The point of rotation.

> **Lever:** A rigid body which rotates around the fulcrum.

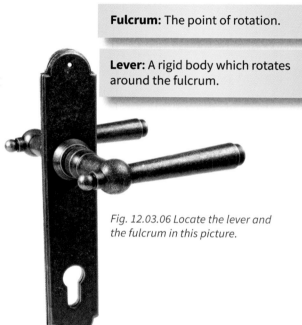

Fig. 12.03.06 Locate the lever and the fulcrum in this picture.

🔍 Investigation 12.03.02: **The law of the lever**

Equipment: Newton weights, metre stick, string, retort stand, paper clips.
Instructions: Design an experiment to investigate the law of the lever.

> #### What did you learn?
> 1. How did you ensure this was a fair test?
> 2. Did you notice any patterns in your data?
> 3. Draw a table with two columns. One column is to note: 'Weight multiplied by distance from fulcrum' of one weight; the other column is to note: 'Weight multiplied by distance from fulcrum' of the other weight. Can you see any pattern forming now?
> 4. What does this pattern tell you about balancing the metre stick?
> 5. Can you make a mathematical formula for what you have found?
> 6. Draw a diagram for each set of the measurements you took. Label which side caused the ruler to move anticlockwise and which side caused the ruler to move clockwise.

Moment of a Force: the force x perpendicular distance from the fulcrum

Moment = force x distance

M = F x d

The unit of a **moment** is the **newton metre** (N m).

You have learned that for a lever to balance, the moments on one side of the lever should be equal to the moments on the other side of the lever. This leads us nicely to a statement made by ancient Greek philosopher Archimedes, defining the Law of the Lever as this:

> *When a lever is balanced, the sum of the clockwise moments is equal to the sum of the anticlockwise moments and the forces up equal the forces down.*

In short, for an object to be balanced:

Clockwise Moments = Anticlockwise Moments

Forces up = Forces down

Question: Two people sit on a see-saw. One weighs 55 kg and sits 2 m from the fulcrum. The other weighs 45 kg. Where should this second person sit in order to balance the see-saw?

Formula: We can see the see-saw is not balanced.

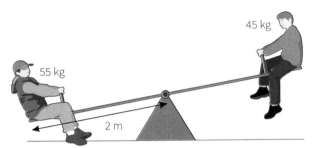

Fig. 12.03.08 *Where should the person weighing 45 kg sit to balance the see-saw?*

Moment of a force = force x distance from fulcrum

Forces up = Forces down

REMEMBER

So, on the left side of the see-saw we need to calculate the moment of the force. But be careful, as we don't have force, only mass, so we need to calculate force:

F = ma

F = 55 kg x 10 m/s^2

F = 550 N

We can now find the moments on the left:

M = F x d

M = 550 N x 2 m

M = 1100 N m

We now know that on the left the total forces down = 1100 N m. So if we want to balance this on the right we need to move the person so they exert 1100 N m.

We have M = 1100 N m, and we have the second person's mass, which is 45 kg.

First find their force:

F = ma

F = 45 kg x 10 m/s^2

F = 450 N

Plug this into the moment formula:

M = F x d

1100 N m = 450 N x d

d = 1100 N m/450 N

d = 2.44 m

So Person 2 will need to sit 2.44 m away from the fulcrum to balance the see-saw.

Fig. 12.03.09 *'Give me a place to stand, and I shall move the Earth with it'– Archimedes (third century BC).*

PHYSICS

WHAT I HAVE LEARNED...

- There are three states of equilibrium:
  - Stable
  - Unstable
  - Neutral.
- An object is stable when it has:
  - A wide base
  - A low centre of gravity.
- Centre of gravity is the point at which all the weight appears to act.
- The point of rotation is called the fulcrum.
- The lever is a rigid body which rotates around the fulcrum.
- Moment = force x distance from fulcrum.
- Law of the Lever states:
  - Clockwise moments = Anticlockwise moments
  - Forces up = Forces down.

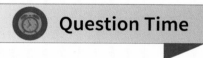

Question Time

Copy and Complete

In this unit I learned that the _____ is the point at which the mass appears to act. This means I can _____ an object at this point. For an object to balance the _____ up must equal the _____ down. I also learned that there are _____ states of _____: stable, _____ and _____. For an object to be stable it must have a _____ base and a low _____ _____ _____. Finally, I learned that a _____ is a _____ body and that the _____ is the point of rotation of this body.

Questions

1. What is the moment of a force?
2. Calculate the moment when a force of 5 N is placed 1 m from the fulcrum.
3. A door handle experiences a moment of 5 N m when the lever is rotated 20 cm from the fulcrum. What force is exerted on the door handle.

4. *Fig. 12.03.10* shows a metre stick suspended from its centre of gravity. A force of X N acts on the stick at the 20 cm mark and a force of 4 N acts on the stick at the 70 cm mark. The metre stick is balanced horizontally. Calculate force F. (*JC HL 2013*)

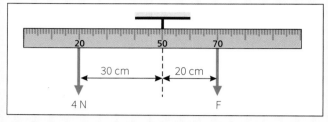

Fig. 12.03.10 Calculate force F in this instance.

5. Give one everyday application of levers. (*JC HL 2013*)
6. The door handle in *Fig. 12.03.11* is an application of a lever. The labels and arrows show three points. Which of the points, A, B and C, represent:
   (i) the fulcrum (turning point)?
   (ii) the point where the smallest force will open the door lock? (*JC HL 2011*)

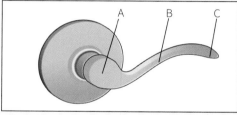

Fig. 12.03.11 Door handle as an application of a lever.

7. A uniform metre stick, suspended at its mid-point, is balanced as shown in *Fig. 12.03.12*. Calculate force X. (*JC HL 2010*)

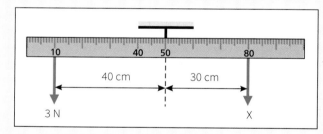

Fig. 12.03.12 Calculate the force X in this instance.

Inquiry

A If the moon is your fulcrum, **calculate** how far away you would have to be in order to lift Mars.

B The Guinness World Records Heaviest Man wants you to build him a see-saw so that he can play on this see-saw with other people. **Design** a see-saw capable of this task and show all calculations.

13.1

Density and Flotation

KEYWORDS

buoyant force
compound unit
density
flotation
mass
volume

LEARNING INTENTIONS

At the end of this unit you should:

1. Understand that density is the measure of mass in a solid/liquid per unit volume.
2. Be able to compare densities of different solids/liquids.
3. Be able to determine the flotation for a variety of solids and liquids in water and other liquids.

PHYSICS

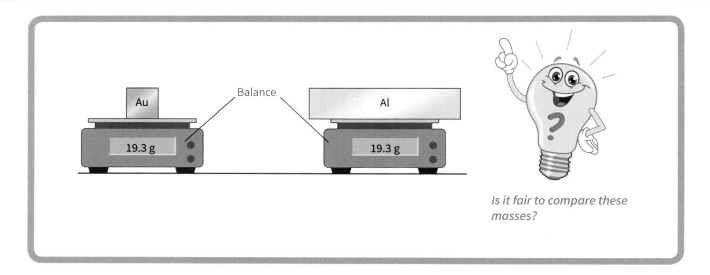

Is it fair to compare these masses?

Density

As we discussed in *Unit 12.1*, the **mass** of an object is the amount of matter it contains, and that mass remains constant. However, if we want to make fair comparisons between different objects, we can't do that based on their mass alone. For instance, the **volume** over which that mass is spread plays a big role in fair comparisons. One such property that all physical objects have is **density**. Density is a **compound unit**. This means it combines several properties of an object which allows us to compare objects fairly. In this instance, density combines the mass of the object and its volume.

> **Density:** The mass per unit volume of a substance.

All objects have density. We measure density in kg/m^3 or g/cm^3. The mass of $1\ cm^3$ of a substance is called its density.

So how are objects more dense than others? Recall in *Unit 7.1* that we discussed the atom. In more dense objects, atoms are packed much tighter together. This means more atoms (and therefore more mass) can fit into the same amount of space.

Remember that density is a compound unit, so if we wish to calculate the density of an object we need to know the two basic measurements first, i.e. mass and volume, and then we can use the following formula:

Density = Mass/Volume

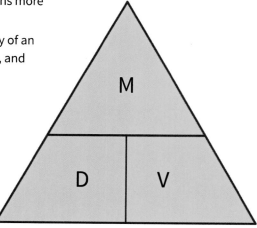

Fig. 13.01.01 The Density Triangle.

✓ Checkpoint 1

(a) What is the density of a block of wood with a mass of 100 g and a volume of 200 cm^3?

(b) What is the density of a bar of gold with a mass of 386 g and a volume of 20 cm^3?

(c) What mass of gold would be contained in 12 cm^3?

(d) Limestone has a density of 1.96 kg/m^3. Calculate the volume of a rock of limestone with a mass of 2.25 kg.

How to Find the Density of an Object

🔍 Investigation 13.01.01: **Finding the density of an object**

Equipment: Graduated cylinder, overflow can, a stone, a block of wood, newton weights and a mass balance.

Instructions: Using the equipment as listed, design an investigation to find the density of a rock and a block of wood.

> **What did you learn?**
> 1. How did you ensure this was a fair test?
> 2. Can you describe any pattern or relationship from your observations?

Comparing Densities

Remember our lightbulb question: was it fair to compare these masses? No, it was not a fair comparison. The masses may be the same, but the volumes are completely different. In order to make fair comparisons we need to ensure both volumes are the same. This allows us to make a fair comparison between the masses, as depicted in *Fig. 13.01.02*.

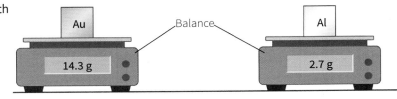

✅ **Checkpoint 2**

Fig. 13.01.02 A fair comparison of these two metals.

Copy and complete *Table 13.01.01*, ticking the variables that should stay the same and putting an *x* where the variables can be different, with Object 1 being the gold and Object 2 the aluminium as depicted in *Fig. 13.01.02*.

Comparison of	Mass of Object 1	Mass of Object 2	Volume of Object 1	Volume of Object 2
Mass				
Density				
Volume				

Table 13.01.01.

🔍 Investigation 13.01.02: **Finding the density of a liquid**

Equipment: Beaker, water, mass balance.

Instructions: Using the equipment as listed, design an investigation to measure the density of a liquid and compare the densities of each liquid. You can also find the density of these other liquids: oil, ethanol, any fizzy drink, salt-water.

> **What did you learn?**
> 1. How did you ensure this was a fair test?
> 2. How did you compare the densities of each liquid?

PHYSICS

Practical Applications of Density

The most practical application of density is **flotation**. Water has a density of 1 g/cm³. This means each cm³ of water has a mass of 1 g. This is why cork floats in water and why some woods also float. It is also why balloons that we want to float are filled with helium. Helium is much lighter than air and so it 'rises' or floats in air.

Cork is gathered from the bark of the cork oak tree, which is typically found in Portugal. As you learned in *Unit 1.1* and *Unit 1.2*, Robert Hooke examined the bark of this tree, which led to the discovery and naming of the cell.

Flotation: The action of floating in a liquid or gas.

Fig. 13.01.03 *Why do you think a helium balloon floats in air and a cork floats in water?*

Did you know?
Archimedes of Syracuse, a famous Ancient Greek scientist, first described a buoyant force and displacement in his book *On Floating Bodies*. He stated that an object immersed in a fluid experiences a buoyant force equal to the weight of the fluid it displaces. The buoyant force is the upward force exerted by a fluid that opposes the weight of the immersed object. As we know, if an object is less dense than the liquid it is in, it will float.

Investigation 13.01.03: **Sink or float?**

Equipment: Mass balance, graduated cylinder, salt and overflow can, oil, full cans of regular and diet fizzy drink, empty can of fizzy drink, ice.

Instructions: Design an investigation to show whether ice, oil, a full can of regular fizzy drink, a full can of diet fizzy drink, an empty can of fizzy drink and some materials of your choosing sink or float in water.

What did you learn?
1. How did you ensure this was a fair test?
2. Construct a table which clearly presents your data and findings.
3. Describe all differences between the full cans of fizzy drink (regular and diet) and the empty can of fizzy drink.
4. Describe all differences between the regular can and diet can of fizzy drink.
5. Suggest a reason why ice did/didn't float in water.

Buoyancy

Fig. 13.01.04 shows how an oil tanker sinks lower in the water as it is filled. The force of the sea upwards is called the buoyant force (as indicated by the orange arrow).

Density of object > Density of liquid = Object sinks

Density of object < Density of liquid = Object floats

> **Buoyant Force:** The upward force in a fluid that opposes the weight of an object immersed in the fluid.

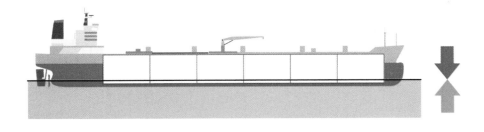

The oil tanker creates a downward force, or pressure, which increases as it is filled. The force of the tanker increases because it stays the same size but is being filled with oil. This increases the amount of matter in the space taken up by the tanker, and so this increases the overall density of the tanker.

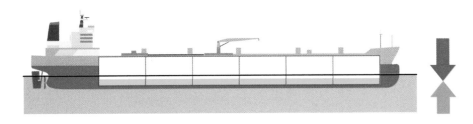

The tanker will only sink below the water when its overall density is more than the water it sits in. Even if all the oil tanks are full, the ship still has many air pockets so its overall density is less than the water it floats in. (Liquids are usually more dense than gases.)

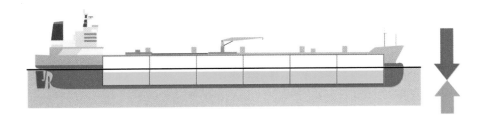

If this tanker was a model sitting in a bathtub, its displacement would be the rise in the water level caused by the downward force of the oil tanker.

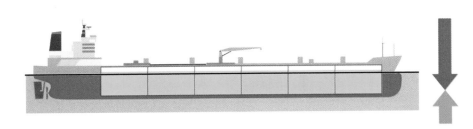

The amount of force exerted by any object that floats depends on its mass. If its mass changes, then its density changes automatically. A change in density will affect how well an object sinks or floats. If its density is greater than the liquid it is in, it will sink. If its density is less than the liquid it is in, it will float.

Fig. 13.01.04 Oil tanker indicating buoyancy.

PHYSICS

WHAT I HAVE LEARNED...

- Density is the mass per unit volume of a substance.
- Density is measured in g/cm³ or kg/m³.
- When placed in a liquid, an object will sink if its density is more than that of the liquid.
- When placed in a liquid, an object will float if its density is less than that of the liquid.
- The buoyant force is the upward force that opposes the weight of the body immersed in the fluid.

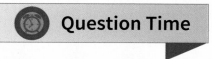

Question Time

Copy and Complete

In this unit I learned that density is the _____ per unit _____ of a substance. The unit for density is the ____/____ or the ____/____. All physical substances have a _____. What causes the density of an object is the packing of ____/____ in the substance. A denser object has more ____/____ packed _____, whereas a less dense object has less ____/____ packed _____. To calculate density we need to find the object's _____ and _____. Once we have these we can use the formula *density* = _____ / _____. For an object to float in a liquid the _____ of the object needs to be _____ than that of the liquid. For example, _____ floats in water whereas _____ does not.

Questions

1. Describe how you would measure the density of the following:
   (a) A block of wood with a mass of 2000 g
   (b) Paraffin oil.
2. Find the density of a block of wood with a volume of 400 cm³ and a mass of 360 g.
3. Find the volume of a piece of lead with a mass of 90 g.
4. What volume does 67 g of mercury have?
5. Which of the following will float in liquid mercury (density 13.6 g/cm³):
   (a) Gold (density 19.3 g/cm³)
   (b) Aluminium (density 2.7 g/cm³)
   (c) Iron (density 7.9 g/cm³)
   (d) Silver (density 9.32 g/cm³)
   (e) Copper (density 8.94 g/cm³)
   (f) Tungsten (density 19.3 g/cm³).

6. *Fig. 13.01.05* shows the cargo hold in a large ship filled in three different ways. Ship captains are careful about how they load their ships as the weight distribution can contribute to how easy or difficult it is to manoeuvre the ship, or indeed may contribute to the sinking of the ship in a heavy storm. In such a storm, which arrangement of the cargo is more likely to 'turn turtle' (turn upside down) and sink? Which cargo arrangement makes it easier to steer the ship? Justify your answer.

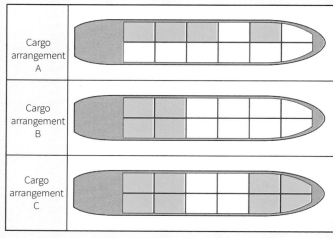

Fig. 13.01.05 Cargo ship with three different arrangements of load.

7. Submarines dive and submerge by changing their density, which changes their buoyancy. They do this by filling or emptying ballast tanks in their hull. In *Fig. 13.01.06,* diagram A shows a submarine on the surface, while diagram B shows a submarine submerged at depth. What is happening to the submarine in diagram C? Give reasons for your answer.

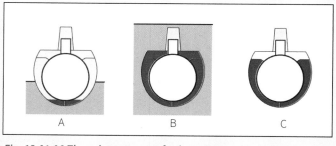

Fig. 13.01.06 The submergence of submarines.

Inquiry

A   A tiara – deemed to be priceless – has been stolen from the Natural History Museum. Several days later, police find the tiara, along with two exact replicas, in a home not far from the museum. You speak with the archaeologist at the museum, who informs you that the real tiara is made of cubic zirconia. As a member of the police investigatory team, **devise** an experiment to test which tiara is the real one. You must include all your research as well as experimental methodologies. Keep in mind that you will not be carrying out this experiment, only devising it for someone else to carry out, so you need to clearly outline every step involved in the experiment as well as any equipment needed.

B   **Investigate** the relationship between the mass and volume of an object.

C   **Research** how big oil tankers float when at sea and **present** this information in a PowerPoint presentation or on a poster.

D   Milk is very important to the development of young children. It is generally recommended that they be given whole-fat milk, as young children need the fat content and other valuable nutrients such milk provides. You are given three label-free containers of milk and told that one is whole fat milk, one is 2% fat milk and one is 1% fat milk. Using the knowledge gained in this unit, **design** an investigation to determine which milk is which.

14.1 Electricity

Learning Outcomes

PWLO 1. Select and use appropriate measuring tools.
PWLO 2. Identify and measure/ calculate length, mass, time, temperature, area, volume, density, speed, acceleration, force, **potential difference, current, resistance** and electrical power.
PWLO 5. Design and build simple electronic circuits.

 Teacher's reference

KEYWORDS

circuit
conductor
electric current
electrolysis
electrolyte
electromotive force
insulator
Ohm's Law
parallel
potential difference
resistance
schematic
series
static electricity
voltage

LEARNING INTENTIONS

At the end of this unit you should:

1. Be able to classify materials as conductors or insulators.
2. Be able to use appropriate instruments to measure current, potential difference (voltage) and resistance.
3. Be able to explain the relationship between current, potential difference and resistance.
4. Be able to perform simple calculations based on the relationship between current, potential difference (voltage) and resistance.
5. Be able to describe the heating effect, the chemical effect and the magnetic effect of an electric current, and identify everyday applications of these, including the action of a fuse.
6. Be able to set up simple series and parallel circuits containing a switch and two bulbs.

Electricity

Electricity is essential to our everyday lives. Without it we would not be able to charge our phones, turn on our kettles, power our schools or even produce this book. However, there was a time when electricity was not around. Electricity, as it currently is, was not discovered until 1800 by Italian physicist, Alessandro Volta. He stacked copper (Cu) and zinc (Zn) plates in acid and discovered that it produced a steady flow of electricity. It was this invention that sparked the generation of electricity as we know it today.

Fig. 14.01.01 Alessandro Volta (1745–1827).

Why do wires glow red hot when electricity passes through them?

Fig. 14.01.02 The electrifying torpedo fish.

Did you know?
Volta got his idea for stacking the zinc and copper plates in acid by dissecting a torpedo fish (also known as an electric ray). Torpedo fish have two organs on either side of their brain which consist of millions of jelly-like plates stacked up.

Current electricity is one form of energy, but there is another form of electricity called **static electricity**. Unlike current electricity (which is what we will be looking at), static – as the name suggests – does not move.

R Did you know?
Static electricity can be easily created by rubbing a balloon against your head or rubbing a pen against your jumper and trying to pick up a small piece of paper.

Current Electricity

So what is current electricity? How does it work? We must look back to atoms again. Recall that an atom is made up of different sub-atomic particles, one of which, the electron, contains a negative electrical charge. Electricity works on the principle of the flow of these negative charges. This flow of charge is called a **current** and is given the symbol I. The unit of current is the ampere, also known as amp, and the symbol for amp is A.

R Imagine this: You have a small pipe and you place it flat on the ground (this is your wire). Grabbing some marbles (your 'charge carriers'), you roll one marble through the pipe. So when you roll one charge carrier (marble) through the wire (pipe), you now have a current. The more charge carriers (marbles) you have going through the wire (pipe), the higher the current.

Current: The flow of charged particles. Symbol: I. Unit: amp (A).

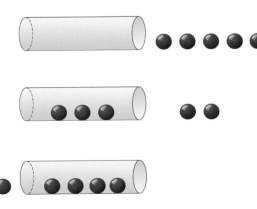

Fig. 14.01.03 Current: the flow of charged particles.

Conductors and Insulators

Not all substances will allow electricity to flow through them. For example, if we try to pass an **electric current** through wood, nothing will happen, whereas electric current will pass through metal (*Fig. 14.01.04*). We classify any object which allows electric current to easily pass through as a **conductor**, whereas any object which does not allow electric current to easily pass through is called an **insulator**. It is important to remember that an insulator is just a poor conductor and not something completely different to a conductor.

REMEMBER

Current is the flow of charge carriers (for example, the electron) flowing through the wire. The unit of current is the ampere (or the amp) (A).

Conductor: An object or substance that electric current passes through easily.

Insulator: An object or substance that electric current cannot pass through easily.

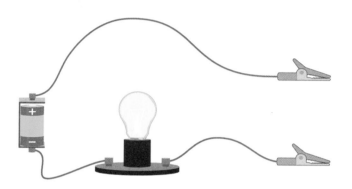

Fig. 14.01.04 Passing an electrical current through an object.

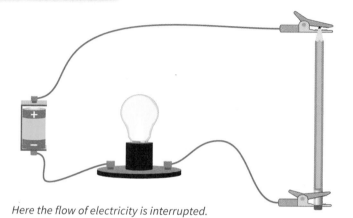

Here the flow of electricity is interrupted.

How Do the Charge Carriers Flow Through the Wires?

You might next wonder how the charge is carried along the wire/circuit? This is a very good question, but first we must understand the following: *Fig. 14.01.05* shows two identical **circuits** – one where the light is not lighting, the other where it is. A circuit is a connection between electrical components (i.e. the wire, pencil and bulbs) and a source (the battery).

Circuit: A connection between electrical components and a power source.

Incomplete circuit

Complete circuit

Fig. 14.01.05 On the right we have a complete circuit as all terminals are connected in a loop back to the battery. On the left we have an incomplete circuit as there isn't a complete loop back to the terminal.

In order for any electric current to flow we must have a complete circuit. This means that the wires must start at the source and end at the source. If the circuit is not complete, no current flows through the circuit and the bulb does not light.

Electromotive Force/Potential Difference/Voltage

Now that we know this, we can explain how an electric current goes through these circuits. If you look at the top of a 9V battery, you will notice two little bumps. These bumps are called terminals and are labelled positive (+) and negative (–). The negative terminal contains all of the negative charge carriers. The positive terminal contains positive charges. You've heard the phrase opposites attract? In *Unit 7.3* we noted that positive ions attract negative ions. The same goes for electricity. We have negative charge carriers in the – terminal and they want to find the positive ones in the + terminal. This force of attraction causes the negative charge carriers to move through the wires to find the positive ones (*Fig. 14.01.07*). This is called the **Electromotive Force** (**voltage**), or EMF. The unit is the volt (V). In batteries the negative charge carriers are in fact electrons.

Fig. 14.01.06 A 9V battery.

> **Be aware:**
> It is more common to call EMF potential difference or voltage. For the rest of this unit we will call it voltage or EMF.

> **Electromotive Force (Voltage):** The work done to bring one charge carrier from the negative terminal to the positive one. Unit: volt (V).

So an electric current will go through a circuit under these conditions:

1. We have a complete circuit
2. When the EMF is enough to move the charge carriers in that circuit between the – and + terminals.

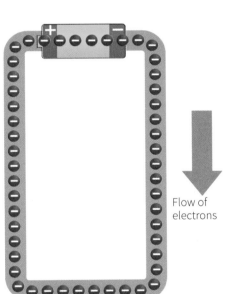

Fig. 14.01.07 The flow of electrons from the negative terminal of the battery to the positive terminal of the same battery.

Flow of electrons

> **R Did you know?**
> Scientist now know that charge carriers flow from – to +. But this wasn't actually discovered until much later on because we did not understand the nature of the electron. Therefore we still refer to the flow of 'conventional' current as from + to –.

PHYSICS

Resistance

We have spoken about conductors and insulators, but do all conductors allow current to flow through them at the same rate?

Some conductors allow the electrons to flow through them with great ease (for example, copper). However, others such as brass and bronze do not allow the electrons to flow through them easily. This brings us to what is known as **resistance**. The unit of resistance is the Ohm (Ω).

To understand resistance, imagine yourself walking down your school corridor. When it is empty you can walk through it with ease. But what happens when students spill out of class and start walking against you? You begin to bump off them and slow down. This is the idea of resistance.

> **Resistance:** The ability of a material to resist the flow of electric current. Unit: Ohm (Ω).

Each material has a built-in level of resistance to electrical current, which slows down the flow of electrons. The higher the resistance, the harder it is for the electrons to flow though the material.

Some materials have such a high resistance that the electrons begin to give off heat energy. When these electrons are slowed down, the energy they have must go somewhere (according to the Law of Conservation of Energy). This is why the electrons start to give off heat energy.

This is how the heating coils in kettles and washing machines work. Indeed, in the old filament lightbulbs, a lot of the energy produced by the electrons was in fact turned into heat energy, because the metal used in the bulbs had a very high resistance. Nowadays we use what are called 'energy-saving' lightbulbs, where more light energy is produced as opposed to heat energy.

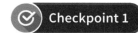
Checkpoint 1

(a) **What is an electric current?**
(b) **What is a conductor?**
(c) **What is an insulator?**
(d) **What are the charged carriers in a battery?**
(e) **What is another name for potential difference?**
(f) **What is electromotive force?**
(g) **In which direction does actual current flow?**

Effects of Current

R 1. Heating Effect

As we have mentioned, the old filament bulbs used to become hot when turned on This is because the wires used in the bulbs, typically Tungsten, had a very high resistance. As a result, most of the energy was converted into heat energy and very little was converted into light energy. This is an example of the **heating effect** of electric current.

Fig. 14.01.08 Old filament lightbulbs (left) used to convert most of their electricity into heat energy and very little into light. To combat this, 'energy-saving' lightbulbs were created. Compact Fluorescent Lamps (CFL) use one-fifth of the energy of old filament bulbs while giving out the same amount of light. They also last 8–15 times longer.

2. Magnetic Effect

If you just connect a battery with wires and place a compass near the wires, you will notice something strange. The compass will deflect when it comes near the wire. This means that the wire is producing a magnetic field.

An amazing application of this magnetic effect is the Magnetic Levitation (MagLev) train in Shanghai, China (*Fig. 14.01.09 (a)*). Using the magnetic effect, the MagLev train travels along guiding rails using magnets to create not only lift but also propulsion (forward movement). As well as this, because it is not in contact with the ground or guiding rails, there is a reduction in friction, allowing the train to reach a whopping 430 km/h (its safe operational speed). It covers its full journey, a distance of 30.5 km, in just eight minutes!

Fig. 14.01.09 (b) The magnetic effect is also seen in scrapyards where large amounts of metal can be moved about.

Fig. 14.01.09 (a) The amazing MagLev Train in operation.

🔍 **Investigation 14.01.01: The magnetic effect of current**

Equipment: Power supply, wires, resistor, crocodile clips, compass.
Instructions: Design an investigation to discover what effect a wire carrying electricity might have.

> **What did you learn?**
> What effect, if any, did you notice? What does this tell us?

ℝ 3. Chemical Effect

When current is passed through acidified water, the water is chemically broken down into hydrogen and oxygen gas. This is called **electrolysis**. The electric current is able to break down the H_2O (water) and charge can then be conducted through the liquid. Conduction is possible in other liquids such as nitric acid, and hydrochloric acid, and these liquids allow current to flow through them. This is because when electricity is passed through these liquids, they decompose and create ions, which are able to conduct electricity.

These types of liquids are called **electrolytes**.

A **Hofmann Voltameter** is used to split water into hydrogen and oxygen.

> You can see a Hofmann Voltameter in action by following this link: https://www.youtube.com/watch?v=EE58a5fN468

> **Electrolysis:** The breaking down of water into hydrogen and oxygen by the application of a current.

> **Electrolyte:** A liquid which conducts electricity through the movement of ions created by electrolysis.

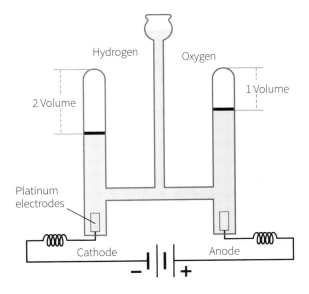

Fig. 14.01.10 Diagram of a Hofmann Voltameter.

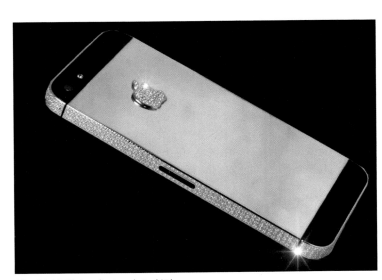

Fig. 14.01.11 An electroplated iPhone.

There are many practical applications of electrolysis, but one you may all be familiar with is **electroplating**. Electroplating uses the movement of these electrolytes to coat a material a different colour. A famous example of this is Apple's gold iPhone.

 Checkpoint 2

(a) **Name the three effects of electric current.**
(b) **Pick two of these effects and describe how to demonstrate them.**
(c) **Give an everyday example of one of the effects.**

PHYSICS

Building Circuits and Measuring Voltage, Resistance and Current

Drawing all the components in a circuit correctly can become very difficult, so scientists agreed on a set of symbols, known as **circuit symbols**. An agreed set of symbols means that fewer mistakes will be made and everyone using them understands each other.

Circuit symbols can be put together in a circuit diagram, called a **schematic**. Engineers and electricians use these diagrams when they are working; otherwise the drawings for real-life versions of complicated circuits would simply be too big to carry around.

Table 14.01.01 gives a complete table of the components of a circuit you will need to know.

Component	Symbol	Measures	What it does
Battery			Produces an EMF for the circuit
Wire			Provides conduction for charge carries
Switch			Breaks/connects a circuit
Bulb			Produces light when connected in a closed circuit
Resistor			A fixed value resistance
Voltmeter		Voltage	Connected in parallel (across an object); measures the potential difference across that object
Ammeter		Current	Connected in series, it measures the current of a circuit
Variable resistor		Resistance	Increases/decreases the resistance of the resistor
Diode			A device that allows current to flow in one direction only
Light emitting diode (LED)			A diode which gives off light when current is flowing through it
Light dependent resistor (LDR)			A resistor whose resistance depends on the amount of light shining on it

Table 14.01.01 Circuit components and their symbols.

Series Circuit

A circuit is said to be in **series** when the current has to flow through each component one after the other in order to complete the circuit (*Fig. 14.01.12*).

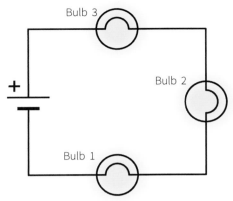
Fig. 14.01.12 A circuit in series.

 Investigation 14.01.02: **The effect of adding bulbs to a series circuit**

Equipment: Suitable filament bulbs (at least three), wires, crocodile clips, 9V battery, switch.

Instructions: Using the equipment as listed, design and carry out an investigation to demonstrate the effect of adding several bulbs to a series circuit.

What did you learn?
1. What did you notice happened as you added bulbs to the circuit?
2. Compare the effect when there is one bulb, a second bulb and a third bulb added. What did you find?
3. What conclusion can you draw about the effect of adding bulbs in a series circuit?

Parallel Circuit

A circuit is said to be in **parallel** when the current does not have to flow through each component one after the other in order to complete the circuit (*Fig. 14.01.13*). This means that each component is connected independently of the others, which has a very interesting side-effect.

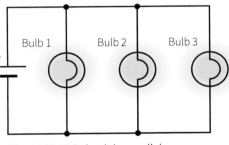
Fig. 14.01.13 A circuit in parallel.

 Investigation 14.01.03: **The effect of adding bulbs in parallel**

Equipment: Suitable filament bulbs (at least three), wires, crocodile clips, 9V battery, switch.

Instructions: Using the materials above, design and carry out an investigation on the effect adding several bulbs to a parallel circuit has on the circuit. In your investigation, ensure you measure voltage, current and resistance.

What did you learn?
1. Did you notice any effect when bulbs were added in parallel?
2. Discuss what effects you observed on the current, voltage and resistance when bulbs were added in parallel.
3. What conclusion can you draw about the effect of adding bulbs in parallel circuits?
4. Compare and contrast the effects of adding bulbs between series and parallel circuits.

PHYSICS

The Relationship Between Current, Voltage and Resistance

Recall that:

- **Current** (*I*) is the flow of charged particles. Its unit is the amp (A).
- **Electromotive force** (voltage) is the force of attraction between the two terminals of a source. Its unit is the volt (V).
- **Resistance** is a material's ability to resist the flow of current in it. Its unit is the Ohm (Ω).

🔍 Investigation 14.01.04: **The relationship between voltage and current**

Equipment: Voltmeter (used to measure voltage), resistor, power supply, wires, crocodile clips, variable resistor (if not built into power supply) and ammeter (used to measure current).

Instructions: Design an investigation using the equipment as listed to find out if there is a relationship between voltage and current.

> **What did you learn?**
> 1. Construct a table with your data.
> 2. Represent this information on a graph.
> 3. What does your graph tell you about the relationship between voltage and current?

In 1827, Georg Ohm was able to find a link between the current flowing through a battery and its **voltage**. To do this he used a constant which he called **resistance**. This is why the unit of resistance is called the Ohm. This discovery led to one of the most useful laws in electricity, called **Ohm's Law**. This law describes the relationship between voltage and current, and is written as:

$$R = \frac{V}{I}$$

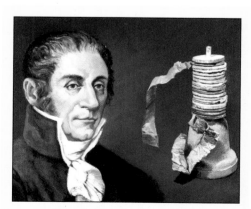

Alessandro Volta (1745–1827)

André-Marie Ampère (1775–1836)

Georg Ohm (1789–1854)

Fig. 14.01.14 The scientists whose names are given to the basic units of electricity because their experiments help to improve the understanding of electricity, how it worked and could be used. Volta gave his name to the volt, Ampere gave his name to the amp and Ohm to the ohm!

When Ohm carried out his own version of this experiment, he found that the voltage is directly proportional to the current in the wire. So when voltage is increased each time by a fixed amount, the current increases by a fixed amount (similar to *Table 14.01.02*).

When Ohm plotted his current and voltage measurements on a graph, he got a straight line. When this straight line passes through the origin we get a unique relationship which is referred to as being **directly proportional**. This means that the two properties maintain a constant ratio. After many years it was found that this ratio could be described by a constant. In the case of Ohm's Law, this constant is called **resistance**.

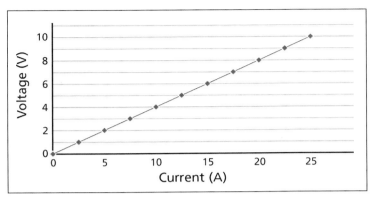

Table 14.01.02.

So using the readings as depicted in *Table 14.01.02*, Ohm would have divided the voltage by a matching current. For this graph the answer is 0.8 Ω. This means that every time Ohm increased the current by 2 A, the voltage increased by 1.6 V. This means that multiplying the current by the resistance allows you to calculate the voltage. Also, dividing the voltage by the resistance will give you the current.

Ohm's work showed that the relationship between resistance, current and voltage is the same even if each experiment gives a different set of voltages and currents.

Calculating Resistance	Calculating Voltage	Calculating Current
V = 40 V	I = 2 A	V = 3.5 V
I = 8 A	R = 0.8 Ω	R = 2 Ω
$R = \dfrac{V}{I}$	V = IR	$I = \dfrac{V}{R}$
$= \dfrac{40}{8}$	$= 2 \times 0.8$	$= \dfrac{3.5}{2}$
= 5 Ω	= 1.6 V	= 1.75 A

Fig. 14.01.15 Ohm's examples of how to calculate voltage, current and resistance using

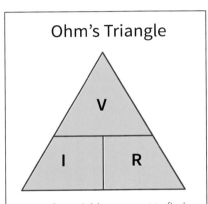

Ohm's Triangle

Cover the variable you want to find and perform the resulting calculation (Multiplication/Division) as indicated.

Fig. 14.01.16 Ohm's Law Triangle.

PHYSICS

WHAT I HAVE LEARNED...

- Current (*I*) is the flow of charged particles and its unit is the amp (A).
- Voltage is the force of attraction between the two terminals of a source. The unit is the volt (V).
- Resistance is a material's ability to resist the flow of current in it. The unit is the ohm (Ω).
- Conductors allow current to flow through them easily.
- Insulators do not allow current to flow through them easily.
- We must have a complete circuit for current to flow through it.
- A series circuit is when components are connected one after the other.
- A parallel circuit is when components are connected side by side.
- The relationship between voltage and current is also known as Ohm's Law.
- Ohm's Law states that the voltage and current are directly proportional.
- When resistors are added in series their resistance is added together.

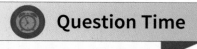

Question Time

Copy and Complete

In this unit I learned that _____ is the flow of _____ particles. In order to make these _____ particles flow there needs to be a P_____ d_____. P_____ d_____ is also known as voltage. This voltage is the force of _____ between two _____ in a battery. It is this force which causes the _____ _____ to flow through a circuit. I also learned that in order for charged particles to flow in a circuit, we must have a _____ circuit. This means that all wires are connected to each component and connected to both terminals of the _____. I also learned that not all materials will allow _____ to flow through them. When current does not flow through a material easily it is called an _____; whereas if it does allow current to flow through it easily it is called a _____. This property of materials is called _____ and its unit is the _____. There are two types of complete circuits. _____circuit is when the current has to _____ through the _____ one after another. _____ circuits are when the current _____ _____ have to flow through all the components one after another. I also learned another key relationship between _____ and _____. This is commonly known as _____ Law. This relationship states that _____ is directly _____ to the _____ and this gives us our physical constant of _____.

Questions

1. What are the three effects of electric current?
2. Which effect is the Hofmann Voltameter associated with?
3. How do you test if a current carrying wire produces a magnetic field?
4. What is the relationship between the voltage and current in a circuit?
5. What instrument would you use to measure current?
6. What instrument would you use to measure voltage?
7. Calculate the current of the circuit as shown in *Fig. 14.01.17*.

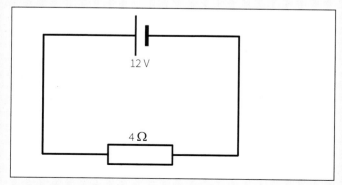

Fig. 14.01.17 Calculate the current of the circuit shown.

8. If we have a complete series circuit with a 2 Ω and 5 Ω resistor connected in series, what is the total resistance of this circuit?

9. A science student investigated the relationship between voltage and current for a resistor, as detailed in *Table 14.01.03*.

Voltage (V)	0	0.22	0.40	0.58	0.80
Current (I)	0	0.20	0.40	0.60	0.80

Table 14.01.03.

(i) Draw a graph of voltage versus current.
(ii) Describe clearly the relationship between voltage and current shown by the graph you have drawn.
(iii) Use the graph to calculate the resistance of the resistor used in this experiment.

10. *Fig. 14.01.18* shows the circuit used by the student to perform this experiment. Two meters were used, one to measure voltage and the second to measure current.

(i) Ⓡ Copy and complete *Fig. 14.01.18* by entering the symbols for both meters in the circuit diagram, each one in the appropriate circle.
(ii) How was the voltage/current varied when doing this investigation? (*JC HL 2013*)

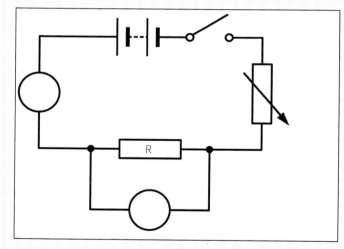

Fig. 14.01.18.

Inquiry

A   Using PhET Simulations or the actual physical
    components, **build** a series and a parallel circuit and
    complete the following tasks:
    (i)   **Compare** the brightness of:
          (a) Two bulbs in a series circuit to two bulbs
               in a parallel circuit
          (b) Three bulbs in a series circuit to three bulbs in
               a parallel circuit.
    (ii) **Design** a circuit such that when one bulb blows,
          the rest stay lit.
    (iii) **Compare** the current of:
          (a) Two bulbs in a series circuit to two bulbs in a
               parallel ciruit
          (b) Three bulbs in a series circuit to three bulbs in
               a parallel circuit.

B   A diode is a specialised electronic component made
    up of two terminals: the negative cathode and the
    positive anode. The primary function of a diode is
    to restrict current flow to one direction. When current
    is allowed to flow through the diode, it is said to be in
    forward bias. When current is not allowed to flow, it is
    said to be in reverse bias. **Prepare** a PowerPoint/video
    presentation discussing the following points:
    (i)   what diodes are typically made of
    (ii) how to tell if a diode is in forward or reverse
          bias (include photos or a video of setting up the
          demonstration)
    (iii) common uses of diodes
    (iv) how diodes affect Alternating Current
    (v)   when it is connected correctly it allows current to
          flow through it.

C   If a large electromagnetic pulse hit our planet, could
    we survive it? Where could such a pulse naturally
    occur in our universe? **Create** a poster on this subject.

PHYSICS

14.2

Electricity in the Home

Learning Outcomes

PWLO 2. Identify and measure/ calculate length, mass, time, temperature, area, volume, density, speed, acceleration, force, potential difference, current, resistance and **electrical power.**

NSLO 6. Conduct research relevant to a scientific issue, evaluate different sources of information including secondary data, understanding that a source may lack detail or show bias.

NSLO 7. Organise and communicate research and investigative findings in a variety of ways fit for purpose and audience, using relevant scientific terminology and representations.

NSLO 9. Research and present information on the contribution that scientists make to scientific discovery and invention, and its impact on society.

(R) Teacher's reference

KEYWORDS

alternating current
direct current
earth
electrical power
fuse
kilowatt-hour
live
Miniature Circuit
  Breakers (MCB)
neutral
Residual Current Device
  (RCD)
ring circuit

LEARNING INTENTIONS

At the end of this unit you should:

1. Be able to explain how a ring circuit works.
2. Be able to distinguish between direct and alternating current.
3. Know that the voltage of the mains supply is 230 volts a.c.
4. Be able to recall that the unit of electrical energy used by electricity supply companies is the kilowatt-hour.
5. Be able to calculate the cost of using common electrical appliances, based on their power rating.
6. Be able to explain how to wire a plug correctly.
7. Be able to explain the safety role of a fuse in domestic electrical circuits.
8. Be able to explain the safety role of circuit breakers in domestic electrical circuits.

Electricity in the Home

In every home a **ring circuit** is used. This ring circuit consists of parallel circuits for lighting and other connections. A typical ring circuit consists of the following:

- **Live** and **neutral** wires for carrying the electric current.
- **Earth** wire for safely earthing the appliance if a fault develops.
- **Fuses**, **Residual Current Device (RCD)** or **Miniature Circuit Breakers (MCB)** (only plugs have fuses on the live wire to protect the circuit from overloading).
- Sockets as points to connect to the electric current.

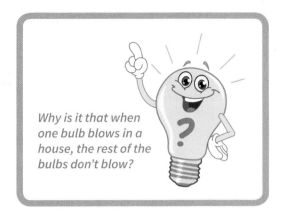

Why is it that when one bulb blows in a house, the rest of the bulbs don't blow?

1

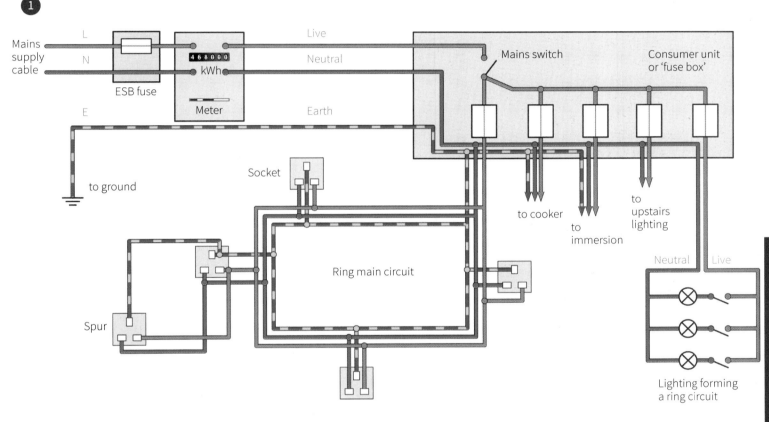

2

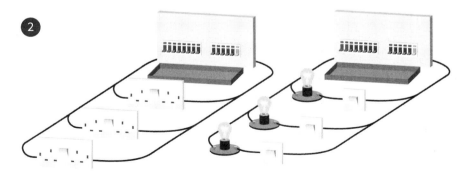

Fig. 14.02.01 These two diagrams demonstrate two simple versions of the ring circuits in your home. You can clearly see how each socket and bulb are connected in parallel.

PHYSICS

Electrical Safety Features in a Home

Fuses

A fuse is a safety feature designed into plugs. It consists of a thin metal wire which heats up, and when too large a current passes through the fuse, it melts. This is why you have different fuse ratings like 1 A, 2 A, 5 A, etc. (with A standing for amp). This means that a 2 A fuse will melt when more than 2 A is passed through the fuse. When the metal wire melts, it breaks the circuit, preventing electrocution and fire.

If a fuse breaks, you must replace it with a fuse of the same rating. If you use a lower rating, the fuse will blow again too soon. If you use a higher fuse rating, it will not melt in time and a fire can occur.

Fuses (as seen in *Fig. 14.02.02*) are connected to the live wire. This is because the electric current enters the home through the live wire. The current then goes through the appliance and leaves via the neutral wire.

Fig. 14.02.02 Fuses normally have a white ceramic shell filled with sand through which the fuse wire is threaded. If a fuse wire burns out, this means that there is no oxygen available and neither material is flammable. Glass-walled fuses are filled with inert gas.

Plugs

If you open up a plug you will see the following:

- A brown wire, called the live wire. This is connected to the fuse in the plug and is responsible for carrying the electric current to the appliance.
- A blue wire, called the neutral wire. This is connected to the left of the plug and carries the electric current back from the appliance.
- A yellow and green wire, called the earth wire. This wire is connected to the metal casing of the appliance and runs to a metal plate found in the ground.

Earthing is the process of connecting part of the circuit to the ground, and is mainly found in appliances that are made of metal. This is because if an excess current passes through the appliance and a person touches the metal, they would be electrocuted. Instead, the earth acts as a conductor and takes the charge to a metal plate located safely under the home.

Earthing: The connection of an electrical device with the ground.

Investigation 14.02.01: **Wiring a plug**

Equipment: Plug, fuse, earth, live and neutral wire.

Instructions: Using the equipment as listed and the knowledge you have gained so far, and referring to the diagrams below, connect the earth, live and neutral wires to their correct places and connect a fuse.

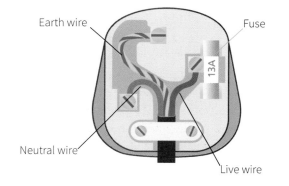

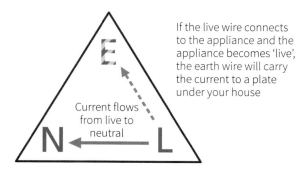

If the live wire connects to the appliance and the appliance becomes 'live', the earth wire will carry the current to a plate under your house

Circuit Breakers

All modern houses now have circuit breakers instead of fuses on their ring circuits. Unlike fuses, once these 'trip' you can simply reset them rather than having to replace them. You can find circuit breakers in the distribution box, which is typically near the front door.

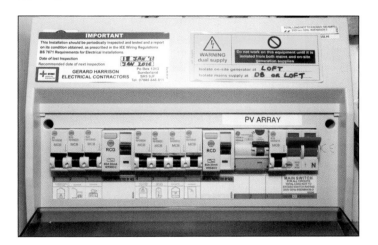

Fig. 14.02.03 A distribution box (left) and a circuit breaker.

How circuit breakers work

Inside a circuit breaker (CB) there are several important objects. From top to bottom, they are: the entrance terminal, stationary contact, moving contact, switch, catch, electromagnet and exit terminal. When current flows normally through the CB it looks exactly like *Fig. 14.02.04*. The exit terminal generates an electromagnetic field (remember from *Unit 14.1*, magnetism is an effect of current passing through a wire). When current through the CB decreases, the electromagnet gets weaker, which doesn't cause any issues. However, when the current becomes too large, the exit terminal electromagnetic field becomes strong enough to pull the electromagnet down towards it, moving the catch and moving contact, which breaks the circuit and trips the switch. This can be seen in *Fig. 14.02.05*.

Notice how the catch has moved towards the left of the CB, which has caused the moving contact to break contact with the stationary contact. This has broken the circuit. The circuit can easily be reset by flipping the switch back to its original position.

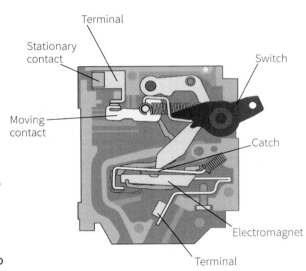

Fig. 14.02.04 Inside a circuit breaker.

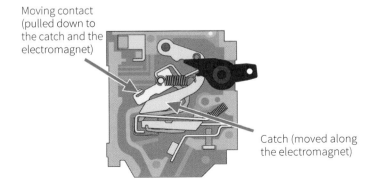

Fig. 14.02.05 A tripped circuit.

Residual Current Devices

A lot of homes have electric showers. Have you ever considered how dangerous these are? We're mixing water with electricity!

Fortunately an extremely sensitive circuit breaker is connected to electric showers. These are called Residual Current Devices (RCDs) and can detect changes as small as 0.05 A in the current. If a change of this size is detected, the RCD will trip and shut off the shower. Just like the circuit breakers, these RCDs can be reset by flipping the switch in your distribution box.

PHYSICS

Checkpoint 1

(a) What is the name of the circuit to which lights in your home are connected?

(b) What is the biggest advantage of connecting lights in this type of circuit?

(c) Draw a fully labelled diagram of a plug and write a brief sentence about the flow of current through the plug.

(d) Name the safety feature found in plugs.

(e) What does RCD stand for?

(f) At home, check the distribution box. Draw a diagram of what it looks like and take note of any labels on the circuit breakers such as which room or which device they control.

Measuring the Cost of Electricity in Our Homes

How is the amount of electricity we use in our homes measured? The major electrical companies use a unit called the **kilowatt-hour** (kW h). Remember that the watt is the unit of power. So 1 kW = 1000 W.

Formula: The kilowatt-hour, therefore, is the electrical energy used by a 1 kW appliance for one hour. For example, if you have a 3 kW appliance and run it for one hour you use:

3 kW x 1 h = 3 kW h

If you have a 4 kW appliance and run it for 24 hours you get:

4 kW x 24 h = 96 kW h

At the moment, one kW h costs around 0.20c (20 cents). So to calculate the cost of running an appliance, we multiply kW h by cost per kW h. Applying this to the two examples above:

1. A 3 kW appliance running for one hour:

   3 kW x 1 h = 3 kW h x 0.20 = 0.60c

2. A 4 kW appliance running for 24 hours:

   4 kW x 24 h = 96 kW h x 0.20 = €19.20c

Electrical Power

We know that appliances such as kettles and toasters convert electrical energy to heat energy. However, a kettle has more **electrical power** than a toaster because it has a greater ability to convert electrical energy to heat energy. Most kettles have a power rating of between 2 kW and 3 kW. This means that a kettle can convert 2000 J of electrical energy into heat energy per second.

You can find the power rating of any appliance on the device. Sometimes it can be found on a sticker somewhere on the base of the device. If we want to calculate the power of an appliance we use the formula:

Power (*W*) = Current (*I*) x Voltage (*V*)

You should note that the mains voltage is 230 V so you have no need to work out the voltage.

AC/DC: Alternating Current and Direct Current

You now know that electrons flow from the negative terminal to the positive terminal in the case of batteries (recall that electrons have a minus charge and opposite charges attract). This one-directional movement is called **Direct Current** (DC), as seen in *Fig. 14.02.06*. Most battery-operated devices such as TV remotes run on direct current. However, electric companies do not supply DC current directly to our homes. Rather, they supply an **Alternating Current** (AC) through power lines, as seen all over the country, as it is the much cheaper option. This is partly because DC current would heat up power lines too much and a lot of the energy would be lost to heat. AC does have this problem, but the heat loss is small compared to the heat lost via DC. This is why birds stand on these lines: the small amount of heat keeps their feet warm!

Alternating current, as the name suggests, changes. In fact, it changes 100 times per second. But what change does it undergo? The change is in terms of its charge, going from positive to negative. This does not mean that the current doesn't move or that its overall charge is zero. It means that as the current flows from one point to another, the charge changes from positive to negative and back again. Looking again at *Fig. 14.02.06*, the graph on the right is what AC current looks like when it is plotted. Here we can see the charge going from a neutral to a positive charge, back to neutral towards negative and eventually back to neutral; and the cycle continues.

Since AC flows into our homes and most of our appliances need DC, these appliances are fitted with a rectifier, which converts AC to DC.

Alternating Current: Changes its charge many times a second as it travels around a circuit.

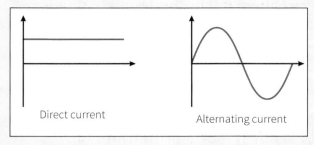

Fig. 14.02.06 Direct current (left) and alternating current (right).

Direct Current: Travels around a circuit in one direction only.

Fig. 14.02.07 Birds warming their feet.

PHYSICS

WHAT I HAVE LEARNED...

- Ring circuits are used in homes.
- A fuse is a thin metal wire which melts when excessive current flows through it.
- A circuit breaker is found in most modern homes and is more effective than a fuse.
- Plugs contain three wires:
  - Live (brown), which is connected to the fuse and carries the electricity
  - Neutral (blue), which is connected to the left side of the plug
  - Earth (green/yellow), which is connected to a metal plate in the ground to ensure the appliance doesn't become 'live' when a fault develops.

- The unit of electricity is the kW h.
- Electrical power is calculated by multiplying the voltage by the current.
- Electrical power is measured in watts.
- Direct current flows in one direction only.
- Alternating current flows in one direction for 1/100th of a second and then in the opposite direction for the next 1/100th of a second.

Question Time

Copy and Complete

In this unit I learned that _____ circuits are used in the home. I also learned about the key safety features in a home. First I learned about the _____, which is a thin _____ _____ found in a plug. When excessive _____ flows through the _____, the metal wire breaks and this breaks the _____. I also learned about the plug and the wires inside a plug. The _____ wire is called the _____ _____ and this is attached to the fuse. The _____ wire is called the_____ _____ and is found on the left of the plug. The __/__ wire is called the _____ _____ and this is another safety feature. If a fault develops, this wire is connected to a metal plate found under the _____ and the current flows through it rather than the appliance. Another safety feature is the circuit _____, which you can find in any modern home. These are more sensitive than fuses and more practical. This is because instead of melting, it simply _____ and it can be easily reset. I also learned how to calculate the cost of electricity in my home. The unit used by electric companies to measure electricity use is the _____ _____. Once I know how many _____ are used I simply multiple it by the cost of each unit. I can find the _____ rating of each appliance and use this to estimate the cost of running the appliance for a set amount of time. Finally I learned the difference between __/____ ____ and __/____ ____current. _____ flows in one direction whereas _____ changes direction every 1/100th of a second.

Questions

1. Explain the difference between AC and DC currents.
2. What type of circuit is built in a home?
3. Name the safety features of a plug.
4. What is a fuse used for and how does it work?
5. Draw a labelled diagram of a plug and explain each feature.
6. A portable heater has a power rating of 2500 W.
   (i) What is its rating in kW?
   (ii) How many units of electricity does it use in two hours?
   (iii) How many units of electricity does it use in five hours?
   (iv) If electricity costs 20c per unit, what does it cost to run the heater for two hours and five hours?
7. An appliance with a power rating of 600 W cost €3.25 to run. How long was the appliance left running for?
8. You buy a second-hand immersion heater and want to know its power rating. You look at the plug and discover there is a 13 A fuse in it. Calculate the power rating (*Hint:* Mains voltage is 230 V).
9. Copy and complete *Table 14.02.01*, keeping in mind Mains voltage is 230 V.

Appliance	Power rating	Current	Cost to run for 1 hour	Cost to run for 8 hours	Suggested fuse rating
TV	1800 W				
Kettle	1.2 kW				
Hair dryer	545 W				
High-end computer	850 W				
Bedside lamp	80 W				
Toaster	600 W				

Table 14.02.01.

Inquiry

A **Research** James Prescott Joule or James Watt and **present** information on a poster or in a presentation about their lives, work in physics and major accomplishments.

B **Investigate** the factors that affect the heat loss of electric current (time, mass, size of current, etc.) and **present** your information in a PowerPoint presentation.

C **Research** and **create** a short video describing the effects of electrocution on the human body.

D **Prepare** a safety talk on electrical safety issues and the risk of electrocution, as well as what you would do and what precautions you would take if you saw someone being electrocuted.

E Electric current can be used to restart the human heart. **Research** how this can be done and **describe** in detail one such device.

F Ⓡ You are designing a new bungalow.
   (i) Draw the ring circuit needed for your bungalow.
   (ii) Suggest where the sockets should go.
   (iii) Where these sockets are suggested, give an example of what you expect to be plugged in here and suggest which fuse(s) these plugs would have.
   (iv) Suggest where you would install the circuit breaker box in this home.
   (v) Draw the lighting circuit(s) needed to light each room in the house.

G Newer metallic devices no longer include earth wires, instead being 'doubly insulated'. **Research** what this means and how it is different from having an earth wire only.

15.1

Origins of the Universe

Learning Outcomes

ESLO 2. Explore a scientific model to illustrate the origin of the universe.

NSLO 1. Appreciate how scientists work and how **scientific ideas are modified over time.**

NSLO 9. Research and present information on the contribution that scientists make to **scientific discovery** and invention, and its impact on society.

(R) Teacher's reference

KEYWORDS

Big Bang
black hole
celestial bodies
electromagnetic force
fundamental forces
  of nature
fundamental particles
gravitational force
heliocentrism
mass density
orbits
singularity
solar nebula
strong nuclear force
weak nuclear force

LEARNING INTENTIONS

At the end of this unit you should:
1. Be able to describe how the Big Bang Theory explains the origins of the universe.
2. Be able to give evidence to support the Big Bang Theory.
3. Know the four fundamental forces of nature.

EARTH & SPACE

In The Beginning ...

Nearly 14 billion years ago, it is believed space, time, matter and energy came into existence. This moment is called the **Big Bang** and is currently the leading model which describes the origins of the universe.

But before we discuss the Big Bang, we should note that many models were developed along the way. Let us examine some of the theories which led to the development of our understanding of our universe.

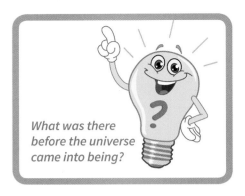

What was there before the universe came into being?

Theory 1: Aristotle and Geocenterism

In the fourth century BC, Greek philosopher Aristotle put forward his theory of a geocentric universe in which the earth was fixed at the centre, surrounded by **celestial bodies** in the sky. Aristotle also stated his belief that the universe was static and unchanging in size throughout all eternity. He also proposed five elements: earth, fire, water, air and aether (the darkness that fills the universe) and that everything in the universe was made up of one of these five elements, or some combination of them. He believed that these five elements were acted on by two forces: gravity and levity (the tendency of air and fire to rise, in a sense the opposite of gravity).

Celestial Body: Any natural object outside of Earth's atmosphere, e.g. the moon, other planets, stars, etc.

Theory 2: The Copernican Universe

Fig. 15.01.01 Nicolaus Copernicus (1473–1543).

Polish astronomer Nicolaus Copernicus was the first scientist to describe the motions of celestial bodies without placing the earth at the centre of the universe. He used the idea of **Heliocenterism**, which put the sun at the centre of the universe ('helios' is the Greek word for sun and 'centric' means 'at the centre'. According to this theory, the celestial bodies all travelled around the sun in fixed circular tracks called **orbits**.

Publishing his findings in 1543, Copernicus is often credited with sparking the birth of modern cosmology (the study of the universe). This period is sometimes referred to as the 'Copernican Revolution'. In 1605, Johannes Kepler refined Copernicus's original theory of circular orbits and proposed that the planets actually move in elliptical orbits.

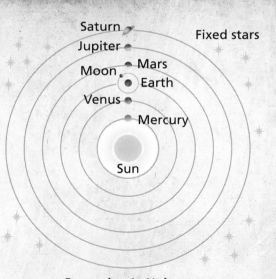

Copernicus's Universe

Fig. 15.01.02 Artist's illustration of Copernicus's Heliocentric Universe. Notice that the orbits are circular.

Theory 3: The Newtonian/Einsteinian Universe

Later in the seventeenth century, Isaac Newton weighed in and proposed his own model of the universe. His was the first to incorporate the existence of forces between planets in the form of gravity, as well as proposing that the universe is static and infinite, upholding what Aristotle had proposed. This remained unchallenged until the early twentieth century when two scientists, Albert Einstein and Edwin Hubble, made progress in our understanding of the universe.

When Einstein proposed his general relativity equation, one consequence was a prediction that the universe would collapse in on itself. This was obviously not the case, so Einstein suggested that adding a cosmological constant (i.e. the universe is static and unchanging) to his equation would solve the contradiction. However, several years later, Edwin Hubble proved that the universe was in fact expanding! This evidence meant that Einstein had to reject his own model of the universe.

The constant search for evidence to prove a model of the universe has lead cosmologists, astronomers, scientists and philosophers to the idea of the **Big Bang Theory**.

The never-ending interest and work of cosmologists and astronomers, scientists and philosophers, has led us to where we are today, with the discovery of and further exploration into the Big Bang Theory, how it happened and what it means for the universe.

 **Checkpoint 1**

Create a timeline/drawing outlining the progression of the model of the universe over time, giving examples of scientists who contributed to the development of these models.

The Big Bang

Let us imagine going back in time to a split second before the Big Bang. What would we have seen? Unimaginable amounts of mass in an unimaginably small volume. As we learned in *Unit 13.1*:

Density = Mass/Volume

So if we have massive amounts of matter in a really, really small volume, then the density is even more unimaginably dense. Think of it this way: it would be like trying to roll everything in the universe back into a single point (much smaller than a full stop), billions of times smaller than that of an atom. That is what we think the universe was like a split second before the Big Bang.

A Common Misconception

Before we examine the Big Bang, we must address one misconception: the Big Bang was actually not a bang, but rather a rapid and sudden expansion. This will become clearer as this unit progresses.

We also need to keep in mind that a lot of what we will discuss is a working theory. This means that it is unproven, but so far best fits the evidence we have. We don't actually know what the universe looked like at these particular points in time. However, this makes it a lot more interesting, as you will be developing your own interpretations of what the universe may have looked like billions of years ago.

Before the Bang

The Big Bang Theory proposes that in this split second before the Big Bang, there was a **black hole**, which is a region of space where the gravitational pull is so intense not even light can escape. At the centre of this black hole was a **singularity** – a single hot, condensed point containing all matter in the universe. In addition, there was a single force which later split into the **four fundamental forces** (gravitational, strong, weak and **electromagnetic forces**).

Fig. 15.01.03 Artist's impression of the Big Bang.

EARTH & SPACE

A split second later after the Big Bang, the universe started expanding, matter was created from the energy of the singularity and **fundamental particles**, such as protons and neutrons. From here on, the universe started to expand and the temperature of the universe began to decrease.

We will now explore some of the main events of the last 13.7 billion years!

Checkpoint 2

Can you think of reasons why, just after the Big Bang, the universe started to expand and the temperature decrease? *Hint:* **You may need to revisit** *Units 11.1* **and** *11.2.*

Timeline of the Big Bang

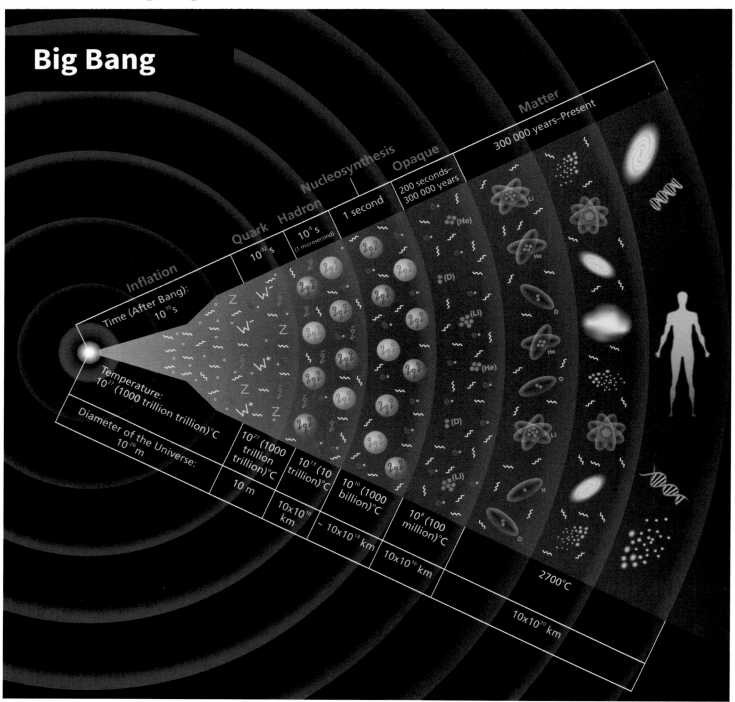

Fig. 15.01.04 Timeline of the Big Bang.

1. The Planck Era

This is the only part of the model that scientists cannot describe. No one knows what happened in this era.

2. The Grand Unified Theory Era

Name of Force	Strength (relative to the strongest force)	Purpose	Range of Force
Strong nuclear force	1 (the strongest force)	Holds protons and neutrons together in atomic nuclei	10^{-15} m
Electromagnetic force	1/137	Force of repulsion between atoms	Infinity
Weak nuclear force	10^{-6}	Similar to strong nuclear force but acts over a much smaller distance	10^{-18} m
Gravity	6×10^{-39}	The force of attraction between objects in the universe	Infinity

During this era, gravity split from the other three fundamental forces of nature, leaving us with **1. Gravitational Force** (comprising **gravity**); and **2. Grand Unified Force** comprising **strong nuclear force, weak nuclear force** and **electromagnetic force**).

3. The Inflation Era

Diameter of the Universe	Temperature	Time (After Bang)
10–26 m	10^{27} (one thousand trillion trillion) °C	10^{-35} s

During this era, the universe began its expansion. In this short space of time it went from being billions of times smaller than that of a proton typically found in atoms to being roughly the size of a GAA pitch.

4. The Quark Era

Diameter of the Universe	Temperature	Time (After Bang)
10 m	10^{27} °C	10^{-32} s

R During this era, sub-atomic particles – such as protons, neutrons and electrons – were created, as well as their anti-particles. Anti-particles have the same mass, but the opposite charge. For example, an electron is negatively charged so the anti-electron (also known as the positron) is positive in charge. They then collided together and produced energy and more subatomic particles.

5. The Hadron Era

Diameter of the Universe	Temperature	Time (After Bang)
10×10^{10} m	10^{13} (10 trillion) °C	10^{-6} s (1 microsecond)

During this era, protons and neutrons were created. These were formed because the universe had cooled enough for them to develop. These were the first protons and neutrons, and when they collided, atomic nuclei were formed.

Fundamental Forces of Nature: Gravity; strong nuclear; weak nuclear; electromagnetic.

Grand Unified Force: Comprises the strong nuclear force, weak nuclear force and electromagnetic force.

EARTH & SPACE

405

6. The Nucleosynthesis Era

Diameter of the Universe	Temperature	Time (After Bang)
~10 x 10^{14} km	10^{10} (1000 billion) °C	1 s

At this stage the neutrons began converting into protons. This meant there was an abundance of protons. So the neutrons joined with the protons and became the first helium nuclei. This happened roughly 100 seconds after the Big Bang started!

7. The Opaque Era

Diameter of the Universe	Temperature	Time (After Bang)
10 x 10^{16} km	10^{8} (100 billion) °C	200 seconds–300 000 years

So-named because of the 'foggy' appearance of the universe during this time due to the massive amount of interactions between electrons, protons, neutrons and helium nuclei. The Opaque Era stretched from 200 seconds to 300 000 years after the Big Bang. Near the end of this era there were more free protons (protons which were not combined with neutrons) produced. This set the stage for the first atoms to form. Hydrogen, helium and lithium were produced.

8. The Matter Era

Diameter of the Universe	Temperature	Time (After Bang)
10 x 10^{20} km	2700 °C	300 000 years–present

Our current era. Following on from the end of the Opaque Era, the first atoms began forming around 300 000 years after the Big Bang. More and more elements began forming, and as a result, stars and planets began to form from the space dust (**solar nebula**).

Checkpoint 3

(a) List the eight eras of the Big Bang.
(b) Create your own timeline of the Big Bang, highlighting the eras and describing the major changes that occurred during each.

Evidence Supporting the Big Bang Theory

A significant amount of evidence has been found to support the Big Bang theory as the origin of our universe.

Fig. 15.01.05 George Gamow.

Radiation

The strongest evidence for the Big Bang Theory is the presence of the radiation it left. Known as Cosmic Microwave Background Radiation (CMBR), and predicted by George Gamow in 1948, CMBR is known as the oldest light in the universe. Its discovery twelve years after Gamow had predicted it meant the Big Bang Theory could be confirmed.

Fig. 15.01.06 Albert Einstein.

Did you know?

On 11th February 2016, the final piece of Einstein's Theory of General Relativity was proven. Physicists in the Laser Interferometer Gravitational-Wave Observatory (Ligo) discovered and so proved the existence of gravitational waves when two massive black holes collided. Einstein had predicted their existence, saying that we could detect information from the universe through these waves. Up until now, we have used light to detect astronomical events such as stars dying, black holes forming, etc. The problem with this is the light can get lost/blocked by space dust or other celestial bodies. However, these gravity waves perfectly transmit all of the information. This is a huge development because now we may finally discover what happened at the early stages of the Big Bang.

Expansion and General Relativity

As we read earlier, Einstein put forward a theory for the model of the universe which incorporated his theory of general relativity and introduced a cosmological constant.

In his model, the universe was static; however, Edwin Hubble proved that the universe was expanding by measuring the velocity of distant celestial bodies, and found that they were actually moving away from us! This was significant as it made Einstein re-evaluate his model of the universe and his theory of general relativity. Eventually, Einstein's theory of general relativity was able to prove beyond any doubt that the universe cannot stay the same size and, as such, must be expanding.

Fig. 15.01.07 Heinrich Wilhelm Olbers.

The Dark Night Sky

Heinrich Wilhelm Olbers looked up into the night sky and wondered why there were dark patches if the universe was supposed to be a static entity – if it were static and not expanding, there would be much less space between objects and so the night sky would be much brighter. Therefore, he surmised that the 'dark night sky' proved the universe was expanding. This became known as 'Olbers' Paradox'.

Investigation 15.01.01: Modelling the expansion of the universe

Equipment: Round balloon, masking tape, pencil/pen, clothes-peg and tape measure (or a piece of twine to be measured against a metre stick).

Instructions: Using the equipment as listed, and following the method described, develop a model showing the expansion of the universe.

1. Blow up the balloon part way and peg the mouthpiece shut so no air escapes.
2. Tear off three (or more) small pieces of masking tape and label them A, B, C, etc.
3. Place the labels in three separate places on the balloon. These now represent the galaxies.
4. Measure the distances between each galaxy as well as the circumference of the balloon at its widest point. This is similar to finding the size of the universe at this stage.
5. Blow the balloon up by a fraction, and measure the circumference and distances between the galaxies again.
6. Repeat Step 5 a few more times.

What did you learn?

Using *Table 15.01.01*, fill in with the data you collected from your measurements.

Balloon	Changes in Distances Between Galaxies as the Universe Expands			
	Circumference	A → B	B → C	C → A
Round 1				
Round 2				
Round 3				
Round 4				

Table 15.01.01.

EARTH & SPACE

ill the Universe Last Forever?

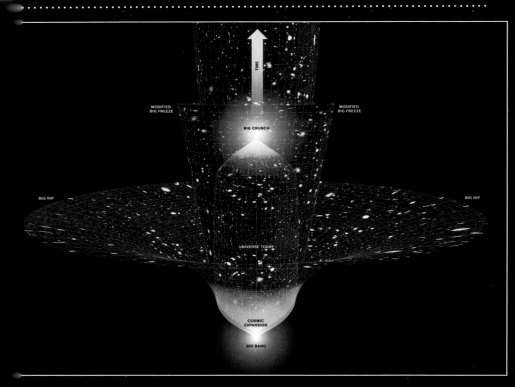

Maybe. Realistically, however, the universe will come to an end in one of two ways:

1. The Big Crunch

or

2. The Big Chill

The one factor that will determine the fate of our universe is its **mass density**. We will now examine the two realistic possibilities.

The Big Crunch

is is the exact opposite of the Big Bang. Instead of expanding as it currently does, the iverse contracts (gets smaller) ... instantly. All matter in the universe will lapse into an infinitely hot, dense singularity. For this to happen, the mass density of e universe would have to be above a critical number. Current research indicates that r universe's mass density is roughly equal to this critical value. So that means that 'll escape death by spontaneous crushing ... which is good news!

2. The Big Chill

This is the more likely cause of the demise of our universe. For this doomsday event to occur, the mass density of our universe would have to be equal to or smaller than the critical value. Current research suggests that the mass density of our universe is just about equal to the critical number (9.47×10^{-27} kg/m^3).

As you can see from the eras of the Big Bang, the universe got considerably larger, but it also got considerably colder. This will be a slow death. It would take over 1 *trillion* years for galaxies to stop producing new stars. All matter will be kept inside the dead stars and eventually become black holes, swallowing up any nearby matter. These black holes will then evaporate, emitting radiation and fundamental particles. Eventually the universe will be dark, cold and empty. In total, this process would take up to 10^{100} years. The good news is that you'll be long gone by this time and won't have to suffer the fate of the Big Chill!

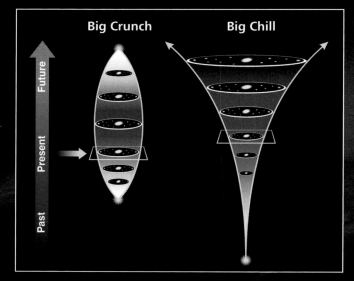

Fig. 15.01.08 The Big Crunch vs the Big Chill.

Problems with the Big Bang Theory

While the Big Bang Theory goes a long way towards describing our universe, its development, the creation of planets, galaxies and the laws of nature, etc., it does not explain everything.

One thing to bear in mind is that the Big Bang Theory is just that – a theory. In science, this means that an idea has been well supported with repeated testing and explains a phenomenon very well. However, a theory is only valid so long as it is not disproven. This reinforces the idea that science is tentative and can be changed should new evidence suggest an idea is wrong. Science is all about accepting change. In fact, a good scientist sets out to disprove his or her claims, because only by failing to disprove something have we succeeded in proving something else. This means that, for the Big Bang Theory, we have yet to disprove it, but it does have its problems.

 1 *'Energy is neither created nor destroyed; it is converted from one form to another.'*

You should have learned this off by heart by this stage. But believe it or not, the Big Bang Theory actually violates this law. If we are to believe the universe was created from nothing as such, then it does not obey the law of conservation of energy. However, some supporters of the Big Bang Theory claim this criticism is unnecessary. They suggest that the Big Bang Theory does not deal with the creation of the universe, but rather its *evolution*.

 2 *'Nothing can travel faster than the speed of light.'*

If we follow the timeline of the early inflation of the universe, we will find that the expansion of the universe is quicker than the speed of light, which violates the laws of general relativity which states that nothing can travel faster than the speed of light. However, some people have suggested that since it was the start of the universe, the laws governing faster-than-light travel did not apply then.

Also, the Big Bang Theory is not the only theory which explains the origins of our universe. Other models include:

1. The Steady State Model

Suggests that the universe had and always will have the same density. This means that the universe generates matter to keep the density constant.

2. The Ekpyrotic Model

Suggests that the creation of our universe is the result of two three-dimensional worlds colliding in a hidden fourth dimension.

3. The Many Worlds Theory

While this theory does not set out to explain the origins of our universe, it does have an interesting consequence. The Many Worlds Theory is an interpretation of advanced physics (quantum mechanics). It states that all possible alternative outcomes can and have happened. Imagine this: you toss a coin and it lands on heads. In the Many Worlds Theory, another 'you' did the same coin toss and it landed on tails. Essentially, this theory suggests that when a choice must be made, in an alternative universe you made the other choice. So every time you made a choice, you created an alternate universe where you did the opposite ...

WHAT I HAVE LEARNED...

- The Big Bang Theory is currently the scientifically accepted model describing the origin of the universe.

- In the beginning, the universe was a small point inside a black hole, called a singularity. This singularity was infinitely hot and unimaginably dense. Suddenly the universe started expanding and cooling as a result of the Big Bang.

- There are eight key eras following the Big Bang: the Planck Era, the Grand Unified Theory Era, the Inflation Era, the Quark Era, the Hadron Era, the Nucleosynthesis Era, the Opaque Era and the Matter Era.

- The first atom appeared at the end of the Opaque Era and beginning of the Matter Era.

- There is evidence to support the Big Bang Theory, such as the discovery of Cosmic Microwave Background Radiation and Olbers' Paradox.

- The universe will more than likely end in one of two ways: the Big Crunch or the Big Chill.

- The Big Crunch would be like a reverse Big Bang, where all matter in the universe would spontaneously condense into a singularity. However, research suggests that the Mass–Energy density of our universe is not above the critical value for this to occur.

- The Big Chill would be a consequence of the expansion and subsequent cooling of the universe. Matter would be locked in dead stars and planets, causing black holes, which would eventually evaporate and leave nothing but a cold, dark universe. Research suggest this is the most likely event to occur as the Mass–Energy density of our universe is equal to the critical value.

Question Time

Copy and Complete

In this unit I learned that the origin of the universe occurred from a ____ _____. This took place from a s_____ which is infinitely h_____ and _____. Rapid _____ occurred nearly __ billion years ago creating matter, t_____ and space. There were _____ eras after the Big Bang. The first era is known as the _____ era and is still a mystery to scientists. The next era saw _____ force breaking away from the _____ fundamental forces of _____. This was known as the _____ _____ _____ era. During the _____ era the universe started to expand. From then on the other eras saw the production of

p_____, n_____ and h_____ _____. It wasn't until the end of the _____ era and start of the _____ era that the first _____ began to form. This lead to the formation of s_____ and other elements, giving us the universe as we know it today.

Questions

1. What is the currently accepted scientific model used to explain the origins of the universe?
2. Which part of a black hole is the Big Bang speculated to have occurred from?
3. Do scientists know everything about the Big Bang? If your answer is no, justify your answer.
4. When did the first protons or neutrons appear?
5. When did the first nuclei form?
6. During which era did the first atom form?
7. What are the four fundamental forces of nature?
8. Which era are we currently in?
9. What is the likeliest cause of the end of our universe?
   (i) What will happen?
   (ii) How will it happen?
   (iii) What condition is necessary for this event to happen?

Inquiry

A   In the Big Crunch Theory, the return of the universe to a singularity was mentioned. In groups, **research** and **present** your findings on white holes and their role in creating our universe and other universes (multiverse).

B   Two popular conspiracies explaining our origins in the universe are:
   1. 'We are digital simulations running on vast computers'
   2. 'We are a failed or on-going alien experiment'
   Research one of the conspiracies and clearly present your position regarding it, with data supporting your position.

C   There are several models which try to explain the origins of our universe. **Research** one of these models and **develop** a paragraph explaining:
   1. How it describes the origins of the universe
   2. How it differs from the Big Bang Theory
   3. Problems with this theory.

D   Edwin Hubble discovered that the <u>Doppler Shift</u> and the <u>Redshift</u> concern celestial bodies moving away from the earth. **Design** a poster to explain the difference between the two underlined terms.

E   Using the balloon model to explain the expansion of the universe, **write** a narrative discussing the timeline of the Big Bang.

15.2 Astronomy

Learning Outcomes

ESLO 1. Describe the relationships between various celestial objects including moons, asteroids, comets, planets, stars, solar systems, galaxies and space.

ESLO 3. Interpret data to compare the earth with other planets and moons in the solar system with respect to properties including mass, gravity, size and composition.

NSLO 7. Organise and communicate research and investigative findings in a variety of ways fit for purpose and audience, using relevant scientific terminology and representations.

Ⓡ Teacher's reference

KEYWORDS

astronomy	meteor
asteroid	meteorite
celestial bodies	meteoroid
comet	moon
Earth	natural
exoplanets	satellites
galaxies	nuclear fusion
gravitationally	planetary
independent	system
habitable zone	primary
Halley's Comet	protostars
heliocentric	short period
system	comet
high mass stars	solar nebula
intermediate–	solar system
long period	spectral type
comet	spiral galaxy
Kuiper belt	sun
low mass stars	sun-like stars
luminosity	tidally locked
main belt	

LEARNING INTENTIONS

At the end of this unit you should:

1. Be able to distinguish between the different celestial bodies.
2. Be able to describe how stars, moons and planets behave in relation to each other and more widely in their planetary systems.
3. Be able to recall the differences between each of the eight planets of our solar system.
4. Be able to differentiate between comets, asteroids, meteors, meteorites and meteoroids.

EARTH & SPACE

You Are Made From Stardust!

Did you realise that you, everyone and everything around you is made from stardust? The same stardust as is found in planets, stars and other objects in our universe. Everything you see on **Earth** – the animals, your friends, the trees – were all formed from dead stars. How do we know this? Through the study of **astronomy**.

Astronomy is the study of **celestial bodies** (objects in space), such as planets, stars, **galaxies, moons, asteroids** and **comets**. Astronomy is different to cosmology (the study of the universe), as cosmologists concern themselves with studying the universe as a whole and not its individual parts.

In groups, write a list of why there might or might not be life on other planets.

Celestial Bodies

 **Checkpoint 1**

There are several types of celestial bodies that we will cover in this unit. However, what we will cover here is only a tiny slice of the fascinating universe out there to be studied.

Individually or in pairs, list as many celestial bodies as you can, and where possible give an example (e.g. a planet is an example of a celestial body, and Earth is an example of a planet).

Galaxies

Galaxies are gravitationally bound systems which contain stars, planets, dark matter, moons, nebula, black holes, white dwarf stars and red dwarf stars. These systems can have many different shapes. Our own galaxy, the Milky Way, is an example of a **spiral galaxy**. Spiral galaxies comprise roughly 30 per cent of known galaxies out there. These galaxies are defined by their spiral arms, which are caused by the slower rotation of objects further away from the centre of the galaxy, and the faster rotation of objects closer to the centre.

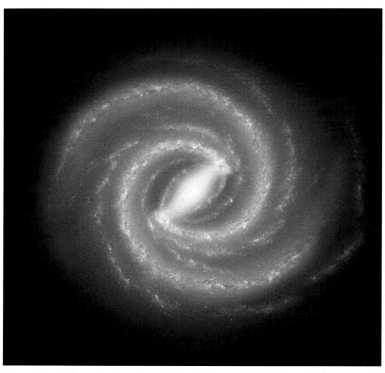

Planets

Planets are celestial bodies with three defining characteristics:

1. Massive enough to be rounded by its own gravity
2. Not massive enough to cause fusion (*Unit 11.1*)
3. **Gravitationally independent** of their neighbours.

There are eight planets in our **solar system**. Starting closest the **sun**, they are:

1. Mercury
2. Venus
3. Earth
4. Mars
5. Jupiter
6. Saturn
7. Uranus
8. Neptune

Fig. 15.02.01 The galaxy to which we belong – the Milky Way.

REMEMBER

An easy mnemonic (a clever sentence or rhyme) to remember this is:

My **V**ery **E**xcited **M**other **J**ust **S**erved **U**s **N**achos (**M**ercury, **V**enus, **E**arth, **M**ars, **J**upiter, **S**aturn, **U**ranus and **N**eptune)

Fig. 15.02.02 A complete family portrait of all eight planets.

Did you know?
Discovered in 1930, Pluto was originally considered the ninth planet in our solar system. However, over the next seventy-five years, numerous celestial bodies similar in composition to Pluto were discovered. This left the International Astronomical Union with no choice but to redefine what constituted a 'planet', and as such Pluto was demoted to the status of 'dwarf planet'. It is, however, the second largest object in the **Kuiper belt**, a region of asteroids beyond Neptune, so it has that going for it!

Planets are believed to have been formed from the same space dust (or **solar nebula** as it is sometimes known) that formed our sun, containing helium, hydrogen and other elements in trace (extremely small) amounts. Over millions of years, the force of gravity clumped together lumps of solar nebula, which kept growing in size until eventually they became the planets we know today.

You will be expected to be able to discuss, compare and give similarities of the planets in our solar system. *Table 15.02.01* gives you all the information you need to know.

Fig. 15.02.03 Artist's impression of solar nebula.

EARTH & SPACE

Name	Class	Mass	Gravity	Diameter	Composition	Atmosphere	Surface Temperature	Rotation	Number of Moons	Length of Year
Sun	Star	1.989×10^{30} kg	274 m/s^2	1.4×10^6 km	Plasma gas / Helium (created from fusion) / Hydrogen	None present	5500°C	25 Earth days	0	
Mercury	Planet	328.5×10^{21} kg	3.7 m/s^2	4875 km	Rich in iron	Oxygen (52%) / Sodium (39%) / Helium (8%) / Potassium and other gases (1%)	-180°C–430°C	59 Earth days	0	88 days
Venus	Planet	4867×10^{24} kg	8.87 m/s^2	12 104 km	Similar to Earth / Iron and nickel core	Carbon dioxide (96.5%) / Nitrogen and trace gases (3.5%)	464°C	243 Earth days	0	224.7 days
Earth	Planet	5.972×10^{24} kg	9.81 m/s^2	12 756 km	Iron and nickel core / Rocks rich in magnesium	Nitrogen (78.1%) / Oxygen (20.9%) / Argon and trace gases (1%)	15°C	24 hours	1	365.25 days
Earth's Moon	Moon	7.35×10^{22} kg	1.62 m/s^2	3476 km	Calcium-rich core	Neon (29%) / Helium (25.8%) / Hydrogen (22.6%) / Argon (20.6%) / Trace gases (2%)	-150°C–120°C	27.32 Earth days	0	
Mars	Planet	639×10^{21} kg	3.71 m/s^2	6780 km	Small solid iron core	Carbon dioxide (95.3%) / Nitrogen (2.7%) / Argon (1.6%) / Oxygen, carbon monoxide and trace gases (0.4%)	-125°C–25°C	24.63 hours	2	687 days
Jupiter	Planet (Gas giant)	1.898×10^{27} kg	24.92 m/s^2	142 984 km	Hydrogen and helium gases / Hydrogen can also be found in liquid and solid form	Hydrogen (89.8%) / Helium, methane and ammonia (10.2%)	-110°C	9.93 hours	64	11.86 years
Saturn	Planet	568.3×10^{24} kg	10.44 m/s^2	120 563 km	Core of rock and ice / Liquid hydrogen and helium	Hydrogen (96.3%) / Helium and trace gases (3.7%)	-140°C	10.66 hours	62	29.46 years
Uranus	Planet	86.81×10^{24} kg	8.87 m/s^2	51 118 km	Water, methane and ammonia ices / Atmosphere consists of hydrogen, helium and other gases	Hydrogen (82.5%) / Helium (15.2%) / Methane (2.3%)	-220°C	17.24 hours	27	84 years

Name	Class	Mass	Gravity	Diameter	Composition	Atmosphere	Surface Temperature	Rotation	Number of Moons	Length of Year
Neptune	Planet	102.4 x 10^{24} kg	1.13 m/s²	49 532 km	Core made of rock and ice	Hydrogen (79%)	-218°C	16.11 hours	14	164.8 years
					A layer of ice containing water, methane and ammonia	Helium (18%)				
						Methane and trace gases (3%)				
Pluto	Dwarf Planet	1.305 x 10^{22} kg	0.658 m/s²	2372 km	Frozen nitrogen	Nitrogen	-229°C	6.39 days	5	247.68 years
					Water ice	Methane				
					Rock	Carbon Monoxide				

Table 15.02.01.

Let us look at **Earth** in *Table 15.02.01* The mass of the earth is approximately 6 x 10^{24} kg, that is 6 000 000 000 000 000 000 000 000 kg, or six septillion kilograms.

There are two pieces of new information in *Table 15.02.01* you need to understand.

Rotation: How long a planet takes to do a full rotation on its axis (i.e. spin around 360°). In the case of Earth, this is twenty-four hours.

Length of Year (Orbital Period): This is how long the planet takes to do one full revolution around the sun on an elliptical (stretched circle) pathway. In the case of Earth, that is 365.25 days. That extra 0.25 is where we get our leap year from. Rather than add an extra quarter of a day every year, we simply add a new full day every four years.

✅ Checkpoint 2

(a) Which planet has the greatest mass?

(b) Which planet has the longest day?

(c) Name two or three elements that are common to nearly all.

(d) Suggest a reason why Mercury is the hottest planet in the solar system and why Neptune is the coldest planet (*remember:* Pluto is not a planet!).

(e) In the spaces given at the end of *Table 15.02.01*, add in two moons from any of the planets listed and complete all the details.

(f) Develop your own mnemonic device to remember the order of the planets from the sun.

EARTH & SPACE

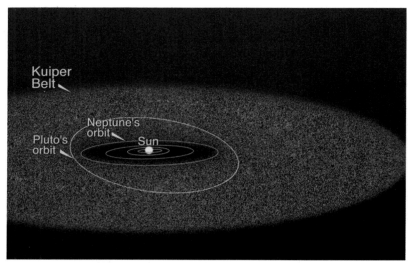

Fig. 15.02.04 The Kuiper belt.

Fig. 15.02.05 The first close-up picture of Pluto sent back from the New Horizons spacecraft in 2015. People have noted that the clearing on the face of the planet resembles the outline of the Disney character, Pluto, while others think it looks like a heart.

Exoplanets – Our Future Home Planets and the Search for Extra-Terrestrial Intelligence

Exoplanets are planets which orbit a star other than our sun. Almost 2000 exoplanets have been discovered by the Kepler space telescope. Particular interest is placed on those planets which lie within the **habitable zone** or 'Goldilocks Zone' (a 'just right' zone!) of their star. This is a region in space in which a planet will be able to support liquid water.

Given the importance of water as a liquid in Earth's life support, the liquid water condition is considered vital to support any extra-terrestrial life. It is currently estimated that there might be as many as 40 billion Earth-like planets orbiting the habitable zone in the Milky Way alone!

The first discovery of an exoplanet with a similar radius to that of Earth and within the habitable zone of a star was Kepler-186f. It is not thought that Kepler-186f harbours extra-terrestrial life, as two studies by SETI (Search for Extra-Terrestrial Intelligence – an organisation whose mission is to 'explore, understand and explain the origin, nature and prevalence of life in the universe') found no evidence of activity on the planet.

Fig. 15.02.06 A habitable zone around a star.

Did you know?

On 23 July 2015, the first candidate for harbouring extra-terrestrial life was discovered, Kepler-452b, or 'Earth 2.0' as the media called it. At 1400 light-years from Earth, Kepler-452b orbits its own 'sun', which is 4% bigger and 10% brighter than ours. Kelper-452b is 1.6 times the size of Earth. Unfortunately, none of us will ever travel there because it would take 1400 years to get there, and that's only if we travel at the speed of light!

Fig. 15.02.07 Size comparison of Kelper-438b (left) to Earth (right).

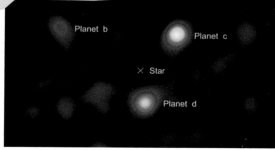

Fig. 15.02.08 The star HR8799 (marked with the x) is 120 light years away from Earth. The three planets orbiting it are called HR8799 b, c and d. This is the first image of exoplanets captured with a relatively small telescope (a 1.5-metre lens).

Stars

Stars are formed by the condensing (shrinking) of solar nebula into a tight cluster. This creates high pressures and temperatures, which starts a nuclear fusion reaction. The main reaction which the star undergoes is the conversion of hydrogen to helium (**nuclear fusion**). The energy generated from the fusion of hydrogen and helium is then pushed out of the core and radiates into space in the form of an electromagnetic wave (see *Unit 11.2*). This is why we can feel the heat from the sun, and as we have learned from previous units, this energy is vital to the basic functions of life on Earth.

This causes massive pressure to be exerted outwards from the core, meaning that if no equal force was exerted inwards towards the core of the star, the star would continue to grow outwards. As you learned in *Unit 12.1*, Newton's Third Law of Motion states: 'For every action there is an equal and opposite reaction.' Stars are no exception to this law. To stop a star from continuously growing, gravity is exerting an equal force (equal to the pressure from the star) inwards towards the core of the star. This allows the star to remain stable.

Stars can be categorised into seven different classes called **spectral types**. Spectral types are determined by their colour, which indicates which elements are being created and used in the fusion process, as well as providing us with an indication of the surface temperature.

> **Stars:** Enormous gaseous celestial bodies which generate energy by nuclear fusion. Emit light and heat energy because of this generation of energy.

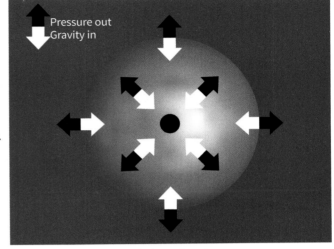

Fig. 15.02.09 The pressure balance in a star.

Type	Prominent spectral lines	Colour		Average temperature	Example
O	He^+, He, H, O^{2+}, N^{2+}, C^{2+}, Si^{3+}	Blue	●	45 000°C (80 000°F)	Gamma Velorum
B	He, H, C^+, O^+, N^+, Fe^{2+}, Mg^{2+}	Bluish white	○	30 000°C (55 000°F)	Rigel
A	H, ionized metals	White	○	12 000°C (22 000°F)	Sirius
F	H, Ca^+, Ti^+, Fe^+	Yellowish white	○	8 000°C (14 000°F)	Procyon
G	Ca^+, Fe, Ti, Mg, H, some molecular bands	Yellow	○	6 500°C (12 000°F)	The Sun
K	Ca^+, H, molecular bands	Orange	●	5 000°C (9 000°F)	Aldebaran
M	TiO, Ca, molecular bands	Red	●	3 500°C (6 500°F)	Betelgeuse

> Stars are classified by their colour and their temperature. There are seven main types of stars. In order of decreasing temperature, they are: O, B, A, F, G, K and M. Try making up a mnemonic to remember them.

Table 15.02.02 Stellar spectral chart. Looking at the chart, can you identify what type of star our sun is?

Luminosity

Another characteristic of stars is their **luminosity**. This is their brightness and is calculated as the total energy radiated per second by the star. Luminosity is generally given by comparing the brightness of others stars to our own sun. We use a range of less than one ten-thousandth the brightness of our sun to over one million times brighter than our sun.

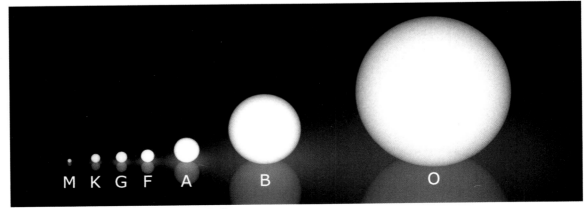

Fig. 15.02.10 Size comparison of different types of stars.

EARTH & SPACE

The Life of a Star

When the interstellar clouds between stars become condensed due to the influence of gravity, hydrogen molecules begin to form. As this process continues, the cloud gains more mass. If the cloud reaches a certain mass, the force of gravity will cause the gas to collapse and different parts of the cloud will clump together and form **protostars** (baby stars). These protostars will continue to collapse, resulting in a rise in temperature and pressure. Here, two things can occur:

1
The mass of the protostar is great enough to begin generating nuclear (fusion) reactions, with this reaction becoming a self-sustaining chain reaction.

2
The mass of the protostar is too small to generate nuclear reactions and it becomes a brown dwarf.

Fig. 15.02.11 A brown dwarf star.

If the protostar begins to generate nuclear reactions, it moves on to the next phase. The gas that was used to build the protostar starts to rotate and begins to speed up, causing it to be pulled inward, before joining the core. Eventually, the protostar becomes a main sequence star (stable star). It is at this stage that the helium and other products generated by the nuclear reactions thrown out by the star can generate new planets.

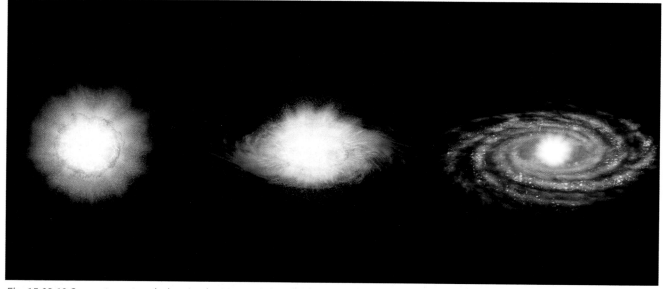

Fig. 15.02.12 Computer artwork showing how a star is formed from the condensation of swirling dust and gas. Stars form when this dust begins to clump together under the influence of their own gravity.

The Death of a Star

When a star has exhausted the hydrogen in its core, it will start to fuse the heavier elements in its outer layers. Depending on the size of the star, the outcomes can be very different.

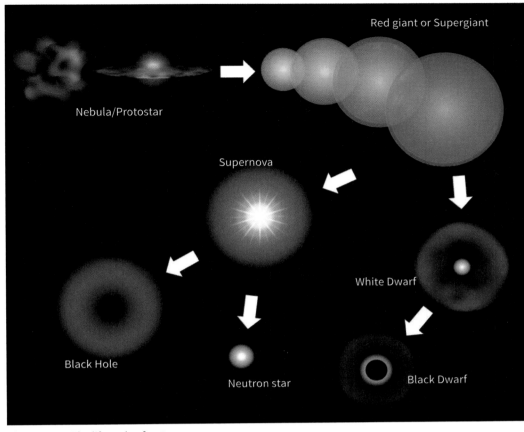

Fig. 15.02.13 The life cycle of a star.

Low Mass Stars

When a star with a mass of less than half that of our sun has used up all its hydrogen, it will begin to convert the hydrogen in its atmosphere into helium. The star does not have enough pressure or temperature for fusion to continue, and eventually the star will cool and fade into a small black dwarf star.

Sun-Like Stars

When the hydrogen is exhausted, these stars fuse the elements found in their outer shells and eventually become a red giant with some planetary nebula (space dust). These stars do have enough pressure and temperature to fuse the helium core, and so begin expanding again, before finally collapsing into a white dwarf.

Our Sun

Our sun was born about 4.6 billion years ago, spending nearly 100 000 years as a protostar before becoming the sun as we know it a few million years later. Our sun converts 600 million tonnes of hydrogen into helium every second, generating 4×10^{27} W (watts) of energy. But what will happen to our sun in billions of years' time? It has been estimated that the sun has about 7 billion years' worth of fuel left.

In roughly 1 billion years, the sun will produce about 10% more energy than it does now. This energy will evaporate all the water vapour in our atmosphere.

In 3.5 billion years, the sun will be producing 40% more energy and this will result in our oceans boiling and evaporating into space. At this stage the earth will resemble a modern-day Venus.

In roughly 6 billion years, the sun's core will contain so much helium that it will collapse under its own weight. It will then grow in size, easily consuming Mercury and Venus. Many scientists predict it will also expand as far as Earth and destroy our planet.

Then, after millions of years, the sun will begin to fuse the helium into carbon and will eventually become a white dwarf star.

High Mass Stars

Similar to the death of sun-like stars, **high mass stars** will undergo contraction and expansion many times, depending on their mass. They can produce supergiant stars which have an iron core. If this giant's mass is still over 1.4 times greater than the mass of the sun, it will collapse to become a neutron star. If the mass of the supergiant is over three solar masses, then it will collapse to become a black hole.

Fig. 15.02.14 In roughly 7 billion years, the sun will have spent its nuclear fusion fuel, expanded, destroyed Mercury, Venus and possibly Earth, before settling down to become a white dwarf star.

Investigation 15.02.01: Measuring the diameter of the sun and the moon

Equipment: Cardboard with a 2 x 2 cm square cut from its centre, aluminium foil, pin, white paper, clear view of the sun and the moon.

Instructions: Using the equipment as listed and the formula, plan an investigation to approximate the diameter of the sun and the moon.

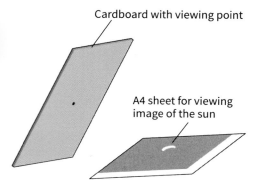

Cardboard with viewing point

A4 sheet for viewing image of the sun

$$\frac{\text{Diameter of the image of the sun}}{\text{Distance from the pinhole to the paper}} \times \text{Distance from Earth to the sun} = \text{Diameter of the sun}$$

What did you learn?
How did you know when to measure the distance of the image on the paper?

Investigation 15.02.02: Examining the detail of the sun

Equipment: Binoculars, clear view of the sun, projector screen/paper, mirror.

Instructions: Using the equipment as listed, design an investigation to examine some finer details of the sun.

N.B.
Do not use the binoculars to look directly at the sun!

What did you learn?
1. How did you ensure that only the image of the sun was produced onto the screen?
2. What safety precautions did you take to ensure you did not look directly at the sun?
3. Draw a diagram of what details you were able to see of the sun.

Checkpoint 3

Write a paragraph describing the life and death of a star. Be sure to include how a star remains stable.

Moons

In our solar system alone, there are 173 known **natural satellites** (moons). Moons are thought to be created from the same solar nebula used in creating their **primary**. Moons are generally **tidally locked** (gravitationally locked) to their primary. This means that the same side of the moon faces the planet at all times. In the case of Earth's moon: it takes the moon approximately thirty days to spin on its axis, which, as it so happens, is also the amount of time it takes to orbit the earth.

There is only one exception to this rule: Hyperion, Saturn's natural satellite, rotates chaotically due to the gravitational influence of Titan (Saturn's other, much larger moon).

Moons: Celestial bodies that orbit another body, called its 'primary', e.g. a planet. Also known as satellites.

Fig. 15.02.15 Scale of moons in comparison to Earth.

The earth's moon has an effect on its tides. As the moon orbits the earth, its gravity influences the water on Earth. At the point underneath the moon the water is slightly pulled towards the moon (this is called a swell). Recall Newton's third law of motion: for every action there is an equal and opposite reaction. So, there is another bulge on the far side of the earth, which is moving away from the moon. As the earth rotates on its axis, tides are produced. This is where we get the term 'high tide' from. It is the point where the moon is directly over a geographic location.

You can look online and find the times for high tide for your closest beach.

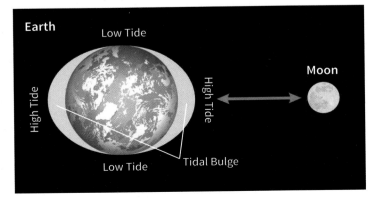

Fig. 15.02.16 The effect of the moon on Earth's tides.

EARTH & SPACE

teroids and Comets

eroids

eroids are remnants of a failed attempt to form a planet. These failed planets are
and dusty and are too small to have their own atmosphere. To date, 200 000 have
n discovered, but it is believed that there are in excess of over a billion asteroids.
st asteroids are found in a region between Mars and Jupiter called the **main belt**.

eroids are divided into three categories:

Carbonaceous (C-Type) (contains carbon)
Silicaceous (S-Type) (contains silicon)
Metallic (M-Type) (contains mainly heavier metals)

Did you know?
s is the largest asteroid
solar system but it is so
that it can be classified
as a dwarf planet!

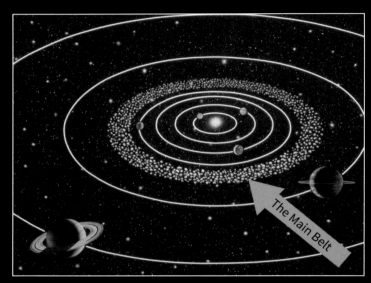

Fig. 15.02.17 The main belt.

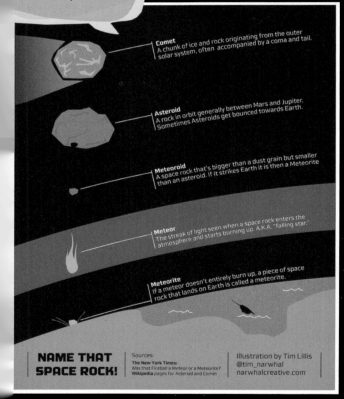

Comet
A chunk of ice and rock originating from the outer
solar system, often accompanied by a coma and tail.

Asteroid
A rock in orbit generally between Mars and Jupiter.
Sometimes Asteroids get bounced towards Earth.

Meteoroid
A space rock that's bigger than a dust grain but smaller
than an asteroid. If it strikes Earth it is then a Meteorite

Meteor
The streak of light seen when a space rock enters the
atmosphere and starts burning up. A.K.A. "falling star."

Meteorite
If a meteor doesn't entirely burn up, a piece of space
rock that lands on Earth is called a meteorite.

NAME THAT SPACE ROCK!

Sources:
The New York Times:
Was that Fireball a Meteor or a Meteorite?
Wikipedia pages for Asteroid and Comet

Illustration by Tim Lillis
@tim_narwhal
narwhalcreative.com

Fig. 15.02.18 The different types of comets, asteroids and meteors.

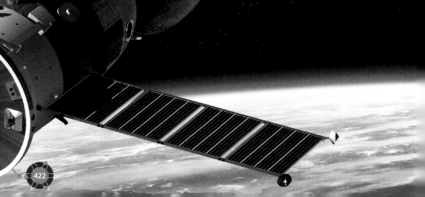

Fig. 15.02.19 As depicted in the Bayeux Tapestry, we can see onlookers on the left pointing at Halley's Comet shooting across the sky.

Comets

Short Period Comets: Comets that orbit the sun roughly every seven years. This is due to the gravitational influence of Jupiter.

Intermediate–Long Period Comets: Comets with an orbital period greater than twenty years (such as **Halley's Comet**).

Fig. 15.02.20 A crater.

Meteors, Meteoroids and Meteorites

- **Meteor:** The flash of light produced when celestial debris enters the earth's atmosphere.
- **Meteoroid:** Celestial debris that has entered the earth's atmosphere. These usually burn up upon entering our atmosphere.
- **Meteorite:** Any remaining small fragment which has not been burned up as a result of entering our atmosphere.

Planetary Systems and Gravity

The final celestial body we will examine isn't actually a 'celestial body' at all but rather the culmination of everything we have looked at so far, explaining how it all links together. It is well known that we are located in a **planetary system** we call our 'solar system'. In our solar system, we have:

- A star around which all celestial bodies orbit (the sun)
- Eight planets and their natural satellites
- Asteroids
- Dwarf planets.

There are other planetary systems in the universe. A planetary system is a system of celestial bodies which all orbit around a star.

Did you know?

In February 2013, a meteorite entered Earth's atmosphere over the Ural region in Russia. The object travelled at a speed of 60 000 km/h and was brighter than the sun. It exploded at about 30 km above the ground. This caused a massive shockwave, which produced roughly 25 times the kinetic energy of the atomic bomb detonated over Hiroshima. Luckily all this happened in a very large, remote area.

Fig. 15.02.21 The meteorite just before crashing in remote Russia.

Many scientists believe that our solar system was formed around 4.6 billion years ago from a massive cloud of gas and dust (solar nebula). Over millions of years, this gas flattened due to gravity, and at the centre of this gas cloud it reached huge temperatures and began to form our sun. The rest of our celestial bodies were then created from the remaining cloud of gas and dust.

At the centre of our solar system is a star, and all planetary bodies orbit this star. This is referred to as a **heliocentric system**. Nicolaus Copernicus was the first scientist to mathematically predict this. His work would later be relied on by Isaac Newton to further develop physics. Newton was the first to suggest that there was a force between the planets: gravity. He suggested that the orbits of the earth, sun and other planetary bodies were kept constant due to gravity. This explains why we are able to predict the orbits of the planets in our solar system.

Gravity
Gravity is a force of attraction. Believe it or not, gravity does attract us to each other, but because we're so small we don't feel it. Instead we experience the pull of gravity towards the centre of the earth.

The magnitude of this force
In space we are dealing with massive objects like planets and stars, so the force of the attraction of gravity is much stronger than we experience here on Earth. This is why the moon is locked to the earth. The gravity of the earth is pulling the moon towards the earth.

The mass of the object
The more massive an object, the more gravity it 'exerts', in other words, the more 'attractive it is'. Since the sun is the largest celestial body in our solar system, it attracts all the other planets and moons as well as asteroids such as Halley's Comet.

Orbits
This means the earth is being pulled towards the sun and this creates its orbit.

The Orbit of the Moon around the Earth
Why is it that the moon doesn't just crash into the earth or the earth crash into the sun if it's attracted to it? This is a very difficult concept to grasp. Imagine this.

Find this video on YouTube to learn more about this: https://wwwyoutube.com/watch?v=2Wgijlb4DJM

You throw a tennis ball out your bedroom window. What happens? No matter how far or fast you throw it, it will eventually fall down to the ground, because of gravity.

Now imagine you are standing on the top of a very tall building and you throw the same tennis ball as fast/far as possible. What will happen? The ball will travel further, but it will still fall to the ground.

Now imagine standing on the top of Mount Everest and throwing the ball. Its movement will look somewhat like the above image.

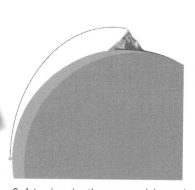

So let us imagine the moon and the earth. You are correct to believe that the moon is falling towards the earth. However, the moon is far enough away and moving fast enough that 'down' is never the same direction! Gravity is pulling the moon towards Earth but the speed of the fall is creating the flight path we've seen in the first three images. So with the right amount of speed, the moon 'falls' towards the earth but never crashes. This is known as its orbit, and works the same for planets around the sun.

WHAT I HAVE LEARNED...

- Galaxies are gravitationally bound systems which contain stars, planets, dark matter and more.
- A planet is defined by three characteristics:
  - Massive enough to be rounded by its own gravity
  - Not massive enough to cause fusion
  - Are gravitationally independent of its neighbours.
- There are eight planets in our solar system: Mercury, Venus, Earth, Mars, Jupiter, Saturn, Uranus and Neptune. (Pluto was originally considered to be a planet.)
- The creation of our sun, planets and moons can be attributed to space nebula (space gases and clouds).
- Exoplanets are similar in set-up to that of earth: they contain a planet in the habitable zone of a star. This allows liquid water to exist on the planet which is necessary for life to exist.
- Stars are formed when hot mass is condensed at massive pressures causing nuclear reactions. The production of gases causes the star to grow and gravity equalises this pressure to make the star stable.
- Moons are known as natural satellites and orbit another celestial body known as their 'primary'.
- Asteroids are remnants of a failed attempt to form a planet; most of them can be found in the main belt between Mars and Jupiter.
- There are three types of asteroids:
  - Carbonaceous (C-Type)
  - Silicaceous (S-Type)
  - Metallic (M-Type)
- Comets are small bodies of ice which produce bright clouds of dust and gases when they get close to the sun.
- There are two types of comets:
  - Short Period Comets: Comets that orbit the sun roughly every seven years. This is due to the gravitational influence of Jupiter.
  - Intermediate–Long Period Comets: Comets with an orbital period greater than twenty years (such as Halley's Comet).
- Meteor: The flash of light produced when celestial debris enters the earth's atmosphere.
- Meteoroid: Celestial debris that has entered the earth's atmosphere. These usually burn up upon entering our atmosphere.
- Meteorite: Any remaining small fragment which has not been burned up as a result of entering our atmosphere.
- A planetary system is a system of celestial bodies which all orbit around a star.

Question Time

Copy and Complete

In this unit I learned that there are many celestial bodies in our universe. All of these celestial bodies can be found in giant gr_____ bound systems called _____. These contain planets, _____, dark _____ and much more. I also learned that there are three defining characteristics of a _____. First it must be _____ enough to be rounded by its own _____. Second, it must not be massive enough to cause _____, and finally it must be gravitationally _____ of its _____. There are eight planets in our solar system. Starting with the closest to the sun we have _____, _____, _____, _____, _____, _____, _____ and _____. _____ was considered a planet, but is now considered a _____ planet. The creation of all celestial bodies in our solar system can be attributed to solar _____. In the search for an understanding of our universe we have discovered other planets similar to earth called _____. These planets lie within the _____ _____ of its nearest star, which is important as it means _____ _____ could be present on the planet, which is necessary for _____ to exist. Other celestial bodies that exist in the universe include **a**_____ and **c**_____. There are three classes of _____. These are: Carbonaceous (__-____), Silicaceous (__-____) and _____ (M-Type). _____ are the remnants of a _____ attempt to form a _____ and are mainly found in the _____ belt between Mars and _____. _____ are small bodies of _____ which produce bright clouds of _____ and _____ when they get close to the _____. _____ only have two classes, _____ period comets and _____–long period comets, such as _____ _____.

Questions

1. From what are our stars and planets made?
2. What is the name of the zone around a star in which it is possible that liquid water can exist on a planet?
3. Our galaxy, the Milky Way, is an example of what?
4. What is the biggest asteroid in our solar system called?
5. In what belt can you find the majority of asteroids?
6. Pluto is the largest celestial body in what belt?
7. In your own words, explain how a star is formed, and how it maintains its size.
8. Write a paragraph explaining how a star dies.

EARTH & SPACE

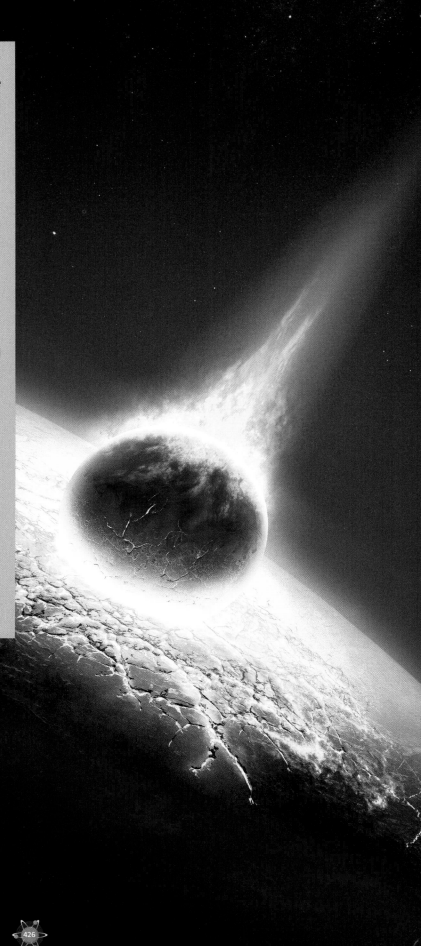

Inquiry

A There are over two hundred moons in our solar system. Using *Table 15.02.01* as a template, **create** your own table of five moons from Jupiter, Saturn, Uranus, Neptune and Pluto. The following information must be provided. Add more if you wish.

- Name
- Planet it orbits (its primary)
- Mass
- Gravity
- Diameter
- Atmosphere
- Surface temperature
- Time taken to orbit its primary

B **Create** a model of one of the following:

(a) The solar system

(b) The life cycle of a star

In your model, try to keep scale in mind, i.e. Pluto should not be the same size as Jupiter nor the moon the same size as the sun or Earth. You may use whatever materials you wish, or if you prefer, you may construct the model using a computer.

C NASA, the Russian Federal Space Agency, the Indian Space Research Organisation and the European Space Agency have all launched many unmanned probes into space to examine our neighbourhood planets. **Research** one of these missions and **present** your research in an appropriate manner.

D **Research** the other types of galaxy shapes and **list** the names of other spiral galaxies.

E **Research** and **present** a poster on the effect an asteroid would have if it impacted Earth.

15.3

The Sun–Earth–Moon Model

Learning Outcomes

ESLO 4. Develop and use a model of the earth–sun–moon system to describe predictable phenomena observable on Earth, including seasons, lunar phases and eclipses of the sun and moon.

NSLO 7. Organise and communicate research and investigative findings in a variety of ways fit for purpose and audience, using relevant scientific terminology and representations.

R Teacher's reference

KEYWORDS

first quarter moon
full moon
last quarter moon
lunar eclipse
lunar phases
new moon
non-luminous object
partial eclipse
solar eclipse
sun–earth–moon model
tidally locked
total eclipse

LEARNING INTENTIONS

At the end of this unit you should:
Be able to describe the sun–earth–moon model and how it influences our seasons, the tides of the oceans and other astronomical phenomena.

EARTH & SPACE

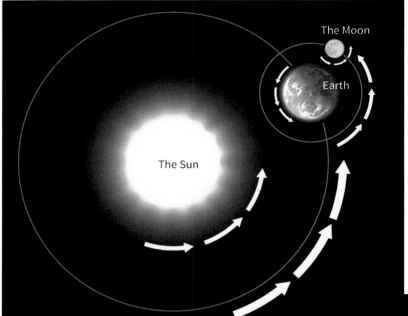

A Unique Relationship

The sun and moon both have a part to play in life on Earth. The sun provides energy and light, the moon provides the tidal movement. But did you know that both the moon and sun have much larger effects on Earth; they influence our seasons, day and night cycles and even eclipses. There is a unique relationship between the earth, the sun and the moon.

Fig. 15.03.01 The sun–earth–moon Model. The arrows indicate the rotation of the celestial body as well as its orbit.

Seasons and Why They Change

The earth is tilted at an angle of 23.5 degrees. Because of this, one half of the earth is facing the sun for half of the year while the other is not. This creates our seasons. From March until September, the northern hemisphere (our hemisphere) experiences more sunlight (spring and summer). From March until June (summertime), the hours of daylight increase, reaching a maximum on June 21, which is known as the 'summer solstice' (the longest day of the year).

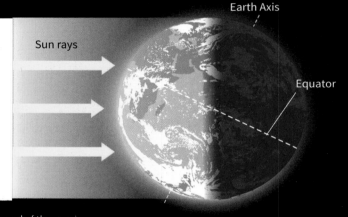

Fig. 15.03.02 An example of how the sunlight falls on the nothern hemisphere.

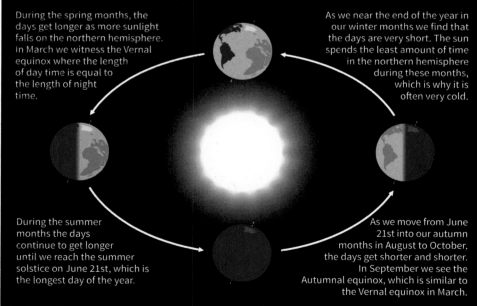

During the spring months, the days get longer as more sunlight falls on the northern hemisphere. In March we witness the Vernal equinox where the length of day time is equal to the length of night time.

As we near the end of the year in our winter months we find that the days are very short. The sun spends the least amount of time in the northern hemisphere during these months, which is why it is often very cold.

During the summer months the days continue to get longer until we reach the summer solstice on June 21st, which is the longest day of the year.

As we move from June 21st into our autumn months in August to October, the days get shorter and shorter. In September we see the Autumnal equinox, which is similar to the Vernal equinox in March.

Fig. 15.03.03 The seasonal cycle of our earth.

During the winter months (October to February), the earth's tilt is such that the northern hemisphere receives less sun rays. Consequently, it gets colder and the days are shorter until we reach the winter solstice (shortest day of the year). The solstices are the days when the earth has maximum tilt either towards or away from the sun.

Lunar Phases

When you look up at a clear sky, you can see the moon. However, depending on the time of the month, you may see a different phase of the moon. In *Unit 15.2* we noted that the earth and moon are **tidally locked**. This means that from our position on Earth, we are always looking at the same face of the moon.

As the earth and moon rotate around the sun, the sunlight illuminates different amounts of the moon's surface. There are several **lunar phases**: **New Moon**, **First Quarter Moon**, **Full Moon** and **Last Quarter Moon**. A full lunar phase takes just under thirty days to complete.

Did you know?

Nowadays the phrase 'once in a blue moon' refers to the rare occurrence of having two full moons in one month, one at the start and one at the end. This happens mainly because the lunar phase is 29.53 days. The last 'blue' moon (the moon doesn't actually turn blue!) occurred in July 2015. They occur every two to three years

Phase	Description	Image
New Moon	This is the first lunar phase. It occurs when the moon and sun are in front of the earth. Since all the light is hitting the back of the moon, we don't see it. (You can just make out a faint outline on the right of the image.)	
First Quarter Moon	The moon has moved and the sunlight has uncovered the first quarter of the right-hand side of the moon. We always see the uncovering of the moon from right to left.	
Full Moon	The earth is now between the moon and the sun. The moon is behind the earth and receives the maximum amount of sunlight from the sun.	
Last Quarter Moon	The moon now begins to move back towards the front of the earth. As this happens, less light hits the surface of the moon. When we look at the moon, we see the light fade from right to left until it goes to a 'crescent moon', and finally back to a New Moon and the beginning of another cycle.	

 Checkpoint 1

Draw a diagram showing the lunar phases as they appear in space. You must include the following items: the sun, earth and moon.

EARTH & SPACE

Investigation 15.03.01: Investigating the lunar phases

Equipment: Paper plates, scissors, colouring pens and any other equipment you think will help.
Instructions: Using the equipment as listed, represent the lunar phases.

Eclipses

An eclipse is when a celestial body is temporarily obscured, either by passing into the shadow of another body, or by having another body pass between it and the observer (you).

There are two types of eclipses: **solar** and **lunar**.

Solar Eclipse

A **solar eclipse** occurs when the moon passes between the sun and the earth. There are two main types of solar eclipses: **total eclipse** and **partial eclipse**.

A **total solar eclipse** occurs when the moon completely covers the sun, leaving only a small outer ring of the sun visible. This creates a shadow on the earth and can last for up to seven and a half minutes.

The Sun and Your Eyes

Looking directly at the sun at any time can permanently damage your eyes. You must never look directly at a solar eclipse. During an eclipse, since it gets dark, your pupils dilate to increase the amount of light entering into your eye. If you look directly at the eclipse, the sudden influx of light into your retina as the eclipse moves away can permanently blind you. **To view an eclipse, you must look at it indirectly or with special viewing equipment.**

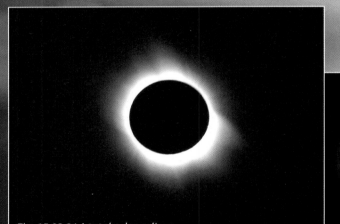

Fig. 15.03.04 A total solar eclipse.

Solar eclipse:
Sun, moon and earth line up, with the moon in the middle

Fig. 15.03.05 What happens to cause a total solar eclipse.

A **partial eclipse** is when the moon and sun are not exactly in line and as a result we don't get total coverage. However, we can get up to 90% coverage. It is still extremely dangerous to look at a partial eclipse directly.

Fig. 15.03.06 A partial solar eclipse.

Lunar Eclipse

A **lunar eclipse** is a little harder to understand. It is when the sun, earth and moon are exactly in line.

The sun emits light in all directions, and because of its size it covers a large area. When the moon passes behind the earth, it generally receives some light, which is why we have our lunar phases. Also, remember that the moon is a **non-luminous object** so it reflects the light from the sun.

However, when the moon, earth and sun are in line, the earth blocks a lot of the light from the sun, creating what is called the 'umbra' (a region where there is little sunlight) and the 'penumbra' (a region where there is no sunlight).

As the moon orbits behind the earth, it passes through the umbra and we see a lunar eclipse.

The moon may even pass slightly (or on very, very rare occasions, totally) through the penumbra, which gives us an even darker lunar eclipse.

Lunar eclipses are safe to look at with the naked eye as the change in light intensity between non-eclipse and eclipse is minimal.

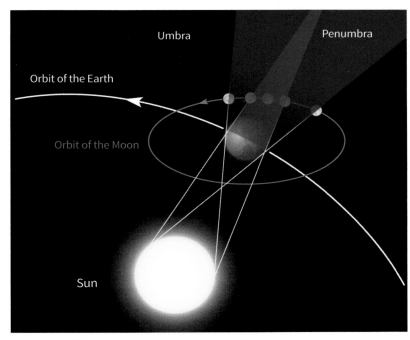

Fig. 15.03.07 What happens to cause a lunar eclipse.

Fig. 15.03.08 A lunar eclipse.

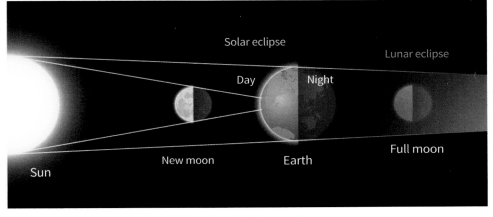

Fig. 15.03.09 The differences between a solar and a lunar eclipse.

Investigation 15.03.02: **Investigating the solar and lunar eclipses**

Equipment: A lamp, ruler, pencil, plain A3 paper, tennis ball, Blu-tack, two table tennis balls, black marker.
Instructions: Using the equipment as listed, investigate the solar and lunar eclipses.

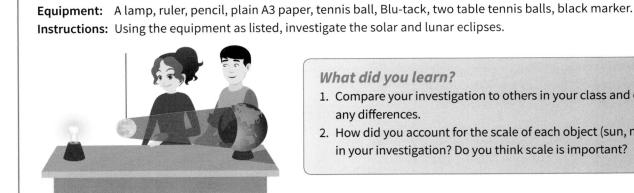

What did you learn?
1. Compare your investigation to others in your class and comment on any differences.
2. How did you account for the scale of each object (sun, moon, earth) in your investigation? Do you think scale is important?

EARTH & SPACE

WHAT I HAVE LEARNED...

- The sun–earth–moon model describes a unique relationship between these celestial bodies.
- The tilt of the earth is responsible for the seasons on Earth.
- Our moon is tidally locked to our planet, so the same face of the moon always faces the earth.
- Our moon has several lunar phases: new moon, first quarter moon, full moon and last quarter moon.
- When the moon passes between the sun and the earth, a solar eclipse occurs.
- When the earth passes between the moon and the sun, we get a solar eclipse.

 ## Question Time

Copy and Complete

In this unit I learned that there is a unique relationship between the sun, _____ and _____ and this is known as the _____–_____–_____ model. This relationship is responsible for the _____ of the sea, the changes in our_____ and other astronomical phenomena such as _____. The _____ occur because our earth has a ____.__ degree _____ about its axis. This _____ means that for one half of the year one _____ of the earth is facing the _____. In the northern hemisphere we face the sun from _____ until _____. Our moon is _____ locked to the earth; this means the same _____ of the moon is always facing us. Another unique aspect of this model is the _____ _____ of our moon. The moon orbits the earth in the same way as the earth orbits the sun. So depending on where the moon, earth and sun are, we will see a different _____ of the _____. There are _____ key _____ phases: new moon, _____ _____ moon, _____ moon and _____ _____ _____. The last characteristic of this model is the occurrence of eclipses. There are two types of eclipse, _____ _____ and _____ _____. A _____ eclipse occurs when the _____ either completely covers the sun or _____ covers it. The result is a shadow cast on Earth and a few minutes of darkness. In a _____ eclipse, the _____ blocks the light from the _____ and as the moon travels through the _____ into the _____ the moon becomes darker and darker.

Questions

1. What are the main lunar phases?
2. What is responsible for the earth's seasons?
3. In your own words, describe how the seasons change.
4. Write a paragraph detailing how a solar eclipse occurs.

Inquiry

A **Create** a **model** of the sun–earth–moon model. Try to keep **scale** in mind, i.e. the moon should not be the same size as the sun or Earth. You may use whatever materials you wish, or you may use a computer to build your model.

B **Research** and **build** your own eclipse-viewing camera.

C **Research** and **design** a poster explaining why some countries use 'daylight savings' and why other countries do not. In your poster, outline the advantages and disadvantages of daylight savings.

D Newgrange in County Meath was built during the Neolithic Era, around 300–2500 BC. **Research** the history behind Newgrange (who built it and why) and **explain** the scientific occurrences associated with Newgrange. **Present** your findings as a presentation/poster.

15.4

Space Exploration

Learning Outcomes

ESLO 8. Examine some of the current **hazards and benefits of space exploration** and discuss the future **role and implications of space exploration in society.**

PWLO 4. Research and discuss **an aspect of modern physics/technologies in terms of scientific, societal and environmental impact.**

NSLO 1. Appreciate how scientists work and **how scientific ideas are modified over time.**

NSLO 4. Produce data (qualitatively/ quantitatively); **critically analyse data to identify patterns and relationships**; identify anomalous observations; **draw and justify conclusions.**

NSLO 7. Organise and communicate research and investigative findings **in a variety of ways fit for purpose and audience, using relevant scientific terminology and representations.**

NSLO 9. Research and present information on the **contribution that scientists make to scientific discovery and invention,** and its impact on society.

NSLO 10. Appreciate the role of science in society and its **personal, social and global importance.**

R Teacher's reference

KEYWORDS

ablative	nozzle
heat shield	orbit
astronaut	oxidiser
Blunt Body	payload
Theory	propellant
capsule	re-entry
drogue	rocket
parachute	satellites
escape	solid fuel
velocity	spacecraft
fuel	spaceplane
gravity	stage
liquid fuel	staging
manned	thrust
microgravity	unmanned

LEARNING INTENTIONS

At the end of this unit you should:

1. Know the differences between solid and liquid fuel rockets.
2. Be able to explain how rocket staging works.
3. Explain that there are different types of manned spacecraft.
4. Know the advantages and disadvantages of manned and unmanned missions.
5. Know and explain some of the challenges of space travel.
6. Know about some of the technologies developed from space travel research.
7. Know some of the arguments in favour of and against space exploration.

EARTH & SPACE

Why Explore Space?

> *'Nothing is so dangerous to the progress of the human mind than to assume that our views of science are ultimate, that there are no mysteries in nature, that our triumphs are complete and there are no new worlds to conquer.'*
>
> Humphry Davy

Humphry Davy, who discovered six elements and invented a coalminer's lamp, believed in the development of science through exploration and investigations. This quote from him is one answer to the question 'Why explore space?'

While many would say that developing scientific knowledge is a good enough reason, there are other reasons:

- To develop more technologies and skills
- To investigate whether other planets can be colonised for living
- To mine asteroids and comets for precious or unusual metals and minerals
- To explore other celestial bodies and so learn more about our own planet and how to care for it.

Many argue, however, that all of these aims can be achieved without humans having to leave Earth. They believe that robotic probes can do all this exploration, at a smaller cost and without the danger to human life that comes with space exploration.

Others argue that considering how much of Earth has yet to be explored, especially under our seas and oceans, what point is there in space exploration? As well as that, they believe that the vast sums of money needed for space exploration could be better spent on providing aid to those living in absolute poverty in our world.

The decision to carry out space exploration or not is an ethical question, whereby competing aims have to be balanced for the good of all. As the USA, China and India prepare for **manned** Moon and Mars missions, this ethical question will become more obvious in the near future.

The History of Rockets

The first record of a **rocket**-type device was in 1232, when arrows with simple solid fuel devices attached were fired at Mongol invaders to drive them out of China. The Mongols went on to use these new weapons in their own invasion of other lands. In 1780, Hyder Ali, the ruler of the kingdom of Mysore in India, used rockets to defeat the British army at the Battle of Pollilur. Just as the Mongols learned from defeat, Sir William Congreve developed rockets based on these Mysore rockets that were later used in the wars against the armies of Napoleon.

By the end of the eighteenth century, writers Jules Verne and H. G. Wells had imagined rockets being used to travel to the moon. George Méliès was inspired by these works to create the silent film, *A Trip to the Moon*. At about the same time, Russian scientist Konstantin Tsiolkovsky not only wrote a book about space exploration by rockets, but calculated the speed a rocket needed to escape the pull of Earth's **gravity**.

 Checkpoint 1

'To explore strange new worlds, to seek new life ... to boldly go where no one has gone before.' This is a quote from *Star Trek*. Give two other reasons why you think that manned space missions should continue and two reasons why they should not.

In the USA, Robert Goddard conducted many experiments in almost complete secrecy from the public, testing solid fuel and **liquid fuel** rockets, as well as proving that rockets could work in a vacuum. Because there is no atmosphere in space, Goddard's work was an important step towards creating a space rocket.

Hermann Oberth wrote on interplanetary travel by rocket, inspiring the Spaceflight Society to be founded in Germany by rocket enthusiasts, one of whom later became chief rocket scientist for both the Nazi rocket programme and the US space programme. In Moscow, Tsiolkovsky inspired another rocket society which later inspired scientists involved in the Russian space programme.

While some theories had been proven by basic research, it was only after World War II that enough focus was put on rockets to develop them as long-range weapons (missiles). Scientists then used this technology to begin exploring space. When the first Nazi rocket weapon was used to attack another country, chief scientist Wernher von Braun supposedly said: '*The rocket worked perfectly, except for landing on the wrong planet.*' He and Russian chief scientist, Sergei Korolev, would later compete during the 'Space Race' to see which of their countries would be the first to land a man on the moon.

Hyder Ali
(1721–1782)

William Congreve
(1772–1828)

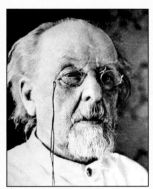

Konstantin Tsiolkovsky
(1857–1935)

Robert H. Goddard
(1882–1945)

Hermann Oberth
(1894–1989)

Checkpoint 2

R Design a timeline of early rocket use up to World War II.

EARTH & SPACE

Timeline of Space Exploration

1932
The German Army begins a rocketry programme.

1933
Wernher von Braun begins working for the German Army. He designs and builds the A1 rocket.

24 October 1946
First photo of Earth from space is taken from a V-2 rocket launched by the US Army.

1st September 1939
Nazi Germany invades Poland. World War II has begun.

8 May 1945
USA begins to evacuate 1500 Nazi military scientists engineers and technicians in 'Operation Paperclip'.

1938
Katyusha rocket launchers are tested by the Russian Army as weapons.

8 September 1944
A4 rockets are now called V-2. First long-range attack rocket is launched at Paris. Wernher von Braun is chief rocket scientist for the German Army.

16 April 1946
US Army test launches a V-2 rocket.

17 September 1947
USSR successfully launches R-1 rocket based on V-2 design. Sergei Korolev is chief scientist.

20 August 1953
US Army successfully launches Redstone rocket based on V-2 design. Wernher von Braun is chief scientist.

2 October 1945
British Army test launches a V-2 rocket.

27 March 1945
Last V-2 rocket used in warfare is launched. 5200 had been built using slave labour, in underground factories.

3 August 1942
A4 rocket becomes the first man-made object in space.

1935
A3 rocket is tested.

1934
A2 rocket is tested.

Wernher von Braun
(1912–1977)

V-2 rockets were Nazi vengeance weapons meant to terrorise civilians and devastate soldiers. Expensive to produce, they had very little effect on the outcome of World War II.

Sergei Korolev
(1907–1966)

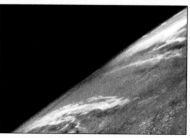

First photo of Earth from space taken from a US Army V-2 rocket.

4 October 1959
Luna 3 takes first images of dark side of the Moon.

25 May 1961
US President John F. Kennedy announces a manned mission to the Moon by the end of 1969.

27 January 1967
Three astronauts die when Apollo 1 capsule goes on fire during a test.

24 December 1968
Earthrise photo is taken on by Apollo 8 astronaut William Anders.

August 1955
The 'Space Race' begins as both the USA and the USSR announce that they each intend to be the first nation to launch an artificial satellite.

4 October 1957
The USSR launches Sputnik 1 the first artificial satellite to go into Earth orbit.

12 April 1961
Yuri Gagarin becomes the first human in space in Vostok 1.

16 June 1963
Valentina Tereshkova is first woman in space in Vostok 6.

24 April 1967
A cosmonaut dies when a parachute fails to open as Soyuz 1 lands.

11 July 1969
Apollo 11 astronauts Neil Armstrong and Buzz Aldrin become the first to set foot on the Moon. Michael Collins remained in orbit around the Moon. Overshooting the intended landing spot, there was less than one minute's worth of fuel left when they landed.

29 July 1958
The National Aeronautics and Space Administration (NASA) is founded.

5 May 1961
Alan Shepard is the first astronaut in space.

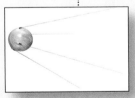
Sputnik 1.

Vostok 1 Mission Patch.

Yuri Gargarin (1934–1968)

Alan Shepard (1923–1998)

Valentina Tereshkova (b. 1937)

The plaque left attached to the Moon lander by the Apollo 11 mission.

Buzz Aldrin (b. 1930)

Neil Armstrong (1930–2012)

Michael Collins (b. 1930)

EARTH & SPACE

Rocket Science

While rockets have existed for a thousand years, the greatest advances in rocket technology and science happened just before World War II. These advances lead to manned spaceflights. Some of the most important elements of these flights were the development of:

- **Propellants**
- Engine **nozzle** sizes and shapes
- Research on **escape velocity** and **rocket staging**
- **Re-entry** technology and techniques.

Propellants

In rocketry, the chemicals used in the rocket engine are called the propellants. When reacted, the propellants create a lot of exhaust gases, which move at great speed out of the engine and with a lot of force.

The force of the gases hitting the ground below them causes a reaction force called thrust (see *Unit 12.1*) The more thrust a fuel creates, the better the propellant. But a few other factors are also important:

- Is the propellant too reactive to store safely or sit in a fuel tank near a hot engine?
- How much thrust (force) does one kilogram of fuel produce?
- Can the fuels react in space where no oxygen is available?

To operate in a space rocket, fuels normally come in two parts: the fuel and an **oxidiser**. On Earth, oxygen chemically combines with fuel to allow combustion to happen. As there is no atmosphere in space, there is no oxygen, so an **oxidiser** is needed to produce a similar reaction. Oxidisers get their name from acting in a similar way to oxygen by releasing energy during a chemical reaction.

Solid fuels give the greatest amount of thrust for their mass, but once a solid fuel is ignited it cannot stop. Solid fuel rockets are normally used for missiles, launching satellites, or to boost other rocket engines for a short period.

Liquid fuels can be controlled by switching on and off the flow of either fuel or oxidiser. The most efficient liquid fuel to use is liquid hydrogen with liquid oxygen as the oxidiser. This is a clean burn without environmental pollution and provides an enormous amount of thrust. The main engines of the Space Shuttle used this propellant mixture. The main fuel tank of the shuttle also had solid rocket boosters attached to it, which provided most of the lift-off thrust and were jettisoned (cast off to lighten the load) shortly after lift-off.

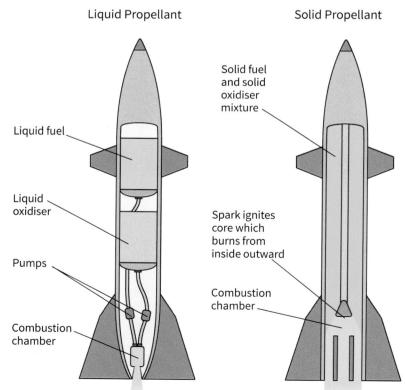

Fig. 15.04.01 Comparing liquid fuel and solid fuel rockets.

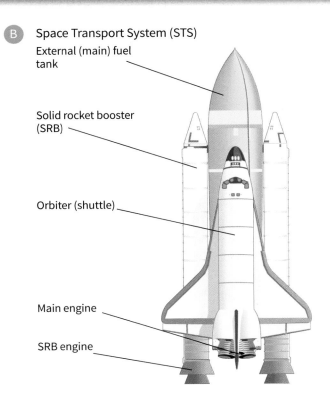

B   Space Transport System (STS)

External (main) fuel tank

Solid rocket booster (SRB)

Orbiter (shuttle)

Main engine

SRB engine

Fig. 15.04.02 (a) The main engines and SRB engines at full throttle shortly after lift-off; (b) the Space Transport System; (c) a close-up of a main engine burning hydrogen.

Investigation 15.04.01: **Investigating thrust**

Equipment: Fishing line (or thin string), drinking straw, sticky tape, small plastic (or paper) cup, paperclips, long balloon, bulldog clip.

Instructions: Using the equipment as listed, and referring to the diagram, design an investigation that tests thrust from a balloon when different amounts of paperclips are added to the plastic/paper cup.

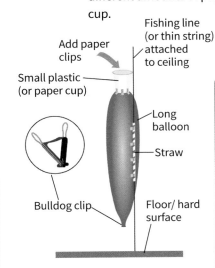

Add paper clips

Fishing line (or thin string) attached to ceiling

Small plastic (or paper cup)

Long balloon

Straw

Bulldog clip

Floor/ hard surface

What did you learn?

1. How was thrust created in this experiment?
2. What factors affect the amount of thrust generated?
3. Can you suggest how to carry out this investigation as a fair test, using only one balloon?
4. How could you make sure that each test launch is a fair test if you use different balloons each time?
5. What factor affected the speed of lift-off and final height above the launch site? Justify your answer.

EARTH & SPACE

Fig. 15.04.03 Swedish steam turbine engineer,
Gustaf de Laval (1845–1913).

Nozzle Shape and Size

Robert Goddard was the first to realise the importance of nozzle design in rocketry. He discovered that a nozzle invented by Swedish engineer Gustaf de Laval to increase steam pressure in turbines could be used to increase the efficiency of rockets.

Goddard knew that if the exhaust outlet from the rocket's combustion chamber could be narrowed, exhaust pressure would automatically increase. Increasing and decreasing the amounts of fuel or oxidiser would in turn increase the amount of gases trying to escape, so this is also a way of controlling the exhaust pressure and the thrust a rocket engine could produce.

🔍 Investigation 15.04.02: **Investigating the vinegar rocket**

Equipment: Small plastic bottle with pull-top lid, rubber/cork stopper, three pencils (or barbeque skewers), sticky tape, baking soda, tissue paper, teaspoon, bulldog clip, 100 ml distilled (white) vinegar.

Instructions: Using the equipment as listed, and referring to the diagram, build a vinegar rocket. Test two versions, one using a rubber stopper and another using a pull-top cap. Place your baking soda into the tissue parcel.

Rubber stopper/
cork stopper

Pull-top cap

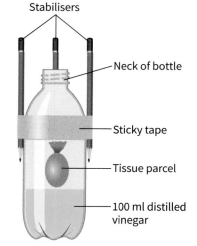

Stabilisers

Neck of bottle

Sticky tape

Tissue parcel

100 ml distilled vinegar

What did you learn?

1. Would you describe this as a liquid-fuel or solid-fuel rocket? Justify your answer.
2. What factors affect how fast the reaction between the vinegar and baking soda happens?
3. What substance provides the thrust for the rocket launch?
4. Why is the baking soda placed in the tissue paper?
5. In each version of the rocket, are different nozzles used? Explain why.
6. Which version of the rocket do you think will perform better? Explain why.
7. Did you observe a difference between the two versions? Suggest reasons why your observations did or did not match what you expected.

✓ Checkpoint 3

(a) Based on your investigations (testing thrust and the vinegar rocket), why should rocket scientists choose fuels that don't react too quickly?

(b) If thrust was created slowly, would a rocket launch? Explain.

Escape Velocity and Rocket Staging

In 1903, Konstantin Tsiolkovsky calculated the **escape velocity** for a rocket. The escape velocity is the speed a rocket needs to achieve to escape the force of Earth's gravity. The higher the speed of an object, the more force it has as its moves, so this counteracts the force of gravity.

There is a well-known need for speed to counteract the effects of gravity. It was often observed that cannonballs failed to reach their target due to the lack of gun powder. We can also see examples of this in sport; in Gaelic football, a hand pass to a team-mate will fail if there is not enough force used to increase the speed of the ball, even if the player aims well; basketball players know that a 'chest pass' combines force and speed to create accurate ball passing from player to player.

Because the earth is so massive compared to any object on or near it, its force of gravity is also huge. A small object has to move very fast to escape the effects of Earth's gravity. *Fig. 15.04.04* shows the cannonball thought experiment. If there is not enough force pushing the cannonball fast enough, it will eventually curve towards the earth; if it gains enough speed it can go into **orbit** around the earth; if it gains more speed it will break orbit and escape the effects of Earth's gravity. Most orbiting objects eventually fall back to Earth if their orbit decays because Earth's gravity is a constant force and satellites eventually run out of fuel.

Sending men to the moon requires a huge amount of thrust to get the **spacecraft** airborne, into orbit and then out of orbit on its way to the moon, especially considering how heavy a rocket and its fuel can be. To get around these problems, staging is used. As the fuel in each **stage** is used up, that stage is jettisoned, and the rocket motors for the next stage start up. Because the rocket is becoming physically smaller as it rises, each stage needs less fuel and smaller engines are needed.

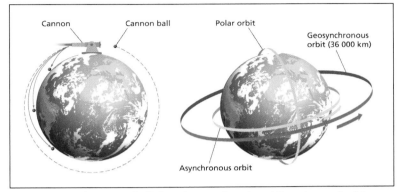

Fig. 15.04.04 The cannonball thought experiment and three types of orbit. Objects in polar orbit circle the planet from pole to pole. Asynchronous objects orbit close in and are either faster or slower than the speed of the earth's rotation. Geosynchronous objects match the earth's rotation, so move across the sky to end up at the same point at the same time each day.

Apollo

Emergency escape system

Command module (Apollo capsule)

Service module

Lunar module/ lunar rover

Stage 3
Liquid O_2 and liquid H_2, one J-1 engine

Stage 2
Liquid O_2 and liquid H_2, one J-1 engine

Saturn V rocket

Stage 1
Liquid O_2 and kerosine, five F-1 engines

F-1 engine

Human to scale

How staging worked in the Saturn V rocket

STAGE 1
• Lifts rocket into upper atmosphere to 67 km
• Jettisoned 2 min 42 s after launch
• Falls into Atlantic Ocean

STAGE 2
• Engines start 3 min 12 s after launch
• Lifts rocket out of atmosphere to 176 km
• Separates 9 min 9 s after launch
• Falls into the Atlantic Ocean

STAGE 3
• Engines ignite 9 min 19 s after launch
• Lifts the rocket to 191.2 km and into a stable orbit
• Reignites 2 h 44 min 16 s after launch
• Reaches escape velocity and heads for the Moon (translunar injection)
• 4 h 17 min 3 s after launch, the Apollo capsule modules separate from the third stage and continue to the Moon

Most of the third stages from the manned missions continued moving into space as junk, but on 3 September 2002, amateur astronomer Bill Yeung found the Apollo 12 third stage in Earth orbit thirty-three years after it had been launched.

Fig. 15.04.05 The Saturn V rocket was the largest rocket ever sent into space. It took humans to the moon. Its chief designer, Wernher von Braun, hoped to adapt and improve it for missions to Mars also.

EARTH & SPACE

Investigation 15.04.03: Rocket staging

Instructions: Using the equipment from the rocket thrust investigation, set up an investigation as shown in the diagram. Test the rocket staging horizontally without any **payload** and vertically with payload.

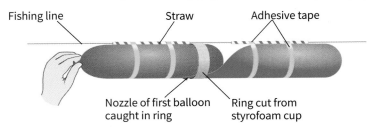

Fishing line   Straw   Adhesive tape

Nozzle of first balloon caught in ring   Ring cut from styrofoam cup

What did you learn?

1. What factors affect the amount of thrust generated?
2. Can you suggest how to carry out this investigation as a fair test, using two balloons?
3. Should the two stages (balloons) be attached together before taping to the straws? Explain.
4. How could you make sure that each test launch is a fair test each time if you carry out the test more than once?
5. Do the results of your test prove that rocket staging works? Justify your answer.

Did you know?
Close-ups of space rocket launches often show snow or ice falling as launch begins. This happens because liquid oxygen is formed by cooling oxygen gas until it becomes a liquid. The coldness of the fuel's tanks causes water in the air near them to form ice on the outside of the rocket (condensation). This ice layer falls off as the rocket begins to move.

Checkpoint 4

(a) What is 'escape velocity'?

(b) (R) Using a diagram, explain what 'staging' in a rocket means.

Re-Entry

The fact that Earth has an atmosphere can create friction problems for all spacecraft as they try to land. Three factors are taken into consideration regarding how a spacecraft cuts through the atmosphere and lands:

- The shape of its nose
- The angle of attack
- The re-entry angle.

Nose Shape

When making a paper aeroplane, we all know that a sharp or pointed nose allows it to fly through the air better because it cuts through the particles in the air. In 1951, Harvey Allen and Alfred Eggers discovered that this was untrue for high-speed objects. What they discovered became known as the **Blunt Body Theory**.

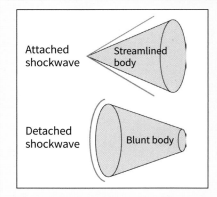

Attached shockwave   Streamlined body

Detached shockwave   Blunt body

Harvey Allen (1910–1977)

Alfred Eggers (1922–2006)

Fig. 15.04.06 The Blunt Body Theory and the men who discovered it, Harvey Allen and Alfred Eggers.

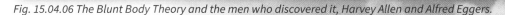

Allen and Eggers discovered that the shockwave from a blunt body created a cushion of air which helped to reduce the amount of air friction on the object, greatly reducing the amount of heat running up the side of the body. These discoveries lead to **ablative heat shielding** on the base of capsules and on the underside of the shuttle. This means that the heat shield or its surface layer is allowed to burn off the spacecraft. When this happens, most of the heat of re-entry is lost so the spacecraft itself does not burn up.

Angle of Attack

Spacecraft have to take an angle of attack so that the ablative heat shielding can give maximum heat protection on re-entry. This means that the front edge of the spacecraft has to tilt upwards so the base of it can act like a blunt body.

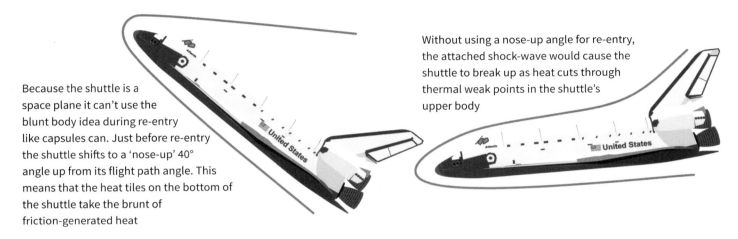

Because the shuttle is a space plane it can't use the blunt body idea during re-entry like capsules can. Just before re-entry the shuttle shifts to a 'nose-up' 40° angle up from its flight path angle. This means that the heat tiles on the bottom of the shuttle take the brunt of friction-generated heat

Without using a nose-up angle for re-entry, the attached shock-wave would cause the shuttle to break up as heat cuts through thermal weak points in the shuttle's upper body

Fig. 15.04.07 The shuttle lifts its nose at an angle as it re-enters the atmosphere at 28 000 km/h!

Re-Entry Angle

To cut through the outer atmosphere, spacecraft must pierce it at an angle of 6.2°. If the angle is 5.5° or less, the spacecraft will skip off the top of the atmosphere like a stone skipping across water. If the angle is more than 6.9°, so much friction will be created that the ablative heat shielding will not work and the spacecraft will burn up.

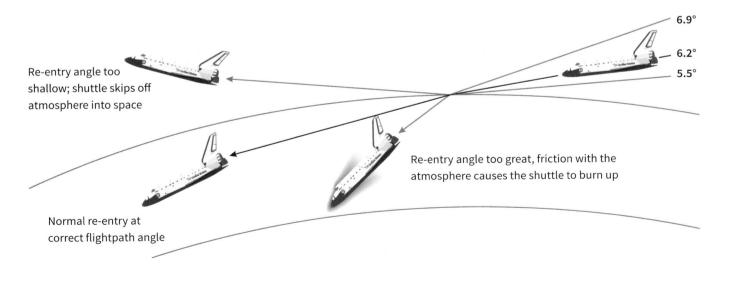

6.9°

6.2°

5.5°

Re-entry angle too shallow; shuttle skips off atmosphere into space

Re-entry angle too great, friction with the atmosphere causes the shuttle to burn up

Normal re-entry at correct flightpath angle

Fig. 15.04.08 The space shuttle re-entry angle.

EARTH & SPACE

Investigation 15.04.04: Examining angles of attack

Equipment: A sheet of newspaper, four lengths of string, sticky tape, a ruler, a protractor, a regularly-shaped object.

Instructions: Using the equipment as listed, design a parachute that holds the object at a specific angle of attack. Drop the object from a height and observe what happens.

> *What did you learn?*
> 1. How can you make this a fair test?
> 2. What conclusion can you make from your observations?

 Investigation 15.04.05: Examining re-entry angles

Instructions: Mark a '+' on a piece of graph paper where a vertical and a horizontal line meet. Using a protractor and ruler, draw three angles 5.5°, 5.2° and 6.9°. Place some Blu-tack on the '+'. Use three long pieces of string attached to the Blu-tack to extend your angles as far as you can.

> *What did you learn?*
> 1. How can you make this a fair test?
> 2. Is it easy for shuttle pilots and navigators to make a mistake about the re-entry angle?

 Checkpoint 5

Imagine this scenario: to stop a 1.5 km-wide meteor from hitting Earth, a missile was used to crash into it, explode and change its angle. Write a brief explanation about why changing the angle of the meteor could save the planet.

Spacecraft: Capsules or Spaceplanes?

R Manned spacecraft exist in two main types: reusable and non-reusable. Manned spacecraft that are one-use crafts are called **capsules**. Reusable spacecraft are **spaceplanes**. Suggestions have been made for reusable spacecraft that are not spaceplanes but none have been built or successfully tested yet. Spaceplanes other than the Shuttle or Buran have not been tested either.

R Most of the Apollo missions were launched using a Saturn V rocket. The Saturn V rocket is the largest and most powerful rocket to be used to launch humans into space. The N1 was a Russian rocket designed to bring cosmonauts to the moon, but all its **unmanned** launches ended in failure.

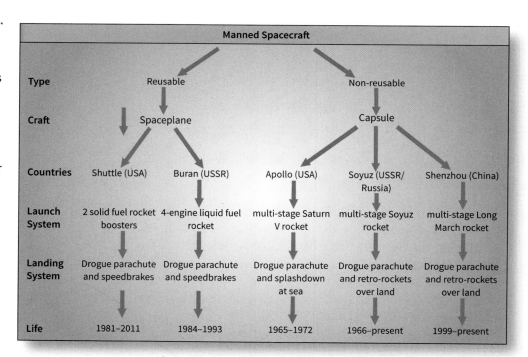

	Manned Spacecraft				
Type	Reusable		Non-reusable		
Craft	Spaceplane		Capsule		
Countries	Shuttle (USA)	Buran (USSR)	Apollo (USA)	Soyuz (USSR/ Russia)	Shenzhou (China)
Launch System	2 solid fuel rocket boosters	4-engine liquid fuel rocket	multi-stage Saturn V rocket	multi-stage Soyuz rocket	multi-stage Long March rocket
Landing System	Drogue parachute and speedbrakes	Drogue parachute and speedbrakes	Drogue parachute and splashdown at sea	Drogue parachute and retro-rockets over land	Drogue parachute and retro-rockets over land
Life	1981–2011	1984–1993	1965–1972	1966–present	1999–present

To land, the Apollo capsules had to free-fall through the atmosphere using a **drogue parachute** to slow them down before they landed in water. Soyuz and Shenzhou capsules use retro-rockets to slow the last part of the landing as they land on ground.

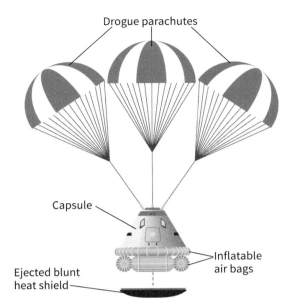

Drogue parachutes

Capsule

Ejected blunt heat shield

Inflatable air bags

Fig. 15.04.09 The drogue parachutes on a capsule as it lands and the splashdown of the Apollo 11 capsule.

NASA's Space Transport System (STS) used an orbiter (shuttle), external main tank and solid rocket boosters (SRBs) as a reusable system. It became known as the 'Space Shuttle' and was even copied by the Russian space programme in 1988 when they flew 'Buran'. It stopped flying in 2011 after thirty years in use.

A

B

Fig. 15.04.10 (a) The drogue parachute deploys on a space shuttle as it lands; (b) Artist's impression of the suggested MAKS spaceplane taking off from an An-225 aeroplane. The An-225 was specially built to carry the Buran shuttle piggy-back from its Moscow factory to the Baikonur Cosmodrome.

Currently there are only two experimental unmanned spaceplanes that have flown: the X-37B for the US Air Force and the IXV for the European Space Agency. Roscomos, the Russian space agency, has proposed the MAKS system, where a spaceplane launches off the back of an An-225 aeroplane. A number of private space exploration firms, like SpaceX, have suggested spaceplanes, but none have been launched into space, i.e. more than 100 km above the earth's surface.

There are advantages and disadvantages to both type of spacecraft, as summarised in *Table 15.04.01* overleaf.

EARTH & SPACE

Type	Avantages	Disavantages
Capsule	• Easier to build • Cheaper to build • More simple to operate • Can land on water/land	• Small crew • Small or no cargo • Free-fall landing • Needs staged rockets to launch • Expensive to launch • Not reusable • Needs a rocket to launch
Spaceplane	• Reusable • Larger • Don't need staged rockets • Can land on existing long runways • Can carry a large crew • Can carry a large cargo	• Difficult to build • Complex to operate • Expensive to build • Expensive to run • Can't land on water • Needs a rocket to launch • Needs a long flat surface to land

Table 15.04.01.

Did you know?
Shannon Airport was an emergency landing site for the Space Shuttle.

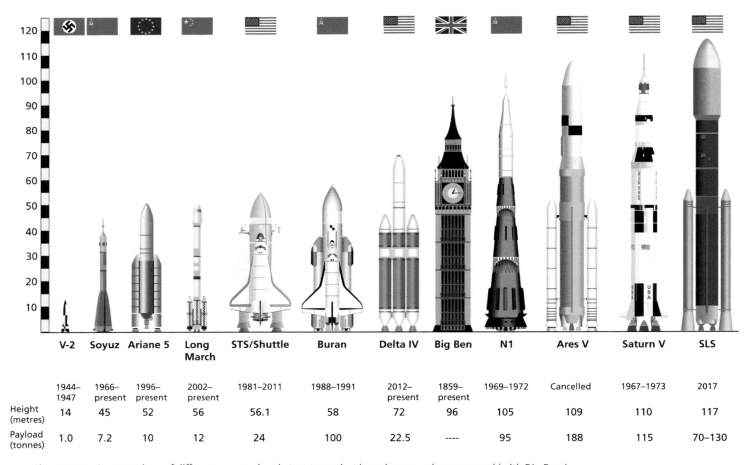

	V-2	Soyuz	Ariane 5	Long March	STS/Shuttle	Buran	Delta IV	Big Ben	N1	Ares V	Saturn V	SLS
	1944–1947	1966–present	1996–present	2002–present	1981–2011	1988–1991	2012–present	1859–present	1969–1972	Cancelled	1967–1973	2017
Height (metres)	14	45	52	56	56.1	58	72	96	105	109	110	117
Payload (tonnes)	1.0	7.2	10	12	24	100	22.5	----	95	188	115	70–130

Fig. 15.04.11 A comparison of different manned rocket systems that have been used or proposed (with Big Ben in the middle for scale comparison!).

✓ **Checkpoint 6**

(a) List the two most important advantages a spaceplane has over a capsule. Justify your answer.

(b) *Fig. 15.04.12* shows a specially converted Boeing 747 Jumbo Jet being used as a shuttle carrier to move the shuttle from its landing site to its repair site. Explain how this is an advantage or disadvantage compared to a capsule?

Fig. 15.04.12 A specially converted Boeing 747 Jumbo Jet.

® Challenges and Risks of Space Travel

Apollo 13 is a space mission that shows some of the greatest difficulties in space travel. Fifty-six hours after launch and 322 000 km from Earth, exposed wires in an oxygen tank caused an explosion that left three **astronauts** without enough electrical power or oxygen to return home using normal procedures. Bringing these men home to Earth involved a DIY solution to counteract failing oxygen scrubbers, extreme temperatures and a lack of fuel. An untried gravity assist manoeuvre was used to slingshot Apollo 13 around the moon and back to Earth – and it worked.

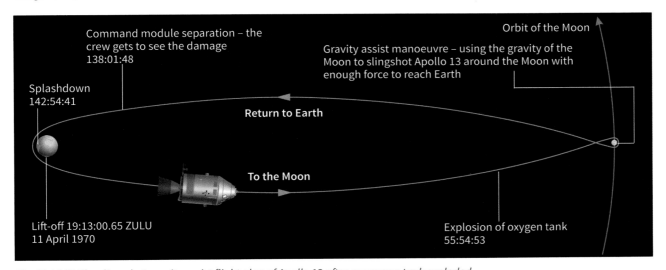

Fig. 15.04.13 The sling-shot gravity assist flight plan of Apollo 13 after an oxygen tank exploded.

The Apollo 13 incident is a spectacular example of the risks of space travel and has made many people question the advantages and disadvantages of space-flight. Space crew face many hazards when in space, and in response to these hazards, potential or otherwise, a huge amount of research has taken place that has led to new technologies and devices for the common good. However, many argue that these benefits do not outweigh the dangers of space exploration.

Fig. 15.04.14 A photo of the damaged Service Module after the Command Module (capsule) detached before the gravity slingshot manoeuvre.

EARTH & SPACE

Some of the Challenges of Space Travel and Exploration

Risks to Society	Risks to Astronauts
• Explosion or break-up of rockets over cities or towns	• Water supply
• Environmental damage from rocket break-ups	• Sufficient food when only limited weight can be carried
• Environmental damage caused by propellants	• Extreme temperatures from –120° C up to +120° C
• Microbial infection of Earth	• Loss of muscle and bone mass
• Diversion of expertise from other important activities	• Motion sickness
• Money not spent on other more important research	• Eye damage
• Use of materials and resources that could be used elsewhere	• DNA/cancer risks due to radiation
• Aggressive competition between countries over technology (Space Race/Cold War)	• Micro-meteor strikes puncturing the spacecraft
• Militarisation of space	• 'Cabin fever' due to isolation in space/living in a confined space
• Space debris	• Back pain
	• Launch failure or explosion
	• Re-entry burn-up or skipping
	• Decompression sickness

Manned Apollo missions involved 5.6 million pieces of machinery working to 99.996% perfection, which meant that engineers expected about 1000 faults every time there was an Apollo mission. There were only 150 on average, but these faults were non-critical.

This means that because most parts and systems had built-in back-ups, a certain number of faults could happen without creating a risk to the astronauts. However, when the *Challenger* shuttle exploded shortly after launch, killing all seven crew, it showed that if a critical part failed, the consequences could be fatal. In this instance, a rubber seal had failed, allowing hot, explosive gases to leak.

Fig. 15.04.15 *At 16:39 on 28 January 1986, the space shuttle Challenger exploded seventy-three seconds after launch. A camera caught a puff of grey smoke 0.0678 seconds after lift-off ignition – the first sign that hot gases were starting to leak. All seven crew members were killed.*

 Checkpoint 7

(a) What sort of objects make up space debris?

(b) What are the possible dangers of space debris?

(c) Why do you think the first men on the moon were placed in quarantine for three weeks after they landed back on Earth? Was this a good idea?

Space Technology Spin-Offs

Technology and equipment created for space exploration – developed to protect astronauts, make equipment light-weight and accurate and improve the efficiency of their equipment and rockets – has led to the development of common and everyday objects. One of the most beneficial is artificial satellite technology, which has improved weather and environmental monitoring and communications, as well as having led to the development of the GPS system.

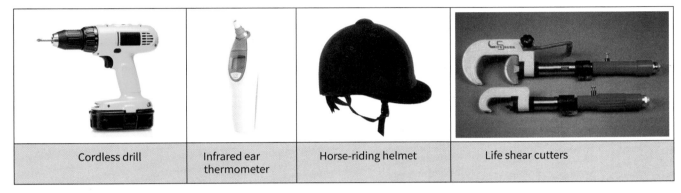

Cordless drill	Infrared ear thermometer	Horse-riding helmet	Life shear cutters

Fig. 15.04.16 Some of the spin-off technology from space exploration.

- Cordless drills were created so astronauts could work outside spacecraft without needing a cable, which took up valuable space and weighed a lot.
- Infrared temperature detectors were perfected and miniaturised as ear thermometers.
- Freeze-dried and enriched food techniques were created so astronauts could carry enough food without it weighing too much.
- Kevlar material was originally invented as lightweight protective material for spacesuits but it is now used in protective helmets.
- Microgravity caused liquids to pool in the wrong places in astronauts' bodies and created problems in their heart muscles. The development of technologies to protect astronauts from these problems influenced modern heart pumps and post-birth pressure garments.
- Life shears – used to free trapped accident victims from vehicle wreckage – were first designed to separate rocket stages quickly.

Space Travel – Examining the Benefits

Technology used in everyday life (e.g. MRI machines) has vastly improved as a result of developments in machinery and systems used in space exploration. It is likely that the need to develop better technology for space exploration will continue and so benefit everyday life, but is the benefit enough when weighed up against the cost of space exploration and the risks involved in it?

In recent decades the satellites and measuring technology developed from space exploration has allowed us to begin to understand how climate change has happened and what we can do to reduce its effects. In combination with the insights from studying other planets, this may be the most important benefit humanity gets from exploring outside our atmosphere. In the centuries to come, it may help humans survive changes to Earth's climate and ecosystems.

It is estimated that Earth will reach its maximum sustainable population by 2100, in which case humanity will need to expand its living space to other planets. Learning to explore our solar system may teach us how to set up colonies on other planets.

An important ethical question is why has so much money been spent on space exploration, when so many people live without enough food, medicines, clean water and education? Maybe a better question to ask would be why so much money is spent on war when space exploration technology could open new worlds to humanity, protect us from meteor and asteroid collisions, and make everyday life easier. It is estimated that the USA, for example, has spent almost $550 billion on space exploration in the past seventy years, but it also spends up to $600 billion a year on war. Some believe that much of world poverty could be eliminated with the money spent by the USA on wars in a single year.

WHAT I HAVE LEARNED...

- The differences between solid and liquid fuel rockets
- How rocket staging works
- The advantage and disadvantages of different types of manned spacecraft
- Ablative heat shielding and the Blunt Body Theory
- The angle of attack
- The re-entry angle
- The advantages and disadvantages of manned and unmanned missions
- Some of the challenges of space travel
- Some of the spin-off technologies of space travel
- Some of the reasons for and against space exploration.

Question Time

Copy and Complete

I learned that rockets use either _____ or _____ fuels. The _____ allows the fuel to react in space when there is no oxygen. The chemicals used in rocket engines are called _____. The force created by these chemicals which lifts a rocket is called _____. The shape of the engine_____ can increase or decrease the amount of thrust. Spaceplanes and _____ are the two main types of _____ spacecraft. Unmanned spacecraft are called _____. Passing from space into the atmosphere is called _____. Spacecraft have to enter the atmosphere 'nose-up' this means that they have an angle of _____. Spacecraft are protected from burning up by _____ heat _____. The parachutes that slow down spacecraft when landing are called _____ parachutes. The low level of gravity in space is called _____. Using the gravity of a planet to speed up or slow down a spacecraft is called a _____ assist or _____.

Questions

1. A special plane called the Antonov An-225 was built to transport the Buran shuttle piggy-back from its factory to the launch site. Explain why you think this is or is not an example of a space exploration spin-off.

Fig. 15.04.17 Buran on the back of an An-225 at the Paris Air Show, 1983.

2. Spacesuits have many layers of material to help insulate astronauts from the cold.
    (i) How do these layers protect against extreme cold?
    (ii) Explain how this might make it more difficult for astronauts to use?
    (iii) Spacesuits also protect astronauts form other things. Name and explain one.
3. Why do you think food is freeze-dried for space missions?
4. Hydrogen fuel cells (see *Unit 9.2*) provide drinking water for space missions. Why can't water used for washing and hygiene be recycled for drinking?

Inquiry

A **Design** a labelled poster of a spacesuit, explaining how it protects astronauts when they are outside their spacecraft. Note any disadvantages.

B 'The Earth is the cradle of humanity, but one cannot live in the cradle forever' (*Konstantin Tsiolkovsky*).
Consider this quote when debating the arguments for and against space exploration.

C Operation Paperclip was a secret programme to recruit Nazi scientists after World War II. Wernher von Braun was one of these scientists. Based on your research, **state** whether you agree or disagree with the aims of *Operation Paperclip*. Give reasons for your answer.

D *Fig. 15.04.18* shows the location of five spaceports currently in use. Research the advantages and disadvantages of their locations and decide which location is the best, giving reasons.

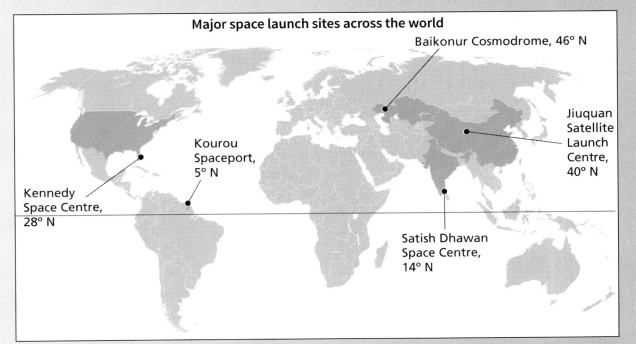

Major space launch sites across the world

Baikonur Cosmodrome, 46° N

Jiuquan Satellite Launch Centre, 40° N

Kourou Spaceport, 5° N

Kennedy Space Centre, 28° N

Satish Dhawan Space Centre, 14° N

Fig. 15.04.18 The location of five spaceports currently in use.

EARTH & SPACE

Cycles of Matter

Learning Outcomes

ESLO 5. Describe the cycling of matter, including that of carbon compounds and water, associating it with biological and atmospheric phenomena.

ESLO 7. Illustrate how Earth processes and human factors influence the Earth's climate; evaluate effects of climate change and initiatives that attempt to address those effects.

NSLO 2. Recognise questions that are appropriate for scientific investigation, pose testable hypotheses and evaluate and compare strategies for investigating hypotheses.

NSOL 3. Design, plan and conduct investigations; explain how reliability, accuracy, precision, fairness, safety, ethics and a selection of suitable equipment have been considered.

NSLO 4. Produce and select data (qualitatively/quantitatively); critically analyse data to identify patterns and relationships; identify anomalous observations; draw and justify conclusions.

NSLO 5. Review and reflect on the skills and thinking used in carrying out investigations, and apply learning and skills to solving problems in unfamiliar contexts.

NSLO 7. Organise and communicate research and investigate findings in a variety of ways fit for purpose and audience, using relevant scientific terminology and representations.

R Teacher's reference

KEYWORDS

biomass
carbon
climate change
condensation
cycle
cycling of matter
decay
deforestation
evaporation
fossil fuels
greenhouse effect
matter
micro-organisms
nitrogen
precipitation
recycled
run-off
transpiration
water

LEARNING INTENTIONS

At the end of this unit you should:

1. Be able to understand the importance of the earth's atmosphere and what gases it is made up of.
2. Know what matter is and that matter is transferred from one living thing to another and between a living thing and their environment.
3. Be able to describe how matter is used and returned to the atmosphere.
4. Be able to describe the carbon and water cycles.
5. Know the four processes in the water cycle.
6. Understand the human impact on the cycling of matter.
7. Be able to put forward ideas on how to reduce the factors of climate change.

How Does Earth Support Life?

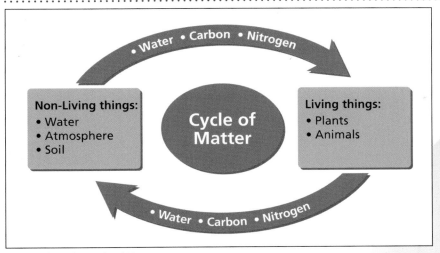

Fig. 16.01.01 The Cycle of Matter.

Earth supports life by the **cycling of matter**. Matter is anything that takes up space and has mass (see *Unit 6.1*). The movement of three chemicals – **water**, **carbon** and **nitrogen** – is very important for life on Earth. These chemicals move from living things to non-living things and back to living things.

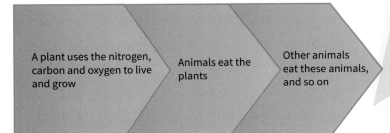

A plant uses the nitrogen, carbon and oxygen to live and grow → Animals eat the plants → Other animals eat these animals, and so on

But it doesn't stop there.

Some of the matter is returned to the non-living part of the biosphere: the atmosphere when animals release carbon dioxide as a gas and when plants and animals die and **decay**. When death or decay happens, **micro-organisms** break down the dead organism and matter is released back into the soil. We can therefore say that matter is **recycled**.

This is what we know as the cycling of matter. It is a continuous **cycle** so the total amount of matter changes very little. In this unit we will look at the water and carbon cycles.

Cycles of Matter	Brief Explanation
Water Cycle	The movement of water has no starting point: it travels in a continuous cycle, from the land to the air, the air to the land and to the sea, and so on.
Carbon Cycle	Carbon moves from the atmosphere into the food chain, and back again into the atmosphere.
Nitrogen Cycle	Nitrogen moves from the atmosphere into the food chain, and back again to the atmosphere.

Table 16.01.01 Cycles of Matter.

 **Checkpoint 1**

(a) **Explain what matter is.**

(b) **Why do all living things depend on the cycling of matter?**

EARTH & SPACE

The Water Cycle

70% of the earth is covered in water.

3% is left as fresh water BUT 2% of this is ice.

1% is left for human consumption.

97% of this water is in seas and oceans.

Do we look after our share of water?

When it rains, what happens to the water? What happens when it evaporates into the air?

Did you know?
A person can only live for three days without water.

Every living thing needs water to survive. The earth has a certain amount of water, which is continuously recycled. The water that we have today will be the same water in ten, fifty, 100 or 1000 years' time.

R What Happens During the Water Cycle?

Water is constantly moving. The sun provides the energy that powers the water cycle.

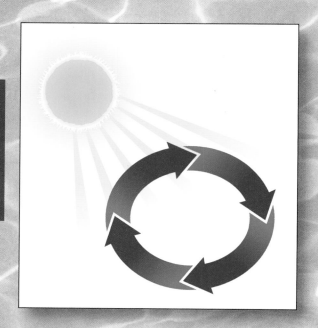

The Process: Evaporation

What is happening?
The water on Earth changes from being a liquid into a gas (water vapour).

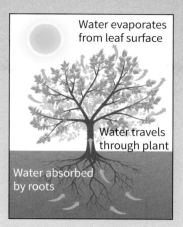

Water evaporates from leaf surface

Water travels through plant

Water absorbed by roots

The Process: Transpiration

What is happening?
Water vapour is released into the air from the leaves of plants.

The Process: Condensation

What is happening?
Water vapour cools, turns into liquid droplets forming clouds.

Rain   Snow   Sleet   Hail

The Process: Precipitation

What is happening?
The water droplets in the clouds become bigger and can fall to the ground as rain, snow, sleet or hail.

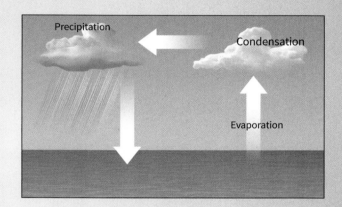

Precipitation   Condensation

Evaporation

Where does the water that is not in the oceans or in plants go?

The Process: Run-off

What is happening?
Water moves across the surface of the ground and runs into ponds, rivers and seas.

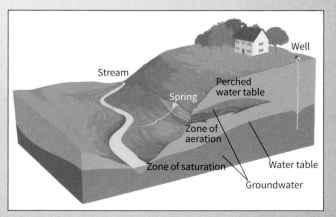

Well

Stream

Spring

Perched water table

Zone of aeration

Zone of saturation

Water table

Groundwater

The Process: Groundwater

What is happening?
Water seeps through the spaces in rocks or soil, soaking into the ground.

Now knowing the processes shown on the previous page, take a look at *Fig. 16.01.02.*

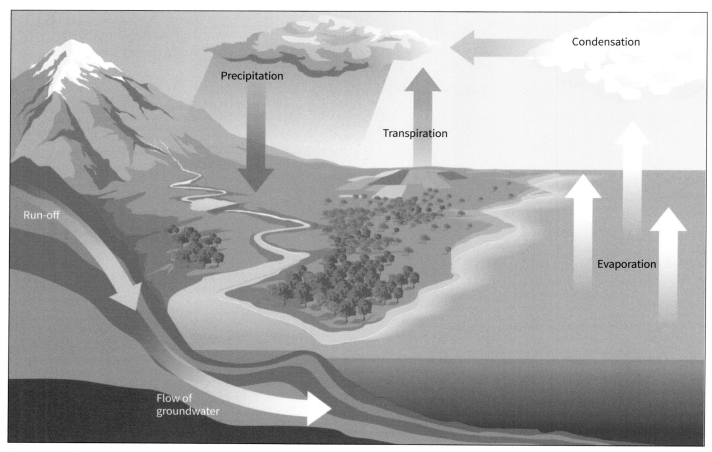

Fig. 16.01.02 The water cycle.

No water is wasted or lost in nature's cycle: it simply changes form, eventually making its way back into the atmosphere.

⊘ Checkpoint 2

(a) List the four processes of the water cycle.

(b) Does water disappear when used? Explain.

(c) Wally is a tiny water droplet who has just been evaporated. He wants to return to the leaf of the oak tree he was hanging out on with his friends. Apply the processes of the water cycle to tell Wally how he is going to get back to the tree. You can used a diagram to help you explain the story to him.

  (i) Tell him what forms he might take along the way.

  (ii) Tell him what will happen when he meets some animals, and how he will survive this.

🔍 Investigation 16.01.01: **Create a model that demonstrates the water cycle**

Equipment: Large transparent box/large lunch box, a clock glass or evaporating dish, strong paper towels (four sheets), lamp/direct sunlight at a window, permanent marker, food colouring (optional), water, two zip-lock sandwich bags, ice.

Instructions: Using the equipment as listed, plan and design an experiment to demonstrate the water cycle.

What did you learn?

1. What is the job of the sun/lamp in your water cycle?
2. Suggest what would be the effect of having different water volumes?
3. What happens to the water in your model?
4. What is the purpose of the paper towels?
5. How does the water become precipitation?
6. Is there a way you could improve your model? *Hint:* Think about the processes of the water cycle and what causes them to happen.

The Earth's Atmosphere

Earth is surrounded by a layer of gases called its 'atmosphere'. The two main gases in the atmosphere are nitrogen and oxygen. Other gases are present in small amounts, such as carbon dioxide, water vapour and noble gases.

As you can see from the pie chart, there is virtually no carbon dioxide in the atmosphere, contrary to what you might think. This is because carbon dioxide is locked away in **fossil fuels**, in sedimentary rocks and in **biomass** (living plants). Let us explain by looking at the **carbon cycle**.

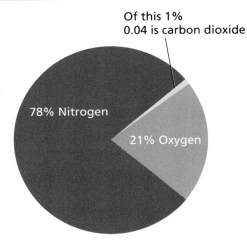

Of this 1%
0.04 is carbon dioxide

78% Nitrogen

21% Oxygen

The Carbon Cycle

The carbon cycle is the movement of carbon through the ecosystems: from the atmosphere, through the food chains, and back to the atmosphere.

Fossil fuels such as coal, oil and natural gas are made up of decayed plants and animals. Carbon is present in these decayed parts. When the fossil fuel is burned, carbon dioxide is released.

Carbon is also part of the fats, carbohydrates and protein that you eat. Plants contain carbon, so when humans and other animals eat these plants, the carbon is passed on. We then respire and release this carbon into the atmosphere as carbon dioxide.

Animals (through respiration) and industry (through the burning of fuels) *release* carbon dioxide into the atmosphere. Only plants *use* and *remove* carbon dioxide. Take a look at *Fig. 16.01.03* to see how trees recycle carbon.

With the increase in carbon dioxide emissions – from industry as well as other sources – the atmosphere is heating up. This is known as 'global warming' and is leading to **climate change**.

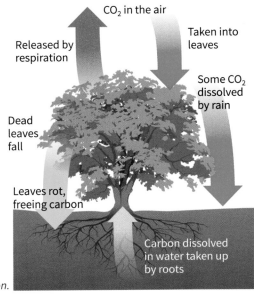

CO_2 in the air

Released by respiration

Taken into leaves

Some CO_2 dissolved by rain

Dead leaves fall

Leaves rot, freeing carbon

Carbon dissolved in water taken up by roots

Fig. 16.01.03 How a tree recycles carbon.

EARTH & SPACE

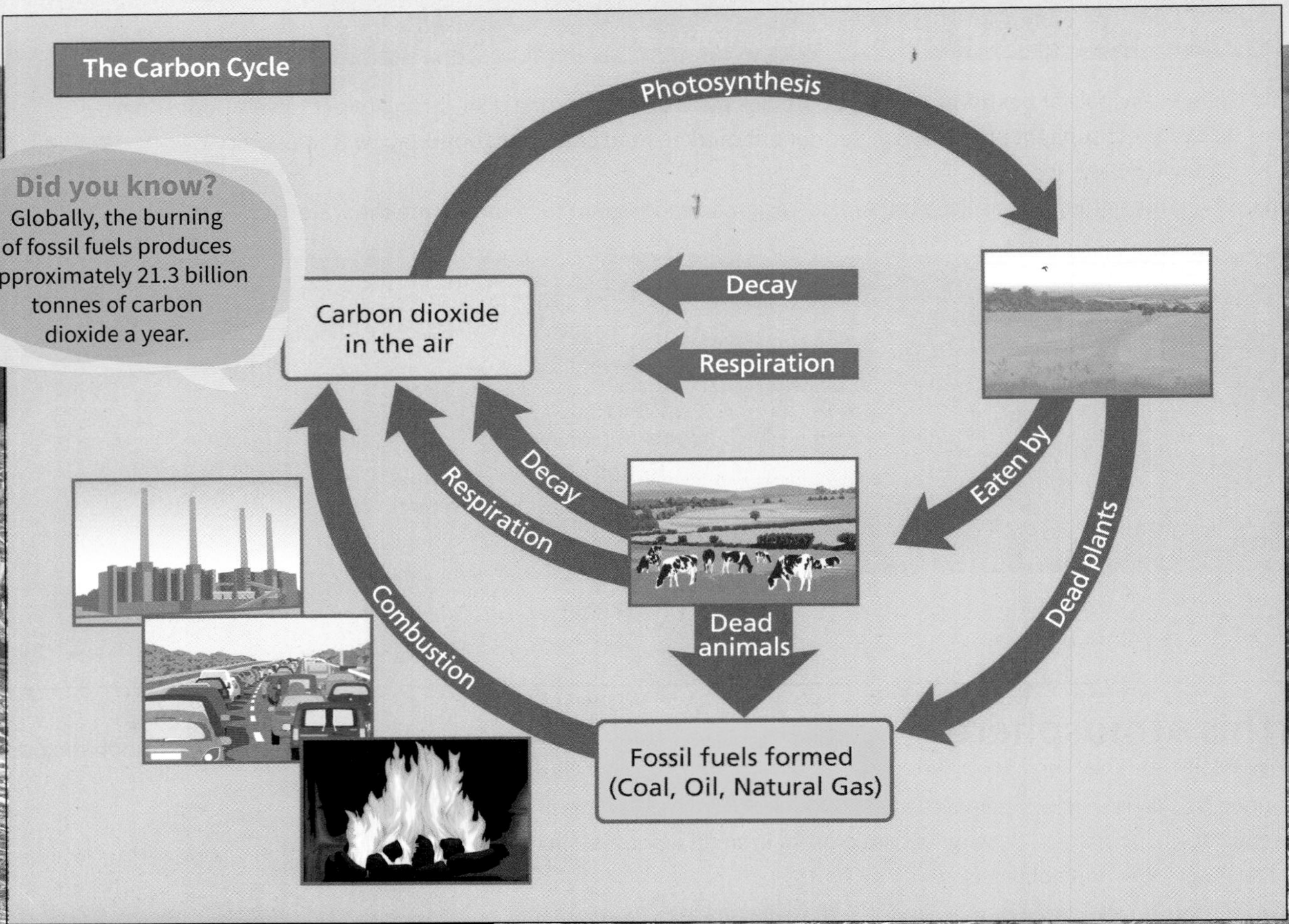

The Carbon Cycle

Photosynthesis

Did you know?
Globally, the burning of fossil fuels produces approximately 21.3 billion tonnes of carbon dioxide a year.

Carbon dioxide in the air

Decay

Respiration

Decay

Respiration

Combustion

Eaten by

Dead plants

Dead animals

Fossil fuels formed (Coal, Oil, Natural Gas)

Fig. 16.01.04 The carbon cycle.

The Impact of Humans on the Carbon Cycle

One of Earth's natural phenomena is the **greenhouse effect**. By this effect, the earth's gases are trapped within the atmosphere and the temperature is kept steady and within limits. However, human industry and activity has added to the amount of carbon dioxide in the atmosphere, which has increased the amount of gases/heat being trapped by the atmosphere, leading to global warming. Two ways in which humans have impacted on the carbon cycle are through:

1. **Deforestation**
2. The burning of fossil fuels.

Fig. 16.01.05 Deforestation – where huge areas of land are cleared to facilitate road-building or agriculture, to supply timber or to support industry.

 **Checkpoint 3**

Copy and complete *Table 16.01.02* regarding the effect of human actions on the environment.

How?	Explanation	The Effect on the Atmosphere
Deforestation	The cutting down of vast acres of trees (plants) for roads, timber, industry, houses and agriculture	These trees are no longer recycling carbon (taking carbon out of the air and producing oxygen) ...
Factories	Burning of fossil fuels to power industry	
Cars		Cars burn fossil fuels which ...
Flights		
Fires		

Table 16.01.02 Human impacts on the carbon cycle.

🔍 **Investigation 16.01.02: Showing the importance of plants/trees to our water supplies**

Equipment: Three 2-litre empty plastic bottles and caps, three 1-litre bottles or smaller, soil, cress or radish seeds (alternatively, plants ready to be transplanted), water, knife, string.

Instructions: Design and plan an investigation to show the importance of trees and plants to our soil.

What did you learn?
1. Why does the third bottle contain only soil?
2. Why is it important to add water to all bottles and not just the bottle with the seeds?
3. What type of water do you think will come from the three bottles? Explain.

The Impact of Humans on the Water Cycle

Water is necessary for human survival. However, human activity impacts negatively on the water cycle in a number of ways, whether it is by interrupting the natural, necessary flow of it, causing pollution to it, or wasting it. Some ways in which humans have impacted on the water cycle include:

- Diverting freshwater from streams and lakes for urban supply.
- Using freshwater for the production of food (see *Fig. 16.01.06* for the amount of water it takes to manufacture certain food items).
- Spraying water (irrigation) on land when rain water is in short supply.
- Spraying plants with pesticides, which soak into the soil and so into the water system.
- Wasting water within the home.
- Deforestation (soil erosion).

EARTH & SPACE

Water Footprint (total amount of water needed to make an item)

= **1800** litres — A chocolate bar needs 1800 litres **of water**

= **220** litres — A glass of milk needs 220 litres **of water**

= **140** litres — A cup of tea needs 140 litres **of water**

= **2400** litres — A hamburger needs 2400 litres **of water**

= **5** litres — A 1-litre bottle of water needs 5 litres **of water**

Fig. 16.01.06.

⊘ Checkpoint 4

(a) Scientists have being monitoring carbon dioxide levels in the atmosphere. Discuss or write a few sentences on what you think scientists have concluded in their research. (*Hint:* See *Units 9.2* and *9.3.*)

(b) How does our use of water have an effect on the water cycle?

(c) How are the carbon and water cycles similar?

Fig. 16.01.07 Volcanic eruptions are another example of a natural occurrence which can cause widespread damage and impact on the cycle of matter.

The Impact of Nature on the Cycle of Matter

Natural events occur which have a major impact on life on Earth. Floods and droughts, for example, cause major devastation to regions and the people living in them. As well as the immediate devastation, matter gets destroyed and so is not available in the long run to return to the environment or the atmosphere.

Climate Change

Climate change refers to global changes in weather patterns, such as in the:

- average temperature of an environment
- average rainfall
- level of air and water pollution.

In Ireland and other countries, these changes lead to:

- more storms
- more floods
- more droughts.

These changes then affect habitats, which affects the animals and plants that live in them, and subsequently humans, as we rely on these habitats and their animal and plant life to survive.

Do we see the effects of climate change in Ireland? The worsening and more frequent flooding that parts of Ireland have experienced in recent years has been attributed to climate change. The farming industry has also been affected; changes in temperature and rainfall patterns mean it is becoming increasingly difficult to rely on the weather when planting, cultivating and harvesting crops. This is an effect being felt worldwide by the food industry, which has seen not only a decrease in crop production but also a decline in the quality of food being produced.

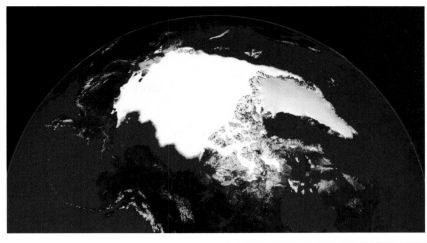

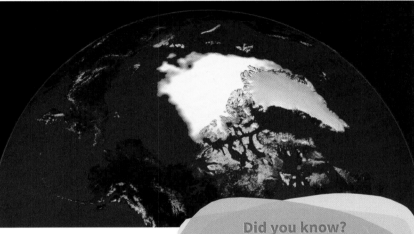

Fig. 16.01.08 The visual impact of climate change over time. The amount of ice surrounding the Arctic has visibly reduced.

Did you know?
Climate change means long-term changes to weather patterns. Global warming can be a short-term issue if the world's governments agree to specific measures to reduce their carbon emissions (e.g. reduce their fossil fuel consumption), but if it lasts much longer, it will cause long-term and irreversible damage.

✅ **Checkpoint 5**

The rate of change being experienced by the earth's varying climates is greater than in the past. The carbon and water cycles have contributed to this climate change. Why do you think the earth's climate has changed?

Fig. 16.01.09 Composting is one small way you can contribute to a reduction in greenhouse gases and so reduce the rate of climate change.

How to Protect Against Climate Change

- Reduce the amount of trees being cut down.
- Dispose of waste properly.
- Composting (no greenhouse gases produced).
- Find alternative fuel sources other than fossil fuels.
- Reduce use of fertilisers and pesticides.
- Use energy efficiently.

Reduce ● Reuse ● Recycle

EARTH & SPACE

 **Checkpoint 6**

(a) Climate change causes more floods, droughts and storms. What direct affect do these events have on habitats?

(b) Why are prices for certain food items increasing?

(c) Why are scientists urging us to reduce the amount of greenhouse gases in the atmosphere?

(R) Initiatives Aimed at Addressing Climate Change

The drive is now on worldwide to deal with climate change and its effects. While the world's main powers meet in attempts to agree on emission reduction targets – a difficult task – individual countries have decided on initiatives to play their part in combating climate change.

- In **Australia**, fines have been imposed on the top 500 environment polluters. The government has set a goal of reducing carbon emissions by 5% on 2000 levels by 2020.
- **Brazil** – a culprit in deforestation with the massive destruction of the vital Amazon forest – aims to cut its rate of deforestation by 80% by 2020.
- The **EU** and its twenty-eight member states have pledged to reduce its emissions by 20% on 1990 levels by 2020.
- In **Malawi**, the drive has been towards improving crop diversity.
- **Ethiopia** is focusing on promoting land conservation.

Here in **Ireland**, the focus has been on changing the energy we use and the way we travel. The Environmental Protection Agency (EPA) works on our behalf to implement positive changes to safeguard our environment, focusing on:

- Increasing the amount of electricity generated by renewable sources
- Using waste biomass in energy production
- Introducing biomass heating in schools
- Combating deforestation by promote tree-planting
- Promoting a climate change awareness campaign
- Promoting the use of fuel-efficient cars
- Investing in public transport to reduce the amount of traffic on the road
- Imposing building regulations on energy consumption

WHAT I HAVE LEARNED...

- The earth's atmosphere is made up of two main gases, nitrogen and oxygen, with other gases being present in small amounts.
- A cycle of matter exists, e.g. the water cycle and the carbon cycle.
- Matter is transferred from one living organism to another and then back into the environment. Plants are eaten by animals, which are eaten by other animals and by humans, who excrete and respire to release matter back into the environment.
- If too much carbon dioxide is present in the atmosphere, its temperature will increase.

- The four processes within the water cycle are evaporation, transpiration, condensation and precipitation.
- Human activities can negatively affect our carbon and water cycles by adding more carbon to the atmosphere, which leads to an increase in the atmosphere's temperature.
- Taking from the water cycle and polluting it has negative effects on its availability and quality.
- It is important to address the factors that cause climate change on a national and global level.

Question Time

Copy and Complete

In this unit I learned that matter is _____, _____ and _____. Matter works in a _____ where it is transferred from one living organism to _____ and also into the atmosphere. In the water cycle there are four processes that happen: _____, transpiration, _____ and precipitation. No water is lost: it just changes from a liquid to a _____ and back again. Carbon is transferred through the food _____: from the plant to the animal and from one _____ to another. When a plant or animal dies, the _____ that is inside them is released back into the _____ or atmosphere. Climate change is the changes to the _____ patterns, such as the average temperature, _____ and the amount of _____ and _____ pollution. Due to climate change, farmers in Ireland do not know when to sow seeds, or _____ their crops. We can protect against climate change by r_____, _____ and _____.

Questions

1. Make a list of reasons why forest areas are being cut down at such a high rate.
2. How does deforestation directly affect the levels of greenhouse gases?
3. 'Burning fossil fuels is the biggest contributor to the increased levels of carbon dioxide.' Explain this statement.
4. How is rain formed?
5. Where does rainwater go?
6. Why do all living things depend on water? (*Hint:* See *Units 6.2* and *8.3*.)
7. Name and describe what is happening at each stage numbered in *Fig. 16.01.10*.

Fig. 16.01.10.

8. Explain how the human activity being carried out in *Fig. 16.01.11* could contribute positively as well as negatively to the life of a community.

Fig. 16.01.11.

Inquiry

A **Prepare** a leaflet for distribution to your school community raising awareness of the water footprint of certain foods.

B **Choose** one way in which human activity is having an impact on the water cycle and **prepare** a poster on this negative impact.

C Some scientists state that climate change is a result of an increase in human activity. **Research** or **discuss** this point and put forward a debate evaluating the link between climate change and human activity.

D **Create** a poster that is a step-by-step guide as to how we can reduce climate change (mention any positive daily actions that could be undertaken).

16.2

Cycles of Energy

Learning Outcomes

ESLO 6. Research different energy sources; formulate and communicate an informed view of ways that current and future energy needs on Earth can be met.

NSLO 2. Recognise questions that are appropriate for scientific investigation; pose testable hypotheses and evaluate and compare strategies for investigating hypotheses.

NSLO 3. Design, plan and conduct investigations; explain how reliability, accuracy, precision, fairness, safety, ethics and a selection of suitable equipment have been considered.

NSLO 4. Produce and select data (qualitatively/quantitatively); critically analyse data to identify patterns and relationships; **identify** anomalous **observations**; draw and justify conclusions.

NSLO 5. Review and reflect on the skills and thinking used in carrying out investigations, and apply learning and skills to solving problems in unfamiliar contexts.

NSLO 7. Organise and communicate research and investigate findings in a variety of ways fit for purpose and audience, using relevant scientific terminology and representations.

PWLO 6. Explain energy conservation and analyse natural processes in terms of energy **changes** and dissipation.

PWLO 8. Research and discuss the ethical and sustainability issues that arise from generation and consumption of electricity.

Ⓡ Teacher's reference

KEYWORDS

biofuels
biomass
conserve
dam
fermented
fossil fuels
geothermal
hydro-electric
hydrogen
methane
non-renewable
nuclear
renewable
sustainable

LEARNING INTENTIONS

At the end of this unit you should:
1. Understand the differences between energy sources: non-renewable and renewable.
2. Be able to explain the effect of non-renewable energy sources on the environment.
3. Understand what will happen non-renewable energy sources in Ireland and globally.
4. Understand the need to conserve energy and identify where energy may be wasted.

Energy and You

Energy causes things to happen. It powers things. Think of all the times you have flicked a switch to turn something on: the television, the hairdryer, the computer, the kettle, the light switch in your bedroom. Think of when fuel has been burned to produce heat in your house or to power your family's car. Each time you did any of these things, you needed and used energy.

We obtain most of our energy from the burning of coal, oil and natural gas. A car uses petrol or diesel, which come from oil. The electricity that powers your house or school comes from power stations that burn coal, oil or natural gas to produce the electricity. Other sources are increasingly being used to power electricity globally – solar, wind, wave and hydro-electric – but we still predominantly use fossil fuels to produce our energy.

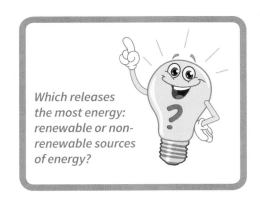

Which releases the most energy: renewable or non-renewable sources of energy?

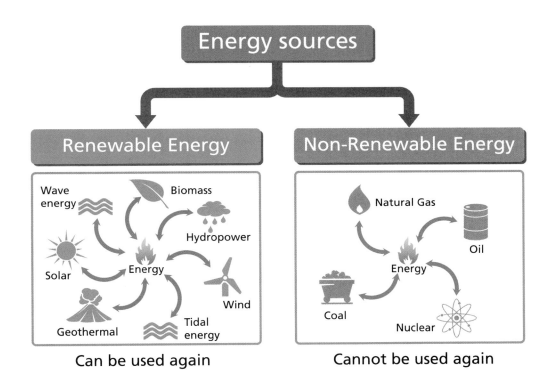

Can be used again

Cannot be used again

Non-Renewable Energy vs Renewable Energy

Before considering what energy source to use, we must think about what happens during the process of turning a particular source into the energy we need. Take a look at the headings in *Table 16.02.01* overleaf. Which source do you think is the most viable option for Ireland?

EARTH & SPACE

	Sustainability	Can they be used again	Damage to atmosphere	Availability	Damage to area/habitat when built	Initial costs	Energy amounts	Weather dependent	Ireland's use of these energy sources
Non-renewable	*The Cons of Non-Renewable*					*The Pros of Non-Renewable*			
	Limited supply; will run out; used quicker than they can be replaced	Once used, cannot be reused	Release carbon dioxide (a greenhouse gas) and other pollutants	Only in some areas and some countries	Some damage	Low in comparison to renewable set-up costs	Very high	Does not rely on the weather	91.7%

	Sustainability	Can they be used again	Damage to atmosphere	Availability	Damage to area/habitat when built	Initial costs	Energy amounts	Weather dependent	Ireland's use of these energy sources
Renewable	*The Pros of Renewable*					*The Cons of Renewable*			
	Always replenished; will never run out	Always replenished; will never run out; once used, can be reused	No damage; a clean energy (however, if biomass is burned it results in air pollution)	Everywhere	Some damage but not as much as non-renewables	Expensive to install or build (but maintenance costs are low)	Energy amounts produced are low	Energy amounts depend on the weather, which reduces their reliability, e.g. wind turbines need a certain wind speed to rotate	6.8%

Table 16.02.01 Non-renewable vs renewable energy sources.

Oil: A Non-Renewable Source

When we fill a car with petrol (made from oil) and drive the car, the fuel is being used. The petrol used to drive the car is used up in the car's engine and cannot be used again. The petrol tank will become empty and will have to be refilled. This non-renewable source is derived from fossil fuels, which were produced over millions of years by the death, decay and fossilisation of dead plants and animals.

Solar Energy: A Renewable Source

When solar panels absorb heat energy from the sun, this energy can be used to heat water. Heat energy from the sun can be used again, and more water can be heated up.

What Do Scientists Think?

Scientists believe that climate change is happening at a faster rate today in comparison to the last few hundred years. In *Unit 16.1,* we looked at the negative effects of burning fossil fuels, which is leading to an increase in greenhouse gas emissions. Scientists cannot accurately predict the long-term effects of global warming, but they say it will be damaging to us, other animals and plants.
The focus therefore is on developing and using renewable energy. This will reduce the amount of greenhouse gases in the atmosphere, which in turn will reduce our contribution to climate change.

Non-renewable: Where an energy source is used and cannot be used again.

Renewable: Where an energy source is used and can be used again.

⊘ Checkpoint 1

(a) Name two types of energy sources and explain the difference between them.
(b) Coal, oil and natural gas are examples of what kind of energy?
(c) List five sources of energy that can be reused.
(d) Why is there a move in Ireland and globally to use sources of energy that can be reused?

® A Closer Look at Renewable Energies

Wave Energy

The waves at sea hold a lot of energy. This energy is harnessed to drive a turbine and make electricity.

How does it work?

There are several ways of getting energy from waves. Two examples are:

1. Floating: A wave energy machine floats out at sea. The waves move parts of the machine, causing an internal generator to spin, which then produces electricity. Example: the Pelamis in Scotland (*Fig. 16.02.01*).
2. Fixed: Water enters a chamber and its movement turns a turbine, which is linked to a generator that produces electricity (*Fig. 16.02.02*).

Did you know?
The Pelamis is longer than a football pitch.

Fig. 16.02.01 The floating Pelamis.

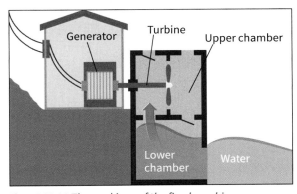

Fig. 16.02.02 The workings of the fixed machine.

Advantages

- Renewable – it will never run out
- Reliable
- Maintenance costs are low
- No fuel costs needed to run
- No pollutants given off
- Large amounts of energy can be produced – with strong waves

Disadvantages

- Expensive to build
- May damage marine life
- Some can be noisy

Solar Energy

Solar energy is energy from the sun. The sun gives out heat and light energy, which are both used.

How does it work?

The sun's energy is captured and can then be used in many different ways.

1. Solar cells in panels are used to convert sunlight directly into electricity.
2. A building is designed purposely to use the sun's heat energy.
3. The sun's energy can be used to provide hot water for buildings (including heating).

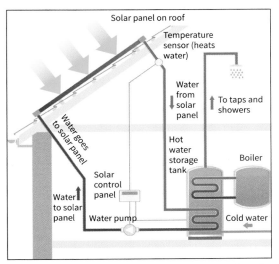

Fig. 16.02.03 Solar energy being transferred and used to heat a tank of water.

Fig. 16.02.04 A solar-powered battery charger.

Advantages

- Renewable – it will never run out
- Easy to install
- Maintenance costs are low
- No fuel costs needed to run
- No pollutants given off
- Remote or valley areas can have access to electricity

Disadvantages

- Can be unreliable as is weather-dependent
- No sunlight or energy captured at night
- Expensive to install

EARTH & SPACE

Tidal Energy

Electricity is generated from the movement of the tides. (Note that wave and tidal energy are not the same thing.)

How does it work?
They are several ways of getting energy from waves. Two examples are:

1. A barrage: Like a dam, it has a well to collect the water. A turbine underneath the dam turns with the power of the tides and causes a generator to work, which makes electricity.
2. A turbine: An underwater device, the turbine works on the flow of water through it. It is linked to a generator, which produces electricity.

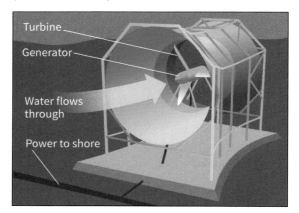

Fig. 16.02.05 *How a tidal turbine machine works.*

Fig. 16.02.06 *Tidal turbine machine being installed.*

Advantages
• Renewable – it will never run out
• Maintenance costs are low
• No fuel costs needed to run
• No pollutants given off
• Turbine is installed deep in the seabed and moves slowly, so avoids harm to marine life

Disadvantages
• Expensive to install
• Barrage can negatively affect the environment
• Some can be noisy

Biomass Energy

Biomass is plant and animal matter such as the wood from trees, food waste from farms or restaurants, or sewage from farms.

How does it work?

1. Plants: trees grown just for fuel purposes are burned.
2. Wood chips or sawdust from trees are burned, with the heat energy used to heat water or generate electricity.
3. Waste material rots, giving off methane gas. The gas is collected and used to make steam, which moves a generator, which makes electricity.
4. The waste material is burned, which produces heat energy, which is then harnessed to produce electricity.

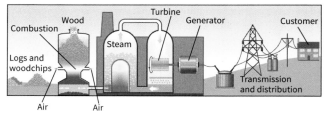

Fig. 16.02.07 *The workings of a biomass plant.*

Fig. 16.02.08 *A biomass plant in Co. Offaly.*

Advantages
• Renewable – it will never run out
• Fuel sources are cheap
• Waste at landfill sites can be used
• Methane gas is used rather than being released into the air

Disadvantages
• Air pollution as carbon dioxide is released
• Trees are cut down so habitats are lost
• Costs can be high as trees need to replanted

Wind Energy

Wind energy is harnessed by wind turbines. The energy is produced when the wind turbine blades rotate. Wind speed increases higher above the ground, so wind turbines are tall or placed on hills. Wind speed is also higher in areas where there are no buildings to disrupt the flow. Therefore, wind turbines are usually in open areas or at sea.

How does it work?
At the top of the wind turbine there is a shaft and a generator. The force of the wind causes the blades of the rotor to spin, which causes the shaft to work the generator. The generator produces electricity as it works.

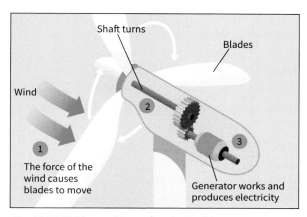

Fig. 16.02.09 The workings of a wind turbine.

Fig. 16.02.10 Carnsore Windfarm, Co. Wicklow.

Advantages
- Renewable – it will never run out
- Maintenance costs are low
- No fuel costs needed to run
- No pollutants given off
- The land on which the wind turbine is built can also be used for agriculture

Disadvantages
- Large and noisy
- A danger to birds or bats
- Does not work without wind
- Not all areas are suitable
- Expensive
- Wind turbines can be unsightly

Hydroelectric Energy

Hydroelectric energy is electricity created from the force of flowing water. It is sometimes called 'hydropower'.

How does it work?
1. Hydroelectric dams: Water from rivers (usually fast-flowing) is collected in a reservoir (a dam) which creates water pressure. Water flows down pipes under pressure, past a turbine, which turns to work a generator, which produces electricity.
2. Pumped station: Two reservoirs are needed, the first situated at a higher level than the second. The water then flows down pipes under pressure, which turns a turbine, which works a generator, which produces electricity.

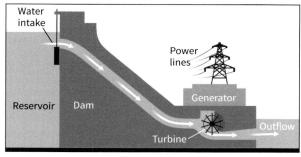

Fig. 16.02.11 The workings of a hydroelectric power plant.

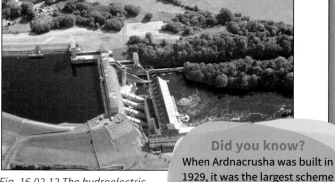

Fig. 16.02.12 The hydroelectric power plant at Ardnacrusha, on the River Shannon.

Did you know?
When Ardnacrusha was built in 1929, it was the largest scheme of its kind in the world. It is Ireland's largest generating unit using renewable energy.

Advantages
- Renewable – it will never run out
- Cheap to run
- No fuel costs needed to run
- No pollutants given off
- Water can be stored at the dam – this deals with constant and often high demands on electricity
- Recreational: Boating and fishing trips can be taken on reservoirs

Disadvantages
- Expensive to build
- Wildlife and environment can be affected
- Flooding can occur
- Homes can be lost due to construction or flooding
- Can only be built in certain places

EARTH & SPACE

Geothermal Energy

This is the heat energy that is naturally found in the earth's core and used to make electricity. This heat rises out of the ground either as a liquid or a gas.

How does it work?

A liquid (hot water) or a gas (steam) rises to the surface and turns a turbine, which works a generator, which produces electricity. The water goes through a cooling station and returns underground.

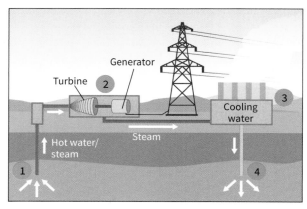

Fig. 16.02.13 The workings of a geothermal site.

Fig. 16.02.14 A geothermal power plant.

Advantages
- Renewable – it will never run out
- Cheap to run
- No fuel costs
- No pollutants given off
- Temperatures below ground level are constant so heat energy is produced consistently
- Can be used to heat water directly

Disadvantages
- Expensive to build
- Pipes can corrode
- Can only be built in suitable areas

 Checkpoint 2

(a) Why do we use non-renewable energy sources when the evidence proves that renewable is better?

(b) Do any of the renewable sources become non-renewable?

(c) What disadvantage is common to most of the renewable sources of energy?

(d) Give one advantage and one disadvantage of using solar, wind and hydroelectric energy.

(e) Give one disadvantage of using wave, geothermal and biomass energy.

(f) Suggest one source of renewable energy that you think Ireland should invest more money into. Support your choice with an explanation.

Conserving Energy

Conserving energy means reducing our energy waste and managing our energy sources wisely. We need to think about the energy needs of future generations.

The Sustainable Energy Authority of Ireland (SEAI) released figures as depicted in the chart below on Ireland's use of energy sources. Peat is considered a non-renewable source of energy, but it is not used throughout Europe, so it is not often displayed in global statistics. The total amount of energy used from renewable sources is 6.8%. This is the figure that Ireland wants to increase

Ireland's energy sources

0.4%   1.4%
6.8%
5.4%
9.9%
47%
29%

- Oil
- Natural gas
- Coal
- Peat
- Renewables
- Wastes
- Electrical import

- Most of Ireland's power stations make electricity by burning fossil fuels. Our target is to have 40% of our electricity generated from renewable sources.

- By using renewable sources of energy, Ireland can become more self-sustainable. At present, we import most of our fossil fuels.

Think About It

How do you use or waste energy? How does your school use or waste energy? How do local businesses use or waste energy?

- Analyse how you travel. Do you use a renewable or non-renewable source?
- Have you burned a fossil fuel unnecessarily at home?
- Is your house insulated?
- Is the boiler insulated?
- Have you ever left the television on when not watching it, or left a light switched on in a room when not in it?

Small changes make a big difference to our energy consumption.

 **Checkpoint 3**

(a) Why is it important to conserve energy?
(b) *Table 16.02.02* displays information from the SEAI regarding where Ireland's energy needs go.
   (i) **Display the information in the table on a graph.**
   (ii) **Which percentage are you surprised with? Why?**

Energy need	Amount
Agri/Fisheries	2.3%
Transport	32.7%
Industry	23.7%
Residential	26.8%
Services	14.5%

Table 16.02.02 Ireland's energy needs.

Alternative Energy Sources and Supplies

By increasing our use of renewable resources, we can achieve a more secure and stable energy supply for the future. Ireland has a lot of renewable sources of energy, but currently we only utilise a small amount.

Did you know?
A race car has been developed which is powered by waste from chocolate. It can reach up to 135 mph!

Ⓡ Biofuels

Also known as biomass energy or bio-energy. As we have discussed, biofuels are energy sources made from living things or the waste produced by living things. They are therefore a renewable energy source. Biofuels are a possible replacement for diesel and petrol.

Fig. 16.02.15 A car powered by waste.

There are two main sources for the generation of biofuels:

1. **Crops**
- Crops or plants are grown specifically to be used as an energy source, for example: wood, sugar beet and oilseed rape.
- Crops can be fermented to produce ethanol, which is very similar to petrol.
- However, growing crops specifically for this purpose reduces the amount of farmland available for the production of food, and thus impacts on food supplies.

2. **Waste**
- Already in development through the burning of bark and sawdust, but food, farm and plant waste can also be used.
- Food wastes such as oil can be used to produce biodiesel, and is in use in Germany and Austria.
- The methane released from farm or crop waste or sewage plants can be burnt and steam produced. This steam can then turn a turbine to generate electricity or heat energy.

How does the burning of the fuel result in the production of energy? The fuel burns with oxygen; this burning is combustion, which releases carbon dioxide, water and energy. Heat energy is produced.

The fuel + oxygen = carbon dioxide + water + energy

EARTH & SPACE

Checkpoint 4

(a) List two ways to produce bio-energy.

(b) Explain how burning a fuel can produce energy.

Hydrogen Fuel

This is when hydrogen gas is used as a fuel and converted into electricity to power vehicles, for example. Think of a normal car: when it is low on fuel, it is refilled. In the case of hydrogen fuel, when the vehicle is low, it is filled with hydrogen.

How does it work?

Hydrogen fuel works in two ways.

1. Hydrogen is burned to produce energy directly in an engine. Water is the product.

   Hydrogen + Oxygen = Water

2. Hydrogen fuel cells: In cells, the hydrogen reacts with the oxygen but it is not burned. The energy that is produced powers an electric motor.

Advantages

- No carbon dioxide or other pollutants are released into the environment – is a 'clean energy'
- Efficient, noiseless process
- The size of the fuel cell can be changed to suit the need

Disadvantages

- Hydrogen is flammable, so structures have to be put in place so it does not ignite
- Hydrogen is sourced from burning fossil fuels, which, as we know, are non-renewable sources – this therefore defeats the purpose of proposing this as an alternative fuel source
- The fuel cells are currently expensive

WHAT I HAVE LEARNED...

- Energy sources are either non-renewable or renewable.
- Non-renewable sources are coal, oil and natural gas. They cannot be used again and cause pollution by releasing gases into the atmosphere.
- Coal, oil and natural gas are fossil fuels.
- Renewable source of energy are energy sources that can be reused. Examples are: wave, solar, tidal, biomass, wind, hydroelectric and geothermal.
- To 'conserve energy' means to use our energy sources wisely and not waste energy.

Question Time

Copy and Complete

In this unit I learned that energy _____ things. Energy sources are either _____ or___-_____. Renewable means they _____ be used again, non-renewable sources _____ be _____ again. Coal, _____, _____ _____ and nuclear are examples of non-renewable energy. When non-renewable energies are burned to release their energy, they give off _____ that damage our atmosphere. An example is _____ _____. Too much carbon dioxide is _____ for our environment; it is one of the _____ gases and contributes to _____ warming. Renewable energy examples are wind, wave, tidal, _____, biomass, _____ and _____ . A lot of the renewable energies use the energy to turn turbines, to work a _____ that then produces _____. The advantages of using renewable energy is that they are _____, never run out, no _____ are given off and therefore no damage is caused to the _____. We must _____

Questions

1. Why are fossil fuels running out?
2. Write a short paragraph on why the use of renewable sources of energy is better than using non-renewable sources.
3. Suggest why it is important that energy sources are sustainable, in your opinion.
4. Why is Ireland a good place for wind energy?
5. Suggest ways in which your school could conserve its use of energy. Put together a short-term and a long-term plan.
6. Why is it essential to find alternative energy sources?

Inquiry

A   Nuclear energy is an example of an energy source. It is the only electricity-production source that creates large amounts of energy or power. It is reliable and does not give off greenhouse gases.
Research and **write** a short paragraph on why nuclear energy is not in greater use across the world.

B   Nuclear energy is energy in the nucleus of cells. Today's nuclear power plants use fission to release the energy. **Research** how this process works. (*Hint: See Unit 11.1.*)

C   Solar energy can be used in many ways. **Research** how the design of a building can use and make the most of the sun as a source of energy.

D   **Carry out** a renewable energy survey across your year group to see who may already be using renewable energy sources.

EARTH & SPACE

Index

Page numbers **bolded** and set in *italic* indicate photographs